Teachers of singing, and others who are desirous to promote the cause of music, can employ no means so effectual as the circulation of the Harp. The book will recommend itself to those who will examine it. The sale of seventeen thousand copies in a short time, is good evidence of its merit.

Persons who order the above work must be very particular, and specify whether the *round* or *patent* edition is wanted.

SPELLING AND READING COURSE.*

Eclectic Primer, with Pictures. Price 6 cents.
Eclectic Spelling Book, on a new plan.
Eclectic First Reader. Price 19 cents.
Eclectic Second Reader. Price 25 cents.
Eclectic Third Reader. Price 38 cents.
Eclectic Fourth Reader. 324 pages.

The above Readers are by W. H. McGuffey, President of Cincinnati College,—late Professor in Miami University, Oxford. In preparing the first two books, President McGuffey has taken a class of young pupils into his own house, and has taught them spelling and reading, for the express purpose of being able to judge with the greatest accuracy of the best method of preparing the "Readers." The Lessons and Stories which he has adopted in the First and Second Books, are probably the most simple, and yet the most instructive, amusing, and beautiful for the young mind that can be found in our language. The Third and Fourth Books, being in regular gradation above the First and Second, are made up of beautiful and chaste selections from prose and poetry: the whole forming a progressive series (of excellent moral tendency) peculiarly adapted to the purpose of instruction.

See notice of **ARITHMETICAL COURSE,** on the fourth page of this Reader.

JUVENILE MUSIC.

MASON'S YOUNG MINSTREL, a new collection of Juvenile Songs, with appropriate music— prepared for the Eclectic Series.

The Public have long demanded a *new* Collection of Juvenile Music; and in obedience to this call, Mr. Mason, Professor in the Academy of Music, has prepared the "YOUNG MINSTREL."

The work will be found peculiarly adapted to Juvenile Singing Schools, Common Schools, Families, and Sabbath Schools. The author has been careful to adopt nothing that would not be decidedly of a direct moral tendency, and he has most happily succeeded in combining pure moral sentiment with amusement. In the department of Juvenile Song, it is believed the volume is the most valuable and interesting one extant.

(* Actual 1838 retail prices)

THE

ECLECTIC FOURTH READER:

CONTAINING

ELEGANT EXTRACTS IN PROSE AND POETRY,

FROM THE BEST

AMERICAN AND ENGLISH WRITERS.

WITH

COPIOUS RULES FOR READING,

AND

DIRECTIONS FOR AVOIDING COMMON ERRORS.

BY WILLIAM McGUFFEY,
President of Cincinnati College—Late Professor in Miami University, Oxford.

Enlarged, Improved, and Stereotyped.

SIXTH EDITION.

— 1838 —

CINCINNATI:
PUBLISHED BY TRUMAN AND SMITH.

ROMAN NUMERALS EXPLAINED.

A numeral is a symbol meaning number. Our system of counting is believed to have begun by people counting on their fingers. Both the Arabic (1, 2, 3, 4, etc.) and the Roman (I, II, III, IV, etc.) are believed to have started this way. The word digit, meaning number, is from the Latin word digitus, meaning finger. The number V (5) seems to be representative of an open hand; and, the number X (10) seems to be like two open hands.

In earlier days, our forefathers used the Roman system to indicate chapter headings in books. To help you understand those numbers more easily you may refer to the chart below:

Roman	Arabic	Roman	Arabic	Roman	Arabic
I	1	XI	11	XXX	30
II	2	XII	12	XL	40
III	3	XIII	13	L	50
IV	4	XIV	14	LX	60
V	5	XV	15	LXX	70
VI	6	XVI	16	LXXX	80
VII	7	XVII	17	XC	90
VIII	8	XVIII	18	C	100
IX	9	XIX	19	D	500
X	10	XX	20	M	1000

Entered according to Act of Congress, in the year 1837
By TRUMAN & SMITH,
In the Clerk's Office for the District Court of Ohio.

ISBN 0-88062-005-6
Printed in the United States of America

PRESENT PUBLISHER'S PREFACE.

Out-of-print for over 125 years, the *original* McGuffey's Eclectic Readers are considered educational classics. These books are world renowned for their teaching of reading through the integration of faith with learning.

William Holmes McGuffey, outstanding 19th century educator and preacher, combined both of his God-given talents in the preparation of these early textbooks. Millions of copies were sold in their *original* Christ-centered form. The character of our Nation was molded in an upright manner through the repeated use of these textbooks over several generations.

In order to capture the true spirit of the *original* McGuffey's Eclectic Readers we have made no major content changes. While this edition of the *authentic* Readers is being presented in a more easily readable form, the stories and poems appear as they did in the first edition.

Slight changes have taken place for the sake of clarification. Those changes are as follows: a. some punctuation has been changed to keep it consistent with current usage; b. many words which used to be hyphenated are now shown as one word; c. the following lesson has been omitted because it was not appropriate today: XVIII, and the last half of paragraph 11 in lesson VII.

The Publisher wishes to express his heart-felt appreciation to the staff of the Special Collections Library at Miami University, Oxford, Ohio, for its cooperation in researching the *authenticity* of this book. Additionally, we desire to thank Dr. John H. Westerhoff, III, for his inspiration in promoting the republishing of the *original* works and Bohn Printing for their untiring efforts in typesetting the Readers.

It is indeed an honor and distinct pleasure to return the *original* McGuffey's Eclectic Readers to you. The content of this series will help you develop outstanding reading skills, Christ-centered character, a love for good literature, and impressive speaking abilities. I am sure you will find the *original* McGuffey's Eclectic Readers to be a valuable teaching tool whether they are used in the public school, Christian school, or for those who choose to teach their children at home.

George M. Mott, President
MOTT MEDIA, INC.

ECLECTIC SERIES OF SCHOOL BOOKS.

THE ECLECTIC SERIES has been undertaken by a few untiring laborers in the cause of education, for the purpose of furnishing a complete, *uniform* and *improved* set of school books, commencing with the alphabet. The books are commended by intelligent teachers.

ARITHMETICAL COURSE.

RAY'S ECLECTIC ARITHMETIC, on the inductive and analytic methods of instruction. Designed for common schools and academies. By Joseph Ray, Professor or Mathematics in Woodward College, and late Teacher of Arithmetic in that Institution. Stereotyped.

RAY'S LITTLE ARITHMETIC, containing intellectual exercises for young beginners, and designed to precede the "ECLECTIC ARITHMETIC." Prepared expressly for the Eclectic Series. Stereotyped.

RAY'S TABLES AND RULES IN ARITHMETIC. For young children. Prepared for the Eclectic Series. Stereotyped.

This system of Arithmetic is the result of many years' labor, which the author entered upon (in compliance with the earnest solicitation of many friends of education,) with a view of preparing a *standard* work, which would justify *general* use in schools. The effort has proved completely successful. The ease and rapidity with which even very young pupils can learn arithmetic from these books is highly gratifying. The author is a practical, ingenious and successful teacher. He has instructed children and youth of all ages and grades; and well knows what a school book ought to be.

READING COURSE.

THE ECLECTIC READERS, by Mr. McGuffey (advertised on the first page of this volume), were much needed. They have already been widely introduced into schools of the city and country. Numerous instructors, who are *practically* acquainted with their merits, from having *used* them with great success in teaching, pronounce them unequaled aids to the young learner, in this important branch of a primary education. *Forty thousand* copies of these READERS have been sold in a few months.

PREFACE.

This volume completes the series of "Eclectic Readers." It treads in the steps of its predecessors, so far as principle is concerned. The main difference between this and the "Third Eclectic Reader" is, that the rules are more specific—the exemplifications more numerous—the list of errors more extended—and the interrogations more copious, embracing a wider range, and requiring a more vigorous exercise of thought, in order to reach intelligent, and intelligible answers.

The selections for the present volume, are of a higher grade of literary and intellectual excellence. The mind of the pupil is presumed to have improved, and expanded, as he advanced through the preceding numbers of the "Series," or its equivalent in other books. In this therefore, he is to expect, that higher claims will be made upon his powers of thought; and larger contibutions be levied upon what he may, (or ought to) have learned from other sources.

All he knows, and, not infrequently, more than he knows, will be put in requisition by the questions appended to the lessons here presented. It is deliberately intended to lead the mind of the pupil, as often as practicable, beyond the pages of the book in his hands. Let him not think this unfair. Nor will he, for a moment, entertain such an opinion, if his mind is sufficiently active and vigorous to take delight in new efforts, and fresh acquisitions.

We often seem to make *discoveries*; and certainly do make advances in knowledge, by being somewhat importunately interrogated upon topics, with which our previous acquaintance was neither accurate nor extensive. It rouses the mind to successful effort, and often strikes out new and brilliant views of a familiar subject. And who, that has made one acquisition of this kind, does not desire frequently to repeat the experiment?

It may even happen, that some of the questions cannot at once be intelligently answered by the *instructor*. And what then? Is a teacher never to admit that there are some things which he does not know? Does not sound instruction require that the habit of *setting* bounds to our speculations, and of confessing that there *are* bounds to our acquisitions, should be early, and strongly formed? The teacher who *never* dares to say "I do not know" in reply to the questions of his pupil, must be conscious of extreme ignorance. "He must be poor indeed, who would be

bankrupted by the loss of a farthing." Narrow indeed must be
the views of that pupil who should suppose that "all knowledge"
was possessed by his teacher, however much that teacher might
seem to know.

Still there is nothing to be met with, in the following pages,
but what an intelligent teacher of a "common school" might be
expected to know, or might, at least, easily acquire. Let him not
be ashamed to learn. It is no disgrace to be ignorant; but, to be
content to remain so, *is* a disgrace. Let the teacher have recourse
to those sources of information, from which it may most readily
be obtained; and his credit will not suffer by the fact being known.
No one is fit to teach, who is too proud, too old, too indolent,
or too wise to learn. Nothing is so well taught as that which the
teacher has most recently acquired. The business of instruction
never goes more pleasantly, nor more profitably on, than when
teacher and pupil advance together; and it admits of debate,
whether it is more desirable, that, in order to this, the teacher
should *return* for his pupil; or *start* only so far in advance of him,
as to be his conductor. He is not the best pilot, who has most
frequently traveled the road; but he who can most safely,
pleasantly, and expeditiously conduct you to your journey's end.
This book is intended to aid and stimulate the *teacher*, as well
as the *pupil.*

The author ventures to predict, that if any of the lessons shall
be found unintelligible to the younger class of readers, it will not
be those of the highest character for thought and diction; and
especially in the selections from poetry. He has long been of the
opinion that a mischievous error pervades the public mind, on
the subject of the juvenile understanding. Nothing is so difficult
to be understood as "nonsense." Nothing is so clear and easy
to be comprehended as the simplicity of wisdom.

It may perhaps be expected, that the author should here add
something in explanation of the principle, or in defense of the
plan which he has adopted, and pursued in the series of books,
of which this professes to be the last. But, as in every instance
of intelligent criticism which has met his eye, both plan and
principle have been approved and commended, he infers that both
have been understood, and that neither requires to be explained
or defended here.

Much has, at times, been said and written against the use of
cuts, or *Pictures* as employed in books for children, such as the
First and Second Eclectic Readers. But the author cannot bring
himself to believe, that those who employ this declamation, can
mean anything more than that pictures are liable to *abuse*, in

the business of instruction. And what is there that is not liable to abuse?

There is no person but the veriest smatterer in the business of education, who does not see at once, that visible delineations are indispensable in every grade of education, from the primer to the Principia. What are maps in Geography, or cuts in Natural History, or diagrams in Geometry, but visible delineations on precisely the same *principle* with pictures and cuts in elementary books for children?

On the subject of *Questions* appended to the lessons, there is, and can be, but one opinion amongst the intelligent in community. Where answers are furnished to every question the memory alone will be cultivated. But no teacher can give instruction without *asking questions*.

The compiler will rejoice to know, that those who use his books, ask more intelligent questions, and in much greater numbers, than are to be found in the pages before them. This is the very design of that part of his labors. His wish is, to incite the teacher to the interrogative method *orally*, and then he cares not whether he asks a single question that is printed in the book. Still, he believes that some teachers may be found, who are not too wise to be *assisted* in this manner; and who may not only need, but feel that they need such suggestions as are furnished in the questions.

The *Errors* marked in pronunciation are such as more frequently occur in reading and in common conversation; and are sometimes heard even in literary society, and in addresses to the public from literary men. A variety of mispronunciation is sometimes given on the same word; because such variety prevails in the community. But what has been done in this, as in everything else, must be taken as an incipient attempt at correcting the errors, and supplying the defects that exist, and prevail, to the detriment not only of elegance, but of accuracy in our oral and literary communication with our fellow citizens.

In conclusion, the author begs leave to state, that the whole series of "Eclectic Readers" is his own. In the preparation of the rules, etc., for the present volume he has had the assistance of a very distinguished Teacher, whose judgment and zeal in promoting the cause of education have often been commended by the American people. In the arrangement of the series generally, he is indebted to many of his friends for valuable suggestions, and he takes this opportunity of tendering them his thanks for the lively interest they have manifested for the success of his undertaking.

From no source has the author drawn more copiously, in his selections, than from the sacred Scriptures. For this, he certainly apprehends no censure. In a Christian country, that man is to be pitied, who at this day, can honestly object to imbuing the minds of youth with the language and spirit of the Word of God.

The student of the Bible will, it is believed, be pleased to find a specimen of the elegant labors of Bishop Jebb, and some specimens of sacred poetry as arranged by Dr. Coit, in which the exact words of our authorized translation are preserved, while the poetic order of the original is happily restored.

With these somewhat extended prefatory remarks, the volume is respectfuly submitted to the judgment of the public.

SECOND EDITION.—This second edition is considerably enlarged; and, it is hoped, somewhat improved. The volume is now stereotyped, and will not be subjected to alterations in subsequent editions.

Cincinnati, 1837.

CONTENTS.

PROSE.

LESSON.   PAGE.

I.—Remarkable Preservation 1
II.—The Maniac 7
III.—Scene at the Sandwich Islands 9
IV.—Contrasted Soliloquies 14
V.—On Letter Writing 18
VII.—The Whale Ship 27
IX.—Death at the Mirror 34
X.—Death of Absalom 37
XII.—The Intemperate Husband 45
XIII.—The Intemperate Husband (cont.) 49
XV.—On Elocution and Reading 56
XVI.—Necessity of Education 59
XVII.—Necessity of Education (cont.) 62
XVIII.—The Scriptures and the Savior 65
XIX.—Washington's Birthday 67
XXI.—Niagara Falls 72
XXIII.—Character of Wilberforce 81
XXVI.—Speech of Logan, Chief of
the Mingoes .88
XXVII.—The Alhambra by Moonlight 90
XXVIII.—Portrait of a Patriarch 93
XXIX.—An End of all Perfection 95
XXXI.—Character of Mr. Brougham 101
XXXII.—Elevated Character of Woman 104
XXXIV.—Modes of Writing 110
XXXVII.—Criminality of Dueling 118
XXXVIII.—Character of Napoleon Bonaparte . . .121
XXXIX.—The Field of Waterloo 124
XL.—The Splendor of War 126
XLI.—The Best of Classics 129
XLII.—The New Song 131

XLIII.—The Deluge 132
XLV.—External Appearance of England 137
XLVII.—Character of the Puritan Fathers
      of New England 145
XLVIII.—Character of the Puritan Fathers
      of New England (cont.)........... 149
XLIX.—Decisive Integrity 154
LI.—The Steam Boat on Trial.......... 160
LII.—Paine's Age of Reason 165
LIV.—The Righteous never Forsaken...... 170
LV.—Religion the only Basis of Society ... 174
LVI.—Benevolence of the Supreme Being .. 176
LVII.—Love of Applause 178
LIX.—Ludicrous Account of
      English Taxes 185
LX.—Christ and the Blind Man 187
LXII.—The Horrors of War 192
LXIII.—The Bible 196
LXIV.—Tit for Tat...................... 198
LXV.—Political Corruption 201
LXVI.—The Blind Preacher 204
LXIX.—America 213
LXXI.—View from Mount Etna 217
LXXII.—Sublime Virtues Inconsistent
      with Infidelity 221
LXXIV.—Parallel between Pope and Dryden .. 226
LXXV.—Happy Consequences of
      American Independence 229
LXXVII.—Evils of Dismemberment.......... 235
LXXVIII.—No Excellence without Labor 238
LXXX.—A Plea for Common Schools 242
LXXXII.—Omnipresence of God............. 250
LXXXIII.—Henry Martyn and Lord Byron 251
LXXXV.—Chesterfield and Paul............. 262
LXXXVII.—Effects of Gambling.............. 266
LXXXVIII.—Effects of Gambling (cont.) 270
XCI.—The Wife 281
XCII.—Duty of the American Orator 283
XCIII.—The Patriotism of
      Western Literature 289

XCV.—Rebellion in Massachusetts
        State Prison 297
XCIX.—Charles de Moor's Remorse 311
C.—Value of Mathematics 313
CI.—Value of Mathematics (cont.) 316
CIII.—Capturing the Wild Horse 322
CVII.—Egyptian Mummies, Tombs,
        and Manners 338
CIX.—On the Value of Studies 348
CX.—Natural Ties among the
        Western States 350
CXI.—The Venomous Worm 355
CXIII.—Benefits of Literature 358
CXVIII.—The Vision of Mirza 385
CXX.—Ladies' Headdresses 393
CXXII.—Reflections in Westminster Abbey . . . 399
CXXIII.—The Journey of a Day: A Picture
        of Human Life 402
CXXVIII.—The Celestial City 417

POETRY.

VI.—Ginevra 24
VIII.—The Winged Worshipers 32
XI.—Absalom 42
XIV.—God's First Temples 52
XX.—Nature and Revelation 70
XXII.—Niagara Falls 78
XXIV.—Pleasure in Affliction 83
XXV.—Make Way for Liberty 85
XXX.—A Rest for the Weary 98
XXXIII.—The Passions 107
XXXV.—Joyous Devotion 114
XXXVI.—A Night Scene in Turkey 116
XLIV.—A Hebrew Tale 134
XLVI.—Vision of a Spirit 143
L.—On the Being of a God 157

LIII.—Divine Providence 168
LVIII.—Scripture Lesson.................182
LXI.—The Ocean 190
LXVII.—Apostrophe to Light 209
LXVIII.—Procrastination 211
LXX.—Thirsting after Righteousness 216
LXXIII.—The Alps 224
LXXVI.—Satan and Death at
the Gate of Hell 232
LXXIX.—Thoughts in a Place of
Public Worship 240
LXXXI.—Midnight Musings 248
LXXXIV.—Byron........................259
LXXXVI.—Henry First after the Death
of his Son....................264
LXXXIX.—The Miser 277
XC.—True Wisdom 279
XCIV.—Rome 292
XCVI.—Prince Arthur 303
XCVII.—The Child's Inquiry 308
XCVIII.—Christian Hymn of Triumph;
from "The Martyr of Antioch." ...309
CII.—Washing Day 319
CIV.—The Gods of the Heathen 328
CV.—The Fall of Babylon 330
CVI.—Antony's Oration over
Caesar's Dead Body 334
CVIII.—Address to the Mummy in
Belzoni's Exhibition, London 345
CXII.—The Better Land.................357
CXIV.—Thalaba among the Ruins
of Babylon 364
CXV.—William Tell....................367
CXVI.—William Tell (cont.) 372
CXVII.—William Tell (cont.) 380
CXIX.—A Dirge 391
CXXI.—Apostrophe to the Ocean 397
CXXIV.—Morning.......................407
CXXV.—Woe to Ariel 409
CXXVI.—The Proverbs of Solomon 411
CXXVII.—Comfort ye my People 413
CXXIX.—America.—National Hymn 422

SUGGESTIONS TO TEACHERS.

To read with a loud and full tone, to pronounce every syllable properly and distinctly, and to mind the pauses;—are the three most difficult points to be gained in making good readers. If these three things are attained, the various intonations that express sentiment will generally follow, as soon as pupils have knowledge enough to understand the sense, and will give their attention to it.

There are no general rules for modulating the tones and manner, with reference to the sense, that can be of much service in a reading book for schools. This work contains all the other rules that can be of much practical use to teachers.

If teachers will classify with reference to particular defects in reading, it will much abridge the labor of teaching. Let all who read in a low and feeble voice be put in one class and practised with reference to this fault till it is conquered.

Let all who clip their words or pronounce indistinctly be put in another class, and practice on those rules in the book intended to correct this fault.

Let all who read too fast, and disregard the stops, be put in a class and special attention be paid to this fault.

The great maxim of good teaching in reading is, to take *one thing at a time,* and to persevere in *repetition,* till the object aimed at is attained.

It is with reference to this, that the most important rules are repeated in successive lessons.

If the pupils are required to criticize each other's reading—to point out mispronunciation or the omissions of syllables, it sustains the interest of the exercise, and makes all more careful when called to read themselves.

The plan of having the pupils *go up toward the head of the class* as they correct faults, thus stimulating attention in the listeners and care in the reader, will sometimes be found useful.

But while one thing should be prominently attended to at a time many things may be joined collaterally, if proper pains be taken.

Let a class be called to read. The teacher requires the pupils to pay particular attention to *emphasis.* But he may, at the same time, direct them to stand at different distances while they read lessons; and thus secure a proper attention to force or loudness of utterance.

Let the teacher sometimes place his class as far from his desk as the room will permit, and require the lesson to be read in a suppressed tone, but so distinctly as to be audible throughout the room; and in this way he will most effectually secure distinct articulation. Those readers who have feeble voices are generally most remarkable for their distinctness of utterance; while those speakers and readers who have strong voices, as a general thing, articulate badly.

But this book is designed for other purposes than merely to teach the pupil to read. The selections have been made with a constant reference to the improvement of the *mind* as well as to the cultivation of the voice. Many of the lessons require thought, in order to be appreciated, and before they can be comprehended. Some of these require an extensive range of reading and deep reflection, to enable the reader fully to understand the allusions, to enter into the spirit, and to realize the excellence of the extracts.

Let the *teacher* then *study* the lessons as well as the pupils. Let him require, that the substance of what has been read be continuously narrated by the pupil *without* recurrence to the book. Let him direct that this be *written down* without the aid of a dictionary or grammar, and with no other appliances at hand than pen, ink, and paper. Let each pupil be so situated that he can derive no assistance from his fellow pupil; and then let the narratives, both oral and written, be the subject of severe but candid criticism by the teacher and the other pupils, as to the style, pronunciation, grammar and penmanship.

Let the teacher sometimes read aloud a lesson to his class, having previously removed every means of taking *notes* while he reads—and then let him require each pupil within a given, but sufficient time, to render in writing and from recollection, an abstract of what he has read.

This exercise improves the attention, practices the pen, gives fluency of expression, and a readiness of employing the ideas gained in reading, as capital of our own; and will be found highly interesting to the pupils and highly improving in a greater variety of ways than many other highly approved methods of recitation.

ECLECTIC FOURTH READER.

LESSON I.

RULE.—Be careful to pronounce every syllable distinctly, and not to join the words together. Nothing is more important to good reading than attention to this rule, and yet most young readers violate it.

EXERCISES UNDER THE RULE. To be read over several times by all the pupils.

In the following exercises difficult sounds have been introduced, which are commonly spoken indistinctly or entirely omitted. Let every pupil, before commencing the reading lesson, read them over several times slowly and distinctly. The difficult sounds are put in Italics.

He was *incapable of* it. (Here take care not to join *ble* and *of.*)

He was *amiable, respectable, formidable, unbearable, intolerable, unmanageable, terrible.* (Here the sound *ble* must be fully sounded.)

He was *branded* as a traitor.

Thou *prob'st* my wound.

He was *stretched on* the floor.

But *Ruth clave* unto her.

The above rule is so important, that the first twelve lessons will all be under it.

Remarkable Preservation.
PROF. WILSON.

1. You have often asked me to describe to you on paper an event in my life, which thirty years later, I cannot look back to without horror. No words can give an adequate image of the miseries I suffered during that fearful night; but I shall try to give you something like a faint shadow of them, that from it your soul may conceive what I must have suffered.

2. I was, you know, on my voyage back to my native country after an absence of five years spent

in unintermitting toil in a foreign land, to which I had been driven by a singular fatality. Our voyage had been most cheerful and prosperous, and on Christmas day we were within fifty leagues of port. Passengers and crew were all in the highest spirits, and the ship was alive with mirth and jollity.

3. The ship was sailing at the rate of seven knots an hour. A strong snowstorm blew, but steadily and without danger, and the ship kept boldly on her course, close reefed, and mistress of the storm. While leaning over the gunwale, admiring the water rushing by like a foaming cataract, by some unaccountable accident, I lost my balance, and in an instant fell overboard into the sea.

4. I remember a convulsive shuddering all over my body, and a hurried leaping of my heart as I felt myself about to lose hold of the vessel, and afterwards a sensation of the most icy chillness, from immersion in the waves, but nothing resembling a fall or precipitation. When below the water, I think that a momentary belief rushed across my mind that the ship had suddenly sunk, and that I was but one of a perishing crew. I imagined that I felt a hand with long fingers clutching at my legs and made violent efforts to escape, dragging after me as I thought, the body of some drowning wretch.

5. On rising to the surface, I recollected in a moment what had befallen me, and uttered a cry of horror, which is in my ears to this day. It often makes me shudder, as if it were the mad shriek of another person in perilous agony! Often have I dreamed over again that dire moment, and the cry I utter in my sleep is said to be something more horrible than a human voice. No ship was to be seen. She was gone forever.

6. The little happy world to which, a moment before, I had belonged, had been swept by, and I felt

that God had flung me at once from the heart of joy, delight, and happiness, into the uttermost abyss of mortal misery and despair. Yes! I felt that the Almighty God had done this—that there was an act, a fearful act of Providence. Miserable worm that I was, I thought that the act was cruel, and a sort of wild, indefinite, objectless rage and wrath assailed me, and took for awhile the place of that first shrieking terror. I gnashed my teeth, and cursed myself—and, with bitter tears and yells, blasphemed the name of God.

7. It is true, my friend, that I did so. God forgave that wickedness. The Being, whom I then cursed, was, in his tender mercy, not unmindful of me,—of me, a poor, blind miserable, mistaken worm. The waves dashed over me and struck me on the face, and howled at me. The winds yelled, and the snow beat like drifting sand into my eyes, and the ship, the *ship* was *gone*, and there was I left to struggle, and buffet, and gasp, and sink, and perish, alone, unseen, and unpitied by man, and, as I thought too, by the everlasting God.

8. I tried to penetrate the surrounding darkness with my glaring eyes, that felt as if leaping from their sockets. I saw, as if by miraculous power, to a great distance through the night—but no *ship*—nothing but white-crested waves, and the dismal noise of thunder.

9. I shouted, shrieked, and yelled, that I might be heard by the crew, until my voice was gone—and that too, when I knew that there were none to hear me. At last I became utterly speechless, and when I tried to call aloud, there was nothing but a silent gasp and convulsion, while the waves came upon me like stunning blows, reiterated, and drove me along, like a log of wood, or a dead animal.

10. All this time I was not conscious of any act of swimming, but I soon found that I had instinctively been exerting all my power and skill, and both were

requisite to keep me alive in the tumultuous wake of the ship. Something struck me harder than a wave. What it was I knew not, but I grasped it with a passionate violence, for the hope of salvation came suddenly over me, and with a sudden transition from despair, I felt that I was rescued.

11. I had the same thought as if I had been suddenly heaved on shore by a wave. The crew had thrown overboard everything they thought could afford me the slightest chance of escape from death, and a hencoop had drifted towards me. At once all the stories I had even read of mariners miraculously saved at sea rushed across my recollection. I had an object to cling to, which I knew would enable me to prolong my existence.

12. I was no longer helpless on the cold weltering world of waters, and the thought that my friends were thinking of me, and doing all they could for me, gave to me a wonderful courage. I may yet pass the night in the ship, I thought, and I looked round eagerly to hear the rush of her prow, or to see through the snow-drift the gleaming of her sails.

13. This was but a momentary gladness. The ship I knew could not be far off, but for any good she could do me, she might as well have been in the heart of the Atlantic Ocean. Before she could have altered her course, I must have drifted a long way to leeward, and in the dim snowy night how was such a speck to be seen? I saw a flash of lightning, and then there was thunder. It was the ship firing a gun to let me know, if still alive, that she was somewhere lying to.

14. But where? I was separated from her by a dire necessity, by many thousand fierce waves that would not let my shrieks be heard. Each succeeding gun was heard fainter and fainter, till at last I cursed the sound that, scarcely heard above the hollow rumbling of the tempestuous sea, told me that the ship was farther

and farther off, until she and her heartless crew had left me to my fate.

15. Why did they not send out all their boats to row round and round all that night through, for the sake of one whom they pretended to love so well? I blamed, blessed, and cursed them by fits, until every emotion of my soul was exhausted, and I clung in sullen despair to the wretched piece of wood that still kept me from eternity.

16. Everything was now seen in its absolute dreadful reality. I was a castaway—no hope of rescue. It was broad daylight, and the storm had ceased, but clouds lay round the horizon, and no land was to be seen. What dreadful clouds! Some black as pitch, and charged with thunder, others like cliffs of fire, and here and there all streamered over with blood. It was indeed a sullen, wrathful, and despairing sky.

17. The sun itself was a dull brazen orb, cold, dead, and beamless. I saw three ships afar off, but all their heads were turned away from me. For whole hours they would adhere motionless to the sea, while I drifted away from them, and then a rushing wind would spring up, and carry them, one by one, into the darkness of the stormy distance. Many birds came close to me, as if to flap me with their large spreading wings, screamed round and round me, and then flew away in their strength, and beauty, and happiness.

18. I now felt myself indeed dying. A calm came over me. I prayed devoutly for forgiveness of my sins, and for all my friends on earth. A ringing was in my ears, and I remember only the hollow fluctuations of the sea with which I seemed to be blended, and a sinking down and down an unfathomable depth, which I thought was Death, and into the kingdom of the eternal Future.

19. I awoke from insensibility and oblivion with a hideous, racking pain in my head and loins, and in

a place of utter darkness. I heard a voice say, "Praise the Lord." My agony was dreadful, and I cried aloud. Wan, glimmering, melancholy lights kept moving to and fro. I heard dismal whisperings, and now and then a pale silent ghost glided by. A hideous din was over head, and around me the fierce dashing of the waves. Was I in the land of spirits?

20. But, why strive to recount the mortal pain of my recovery, the soul-humbling gratitude that took possession of my being? I was lying in the cabin of a ship and kindly tended by a humane and skillful man. I had been picked up, apparently dead, and cold. The hand of God was there. Adieu, my dear friend. It is now the hour of rest, and I hasten to fall down on my knees before the merciful Being who took pity upon me, and who, at the intercession of our Redeemer, may, I hope, pardon all my sins.

QUESTIONS.—1. Narrate this story in your own language. 2. What were the Professor's feelings when he first fell into the water? 3. What did he imagine was clutching at his heels? 4. How did he act upon rising to the surface? 5. How did he escape a watery grave?

ERRORS.—*Ad-e-quit* for ad-e-quate; *vo-ige* for voy-age; *cussed* for curs-ed.

SPELL AND DEFINE.—(1) adequate; (2) unintermitting, passengers; (3) gunwale (pronounced gun-nel), unaccountable; (4) shuddering, immersion, precipitation, momentary, clutching; (6) uttermost, shrieking; (7) unmindful; (8) surrounding, miraculous; (10) instinctively; (11) overboard; (13) leeward; (14) tempestuous; (16) streamered; (18) fluctuations, unfathomed.

LESSON II.

RULE.—Be careful to pronounce every syllable distinctly, and not to join the words together.

EXERCISES UNDER THE RULE. To be read over several times by all the pupils.

The *ribs of death*.

Can you *cry crackers, crime, cruelty, crutches?*

The *orb'd moon*.

It was the worst *act* of all *acts*.

It was a *mixed government*.

The *idle spindle*. Long *droves of cattle*.

Their *deeds show* their feelings.

The *length and breadth, and height, and depth,* of the thing.

It was *highly and holily* done.

The Maniac.—ANONYMOUS.

1. A gentleman who had traveled in Europe relates that he one day visited the hospital of Berlin, where he saw a man whose exterior was very striking. His figure, tall and commanding, was bending with age, but more with sorrow. The few scattered hairs which remained on his temples were white, almost as the driven snow, and the deepest melancholy was depicted in his countenance.

2. On inquiring who he was and what brought him there, he startled, as if from sleep, and after looking round him, began with slow and measured steps to stride the hall, repeating in a low but audible voice, "Once one is two, once one is two."

3. Now and then he would stop and remain with his arms folded on his breast, as if in contemplation for some minutes. Again resuming his walk, he continued to repeat, "Once one is two; once one is two." His story, as our traveler understood it, was as follows.

4. Conrad Lange, collector of the revenues of the city of Berlin, had long been known as a man whom nothing could divert from the paths of honesty.

Scrupulously exact in all his dealings, and assiduous in the discharge of his official duties, he had acquired the good will and esteem of all who knew him, and the confidence of the minister of finance, whose duty it is to inspect the accounts of all officers connected with the revenue.

5. On casting up his accounts at the close of a particular year, he found a *deficit* of ten thousand ducats. Alarmed at this discovery, he went to the minister, presented his accounts, and informed him that he did not know how it had arisen, and that he had been robbed by some person bent on his ruin.

6. The minister received his accounts, but thinking it a duty to secure a person who might probably be a defaulter, he caused him to be arrested, and put his accounts into the hands of one of his secretaries, for inspection. He returned them the day after, with the information that the deficiency arose from a miscalculation, that in multiplying; Mr. Lange had said, *once one is two*, instead of, *once one is one*.

7. The poor man was immediately released from confinement, his accounts returned, and the mistake pointed out. During his imprisonment, which lasted only two days, he had neither eaten, drunk, nor taken any repose—and when he appeared, his countenance was as pale as death. On receiving his accounts, he was a long time silent; then suddenly awaking as if from a trance, he repeated, "once one is two."

8. He appeared to be entirely insensible of his situation; would neither eat nor drink unless solicited, and took notice of nothing that passed around him. While repeating his accustomed phrase, if anyone corrected him by saying, "once one is *one*," he was recalled for a moment and said,"ah, right, once one *is* one," and then resuming his walk, he continued to repeat, "once one is two." He died shortly after the traveler left Berlin.

9. This affecting story, whether true or untrue, obviously abounds with lessons of instruction. Alas! How easily is the human mind thrown off its "balance," especially when it is stayed on *this world* only—and has no experimental knowledge of the meaning of the injunction of Scripture to cast all our cares upon Him who careth for us, and who heareth even the young ravens when they cry.

QUESTIONS.—1. You may sketch the circumstances here narrated. 2. How do you account for the *unhinging* of this man's mind? 3. Is it common that one idea keeps possession of a maniac's mind?

ERRORS.—*Hosp-tal* for hos-pi-tal; *as-sid-di-ous* for as-sid-u-ous; *de-fi-cit* for def-i-cit. (pronounced def-e-cit)

SPELL AND DEFINE.—(1) hospital, commanding, melancholy; (2) measured; (3) contemplation, traveler; (4) assiduous, finance; (6) defaulter, secretaries, miscalculation, multiplying; (7) imprisonment; (8) solicited; (9) experimental.

LESSON III.

RULE.—Be careful to pronounce every syllable distinctly, and not to join the words together.

EXERCISES UNDER THE RULE. To be read over several times by all the pupils.

They *reef'd* the top-sails. No dangers *fright* him.

He *quenched* a flame. She *laughs at* him.

A *frame of adamant. She begged pardon.*

Thou *look'st from* thy throne in the clouds, and laugh'st at the storm.

The *glow-worm* lights her lamp.

The table *groans beneath* its burden.

All clothed in *rags an infant* lay.

The birds were all *fledg'd in* the nest.

Scene at the Sandwich Islands.
STEWART.

1. At an early hour of the morning, even before we had taken our breakfast on board ship, a single islander here or there, or a group of three or four, wrapped in their large mantles of various hues, might be seen winding their way among the groves fringing the bay on the east, or descending from the hills and ravine on the north, towards the chapel. By degrees their numbers increased, until, in a short time, every path along the beach and over the uplands presented an almost uninterrupted procession of both sexes, and of every age, all pressing to the house of God.

2. So few canoes were round the ship yesterday, and the landing-place had been so little thronged, as our boats passed to and fro, that one might have thought the district but thinly inhabited. Now, such mulitudes were seen gathering from various directions that the exclamation, *"What crowds of people! What crowds of people!"* was heard from the quarter-deck to the forecastle.

3. Even to myself it was a sight of surprise; surprise not at the magnitude of the population, but that the object for which they were evidently assembling should bring together so great a multitude. As my thoughts re-echoed the words, "What crowds of people!" remembrances and affections of deep power came over me, and the silent musings of my heart were, "What a change—what a happy change!"

4. At this very place, only four years ago, the known wishes and example of chiefs of high authority, the daily persuasion of teachers, added to motives of curiosity and novelty, could scarcely induce a hundred of the inhabitants to give an irregular,

careless, and impatient attendance on the services of
the sanctuary. But now,

"Like mountain torrents pouring to the main,
From every glen a living stream came forth—
From every hill, in crowds, they hastened down,
To worship Him, who deigns, in humblest fane,
On wildest shore, to meet th' upright in heart."

5. The scene, as looked on from our ship, in the
stillness of a brightly-beaming Sabbath morning, was
well calculated, with its associations, to prepare the
mind for strong impressions on a nearer view, when
the conclusion of our own public worship should allow
us to go on shore. Mr. Goodrich had apprised us that
he had found it expedient to hold both the services
of the Sabbath in the forepart of the day, that all
might have the benefit of two sermons and still reach
their abodes before nightfall. For,

"Numbers dwelt remote,
And first must traverse many a weary mile,
To reach the altar of the God they love."

6. It was arranged, that, on this occasion, the
second service should be postponed until the officers
should be at liberty to leave the ship. It was near 12
o'clock when we went on shore—the captain and first
lieutenant, the purser, surgeon, several of the midshipmen, and me. Though the services had commenced when we landed, large numbers were seen
circling the doors without. As we afterwards found,
this was only from the impracticability of obtaining
places within.

7. The house is an immense structure capable of
containing many thousands, every part of which was
filled, except a small area in front of the pulpit where
seats were reserved for us, and to which we made our
way, in slow and tedious procession, from the difficul-

ty of finding a spot to place even our footsteps, without treading on limbs of the people, seated on their feet, as closely, almost, as they could be stowed.

8. As we entered, Mr Goodrich paused in his sermon, until we should be seated. I ascended the pulpit beside him from which I had a full view of the congregation. The suspense of attention in the people was only momentary, notwithstanding the entire novelty to them of the laced coats, cocked hats, and other appendages of naval uniform. I can scarcely describe the emotions experienced in glancing an eye over the immense number, seated so thickly on the matted floor as to seem literally one mass of heads, covering an area of more than nine thousand square feet. The sight was most striking, and soon became, not only to myself, but to some of my fellow officers, deeply affecting.

9. I have listened with delighted attention to some of the highest eloquence, the pulpits of America and England of the present day can boast. I have seen tears of conviction and penitence flow freely, under the sterner truths of the word of God; but it was left for one at Hido, the most obscure corner of these distant islands, to excite the liveliest emotions ever experienced, and leave the deepest impressions of the extent and unsearchable riches of the gospel, which I have ever known.

10. It seemed, even while I gazed, that the majesty of that Power might be seen rising and erecting to itself a throne, permanent as glorious, in the hearts of these but late utterly benighted and deeply-polluted people. When I compared them, as they had once been known to me, and as they now appeared, the change seemed the effect of a mandate scarcely less mighty in its power, or speedy in its result, than that exhibited when it was said, *"Let there be light," "and there was light!"*

11. The depth of the impression arose from the irresistible conviction that the SPIRIT OF GOD was there. It could have been nothing else. With the exception of the inferior chiefs, having charge of the district, and their dependents, of two or three native members of the church, and of the mission family, scarcely one of the whole multitude was in other than the native dress, the simple garments of their primitive state.

12. In this respect, and in the attitude of sitting, the assembly was purely pagan. But the breathless silence, the eager attention, the half-suppressed sigh, the tear, the various feeling, sad, peaceful, joyous, discoverable in the faces of many—all spoke the presence of an invisible but omnipotent Power—the Power which alone can melt and renew the heart of man, even as it alone first brought it into existence.

13. It was, in a word, a heathen congregation laying hold on the hopes of eternity—a heathen congregation, fully sensible of the degradation of their original state, exulting in the first beams of truth, and in the no uncertain dawning of the Sun of Righteousness: thirsting after knowledge, even while they sweetly drank of the waters of life; and, under the inspiring influence, by every look, expressing the heartfelt truth—"Beautiful on the mountains are the feet of him that bringeth good tidings; that bringeth good tidings of good, that publisheth SALVATION!"

14. The simple appearance and yet Christian deportment of that obscure congregation, whom I had once known, and at no remote period, only as a set of rude, licentious, and wild pagans, did more to rivet the conviction of the divine origin of the Bible, and of the holy influences by which it is accompanied to the hearts of men, than all the arguments, and apologies, and defences of Christianity I ever read.

15. An entire moral reformation has taken place.

Instruction of every kind is eagerly and universally
sought, and from many a humble dwelling, now

"Is daily heard
The voice of prayer and praise to Jacob's God:
And many a heart in secret heaves the sigh,
To Him who hears, well pleased, the sigh
   contrite."

QUESTIONS.—1. Where are the Sandwich Islands?   2. What
is the degree of population?   3. What change has taken place
in the moral character of the population and in how long a
time?   4. To what is this change to be attributed?   5. Give your
own description of this.

ERRORS.—*A-fore* for be-fore; *dur-rec-tions* for di-rec-tions; *cep-
tions* for ex-cep-tions; *pul-lu-ted* for pol-lu-ted.

SPELL AND DEFINE.—(1) uninterrupted, procession;
(2) multitudes; (3) remembrances, re-echoed, assembling;
(4) hundred, irregular, inhabitants;   (5) associations, apprized,
nightfall;   (6) postponed, midshipmen, impracticability;
(8) congregation, appendages;

LESSON IV.

RULE.—Be careful to pronounce every syllable distinctly, and
not to join the words together.

EXERCISES UNDER THE RULE. To be read over several
times by all the pupils.

My *Uncle Toby* was *racked with* pain.

Racked with whirlwinds.

Victory will weaken the enemy.

Think'st thou so meanly of me?

On *the River Elbe.* We saw *the Elk.*

And he cried, *hold, hold, hold.*

The *wolf who howl's his* watch.

Fall'n, fall'n, fall'n, fall'n, fall'n, from his high estate.

There was no *help for* it.

He *watch'd and wept,* he *felt and pray'd* for all.

It was a *willfully false* account.

Contrasted Soliloquies.—JANE TAYLOR.

1. "Alas!" exclaimed a silver-headed sage, "how narrow is the utmost extent of human science!—how circumscribed the sphere of intellectual exertion! I have spent my life in acquiring knowledge, but how little do I know! The farther I attempt to penetrate the secrets of nature, the more I am bewildered and benighted. Beyond a certain limit, all is but confusion or conjecture, so that the advantage of the learned over the ignorant consists greatly in having ascertained how little is to be known.

2. "It is true that I can measure the sun and compute the distances of the planets. I can calculate their periodical movements, and even ascertain the laws by which they perform their sublime revolutions, but with regard to their construction, and the beings which inhabit them, what do I know more than the clown?

3. "Delighting to examine the economy of nature in our own world, I have analyzed the elements and have given names to their component parts. Yet, should I not be as much at a loss to explain the burning of fire, or to account for the liquid quality of water, as the vulgar who use and enjoy them without thought or examination?

4. "I remark that all bodies, unsupported, fall to the ground, and I am taught to account for this by the law of gravitation. What have I gained here more than a term? Does it convey to my mind any idea of the nature of that mysterious and invisible chain which draws all things to a common center? I observe the effect, I give a name to the cause, but can I explain or comprehend it?

5. "Pursuing the track of the naturalist, I have learned to distinguish the *animal, vegetable* and *mineral* kingdoms, and to divide these into their

distinct tribes and families; but can I tell, after all this toil, whence a single blade of grass derives its vitality? Could the most minute researches enable me to discover the exquisite pencil that paints and fringes the flower of the field? Have I ever detected the secret that gives their brilliant dye to the ruby and the emerald, or the art that enamels the delicate shell?

6. "I observe the sagacity of animals. I call it *instinct*, and speculate upon its various degrees of approximation to the reason of man. After all, I know as little of the cogitations of the brute as he does of mine. When I see a flight of birds overhead, performing their evolutions, or steering their course to some distant settlement, their signals and cries are as unintelligible to me as are the learned languages to the unlettered rustic. I understand as little of their policy and laws as they do of Blackstone's Commentaries.

7. "Leaving the material creation, my thoughts have often ascended to loftier subjects, and indulged in *metaphysical* speculation. Here, while I easily perceive in myself the two distinct qualities of matter and mind, I am baffled in every attempt to comprehend their mutual dependence and mysterious connection. When my hand moves in obedience to my will, have I the most distant conception of the manner in which the volition is either communicated or understood? Thus, in the exercise of one of the most simple and ordinary actions, I am perplexed and confounded if I attempt to account for it.

8. "Again, how many years of my life were devoted to the acquisition of those *languages*, by the means of which I might explore the records of remote ages, and become familiar with the learning and literature of other times! What have I gathered from these, but the mortifying fact that man has ever been struggling with his own impotence, and vainly endeavoring to

overleap the bounds which limit his anxious inquiries?

9. "Alas! Then, what have I gained by my laborious researches, but a humbling conviction of my weakness and ignorance? How little has man, at his best estate, of which to boast! What folly in him to glory in his contracted power, or to value himself upon his imperfect acquisitions!"

10. "Well," exclaimed a young lady, just returned from school, "my education is at last finished!— Indeed, it would be strange, if, after five years' hard application, anything were left incomplete. Happily, *that* is all over now and I have nothing to do but to exercise my various accomplishments.

11. "Let me see!—As to *French*, I am complete mistress of that, and speak it, if possible, with more fluency than English. *Italian* I can read with ease, and pronounce very well. As well, at least, as any of my friends, and that is all one need wish for in Italian. *Music* I have learned until I am perfectly sick of it. Now that we have a grand piano, it will be delightful to play when we have company. I must still continue to practice a little, the only thing, I think, that I need now to improve myself in. Then there are my Italian songs which everybody allows I sing with taste. As it is what so few people can pretend to, I am particularly glad that I can.

12. "My *drawings* are universally admired— especially the shells and flowers, which are beautiful, certainly. Besides this, I have a decided taste in all kinds of fancy ornaments. Then my *dancing* and *waltzing*—in which our master himself owned that he could take me no farther—just the figure for it, certainly; it would be unpardonable if I did not excel.

13. "As to *common* things, *geography* and *history*, and *poetry*, and *philosophy*—thank my stars, I have got through them all so that I may consider myself not only perfectly accomplished, but also thoroughly

well informed. Well, to be sure, how much I have worked through! The only wonder is that one head can contain it all!''

QUESTIONS.—1. What is the subject of this lesson? 2. What is meant by "Soliloquies?" 3. What soliloquies are here contrasted? 4. What is the substance of the old man's soliloquy? 5. What is the substance of the young lady's? 6. Which reasons most correctly, the old man or the young lady? 7. What feeling is manifested by the old man in view of his attainments? 8. What by the young lady?   9. If we are truly wise, will we be vain?

ERRORS.—*Nar-rer* and *nar-ry* for nar-row; *be-yund* for be-yond; *cal-kil-ate* for cal-cu-late; *in-joy* for en-joy; *Black-stun* for Blackstone; *ed-e-ca-tion* for ed-u-ca-tion; *flu'n-cy* for flu-en-cy; *jog-ra-phy* for ge-og-ra-phy; *his-try* for his-to-ry; *kin* for can.

SPELL AND DEFINE.—(1) circumscribed, intellectual, penetrate, conjecture, ascertained; (2) compute, ascertain, revolutions, construction; (3) economy, analyzed, component; (4) gravitation; (5) exquisite, animal, vegetable, mineral, vitality, enamels; (6) sagacity, instinct, approximation, cogitation, unintelligible; (7) metaphysical, volition; (10) incomplete; (11) fluency; (12) waltzing.

LESSON V.

RULE.—Be careful to pronounce every syllable distinctly, and not to join the words together.

EXERCISES UNDER THE RULE. To be read over several times by all the pupils.

It was a species of *calx, which* he showed me.

The word *filch is* of doubtful derivation.

If thou *fall'st*, thou *fall'st* a blessed martyr.

Health is indispensable to the soldier.

Those who lie *entombed in* the cemetery.

The *attempt and* not the deed confounds us.

But truth *and* liberty *and* virtue would fall with him.

The *song began* from Jove.

Do you mean *plain* or *playing*?

On Letter Writing.—BLACKWOOD.

1. Epistolary as well as personal discourse is, according to the mode in which it is carried on, one of the pleasantest or most irksome things in the world. It is delightful to drop in on a friend without the solemn prelude of invitation and acceptance—to join a social circle, where we may suffer our minds and hearts to relax and expand in the happy consciousness of perfect security from invidious remark and carping criticism. We may give the reins to the sportiveness of innocent fancy, or the enthusiasm of warmhearted feeling. We may talk sense or nonsense, (I pity people who *cannot* talk nonsense,) without fear of being looked into icicles by the coldness of unimaginative people, living pieces of clockwork, who dare not themselves utter a word, or lift up a little finger, without first weighing the important point in the hair balance of propriety and good breeding.

2. It is equally delightful to *let* the pen talk freely, and unpremeditatedly, and to one by whom we are sure of being understood, but a formal letter, like a ceremonious morning visit, is tedious alike to the writer and receiver—for the most part spun out with unmeaning phrases, trite observations, complimentary flourishes, and protestations of respect and attachment, so far not deceitful, as they never deceive anybody. Oh the misery of having to compose a set, proper, well worded, correctly pointed, polite, elegant epistle!—One that must have a beginning, a middle, and an end, as methodically arranged and portioned out as the several parts of a sermon under three heads, or the three gradations of shade in a schoolgirl's first landscape!

3. For my part, I would rather be set to beat hemp, or weed in a turnip field, than to write a letter exactly every month, or every fortnight, at the precise point

of time from the date of our correspondent's last
letter, that he or she wrote after the reception of
ours—as if one's thoughts bubbled up to the wellhead,
at regular periods, a pint at a time, to be bottled off
for immediate use. Thought! What has thought to do
in such a correspondence? It murders thought,
quenches fancy, wastes time, spoils paper, wears out
innocent goose-quills—"I'd rather be a kitten, and cry
mew, than one of those same" prosing lettermongers.

4. Surely in this age of invention something may
be struck out to obviate the necessity (if such
necessity exists) of so tasking—degrading the human
intellect. Why should not a sort of mute barrel organ
be constructed on the plan of those that play sets of
tunes and country dances, to indite a catalogue of
polite epistles calculated for all the ceremonious observances of good breeding? Oh the unspeakable relief
(could such a machine be invented) of having only to
grind an answer to one of one's "dear five hundred
friends!"

5. Or, suppose there were to be an epistolary steam-
engine—ay, that's the thing—steam does everything
nowadays. Dear Mr. Brunel, set about it, I beseech
you, and achieve the most glorious of your undertak-
ings. The block-machine at Portsmouth would be
nothing to it—*that* spares manual labor—this would
relieve mental drudgery, and thousands yet unborn
- - - But hold! I am not so sure the female sex in
general may quite enter into my views of the subject.

6. Those who pique themselves on the elegant style
of their billets, or those fair scribblerinas just emancipated from boarding school restraints, or the
dragonism of their governess, just beginning to taste
the refined enjoyments of sentimental, confidential,
soul-breathing correspondence with some Angelina,
Seraphina, or Laura Matilda; to indite beautiful lit-

tle notes, with long-tailed letters, upon vellum paper, with pink margins sealed with sweet mottoes, and dainty devices, the whole deliciously perfumed with musk and attar of roses—young ladies who collect "copies of verses," and charades—keep albums—copy patterns—make bread seals—work little dogs upon footstools, and paint flowers without shadow. Oh, no, the epistolary steam engine will never come into vogue with those dear creatures. *They* must enjoy the "feast of reason, and the flow of soul," and they must write. Yes, and how they *do* write!

7. But for another genus of female scribes— unhappy innocents! Who groan in spirit at the dire necessity of having to hammer out one of those aforesaid terrible epistles. They, in due form, date the gilt-edged sheet that lies outspread before them in appalling whiteness, having also felicitously achieved the graceful exordium, "My dear Mrs. P." or "My dear Lady V." or "My dear—anything else," feel that they are *in for it*, and must say something. Oh, that something that must come of nothing! those bricks that must be made without straw! those pages that must be filled with words! Yea, with words that must be sewed into sentences! Yea, with sentences that must *seem* to mean something, the whole to be tacked together, all neatly fitted and dovetailed so as to form one smooth, polished surface!

8. What were the labors of Hercules to such a task! The very thought of it puts me into a mental perspiration, and, from my inmost soul, I compassionate the unfortunates now (at this very moment, perhaps,) sitting perpendicular in the seat of torture, having in the right hand a fresh-nibbed patent pen, dipped ever and anon into the ink-bottle, as if to hook up ideas, and under the outspread palm of the left hand a fair sheet of best Bath post, (ready to receive thoughts

yet unhatched,) on which their eyes are riveted with a stare of disconsolate perplexity infinitely touching to a feeling mind.

9. To such unhappy persons, in whose miseries I deeply sympathize - - - have I not groaned under similar horrors, from the hour when I was first shut up (under lock and key, I believe,) to indite a dutiful epistle to an honored aunt? I remember, as if it were yesterday, the moment when she who had enjoined the task entered to inspect the performance, which, by her calculation, should have been fully completed. I remember how sheepishly I hung down my head when she snatched from before me the paper, (on which I had made no further progress than "My dear *ant*,") angrily exclaiming, "What, child! have you been shut up here three hours to call your aunt a pismire?" From that hour of humiliation I have too often groaned under the endurance of similar penance, and I have learned from my own sufferings to compassionate those of my dear sisters in affliction. To such unhappy persons, then, I would fain offer a few hints, (the fruit of long experience,) which, if they have not already been suggested by their own observation, may prove serviceable in the hour of emergency.

10. Let them - - - or suppose I address myself to *one* particular sufferer—there is something more confidential in that manner of communicating one's ideas. As Moore says, "Heart speaks to heart"—I say, then, take always special care to write by candlelight, for not only is the apparently unimportant operation of snuffing the candle in itself a momentary relief to the depressing consciousness of mental vacuum, but not unfrequently that trifling act, or the brightening flame of the taper, elicits, as it were, from the dull embers of fancy, a sympathetic spark of fortunate conception. When such a one occurs, seize it quickly and dexterously, but, at the same time, with such

cautious prudence, as not to huddle up and contract in one short, paltry sentence, that which, if ingeniously handled, may be wire-drawn, so as to undulate gracefully and smoothly over a whole page.

11. For the more ready practice of this invaluable art of dilating, it will be expedient to stock your memory with a large assortment of those precious words of many syllables that fill whole lines at once, "incomprehensibly, amazingly, decidedly, solicitously, inconceivably, incontrovertibly." An opportunity of using these is, to a distressed spinner as delightful as a copy all m's and n's to a child. "Command you may, your mind from play." They run on with such delicious smoothness! * * * *

QUESTIONS.—1. Upon what does the pleasure of epistolary and social discourse depend? 2. What is meant by talking *nonsense*? 3. What is the intention of the writer of this piece? 4. From whom does the author quote in the sentence, "Heart speaks to heart."

ERRORS.—*Pre-lude* for prel-ude; '*xac-ly* for ex-act-ly; *sued* for sewed (pronounced sude); *Herc-les* for Her-cu-les; *per-tic-lar* for par-tic-u-lar.

SPELL AND DEFINE.—(1) epistolary, invidious, enthusiasm, nonsense, unimaginative; (3) wellhead, correspondent, lettermonger; (4) invention; (5) manual; (6) scribblerinas, emancipated; (7) genus; (8) mental, compassionate, disconsolate; (9) humiliation; (10) elicits, communicating, dilate.

LESSON VI.

RULE.—Be careful to pronounce every syllable distinctly and not to join the words together.

EXERCISES UNDER THE RULE. To be read over several times by all the pupils.

The *range of* the valleys is his.

He was the *first ambassador sent.*

Swords and pens were both employed.

I do not *flinch from* the argument.

He never *winced, for* it hurt him not

Do not *singe your* gown.

Pluck'd from its native tree.

Nipt in the bud.

Thou *found'st me* poor, and *keep'st me* so.

Ginevra.—ROGERS.

1. If ever you should come to Modena,
    Stop at a palace near the Reggio-gate,
    Dwelt in of old by one of the Donati.
    Its noble gardens, terrace above terrace,
    And rich in fountains, statues, cypresses,
    Will long detain you—but, before you go,
    Enter the house—forget it not, I pray you—
    And look awhile upon a picture there.

2. 'Tis of a lady in her earliest youth,
    The last of that illustrious family;
    Done by Zampieri—but by whom I care not.
    He, who observes it—ere he passes on,
    Gazes his fill, and comes and comes again,
    That he may call it up when far away.

3. She sits, inclining forward as to speak,
    Her lips half open, and her finger up,
    As though she said, "Beware!" Her vest of gold
    Broidered with flowers and clasped from head
        to foot
    An emerald stone in every golden clasp;
    And on her brow, fairer than alabaster,
    A coronet of pearls.

4. But then her face,
   So lovely, yet so arch, so full of mirth,
   The overflowings of an innocent heart—
   It haunts me still, though many a year has fled,
   Like some wild melody!

5. Alone it hangs
   Over a mouldering heirloom; its companion,
   An oaken chest, half-eaten by the worm,
   But richly carved by Antony of Trent
   With scripture-stories from the life of Christ;
   A chest that came from Venice, and had held
   The ducal robes of some old ancestors—
   That by the way—it may be true or false—
   But don't forget the picture; and you will not,
   When you have heard the tale they told me there

6. She was an only child—her name Ginevra,
   The joy, the pride of an indulgent father;
   And in her fifteenth year became a bride,
   Marrying an only son, Francesco Doria,
   Her playmate from her birth, and her first love.

7. Just as she looks there, in her bridal dress,
   She was, all gentleness, all gayety,
   Her pranks the favorite theme of every tongue.
   But now the day was come, the day, the hour;
   Now, frowning, smiling for the hundredth time,
   The nurse, that ancient lady, preached deco'rum;
   And, in the luster of her youth, she gave
   Her hand, with her heart in it, to Francesco.

8. Great was the joy; but at the nuptial feast,
   When all sat down, the bride herself was wanting.
   Nor was she to be found! Her father cried,
   " 'Tis but to make a trial of our love!"
   And filled his glass to all; but his hand shook,
   And soon from guest to guest the panic spread.

9. 'Twas but that instant she had left Francesco,
   Laughing and looking back and flying still,
   Her ivory tooth imprinted on his finger.
   But now, alas! she was not to be found;
   Nor from that hour could anything be guessed,
   But that she was not!

10. Weary of his life,
    Francesco flew to Venice, and embarking,
    Flung it away in battle with the Turk.
    Donati lived—and long might you have seen
    An old man wandering as in quest of something,
    Something he could not find—he knew not what.
    When he was gone, the house remained awhile
    Silent and tenantless—then went to strangers.

11. Full fifty years were past, and all forgotten,
    When on an idle day, a day of search
    Mid the old lumber in the gallery,
    That mouldering chest was noticed; and 'twas
        said
    By one as young, as thoughtless as Ginevra,
    "Why not remove it from its lurking-place?"
    'Twas done as soon as said; but on the way
    It burst, it fell; and lo! a skeleton
    With here and there a pearl, an emerald-stone,
    A golden clasp, clasping a shred of gold.
    All else had perished—save a wedding ring,
    And a small seal, her mother's legacy,
    Engraven with a name, the name of both—
    "Ginevra."

12. —There then had she found a grave!
    Within that chest had she concealed herself,
    Fluttering with joy, the happiest of the happy;
    When a spring lock, that lay in ambush there,
    Fastened her down forever!

QUESTIONS.—1. Where is Modena? 2. Who was the painter of the picture? 3. Describe the attitude and dress. 4. What lies beneath the picture? 5. Relate the story which gives interest to the chest and picture.

ERRORS.—*Reg-gi-o* for Red-ge-o; *hont* for haunt (pronounced hant); *an-cient* for an-cient; *sred* for shred.

SPELL AND DEFINE.—(1) statues, terrace, cypresses; (2) illustrious; (3) broidered, emerald; (4) overflowing; (5) mouldering, ancestors, heirloom; (6) indulgent; (7) ancient; (8) nuptial; (9) imprinted; (10) embarking; (11) engraven, emerald; (12) ambush.

LESSON VII.

RULE.—Be careful to pronounce every syllable distinctly, and not to join the words together.

EXERCISES UNDER THE RULE. To be read over several times by all the pupils.

We constructed *an arc* and began the problem.

The *surf beat* heavily.

Arm! warriors, arm!

Return to thy dwelling, *all lovely return.*

Weave the warp and *weave the woof.*

Lend me *Smith's Thucydides.*

Thou tear'st my heart asunder.

I give my hand and *heart too to* this vote.

The Whale Ship.—PROV. LIT. JOURNAL.

1. They who go down to the sea in ships pursue a perilous vocation, and well deserve the prayers which are offered for them in the churches. It is a hard life—full of danger, and of strange attraction. The seaman rarely abandons the glorious sea. It requires, however, a pretty firm spirit, both to brave the ordinary dangers of the deep, and to carry on war with its

mightiest tenants. Yet it is a service readily entered
upon, and zealously followed, though indisputably the
most laborious and most terrific of all human pursuits. Well might Burke speak glowingly of that
hardy spirit of adventure which had pursued this
gigantic game, from the constellations of the north
to the frozen serpent of the south.

2. The most common accident to which whalemen
are exposed is that of being 'stove,' as they express
it, by the huge animal, before they can back out from
their dangerous proximity. A slight tap of his tail is
quite sufficient to shiver a common whaleboat to
atoms. If this danger be escaped, the whale, with the
harpoon in his hide, sinks beneath the sounding of
the deep-sea lead. Not long will he stay at the bottom. He rises for air, and this is a signal for the
renewal of the battle. The boat is drawn up, and the
lance is buried in his giant body. Not safe is the game
until it is fairly bagged. Often, in the moment of victory, the vanquished leviathan settles quietly down
in the deep sea, and no tackle can draw him up. The
curses of the exhausted seamen are 'not loud, but
deep.'

3. On the twenty-eighth of May, 1817, the Royal
Bounty, an English ship, fell in with a great number
of whales. There was neither ice nor land in sight, The
boats were manned and sent in pursuit. After a chase
of five hours, a harpooner, who had rowed out of sight
of the ship, struck one of the whales. This was about
four o'clock in the morning. The captain directed the
course of the ship to the place where he had last seen
the boats, and at about eight o'clock got sight of the
boat which displayed the signal for being fast. Soon
after, another boat approached the first, and struck
a second harpoon.

4. By mid-day, two more harpoons were struck,
but such was the astonishing vigor of the whale, that

although it constantly dragged through the water from four to six boats, together with sixteen hundred fathoms of line, yet it pursued its flight nearly as fast as a boat could row. Whenever a boat passed beyond its tail, it would dive. All endeavors to lance it were therefore in vain. The crews of the loose boats then moored themselves to the fast boats. At eight o'clock in the evening, a line was taken to the ship, with a view of retarding its flight, and topsails were lowered, but the harpoon 'drew.' In three hours, another line was taken on board, which immediately snapped.

5. At four in the afternoon of the next day, thirty-six hours after the whale was struck, two of the fast lines were taken on board the ship. The wind blowing a moderately brisk breeze, the topgallant sails were taken in, the courses hauled up, and the topsails clewed down. In this situation she was towed directly to windward during an hour and a half, with the velocity of from one and a half to two knots. Then though the whale must have been greatly exhausted, it beat the water with its fins and tail so tremendously that the sea around was in a continual foam and the most hardy seamen scarcely dared to approach it. At length, at about eight o'clock, after forty hours of incessant exertion, this formidable and astonishingly vigorous animal was killed.

6. But the most strange and dreadful calamity, that ever befell the wanderers of the sea, in any age, was that which happened in 1820, to the ship Essex, of Nantucket. Some of those who survived the terrible catastrophe are yet alive, and bear their united testimony to the truth of the statements which one of them has published. It is a story which no man, for any conceivable purpose, would be likely to invent. The captain of the Essex is yet living upon his native island, and it is a fact filled with meaning, that, so vivid, to this day, is his recollection of the horrors

which he witnessed, that he is never heard to mention the subject, and nothing can induce him to speak of it. He has abandoned the sea forever. The story bears the marks of truth upon it. It may be briefly told.

7. The Essex, a sound and substantial ship, sailed for the Pacific Ocean, on a whaling voyage, from Nantucket, on the 12th of August, 1820. On the 20th of November, a shoal of whales was discovered. Three boats were manned and sent in pursuit. The mate's boat was struck by a whale, and he was obliged to return to the ship to repair the damage. While thus engaged, a sperm whale, eighty-five feet long, broke water about twenty rods from the ship, on her weather bow. He was going at the rate of three knots an hour, and the ship at the same rate, when he struck the bows of the vessel just forward of the chains.

8. The shock produced by the collision of two such masses of matter in motion, may well be imagined. The ship shook like a leaf. The whale 'dove,' passed under the vessel—grazed her keel—and appeared at the ship's length distant, lashing the sea with his fins and tail, as if suffering the most horrible agony. He was evidently hurt by the collision, and rendered frantic with rage. In a few minutes he seemed to recover himself, and started, with great speed, directly across the bows of the vessel to windward. Meantime the hands on board discovered the vessel to be gradually settling down by the bows, and the pumps were to be rigged. While engaged in fixing the pumps, one of the men exclaimed, 'Here he comes upon us again!'

9. The whale had turned, at the distance of one hundred rods from the ship, and was making for her with double his former speed. His pathway was white with foam. He struck her bow, and the blow shook every timber in the ship. Her bows were stove in. The whale dove under the vessel and disappeared. The

vessel immediately filled; and the crew took to the boat that had returned. All this was transacted in the space of a few minutes. The other boats rowed up, and when they came together—when a sense of their loneliness and helplessness came over them—no man had the power of utterance. They were in the midst of the 'illimitable sea'—far, far from land—in open whaleboats, relying only on God for succor, in this hour of their utmost need.

10. They gathered what they could from the wreck. The ship went down, and on the 22nd of November, they put away for the coast of South America—distant two thousand miles! How their hearts must have died within them, as they looked at the prospect before and around them! After incredible hardships and sufferings, on the 20th of December, they reached a low island. It was a mere sandbank, almost barren, which supplied them with nothing but water. On this island, desolate as it was, three of the men chose to remain, rather than to commit themselves again to the uncertain chances of the sea.

11. On the 27th of December, the three boats, with the remainder of the men, started in company from the island for Juan Fernandez, a distance of two thousand five hundred miles! On the 12th of January, the boats parted company in a gale.

12. The mate's boat was taken up by the Indian, of London, on the 19th of February, *ninety-three days* from the time of the catastrophe, with three living men of that boat's crew. The captain's boat was taken up on the 23rd of February, by the Dauphin, of Nantucket. The other boat was never heard from. The three men who were left on the island were saved by a ship which was sent for their deliverance. No wonder that the heart of that brave man recoils and shudders when this terrific scene is forced upon his recollection.

QUESTIONS.—1. What is the character of the seaman's profession? Particularly of the whalemen? 2. What are the most common accidents to which whalers are liable? 3. How do they often lose their game when vanquished? 4. How long was the whale first mentioned (3-5) in being vanquished? 5. At what rate was he able to draw the ship through the water? 6. Can you give a sketch of what occurred to the ship Essex in 1820? 7. Narrate the adventures and fate of the crew, after the destruction of their vessel.

ERRORS.—*Ord-na-ry* for or-di-na-ry; *pur-ty* or *per-ty* for pretty; *vict-ry* for vic-to-ry.

SPELL AND DEFINE.—(1) zealously, indisputably, glowingly, gigantic, constellations; (2) proximity, vanquished, leviathan; (3) approached, harpoon; (4) fathoms, moored, retarding; (5) moderately, topgallant, clewed, windward, exhausted, tremendously, incessant, formidable.

LESSON VIII.

. RULE.—Be careful to pronounce every syllable distinctly, and not to join the words together.

EXERCISES UNDER THE RULE. To be read over several times by all the pupils.

We saw a *large dead fish, floating*.

And he *slew him.*

Every *man's house is* his castle.

This meteorous vapor is called *"Will o' the wisp."*

I thrust three thousand thistles through the thick of my thumb.

Braid broad braids, my *brave babes.*

We never *swerved*, but lost our *swivel* gun.

The Winged Worshipers.—SPRAGUE.

[Addressed to two swallows, that flew into Church during Divine Service.]

1. Happy, guiltless pair,
   What seek ye from the fields of heaven?
   Ye have no need of prayer,
   Ye have no sins to be forgiven.

2. Why perch ye here,
   Where mortals to their Maker bend?
   Can your pure spirits fear
   The God ye never could offend?

3. Ye never knew
   The crimes for which we come to weep:
   Penance is not for you,
   Bless'd wand'rers of the upper deep.

4. To you 'tis given
   To wake sweet nature's untaught lays;
   Beneath the arch of heaven
   To chirp away a life of praise.

5. Then spread each wing,
   Far, far above, o'er lakes and lands,
   And join the choirs that sing
   In yon blue dome not reared with hands.

6. Or if ye stay
   To note the consecrated hour,
   Teach me the airy way,
   And let me try your envied power.

7. Above the crowd,
   On upward wings could I but fly,
   I'd bathe in yon bright cloud,
   And seek the stars that gem the sky.

8. 'Twere heaven indeed,
   Through fields of trackless light to soar,
   On nature's charms to feed,
   And nature's own great God adore.

QUESTIONS.—1. On what occasion was this poem written? 2. We address letters to our friends—was this addressed to the birds in the same sense? 3. Do you discover any beautiful expressions in this lesson? 4. Point them out.

ERRORS.—*Par* for pair; *prar* for pray-er; *en-vide* for en-vi-ed.

SPELL AND DEFINE.—(1) guiltless; (2) perch; (3) penance; (4) untaught; (5) choirs; (6) consecrated; (8) trackless.

LESSON IX.

RULE.—Be careful to pronounce every syllable distinctly, and not to join the words together.

EXERCISES UNDER THE RULE. To be read over several times by all the pupils.

The bell *tinkles*; the man *truckles* to power.

Thou *chuckl'dst* over thy gains too soon.

It was *barb'd* and *bulb'd*.

The *bulbs* are sprouting.

The pert fairies and the dapper *elves*.

Is this *delft*, or *delf ware*?

The *costliest silks* are there.

Overwhelm'd with whirlwinds and tempestuous fire.

Death at the Mirror
DIARY OF A PHYSICIAN.

1. "What can Charlotte be doing all this while?" inquired her mother. She listened—"I have not heard her moving for the last three quarters of an hour! I will call the maid and ask." She rang the bell, and the servant appeared.

2. "Betty, Miss Jones is not gone yet, is she? Go up to her room, Betty, and see if she wants anything, and tell her it is half past nine o'clock," said Mrs. Jones. The servant accordingly went up stairs, and

knocked at the bedroom door, once, twice, thrice, but received no answer. There was a dead silence, except when the wind shook the window. Could Miss Jones have fallen asleep? Oh, impossible!

3. She knocked again, but as unsuccessfully as before. She became a little flustered; and after a moment's pause opened the door and entered. There was Miss Jones sitting in front of her mirror. "Why ma'am!" commenced Betty in a petulant tone, walking up to her, "here have I been knocking for these five minutes, and"—Betty staggered, horror struck, and uttering a loud shriek, alarmed Mrs. Jones, who instantly tottered up stairs, almost palsied with fright. Miss Jones was dead!

4. I was there within a few minutes, for my house was not more than two streets distant. It was a stormy night in March; and the desolate aspect of things without—deserted streets—the dreary howling of the wind; and the incessant pattering of the rain—contributed to cast a gloom over my mind, when connected with the intelligence of the awful event that had summoned me out, which was deepened into horror by the spectacle I was doomed to witness.

5. On reaching the house, I found Mrs. Jones in violent hysterics, surrounded by several of her neighbors who had been called to her assistance. I went quickly to the scene of death, and beheld what I never shall forget.

6. The room was occupied by a white-curtained bed. There was but one window, and before it was a table, on which stood a looking glass, hung with a little white drapery; and various paraphernalia lay scattered about—pins, brooches, curling papers, ribbons, gloves, etc.

7. An arm chair was drawn to this table, and in it sat Miss Jones, stone dead. Her head rested upon her right hand, her elbow supported by the table; while

her left hung down by her side, grasping a pair of curling irons. Each of her wrists was encircled by a showy gilt bracelet.

8. She was dressed in a white muslin frock, with a little bordering of blonde. Her face was turned towards the glass, which by the light of the expiring candle, reflected with frighful fidelity the clammy, fixed features, daubed with rouge and carmine—the fallen lower jaw—and the eyes directed full into the glass, with a cold stare, that was appalling.

9. On examining the countenance more narrowly, I thought I detected the traces of a smirk of conceit and self-complacency, which not even the palsying touch of death could wholly obliterate. The hair of the corpse, all smooth and glossy, was curled with elaborate precision; and the skinny sallow neck was encircled with a string of glistening pearls. The ghastly visage of death thus leering through the tinselry of fashion—the "vain show" of artificial joy—was a horrible mockery of the fooleries of life!

10. Indeed it was a most humiliating and shocking spectacle. Poor creature! Struck dead in the very act of sacrificing at the shrine of female vanity!

11. On examination of the body, we found that death had been occasioned by disease of the heart. Her life might have been protracted, possibly for years, had she but taken my advice, and that of her mother.

12. I have seen many hundreds of corpses, as well in the calm composure of natural death, as mangled and distorted by violence; but never have I seen so startling a satire upon human vanity, so repulsive, unsightly, and loathsome a spectacle, as a *corpse dressed for a ball*!

QUESTIONS.—1. Narrate, in a few words, the story which you have been reading. 2. What was the true cause of this young

lady's death? 3. Is it common for persons to die suddenly?
4. As no one knows the time of his death, how should all live?
5. What is the reason given in the Bible for obeying parents?
6. Is a ballroom a suitable place to prepare for death?

ERRORS.—*Yit* for yet; *con-trib-it-ed* for con-trib-u-ted;
mus-ling for mus-lin; *nat-er-al* for nat-u-ral.

SPELL AND DEFINE.—(2) impossible; (3) unsuccessfully,
petulant, shriek, palsied; (4) desolate, incessant; (5) hysterics;
(6) drapery, paraphernalia; (7) encircled; (9) obliterate,
elaborate, precision, artificial; (10) humiliating; (11) protracted;
(12) corpse.

LESSON X.

RULE.—Be careful to pronounce every syllable distinctly and
not to join the words together.

EXERCISES UNDER THE RULE. To be read over several
times by all the pupils.

He was *burn'd in* the hand.

He *learned* the art of war in Spain.

A song *bursts* from the groves.

Earth's ample breast.

The *busts of* Fox and Pitt were there.

The *songs broke* the stillness of the night.

A *rat ran over the roof of the house.*

With a *raw lump of liver in his mouth.*

Death of Absalom.—BIBLE.

1. David numbered the people that were with him,
and set captains of thousands and captains of hundreds over them.

2. And David sent forth a third part of the people
under the hand of Joab, and a third part under the
hand of Abishai the son of Zeruiah, Joab's brother,
and a third part under the hand of Ittai the Gittite.
The king said unto the people, "I will surely go forth
with you myself also."

3. But the people answered, "Thou shalt not go forth: for if we flee away, they will not care for us; neither if half of us die, will they care for us; but now thou art worth ten thousand of us: therefore now it is better that thou succor us out of the city."

4. The king said unto them, "What seemeth you best I will do." The king stood by the gate side, and all the people came out by hundreds and by thousands.

5. The king commanded Joab and Abishai and Ittai, saying, "Deal gently for my sake with the young man, even with Absalom." All the people heard when the king gave all the captains charge concerning Absalom.

6. So the people went out into the field against Israel, and the battle was in the wood of Ephraim;

7. Where the poeple of Israel were slain before the servants of David, and there was there a great slaughter that day of twenty thousand men.

8. For the battle was there scattered over the face of all the country: and the wood devoured more people that day than the sword devoured.

9. Absalom met the servants of David, and Absalom rode upon a mule. The mule went under the thick boughs of a great oak, and his head caught hold of the oak, and he was taken up between the heaven and the earth; and the mule that was under him went away.

10. A certain man saw it, and told Joab, and said, "Behold, I saw Absalom hanged in an oak."

11. Joab said unto the man that told him, "Now behold, thou sawest him, and why didst thou not smite him there to the ground? And I would have given thee ten shekels of silver, and a girdle."

12. And the man said unto Joab, "Though I should receive a thousand shekels of silver in my hand, yet would I not put forth my hand against the king's son:

for in our hearing the king charged thee and Abishai and Ittai, saying, 'Beware that none touch the young man Absalom.'

13. "Otherwise I should have wrought falsehood against mine own life: for there is no matter hid from the king, and thou thyself wouldst have set thyself against me."

14. Then said Joab, "I may not tarry thus with thee." He took three darts in his hand, and thrust them through the heart of Absalom, while he was yet alive in the midst of the oak.

15. Ten young men that bare Joab's armor compassed about and smote Absalom, and slew him.

16. Joab blew the trumpet, and the people returned from pursuing after Israel; for Joab held back the people.

17. They took Absalom, and cast him into a great pit in the wood, and laid a very great heap of stones upon him, and all Israel fled everyone to his tent.

18. Now Absalom in his lifetime had taken and reared up for himself a pillar, which is in the king's dale; for he said, I have no son to keep my name in remembrance, and he called the pillar after his own name; and it is called unto this day, Absalom's Place.

19. Then said Ahimaaz the son of Zadok, "Let me now run, and bear the king tidings, how that the Lord hath avenged him of his enemies."

20. Joab said unto him, "Thou shalt not bear tidings this day, but thou shalt bear tidings another day: but this day thou shalt bear no tidings, because the king's son is dead."

21. Then said Joab to Cushi, "Go tell the king what thou hast seen," and Cushi bowed himself unto Joab, and ran.

22. Then said Ahimaaz, the son of Zadok, yet again to Joab, "But howsoever, let me, I pray thee, also run after Cushi." Joab, said, "Wherefore wilt thou run,

my son, seeing that thou hast no tidings ready!"

23. "But howsoever," said he, "let me run," and he said unto him, "Run." Then Ahimaaz ran by the way of the plain, and overran Cushi.

24. David sat between the two gates: and the watchman went up to the roof over the gate unto the wall, and lifted up his eyes, and looked, and behold a man running alone.

25. The watchman cried, and told the king, and the king said, "If he be alone there is tidings in his mouth." He came apace, and drew near.

26. The watchman saw another man running: and the watchman called unto the porter, and said, "Behold, another man running alone." And the king said, "He also bringeth tidings."

27. The watchman said, "Methinketh the running of the foremost is like the running of Ahimaaz the son of Zadok." The king said, "He is a good man, and cometh with good tidings."

28. Ahimaaz called, and said unto the king, "All is well." He fell down to the earth upon his face before the king, and said, "Blessed be the Lord thy God, which hath delivered up the men that lifted up their hand against my lord the king."

29. The king said, "Is the young man Absalom safe?" And Ahimaaz answered, "When Joab sent the king's servant, and me thy servant, I saw a great tumult, but I knew not what it was."

30. The king said unto him, "Turn aside and stand here, and he turned aside, and stood still."

31. Behold, Cushi came; and Cushi said, "Tidings my lord the king; for the Lord hath avenged thee this day of all them that rose up against thee."

32. The king said unto Cushi, "Is the young man Absalom safe?" And Cushi answered, "The enemies of my lord the king, and all that rise against thee to do thee hurt, be as that young man is."

33. The king was much moved, and went up to the chamber over the gate, and wept; and as he went, thus he said, "O my son Absalom! my son, my son Absalom! Would God I had died for thee, O Absalom, my son, my son!"

QUESTIONS.—1. What three oficers did David appoint over the host? 2. Why did not David himself go forth to the battle? 3. What charge did David give to the three officers respecting Absalom? 4. What was the result of the battle? 5. What was the fate of Absalom? 6. What motives probably influenced Joab to such a course of cruelty? 7. What was the effect of the news of Absalom's death upon king David?

ERRORS.—*Pil-lur* for pil-lar; *hend* for hand; *cum-man-did* for com-mand-ed; *Ab-s'lom* for Ab-sa-lom; *rar-ed* for rear-ed; *ti-dins* for ti-dings; *sar-vant* for ser-vant.

SPELL AND DEFINE.—(1) thousands; (3) succor; (5) concerning; (6) Ephraim; (7) slaughter; (11) shekels; (13) otherwise; (15) compassed; (18) remembrance; (19) Ahimaaz; (25) watchman; (27) methinketh; (29) tumult; (31) avenged.

LESSON XI.

RULE.—Be careful to pronounce every syllable distinctly and not to join the words together.

EXERCISES UNDER THE RULE. To be read over several times by all the pupils.

Earth, that entomb'st all that my heart holds dear.

His attempts were fruitless.

Hold off your hands, gentlemen.

The *sounds of horses' hoofs* were heard.

What *want'st thou* here?

It *was wrenched* by the hand of violence.

Their *signed tops*, tho' bare, *still stand.*

The *strength of* his *nostrils is* terrible.

A gentle current *rippled by.*

He *barb'd* the dart.

How do you *like herbs* in your broth?

Thou *barb'st* the dart that *wounds* thee.

Thou *barb'd'st* the dart.

Absalom.—WILLIS.

1. King David's limbs were weary. He had fled
   From far Jerusalem, and now he stood,
   With his faint people, for a little rest
   Upon the shore of Jordan. The light wind
5. Of morn was stirring, and he bared his brow
   To its refreshing breath; for he had worn
   The mourner's covering, and he had not felt
   That he could see his people until now.
   They gathered round him on the fresh green bank
10. And spoke their kindly words; and, as the sun
   Rose up in heaven, he knelt among them there,
   And bowed his head upon his hands to pray.
   Oh! when the heart is full—when bitter thoughts
   Come crowding thickly up for utterance,
15. And the poor common words of courtesy
   Are such a very mockery—how much
   The bursting heart may pour itself in prayer!
   He prayed for Israel; and his voice went up
   Strongly and fervently. He prayed for those

20. Whose love had been his shield; and his deep
    tones
    Grew tremulous. But, oh! for Absalom—
    For his estranged, misguided Absalom—
    The proud, bright being, who had burst away,
    In all his princely beauty, to defy
25. The heart that cherished him—for him he poured,
    In agony that would not be controlled,
    Strong supplication, and forgave him there,
    Before his God for his deep sinfulness.
30. The pall was settled. He who slept beneath
    Was straightened for the grave, and, as the folds
    Sunk to the still proportions, they betrayed
    The matchless symmetry of Absalom.
    His hair was yet unshorn, and silken curls
35. Were floating round the tassels as they swayed
    To the admitted air, as glossy now
    As when, in hours of gentle dalliance, bathing
    The snowy fingers of Judea's girls.
    His helm was at his feet, his banner, soiled
40. With trailing through Jerusalem, was laid,
    Reversed, beside him, and the jeweled hilt,
    Whose diamonds lit the passage of his blade,
    Rested, like mockery, on his covered brow.
    The soldiers of the king trod to and fro,
45. Clad in the garb of battle; and their chief,
    The mighty Joab, stood beside the bier,
    And gazed upon the dark pall steadfastly,
    As if he feared the slumberer might stir.
    A slow step startled him. He grasped his blade
50. As if a trumpet rang; but the bent form
    Of David entered, and he gave command,
    In a low tone, to his few followers,
    Who left him with his dead. The king stood still
    Till the last echo died: then, throwing off
55. The sackcloth from his brow, and laying back
    The pall from the still features of his child,

He bowed his head upon him, and broke forth
In the resistless eloquence of woe:—

1. "Alas! my noble boy! that thou should'st die!
   Thou, who wert made so beautifully fair!
   That death should settle in thy glorious eye,
   And leave his stillness in this clustering hair!
   How could he mark thee for the silent tomb.
   My proud boy, Absalom!

2. "Cold is thy brow, my son! and I am chill,
   As to my bosom I have tried to press thee.
   How was I wont to feel my pulses thrill,
   Like a rich harp-string, yearning to caress thee,
   And hear thy sweet *"my father"* from these dumb
   And cold lips, Absalom!

3. "The grave hath won thee, I shall hear the gush
   Of music, and the voices of the young,
   And life will pass me in the mantling blush,
   And the dark tresses to the soft winds flung,
   But thou no more, with thy sweet voice, shalt
   come
       To meet me, Absalom!

4. "And, oh! when I am stricken, and my heart,
   Like a bruised reed, is waiting to be broken,
   How will its love for thee, as I depart,
   Yearn for thine ear to drink its last deep token!
   It were so sweet, amid death's gathering gloom,
   To see thee, Absalom!

5. "And now, farewell! 'Tis hard to give thee up,
   With death so like a gentle slumber on thee:—
   And thy dark sin!—Oh! I could drink the cup,
   If from this woe its bitterness had won thee.
   May God have called thee, like a wanderer, home,
   My erring Absalom!"

6. He covered up his face, and bowed himself
   A moment on his child: then, giving him
   A look of melting tenderness, he clasped
   His hand convulsively, as if in prayer;
   And, as a strength were given him of God,
   He rose up calmly, and composed the pall
   Firmly and decently, and left him there,
   As if his rest had been a breathing sleep.

QUESTIONS.—1. What had Absalom done to wring the heart of his father? 2. What was the manner of his death? 3. Specify some of the poetic beauties of this piece.

ERRORS.—*Ur-rin* for err-ing; *Job* for Jo-ab; *Is-rel* for Is-ra-el; *wil-ler* for wil-low.

SPELL AND DEFINE.—(7) mourners; (13) bitter; (15) courtesy; (16) mockery; (25) cherished; (26) controlled; (27) misguided, estranged; (31) straightened; (33) matchless, symmetry; (35) tassels; (41) reversed, jeweled, hilt; (47) steadfastly; (55) sackcloth; (58) eloquence; (3) mantling; (6) convulsively.

LESSON XII.

RULE.—Be careful to pronounce every syllable distinctly and not to join the words together.

EXERCISES UNDER THE RULE. To be read over several times by all the pupils.

Many *arks* were seen.

They *bark'd* and howl'd within.

The culprit was *hurl'd* from the rock.

Words, words, words, my lord.

Are the goods *wharf'd*?

It was strongly urg'd upon him.

Remark'd'st thou that?

He *snarls*, but dares not bite.

Arm'd, say ye? Yes, *arm'd*, my lord.

The Intemperate Husband.
SIGOURNEY.

1. There was one modification of her husband's persecutions which the fullest measure of Jane Harwood's piety could not enable her to bear unmoved. This was unkindness to her feeble and suffering boy. It was at first commenced as the surest mode of distressing her. It opened a direct avenue to her heart.

2. What began in perverseness seemed to end in hatred, as evil habits sometimes create perverted principles. The wasted invalid shrunk from his father's glance and footstep, as from the approach of a foe. More than once had he taken him from the little bed which maternal care had provided for him, and forced him to go forth in the cold of the winter storm.

3. "I mean to harden him," said he. "All the neighbors know that you make such a fool of him that he will never to able to earn a living. For my part I wish I had never been called to the trial of supporting a useless boy who pretends to be sick only that he may be coaxed by a silly mother."

4. On such occasions, it was in vain that the mother attempted to protect her child. She might neither shelter him in her bosom, nor control the frantic violence of the father. Harshness, and the agitation of fear, deepened a disease which might else have yielded. The timid boy, in terror of his natural protector, withered away like a blighted flower. It was of no avail that friends remonstrated with the unfeeling parent, or that hoary-headed men warned him solemnly of his sins. *Intemperance* had destroyed his respect for man and his fear of God.

5. Spring at length emerged from the shade of that heavy and bitter winter. But its smile brought no

gladness to the declining child. Consumption fed upon his vitals, and his nights were full of pain.

6. "Mother, I wish I could smell the violets that grew upon the green bank of our old dear home." "It is too early for violets, my child. But the grass is beautifully green around us, and the birds sing sweetly, as if their hearts were full of praise."

7. "In my dreams last night, I saw the clear waters of the brook that ran by the bottom of my little garden. I wish I could taste them once more. And I heard such music, too, as used to come from that white church among the trees, where every Sunday the happy people meet to worship God."

8. The mother knew that the hectic fever had been long increasing, and saw there was such an unearthly brightness in his eye, that she feared his intellect wandered. She seated herself on his low bed, and bent over him to soothe and compose him. He lay silent for some time.

9. "Do you think my father will come?" Dreading the agonizing agitation which in his paroxysms of coughing and pain, he evinced at the sound of his father's well-known footstep, she answered,—"I think not, love. You had better try to sleep."

10. "Mother, I wish he would come. I do not feel afraid now. Perhaps he would let me lay my cheek to his once more, as he used to do when I was a babe in my grandmother's arms. I should be glad to say goodbye to him, before I go to my Savior."

11. Gazing intently in his face, she saw the work of the destroyer, in lines too plain to be mistaken. "My son, my dear son—say, Lord Jesus, receive my spirit." "Mother," he replied, with a sweet smile upon his ghastly features, "he is ready. I desire to go to him. Hold the baby to me, that I may kiss her. That is all. Now sing to me, and oh! wrap me close in your arms, for I shiver with cold."

12. He clung, with a death grasp, to that bosom which had long been his sole earthly refuge. "Sing louder, dear mother,—a little louder,—I cannot hear you." A tremulous tone, as of a broken harp, rose above her grief, to comfort the dying child. One sigh of icy breath was upon her cheek, as she joined it to his—one shudder—and all was over.

13. She held the body long in her arms, as if fondly hoping to warm and restore it to life with her breath. Then she stretched it upon its bed, and kneeling beside it, hid her face in that grief which none but mothers feel. It was a deep and sacred solitude, alone with the dead. Nothing save the soft breathing of the sleeping babe fell upon that solemn pause.

14. Then the silence was broken by a wail of piercing sorrow. It ceased, and a voice arose—a voice of supplication for strength to endure, as "seeing Him who is invisible." Faith closed what was begun in weakness. It became a prayer of thanksgiving to Him who had released the dove-like spirit from the prison-house of pain, that it might taste the peace and mingle in the melody of heaven.

QUESTIONS.—1. What is the subject of this piece?   2. How did the man commence abusing his child?   3. What effect was produced on the health of the child?   4. Can you describe the scene of the deathbed?   5. What did the child dream about? 6. What did he wish to say to his father?

ERRORS.—*Hus-buns* for hus-bands; *fust* for first; *o-pun'd* for o-pen-ed; *rem-on-stra-ted* for re-mon-stra-ted.

SPELL AND DEFINE.—(1) modification, persecutions, unkindness, commenced, distressing; (2) perverseness, principles, maternal; (3) neighbors, supporting, coaxed; (4) harshness, protector, blighted, remonstrated, intemperance; (5) consumption; (8) unearthly, intellect; (9) agonizing, paroxysms, coughing; (14) supplication, thanksgiving.

LESSON XIII.

RULE.—Give a full and prolonged sound to the vowels, yet be careful not to alter their proper sounds.

This rule is intended to correct a very common fault, which makes reading flat, inexpressive, and uninteresting. Some vowel sounds *cannot* be prolonged without altering the proper sound; while others may be lengthened to almost any extent, without any appreciable alteration of sound. Let every pupil repeat these words, giving the vowel sound that is italicized, a long, loud, and full sound, that gradually diminishes in strength.

Hail, all, the, isle, own, how, now, awe, show, do, ooze, eel.

Then let them repeat these sentences several times, prolonging the vowel sounds that are italicized.

Hail holy light. We *praise thee, O Lord God.*

High on a *throne* of *royal state.*

The reader will need to guard against a *drawling* style of reading after these exercises.

The Intemperate Husband.—CONTINUED.

1. She arose from her supplication, and bent calmly over her dead. The thin, placid features wore a smile, as when he had spoken of Jesus. She composed the shining locks around the pure forehead, and gazed long on what was to her so beautiful. Tears had vanished from her eyes, and in their stead was an expression almost sublime, as of one who had given an angel back to God.

2. The father entered carelessly. She pointed to the pallid immovable brow, 'See, he suffers no longer.' He drew near, and looked on the dead with surprise and sadness. A few natural tears forced their way, and fell on the face of the first-born, who was once his pride. The memories of that moment were bitter. He spoke tenderly to the emaciated mother; and she, who a short time before was raised above the sway of grief, wept like an infant, as those few affectionate tones touched the sealed fountains of other years.

3. Neighbors and friends visited them, desirous to console their sorrow, and attended them when they committed the body to the earth. There was a shady and secluded spot, which they had consecrated by the burial of their few dead. There that whole little colony were gathered, and, seated on the fresh grass, listened to the holy, healing words of the inspired volume.

4. It was read by the oldest man in the colony, who had himself often mourned. As he bent reverently over the sacred page, there was that on his brow which seemed to say, 'This has been my comfort in my affliction.' Silver hairs thinly covered his temples, and his low voice was modulated by feeling, as he read of the frailty of man, withering like the flower of grass, before it groweth up; and of His majesty in whose sight 'a thousand years are as yesterday when it is past, and as a watch in the night.'

5. He selected from the words of that compassionate One, who "gathereth the lambs with his arm, and carrieth them in his bosom," who, pointing out as an example the humility of little children, said, "Except ye become as one of these, ye cannot enter the kingdom of heaven," and who calleth all the weary and heavy laden to come unto him, that he may give them rest.

6. The scene called forth sympathy, even from manly bosoms. The mother, worn with watching and weariness, bowed her head down to the clay that concealed her child. It was observed with gratitude by that friendly group, that the husband supported her in his arms, and mingled his tears with hers.

7. He returned from the funeral in much mental distress. His sins were brought to remembrance, and reflection was misery. For many nights, sleep was disturbed by visions of his neglected boy. Sometimes he imagined that he heard him coughing from his low bed, and felt constrained to go to him, in a strange

disposition of kindness, but his limbs were unable to obey the dictates of his will.

8. Conscience haunted him with terrors, and many prayers from pious hearts arose, that he might now be led to repentance. The venerable man who had read the Bible at the burial of his boy, counseled and entreated him, with the earnestness of a father, to yield to the warning voice, and to 'break off his sins by righteousness, and his iniquities by turning unto the Lord.'

9. There was a change in his habits and conversation, and his friends trusted it would be permanent. She who, above all others, was interested in the result, spared no exertion to win him back to the way of truth, and soothe his heart into peace with itself and obedience to his Maker.

10. Yet was she doomed to witness the full force of grief and of remorse upon intemperance, only to see them utterly overthrown at last. The reviving virtue, with whose indications she had solaced herself, and even given thanks that her beloved son had not died in vain, was transient as the morning dew.

11. Habits of industry, which had begun to spring up, proved themselves to be without root. The dead, and his cruelty to the dead, were alike forgotten. Disaffection to the chastened being, who against hope still hoped for his salvation, resumed its dominion.

12. The friends who had alternately reproved and encouraged him, were convinced their efforts had been of no avail. Intemperance, "like the strong man armed," took possession of a soul that lifted no cry to God and girded on no weapon to resist the destroyer.

QUESTIONS.—1. What effect was produced upon the father by the death of his child? 2. What were his friends disposed to hope for? 3. How did intemperance take possession of him?

ERRORS.—*Car-less-ly* for care-less-ly; *col-un-ny* for col-o-ny; *geth-er-ed* for gath-er-ed.

SPELL AND DEFINE.—(1) composed, expression; (2) carelessly, immovable, emaciated, affectionate; (3) committed, secluded, consecrated, inspired; (4) reverently, modulated; (5) compassionate; (6) sympathy; (7) constrained, disposition; (8) venerable, righteousness; (9) permanent; (10) overthrown; (11) disaffection; (12) alternately.

LESSON XIV.

RULE.—Give a full and prolonged sound to the vowels, yet be careful not to alter their proper sounds.

EXERCISES UNDER THE RULE. Repeat these words several times, prolonging the vowel sounds that are italicized.

Day, age, law, awed, father, arm, thee, eel, ooze, thy, isle, thou.
We have err'd and *stray'd* from thy *ways*, like *lost* sheep.
Spare thou those, O God, who *confess* their *faults*.

God's First Temples.—BRYANT.

1. The groves were God's first temples. Ere man
   learned
   To hew the shaft, and lay the architrave,
   And spread the roof above them, ere he framed
   The lofty vault, to gather and roll back

5. The sound of anthems, in the darkling wood,
   Amidst the cool and silence, he knelt down
   And offered to the Mightiest solemn thanks
   And supplication. For his simple heart
   Might not resist the sacred influences,

10. That, from the stilly twilight of the place,
    And from the gray old trunks, that high in
    heaven
    Mingled their mossy boughs, and from the
    sound
    Of the invisible breath, that swayed at once
    All their green tops, stole over them, and bowed

15. His spirit, with the thought of boundless Power
And inaccessible Majesty. Ah, why
Should we, in the world's riper years, neglect
God's ancient sanctuaries, and adore
Only among the crowd, and under roofs
20. That our frail hands have raised! Let me, at least
Here, in the shadow of this aged wood,
Offer one hymn; thrice happy, if it find
Acceptance in His ear.
Father, thy hand
Hath reared these venerable columns; thou
25. Didst weave this verdant roof. Thou didst look
down
Upon the naked earth, and, forthwith, rose
All these fair ranks of trees. They, in thy sun,
Budded, and shook their green leaves in thy
breeze,
And shot towards heaven. The century-living
crow,
30. Whose birth was in their tops, grew old and died
Among their branches; till, at last, they stood,
As now they stand, massy, and tall, and dark,
Fit shrine for humble worshiper to hold
Communion with his Maker. Here are seen
35. No traces of man's pomp, or pride; no silks
Rustle, no jewels shine, nor envious eyes
Encounter; no fantastic carvings show
The boast of our vain race to change the form
Of thy fair works. But thou art here; thou fill'st
40. The solitude. Thou art in the soft winds
That run along the summits of these trees
In music; thou art in the cooler breath,
That from the inmost darkness of the place,
Comes, scarcely felt; the barky trunks, the
ground,
45. The fresh, moist ground, are all instinct with
thee.

Here is continual worship; nature, here,
In the tranquility that thou dost love,
Enjoys thy presence. Noislessly, around
From perch to perch, the solitary bird

50. Passes; and yon clear spring, that, 'midst its
        herbs,
    Wells softly forth, and visits the strong roots
    Of half the mighty forest, tells no tale
    Of all the good it does. Thou hast not left
    Thyself without a witness, in these shades,

55. Of thy perfections. Grandeur, strength, and
        grace,
    Are here to speak of thee. This mighty oak—
    By whose immovable stem I stand, and seem
    Almost annihilated—not a prince,
    In all the proud old world beyond the deep,

60. E'er wore his crown as loftily as he
    Wears the green coronal of leaves, with which
    Thy hand has graced him. Nestled at his root
    Is beauty, such as blooms not in the glare
    Of the broad sun. That delicate forest flower

65. With scented breath, and look so like a smile,
    Seems, as it issues from the shapeless mould,
    An emanation of the indwelling Life,
    A visible token of the upholding Love,
    That are the soul of this wide universe.

70. My heart is awed within me, when I think
    Of the great miracle that still goes on,
    In silence, round me—the perpetual work
    Of thy creation, finished, yet renewed
    Forever. Written on thy works, I read

75. The lesson of thy own eternity.
    Lo! all grow old and die: but see, again,
    How on the faltering footsteps of decay
    Youth presses—every gay and beautiful youth—
    In all its beautiful forms. These lofty trees

80. Wave not less proudly than their ancestors
    Moulder beneath them. O, there is not lost
    One of earth's charms: upon her bosom yet
    After the flight of untold centuries,
    The freshness of her far beginning lies,
85. And yet shall lie. Life mocks the idle hate
    Of his arch enemy Death; yea, seats himself
    Upon the sepulcher, and blooms and smiles—
    And of the triumphs of his ghastly foe
    Makes his own nourishment. For he came forth
90. From thine own bosom, and shall have no end.
    There have been holy men, who hid themselves
    Deep in the woody wilderness, and gave
    Their lives to thought and prayer, till they
        outlived
    The generation born with them, nor seemed
95. Less aged than the hoary trees and rocks
    Around them; and there have been holy men,
    Who deemed it were not well to pass life thus.
    But let me often to these solitudes
    Retire, and in thy presence, reassure
100. My feeble virtue. Here, its enemies,
    The passions, at thy plainer footsteps, shrink,
    And tremble, and are still. O God! when thou
    Dost scare the world with tempests, set on fire
    The heavens with falling thunderbolts, or fill
105. With all the waters of the firmament,
    The swift, dark whirlwind, that uproots the
        woods
    And drowns the villages; when, at thy call,
    Uprises the great deep, and throws himself
    Upon the continent, and overwhelms
110. Its cities; who forgets not, at the sight
    Of these tremendous tokens of thy power,
    His pride, and lays his strifes and follies by?
    O, from these sterner aspects of thy face
    Spare me and mine; nor let us need the wrath

115. Of the mad, unchained elements to teach
Who rules them. Be it ours to meditate,
In these calm shades, thy milder majesty,
And to the beautiful order of thy works,
Learn to conform the order of our lives.

QUESTIONS.—1. What were the most ancient temples of worship? 2. What meditations become the forest scenes? 3. Of what kind of poetic measure is this piece?

ERRORS.—*An-thums* for an-thems; *shad-er* for shad-ow; *ven-r'ble* for ven-e-ra-ble; *cen-try* for cen-tu-ry; *sof-ly* for soft-ly; *an-nih-il-a-ted* for an-ni-hi-la-ted; *co-ro-nal* for cor-o-nal; *in'-stinct* for in-stinct'.

SPELL AND DEFINE.—(2) architrave; (5) darkling; (8) supplication; (9) influences; (10) twilight; (13) invisible; (16) inaccessible; (17) sanctuaries; (33) worshiper; (45) instinct; (47) tranquility; (57) immovable; (58) annihilated; (67) emanation, indwelling; (68) upholding; (87) sepulcher; (104) thunderbolt; (111) tremendous.

LESSON XV.

RULE.—Give a full and prolonged sound to the vowels, yet be careful not to alter their proper sounds.

EXERCISES UNDER THE RULE. Prolong the vowel sounds that are italicized.

War, orb, flows, pure, down, aid, low, save.

These are thy *glorious* works, *parent of good.*

Fairest of *stars! last* in the *train* of *night.*

On Elocution and Reading.

N. A. REVIEW.

1. The business of training our youth in elocution must be commenced in childhood. The first school is the nursery. There, at least, may be formed a distinct

articulation, which is the first requisite for good speaking. How rarely is it found in perfection among our orators! Words, says one, referring to articulation, should "be delivered out from the lips, as beautiful coins, newly issued from the mint, deeply and accurately impressed, perfectly finished, neatly struck by the proper organs, distinct, in due succession, and of due weight." How rarely do we hear a speaker, whose tongue, teeth and lips, do their office so perfectly, as in any wise, to answer to this beautiful description! The common faults in articulation, it should be remembered, take their rise from the very nursery. But let us refer to other particulars.

2. Grace in eloquence—in the pulpit, at the bar—cannot be separated from grace in the ordinary manners, in private life, in the social circle, in the family. It cannot well be superinduced upon all the other acquisitions of youth, any more than that nameless, but invaluable quality, called good breeding. You may, therefore, begin the work of forming the orator with your child, not merely by teaching him to declaim, but what is of more consequence, by observing and correcting his daily manners, motions and attitudes.

3. You can say, when he comes into your apartment, or presents you with something, a book or letter, in an awkward and blundering manner, "Return, and enter this room again," or, "Present me that book in a different manner," or, "Put yourself into a different attitude." You can explain to him the difference between thrusting or pushing out his hand and arm, in straight lines and at acute angles, and moving them in flowing, circular lines, and easy, graceful action. He will readily understand you. Nothing is more true than that "the motions of children are originally graceful;" and it is by suffering them to be perverted, that we lay the foundation for invincible awkwardness in later life.

4. We go, next, to the schools for children. It ought to be a leading object, in these schools, to teach the art of reading. It ought to occupy threefold more time than it does. The teachers of these schools should labor to improve *themselves*. They should feel, that to them, for a time, are committed the future orators of the land.

5. We would rather have a child even of the other sex, return to us from school a first-rate reader, than a first-rate performer on the pianoforte. We should feel that we had a far better pledge for the intelligence and talent of our child. The accomplishment, in its perfection, would give more pleasure. The voice of song is not sweeter than the voice of eloquence, and there may be eloquent readers, as well as eloquent speakers. We speak of *perfection* in this art; and it is something, we must say in defense of our preference, which we have never yet seen. Let the same pains be devoted to reading as are required to form an accomplished performer on an instrument. Let us have—as the ancients had—the formers of the voice, the music-masters of the *reading* voice. Let us see years devoted to this accomplishment, and then we should be prepared to stand the comparison.

6. It is, indeed, a most intellectual accomplishment. So is music, too, in its perfection. We do by no means undervalue this noble and most delightful art, to which Socrates applied himself, even in his old age. But one recommendation of the art of reading is that it requires a constant exercise of mind. It demands continual and close reflection and thought and the finest discrimination of thought. It involves, in its perfection, the whole art of criticism on language. A man may possess a fine genius without being a perfect reader, but he cannot be a perfect reader without genius.

QUESTIONS.—1. When must the business of training in elocution be commenced? 2. What excellent comparison is made use of in illustrating proper enunciation? 3. What is the relative *importance* of good reading? 4. How does the power of reading with perfection, compare with the power of excellent musical performance?

ERRORS.—*a-gin* for a-gain; *or-gins* for or-gans; *ar-tick-e-la-tion* for ar-tic-u-la-tion; *in-tel-le-junce* for in-tel-li-gence; *at-te-toods* for at-ti-tudes; *dif-frunt* for dif-fer-ent.

SPELL AND DEFINE.—(1) elocution, articulation, accurately, succession, description, particulars; (2) eloquence, superinduced, acquisitions, invaluable, consequence; (3) apartment, awkwardness, thrusting, invincible; (4) committed; (5) intelligence, accomplishment, instrument, comparison; (6) intellectual, undervalue, recommendation, discrimination.

LESSON XVI.

RULE.—Give a full and prolonged sound to the vowels, yet be careful not to alter their proper sounds.

EXERCISES UNDER THE RULE. Prolong the vowel sounds that are italicized.

Err, all, age, arm, old, our, eel, boy, isle.

Our *Father*, who *art* in Heaven.

Woe unto *thee Chorazin.*

Woe unto *thee Bethsäida.*

Necessity of Education.—BEECHER.

1. We must educate! We must educate, or we must perish by our own prosperity. If we do not, short will be our race from the cradle to the grave. If in our haste to be rich and mighty, we outrun our literary and religious institutions, they will never overtake us, or only come up after the battle of liberty is fought and lost, as spoils to grace the victory, and as resources

of inexorable despotism for the perpetuity of our bondage.

2. But what will become of the West, if her prosperity rushes up to such a majesty of power, while those great institutions linger which are necessary to form the mind, and the conscience, and the heart of that vast world? It must not be permitted.

3. Yet what is done must be done quickly, for population will not wait, and commerce will not cast anchor, and manufactures will not shut off the steam nor shut down the gate, and agriculture, pushed by millions of freemen on their fertile soil, will not withhold her corrupting abundance.

4. Let no man at the East quiet himself, and dream of liberty, whatever may become of the West. Our alliance of blood, and political institutions, and common interests, is such, that we cannot stand aloof in the hour of her calamity, should it ever come. *Her* destiny is *our* destiny, and the day that her gallant ship goes down, our little boat sinks in the vortex!

5. The motives which call on us to cooperate in this glorious work of consummating the institutions of the West, essential to the perpetuity of her greatness and glory are neither few, nor feeble, nor obscure.

6. All at the West is on a great scale, and the minds and the views of the people correspond with these relative proportions. It is not parsimony which renders momentary aid necessary to the West. It is want of time and assimilation for the consciousness and wielding of her powers. How cheaply can the aid be rendered for rearing immediately the first generation of her institutions! cheaper than we could rear the barracks to accommodate an army for the defense of our liberty, for a single campaign; cheaper than the taxations of crime and its punishment during the same period, in the absence of literary and evangelical influence.

7. Consider, also, that the mighty resources at the West are worse than useless without the supervening influence of the government of God.

8. To balance the temptation of such unrivaled abundance, the capacity of the West for self-destruction, without religious and moral culture, will be as terrific as her capacity for self-preservation, with it, will be glorious.

9. But all the moral energies of the government of God over men, are indissolubly associated with "the ministry of reconciliation." The Sabbath and the preaching of the gospel are Heaven's consecrated instumentality for the efficacious administration of the government of mind in a happy, social state. By these only does the Sun of Righteousness arise with healing in his beams, and ignorance, and vice, and superstition encamp around evangelical institutions, to rush in whenever their light and power is extinct.

10. The great experiment is now making, and from its extent and rapid filling up, is making in the West, whether the perpetuity of our republican institutions can be reconciled with universal suffrage. Without the education of the head and heart of the nation, they cannot be. The question to be decided is, can the nation, or the vast balance power of it be so imbued with intelligence and virtue as to bring out, in laws and their administration, a perpetual self-preserving energy? We know that the work is a vast one, and of great difficulty and yet we believe it can be done.

QUESTIONS.—1. Why is education so necessary in this country? 2. What will, without education, contribute to our downfall? 3. What can save the nation's liberties? 4. Can the nation continue free without the influence of religion? Read and explain the first sentence of paragraph 3. 5. Why is abundance said to be "corrupting?" 6. Why should all cooperate in extending education? 7. Why are the teachers of religion called "the ministry of reconciliation?"

ERRORS.—*Ed-e-cate* for ed-u-cate; *in-ex-ore-a-ble* for in-ex'-o-ra-ble; *in-dis-sol-lu-bly* for in-dis-so-lu-bly; *gov-um-ment* and *gov-er-ment* for gov-ern-ment; *ub-bun-dunce* for a-bun-dance; *ex-pur-ri-ment* for ex-per-i-ment.

SPELL AND DEFINE.—(1) educate, prosperity, resources, inexorable, despotism, perpetuity; (2) conscience, permitted; (3) population, commerce, manufactures, agriculture, corrupting; (4) alliance, calamity, destiny, vortex; (5) co-operate, consummating, essential, obscure; (7) supervening; (8) unrivaled, capacity, terrific, self-preservation; (9) indissolubly, reconciliation, consecrated, instrumentality, efficacious, superstition, evangelical, extinct; (10) suffrage.

LESSON XVII.

RULE.—Give a full and prolonged sound to the vowels, yet be careful not to alter their *proper* sounds.

EXERCISES UNDER THE RULE. Prolong the vowel sounds that are italicized.

Know, free, they, dawn, now, bay, there, shore.
Soothed with the *sound* the *king* grew *vain.*
Roll on, thou *deep* and *dark* blue ocean, *roll.*

Necessity of Education.—CONTINUED.

1. I am aware that our ablest patriots are looking out on the deep, vexed with storms, with great forebodings and failings of heart for fear of the things that are coming upon us, and I perceive a spirit of impatience rising, and distrust in respect to the perpetuity of our republic. I am sure that these fears are well founded, and am glad that they exist. It is the star of hope in our dark horizon.

2. Fear is what we need, as the ship needs wind on a rocking sea after a storm, to prevent foundering. But when our fear and our efforts shall correspond with our danger, the danger is past.

3. For it is not the impossibility of self-preservation which threatens us, nor is it the unwillingness of the nation to pay the price of the preservation, as she has paid the price of the purchase of our liberties.

4. It is inattention and inconsideration, protracted till the crisis is past, and the things which belong to our peace are hid from our eyes. Blessed be God, that the tokens of a national waking up, the harbinger of God's mercy, are multiplying upon us!

5. We did not, in the darkest hour, believe that God had brought our fathers to this goodly land to lay the foundation of religious liberty, and wrought such wonders in their preservation, and raised their descendants to such heights of civil and religious liberty, only to reverse the analogy of His providence, and abandon His work.

6. Though there now be clouds, and the sea roaring, and men's hearts failing, we believe there is light behind the cloud, and that the imminence of our danger is intended, under the guidance of Heaven, to call forth and apply a holy, fraternal fellowship between the East and the West, which shall secure our preservation, and make the prosperity of our nation durable as time, and as abundant as the waves of the sea.

7. I would add, as a motive to immediate action, that if we do fail in our great experiment of self-government, our destruction will be as signal as the birthright abandoned, the mercies abused, and the provocation offered to beneficent Heaven. The descent of desolation will correspond with the past elevation.

8. No punishments of Heaven are so severe as those for mercies abused, and no instrumentality employed in their infliction is so dreadful as the wrath of man. No spasms are like the spasms of expiring liberty, and no wailing such as her convulsions extort.

9. It took Rome three hundred years to die, and our death, if we perish, will be as much more terrific as our intelligence and free institutions have given to us more bone, and sinew, and vitality. May God hide from me the day when the dying agonies of my country shall begin! O, thou beloved land, bound together by the ties of brotherhood and common interest and perils, live forever—one and undivided!

QUESTIONS.—1. Why should men regard the prospects of this nation with *fear*? 2. What can be the advantage of a spirit of fear? 3. Why may we trust that God will not abandon our nation to ruin? 4. What will *ensure* her destruction? 5. Suppose our nation destroyed, how great will be the destruction? 6. What are the most dreadful punishments heaven can inflict upon a nation? 7. How would our destruction compare with that of Rome?

ERRORS.—*Un-wil-lin-ness* for un-wil-ling-ness; *lib-y-ties* for lib-er-ties; *'nal-y-gy* for an-al-o-gy; *im-nunce* for im-mi-nence; *ben-e-fi-cient* for be-nef-i-cent; *spas-um* for spasm; *wail-in'* and *dy-in'* for wail-ing and dy-ing.

SPELL AND DEFINE.—(2) correspond; (3) impossibility; (4) inconsideration, harbinger, multiplying; (5) analogy; (7) birthright; (8) instrumentality, spasm; (9) institutions.

LESSON XVIII.

RULE.—Give a full and distinct sound to the consonants in every syllable.

EXERCISES UNDER THE RULE. Pronounce the following words, sounding the last consonant very distinctly.

or-*b*, ai-*d*, i-*f*, fa-*g*, Geor-*ge*, rich-*er*, a-*ll*, ai-*m*, ow-*n*, ti-*p*, wa-*r*, hi-*ss*, ha-*t*, gi-*ve*, ad-*d*, so-*ng*, brea-*th*, tru-*th*, pu-*sh*, bir-*ch*.

The Scriptures and the Savior.
ROUSSEAU.

1. The majesty of the Scriptures strikes me with astonishment, and the sanctity of the gospel addresses itself to my heart. Look at the volumes of the philosophers, with all their pomp. How contemptible do they appear in comparison to this! Is it possible, that a book at once so simple and sublime, can be the work of man?

2. Can he who is the subject of its history, be himself a mere man? Was his the tone of an enthusiast, or of an ambitious sectary? What sweetness! What purity in his manners! What an affecting gracefulness in his instructions! What sublimity in his maxims! What profound wisdom in his discourses! What presence of mind, what sagacity and propriety in his answers! How great the command over his passions! Where is the man, where the philosopher, who could so live, suffer, and die, without weakness and without ostentation!

3. When Plato described his imaginary good man, covered with all the disgrace of crime, yet worthy of all the rewards of virtue, he described exactly the character of Jesus Christ. The resemblance was so striking, it could not be mistaken, and all the fathers of the church perceived it. What prepossessions, what blindness must it be to compare the son of Sophronius, to the son of Mary! What an immeasurable distance between them! Socrates, dying without pain, and without ignominy, easily supported his character to the last; and if his death, however easy, had not crowned his life, it might have been doubted whether Socrates, with all his wisdom, was anything more than a mere sophist.

4. He invented, it is said, the theory of moral science. Others, however, had before him put it in

practice; and he had nothing to do but to tell what they had done, and to reduce their examples to precept. Aristides had been just, before Socrates defined what justice was; Leonidas had died for his country, before Socrates made it a duty to love one's country. Sparta had been temperate, before Socrates eulogized sobriety; and before he celebrated the praises of virtue, Greece had abounded in virtuous men.

5. But from whom of all his countrymen, could Jesus have derived that sublime and pure morality, of which he only has given us both the precepts and example? In the midst of the most licentious fanaticism, the voice of the sublimest wisdom was heard, and the simplicity of the most heroic virtue crowned one of the humblest of all the multitude.

6. The death of Socrates, peaceably philosophising with his friends, is the most pleasant that could be desired! That of Jesus, expiring in torments, outraged, reviled, and execrated by a whole nation, is the most horrible that could be feared. Socrates in receiving the cup of poison, blessed the weeping executioner who presented it, but Jesus in the midst of excruciating torture, prayed for his merciless tormentors.

7. Yes! If the life and death of Socrates were those of a sage, the life and death of Jesus were those of a God. Shall we say that the evangelical history is a mere fiction—it does not bear the stamp of fiction, but the contrary. The history of Socrates which nobody doubts, is not as well attested as that of Jesus Christ. Such an assertion in fact only shifts the difficulty, without removing it. It is more inconceivable that a number of persons should have agreed to fabricate this book, than that one only should have furnished the subject of it.

8. The Jewish authors were incapable of the diction, and strangers to the morality, contained in the gospel, the marks of whose truth are so striking, so perfectly inimitable, that the inventor would be a more astonishing man than the hero.

QUESTIONS.—1. What was the character of Rousseau? 2. How could an infidel testify thus without renouncing his infidelity? 3. How does Plato's character of what a good man *ought* to be, correspond with what Christ *was*? 4. What differences can you mention between the life and death of Christ and that of Socrates? 5. In what country did Aristides, Leonidas, Plato, and Socrates live? 6. What is the character of each? 7. Is the history of Socrates any better attested than that of Christ? 8. Why is it inconceivable that the book is a fiction? 9. Suppose it an invention of man—which would be the most wonderful, the inventor or the hero?

ERRORS.—*Gaws-p'l* for gos-pel; *Soc-er-tes* for Soc-ra-tes; *so-phist* for soph-ist; *vir-ty-ous* and *var-tu-ous* for vir-tu-ous.

SPELL AND DEFINE.—(1) majesty, astonishment, philosophers, contemptible, comparison; (2) enthusiast, sectary, gracefulness, discourses, sagacity, ostentation; (3) imaginary, resemblance, prepossession, Sophronius, immeasurable; (4) eulogized; (6) outraged, execrated, executioner, excruciating, evangelical; (8) inimitable.

LESSON XIX.

RULE.—Take care not to let the voice grow weaker and weaker as you approach the end of a sentence.

Washington's Birthday.—WEBSTER.

1. The name of Washington is intimately blended with whatever belongs most essentially to the prosperity, liberty, the free institutions, and the renown of our country. That name was of power to rally a nation in the hour of thick-thronging public disasters

and calamities. That name shone amid the storm of war, a beacon light, to cheer and guide the country's friends. It flamed, too, like a meteor to repel her foes.

2. That name, in the days of peace, was a loadstone, attracting to itself a whole people's confidence, a whole people's love, and the whole world's respect. That name, descending with all time, spreading over the whole earth, and uttered in all the languages belonging to the tribes and races of men, will forever be pronounced with affectionate gratitude by everyone, in whose breast there shall arise an aspiration for human rights and human liberty.

3. All experience evinces that human sentiments are strongly influenced by associations. The recurrence of anniversaries, or of longer periods of time, naturally freshens the recollection, and deepens the impression, of events with which they are historically connected. Renowned places, also, have a power to awaken feeling, which all acknowledge. No American can pass by the fields of Bunker Hill, Monmouth or Camden, as if they were ordinary spots on the earth's surface. Whoever visits them feels the sentiment of love of country kindling anew, as if the spirit that belonged to the transactions which have rendered these places distinguished, still hovered around, with power to move and excite all who in future time may approach them.

4. Neither of these sources of emotion equals the power with which great moral examples affect the mind. When sublime virtues cease to be abstractions, when they become embodied in human character, and exemplified in human conduct, we should be false to our own nature if we did not indulge in the spontaneous effusions of our gratitude and our admiration.

5. A true lover of the virtue of patriotism delights to contemplate its purest models; and that love of country may be well suspected, which affects to soar

so high into the regions of sentiment, as to be lost
and absorbed in the abstract feeling, and becomes too
elevated, or too refined, to glow with fervor in the
commendation or the love of individual benefactors.—All this is unnatural.

6. It is as if one should be so enthusiastic a lover
of poetry, as to care nothing for Homer or Milton, so
passionately attached to eloquence, as to be indifferent to Tully and Chatham, or such a devotee to the
arts, in such an ecstacy with the elements of beauty,
proportion, and expression, as to regard the masterpieces of Raphael and Michael Angelo with coldness
or contempt. We may be assured, gentlemen, that he
who really loves the thing itself, loves its finest exhibitions. A true friend of his country loves her friends
and benefactors, and thinks it no degradation to commend and commemorate them.

7. The voluntary outpouring of the public feeling,
made today, from the north to the south, and from
the east to the west, proves this sentiment to be both
just and natural. In the cities and in the villages, in
the public temples, and in the family circles, among
all ages and sexes, gladdened voices today, bespeak
grateful hearts, and a freshened recollection of the virtues of the father of his country.

8. It will be so, in all time to come, so long as public
virtue is itself an object of regard. The ingenuous
youth of America will hold up to themselves the
bright model of Washington's example, and study to
be what they behold. They will contemplate his
character till all its virtues spread out and display
themselves to their delighted vision, as the earliest
astronomers, the shepherds on the plains of Babylon,
gazed at the stars till they saw them form into
clusters and constellations, overpowering at length
the eyes of the beholders with the blaze of a thousand
lights.

QUESTIONS.—1. When is Washington's birthday? 2. In what year was he born? 3. In what year did he die? 4. What has Washington done for us—or in what way are we happier by his career? 5. What is the strength of associations connected with times and places, compared with the strength of those connected with *character*? 6. How must the lover of virtue itself, feel towards all virtuous men? 7. What will be the effect of Washington's character on future generations in America?

ERRORS.—*Wash-in-ton* for Wash-ing-ton; *fu-ter* for fu-ture; *pat-ri-et-ism* for pa-tri-ot-ism; *un-nat-er-al* for un-nat-u-ral.

SPELL AND DEFINE.—(1) intimately, blended, renown, beacon, meteor; (2) loadstone, aspiration; (3) sentiments, associations, recurrence, anniversaries, ordinary; (4) abstractions, embodied, exemplified, spontaneous, effusions, admiration; (5) partriotism, benefactors; (6) enthusiastic, devotee, ecstacy, masterpieces, degradation, commemorate; (7) voluntary; (8) ingenuous, vision, constellations.

LESSON XX.

RULE.—While each pupil reads, let the rest observe, and then mention which syllables were pronounced wrong, and which were omitted or indistinctly sounded.

Nature and Revelation.—BIBLE.

1. The heavens declare the glory of God,
   And the firmament showeth his handywork.
   Day unto day uttereth speech,
   And night unto night showeth knowledge.

2. There is no speech nor language,
   Where their voice is not heard.
   Their line is gone out through all the earth,
   And their words to the end of the world.

3. In them hath he set a tabernacle for the sun,
   Which is as a bridegroom coming out of his
       chamber,
   And rejoiceth as a strong man to run a race.

4. His going forth is from the end of the heaven,
   And his circuit unto the ends of it:
   And there is nothing hid from the heat thereof.

5. The law of the Lord is perfect, converting the soul:
   The testimony of the Lord is sure, making wise the
       simple,
   The statutes of the Lord are right, rejoicing the
       heart.

6. The commandment of the Lord is pure,
       enlightening the eyes.
   The fear of the Lord is clean, enduring forever:
   The judgments of the Lord are true and righteous
       altogether.

7. More to be desired are they than gold, yea, than
       much fine gold;
   Sweeter also than honey and the honeycomb.
   Moreover by them is thy servant warned:
   And in keeping of them there is great reward.

8. Who can understand his errors?
   Cleanse thou me from secret faults,
   Keep back thy servant also from presumptuous
       sins;
   Let them not have dominion over me:

9. Then shall I be upright,
   And I shall be innocent from the great
       transgression.
   Let the words of my mouth, and the meditation of
       my heart,
   Be acceptable in thy sight,
   O Lord, my strength, and my redeemer!

QUESTIONS.—1. What is the character of God, as exhibited by the works of nature?   2. What is the character and influence of the law of God?   3. How can a man be kept from sin?

ERRORS.—*Fir-m'munt* for fir-ma-ment; *lan-guidge* for language; *tab-er-nic-cle* for tab-er-na-cle.

SPELL AND DEFINE.—(1) firmament, handywork; (2) language;   (3) tabernacle, bridegroom;   (4) circuit; (5) testimony;   (6) commandment, enlightening, judgments; (7) honeycomb;   (8) presumptuous;   (9) transgression, meditation, redeemer.

LESSON XXI.

RULE.—Sound the vowels correctly, and very full.

EXERCISES UNDER THE RULE. Prolong the following vowel sounds that are italicized. *a*-we, *a*-ge, *a*-rm, *o*-ld, *o*-r, *ee*-l, *oo*-ze, bu-*oy*, *i*-sle.

These are the only vowel sounds that can be much prolonged without altering their proper sound.

Niagara Falls.—HOWISON.

1. The form of the Niagara Falls is that of an ir-regular semicircle, about three quarters of a mile in extent. This is divided into two distinct cascades by the intervention of Goat Island, the extremity of which is perpendicular, and in a line with the precipice, over which the water is projected. The cataract on the Canada side of the river is called the Horseshoe, or Great Falls, from its peculiar form; and that next the United States, the American Falls.

2. Three extensive views of the Falls may be obtained from three different places. In general, the first

opportunity travelers have of seeing the cataract is from the highroad, which at one point, lies near the back of the river. This place, however, being considerably above the level of the Falls, and a good way beyond them, affords a view that is comparatively imperfect and unimposing.

3. The Table Rock, from which the Falls of the Niagara may be contemplated in all their grandeur, lies on an exact level with the edge of the cataract on the Canada side, and indeed forms a part of the precipice, over which the water rushes. It derives its name from the circumstance of its projecting beyond the cliffs that support it, like the leaf of a table. To gain this position, it is necessary to descend a steep bank, and to follow a path that winds among shrubbery and trees which entirely conceal from the eye the scene that awaits him who traverses it.

4. When near the termination of this road, a few steps carried me beyond all these obstructions, and a magnificent amphitheater of cataracts burst upon my view with appalling suddenness and majesty. However,in a moment, the scene was concealed from my eyes by a dense cloud of spray, which involved me so completely that I did not dare to extricate myself.

5. A mingled and thunder-like rushing filled my ears. I could see nothing, except when the wind made a chasm in the spray, and then tremendous cataracts seemed to encompass me on every side. Below, a raging and foamy gulf, of undiscoverable extent, lashed the rocks with its hissing waves, and swallowed, under a horrible obscurity, the smoking floods that were precipitated into its bosom.

6. At first the sky was obscured by clouds, but after a few minutes, the sun burst forth, and the breeze, subsiding at the same time, permitted the spray to ascend perpendicularly. A host of pyramidal

clouds rose majestically, one after another, from the abyss at the bottom of the Falls! Each, when it had ascended a little above the edge of the cataract, displayed a beautiful rainbow, which in a few moments, was gradually transferred into the bosom of the cloud that immediately succeeded.

7. The spray of the Great Falls had extended itself through a wide space directly over me, and, receiving the full influence of the sun, exhibited a luminous and magnificent rainbow, which continued to over-arch and irradiate the spot on which I stood, while I enthusiastically contemplated the indescribable scene.

8. Any person, who has nerve enough, may plunge his hand into the water of the Great Falls, after it is projected over the precipice, merely by lying down flat, with his face beyond the edge of the Table Rock, and stretching out his arm to its utmost extent. The experiment is truly a horrible one, and such as I would not wish to repeat for, even to this day, I feel a shuddering and recoiling sensation when I recollect having been in the posture above described.

9. The body of water which composes the middle part of the Great Falls is so immense that it descends nearly two-thirds of the space without being ruffled or broken, and the solemn calmness with which it rolls over the edge of the precipice is finely contrasted with the perturbed appearance it assumes after having reached the gulf below. But the water, towards each side of the Falls is shattered the moment it drops over the rock, and loses, as it descends, in a great measure, the character of a fluid, being divided into pyramidal shaped fragments, the bases of which are turned upwards.

10. The surface of the gulf, below the cataract, presents a very singular aspect seeming, as it were, filled with an immense quantity of hoar frost, which

is agitated by small and rapid undulation. The particles of water are dazzlingly white, and do not apparently unite together, as might be supposed, but seem to continue for a time in a state of distinct comminution, and to repel each other with a thrilling and shivering motion, which cannot easily be described.

11. The road to the bottom of the Falls presents many more difficulties than that which leads to the Table Rock. After leaving the Table Rock the traveler must proceed down the river nearly half a mile, where he will come to a small chasm in the bank, in which there is a spiral staircase enclosed in a wooden building. By descending the stair, which is seventy or eighty feet in perpendicular height, he will find himself under the precipice, on the top of which he formerly walked. A high but sloping bank extends from its base to the edge of the river, and on the summit of this there is a narrow slippery path, covered with angular fragments of rock, which leads to the Great Falls.

12. The impending cliffs, hung with a profusion of trees and brushwood, over-arch this road, and seem to vibrate with the thunders of the cataract. In some places they rise abruptly to the height of one hundred feet and display, upon their surfaces, fossil shells, and the organic remains of a former world, thus sublimely leading the mind to contemplate the convulsions which nature has undergone since the creation.

13. As the traveler advances, he is frightfully stunned by the appalling nose. Clouds of spray sometimes envelop him, and suddenly check his faltering steps. Rattlesnakes start from the cavities of the rocks, and the scream of eagles, soaring among the whirlwinds of eddying vapor, which obscure the gulf of the cataract, at intervals announce that the raging waters have hurled some bewildered animal over the precipice. After scrambling among piles of huge

rocks that obscure his way, the traveler gains the bottom of the Falls, where the soul can be susceptible only of one emotion—that of uncontrollable terror.

14. It was not until I had, by frequent excursions to the Falls, in some measure familiarized my mind with their sublimities, that I ventured to explore the recesses of the Great Cataract. The precipice over which it rolls is very much arched underneath, while the impetus which the water receives in its descent, projects it far beyond the cliff, and thus an immense Gothic arch is formed by the rock and the torrent. Twice I entered this cavern and twice I was obliged to retrace my steps, lest I should be suffocated by the blast of dense spray that whirled around me; however, the third time, I succeeded in advancing about twenty-five yards.

15. Here darkness began to encircle me. On one side, the black cliff stretched itself into a gigantic arch far above my head, and on the other, the dense and hissing torrent formed an impenetrable sheet of foam, with which I was drenched in a moment. The rocks were so slippery that I could hardly keep my feet, or hold securely by them while the horrid din made me think the precipices above were tumbling down in colossal fragments upon my head.

16. A little way below the Great Falls, the river is, comparatively speaking, so tranquil, that a ferryboat plies between the Canadian and American shores, for the convenience of travelers. When I first crossed, the heaving flood tossed about the skiff with a violence that seemed very alarming, but, as soon as we gained the middle of the river, my attention was altogether engaged by the surpassing grandeur of the scene before me.

17. I was now in the area of a semicircle of cataracts more than three thousand feet in extent, and floated on the surface of a gulf, raging,

fathomless, and interminable. Majestic cliffs, spendid rainbows, lofty trees, and columns of spray were the gorgeous decorations of this theater of wonders while a dazzling sun shed refulgent glories upon every part of the scene.

18. Surrounded with clouds of vapor, and stunned into a state of confusion and terror by the hideous noise, I looked upwards to the height of one hundred and fifty feet, and saw vast floods, dense, awful, and stupendous, vehemently bursting over the precipice, and rolling down as if the windows of heaven were opened to pour another deluge upon the earth.

19. Loud sounds, resembling discharges of artillery or volcanic explosions, were now distinguishable amidst the watery tumult, and added terrors to the abyss from which they issued. The sun, looking majestically through the ascending spray, was encircled by a radiant halo, while fragments of rainbows floated on every side, and momentarily vanished, only to give place to a succession of others more brilliant.

20. Looking backwards I saw the Niagara River, again becoming calm and tranquil, rolling magnificently between the towering cliffs that rose on either side. A gentle breeze ruffled the waters, and beautiful birds fluttered around, as if to welcome its egress from those clouds, and thunders, and rainbows, which were the heralds of its precipitation into the abyss of the cataract.

QUESTIONS.—1. What is the form and height of Niagara Falls? 2. Is there more than one Falls? 3. What divides it? 4. From what place may the Falls be seen in all their grandeur? 5. Where is Table Rock, and why is it so named? 6. Is there much water? 7. How does it appear below the Falls? 8. What effect is produced upon the mind by the union of all these sights and sounds?

ERRORS.—*Ir-reg-ler* and *un-reg-u-lar* for ir-reg-u-lar; *per-pen-dic-ler* for per-pen-dic-u-lar; *cat-a-rac* for cat-a-ract; *pint* for point; *con-sid-er-bly* for con-sid-er-a-bly; *mag-ni-fic-ient* for mag-nif-i-cent; *tre-men-du-ous* and *tre-men-de-ous* for tre-men-dous; *streetch-ing* for stretch-ing; *sing-ler* for sin-gu-lar; *ma-jes-tic-ly* for ma-jes-ti-cal-ly.

SPELL AND DEFINE.—(1) irregular, semicircle, intervention; (2) extensive, unimposing, opportunity; (3) contemplated, conceal, traverses; (4) termination, amphitheater, appalling; (5) chasm, tremendous, encompass, obscurity; (6) pyramidal, gradually; (7) luminous, irradiate, indescribable; (8) sensation; (9) perturbed; (10) undulations, comminution; (11) spiral; (12) impending, vibrate, convulsion; (13) conscious, uncontrollable; (14) suffocated, impetus; (15) colossal; (16) tranquil; (17) interminable, gorgeous, decoration; (19) halo; (20) egress, herald.

LESSON XXII.

RULE.—Let the pupil stand at a great distance from the teacher, and then try to read so loud and distinctly, that the teacher may hear each syllable.

Niagara Falls.—U. S. REVIEW.

1. Tremendous torrent! for an instant hush
   The terrors of thy voice, and cast aside
   Those wide-involving shadows, that my eyes
   May see the fearful beauty of thy face!
5. I am not all unworthy of thy sight;
   For, from my very boyhood, have I loved,
   Shunning the meaner track of common minds,
   To look on nature in her loftier moods.
   At the fierce rushing of the hurricane,
10. At the near bursting of the thunderbolt,
   I have been touched with joy; and, when the sea,
   Lashed by the wind, hath rocked my bark, and
       showed

Its yawning caves beneath me, I have loved
Its dangers and the wrath of elements.

15. But never yet the madness of the sea
Hath moved me as thy grandeur moves me now.
Thou flowest on in quiet, till thy waves
Grow broken 'midst the rocks; thy current then
Shoots onward, like the irresistible course

20. Of destiny. Ah! terribly they rage—
The hoarse and rapid whirlpools there! My brain
Grows wild, my senses wander, as I gaze
Upon the hurrying waters, and my sight
Vainly would follow, as toward the verge

25. Sweeps the wide torrent—waves innumerable
Meet there and madden—waves innumerable
Urge on and overtake the waves before,
And disappear in thunder and in foam.
They reach—they leap the barrier: the abyss

30. Swallows, insatiable, the sinking waves.
A thousand rainbows arch them, and the woods
Are deafened with the roar. The violent shock
Shatters to vapor the descending sheets:
A cloudy whirlwind fills the gulf, and heaves

35. The mighty pyramid of circling mist
To heaven. The solitary hunter, near,
Pauses with terror in the forest shades.
God of all truth! in other lands I've seen
Lying philosophers, blaspheming men,

40. Questioners of thy mysteries, that draw
Their fellows deep into impiety;
And therefore doth my spirit seek thy face
In earth's majestic solitudes. Even here
My heart doth open all itself to thee.

45. In this immensity of loneliness
I feel thy hand upon me. To my ear
The eternal thunder of the cataract brings
Thy voice, and I am humbled as I hear.
Dread torrent! that with wonder and with fear

50. Dost overwhelm the soul of him that looks
Upon thee, and dost bear it from itself,
Whence hast thou thy beginning? Who supplies,
Age after age, thy unexhausted springs?
What power hath ordered, that, when all thy
    weight
55. Descends into the deep, the swollen waves
Rise not, and roll to overwhelm the earth?
The Lord hath opened his omnipotent hand,
Covered thy face with clouds, and given his voice
To thy down-rushing waters; he hath girt
60. Thy terrible forehead with his radiant bow.
I see thy never-resting water run,
And I bethink me how the tide of time
Sweeps to eternity. So pass of man,—
Pass, like a noon-day dream,—the blossoming
    days,
65. And he awakes to sorrow.
Hear, dread Niagara! my latest voice.
Yet a few years, and the cold earth shall close
Over the bones of him who sings thee now
Thus feelingly. Would that this my humble verse,
70. Might be, like thee, immortal. I, meanwhile,
Cheerfully passing to the appointed rest,
Might raise my radiant forehead in the clouds
To listen to the echoes of my fame.

QUESTIONS.—What is the difference between this lesson and
the last? 2. What is the difference between prose and
poetry? 3. Do the lines in poetry always rhyme? 4. What is
that poetry called which does not? 5. What kind of poetry is
this lesson? 6. What is meant by *feet* in poetic composition?
7. Answer the questions proposed in the 52, 53, 54, 55, and 56
lines. 8. How are Niagara Falls like time?

ERRORS.—*Ter-rus* for ter-rors; *shad-ders* for shad-ows; *har-ri-cane* for hur-ri-cane; *ph'los'pher* for phil-os-o-pher; *ap-pint-ed*
for ap-point-ed; *e-choes* for ech-oes; *bust-ing* for burst-ing.

SPELL AND DEFINE.—(5) unworthy; (13) yawning; (16) grandeur; (19) irrestible; (25) innumerable; (30) insatiable; (35) pyramid; (39) philosophers; (43) majestic; (45) immensity; (50) overwhelm; (53) unexhausted; (55) swollen; (57) omnipotent; (60) radiant; (70) immortal.

LESSON XXIII.

RULE.—Let every pupil notice, as each one reads, when the final consonant of any word is joined to the vowel of the next word.

Character of Wilberforce.—ANONYMOUS.

1. The speeches of Mr. Wilberforce, are among the very few good things now remaining in the British Parliament: his diction is elegant, rich, and spirited; his tones are so distinct and so melodious, that the most hostile ear hangs on them delighted. Then his address is so insinuating, that if he talked nonsense, you would feel yourself obliged to hear him. I recollect when the house had been tired night after night, with discussing the endless questions relating to Indian policy, when the commerce and finances and resources of our oriental empire had exhausted the lungs of all the speakers, and the patience of all the auditors— at that period Mr. Wilberforce, with a just confidence in his powers, ventured to broach the subject of Hindu conversion.

2. He spoke three hours, but nobody seemed fatigued: all, indeed, were pleased, some with the ingenious artifices of his manner, but most with the glowing language of his heart. Much as I differed from him in opinion, it was impossible not to be delighted with his eloquence: and I felt disposed to agree with him, that much good must arise to the human mind, by being engaged in a controversy which will exercise most of its faculties.

3. Mr. Wilberforce is now verging towards age,* and speaks but seldom; he, however, never speaks without exciting a wish that he would say more; he maintains, like Mr. Grattan, great respectability of character, by disdaining to mix in the daily paltry squabbles of party: he is no hunter after place.

4. I confess I always look with equal respect and pleasure on this eloquent veteran, lingering among his bustling, but far inferior posterity; and well has he a right to linger on the spot where he achieved one of the greatest laurels that ever brightened in the wreath of fame: a laurel better than that of the hero, as it is not stained with blood or tears, better than that of the statesman who impoves the civilization of his country, inasmuch as to create is better than to improve.

5. The man whose labors abolished the Slave Trade, at one blow struck away the barbarism of a hundred nations, and elevated myriads of human beings, degraded to the brute, into all the dignified capacities of civilized man. To have done this is the most noble, as it is the most useful work, which any individual could accomplish.

QUESTIONS.—1. What were the characteristics of Wilberforce's style? 2. When was this piece written? 3. What anecdote is given concerning the "Hindu conversion?" 4. What great achievement has immortalized the name of Wilberforce?

ERRORS.—*Spr-it-id* for spir-it-ed; *in-sin-i-a-tin* for in-sin-u-a-ting; *rec'-lect* for rec-ol-lect; *Hin-dooz* for Hindus.

SPELL AND DEFINE.—(1) parliament, elegant, insinuating, discussing, commerce, confidence; (2) ingenious, impossible; (3) respectability, squabbles; (4) civilization; (5) barbarism, accomplish.

---

* Written in 1814 or 1815.

LESSON XXIV.

RULE.—Sound the vowels correctly and very full.

EXERCISES UNDER THE RULE. Prolong the following vowel sounds that are italicized.—*a*-ge, *a*-we, *a*-rm, *o*-ld, *ou*-r, *ee*-l, *oo*-ze, bu-*oy*, *i*-sle.

Pleasure in Affliction.—AKENSIDE.

1.   *   *   *   Behold the ways
Of heaven's eternal destiny to man,
Forever just, benevolent and wise:
That virtue's awful steps, howe'er pursued,
5. By vexing fortune, and intrusive pain,
Should never be divided from her chaste,
Her fair attendant, pleasure. Need I urge
Thy tardy thought through all the various round
Of this existence, that thy softening soul
10. At length may learn what energy the hand
Of virtue mingles in the bitter tide
Of passion, swelling with distress and pain,
To mitigate the sharp, with gracious drops
Of cordial pleasure? Ask the faithful youth,
15. Why the cold urn of her whom long he loved,
So often fills his arms; so often draws
His lonely footsteps at the silent hour,
To pay the mournful tribute of his tears?
Oh! he will tell thee that the wealth of worlds
20. Should ne'er seduce his bosom to forego
That sacred hour, when, stealing from the noise
Of care and envy, sweet remembrance soothes,
With virtue's kindest looks, his aching breast,
And turns his tears to rapture. Ask the crowd
25. Which flies impatient from the village-walk
To climb the neighboring cliffs, when far below,
The cruel winds have hurled upon the coast
Some helpless bark; while sacred pity melts
The general eye, or terror's icy hand

30. Smites their distorted limbs and horrent hair;
    While every mother closer to her breast
    Catches her child, and pointing where the waves
    Foam through the shattered vessel, shrieks aloud,
    As one poor wretch that spreads his piteous arms
35. For succor, swallowed by the roaring surge;
    As now another, dashed against the rock,
    Drops lifeless down: O deemest thou indeed
    No kind endearment here by nature given
    To mutual terror and compassion's tears?
40. No sweetly melting softness, which attracts
    O'er all that edge of pain, the social powers
    To this, their proper action, and their end?

QUESTIONS.—1. What is the subject of this lesson? 2. What
two instances are there (lines 3-7) of the figure of speech called
personification? 3. From line 7 to 14 is one question: what is
the sense of it in a few words? 4. What is the pleasure enjoyed
by the youth bereaved of a friend, even in mourning at the
grave? 5. What is the pleasure felt in viewing the horrors of a
shipwreck?

ERRORS.—*Of'n* for of-ten; *a'ms* for arms; *trib-it* for trib-ute;
koind-est and *kynd-est* for kind-est; *rap-chur* for rap-ture.

SPELL AND DEFINE.—(2) destiny;   (3) benevolent;
(5) intrusive; (9) existence, softening; (10) energy; (13) mitigate;
(14) cordial;   (18) mournful;   (22) remembrance;   (24) rapture;
(26) neighboring; (30) horrent; (37) deemest; (38) endearment;
(39) compassion.

LESSON XXV.

RULE.—In reading poetry, be careful not to join the final consonant of one word to the vowel of the next word.

EXAMPLE.—Loud as his thunder shout his praise
And sound it lofty as his throne.

The following way of reading it, shows the fault to be remedied, by observing the rule.

Lou das his thunder shout his praise
And soun dit lofty as his throne.

Make Way for Liberty.—MONTGOMERY.

At the battle of Lompach, A.D. 1315, between the Swiss and Austrians, the latter having obtained posession of a narrow pass in the mountains, formed a serried phalanx with presented spears. Until this was broken, the Swiss could not hope to make a successful attack. At last, Arnold Winkelried, leaving the Swiss ranks, rushed upon the Austrian spears, and receiving in his body as many points as possible, made a breach in the line, which resulted in the complete rout of the Austrian army.

1. "Make way for Liberty!"—he cried;
   Made way for Liberty, and died!
   In arms the Austrian plalanx stood,
   A living wall, a human wood!
   A wall, where every conscious stone
   Seemed to its kindred-thousands grown;
   A rampart all assaults to bear,
   Till time to dust their frames should wear;
   A wood, like that enchanted grove,
   In which with friends Rinaldo strove,
   Where every silent tree possessed
   A spirit prisoned in his breast,
   Which the first stroke of coming strife
   Would startle into hideous life:
   So dense, so still, the Austrians stood,
   A living wall, a human wood!
   Impregnable their front appears,
   All horrent with projected spears,

Whose polished points before them shine,
From flank to flank, one brilliant line,
Bright as the breakers' splendors run
Along the billows, to the sun.

2. Opposed to these, a hovering band,
Contending for their native land:
Peasants, whose new-found strength had broke
From manly necks the ignoble yoke,
And forged their fetters into swords,
On equal terms to fight their lords;
And what insurgent rage had gained,
In many a mortal fray maintained:
Marshaled once more at freedom's call,
They came to conquer or to fall,
Where he who conquered, he who fell,
Was deemed a dead, or living Tell!
Such virtue had that patriot breathed,
So to the soil his soul bequeathed,
That wheresoe'er his arrows flew,
Heroes in his own likeness grew,
And warriors sprang from every sod
Which his awakening footsteps trod.

3. And now the work of life and death
Hung on the passing of a breath;
The fire of conflict burned within;
The battle trembled to begin;
Yet while the Austrians held their ground,
Point for attack was nowhere found;
Where'er the impatient Switzers gazed,
The unbroken line of lances blazed;
That line 'twere suicide to meet,
And perish at their tyrants' feet;
How could they rest within their graves,
And leave their homes, the homes of slaves?
Would they not feel their children tread
With clanking chains above their head?

4. It must not be: this day, this hour,
Annihilates the oppressor's power;
All Switzerland is in the field,
She will not fly, she cannot yield.
She must not fall; her better fate
Here gives her an immortal date.
Few were the numbers she could boast;
But every freeman was a host
And felt as though himself were he,
On whose sole arm hung victory.

5. It did depend on *one* indeed;
Behold him,—Arnold Winkelried!
There sounds not to the trump of fame
The echo of a nobler name.
Unmarked he stood amid the throng,
In rumination deep and long,
Till you might see with sudden grace,
The very thought come o'er his face;
And by the motion of his form,
Anticipate the bursting storm;
And by the uplifting of his brow
Tell where the bolt would strike, and how.

6. But, 'twas no sooner thought than done;
The field was in a moment won:
"Make way for Liberty!" he cried,
Then ran, with arms extended wide,
As if his dearest friend to clasp,
Ten spears he swept within his grasp:
"Make way for Liberty!" he cried,
Their keen points met from side to side;
He bowed among them like a tree,
And thus made way for Liberty.
Swift to the breach his comrades fly;
"Make way for Liberty!" they cry,
And through the Austrian phalanx dart,
As rushed the spears through Arnold's heart;

While instantaneous as his fall,
Rout, ruin, panic, scattered all:
An earthquake could not overthrow
A city with a surer blow.
Thus Switzerland again was free;
Thus Death made way for Liberty!

QUESTIONS.—1. When, and between whom, did the battle
of Lempach take place? 2. How were the Austrians drawn
up? 3. What was the necessity for the self-sacrifice of
Winkelried? 4. How did it result? 5. Who was Rinaldo?
6. How many spears did Winkelried receive in his body? 7. Is
war justifiable?

ERRORS.—*As-sults* for as-saults; *sper-et* for spir-it; *pat-ri-ot*
for pa-tri-ot.

SPELL AND DEFINE.—(1) phalanx, rampart, impregnable,
horrent, breakers; (2) peasants, insurgent; (5) rumination;
(6) instantaneous.

LESSON XXVI.

RULE.—Sound the vowels correctly and very full.
EXERCISES UNDER THE RULE. Prolong the following
vowel sounds that are italicized.—*a*-ge, *a*-we, *a*-rm, *o*-ld, *o*-ur,
ee-l, bu-*oy*, *i*sle.

Speech of Logan, Chief of the Mingoes.
JEFFERSON.

1. I may challenge the whole of the orations of
Demosthenes and Cicero, and, indeed, of any more
eminent orators, if Europe, or the world, has furnished
more eminent, to produce a single passage superior
to the speech of Logan, a Mingo chief, delivered to
Lord Dunmore, when governor of Virginia. As a
testimony of Indian talents in this line, I beg leave

to introduce it by first stating the incidents necessary for understanding it.

2. In the spring of the year 1774, a robbery was committed by some Indians upon certain land adventurers on the Ohio river. The whites in that quarter, according to their custom, undertook to punish this outrage in a summary way. Captain Michael Cresap and one Daniel Greathouse, leading on these parties, surprised, at different times, traveling and hunting parties of the Indians who had their women and children with them, and murdered many. Among these were unfortunately the family of Logan, a chief celebrated in peace and war, and long distinguished as the friend of the whites.

3. This unworthy return provoked his vengeance. He accordingly signalized himself in the war which ensued. In the autumn of the same year a decisive battle was fought at the mouth of the Great Kenhawa, between the collected forces of the Shawnees, the Mingoes, and the Delawares, and a detachment of the Virginia militia. The Indians were defeated, and sued for peace. Logan, however, disdained to be seen among the suppliants, but, lest the sincerity of a treaty, from which so distinguished a chief absented himself, should be distrusted, he sent, by a messenger, the following speech to be delivered to Lord Dunmore.

4. "I appeal to any white man to say if ever he entered Logan's cabin hungry, and he gave him not meat; if ever he came cold and naked, and he clothed him not. During the course of the last long and bloody war, Logan remained idle in his cabin, an advocate for peace. Such was my love for the whites, that my countrymen pointed as they passed, and said, 'Logan is the friend of the white men.' I had even thought to live with you, but for the injuries of one man. Colonel Cresap, last spring, in cold blood, and unprovoked, murdered all the relatives of Logan, not

sparing even the women and children. There runs not a drop of my blood in the veins of any living creature. This called on me for revenge. I have sought it. I have killed many. I have fully glutted my vengeance. For my country, I rejoice at the beams of peace, but do not harbor a thought that mine is the joy of fear. Logan never felt fear. He will not turn on his heel to save his life. Who is there to mourn for Logan? Not one.''

QUESTIONS.—1. Who was Demosthenes? 2. Cicero? 3. When was Dunmore Governor of Virginia? 4. Who undertook to punish the Indians? 5. Whose family was killed? 6. Where was a decisive battle fought 7. Where does the Kenhawa rise? 8. Did Logan appear among the suppliants?

ERRORS.—*Vir-gin-ny* for Vir-gin-i-a; *pint-ed* for point-ed; *wee-men* for wo-men (pronounced*wim-men*); *De-mos-theens* for De-mos-the-nes; *cab'n* for cab-in; *murn* for mourn.

SPELL AND DEFINE.—(1) challenge; (2) outrage, summary; (3) signalized, detachment; (4) glutted, harbor.

LESSON XXVII.

RULE.—When two or more consonants come together, let the pupil be careful to *sound every one distinctly.*
EXERCISES UNDER THE RULE.

He clenched his *fists.*
He *lifts* his awful form.
He makes his *payments.*
Thou *smoothed'st* his rugged path.
The *president's speech.*

The Alhambra by Moonlight.—IRVING.

1. I have given a picture of my apartment on my first taking possession of it. A few evenings have produced a thorough change in the scene and in my feelings. The moon, which then was invisible, has gradually gained upon the nights, and now rolls in full splendor above the towers, pouring a flood of tempered light into every court and hall. The garden beneath my window is gently lighted up. The orange and citron trees are tipped with silver. The fountain sparkles in the moonbeams, and even the blush of the rose is faintly visible.

2. I have sat for hours at my window, inhaling the sweetness of the garden, and musing on the checkered features of those whose history is dimly shadowed out in the elegant memorials around. Sometimes I have issued forth at midnight when everything was quiet, and have wandered over the whole building. Who can do justice to a moonlight night in such a climate, and in such a place! The temperature of an Andalusian midnight in summer is perfectly ethereal. We seem lifted up into a purer atmosphere. There is a serenity of soul, a buoyancy of spirits, an elasticity of frame, that render mere *existence* enjoyment. The effect of moonlight, too, on the Alhambra, has something like enchantment. Every rent and chasm of time, every mouldering tint and weather stain, disappears. The marble resumes its original whiteness; the long colonnades brighten in the moonbeams; the halls are illuminated with a softened radiance, until the whole edifice reminds one of the enchanted palace of an Arabian tale.

3. At such a time, I have ascended to the little pavilion, called the queen's toilette, to enjoy its varied and extensive prospect. To the right, the snowy summits of the Sierra Nevada would gleam, like silver

clouds, against the darker firmament, and all the outlines of the mountain would be softened, yet delicately defined. My delight, however, would be to lean over the parapet of the Tocador, and gaze down upon Granada, spread out like a map below me, all buried in deep repose, and its white palaces and convents sleeping, as it were, in the moonshine.

4. Sometimes I would hear the faint sounds of castanets from some party of dancers lingering in the Alameda. At other times, I have heard the dubious tones of a guitar, and the notes of a single voice rising from some solitary street, and have pictured to myself some youthful cavalier, serenading his lady's window, a gallant custom of former days, but now sadly on the decline, except in the remote towns and villages of Spain.

5. Such are the scenes that have detained me for many an hour, loitering about the courts and balconies of the castle, enjoying that mixture of reverie and sensation which steal away existence in a southern climate, and it has been almost morning before I have retired to my bed, and been lulled to sleep by the falling waters of the fountain of Lindaraxa.

QUESTIONS.—1. What and where is the Alhambra?   2. What are castanets?   3. What is the natural instrument of the Spaniards?   4. Where is Andalusia?

ERRORS.—*Firm-'ment* for fir-ma-ment; *dub-'us* for du-bi-ous.

SPELL AND DEFINE.—(1) apartment, splendor; (2) inhaling, checkered, memorials, enchantment, colonnades, buoyancy; (3) pavilion, varied, firmament, palaces; (4) castanets, cavalier, serenading;   (5) reverie, Lindaraxa.

LESSON XXVIII.

RULE.—Be careful to read the *last words* of every sentence with a slow and full tone.

Portrait of a Patriarch.—ADDISON.

1. I cannot forbear making an extract of several passages, which I have always read with great delight, in the book of Job. It is the account which that holy man gives, of his behavior in the days of his prosperity, and, if considered only as a human composition, is a finer picture of a charitable and good-natured man than is to be met with in any other author.

2. "Oh that I were as in months past, as in the days when God preserved me, when his candle shined upon my head, and when, by his light, I walked through darkness; when the Almighty was yet with me; when my children were about me; when I washed my steps with butter, and the rock poured out rivers of oil.

3. "When the ear heard me, then it blessed me, and when the eye saw me, it gave witness to me, because I delivered the poor that cried, and the fatherless, and him that had none to help him. The blessing of him that was ready to perish came upon me, and I caused the widow's heart to sing for joy. I was eyes to the blind, and feet was I to the lame. I was a father to the poor, and the cause which I knew not I searched out.

4. "Did not I weep for him that was in trouble? Was not my soul grieved for the poor? Let me be weighed in an even balance that God may know mine integrity. If I did despise the cause of my manservant or of my maidservant, when they contended with me, what then shall I do when God riseth up, and

when he visiteth, what shall I answer him? Did not he that made me make him also?

5. "If I have withheld the poor from their desire, or have caused the eyes of the widow to fail, or have eaten my morsel myself alone, and the fatherless hath not eaten thereof. If I have seen any perish for want of clothing, or any poor without covering; if his loins have not blessed me, and if he were not warmed with the fleece of my sheep; if I have lifted up my hand against the fatherless, when I saw my help in the gate; then let mine arm fall from my shoulder blade, and mine arm be broken from the bone.

6. "I rejoiced not at the destruction of him that hated me, nor lifted up myself when evil found him. Neither have I suffered my mouth to sin, by wishing a curse to his soul. The stranger did not lodge in the street, but I opened my doors to the traveler. If my land cry against me, or the furrows thereof complain, if I have eaten the fruits thereof without money, or have caused the owners thereof to lose their life, let thistles grow instead of wheat, and cockle instead of barley."

QUESTIONS.—1. What character is here described?   2. What is a Patriarch?   3. Considered merely as an uninspired composition, how does this compare with all others?

ERRORS.—*Char-i-tub-ble* for char-i-ta-ble; *sev-rel* for sev-e-ral.

SPELL AND DEFINE.—(1) composition, charitable; (2) almighty; (3) fatherless; (4) weighed; (5) shoulder blade; (6) destruction, cockle.

LESSON XXIX.

RULE.—Pronounce the vowels fully, and give them the proper sound.

EXERCISES UNDER THE RULE. Sound the following vowels long and full.—*e*-rr, *a*-ll, *o*-r, *a*-ge, *e*-dge, *a*-rm, *a*-t, *o*-ld, *our*, *ee*-l, *i*-t, *ooze*, p-*u*-ll, b-*oy*, *i*-sle.

An End of all Perfection.
MRS. SIGOURNEY.

1. I have seen man in the glory of his days and the pride of his strength. He was built like the tall cedar that lifts its head above the forest trees, like the strong oak that strikes its root deeply into the earth. He feared no danger, he felt no sickness. He wondered that any should groan or sigh at pain. His mind was vigorous, like his body; he was perplexed at no intricacy; he was daunted at no difficulty; into hidden things he searched, and what was crooked he made straight.

2. He went forth fearlessly upon the face of the mighty deep. He surveyed the nations of the earth; he measured the distances of the stars, and called them by their names. He gloried in the extent of his knowledge, in the vigor of his understanding, and strove to search even into what the Almighty had concealed. When I looked on him I said,"What a piece of work is man! how noble in reason! how infinite in faculties! in form and moving how express and admirable! in action how like an angel! in apprehension how like a God!"

3. I returned—his look was no more lofty, nor his step proud; his broken frame was like some ruined tower; his hairs were white and scattered; and his eye gazed vacantly upon what was passing around him. The vigor of his intellect was wasted, and of all that he had gained by study, nothing remained. He feared when there was no danger, and when there was no

sorrow he wept. His memory was decayed and treacherous, and showed him only broken images of the glory that was departed.

4. His house was to him like a strange land, and his friends were counted as his enemies. He thought himself strong and heathful while his foot tottered on the verge of the grave. He said of his son, "He is my brother;" of his daughter, "I know her not;" and he inquired what was his own name. One who supported his last steps, and ministered to his many wants, said to me, as I looked on the melancholy scene, "Let thine heart receive instruction, for thou hast seen an end of all earthly perfection."

5. I have seen a beautiful female treading the first stages of youth, and entering joyfully into the pleasures of life. The glance of her eye was variable and sweet, and on her cheek trembled something like the first blush of the morning. Her lips moved, and there was harmony, and when she floated in the dance, her light form, like the aspen, seemed to move with every breeze. I returned, but she was not in the dance. I sought her in the gay circle of her companions, but I found her not.

6. Her eye sparkled not there—the music of her voice was silent—she rejoiced on earth no more. I saw a train, sable and slow-paced, who bore sadly to an open grave what once was animated and beautiful. They paused as they approached, and a voice broke the awful silence: "Mingle ashes with ashes, and dust with its original dust. To the earth whence it was taken, consign we the body of our sister." They covered her with the damp soil and the clods of the valley. Yet one sad mourner lingered, to cast himself upon the grave, and as he wept he said, "There is no beauty, or grace, or loveliness, that continueth in man, for this is the end of all his glory and perfection."

7. I have seen an infant with a fair brow, and a frame like polished ivory. Its limbs were pliant in its sports. It rejoiced, and again it wept, but whether its glowing cheek dimpled with smiles, or its blue eye was brilliant with tears, still I said to my heart, "It is beautiful." It was like the first pure blossom, which some cherished plant had shot forth, whose cup is filled with a dewdrop, and whose head reclines upon its parent stem.

8. I again saw this child when the lamp of reason first dawned in its mind. Its soul was gentle and peaceful. Its eye sparkled with joy, as it looked round on this good and pleasant world. It ran swiftly in the ways of knowledge. It bowed its ear to instruction; it stood like a lamb before its teachers. It was not proud, or envious, or stubborn, and it had never heard of the vices and vanities of the world. When I looked upon it, I remembered that our Savior had said, "Except ye become as little children, ye cannot enter into the kingdom of heaven."

9. But the scene was changed, and I saw a man whom the world called honorable, and many waited for his smile. They pointed out the fields that were his, and talked of the silver and gold that he had gathered. They admired the stateliness of his domes, and extolled the honor of his family. His heart answered secretly, "By my wisdom have I gotten all this;" so he returned no thanks to God, neither did he fear nor serve him.

10. As I passed along, I heard the complaints of the laborers who had reaped down his fields, and the cries of the poor, whose covering he had taken away, but the sound of feasting and revelry was in his apartments, and the unfed beggar came tottering from his door. But he considered not that the cries of the oppressed were continually entering into the ears of the Most High. When I knew that this man was once the

teachable child that I had loved, the beautiful infant that I had gazed upon with delight, I said in my bitterness, "I have seen an end of all perfection," and I laid my mouth in the dust.

QUESTIONS.—1. What changes pass upon the proudest forms—and the most undaunted intellects—from the lapse of time? 2. What takes the place of childhood and manhood? 3. What becomes of vanity, as time flies past? 4. What becomes of the docility and loveliness of childhood?

ERRORS.—*Bud-dy* for bod-y; *dorn-ted* and *don-ted* for daunted, (pronounced *dant-ed*.)

SPELL AND DEFINE.—(1) perplexed, intricacy; (2) fearlessly, understanding, apprehension; (3) vacantly, intellect, treacherous; (5) joyfully, returned; (6) continueth; (8) envious, stubborn; (9) honorable, extolled; (10) complaints, apartments, tottering, perfection.

LESSON XXX.

RULE.—When anything very solemn or devotional is to be read, there should be a full, solemn tone of voice; the piece should be read slowly, and long pauses should be made at the commas.

A Rest for the Weary.—MONTGOMERY.

1. There is a calm for those who weep,
   A rest for weary pilgrims found,
   They softly lie, and sweetly sleep,
   Low in the ground.

2. The storm that wrecks the wint'ry sky
   No more disturbs their deep repose,
   Than summer evening's latest sigh
   That shuts the rose.

3. I long to lay this painful head
   And aching heart beneath the soil,
   To slumber in that dreamless bed
   From all my toil.

4. For misery stole me at my birth
   And cast me helpless on the wild:
   I perish; O my mother earth,
   Take home thy child.

5. On thy dear lap these limbs reclined,
   Shall gently moulder into thee;
   Nor leave one wretched trace behind,
   Resembling me.

6. Hark! A strange sound affrights mine
   My pulse, my brain runs wild, I rave;
   Ah! Who art thou whose voice I hear?
   I am the Grave!

7. The Grave, that never spake before,
   Hath found at length a tongue to chide:
   Oh listen! I will speak no more:
   Be silent, Pride.

8. Art thou a wretch, of hope forlorn,
   The victim of consuming care?
   Is thy distracted conscience torn
   By fell despair?

9. Do foul misdeeds of former times
   Wring with remorse thy guilty breast?
   And ghosts of unforgiven crimes
   Murder thy rest?

10. Lash'd by the furies of the mind,
    From wrath and vengeance would'st thou flee
    Ah! Think not, hope not, fool, to find
    A friend in me,

11. By all the terrors of the tomb,
    Beyond the power of tongue to tell,
    By the dread secrets of my womb,
    By death and hell,

12. I charge thee live! Repent and pray;
    In dust thine infamy deplore;
    There yet is mercy; go thy way
    And sin no more.

13. Whate'er thy lot, whoe'er thou be,
    Confess thy folly, kiss the rod,
    And in thy chastening sorrows see
    The hand of God.

14. A bruised reed he will not break;
    Afflictions all his children feel,
    He wounds them for his mercy's sake,
    He wounds to heal!

15. Humbled beneath his mighty hand,
    Prostrate his Providence adore:
    Tis done! arise! He bids thee stand,
    To fall no more.

16. Now traveler in the vale of tears!
    To realms of everlasting light
    Through time's dark wilderness of years,
    Pursue thy flight.

17. There is a calm of those that weep,
    A rest for weary pilgrims found:
    And while the mouldering ashes sleep
    Low in the ground;

18. The soul, of origin divine,
    God's glorious image, freed from clay,
    In heaven's eternal sphere shall shine
    A star of day!

19. The sun is but a spark of fire,
     A transient meteor in the sky,
     The soul, immortal as its sire,
     Shall never die.

QUESTIONS.—1. Who is represented as speaking in verse
eighth, and onward? 2. What is a "figure of speech?" 3. What
is that figure of speech called, which represents the grave, or any
inanimate object, as speaking? 4. With what sentiments should
thoughts of death inspire us? 5. Why is death ever
desirable? 6. To what will it introduce us? 7. Is it wise to make
no preparation for death? 8. Should not our *eternal* welfare be
our chief concern in the world?

ERRORS.—*Sof-ly* for soft-ly; *shets* for shuts; *heth* for hath;
lis-sen for lis-ten; *keer* for care; *chas-ning* for chaste-ning; *'um-
bled* for hum-bled; *pur-shue* for pur-sue; *pur-ish* for per-ish; *im-
midge* for im-age.

SPELL AND DEFINE.—(1) pilgrims; (3) dreamless;
(5) reclined, moulder, resembling;   (6) affrights;   (7) chide;
(8) forlorn, victim, consuming, conscience;   (9) remorse;
(10) vengeance;   (11) terrors;   (12) infamy, deplore;
(13) chastening;   (14) afflictions;   (15) prostrate, adore;
(16) realms, everlasting, wilderness, pursue; (17) mouldering;
(18) origin, eternal, sphere;   (19) transient, meteor.

LESSON XXXI.

RULE.—Let every pupil notice, as each one reads, where a
comma is not marked by a proper pause.

Character of Mr. Brougham.

ANONYMOUS.

1. Brougham, is a thunderbolt. He may come in the
dark, he may come at random, his path may be in the
viewless and graspless air; but still give him
something solid, let him come in contact with the

earth, and, be it beautiful or barren, it feels the power of his terrible visitation.

2. You see not, or rather you heed not, the agent which works, but, just as when the arch-giant of physical destroyers rends his way, you see the kingdoms of nature yielding at his approach, and the mightiest of their productions brushed aside as though they were dust, or torn as though they were gossamer.

3. While he raises his voice in the house, while he builds firmly and broadly the bases of his propositions, and snatches from every science a beam to enlarge and strengthen his work, and while he indignantly beats down and tramples upon all that has been reared by his antagonist, you feel as if the wind of annihilation were in his hand, and the power of destruction in his possession.

4. There cannot be a greater treat than to hear Brougham upon one of those questions which give scope for the mighty swell of his mind, and which permit him to launch the bolts of that tremendous sarcasm, for which he has not now, and perhaps never had, an equal in the house. When his display is a reply, you see his long and lathy figure drawn aside from others, and coiled up within itself like a snake, and his eyes glancing from under the slouched hat, as fiery and as fatal as those of the basilisk. You mark the twin sisters of irony and contempt, playing about the tense and compressed line of his mouth.

5. Up rises the orator, slowly and clumsily. His body, swung into an attitude which is none of the most graceful. His long and sallow visage seems lenghtened and deepened in its hue. His eyes, his nose, and mouth seem huddled together, as, if while he presses every illustration into his speech, he were at the same time condensing all his senses into one.

6. There is a lowering sublimity in his brows, which one seldom sees equaled, and the obliquity of the light shows the organization of the upper and lateral parts of his forehead, proud and palpable as the hills of his native north. His left hand is extended with the palm, prepared as an anvil, upon which he is ever and anon to hammer, with the forefinger of his right, as the preparation to that full swing which is to give life to every muscle, and motion to every limb.

7. He speaks! In the most powerful and sustained, and at the same time, the most close, clear and logical manner, does he demolish the castle which his opponent had built for himself. You hear the sounds, you see the flash, you look for the castle, and it is not. Stone after stone, turret after turret, battlement after battlement, and wing after wing, are melted away, and nothing left, save the sure foundation, upon which the orator himself may build.

8. There are no political bowels in him. He gives no quarter, and no sooner has he razed the fort, than he turns to torture the garrison. It is now that his mock solemnity is something more terrible then the satire of Canning, the glow of Burdett, or the glory of Mackintosh.

9. His features, (which are always grave) assume the very depth of solemnity, and his voice (which is always solemn) falls into that under soprano, (that visionary tone between speech and whisper) which men employ when they speak of their own graves and coffins.

10. You would imagine it not audible, and yet its lowest syllable runs through the house like wildfire. You would think it meant only for the ear of him who is the subject of it, yet it comes immediately, and powerfully, and without the possibility of being forgotten, to everyone within the walls.

11. You would think it the fond admonition of a sainted father to the errors of a beloved son, and yet, it has in reality more of that feeling which the Devil is said to exercise, when he acts as the accuser of the brethren. You may push aside the bright thing which raises a laugh. You may find a cover from the wit which ambles to you on antithesis or quotation, but against the home reproof of Brougham there is no defense, its course is so firm that you cannot dash it aside.

QUESTIONS.—1. To what is Brougham (Broome.) compared? 2. What is the marked attribute of his style? 3. His personal appearance? 4. His manner, voice, gestures, &c.

ERRORS.—*Hed* for had; *lay-thy* for la-thy (lah-thy); *sal-ler* for sal-low.

SPELL AND DEFINE.—(1) thunderbolt, viewless, graspless; (2) arch-giant, mightiest, productions, gossamer; (3) propositions, strengthen, indignantly, antagonist, annihilation; (4) tremendous, sarcasm, slouched, basilisk, compressed; (5) lengthened, huddled, illustration; (6) organization; (7) battlement; (9) visionary; (10) immediately; (11) antithesis.

LESSON XXXII.

RULE.—Be careful to speak such little words as *of, the, a, in, from,* &c., very distinctly, and yet not to hold so long on them as on the other more important words.

Elevated Character of Woman.—CARTER.

1. The influence of the female character is now felt and acknowledged in all the relations of life. I speak not now of those distinguished women who instruct

their age through the public press. Nor of those whose devout strains we take upon our lips when we worship. But of a much larger class, of those whose influence is felt in the relations of neighbor, friend, daughter, wife, mother.

2. Who waits at the couch of the sick to administer tender charities while life lingers, or to perform the last acts of kindness when death comes? Where shall we look for those examples of friendship, that most adorn our nature; those abiding friendships, which trust even when betrayed, and survive all changes of fortune?

3. Where shall we find the brightest illustrations of filial piety? Have you ever seen a daughter, herself perhaps timid and helpless, watching the decline of an aged parent, and holding out with heroic fortitude to anticipate his wishes, to administer to his wants, and to sustain his tottering steps to the very borders of the grave?

4. But in no relation does woman exercise so deep an influence, both immediately and prospectively, as in that of mother. To her is committed the immortal treasure of the infant mind. Upon her devolves the care of the first stages of that course of discipline which is to form of a being, perhaps the most frail and helpless in the world, the fearless ruler of animated creation, and the devout adorer of its great Creator.

5. Her smiles call into exercise the first affections that spring up in our hearts. She cherishes and expands the earliest germs of our intellects. She breathes over us her deepest devotions. She lifts our little hands, and teaches our little tongues to lisp in prayer.

6. She watches over us like a guardian angel, and protects us through all our helpless years, when we know not of her cares and her anxieties on our

account. She follows us into the world of men, and lives in us, and blesses us, when she lives not otherwise upon the earth.

7. What constitutes the center of every home? Whither do our thoughts turn, when our feet are weary with wandering, and our hearts sick with disappointments? Where shall the truant and forgetful husband go for sympathy unalloyed and without design, but to the bosom of her who is ever ready and waiting to share in his adversity or his prosperity? If there be a tribunal where the sins and the follies of a froward child may hope for pardon and forgiveness this side of heaven, that tribunal is the heart of a fond and devoted mother.

8. Finally, her influence is felt deeply in religion. "If Christianity should be compelled to flee from the mansions of the great, the academies of philosophers, the halls of legislators, or the throng of busy men, we should find her last and purest retreat with woman at the fireside. Her last altar would be the female heart; her last audience would be the children gathered round the knees of the mother; her last sacrifice, the secret prayer escaping in silence from her lips, and heard, perhaps, only at the throne of God.

QUESTIONS.—1. What is the influence of female character?   2. What traits of this influence are mentioned in sections 1 and 2?   3. What is the principal sphere of woman's influence?   4. How is her influence, in respect to religion, compared with that of man?

ERRORS.—*Sac-ri-fis* for sac-ri-fice; *hert* for heart; *leg-es-la-ters* for leg-is-la-tors; *chris-chan-i-ty* for chris-ti-an-i-ty; *Gud* for God.

SPELL AND DEFINE.—(1) distinguished, neighbor, daughter;   (2) administer, betrayed;   (3) illustrations; (4) exercise, immediately, prospectively; (5) germs; (6) guardian; (7) truant, disappointments, froward;   (8) academies, philosophers.

LESSON XXXIII.

RULE.—When reading poetry that rhymes, there should be a very slight pause after the words that are similar in sound, though the sense may not require it.

EXAMPLE.—Sweet it is, at eve to rest
On the flowery meadow's breast.

Here a slight pause should be made after the word *rest*, which would not be made if it were prose instead of poetry.

The Passions.—COLLINS.

1. When Music, heavenly maid, was young,
While, yet, in early Greece, she sung,
The Passions oft, to hear her shell,
Thronged around her magic cell;
Exulting—trembling—raging—fainting,—
Possessed beyond the muses painting:
By turns, they felt the glowing mind
Disturbed, delighted, raised, refined;
Till once, 'tis said, when all were fired,
Filled with fury, rapt, inspired,
From the supporting myrtles round,
They snatched her instruments of sound;
And, as they oft had heard, apart,
Sweet lessons of her forceful art,
Each (for madness ruled the hour)
Would prove his own expressive power.

2. First, Fear, his hand, its skill to try,
Amid the chords bewildered laid;
And back recoiled, he knew not why,
E'en at the sound himself had made.

3. Next Anger rushed—his eyes, on fire,
In lightnings owned his secret stings;
In one rude clash he struck the lyre—
And swept, with hurried hand, the strings.

4. With woful measures, wan Despair—
Low sullen sounds his grief beguiled;
A solemn, strange, and mingled air;
'Twas sad, by fits—by starts, 'twas wild.

5. But thou, Oh Hope, with eyes so fair,
What was thy delighted measure!
Still it whispered promised pleasure,
And bade the lovely scenes at distance hail.
Still would her touch the strain prolong;
And from the rocks, the woods, the vale,
She called on Echo still through all her song;
And where her sweetest theme she chose,
A soft responsive voice was heard at every close;
And Hope, enchanted, smiled and waved her
    golden hair.

6. And longer had she sung—but, with a frown,
Revenge impatient rose.
He threw his bloodstained sword in thunder
    down,
And, with a withering look,
The war-denouncing trumpet took,
And blew a blast so loud and dread,
Were ne'er prophetic sounds so full of woe;
And ever and anon, he beat
The doubling drum with furious heat;
And though, sometimes, each dreary pause
    between,
Dejected Pity, at his side,
Her soul-subduing voice applied,
Yet still he kept his wild unaltered mien;
While each strain'd ball of sight seem'd bursting
    from his head.

7. Thy numbers, Jealousy, to nought were fixed—
Sad proof of thy distressful state;
Of differing themes the veering song was mixed;
And now it courted Love—now, raving, called on
    Hate

8. With eyes upraised, as one inspired,
   Pale Melancholy sat retired;
   And, from her wild sequestered seat,
   In notes by distance made more sweet,
   Poured through the mellow horn her pensive soul,
   And dashing soft from rocks around,
   Bubbling runnels joined the sound:
   Through glades and glooms the mingled
      measures stole,
   Or o'er some haunted streams, with fond delay,
   (Round a holy calm diffusing,
   Love of peace and lonely musing,)
   In hollow murmurs—died away.

9. But, oh, how altered was its sprightlier tone,
   When Cheerfulness—a nymph of healthiest hue—
   Her bow across her shoulder flung,
   Her buskins gemmed with morning dew,
   Blew an inspiring air, that dale and thicket rung!
   The hunter's call, to Faun and Dryad known.
   The oak-crowned sisters and their chaste-eyed
      queen,
   Satyrs and sylvan boys were seen,
   Peeping from forth their alleys green:
   Brown Exercise rejoiced to hear,
   And Sport leaped up and seized his beechen
      spear.

10. Last came Joy's ecstatic trial:—
    He with viny crown advancing,
    First to the lively pipe his hand addressed;
    But soon he saw the brisk awakening viol,
    Whose sweet, entrancing voice he loved the best.
    They would have thought, who heard the strain,
    They saw in Tempe's vale her native maids,
    Amidst the festal-sounding shades,
    To some unwearied minstrel dancing:
    While, as his flying fingers kissed the strings,

Love framed with Mirth a gay fantastic round,
(Loose were her tresses seen, her zone unbound,)
And he, amidst his frolic play,
As if he would the charming air repay,
Shook thousand odors from his dewy wings.

QUESTIONS.—1. What is that figure of speech, by which passions, &c., are addressed as animated beings? 2. What is meant by "shell" in line 3? 3. What is this ode intended to illustrate? 4. Who were the Fauns and Dryads? 5. What do you know of Tempe's vale?

ERRORS.— '*Zult-in*' for ex-ult-ing; *per-sess-ed* for pos-sess-ed; *ris-pan-sive* for re-spon-sive; *hont-ed* for haunt-ed.

SPELL AND DEFINE.—(1) passions, expressive; (2) recoiled; (4) beguiled; (5) enchanted; (6) revenge; (8) sequestered; (9) nymph; (10) ecstatic, entrancing, tresses, festal, fantastic.

LESSON XXXIV.

RULE.—Avoid reading in a monotonous way, as if you were not interested, and did not understand what is read.

Modes of Writing.—MONTGOMERY.

1. That the art of writing was practised in Egypt before the emancipation of the Israelities, appears almost certain from their frequent and familiar mention of this mode of keeping memorials. When the people had provoked the Lord to wrath, by making and worshiping the golden calf, Moses, interceding in their behalf, says, "Yet now, if thou wilt forgive their sin; and if not, blot me, I pray thee, out of thy book which thou hast written. And the Lord said unto Moses, Whosoever sinneth, him will I blot out of my book."

2. The allusion here is to a table of genealogy, the muster roll of an army, a register of citizenship, or even to those books of chronicles which were kept by order of ancient oriental princes, of the events of their reigns, for reference and remembrance.

3. Besides, such a mode of publishing important documents is alluded to, not merely as nothing new, but as if even the common people were practically acquainted with it. "And thou shalt bind them (the statutes and testimonies of the Lord) as a sign upon thine hand, and they shall be as frontlets between thine eyes, and thou shalt write them upon the posts of thine house, and upon all thy gates." There are various parallel passages which no caviling of commentators can convert from plain meaning into paradox.

4. But not the Egyptians and Hebrews alone possessed this invaluable knowledge at the time of which we speak (from fourteen to seventeen hundred years before Christ;) we have direct and incidental testimony, both in sacred and profane history, that the Phenicians, Arabians, and Chaldeans were instructed in the same. The book of Job lays the scene and the season of his affliction about this era, and in the north of Arabia.

5. That extraordinary composition, extraordinary indeed, whether it be regarded as an historical, dramatic, or poetic performance, contains more curious and minute information concerning the manners and customs, the literature and philosophy, the state of arts and sciences, during the patriarchal ages, than can be collected in scattered hints from all later works put together.

6. In reference to the art and the materials of writing then in use, we meet with the following sublime and affecting apostrophe—"Oh, that my words were now written! Oh, that they were printed (*impress-*

ed or traced out) in a book! That they were graven
with an iron pen and lead, in the rock forever!"

7. The latter aspiration probably alludes to the
very ancient practice of hewing characters into the
faces of vast rocks, as eternal memorials of persons
and events. It is said by travelers whose testimony
seems worthy of credence, that various fragments of
such inscriptions, now utterly undecipherable, may
be seen to this day in the wilderness of Arabia Petrea,
monuments at once of the grasp and the limitation
of the mental power of man, thus making the hardest
substances in nature the depositories of his thoughts,
and yet betrayed in his ambitious expectation of so
perpetuating them.

8. The slow influences of the elements have been
incessantly, though insensibly, obliterating what the
chisel had ploughed into the solid marble, till at length
nothing remains but a mockery of skeleton letters,
so unlike their pristine forms, so unable to explain
their own meaning, that you might as well seek
among the human relics in a charnel-vault the
resemblances of the once living personages, or invoke
the dead bones to tell their own history, as question
these dumb rocks concerning the records engraven
on them.

9. The passage just quoted shows the state of
alphabetical writing in the age of Job. According to
the best commentators, he describes three modes of
exercising it: "O that my words were now written,
traced out in characters, in a book composed of palm-
leaves, or on a roll of linen! O that they were engraven
with a pen of iron on tablets of lead, or indented in
the solid rock to endure to the end of time!"

10. Arguing against the perverse sophistry of his
friends that he *must* have been secretly a wicked man,
because such awful calamities, which they construed
into divine judgments, had befallen him; so fast does

he hold his integrity, that, not only with passing words, liable to be forgotten as soon as uttered, does he maintain it; but by every mode that could give his expressions publicity and ensure them perpetuity, he longs that his confidence in God to vindicate him might be recorded, whatever might be the issue of those evils to himself, even though he were brought down by them to death and corruption, descending not only with sorrow, but with ignominy to the grave. For saith he, "I know that my Redeemer liveth, and that He shall stand at the latter day on the earth, and though after my skin worms destroy this body, yet in my flesh shall I see God, whom I shall see for myself, and mine eyes shall behold though my veins be consumed within me."

11. Had these words of the patriarch been indeed "engraven with a pen of iron on the rock forever," yet without some more certain medium of transmission to posterity, they would have been unknown at this day, or only speaking in the desert with the voice of silence, which no eye could interpret, no mind could hear.

12. But, being inscribed on materials as frail as the leaves in my hand, yet capable of infinitely multiplied transcription, they can never be lost. For though the giant characters enchased in everlasting flint would ere now have been worn down by the perpetual foot of time, yet, committed with feeble ink to perishable paper, liable "to be crushed before the moth," or destroyed by the touch of fire or water, the good man's hope can never fail, even on earth. It was "a hope full of immortality," and still through all ages, and in all lands, while the sun and moon endure, it shall be said by people of every kindred and nation, and in every tongue spoken under heaven, "I know that my Redeemer liveth."

QUESTIONS.—1. How early does it appear that the art of writing was practiced in Egypt? 2. How does it appear? 3. In the verse quoted (1), to what is allusion made? 4. How many years before Christ was this? 5. What other nations besides the Jews and Egyptians possessed this knowledge? 6. What is said of the book of Job? 7. What ancient practice is referred to in the quotation (6)? 8. Are there any remains of such inscriptions known? 9. What was the state of alphabetic writing at the time of Job? 10. What is the comparative durability of written documents, and monumental inscriptions?

ERRORS.—*Gen-e-ol-o-gy* for gen-e-al-o-gy; *prac-tic'-ly* for prac-tic-al-ly; *pat-re-arch* for pa-tri-arch; *arth* for earth.

SPELL AND DEFINE.—(1) emancipation, memorials; (2) allusion, genealogy, chronicles, citizenship, oriental; (3) documents, practically, acquainted, testimonies, frontlets, caviling, commentators, paradox; (5) extraordinary, composition, dramatic, philosophy, patriarchal; (6) apostrophe; (7) aspiration, credence, fragments, undecipherable, wilderness, depositories, perpetuating; (8) incessantly, obliterating; (10) sophistry.

LESSON XXXV.

RULE.—Do not read poetry with a drawling sing-song tone.

Joyous Devotion.—BIBLE.

1. Praise ye the Lord.
    Praise ye the Lord from the heavens,
    Praise ye him in the heights.
    Praise ye him, all his angels,
    Praise ye him, all his hosts.
    Praise ye him, sun and moon:
    Praise him, all ye stars of light.

Praise him, ye heavens of heavens,
And ye waters that be above the heavens.
Let them praise the name of the Lord,
For he commanded—and they were created.
He hath also established them forever and ever,
He hath made a decree which shall not pass.

2. Praise the Lord from the earth,
Ye dragons, and all deeps:
Fire, and hail; snow, and vapors;
Stormy wind fulfilling his word,
Mountains, and all hills;
Fruitful trees, and all cedars;
Beasts, and all cattle;
Creeping things, and flying fowl,
Kings of the earth, and all people;
Princes, and all judges of the earth;
Both young men and maidens;
Old men, and children:
Let them praise the name of the Lord,
For his name alone is excellent;
His glory is above the earth and heaven.
He also exalteth the horn of his people,
The praise of all his saints;
Even of the children of Israel, a people near unto
    him.
Praise ye the Lord!

QUESTIONS.—1. What is meant by calling upon things inanimate and upon brutes to praise God? 2. What reason is
assigned why God should be universally praised?

ERRORS.—*Osts* for hosts; *cra-ted* for cre-a-ted; *Iz-ral* for Is-
ra-el; *chil-dern* for chil-dren; *ann-gels* for an-gels.

SPELL AND DEFINE.—(1) heavens, commanded,
established; (2) dragons, fulfilling, mountains, exalteth.

LESSON XXXVI.

RULE.—In reading poetry, be careful to avoid that sort of sing-song tone which is made by marking too strongly with the voice the accented syllables.

EXAMPLE.—Sweet *is* the work, my *God* my *King*,
              To *praise* thy *name*, give *thanks* and *sing*.

Read the above example, accenting the italicized words; and the fault which is to be avoided will be perceived.

A Night Scene in Turkey.—BYRON.

1. 'Twas midnight: on the mountains brown
    The cold round moon shone brightly down;
    Blue rolled the ocean, blue the sky
    Spread like an ocean hung on high,
5. Bespangled with those isles of light,
    So wildly, spiritually bright;
    Who ever gazed upon them shining,
    And turned to earth without repining,
    Nor wished for wings to fly away,
10. And mix with their eternal ray?
    The waves on either shore lay there
    Calm, clear, and azure as the air,
    And scarce their foam the pebbles shook,
    But murmured meekly as the brook.
15. The winds were pillowed on the waves,
    The banners drooped along their staves,
    And as they fell, around them furling,
    Above them shone the crescent curling;
    And that deep silence was unbroke
20. Save when the watch his signal spoke,
    Save when the steed neighed oft and shrill,
    And echo answered from the hill,
    And the wide hum of that wild host
    Rustled like leaves from coast to coast,

25. As rose the Muezzin's voice in air
In midnight call to wonted prayer.
It rose, that chanted, mournful strain,
Like some lone spirit's o'er the plain;
'Twas musical, but sadly sweet,

30. Such as when winds and harp strings meet;
And take a long, unmeasured tone,
To mortal minstrelsy unknown:
It seemed to those within the wall,
A cry prophetic of their fall;

35. It struck even the besieger's ear
With something ominous and drear,
An undefined and sudden thrill,
Which makes the heart a moment still;
Then beat with quicker pulse, ashamed

40. Of that strange sense its silence framed;
Such as a sudden passing bell
Wakes, though but for a stranger's knell

QUESTIONS.—1. In this lesson there are many similies. Can you select them? 2. Select a metaphor, and point out the difference between it and the simile? 3. What Mohammedan custom is referred to in lines 25-26?

ERRORS.—*Spir-it-i-al-ly,* and *spir-it-chal-ly,* and *spir-it-chew-al-ly* for spir-it-u-al-ly; *i-ther* or *a-ther* for ei-ther; *az-yer* for a-zure; *pil-ler'd* for pil-low'd; *fur-lin'*, *cur-lin'*, *re-pi-nin'*, *shi-nin'*, &c., for furl-ing, curl-ing, re-pi-ning, shi-ning, &c.; *skyi* for sky.

SPELL AND DEFINE.—(1) midnight; (5) bespangled; (6) spiritually; (8) repining; (12) azure; (14) murmured; (17) furling; (25) muezzins; (27) chanted, mournful; (29) musical; (31) unmeasured; (32) minstrelsy; (34) prophetic; (35) besieger's; (36) ominous; (37) undefined.

LESSON XXXVII.

RULE.—Be careful not to dwell long on the little words like *at, on, in, by, the, a, and,*—and yet take care to pronounce them distinctly.

Criminality of Dueling.—NOTT.

1. Hamilton yielded to the force of an imperious custom. Yielding, he sacrificed a life in which all had an interest—and he is lost—lost to his country—lost to his family—lost to us. For this rash act, because he disclaimed it, and was penitent, I forgive him. But there are those whom I cannot forgive. I mean not his antagonist, over whose erring steps, if there be tears in heaven, a pious mother looks down and weeps.

2. If he be capable of feeling, he suffers already all that humanity can suffer. Suffers, and wherever he may fly will suffer, with the poignant recollection of having taken the life of one who was too magnanimous in return to attempt his own. If he had known this, it must have paralyzed his arm while he pointed at so incorruptible a bosom, the instrument of death. Does he know this now, his heart, if it be not adamant, must soften—if it be not ice, it must melt. . . . . . but on this article I forbear. Stained with blood as he is, if he be penitent, I forgive him— and if he be not, before these altars, where all of us appear as suppliants, I wish not to excite your vengeance, but rather, in behalf of an object rendered wretched and pitiable by crime, to wake your prayers.

3. I have said, and I repeat it, there are those whom I cannot forgive. I cannot forgive that minister at the altar who has hitherto forborne to remonstrate on this subject. I cannot forgive that public prosecutor who,

entrusted with the duty of avenging his country's wrongs, has seen these wrongs, and taken no measures to avenge them. I cannot forgive that judge upon the bench, or that governor in the chair of state, who has lightly passed over such offences. I cannot forgive the public in whose opinion the duelist finds a sanctuary. I cannot forgive you, my brethren, who till this late hour have been silent, while successive murders were committed.

4. No, I cannot forgive you, that you have not in common with the freemen of this state, raised your voice to the powers that be, and loudly and explicitly demanded an execution of your laws—demanded this in a manner, which if it did not reach the ear of government, would at least have reached the heavens, and have pleaded your excuse before the God that filleth them, in whose presence as I stand, I should not feel myself innocent of the blood that crieth against us, had I been silent. But I have not been silent. Many of you who hear me are my witnesses. The walls of yonder temple, where I have heretofore addressed you, are my witnesses, how freely I have animadverted on this subject, in the presence both of those who have violated the laws, and of those whose indispensable duty it is to see the laws executed on those who violate them.

5. I enjoy another opportunity, and would to God, I might be permitted to approach for once the last scene of death. Would to God, I could there assemble on the one side the disconsolate mother with her seven fatherless children and on the other those who administer the justice of my country. Could I do this, I would point them to these sad objects. I would entreat them, by the agonies of bereaved fondness, to listen to the widow's heartfelt groans, to mark the orphan's sighs and tears—and having done this, I would uncover the breathless corpse of Hamilton. I

would lift from his gaping wound his bloody mantle. I would hold it up to heaven before them, and I would ask, in the name of God, I would ask, whether at the sight of it they felt no compunction. You who have hearts of pity—you who have experienced the anguish of dissolving friendship—who have wept, and still weep over the mouldering ruins of departed kindred, you can enter into this reflection.

6. O thou disconsolate widow! Robbed, so cruelly robbed, and in so short a time, both of a husband and a son! What must be the plenitude of thy suffering! Could we approach thee, gladly would we drop the tear of sympathy, and pour into thy bleeding bosom the balm of consolation! But how could we comfort her whom God hath not comforted! To his throne let us lift up our voice and weep. O God, if thou art still the widow's husband, and the father of the fatherless, if, in the fullness of thy goodness, there be yet mercy in store for miserable mortals, pity, Oh pity this afflicted mother, and grant that her hapless orphans may find a friend, a benefactor, a father in thee!

QUESTIONS.—1. To what imperious custom did Hamilton yield? 2. Why does the writer forgive him? 3. What is the duty of the minister, of the public prosecutor, of the judge, of the governor, of the public—in reference to dueling?

ERRORS.—*Ruth-er* for rath-er; *wretch-id* for wretch-ed; *ob-jic* for ob-ject; *breth-ern* for breth-ren; *poig-nant* for poign-ant.

SPELL AND DEFINE.—(1) imperious, disclaimed, antagonist; (2) poignant, magnanimous, paralyzed, incorruptible, vengeance; (3) forborne, prosecutor, sanctuary, successive; (4) explicitly, animadverted, indispensable; (5) opportunity, disconsolate, compunction.

LESSON XXXVIII.

RULE.—When several consonants come together, give the full sound to each of them.

EXAMPLE.—Pronounce the following words, sounding fully the consonants that are italicized.—or-*b'd*, pro-*b'd'st*, trou-*bl'd'st*, trou-*bles*, trou-*bl'st*, ri*bs*, rob-*b'st*, han-*dl'd*, fon-*dl'st*, brea-*dths*, lau-*gh'st*.

Character of Napoleon Bonaparte.
PHILLIPS.

1. He is fallen! We may now pause before that splendid prodigy, which towered amongst us like some ancient ruin, whose frown terrified the glance its magnificence attracted. Grand, gloomy, and peculiar, he sat upon the throne a sceptered hermit, wrapped in the solitude of his own originality. A mind, bold, independent, and decisive—a will, despotic in its dictates—an energy that distanced expedition, and a conscience pliable to every touch of interest, marked the outline of this extraordinary character, the most extraordinary, perhaps, that in the annals of this world, ever rose, or reigned, or fell. Flung into life, in the midst of a revolution that quickened every energy of a people who acknowledge no superior, he commenced his course, a stranger by birth, and a scholar by charity! With no friend but his sword, and no fortune but his talents, he rushed in the list where rank, and wealth, and genius had arrayed themselves, and competition fled from him as from the glance of destiny.

2. He knew no motive but interest, acknowledged no criterion but success. He worshiped no God but ambition, and with an eastern devotion he knelt at the shrine of his idolatry. Subsidiary to this, there was no creed that he did not profess, there was no

opinion that he did not promulgate. In the hope of a dynasty, he upheld the crescent; for the sake of a divorce, he bowed before the cross. The orphan of St. Louis, he became the adopted child of the republic and with a parricidal ingratitude, on the ruins both of the throne and tribune, he reared the throne of his despotism. A professed catholic, he imprisoned the pope; a pretended patriot, he impoverished the country; and, in the name of Brutus, he grasped without remorse, and wore without shame, the diadem of the Caesars!

3. Through this pantomime of policy, fortune played the clown to his caprices. At his touch, crowns crumbled, beggars reigned, systems vanished, the wildest theories took the color of his whim, and all that was venerable, and all that was novel, changed places with the rapidity of a drama. Even apparent defeat assumed the appearance of victory—his flight from Egypt confirmed his destiny—ruin itself only elevated him to empire. But if his fortune was great, his genius was transcendent. Decision flashed upon his councils, and it was the same to decide and to perform. To inferior intellects his combinations appeared perfectly impossible, his plans perfectly impracticable, but, in his hands, simplicity marked their development, and success vindicated their adoption. His person partook the character of his mind—if the one never yielded in the cabinet, the other never bent in the field. Nature had no obstacle that he did not surmount—space no opposition he did not spurn, and whether amid Alpine rocks, Arabian sands, or Polar snows, he seemed proof against peril, and empowered with ubiquity!

4. The whole continent trembled at beholding the audacity of his designs, and the miracle of their execution. Scepticism bowed to the prodigies of his performance. Romance assumed the air of history; nor

was there aught too incredible for belief, or too fanciful for expectation, when the world saw a subaltern of Corsica waving his imperial flag over her most ancient capitals. All the visions of antiquity became commonplaces in his contemplation. Kings were his people—nations were his outposts; and he disposed of courts, and crowns, and camps, and churches, and cabinets, as if they were titular dignitaries of the chessboard! Amid all these changes, he stood immutable as adamant.

5. It mattered little whether in the field or in the drawing-room—with the mob or the levee—wearing the jacobin bonnet or the iron crown—banishing a Braganza, or espousing a Hapsburg—dictating peace on a raft to the Czar of Russia, or contemplating defeat at the gallows of Leipsig—he was still the same military despot!

6. In this wonderful combination, his affectations of literature must not be omitted. The gaoler of the press, he affected the patronage of letters—the proscriber of books, he encouraged philosophy—the persecutor of authors and the murderer of printers, he yet pretended to the protection of learning! The assassin of Palm, the silencer of de Stael, and the denouncer of Kotzebue, he was the friend of David, the benefactor of De Lille, and sent his academic prize to the philosopher of England.

7. Such a medley of contradictions, and at the same time such an individual consistency, were never united in the same character. A royalist—a republican and an emperor—a Mohammedan—a catholic and a patron of the synagogue—a subaltern and a sovereign—a traitor and a tyrant—a Christian and an infidel—he was, through all his vicissitudes, the same stern, impatient, inflexible original, the same mysterious, incomprehensible self—the man without a model, and without a shadow.

QUESTIONS.—1. Of what country was Phillips, the author of this piece? 2. What was his profession? 3. Who was the subaltern of Corsica? 4. What is meant by banishing a Braganza, and espousing a Hapsburg? 5. Who was de Stäel? 6. Kotzebue? 7. David? 8. De Lille?

ERRORS.—*Ex-tra-or-di-na-ry* for ex-traor-di-na-ry; *pat-riot* for pa-triot; *cap-ri-ces* for ca-pri-ces (pronounced *ca-preec-es*); *scep-tik-ism* for skep-ti-cism; *de Stale* for de Stä-el (pronounced *de Stah-el.*)

SPELL AND DEFINE.—(2) dynasty, crescent, promulgate, parricidal, diadem; (3) pantomime, development, ubiquity; (4) prodigies; (7) synagogue.

LESSON XXXIX.

RULE.—Pronounce the consonant sounds very distinctly.
EXAMPLE.—Prolong the consonant sounds that are italicized in the following words.—or-*b*, ai-*d*, a-*ll*, ar-*m*, ow-*n*, so-*ng*, wa-*r*, sa-*ve*, ama-*z*-e.

The Field of Waterloo.—LADY MORGAN.

1. It struck my imagination much, while standing on the last field fought by Bonaparte, that the battle of Waterloo should have been fought on a Sunday. What a different scene did the Scotch Grays and English Infantry present from that which, at that very hour, was exhibited by their relatives, when over England and Scotland each churchbell had drawn together its worshipers! While many a mother's heart was sending up a prayer for her son's preservation, perhaps that son was gasping in agony. Yet, even at such a period, the lessons of his early days might give him consolation, and the maternal prayer might prepare the heart to support maternal anguish.

2. It is religion alone which is of universal application, both as a stimulant and a lenitive, throughout the varied heritage which falls to the lot of man. We know that many thousands rushed into this fight, even of those who had been instructed in our religious principles, without leisure for one serious thought, and that some officers were killed in their dress uniforms! They made the leap into the gulf which divides the two worlds, the present from the immutable state, without one parting prayer, or one note of preparation!

3. As I looked over this field, now green with growing grain, I could mark with my eye, the spots where the most desperate carnage had been. The bodies had been heaped together, and scarcely more than covered and so enriched is the soil, that, in these spots, the grain never ripens. It grows rank and green to the end of harvest. This touching memorial, which endures when the thousand groans have expired, and when the stain of human blood has faded from the ground, still seems to cry to Heaven that there is awful guilt somewhere, and a terrific reckoning for those who caused destruction which the earth could not conceal. These hillocks of superabundant vegetation, as the wind rustled through the grain, seemed the most affecting monuments which nature could devise, and gave a melancholy animation to this plain of death.

4. When we attempt to measure the mass of suffering which was here inflicted, and to number the individuals that fell, considering each who suffered as our fellowman, we are overwhelmed with the agonizing calculation, and retire from the field which has been the scene of our reflections with the simple, concentrated feeling—these armies once lived, breathed and felt like us, and the time is at hand when we shall be like them.

QUESTIONS.—1. Between what powers was the battle of Waterloo fought? 2. On what day? 3. Who were the commanders in chief? 4. Which gained the battle? 5. How did Lady Morgan distinguish those spots where the most desperate carnage had been? 6. What feeling does the sight of the battlefield inspire?

ERRORS.—*La-zure* for lei-sure (pronounced *le-zure*); *rus-sled* for rust-'ed; *mes-ure* for mea-sure; *cac-u-la-tion* for cal-cu-la-tion.

SPELL AND DEFINE.—(1) imagination, maternal, anguish; (2) immutable; (3) carnage, superabundant, vegetation; (4) agonizing.

LESSON XL.

RULE.—When several consonants come together, give the full sound to each of them.

EXAMPLE.—Pronounce the following words, sounding fully the consonants that are italicized.—or-*b'd*, pro-*b'd'st*, trou-*bl'd'st*, trou-*bles*, trou-*bl'st*, ri-*bs*, rob-*b'st*, han-*dl'd*, fon-*dl'st*, brea-*dths*, lau-*gh'st*.

The Splendor of War.—CHALMERS.

1. The first great obstacle to the extinction of war, is, the way in which the heart of man is carried off from its barbarities and its horrors, by the splendor of its deceitful accompaniments. There is a feeling of the sublime in contemplating the shock of armies, just as there is in contemplating the devouring energy of a tempest. This so elevates and engrosses the whole man that his eye is blind to the tears of bereaved parents, and his ear is deaf to the piteous moan of the dying, and the shriek of their desolated families.

2. There is a gracefulness in the picture of a youthful warrior burning for distinction on the field, and lured by this generous aspiration to the deepest of the animated throng, where, in the fell work of death, the opposing sons of valor struggle for a remembrance

and a name. This side of the picture is so much the exclusive object of our regard, as to disguise from our view the mangled carcasses of the fallen, and the writhing agonies of the hundreds and the hundreds more who have been laid on the cold ground, and left to languish and to die.

3. There no eye pities them. No sister is there to weep over them. There no gentle hand is present to ease the dying posture, or bind up the wounds, which, in the maddening fury of the combat, had been given and received by the children of one common father. There death spreads its pale ensigns over every countenance, and when night comes on, and darkness gathers around them, how many a despairing wretch must take up with the bloody field as the untented bed of his last sufferings, without one friend to bear the message of tenderness to his distant home, without one companion to close his eyes.

4. I avow it. On every side of me I see causes at work which go to spread a most delusive coloring over war, to remove its shocking barbarities to the background of our contemplations altogether. I see it in the history which tells me of the superb appearance of the troops, and the brilliancy of their successive charges. I see it in the poetry which lends the magic of its numbers to the narrative of blood, and transports its many admirers, as, by its images, and its figures, and its nodding plumes of chivalry, it throws its treacherous embellishments over a scene of legalized slaughter.

5. I see it in the music which represents the progress of the battle, and where, after being inspired by the trumpet-notes of preparation, the whole beauty and tenderness of a drawing room are seen to bend over the sentimental entertainment. Nor do I hear the utterance of a single sigh to interrupt the death-tones of the thickening contest, and the moans of the

wounded men as they fade away upon the ear, and sink into lifeless silence.

6. All, all goes to prove what strange and half-sighted creatures we are. Were it not so, war could never have been seen in any other aspect than that of unmingled hatefulness, and I can look to nothing but to the progress of Christian sentiment upon earth, to arrest the strong current of its popular and prevailing partiality for war.

7. Then only will an imperious sense of duty lay the check of severe principle, on all the subordinate tastes and faculties of our nature. Then will glory be reduced to its right estimate, and the wakeful benevolence of the gospel, chasing away every spell, will be devoted to simple but sublime enterprises for the good of the species.

QUESTIONS.—1. What are the causes of war? 2. Should all men endeavor to prevent war? 3. Why? 4. What is the first great obstacle to the extinction of war? 5. How do History, Poetry and Music tend to keep alive the spirit of war? 6. Will it be finally extinguished? 7. How do you know? 8. How will it be done?

ERRORS.—*Con'-tem-pla-tin'* for con-tem-pla-ting; *pic-ter* for pic-ture; *wreeth-ing* for wri-thing.

SPELL AND DEFINE.—(1) obstacle, extinction, barbarities, accompaniments, contemplating, devouring, engrosses; (2) gracefulness, remembrance, carcasses, languish; (3) maddening, combat, untented; (4) background, treacherous, embellishments, legalized; (5) sentimental, thickening; (7) subordinate, benevolence, species.

LESSON XLI.

RULE.—Take care not to let the voice grow weaker and weaker as you approach the end of a sentence.

The Best of Classics.—GRIMKE.

1. There is a classic, the best the world has ever seen, the noblest that has ever honored and dignified the language of mortals. If we look into its antiquity, we discover a title to our veneration, unrivaled in the history of literature. If we have respect to its evidences, they are found in the testimony of miracle and prophecy, in the ministry of man, of nature and of angels, yea, even of "God, manifest in the flesh," of "God blessed forever."

2. If we consider its authenticity, no other pages have survived the lapse of time, that can be compared with it. If we examine its authority, for it speaks as never man spoke, we discover that it came from heaven, in vision and prophecy, under the sanction of Him who is Creator of all things, and the Giver or every good and perfect gift.

3. If we reflect on its truths, they are lovely and spotless, sublime and holy, as God himself, unchangeable as his nature, durable as his righteous dominion, and versatile as the moral condition of mankind. If we regard the value of its treasures, we must estimate them, not like the relics of classic antiquity, by the perishable glory and beauty, virtue and happiness of this world, but by the enduring perfection and supreme felicity of an eternal kingdom.

4. If we inquire, who are the men that have recorded its truths, vindicated its rights, and illustrated the excellence of its scheme? From the depth of ages and from the living world, from the populous continent

and the isles of the sea—comes forth the answer—
the patriarch and the prophet, the evangelist and the
martyr.

5. If we look abroad through the world of men, the
victims of folly or vice, the prey of cruelty, of injustice,
and inquire what are its benefits, even in this temporal state, the great and the humble, the rich and
the poor, the powerful and the weak, the learned and
the ignorant reply, as with one voice, that humility
and resignation, purity, order and peace, faith, hope
and charity, are its blessings upon earth.

6. And if, raising our eyes from time to eternity,
from the world of mortals to the world of just men
made perfect, from the visible creation, marvelous,
beautiful and glorious as it is, to the invisible creation of angels and seraphs, from the footstool of God,
to the throne of God himself, we ask, what are the
blessings that flow from this single volume. Let the
question be answered by the pen of the evangelist,
the harp of the prophet, and the records of the book
of life.

7. Such is the best of classics the world has ever
admired; such, the noblest that man has ever adopted
as a guide.

QUESTIONS.—1. What is the antiquity of the Bible?
2. Specify some of the reasons for considering the Bible the best
of classics? 3. How does it differ from other classics of
antiquity?

ERRORS.—*Prof-fe-sy* for proph-e-cy; *cre-a-ter* for cre-a-tor;
e-tar-nal for e-ter-nal.

SPELL AND DEFINE.—(1) classic, antiquity, testimony,
literature; (2) authenticity, authority; (3) unchangeable,
dominion, versatile; (4) illustrated, excellence, patriarch;
(5) resignation; (6) marvelous, beautiful, evangelist.

LESSON XLII.

RULE.—Pronounce the consonant sounds very distinctly.

EXAMPLE.—Prolong the consonant sounds that are italicized.—*b*-old, *d*-eign, *f*-ather, *g*-ather, *j*-oy, *l*-ight, *m*-an, *n*-o, *q*-ueer, p-*r*-ay, *v*-ale, *w*-oe, *y*-ours, *z*-one, *h*-ang.

The New Song.—BIBLE.

1. And they sang a new song, saying, "Thou art worthy to take the book, and to open the seals thereof:

2. For thou wast slain and hast redeemed us to God by thy blood, out of every kindred, and tongue, and poeple, and nation, and hast made us unto our God kings and priests, and we shall reign on the earth."

3. And I beheld, and I heard the voice of many angels round about the throne, and the beasts, and the elders, and the number of them was ten thousand times ten thousand, and thousands of thousands, saying with a loud voice, "Worthy is the Lamb that was slain, to receive power, and riches, and wisdom, and strength, and honor, and glory, and blessing."

4. And every creature which is in heaven, and on the earth, and under the earth, and such as are in the sea, and all that are in them, heard I saying, "Blessing, and honor, and glory, and power, be unto him that sitteth upon the throne, and unto the Lamb, forever and ever."

QUESTIONS.—1. Where is the book of Revelation found? 2. Who wrote it? 3. What is the character and style of this extract? 4. Is it poetical? 5. Wherein? 6. Who is meant by the "Lamb," in verse 3? 7. In what does Christ resemble a lamb?

ERRORS.—*Kin-derd* for kin-dred; *arth* and *airth* and *yirth* for earth; *ann-gels* for an-gels (pronounced *ain-gels*); *beas* for beasts; *thou-san* for thou-sand; *say-in* for say-ing; *strenth* for strength; *cre-tur* and *crit-ter* for crea-ture.

SPELL AND DEFINE.—(1) worthy; (2) redeemed, kindred; (3) elders, thousand, receive.

LESSON XLIII.

RULE.—Pronounce the vowels full, and give them the proper sound.

EXERCISES UNDER THE RULE.—Sound the following vowels long and full.—*e*-rr, *a*-ll, *o*-r, *a*-ge, *e*-dge, *a*-rm, *a*-t, *o*-ld, *ou*-r, *ee*-l, *i*-t, *oo*-ze, p-*u*-ll, b-*oy*, *i*-sle.

The Deluge.—BIBLE.

1. And the Lord said unto Noah, Come thou, and all thy house into the ark, for thee have I seen righteous before me in this generation. Of every clean beast thou shalt take to thee by sevens, the male and his female, and of beasts that are not clean by two, the male and his female.

2. Of fowls also of the air by sevens, the male and the female, to keep seed alive upon the face of all the earth. For yet seven days, and I will cause it to rain upon the earth forty days, and forty nights and every living substance that I have made, will I destroy from off the face of the earth.

3. Noah did according unto all that the Lord commanded him. Noah was six hundred years old, when the flood of waters was upon the earth.

4. Noah went in and his sons, and his wife, and his sons' wives with him, into the ark, because of the waters of the flood. Of clean beasts and of beasts that are not clean, and of fowls, and of everything that creepeth upon the earth there went in two and two unto Noah into the ark, the male and the female, as God had commanded Noah. It came to pass after seven days, that the waters of the flood were upon the earth.

5. In the six hundredth year of Noah's life, in the second month, the seventeenth day of the month, the

same day, were all the fountains of the great deep broken up, and the windows of heaven were opened. And the rain was upon the earth forty days and forty nights.

6. In the self same day entered Noah, and Shem, and Ham, and Japheth, the sons of Noah, and Noah's wife, and the three wives of his sons with them, into the ark. They, and every beast after his kind, and all the cattle after their kind, and every creeping thing that creepeth upon the earth after his kind, and every fowl after his kind, every bird of every sort.

7. And they went in unto Noah into the ark, two and two of all flesh, wherein is the breath of life. They that went in, went in male and female, of all flesh, as God had commanded him, and the Lord shut him in.

8. The flood was forty days upon the earth, and the waters increased, and bare up the ark, and it was lifted up above the earth. The waters prevailed, and were increased greatly upon the earth, and the ark went upon the face of the waters. And the waters prevailed exceedingly upon the earth. All the high hills that were under the whole heavens were covered.

9. Fifteen cubits upward did the waters prevail, and the mountains were covered. All flesh died that moved upon the earth, both of fowl, and of cattle, and of beast, and of every creeping thing that creepeth upon the earth, and every man. All in whose nostrils was the breath of life, of all that was in the dry land, died.

10. And every living substance was destroyed which was upon the face of the ground, both man, and cattle, and the creeping things, and the fowl of the heaven. They were destroyed from the earth, and Noah only remained alive, and they that were with him in the ark. And the waters prevailed upon the earth an hundred and fifty days.

QUESTIONS.—1. From what part of the Bible is this lesson taken? 2. How long has it been since the flood? 3. Why did God send a flood on the earth? 4. Who were saved? 5. Why did God preserve Noah and his family? 6. What were preserved with them? 7. What is the distinction between clean and unclean beasts? 8. How many of each class entered the ark? 9. How old was Noah when the flood came? 10. How long did it continue? 11. How high did the waters rise? 12. What evidence is there in nature of there having been a flood? 13. What does this confirm?

ERRORS.—*Noe-r* for No-ah; *in-ter* for in-to; *liv-in* for liv-ing; *kiv-er-ed* for cov-er-ed; *win-ders* for win-dows; *shet* for shut; *hunderd* for hun-dred.

SPELL AND DEFINE.—(1) righteous; (2) substance; (5) fountains; (8) increased, prevailed, exceedingly; (9) cubits, nostrils; (10) destroyed, remained.

LESSON XLIV.

RULE.—Avoid reading in a faint and low tone.

A Hebrew Tale.—MRS. SIGOURNEY.

1. Twilight was deepening with a tinge of eve,
   As toward his home in Israel's sheltered vales
   A stately Rabbi drew. His camels spied
   Afar the palm trees' lofty heads, that decked
5. The dear, domestic fountain, and in speed
   Pressed, with broad foot, the smooth and dewy
      glade.
   The holy man his peaceful threshold passed
   With hasting step. The evening meal was spread,
   And she, who from life's morn his heart had
      shared,
10. Breathed her fond welcome. Bowing o'er the
      board,
   The blessing of his fathers' God he sought;
   Ruler of earth and sea. Then raising high

The sparkling winecup, "Call my sons," he bade,
"And let me bless them ere their hour of rest."
15. The observant mother spake with gentle voice
Somewhat of soft excuse, that they were wont
To linger long amid the Prophet's school,
Learning the holy law their father loved.
His sweet repast with sweet discourse was blent,
20. Of journeying and return. 'Wouldst thou hadst
    seen,
With me, the golden morning break to light
Yon mountain summits, whose blue, waving line
Scarce meets thine eye, where chirp of joyous
    birds,
And breath of fragrant shrubs, and spicy gales,
25. And sigh of waving boughs, stirred in the soul
Warm orisons. Yet most I wished thee near
Amid the temple's pomp, when the high priest,
Clad in his robe pontifical, invoked
The God of Abraham, while from lute and harp,
30. Cymbal, and trump, and psaltery, and glad
    breath
Of tuneful Levite, and the mighty shout
Of all our people like the swelling sea,
Loud hallelujahs burst. When next I seek
Blest Zion's glorious hill, our beauteous boys
35. Must bear me company. Their early prayers
Will rise as incense. Thy reluctant love
No longer must withhold them: the new toil
Will give them sweeter sleep, and touch their
    cheek
With brighter crimson. Mid their raven curls
40. My hand I'll lay, and dedicate them there,
Even in those hallowed courts, to Israel's God,
Two spotless lambs, well pleasing in his sight.
But yet, methinks, thou'rt paler grown, my
    love!—
And the pure sapphire of thine eye looks dim,

45. As though 'twere washed with tears.'
    —Faintly she smiled,—
    '*One doubt*, my lord, I fain would have thee solve.
    Gems of rich luster and of countless cost
    Were to my keeping trusted. Now, alas!
50. They are demanded. Must they be restored?
    Or may I not a little longer gaze
    Upon their dazzling hues?' His eye grew stern,
    And on his lip there lurked a sudden curl
    Of indignation. 'Doth *my wife* propose
55. *Such doubt?* as if a master might not claim
    His own again? 'Nay, Rabbi, come, behold
    These priceless jewels ere I yield them back.'
    So to their spousal chamber with soft hand
    Her lord she led. There, on a snow-white couch,
60. Lay his two sons, *pale, pale and motionless*,
    Like fair twin-lilies, which some grazing kid
    In wantonness had cropped. 'My sons!—my
        sons!—
    Light of my eyes!'—the astonished father cried,—
    'My teachers in the law!—whose guileless hearts
65. And prompt obedience warned *me* oft to be
    More perfect with my God!—
    To earth he fell,
    Like Lebanon's rent cedar; while his breast
    Heaved with such groans as when the laboring
        soul
70. Breaks from its clay companion's close embrace,
    The mourning mother turned away and wept,
    Till the first storm of passionate grief was still.
    Then, pressing to his ear her faded lip,
    She sighed in tone of tremulous tenderness,
75. '*Thou* didst instruct me, Rabbi, how to yield
    The summoned jewels—See! the Lord did give,
    The Lord hath taken away.'
    'Yea!' said the sire,
    And *blessed be his name*. Even for *thy sake*

80. Thrice blessed be Jehovah.' Long he pressed
On those cold, beautiful brows his quivering lip,
While from his eye the burning anguish rolled;
Then, kneeling low, those chastened spirits
    poured
Their mighty homage forth to God.

QUESTIONS.—1. What is a Rabbi? 2. What was the character of this Rabbi? 3. Where had he been journeying? 4. How do you know he had been at Jerusalem? 5. Where is Jerusalem? 6. How often did the Jews go up to Jerusalem for religious purposes? 7. What had happened during the Rabbi's absence? 8. What had been the character of his sons? 9. How did his wife prepare him to hear of their death? 10. What is the best support in time of trouble and affliction?

ERRORS.—*Hal-le-lu-jah* for hal-le-lu-yah; *hol-low-ed* for hal-low-ed.

SPELL AND DEFINE.—(1) twilight; (7) threshold; (15) observant; (26) orison; (28) pontifical; (30) cymbal, psaltery; (33) hallelujah; (34) beauteous; (36) incense, reluctant; (40) dedicate; (41) hallowed.

LESSON XLV.

RULE.—Let each scholar in the class mention every syllable that is pronounced wrong, as each one reads.

External Appearance of England.
A. H. EVERETT.

1. Whatever may be the extent of the distress in England, or the difficulty of finding any remedies for it, which shall be at once practicable and sufficient, it is certain that the symptoms of decline have not displayed themselves on the surface. No country in Europe, at the present day probably none that ever

flourished at any preceding period of ancient or of modern times ever exhibited so strongly the outward marks of general industry, wealth and prosperity.

2. The misery that exists, whatever it may be, retires from public view. The traveler sees no traces of it except in the beggars, which are not more numerous than they are on the continent, in the courts of justice, and in the newspapers. On the contrary, the impressions he receives from the objects that meet his view are almost uniformly agreeable.

3. He is pleased with the attention paid to his personal accommodation as a traveler, with the excellent roads, and the conveniences of the public carriages and inns. The country everywhere exhibits the appearance of high cultivation, or else of wild and picturesque beauty. Even the unimproved lands are disposed with taste and skill, so as to embellish the landscape very highly, if they do not contribute, as they might, to the substantial comfort of the people.

4. From every eminence, extensive parks and grounds, spreading far and wide over hill and vale, interspersed with dark woods, and variegated with bright waters, unroll themselves before the eye, like enchanting gardens. While the elegant constructions of the modern proprietors fill the mind with images of ease and luxury, the mouldering ruins that remain of former ages, of the castles and churches of their feudal ancestors, increase the interest of the picture by contrast, and associate with it poetical and affecting recollections of other times and manners.

5. Every village seems to be the chosen residence of industry, and her handmaids, neatness and comfort. In the various parts of the island, her operations present themselves under the most amusing and agreeable variety of forms. Sometimes her votaries are mounting to the skies in manufactories of innumerable stories in height, and sometimes diving in

mines into the bowels of the earth, or dragging up drowned treasures from the bottom of the sea.

6. At one time the ornamented grounds of a wealthy proprietor seem to realize the fabled Elysium. Again, as you pass in the evening through some village engaged in the iron manufacture, where a thousand forges are feeding at once their dark red fires, and clouding the air with their volumes of smoke, you might think yourself, for a moment, a little too near some drearier residence.

7. The aspect of the cities is as various as that of the country. Oxford, in the silent, solemn grandeur of its numerous collegiate palaces, with their massy stone walls and vast interior quadrangles, seems like the deserted capital of some departed race of giants. This is the splendid sepulcher, where science, like the Roman Tarpeia, lies buried under the weight of gold that rewarded her ancient services, and where copious libations of the richest Port and Madeira, are daily poured out to her memory.

8. At Liverpool, on the contrary, all is bustle, brick and business. Everything breathes of modern times. Everybody is occupied with the concerns of the present moment excepting one elegant scholar, who unites a singular resemblance to the Roman face and dignified person of our Washington, with the magnificent spirit and intellectual accomplishments of his own Italian hero.

9. At every change in the landscape, you fall upon monuments of some new race of men, among the number that have in their turn inhabited these islands. The mysterious monument of Stonehenge, standing remote and alone upon a bare and boundless heath, as much unconnected with the events of past ages as it is with the uses of the present, carries you back, beyond all historical records, into the obscurity of a wholly unknown period.

10. Perhaps the Druids raised it, but by what machinery could these half barbarians have wrought and moved such immense masses of rock? By what fatality is it, that, in every part of the globe, the most durable impressions that have been made upon its surface were the work of races now entirely extinct? Who where the builders of the pyramids, and the massy monuments of Egypt and India?

11. Who constructed the Cyclopean walls of Italy and Greece, or elevated the innumerable and inexplicable mounds which are seen in every part of Europe, Asia, and America; or the ancient forts upon the Ohio, on whose ruins the third growth of trees is now more than four hundred years old? All these constructions have existed through the whole period within the memory of man, and will continue, when all the architecture of the present generation, with its high civilization and improved machinery, shall have crumbled into dust.

12. Stonehenge will remain unchanged when the banks of the Thames shall be as bare as Salisbury heath. But the Romans had something of the spirit of these primitive builders, and they left everywhere distinct traces of their passage.

13. Half the castles in Great Britain were founded, according to tradition, by Julius Caesar, and abundant vestiges remain, throughout the island, of their walls, forts, and military roads. Most of their castles have, however, been built upon and augmented at a later period, and belong, with more propriety, to the brilliant period of Gothic architecture. Thus the keep of Warwick dates from the time of Caesar, while the castle itself, with its lofty battlements, extensive walls, and large enclosures, bears witness to the age when every Norman chief was a military despot within his own barony.

14. To this period appertains the principal part of the magnificent Gothic monuments, castles, cathedrals, abbeys, priories and churches, in various stages of preservation and of ruin. Some like Warwick and Alnwick castles, like Salisbury cathedral and Westminster abbey, are in all their original perfection; others, like Kenilworth and Canterbury, little more than a rude mass of earth and rubbish; and others again in the intermediate stages of decay, borrowing a sort of charm from their very ruin, and putting on their dark green robes of ivy to conceal the ravages of time, as if the luxuriant bounty of nature were purposely throwing a veil over the frailty and feebleness of art.

15. What a beautiful and brilliant vision was this Gothic architecture, shining out as it did from the deepest darkness of feudal barbarism! Here again, by what fatality has it happened that the moderns, with all their civilization and improved taste, have been as utterly unsuccessful in rivaling the divine simplicity of the Greeks, as the rude grandeur of the Cyclopeans and ancient Egyptians?

16. Since the revival of arts in Europe, the builders have confined themselves wholly to a graceless and unsuccessful imitation of ancient models. Strange, that the only new architectural conception of any value, subsequent to the time of Phidias, should have been struck out at the worst period of society that has since occurred!

17. Sometimes the moderns, in their laborious poverty of invention, heap up small materials in large masses, and think that St. Peter's or St. Paul's will be as much more sublime than the Parthenon, as they are larger. At others, they condescend to a servile imitation of the wild and native graces of the Gothic, as the Chinese, in their stupid ignorance of

perspective, can still copy, line by line, and point by point, a European picture. But the Norman castles and churches, with all their richness and sublimity, fell with the power of their owners at the rise of the Commonwealth.

18. The Independents were levelers of substance as well as form, and the material traces they left of their existence are the ruins of what their predecessors had built. They too, had an architecture, but it was not in wood nor stone. It was enough for them to lay the foundation of the nobler fabric of civil liberty. The effects of the only change in society that has since occurred, are seen in the cultivated fields, the populous and thriving cities, the busy ports, and the general prosperous appearance of the country.

QUESTIONS.—1. What is the appearance of England, as to prosperity. 2. What is the appearance of things in respect to industry, neatness, &c.? 3. What is said of the cities? 4. Stonehenge? 5. How old is the "keep" and the castle of Warwick? 6. Who were the Independents, and what did they do?

ERRORS.—*Suf-face* for sur-face; *ob-jics* for ob-jects; *va-ra-gat-ed* for va-ri-e-gat-ed.

SPELL AND DEFINE.—(1) symptoms, exhibited, prosperity; (2) uniformly; (3) accommodation, picturesque; (4) enchanting, interspersed, feudal, recollections; (5) manufactories, innumerable; (6) ornamented, forges; (7) quadrangles; (8) intellectual, accomplishments; (9) Stonehenge; (13) architecture.

LESSON XLVI.

RULE.—In reading poetry that does not rhyme, there should not be any pause at the end of a line, terminating with an unimportant word, unless the sense requires it.

EXAMPLE.—Ye who have anxiously and fondly watched
Beside a fading friend, unconscious that
The cheeks' bright crimson, lovely to the view,
Like nightshade, with unwholesome beauty
bloomed.

In this example there must be a slight pause at the end of the first line, but none at all at the end of the second.

Vision of a Spirit.—BIBLE.

1. Then Eliphaz the Temanite answered and said,
If we assay to commune with thee, wilt thou be
grieved?
But who can withhold himself from speaking?
Behold! thou hast instructed many,

5. And thou hast strengthened the weak hands.
Thy words have upholden him that was falling,
And thou hast strengthened the feeble knees.
But now it is come upon thee, and thou faintest;
It toucheth thee, and thou art troubled.

10. Is not this thy fear, thy confidence,
Thy hope, and the uprightness of thy ways?
Remember, I pray thee, who ever perished,
being innocent?
Or where were the righteous cut off?
Even as I have seen, they that plow iniquity,

15. And sow wickedness, reap the same.
By the blast of God they perish,
And by the breath of his nostrils are they
consumed,
The roaring of the lion, and the voice of the fierce
lion,
And the teeth of the young lions, are broken.

20. The old lion perisheth for lack of prey,
And the stout lion's whelps are scattered abroad.
Now a thing was secretly brought to me,
And mine ear received a little thereof.
In thoughts from the visions of the night,
25. When deep sleep falleth on men,
Fear came upon me, and trembling,
Which made all my bones to shake.
Then a spirit passed before my face;
The hair of my flesh stood up:
30. It stood still, but I could not discern the form
thereof:
An image was before mine eyes,
There was silence, and I heard a voice, saying,
Shall mortal man be more just than God?
Shall a man be more pure than his Maker?
35. Behold! he put no trust in his servants;
And his angels he charged with folly:
How much less in them that dwell in houses in
clay,
Whose foundation is the dust,
Which are crushed before the moth!
40. They are destroyed from morning to evening:
They perish forever without any regarding it.
Doth not their excellency which is in them go
away?
They die even without wisdom.

QUESTIONS.—1. Who was Eliphaz? 2. What is the amount
of his argument against Job? 3. He is proving that he must have
committed some heinous crime—where does he prove it?

ERRORS.—*Ex-len-cy* and *ex-ce-len-cy* for ex-cel-len-cy; *im-ige*
for im-age.

SPELL AND DEFINE.—(1) commune; (4) instructed;
(5) strengthened; (6) upholden; (11) uprightness; (15) wickedness;
(26) trembling; (38) foundation; (42) excellency.

LESSON XLVII.

RULE.—Where two or more consonants come together, let the pupil be careful to sound every one distinctly.

EXERCISES UNDER THE RULE.

Thou *shed'st* a sunshine on his head.

The brown *forests.*

Hop'st thou for *gifts* like these?

Or ever thou *had'st* formed the earth.

I have received *presents.*

Character of the Puritan Fathers of New England.—GREENWOOD.

1. One of the most prominent features which distinguished our forefathers was their determined resistance to oppression. They seemed born and brought up for the high and special purpose of showing to the world that the civil and religious rights of man, the rights of self-government, of conscience and independent thought, are not merely things to be talked of, and woven into theories, but to be adopted with the whole strength and ardor of the mind, and felt in the profoundest recesses of the heart, and carried out into the general life, and made the foundation of practical usefulness, and visible beauty, and true nobility.

2. Liberty, with them, was an object of too serious desire and stern resolve to be personified, allegorized and enshrined. They made no goddess of it, as the ancients did. They had neither time nor inclination for such trifling; they felt that liberty was the simple birthright of every human creature. They called it so; they claimed it as such; they reverenced and held it fast as the unalienable gift of the Creator, which was not to be surrendered to power, nor sold for wages.

3. It was theirs, as men. Without it, they did not esteem themselves men. More than any other

privilege or possession, it was essential to their happiness, for it was essential to their original nature, therefore they preferred it above wealth, and ease, and country, and, that they might enjoy and exercise it fully, they forsook houses, and lands, and kindred, their homes, their native soil, and their fathers' graves.

4. They left all these. They left England, which, whatever it might have been called, was not to them a land of freedom. They launched forth on the pathless ocean, the wide, fathomless ocean, soiled not by the earth beneath, and bounded, all round and above, only by heaven. It seemed to them like that better and sublimer freedom, which their country knew not, but of which they had the conception and image in their hearts. After a toilsome and painful voyage, they came to a hard and wintry coast, unfruitful and desolate, but unguarded and boundless. Its calm silence interrupted not the ascent of their prayers; it had no eyes to watch, no ears to hearken, no tongues to report of them. Here again there was an answer to their souls' desire, and they were satisfied, and gave thanks. They saw that they were free, and the desert smiled.

5. I am telling an old tale, but it is one which must be told, when we speak of those men. It is to be added that they transmitted their principles to their children, and that, peopled by such a race, our country was always free. So long as its inhabitants were unmolested by the mother country in the exercise of their important rights, they submitted to the form of English government, but when those rights were invaded, they spurned even the form away.

6. This act was the revolution, which came of course, and spontaneously, and had nothing in it of the wonderful or unforeseen. The wonder would have

been if it had not occurred. It was indeed a happy and glorious event, but by no means unnatural, and I intend no slight to the revered actors in the revolution when I assert that their fathers before them were as free as they—every whit as free.

7. The principles of the revolution were not the suddenly acquired property of a few bosoms. They were abroad in the land in the ages before. They had always been taught, like the truths of the Bible. They had descended from father to son, down from those primitive days, when the pilgrim, established in his simple dwelling, and seated at his blazing fire, piled high from the forest which shaded his door, repeated to his listening children the story of his wrongs and his resistance, and bade them rejoice, though the wild winds and the wild beasts were howling without, that they had nothing to fear from great men's oppression and the bishop's rage.

8. Here were the beginnings of the revolution. Every settler's hearth was a school of independence. The scholars were apt, and the lessons sunk deeply, and thus it came that our country was always free. It could not be other than free.

9. As deeply seated as was the principle of liberty and resistance to arbitrary power in the breasts of the Puritans, it was not more so than their piety and sense of religious obligation. They were emphatically a people whose God was the Lord. Their form of government was as strictly theocratical, if direct communication be excepted, as was that of the Jews, insomuch that it would be difficult to say, where there was any civil authority among them entirely distinct from ecclesiastical jurisdiction.

10. Whenever a few of them settled a town, they immediately gathered themselves into a church, and their elders were magistrates, and their code of laws

was the Pentateuch. These were forms, it is true, but forms which faithfully indicated principles and feelings. For no people could have adopted such forms, who were not thoroughly imbued with the spirit, and bent on the practice, of religion.

11. God was their King, and they regarded him as truly and literally so, as if he had dwelt in a visible palace in the midst of their state. They were his devoted, resolute, humble subjects. They undertook nothing which they did not beg of him to prosper. They accomplished nothing without rendering to him the praise. They suffered nothing without carrying up their sorrows to his throne. They ate nothing which they did not implore him to bless.

12. Their piety was not merely external; it was sincere. It had the proof of a good tree, in bearing good fruit. It produced and sustained a strict morality. Their tenacious purity of manners and speech obtained for them, in the mother country, their name of Puritans, which though given in derision, was as honorable an appellation as was ever bestowed by man on man.

13. That there were hypocrites among them is not to be doubted, but they were rare. The men who voluntarily exiled themselves to an unknown coast, and endured there every toil and hardship for conscience' sake, and that they might serve God in their own manner, were not likely to set conscience at defiance, and make the services of God a mockery. They were not likely to be, neither were they, hypocrites. I do not know that it would be arrogating too much for them to say, that on the extended surface of the globe, there was not a single community of men to be compared with them, in the respects of deep religious impressions, and an exact performance of moral duty.

QUESTIONS.—1. What was one of the prominent traits of character of our forefathers? 2. How did they regard liberty? 3. What was their conduct in support of liberty? 4. Why was the revolution a perfectly natural event—or just what might have been expected? 5. From whence were derived the principles of the revolution? 6. How were their systems of government formed? 7. What was the character of their piety? 8. As a community, how will they bear comparison for moral worth, with all other communities past or present?

ERRORS.—*Fe-ters* for fea-tures; *lib-ut-ty* for lib-er-ty; *'steem* for es-teem; *civ-vle* for civ-il.

SPELL AND DEFINE.—(1) prominent, distinguished, determined, self-government; (2) personified, allegorized, enshrined, birthright, unalienable, surrendered; (3) essential; (4) fathomless; (5) transmitted, unmolested; (6) spontaneously; (8) independence; (9) communication, ecclesiastical, jurisdiction, theocratical; (10) immediately, magistrates, Pentateuch; (12) honorable; (13) hypocrites.

LESSON XLVIII.

RULE.—When two or more consonants come together, be careful to sound every one distinctly.

EXERCISES UNDER THE RULE.

Thou *waft'st* the flying ships.

Thou *acknowledgests* thy crime.

Thou *list'nests* to my tale.

It *exists somewhere.*

Thou *knewest* that I was a hard man.

Character of the Puritan Fathers of New England.—CONTINUED.

1. What I would especially inculcate is, that, estimating as impartially as we are able, the virtues and defects of our forefathers' character, we should endeavor to imitate the first and avoid the last.

2. Were they tenderly jealous of their inborn rights, and resolved to maintain them, in spite of the oppressor? Shall we ever be insensible to their value, and part with the vigilance which should watch, and the courage which should defend them? Rather let the ashes of our fathers, which have been cold so long, warm and quicken in their graves, and return embodied to the surface, and drive away their degenerate sons from the soil which their toils and sufferings purchased!

3. Rather let the beasts of the wilderness come back to a wilderness, and couch for prey in our desolate gardens, and bring forth their young in our marts, and howl nightly to the moon amidst the grass-grown ruins of our prostrate cities! Rather let the red sons of the forest reclaim their pleasant hunting grounds, and rekindle their council fires which once threw their glare upon the eastern water, and roam over our hills and plains without crossing a single track of the white man!

4. I am no advocate for war. I abominate its spirit and its cruelties. But to me there appears a wide and essential difference between resistance and aggression. It is aggression, it is the love of arbitrary domination, it is the insane thirst for what the world has too long and too indiscriminately called glory, which lights up the flames of war and devastation.

5. Without aggression on the one side, no resistance would be roused on the other, and there would be no war. If all aggression were met by determined resistance, then, too, there would be no war; for the spirit of aggression would be humbled and repressed. I would that it might be the universal principle of our countrymen, and the determination of our rulers, never to offer the slightest injury, never to commit the least outrage, though it were to obtain territory, or fame, or any selfish advantage.

6. In this respect I would that the example whic. was sometimes set by our forefathers might be altogether forsaken. Let us never forsake their better example of stern resistance. Let us cherish and perpetuate their lofty sentiments of freedom. Let us tread the soil which they planted for us as free as they, or lie down at once beside them.

> "The land we from our fathers had in trust
> We to our children will transmit, or die
> This is our maxim, this our piety,
> And God and nature say that it is just.
> That which we *would* perform in arms, we must!
> We read the dictate in the infant's eye,
> In the wife's smile, and in the placid sky,
> And at our feet, amid the silent dust
> Of them that were before us."

7. Our fathers were pious, eminently so. Let us then forever venerate and imitate this part of their character. When the children of the pilgrims forget that Being who was the pilgrim's Guide and Deliverer, when the descendants of the Puritans cease to acknowledge, and to obey, and love that Being, for whose service the Puritans forsook all that men chiefly love, enduring scorn and reproach, exile and poverty, and finding at last a superabundant reward; when the sons of a religious and holy ancestry fall away from its high communion, and join themselves to the assemblies of the profane, they have stained the luster of their parentage. They have forfeited the dear blessings of their inheritance, and they deserve to be cast out from this fair land without even a wilderness for their refuge. No! Let us still keep the ark of God in the midst of us. Let us adopt the prayer of the wise monarch of Israel, "The Lord our God be with us, as he was with our fathers: let him not leave us, nor forsake us; that he may incline our hearts unto him, to

walk in all his ways, and to keep his commandments, and his statutes, and his judgments, which he commanded our fathers."

8. But our fathers were too rigidly austere. It may be thought, that, even granting this to be their fault, we are so rapidly advancing toward an opposite extreme that anything like a caution against it is out of season and superfluous. Yet I see not why the notice of every fault should not be accompanied with a corresponding caution.

9. That we are in danger of falling into one excess is a reason why we should be most anxiously on our guard at the place of exposure, but it is no reason why another excess should not be reprobated, and pointed out with the finger of warning. The difficulty is, and the desire and effort should be, between these, as well as all other extremes, to steer an equal course, and preserve a safe medium.

10. I acknowledge that luxury, and the blandishments of prosperity and wealth, are greatly to be feared. If our softnesses, and indulgences, and foreign fashions, must inevitably accomplish our seduction, and lead us away from the simplicity, honesty, sobriety, purity, and manly independence of our forefathers, most readily and fervently would I exclaim, Welcome back to the pure old times of the Puritans! Welcome back to the strict observances of their strictest days! Welcome, thrice welcome, to all their severity, all their gloom! For infinitely better would be hard doctrines and dark brows, Jewish Sabbaths, strait garments, formal manners, and a harsh guardianship, than dissoluteness and effeminacy, than empty pleasures and shameless debauchery, than lolling ease, pampered pride, and fluttering vanity, than unprincipled, faithless, corrupted rulers, and a people unworthy of a more exalted government.

11. Is it necessary that we must be either gloomy or corrupt, either formal or profane, either extravagant in strictness, or extravagant in dissipation and levity? Can we not so order our habits, and so fix our principles, as not to suffer the luxuries of our days to choke, and strangle, with their rankness, the simple morality of our fathers' days, nor permit a reverence for their stiff and inappropriate formalities and austerities to overshadow and repress our innocent comforts and delights?

12. Let us attempt, at least, to maintain ourselves in so desirable a medium. Let us endeavor to preserve whatever was excellent in the manners and lives of the Puritans, while we forsake what was inconsistent or unreasonable. Then we shall hardly fail to be wiser and happier, and even better, than they were.

QUESTIONS.—1. What should be especially inculcated in regard to the virtues and the defects of our forefathers' character? 2. How ought we to regard our rights? 3. Is this a spirit of war? 4. Did our fathers never fail in this respect? 5. How shall we regard their piety! 6. What shall we say of their austere and rigid severity? 7. What course ought we to pursue?

ERRORS.—*Lux-er-ies* for lux-u-ries; *in-sen-sub-ble* for in-sen-si-ble; *rep-rub-ba-ted* for rep-ro-ba-ted.

SPELL AND DEFINE.—(1) inculcate; (2) degenerate; (4) abominate, aggression, indiscriminately; (5) countrymen; (7) superabundant; (8) superfluous; (9) reprobated; (10) indulgences, inevitably, accomplish, guardianship, debauchery, unprincipled; (11) extravagant, inappropriate; (12) endeavor, excellent.

LESSON XLIX.

RULE.—Be careful to speak such little words as *the*, *of*, *a*, *in*, *from*, *at*, *by*, very distinctly, and yet not to dwell on them so long as on other more important words.

Decisive Integrity.—WIRT.

1. The man who is so conscious of the rectitude of his intentions, as to be willing to open his bosom to the inspection of the world, is in possession of one of the strongest pillars of a decided character. The course of such a man will be firm and steady, because he has nothing to fear from the world, and is sure of the approbation and support of heaven. While he, who is conscious of secret and dark designs which, if known, would blast him, is perpetually shrinking and dodging from public observation, and is afraid of all around, and much more of all above him.

2. Such a man may, indeed pursue his iniquitous plans, steadily. He may waste himself to a skeleton in the guilty pursuit, but it is impossible that he can pursue them with the same health-inspiring confidence, and exulting alacrity, with him who feels, at every step, that he is in the pursuit of honest ends, by honest means. The clear unclouded brow, the open countenance, the brilliant eye which can look an honest man steadfastly, yet courteously in the face, the healthfully beating heart, and the firm elastic step, belong to him whose bosom is free from guile, and who knows that all his motives and purposes are pure and right.

3. Why should such a man falter in his course? He may be slandered; he may be deserted by the world, but he has that within which will keep him erect, and enable him to move onward in his course, with his eyes fixed on heaven, which he knows will not desert him.

4. Let your first step, then, in that discipline which is to give you decision of character, be the heroic determination to be honest men, and to preserve this character through every vicissitude of fortune, and in every relation which connects you with society. I do not use this phrase, "honest men," in the narrow sense merely of meeting your pecuniary engagements, and paying your debts, for this the common pride of gentlemen will constrain you to do.

5. I use it in its larger sense of discharging all your duties, both public and private, both open and secret, with the most scrupulous, heaven-attesting integrity; in that sense, further, which drives from the bosom all little, dark, crooked, sordid, debasing considerations of self, and substitutes in their place a bolder, loftier, and nobler spirit; one that will dispose you to consider yourselves as born, not so much for yourselves, as for your country, and your fellow-creatures, and which will lead you to act on every occasion sincerely, justly, generously, magnanimously.

6. There is a morality on a larger scale, perfectly consistent with a just attention to your own affairs, which it would be the height of folly to neglect: a generous expansion, a proud elevation and conscious greatness of character, which is the best preparation for a decided course, in every situation into which you can be thrown. It is to this high and noble tone of character that I would have you to aspire.

7. I would not have you to resemble those weak and meager streamlets, which lose their direction at every petty impediment that presents itself, and stop, and turn back, and creep around, and search out every little channel through which they may wind their feeble and sickly course. Nor yet would I have you resemble the headlong torrent that carries havoc in its mad career.

8. But I would have you like the ocean, that noblest emblem of majestic decision, which, in the calmest hour, still heaves its resistless might of waters to the shore, filling the heavens, day and night, with the echoes of its sublime declaration of independence, and tossing and sporting on its bed, with an imperial consciousness of strength that laughs at opposition. It is this depth, and weight, and power, and purity of character, that I would have you resemble. I would have you, like the waters of the ocean, become the purer by your own action.

QUESTIONS.—1. What is the effect of conscious rectitude upon a man? 2. The effect of the want of it? 3. What then should be the first step in the attainment of decision of character? 4. In what two senses may we be considered "honest men?" 5. With what beautiful metaphorical comparison does this piece terminate?

ERRORS.—*Stid-dy* for stead-y; *per-pech-u-al-ly* for per-pet-u-al-ly; *dis-ci-plyne* for dis-ci-pline; *sub-stutes* for sub-sti-tutes; *per-fic-ly* for per-fect-ly.

SPELL AND DEFINE.—(1) rectitude, approbation, perpetually, shrinking, observation; (2) iniquitous, health, inspiring, countenance, courteously; (4) discipline, determination, vicissitude, pecuniary, engagements; (5) scrupulous, heaven-attesting, considerations, magnanimously; (6) consistent; (7) streamlets, impediment; (8) independence, consciousness.

LESSON L.

RULE.—When anything very solemn or devotional is to be read, there should be a full, solemn tone of voice, the piece should be read slowly, and long pauses should be made at the commas.

On the Being of a God.—YOUNG.

1. Retire; the world shut out; thy thoughts call
    home:
    Imagination's airy wing repress;
    Lock up thy senses; let no passion stir;
    Wake all to reason: let her reign alone;
5. Then in thy soul's deep silence, and the depth
    Of nature's silence, midnight, thus inquire,
    As I have done; and shall inquire no more.
    In nature's channel thus the questions run.
    What am I? and from whence? I nothing know,
10. But that I am; and since I am, conclude
    Something eternal: had there e'er been nought,
    Nought still had been: eternal there must be.
    But what eternal? Why not human race?
    And Adam's ancestors without an end?
15. That's hard to be conceived; since every link
    Of that long chained succession is so frail;
    Can every part depend, and not the whole?
    Yet grant it true; new difficulties rise;
    I'm still quite out at sea: nor see the shore.
20. Whence earth, and these bright orbs? Eternal
    too?
    Grant matter was eternal; still these orbs
    Would want some other father; much design
    Is seen in all their motions, all their makes;
    Design implies intelligence and art
25. That can't be from themselves or man; that art
    Man scarce can comprehend, could man bestow
    And nothing greater yet allow'd than man.

Who, motion, foreign to the smallest grain,
Shot through vast masses of enormous weight?
30. Who bid brute matter's restive lump assume
Such various forms, and gave it wings to fly?
Has matter innate motion? then each atom,
Asserting its indisputable right
To dance, would form a universe of dust;
35. Has matter none? Then whence those glorious forms
And boundless flights, from shapeless and reposed?
Has matter more than motion? has it thought,
Judgment and genius? Is it deeply learned
In mathematics? Has it framed such laws,
40. Which but to guess, a Newton made immortal?
If so, how each sage atom laughs at me,
Who think a clod inferior to a man!
If art to form; and counsel to conduct;
Resides not in each block; a Godhead reigns.
45. Grant then invisible eternal mind;
That granted, all is solved; but granting that
Draw I not o'er me a still darker cloud?
Grant I not that which I can ne'er conceive?
A Being without origin or end!
50. Hail human liberty! there is no God!
Yet why on either scheme that knot subsists;
Subsist it must, in God, or human race:
If in the last, how many knots beside,
Indissoluble all? Why choose it there,
55. Where chosen still subsist ten thousand more?
Reject it, where that chosen all the rest
Dispersed leave reason's whole horizon clear?
This is not reason's dictate, reason says
Choose with the side where one grain turns the scale;
60. What vast preponderance is here: can reason
With louder voice exclaim Believe a God?

And reason heard is the sole mark of man.
What things impossible must man think true,
On any other system! and how strange
65. To disbelieve through mere credulity?"
If in this chain Lorenzo finds no flaw,
Let it forever bind him to belief.
And where the link in which a flaw he finds?
Such a God there is, that God how great!

QUESTIONS.—1. What question is discussed in this piece?
2. What inquiry is proposed in lines 9-15? 3. How is that inquiry answered in lines 15-18? 4. Suppose matter to be eternal,
or without beginning, what is still the evidence of a designing
God? 5. What is meant by the question, "Has matter innate
motion?" 6. What would follow from such a supposition? 33-34.
7. Can you state the conclusion of the argument?

ERRORS.—*Thar* for there; *in-til-li-gence* for in-tel-li-gence,
in-dis-pu-tub-ble for in-dis-pu-ta-ble; *pre-pon-der-unce* for
pre-pon-der-ance; *lib-i-ty* for lib-er-ty; *math-a-mat-ics* for
math-e-mat-ics.

SPELL AND DEFINE.—(1) retire;   (2) imagination, repress;
(10) conclude;   (11) eternal;   (16) succession;   (22) design;
(24) intelligence;   (26) comprehend;   (27) allowed;   (28) foreign;
(29) enormous;   (30) restive;   (32) innate;   (33) asserting,
indisputable;   (34) universe;   (36) reposed;   (38) judgment;
(39) mathematics; (42) inferior; (51) subsists; (54) indissoluble;
(57) dispersed; (58) dictate; (60) preponderance;(65) disbelieve,
credulity.

LESSON LI.

RULE.—Be careful not to join the last part of one word to the beginning of the next word.

The Steam Boat on Trial.—ABBOTT.

1. The Bible everywhere conveys the idea that this life is not our home, but a state of probation, that is, of *trial and discipline*, which is intended to prepare us for another. In order that all, even the youngest of my readers, may understand what is meant by this, I shall illustrate it by some familiar examples, drawn from the actual business of life.

2. When a large steamboat is built, with the intention of having her employed upon the waters of a great river, she must be *proved* before put to service. Before trial, it is somewhat doubtful whether she will succeed. In the first place, it is not absolutely certain whether her machinery will work at all. There may be some flaw in the iron, or an imperfection in some part of the workmanship which will prevent the motion of her wheels. Or if this is not the case, the power of the machinery may not be sufficient to propel her through the water with such force as to overcome the current. She may, when brought to encounter the rapids at some narrow passage in the stream, not be able to force her way against their resistance.

3. The engineer, therefore, resolves to try her in all these respects, that her security and her power may be properly *proved* before she is intrusted with her valuable cargo of human lives. He cautiously builds a fire under her boiler. He watches with eager interest the rising of the steam gauge, and scrutinizes every part of the machinery, as it gradually comes under the control of the tremendous power which he is apprehensively applying.

4. With what interest does he observe the first stroke of the ponderous piston—and when, at length, the fastenings of the boat are let go, and the motion is communicated to the wheels, and the mighty mass slowly moves away from the wharf, how deep and eager an interest does he feel in all her movements, and in every indication he can discover of her future success!

5. The engine, however, works imperfectly, as everyone must on its first trial, and the object in this experiment is not to gratify idle curiosity, by seeing that she will move, but to discover and remedy every little imperfection, and to remove every obstacle which prevents more entire success. For this purpose, you will see our engineer examining, most minutely and most attentively, every part of her complicated machinery. The crowd on the wharf may be simply gazing on her majestic progress, as she moves off from the shore, but the engineer is within, looking with faithful examination into all the minutiae of the motion.

6. He scrutinizes the action of every lever and the friction of every joint. Here he oils a bearing, there he tightens a nut. One part of the machinery has too much play, and he confines it—another too much friction, and he loosens it. Now he stops the engine, now reverses her motion, and again sends the boat forward in her course. He discovers, perhaps, some great improvement of which she is susceptible, and when he returns to the wharf and has extinguished her fire, he orders from the machine shop the necessary alteration.

7. The next day he puts his boat to the trial again, and she glides over the water more smoothly and swiftly than before. The jar which he had noticed is gone, and the friction reduced. The beams play more smoothly, and the alteration which he has made

produces a more equable motion in the shaft, or gives greater effect to the stroke of the paddles upon the water.

8. When at length her motion is such as to satisfy him, upon the smooth surface of the river, he turns her course, we will imagine, toward the rapids, to see how she will sustain a greater trial. As he increases her steam, to give her power to overcome the new force with which she has to contend, he watches with eager interest her boiler, inspects the gauge and the safety valves, and, from her movements under the increased pressure of her steam, he receives suggestions for further improvements, or for precautions which will insure greater safety.

9. These he executes, and thus he perhaps goes on for many days, or even weeks, trying and examining, for the purpose of improvement, every working of that mighty power, to which he knows hundreds of lives are soon to be intrusted. This now is probation—*trial for the sake of improvement.* What are its results? Why, after this course has been thoroughly and faithfully pursued, this floating palace receives upon her broad deck, and in her carpeted and curtained cabins, her four or five hundred passengers, who pour along, in one long procession of happy groups, over the bridge of planks;—father and son—mother and children—young husband and wife—all with implicit confidence, trusting themselves and their dearest interests to her power.

10. See her as she sails away—how beautiful and yet how powerful are all her motions! That beam glides up and down gently and smoothly in its grooves, and yet gentle as it seems, hundreds of horses could not hold it still. There is no apparent violence, but every movement is with irresistible power. How graceful is her form, and yet how mighty is the momentum with which she presses on her way.

11. Loaded with life, and herself the very symbol of life and power, she seems something etheral—unreal, which, ere we look again, will have vanished away. Though she has within her bosom a furnace glowing with furious fires, and a reservoir of death—the elements of most dreadful ruin and conflagration—of destruction the most complete, and agony the most unutterable, and though her strength is equal to the united energy of two hundred men, she restrains it all.

12. She was constructed by genius, and has been *tried* and improved by fidelity and skill. One man governs and controls her, stops her and sets her in motion, turns her this way and that, as easily and certainly as the child guides the gentle lamb. She walks over the hundred and sixty miles of her route without rest and without fatigue. The passengers, who have slept in safety in their berths, with destruction by water without, and by fire within, defended only by a plank from the one, and by a sheet of copper from the other, land at the appointed time in safety.

13. My reader, you have within you susceptibilities and powers of which you have little present conception, energies, which are hereafter to operate in producing fullness of enjoyment or horrors of suffering, of which you now can form scarcely a conjecture. You are now on *trial.* God wishes you to prepare yourself for safe and happy action. He wishes you to look within, to examine the complicated movements of your hearts to detect what is wrong, to modify what needs change and to rectify every irregular motion.

14. You go out to try your moral powers upon the stream of active life, and then return to retirement, to improve what is right and remedy what is wrong. Renewed opportunities of moral practice are given you, that you may go on from strength to strength, until every part of that complicated moral machinery,

of which the human heart consists, will work as it ought to work, and is prepared to accomplish the mighty purposes for which your powers are designed. You are *on trial—on probation* now. You will enter upon *active service* in another world.

QUESTIONS.—1. How does the Bible consider this life? 2. What is a state of probation? 3. What is a steam boat? 4. Who invented it? 5. Was Robert Fulton an American? 6. What is meant by proving a steamboat? 7. What is the use of doing it? 8. Is there any resemblance between man and a steamboat? 9. If this life is our state of probation, what will a future state of existence be? 10. What difference is there between man's probation before the "fall" and man's probation now?

ERRORS.—*Des-cip-line* for dis-ci-pline; *sar-vice* for ser-vice; *bi-ler* for boil-er; *some-at* for some-what; *sar-tin* and *cer-ting* for cer-tain; *nar-rer* for nar-row; *tre-men-du-ous* and *tre-men-di-ous* for tre-men-dous; *in-jine* for en-gine; *ur-reg-u-lar* for ir-reg-u-lar; *hun-derd* for hun-dred.

SPELL AND DEFINE.—(1) conveys, probation, discipline, illustrate; (2) machinery, imperfection, workmanship, sufficient; (3) engineer, cautiously, steam gauge, scrutinizes, apprehensively; (4) ponderous, piston; (5) obstacle, minutely, complicated, minutiae; (6) lever, friction, bearing, reverses, alteration; (7) equable; (8) safety valve, pressure; (9) implicit; (10) momentum; (11) ethereal, reservoir, conflagration, unutterable; (12) constructed, fatigue; (13) susceptibilities, conception, conjecture, modify, rectify; (14) renewed.

LESSON LII.

RULE.—Stop at each comma long enough to take breath.

Paine's Age of Reason.—ERSKINE.

1. It seems, gentlemen, this is an age of reason, and the time and the person are at last arrived that are to dissipate the errors that have overspread the past generations of ignorance! The believers in Christianity are many, but it belongs to the few that are wise to correct their credulity! Belief is an act of reason, and superior reason may therefore dictate to the weak. In running the mind along the numerous list of sincere and devout Christians, I cannot help lamenting that Newton had not lived to this day, to have had his shallowness filled up with this new flood of light! But the subject is too awful for irony. I will speak plainly.

2. Newton was a Christian! Newton whose mind burst forth from the fetters cast by nature upon our finite conceptions. Newton whose science was truth, and the foundation of whose knowledge of it was philosophy. Not those visionary and arrogant assumptions which too often usurp its name, but philosophy resting upon the basis of mathematics, which, like figures, cannot lie. Newton who carried the line and rule to the utmost barriers of creation, and explored the principles by which, no doubt, all created matter is held together and exists.

3. But this extraordinary man, in the mighty reach of his mind, overlooked, perhaps, the errors which a minuter investigation of the created things on this earth might have taught him, of the essence of his Creator. What shall then be said of the great Mr. Boyle, who looked into the organic structure of all matter, even to the brute inanimate substances which

the foot treads on. Such a man may be supposed to have been equally qualified with Mr. Paine, to "look through nature up to nature's God."

4. Yet the result of all his contemplation was the most confirmed and devout belief in all which the other holds in contempt as despicable and driveling superstition. This error might, perhaps, arise from a want of due attention to the foundations of human judgment, and the structure of that understanding which God has given us for the investigation of truth.

5. Let that question be answered by Mr. Locke, who was to the highest pitch of devotion and adoration, a Christian. Mr. Locke, whose office was to detect the errors of thinking, by going up to the fountain of thought, and to direct into the proper track of reasoning the devious mind of man, by showing him its whole process, from the first perceptions of sense, to the last conclusions of ratiocination, putting a rein besides upon false opinion, by practical rules for the conduct of human judgment.

6. But these men were only deep thinkers, and lived in their closet, unaccustomed to the traffic of the world, and to the laws which partially regulate mankind. Gentlemen, in the place where you now sit to administer the justice of this great country, above a century ago the never to be forgotten Sir Matthew Hale presided, whose faith in Christianity is an exalted commentary upon its truth and reason, and whose life was a glorious example of its fruits in man. Administering human justice with a wisdom and purity drawn from the pure fountain of the Christian dispensation has been, and will be, in all ages, a subject of the highest reverence and admiration. But it is said by Mr. Paine that the Christian fable is but the tale of the more ancient superstitions of the world, and may be easily detected by a proper understanding of the mythologies of the heathen.

7. Did Milton understand those mythologies? Was he less versed than Mr. Paine in the superstitions of the world? No: they were the subject of his immortal song; and though shut out from all recurrence to them, he poured them forth from the stores of a memory rich with all that man ever knew, and laid them in their order as the illustration of that real and exalted faith, the unquestionable source of that fervid genius, which cast a sort of shade upon all the other works of man.

> "He passed the bounds of flaming space
> Where angels tremble while they gaze;
> He saw, till blasted with excess of light,
> He closed his eyes in endless night."

8. But it was the light of the body only that was extinguished; "the celestial light shone inward, and enabled him to justify the ways of God to man."

9. Thus, gentlemen, you find all that is great or wise, or splendid, or illustrious, among created beings, all the minds gifted beyond ordinary nature, if not inspired by their Universal Author for the advancement and dignity of the world, though divided by distant ages, and by the clashing opinions which distinguish them from one another, yet joining, as it were, in one sublime chorus to celebrate the truths of Christianty, and laying upon its holy altars the never fading offerings of their immortal wisdom.

QUESTIONS.—1. Who and what was Paine? 2. What is said of Newton? 3. What of Boyle? 4. What of Locke? 5. These men, it might be said, were only great thinkers, unacquainted with practical life—Who is next brought forward to meet this?
6. What is Paine's argument in respect to the Bible and heathen mythology? 7. How is it met? 8. What is the argument for Christianity, deduced from the consideration of such individual cases?

ERRORS.—*B'lief* for be-lief; *shal-ler-ness* for shal-low-ness; *i-er-ny* for i-ro-ny; *ex-is's* for ex-ists.

SPELL AND DEFINE.—(1) dissipate, overspread, credulity, shallowness; (2) conceptions, philosophy, assumptions, mathematics, barriers; (3) extraordinary, investigation, organic; (4) contemplation, driveling, superstition; (5) adoration, conclusions, ratiocination, judgment; (6) unaccustomed, commentary, administering, dispensation, mythologies; (7) recurrence, unquestionable; (8) extinguished; (9) illustrious.

LESSON LIII.

RULE.—In reading poetry that does not rhyme, there should be no pause at the end of a line, except when it terminates with an unimportant word, or the sense requires it.

Divine Providence.—BIBLE.

1. Call now, if there be any that will answer thee;
   And to which of the saints wilt thou turn?
   For wrath killeth the foolish man,
   And envy slayeth the silly one.
   I have seen the foolish taking root:
   But suddenly I cursed his habitation.
   His children are far from safety,
   And they are crushed in the gate,
   Neither is there any to deliver them.
   Whose harvest the hungry eateth up
   And taketh it even out of the thorns,
   And the robber swalloweth up their substance.
   Although affliction cometh not forth of the dust,
   Neither doth trouble spring out of the ground:
   Yet man is born unto trouble,
   As the sparks fly upward.

2. I would seek unto God,
And unto God would I commit my cause:
Who doeth great things and unsearchable;
Marvelous things without number:
Who giveth rain upon the earth,
And sendeth waters upon the fields:
To set up on high those that be low;
That those which mourn may be exalted to safety.
He disappointeth the devices of the crafty,
So that their hands cannot perform their
enterprise.
He taketh the wise in their own craftiness:
And the council of the froward is carried headlong
They meet with darkness in the daytime,
And grope in the noonday as in the night.
But he saveth the poor from the sword,
From their mouth, and from the hand of the
mighty
So the poor hath hope,
And iniquity stoppeth her mouth.

3. Behold! happy is the man whom God correcteth:
Therefore despise not thou the chastening of the
Almighty.
For he maketh sore, and bindeth up:
He woundeth, and his hands make whole.
He shall deliver thee in six troubles:
Yea, in seven there shall no evil touch thee.
In famine he shall redeem thee from death:
And in war from the power of the sword.
Thou shalt be hid from the scourge of the tongue:
Neither shalt thou be afraid of destruction when
it cometh.
At destruction and famine thou shalt laugh:
Neither shalt thou be afraid of the beasts of the
earth.
For thou shalt be in league with the stones of the
field:

And the beasts of the field shall be at peace with
thee.
And thou shalt know that thy tabernacle shall be
in peace;
And thou shalt visit thy habitation, and shalt
not sin.
Thou shalt know also that thy seed shall be great,
And thine offspring as the grass of the earth.
Thou shalt come to thy grave in a full age,
Like as a shock of corn cometh in, in his season.
Lo! this, we have searched it, so it is;
Hear it, and know thou it for thy good.

QUESTIONS.—1. What is the destiny of the unrighteous?
2. What advice does Eliphaz give to Job? 3. What is the proper
effect of divine chastisement?

ERRORS.—'Ab-it-a-tion for hab-it-a-tion; cus-sed for curs-ed;
gret for great.

SPELL AND DEFINE.—(1) habitation, crushed, swalloweth,
affliction; (2) unsearchable, marvelous, disappointeth,
enterprise, froward, headlong; (3) correcteth, destruction,
tabernacle.

LESSON LIV.

RULE.—Be careful to speak such little words as by, in, on, a,
and, at, of, etc. very distinctly, and yet not to dwell on them so
long as on other more important words.

The Righteous never Forsaken.
NEW YORK SPECTATOR.

1. It was Saturday night, and the widow of the Pine
Cottage sat by her blazing fagots with her five tattered children at her side, endeavoring by listening
to the artlessness of their prattle, to dissipate the
heavy gloom that pressed upon her mind. For a year,

her own feeble hand had provided for her helpless family, for she had no supporter. She thought of no friend in all the wide, unfriendly world around.

2. But that mysterious Providence, the wisdom of whose ways is above human comprehension, had visited her with wasting sickness, and her little means had become exhausted. It was now, too, midwinter, and the snow lay heavy and deep through all the surrounding forests, while storms still seemed gathering in the heavens, and the driving wind roared amidst the bounding pines, and rocked her puny mansion.

3. The last herring smoked upon the coals before her. It was the only article of food she possessed, and no wonder her forlorn, desolate state brought up in her lone bosom all the anxieties of a mother, when she looked upon her children. No wonder, forlorn as she was, if she suffered the heart swellings of despair to rise, even though she knew that he whose promise is to the widow and to the orphan cannot forget his word.

4. Providence had many years before taken from her her eldest son, who went from his forest home, to try his fortune on the high seas, since which she had heard no note of tidings of him. In her latter time the hand of death deprived her of the companion and staff of her earthly pilgrimage, in the person of her husband. Yet to this hour she had been upborne. She had not only been able to provide for her little flock, but had never lost an opportunity of ministering to the wants of the miserable and destitute.

5. The indolent may well bear with poverty, while the ability to gain sustenance remains. The individual who has but his own wants to supply, may suffer with fortitude the winter of want. His affections are not wounded, his heart not wrung. The most desolate in populous cities may hope, for charity has not quite

closed her hand and heart and shut her eyes on misery.

6. But the industrious mother of helpless and depending children—far from the reach of human charity, has none of these to console her. Such a one was the widow of the Pine Cottage, but as she bent over the fire, and took up the last scanty remnant of food, to spread before her children, her spirits seemed to brighten up, as by some sudden and mysterious impulse, and Cowper's beautiful lines came uncalled across her mind—

> Judge not the Lord by feeble sense,
> But trust him for his grace;
> Behind a frowning Providence
> He hides a smiling face.

7. The smoked herring was scarcely laid upon the table when a gentle rap at the door, and loud barking of a dog, attacted the attention of the family. The children flew to open it, and a weary traveler, in tattered garments, and apparently indifferent health, entered and begged a lodging and a mouthful of food. Said he "it is now twenty-four hours since I tasted bread." The widow's heart bled anew as under a fresh complication of distresses, for her sympathies lingered not round her fireside. She hesitated not even now. Rest and share of all she had she proffered to the stranger. "We shall not be forsaken," said she, "or suffer deeper for an act of charity."

8. The traveler drew near the board, but when he saw the scanty fare, he raised his eyes towards heaven with astonishment—"and is this *all* your store?" said he—"and a share of this do you offer to one you know not? Then never saw I *charity* before! But madam," said he, continuing, "do you not wrong your *children* by giving a part of your last mouthful to a stranger?" "Ah," said the poor widow, and the tear drops gushed into her eyes as she said it, "I have a *boy*, a darling

son, somewhere on the face of the wide world, unless heaven has taken him away, and I only act towards you, as I would that others should act towards him.

9. "God, who sent manna from heaven, can provide for us as he did for Israel—and how should I this night offend him, if my son should be a wanderer, destitute as you, and he should have provided for him a home, even poor as this—were I to turn you unrelieved away."

10. The widow ended, and the stranger, springing from his seat, clasped her in his arms, "God indeed has provided your son a home—and has given him wealth to reward the goodness of his benefactress— my mother! Oh my mother!"

11. It was her long lost son returned to her bosom from the Indies. He had chosen that disguise that he might the more completely surprise his family. Never was surprise more perfect, or followed by a sweeter cup of joy. That humble residence in the forest was exchanged for one comfortable, and indeed beautiful, in the valley. The widow lived long with her dutiful son, in the enjoyment of worldly plenty, and in the delightful employments of virtue, and at this day the passerby is pointed to the willow that spreads its branches above her grave.

QUESTIONS.—1. Can you give a sketch of the widow's history? 2. Can evil ever come from judiciously obeying the dictates of benevolence?

ERRORS.—*Sat-a-dy* for Sat-ur-day; *her-rin'* for her-ring; *for-git* for for-get; *ti-din's* for ti-dings.

SPELL AND DEFINE.—(1) endeavoring, artlessness, supporter; (2) mysterious, comprehension, exhausted, surrounding; (3) anxieties, swellings; (4) providence, pilgrimage; (5) sustenance, individual; (6) frowning; (7) apparently, indifferent, sympathies; (8) astonishment; (9) unrelieved; (10) benefactress; (11) exchanged.

LESSON LV.

RULE.—When two or more consonants come together, let the pupil be careful to sound every one distinctly.

EXERCISES UNDER THE RULE.

It *exists* everywhere.

Thou *smoothed'st* his rugged path.

Thou *sat'st* upon thy *throne.*

Do you see the *bird's nests?*

Thou *call'st* in vain.

Alkaline *earths.*

Religion the only Basis of Society.
CHANNING.

1. Religion is a social concern for it operates powerfully on society, contributing, in various ways, to its stability and prosperity. Religion is not merely a private affair. The community is deeply interested in its diffusion, for it is the best support of the virtues and principles, on which the social order rests. Pure and undefiled religion is to do good, and it follows, very plainly, that, if God be the Author and Friend of society, then, the recognition of him must force all social duty, and enlightened piety must give its whole strength to public order.

2. Few men suspect, perhaps no man comprehends, the extent of the support given by religion to every virtue. No man, perhaps, is aware, how much our moral and social sentiments are fed from this fountain. How powerless conscience would become without the belief of a God. How palsied would be human benevolence were there not the sense of a higher benevolence to quicken and sustain it. How suddenly the whole social fabric would quake, and with what a fearful crash it would sink into hopeless ruin, were the ideas of a supreme Being, of accountableness, and of a future life, to be utterly erased from every mind.

3. Let men thoroughly believe that they are the work and sport of chance; that no superior intelligence concerns itself with human affairs; that all their improvements perish forever at death; that the weak have no guardian, and the injured no avenger; that there is no recompense for sacrifices to uprightness and the public good; that an oath is unheard in heaven; that secret crimes have no witness but the perpetrator; that human existence has no purpose, and human virtue no unfailing friend; that this brief life is everything to us, and death is total, everlasting extinction. Once let them *thoroughly* abandon religion, and who can conceive or describe the extent of the desolation which would follow!

4. We hope, perhaps, that human laws and natural sympathy would hold society together. As reasonably might we believe that were the sun quenched in the heavens, *our* torches would illuminate, and *our* fires quicken and fertilize the creation. What is there in human nature to awaken respect and tenderness, if man is the unprotected insect of a day? What is he more, if atheism be true?

5. Erase all thought and fear of God from a community, and selfishness and sensuality would absorb the whole man. Appetite, knowing no restraint, and suffering, having no solace or hope, would trample in scorn on the restraints of human laws. Virtue, duty, and principle would be mocked and spurned as unmeaning sounds. A sordid self-interest would supplant every feeling, and man would become, in fact, what the theory of atheism declares him to be,—*a companion for brutes.*

QUESTIONS.—1. What is the operation of religion upon society? 2. What would be the effect of the removal of religion, upon the whole fabric of virtue? 3. Why would not human laws and sympathies hold society together?

ERRORS.—*Vir-too* for vir-tue; *reas'-na-bly* for rea-son-a-bly; *room'-nate* for ru-mi-nate.

SPELL AND DEFINE.—(1) contributing, community, diffusion, recognition, enlightened; (2) comprehends, sentiments, powerless, conscience, accountableness; (3) intelligence, recompense, perpetrator; (4) illuminate, unprotected; (5) selfishness, atheism.

LESSON LVI.

RULE.—Be careful to notice every comma, and stop long enough to take breath.

Benevolence of the Supreme Being.
CHALMERS.

1. It is saying much for the benevolence of God to say that a single world, or a single system, is not enough for it—that it must have the spread of a mightier region, on which it may pour forth a tide of exuberancy throughout all its provinces—that, as far as our vision can carry us, it has strewed immensity with the floating receptacles of life, and has stretched over each of them the garniture of such sky as mantles our own habitation—and that, even from distances which are far beyond the reach of human eye, the songs of gratitude and praise may now be arising to the one God, who sits surrounded by the regards of his great and universal family.

2. Now, it is saying much for the benevolence of God to say that it sends forth these wide and distant emanations over the surface of a territory so ample— that the world we inhabit, lying imbedded as it does, amidst so much surrounding greatness, shrinks into a point, that to the universal eye might appear to be almost imperceptible.

3. Does it not add to the power and to the perfection of this universal eye, that at the very moment it is taking a comprehensive survey of the vast, it can fasten a steady and undistracted attention on each minute and separate portion of it? That at the very moment it is looking at all worlds, it can look most pointedly and most intelligently to each of them. That at the very moment it sweeps the field of immensity, it can settle all the earnestness of its regards upon every distinct hand-breadth of that field. That at the very moment at which it embraces the totality of existence, it can send a most thorough and penetrating inspection into each of its details, and into every one of its endless diversities.

4. You cannot fail to perceive how much this adds to the power of the all-seeing eye. Tell me, then, if it does not add as much perfection to the benevolence of God, that while it is expatiating over the vast field of created things, there is not one portion of the field overlooked by it. That while it scatters blessings over the whole of an infinite range, it causes them to descend in a shower of plenty on every separate habitation. That while his arm is underneath and round about all worlds, he enters within the precincts of every one of them, and gives a care and a tenderness to each individual of their teeming population.

5. Oh! Does not the God, who is said to be love, shed over this attribute of his, its finest illustration! When, while he sits in the highest heaven, and pours out his fullness on the whole subordinate domain of nature and of providence, he bows a pitying regard on the very humblest of his children, and sends his reviving spirit into every heart, and cheers by his presence every home, and provides for the wants of every family, and watches every sick bed, and listens to the complaints of every sufferer. While, by his won-

drous mind, the weight of universal government is borne, oh, is it not more wondrous and more excellent still, that he feels for every sorrow, and has an ear open to every prayer!

QUESTIONS.—1. Compared with the whole universe, what is this single world? 2. What must, then, be the benevolence which could create such an universe? 3. What higher idea of the intellectual power, as well as goodness of the Creator, does it excite, to reflect, that not the smallest field of this immeasurable universe, is left unnoticed, or unprovided for? 4. Where is it said that "God is love?"

ERRORS.—*Sys-tum* for sys-tem; *ek-zoo-bur-un-cy* for ex-u-ber-an-cy; *hez* and *hed* for has and had; *im-pre-cep-ti-ble* for im-per-cep-ti-ble; *say-in* for say-ing; *set* for sit; *chil-dern* for chil-dren.

SPELL AND DEFINE.—(1) mightier, exuberancy, immensity, receptacles, garniture, surrounded; (2) emanations, imbedded, surrounding, imperceptible; (3) comprehensive, undistracted, pointedly, intelligently, earnestness, totality, penetrating, inspection, diversities; (4) expatiating, overlooked, teeming, population; (5) illustration, subordinate, government.

LESSON LVII.

RULE.—Do not let the voice grow weaker at the last words of a sentence.

Love of Applause.—HAWES.

1. To be insensible to public opinion, or to the estimation in which we are held by others, indicates anything rather than a good and generous spirit. It is indeed the mark of a low and worthless character, devoid of principle, and therefore devoid of shame. A young man is not far from ruin when he can say, without blushing, I *don't care what others think of me.*

2. To have a proper regard to public opinion is one thing; to make that opinion our rule of action is quite another. The one we may cherish consistently with the purest virtue, and the most unbending rectitude. The other we cannot adopt, without an utter abandonment of principle and disregard of duty.

3. The young man whose great aim is to please, who makes the opinion and favor of others his rule and motive of action, stands ready to adopt any sentiments, or pursue any course of conduct, however false and criminal, provided only that it be popular.

4. In every emergency, his first question is, what will my companions, what will the world think and say of me, if I adopt this, or that course of conduct? Duty, the eternal laws of rectitude, are not thought of. Custom, fashion, popular favor, these are the things that fill his entire vision, and decide every question of opinion and duty.

5. Such a man can never be trusted, for he has no integrity, and no independence of mind, to obey the dictates of rectitude. He is at the mercy of every casual impulse and change of popular opinion. You can no more tell whether he will be right or wrong tomorrow, than you can predict the course of the wind, or what shape the clouds will then assume.

6. What is the usual consequence of this weak and foolish regard to the opinions of men? What the *end* of thus acting in compliance with custom in opposition to one's own convictions of duty? It is to lose the esteem and respect of the very men whom you thus attempt to please. Your defect of principle and hollow heartedness are easily perceived, and though the persons to whom you thus sacrifice your conscience, may affect to commend your complaisance, you may be assured that inwardly they despise you for it.

7. Young men hardly commit a greater mistake than to think of gaining the esteem of others by yielding to their wishes, contrary to their own sense of duty. Such conduct is always morally wrong, and rarely fails to deprive one, both of self respect and the respect of others.

8. It is very common, for young men just commencing business, to imagine that, if they would advance their secular interests, they must not be very scrupulous in binding themselves down to the strict rules of rectitude. They must conform to custom, and if in buying and selling they sometimes say the things that are not true, and do the things that are not honest, why, their neighbors do the same. Verily, there is no getting along without it. There is so much competition and rivalry, and to be *strictly honest*, and yet succeed in business, is out of the question.

9. Now if it were indeed so, I would say to a young man, then, quit your business. Better dig, and beg too, than to tamper with conscience, sin against God, and lose your soul.

10. But, is it so? Is it necessary in order to succeed in business, that you should adopt a standard of morals, more lax and pliable than the one placed before you in the Bible? Perhaps for a time, a rigid adherence to rectitude might bear hard upon you but how would it be in the end? Possibly your neighbor, by being less scrupulous than yourself, may invent a more expeditious way of acquiring a fortune. If he is willing to violate the dictates of conscience; to lie and cheat, and trample on the rules of justice and honesty, he may, indeed, get the start of you, and rise suddenly to wealth and distinction.

11. But would you envy him his riches, or be willing to place yourself in his situation? Sudden wealth, especially when obtained by dishonest means, rarely fails of bringing with it sudden ruin. Those who

acquire it, are of course beggared in their morals, and are often, very soon, beggared in property. Their riches are corrupted, and while they bring the curse of God on their immediate possessors, they usually entail misery and ruin upon their families.

12. If it be admitted then, that strict integrity is not always the shortest way to success, is it not the surest, the happiest and the best? A young man of thorough integrity may, it is true, find it difficult in the midst of dishonest competitors and rivals, to start in his business or profession, but how long, ere he will surmount every difficulty, draw around him patrons and friends, and rise in the confidence and support of all who know him?

13. What, if in pursuing this course, you should not, at the close of life, have so much money by a few hundred dollars? Will not a fair character, an approving conscience, and an approving God, be an abundant compensation for this little deficiency of pelf?

14. O there is an hour coming, when one whisper of an approving mind, one smile of an approving God, will be accounted of more value than the wealth of a thousand worlds like this. In that hour, my young friends, nothing will sustain you but the consciousness of having been governed in life by worthy and good principles.

QUESTIONS.—1. What must be said of a total disregard of public opinion in a young man? 2. What is the effect of making public opinion the rule of life? 3. What erroneous opinion respecting *strict honesty* is common? 4. Is it a well-founded opinion?

ERRORS.—*Wuth-liss* for worth-less; *t'oth-er* for the oth-er; *pop-pel-er* for pop-u-lar.

SPELL AND DEFINE.—(1) insensible, estimation; (2) consistently, unbending, abandonment; (3) criminal; (4) companions; (5) integrity, independence; (6) compliance, hollow-hearted; (8) commencing, neighbors, competition; (9) conscience; (10) adherence, expeditious; (11) beggared; (13) compensation; (14) consciousness.

LESSON LVIII.

RULE.—Sound the vowels correctly and very full.

EXERCISES UNDER THE RULE.—Prolong the following vowel sounds that are italicized.—*a*-ge, *a*we, *o*-ld, *ou*-r, *ee*-l, *oo*-ze, bu-*oy*, *i*sle.

Scripture Lesson.

1. Then the Lord answered Job out of the whirlwind,
   and said,
   Who is this that darkeneth counsel
   By words without knowledge?
   Gird up now thy loins like a man;
   For I will demand of thee, and answer thou me.

2. Where wast thou when I laid the foundations
   of the earth?
   Declare, if thou hast understanding.
   Who hath laid the measures thereof, if thou
   knowest?
   Or who hath stretched the line upon it?
   Whereupon are the foundations thereof fastened?
   Or who laid the cornerstone thereof:
   When the morning stars sang together,
   And all the sons of God shouted for joy?

3. Or who shut up the sea with doors,
   When it brake forth, as if it had issued out of the
   womb?

When I made the cloud the garment thereof,
And thick darkness a swaddling band for it,
And brake up for it my decreed place,
And set bars and doors,
And said, Hitherto shalt thou come, but no
    further:
And here shall thy proud waves be stayed?

4. Hast thou commanded the morning since thy
      days;
   And caused the dayspring to know his place;
   That it might take hold of the ends of the earth,
   That the wicked might be shaken out of it?
   It is turned as clay to the seal;
   And they stand as a garment.
   And from the wicked their light is withholden,
   And the high arm shall be broken.

5. Hast thou entered into the springs of the sea?
   Or hast thou walked in the search of the depth?
   Have the gates of death been opened unto thee?
   Or hast thou seen the doors of the shadow of
      death?
   Hast thou perceived the breadth of the earth?
   Declare if thou knowest it all.

6. Where is the way where light dwelleth;
   And as for darkness, where is the place thereof,
   That thou shouldest take it to the bound thereof,
   And that thou shouldest know the paths to the
      house thereof?
   Knowest thou it, because thou wast then born?
   Or because the number of thy days is great?

7. Hast thou entered into the treasures of the snow?
   Or hast thou seen the treasures of the hail,
   Which I have reserved against the time of
      trouble,
   Against the day of battle and war?

8. By what way is the light parted,
   Which scattereth the east wind upon the earth?
   Who hath divided a watercourse for the
       overflowing of waters,
   Or a way for the lightning of thunder;
   To cause it to rain on the earth, where no man is;
   On the wilderness, wherein there is no man;
   To satisfy the desolate and waste ground;
   And to cause the bud of the tender herb to spring
       forth?

9. Hast thou given the horse strength?
   Hast thou clothed his neck with thunder?
   Canst thou make him afraid as a grasshopper?
   The glory of his nostrils is terrible.
   He paweth in the valley, and rejoiceth in his
       strength;
   He goeth out to meet the armed men.

10. He mocketh at fear, and is not affrighted;
    Neither turneth he back from the sword.
    The quiver rattleth against him,
    The glittering spear and the shield.
    He swalloweth the ground with fierceness and
        rage;
    Neither believeth he that it is the sound of the
        trumpet.
    He saith among the trumpets, Ha! ha!
    And he smelleth the battle afar off,
    The thunder of the captains, and the shouting.

QUESTIONS.—1. Is this poetry?   2. Can you select a
metaphor and a simile, from the many to be found in this lesson?

ERRORS.—*Stun* for stone; *mor-nin'*, *o-ver-flow-in'*, *light-nin'*,
glit-ter-in', *shout-in'*, incorrectly terminated with *in'* for *ing*, entirely destroying the beauty of any passage.

SPELL AND DEFINE.—(1) whirlwind, darkeneth; (2) foundations, whereupon; (3) swaddling band; (4) dayspring, withholden; (5) perceived; (6) shouldest: (8) watercourse, wilderness; (9) grasshopper; (10) affrighted, swalloweth, fierceness.

LESSON LIX.

RULE.—Do not read in a monotonous way, as if you were not interested in what you read.

Ludicrous Account of English Taxes.
BROUGHAM.

1. Permit me to inform you, my friends, what are the inevitable consequences of being too fond of glory. Taxes—upon every article which enters into the mouth, or covers the back, or is placed under the foot—taxes upon everything which it is pleasant to see, hear, feel, smell, or taste—taxes upon warmth, light, and locomotion—taxes on everything on earth, and in the waters under the earth—on everything that comes from abroad, or is grown at home—taxes on the raw material—taxes on every fresh value that is added to it by the industry of man—taxes on the sauce which pampers man's appetite, and the drug which restores him to health—on the ermine which decorates the judge, and the rope which hangs the criminal—on the poor man's salt, and the rich man's spice—on the brass nails of the coffin, and the ribbons of the bride—at bed or board, couchant or levant, we must pay.

2. The school boy whips his taxed top—the beardless youth manages his taxed horse, with a taxed bridle on a taxed road. The dying Englishman, pouring his medicine which has paid seven per cent,

into a spoon that has paid fifteen per cent—flings himself back upon his chintz bed which has paid twenty-two per cent—makes his will on an eight pound stamp, and expires in the arms of an apothecary, who has paid a license of an hundred pounds for the privilege of putting him to death.

3. His whole property is then immediately taxed from two to ten percent. Besides the probate, large fees are demanded for burying him in the chancel. His virtues are handed down to posterity on taxed marble, and he is then gathered to his fathers—to be taxed no more.

4. In addition to all this, the habit of dealing with large sums will make the government avaricious and profuse. The system itself will infallibly generate the base vermin of spies and informers, and a still more pestilent race of political tools and retainers, of the meanest and most odious description, while the prodigious patronage, which the collecting of this splendid revenue will throw into the hands of government, will invest it with so vast an influence, and hold out such means and temptations to corruption, as all the virtue and public spirit, even of republicans, will be unable to resist.

QUESTIONS.—1. Can you enumerate some of the benefits of a system of taxation?   2. What will be the effect of the system upon the probity and purity of government?

ERRORS.—*Lo-cum-o-tion* for lo-co-mo-tion; *sass* for sauce; *whops* for whips; *baird* for beard; *pow-er-ing* for pour-ing; *varment* for ver-min.

SPELL AND DEFINE.—(1) inevitable, consequences, locomotion, pampers, appetite, ermine, decorates, couchant, levant;   (2) schoolboy, beardless, chintz, apothecary;   (3) immediately, probate, chancel;   (4) avaricious, infallibly, generate, prodigious, republicans.

LESSON LX.

RULE.—Pronounce the consonant sounds very distinctly.

EXAMPLE.—Prolong the consonant sounds that are italicized in the following words.—or-*b*, ai-*d*, a-*ll*, ar-*m*, ow-*n*, so-*ng*, wa-*r*, sa-*ve*, ama-*z*—e.

Christ and the Blind Man.—BIBLE.

1. As Jesus passed by, he saw a man who was blind from his birth. His disciples asked him, saying, "Master, who did sin, this man or his parents, that he was born blind?"

2. Jesus answered, "Neither hath this man sinned nor his parents, but that the works of God should be made manifest in him.

3. "I must work the works of him that sent me, while it is day; the night cometh when no man can work. As long as I am in the world, I am the light of the world."

4. When he had thus spoken, he spat on the ground, and made clay of the spittle, and he anointed the eyes of the blind man with the clay, and said unto him, "Go, wash in the pool of Siloam, (which is, by interpretation, Sent.)"

5. He went his way, therefore, and washed, and came seeing. The neighbors therefore, and they which before had seen him, that he was blind, said, "Is not this he that sat and begged?"

6. Some said, "This is he;" others said, "He is like him:" but he said, "I am he." Therefore said they unto him, "How were thine eyes opened?"

7. He answered and said, "A man that is called Jesus, made clay, and anointed mine eyes, and said unto me, 'Go to the pool of Siloam, and wash:' and I went and washed, and I received sight." Then said they unto him, "Where is he?" He said, "I know not."

8. They brought to the Pharisees him that afore time was blind. And it was the Sabbath day when Jesus made the clay, and opened his eyes.

9. Then again the Pharisees also asked him how he had received his sight. He said unto them, "He put clay upon mine eyes, and I washed and do see."

10. Therefore said some of the Pharisees, "This man is not of God, because he keepeth not the Sabbath day." Others said, "How can a man that is a sinner, do such miracles?"

11. There was a division among them. They say unto the blind man again, "What sayest thou of him, that he hath opened thine eyes?" He said, "He is a prophet."

12. But the Jews did not believe concerning him that he had been blind, and received his sight, until they called the parents of him that had received his sight.

13. They asked them, saying, "Is this your son, who ye say was born blind? How then doth he now see?"

14. His parents answered them and said, "We know that this is our son, and that he was born blind. But by what means he now seeth, we know not; or who hath opened his eyes, we know not: he is of age, ask him, he shall speak for himself."

15. These words spake his parents, because they feared the Jews: for the Jews had agreed already, that if any man did confess that he was Christ, he should be put out of the synagogue.

16. Therefore said his parents, he is of age, ask him. Then again called they the man that was blind, and said, "Give God the praise: we know that this man is a sinner."

17. He answered and said, "Whether he be a sinner or no, I know not; one thing I know, that whereas I was blind now I see."

18. Then said they to him again, "What did he to thee? How opened he thine eyes?" He answered them, "I have told you already, and ye did not hear: wherefore would ye hear it again? Will ye also be his disciples?"

19. Then they reviled him, and said, "Thou art his disciple; but we are Moses' disciples. We know that God spake unto Moses: as for this fellow, we know not from whence he is."

20. The man answered and said unto them, "Why, herein is a marvelous thing, that ye know not from whence he is, and yet he hath opened mine eyes."

21. "Now we know that God heareth not sinners: but if any man be a worshiper of God, and doeth his will, him he heareth. Since the world began was it not heard, that any man opened the eyes of one that was born blind. If this man were not of God, he could do nothing."

22. They answered and said unto him, "Thou wast altogether born in sin, and dost thou teach us?" And they cast him out.

23. Jesus heard that they had cast him out; and when he had found him, he said unto him, "Dost thou believe on the Son of God?"

24. He answered and said, "Who is he, Lord, that I might believe on him?" Jesus said unto him, "Thou hast both seen him, and it is he that talketh with thee."

25. He said, "Lord, I believe," and he worshiped him.

26. Jesus said, "For judgment I am come into this world: that they which see not, might see; and that they which see, might be made blind."

27. Some of the Pharisees which were with him heard these words, and said unto him, "Are we blind also?"

28. Jesus said unto them, "If ye were blind, ye

should have no sin: but now ye say, We see; Therefore
your sin remaineth."

QUESTIONS.—1. From what part of the Bible was this lesson
taken?   2. What miracle is recorded in it?   3. Who performed
this miracle?   4. What means did he make use of?   5. Will clay,
prepared in the same manner, restore sight to the blind now?
6. Would it ever, if prepared by any mere man?   7. Was Christ
a mere man?   8. This miracle, and many others, were performed
openly—Why were not the Jews convinced by them, that he came
from God?   9. How did the Jews treat the man whose sight was
restored?   10. Why did they put him out of the synagogue?

ERRORS.—*Heth* for hath; *a-nint-ed* for an-oint-ed; *in-ter-per-ta-
tion* for in-ter-pre-ta-tion; *thar-fore* for there-fore; a-gain, pronounced a-gen; *Phar'-sees* for Phar-i-sees.

SPELL AND DEFINE.—(1) disciple;   (2) manifest;
(4) anointed, interpretation;   (5) neighbors;   (10) miracles;
(11) division, prophet;   (15) synagogue;   (19) reviled;
(20) marvelous;   (22) altogether;   (25) worshiped;   (26) judgment;
(28) therefore.

LESSON LXI.

RULE.—In reading poetry that rhymes, there should be a
slight pause after the words that rhyme, even when the sense
does not require it.

The Ocean.—ANONYMOUS.

1. Likeness of heaven! agent of power!
   Man is thy victim! shipwrecks thy dower!
   Spices and jewels, from valley and sea,
   Armies and banners are buried in thee!

2. What are the riches of Mexico's mines,
   To the wealth that far down in thy deep water
       shines?
   The proud navies that cover the conquering west—

Thou fling'st them to death with one heave of thy
breast!

3. From the high hills that view thy wreck-making
shore,
When the bride of the mariner shrieks at thy roar;
When, like lambs in the tempest, or mews in the
blast,
O'er ridge-broken billows the canvass is cast;

4. How humbling to one with a heart and a soul,
To look on thy greatness and list to its roll;
To think how that heart in cold ashes shall be,
While the voice of eternity rises from thee!

5. Yes! where are the cities of Thebes and of Tyre?
Swept from the nations like sparks from the fire;
The glory of Athens, the splendor of Rome,
Dissolved—and forever—like dew in the foam.

6. But thou art almighty—eternal—sublime—
Unweakened, unwasted—twin brother of time!
Fleets, tempests, nor nations, thy glory can bow;
As the stars first beheld thee, still chainless art
thou!

7. But, hold! when thy surges no longer shall roll,
And that firmament's length is drawn back like a
scroll;
Then—then shall the spirit that sighs by thee now,
Be more mighty—more lasting, more chainless
than thou!

QUESTIONS.—1. How is ocean an "agent of power?"
2. What comparison is made in verse 3, lines 3 and 4? 3. What
sentiments are inspired by viewing the ocean? (verse 4.)
4. How will the soul's duration, and that of the ocean compare?

ERRORS.—*Ship-wracks* for ship-wrecks; *bil-las* for bil-lows;
A-thens for Ath-ens; *Roome* for Rome; *tem-pes's* for tem-pests.

SPELL AND DEFINE.—(1) likeness, shipwrecks; (2) conquering; 3. wreck-making, shrieks, ridge-broken, canvass; (5) dissolved; (6) almighty, eternal, sublime, unweakened, unwasted, chainless; (7) firmaments.

LESSON LXII.

RULE.—Let each pupil in the class observe and mention every syllable that is not sounded as each one reads.

The Horrors of War.—ROBERT HALL.

1. Though the whole race of man is doomed to dissolution, and we are hastening to our long home; yet at each successive moment, life and death seem to divide between them the dominion of mankind, and life to have the larger share. It is otherwise in war; death reigns there without a rival, and without control.

2. War is the work, the element, or rather the sport and triumph of death, who here glories not only in the extent of his conquests, but in the richness of his spoil. In the other methods of attack, in the other forms which death assumes, the feeble, and the aged, who at best can live but a short time, are usually the victims. Here they are the vigorous and the strong.

3. It is remarked by the most ancient of poets that in peace children bury their parents; in war, parents bury their children; nor is the difference small. Children lament their parents, sincerely, indeed, but with that moderate and tranquil sorrow, which it is natural for those to feel who are conscious of retaining many tender ties, many animating prospects.

4. Parents mourn for their children with the bitterness of despair. The aged parent, the widowed mother, loses, when she is deprived of her children, everything but the capacity of suffering. Her heart, withered and desolate, admits no other object,

cherishes no other hope. It is Rachel, weeping for her children, and refusing to be comforted, because they are not.

5. But, to confine our attention to the number of the slain would give us a very inadequate idea of the ravages of the sword. The lot of those who perish instantaneously may be considered, apart from religious prospects as comparatively happy, since they are exempt from those lingering diseases and slow torments to which others are so liable.

6. We cannot see an individual expire, though a stranger, or an enemy, without being sensibly moved and prompted by compassion to lend him every assistance in our power. Every trace of resentment vanishes in a moment. Every other emotion gives way to pity and terror.

7. In the last extremities we remember nothing but the respect and tenderness due to our common nature. What a scene, then, must a field of battle present, where thousands are left without assistance, and without pity, with their wounds exposed to the piercing air, while the blood, freezing as it flows, binds them to the earth, amidst the trampling of horses, and the insults of an enraged foe!

8. If they are spared by the humanity of the enemy, and carried from the field, it is but a prolongation of torment. Conveyed in uneasy vehicles, often to a remote distance, through roads almost impassable, they are lodged in ill-prepared receptacles for the wounded and sick, where the variety of distress baffles all the efforts of humanity and skill, and renders it impossible to give to each the attention he demands.

9. Far from their native home, no tender assiduities of friendship, no well-known voice, no wife, or mother, or sister, is near to soothe their sorrows, relieve their thirst, or close their eyes in death! Unhappy man! and must you be swept into the grave unnoticed and

unnumbered, and no friendly tear be shed for your sufferings, or mingled with your dust?

10. We must remember, however, that as a very small proportion of military life is spent in actual combat, so it is a very small part of its miseries which must be ascribed to this source. More are consumed by the rust of inactivity than by the edge of the sword. Confined to a scanty or unwholesome diet, exposed in sickly climates, harassed with tiresome marches and perpetual alarms, their life is a continual scene of hardships and dangers. They grow familiar with hunger, cold and watchfulness. Crowded into hospitals and prisons, contagion spreads amongst their ranks, till the ravages of disease exceed those of the enemy.

11. We have hitherto only adverted to the sufferings of those who are engaged in the profession of arms, without taking into our account the situtation of the countries which are the scenes of hostilities. How dreadful to hold everything at the mercy of an enemy, and to receive life itself as a boon dependent on the sword!

12. How boundless the fears which such a situation must inspire, where the issues of life and death are determined by no known laws, principles or customs, and no conjecture can be formed of our destiny, except so far as it is dimly deciphered in characters of blood, in the dictates of revenge, and the caprices of power!

13. Conceive but for a moment the consternation which the approach of an invading army would impress on the peaceful villages in our own neighborhood. When you have placed yourselves for an instant in that situation, you will learn to sympathize with those unhappy countries which have sustained the ravages of arms. But how is it possible to give you an idea of these horrors!

14. Here you behold rich harvests, the bounty of heaven, and the reward of industry, consumed in a moment, or trampled under foot, while famine and pestilence follow the steps of desolation. There the cottages of peasants given up to the flames, mothers expiring through fear, not for themselves, but their infants; the inhabitants flying with their helpless babes in all directions, miserable fugitives on their native soil!

15. In another you witness opulent cities taken by storm. The streets, where no sounds were heard but those of peaceful industry, filled on a sudden with slaughter and blood, resounding with the cries of the pursuing and the pursued, the palaces of nobles demolished, the houses of the rich pillaged, and every age, sex, and rank, mingled in promiscuous massacre and ruin!

QUESTIONS.—1. In peace, does life or death reign? 2. How is it in war? 3. What is the difference between war and peace, according to the ancient poet? 4. Who are victims of war besides those killed outright? 5. Mention some of the most prominent evils of war.

ERRORS.—*Meth-ids* for meth-ods; *par-rents* for pa-rents; *chur-ish-es* for cher-ish-es.

SPELL AND DEFINE.—(1) dissolution, successive; (2) vigorous; (5) inadequate, instantaneously; (6) resentment; (8) prolongation; (9) unnumbered; (10) unwholesome, contagion.

LESSON LXIII.

RULE.—Be careful to read the last words of every sentence in as full and loud a tone as the first part.

The Bible.—GRIMKE.

1. The Bible is the only book which God has ever sent, the only one he ever will send, into this world. All other books are frail and transient as time, since they are only the registers of time. The Bible is durable as eternity, for its pages contain the records of eternity.

2. All other books are weak and imperfect like their author, man. The Bible is a transcript of infinite power and perfection. Every other volume is limited in its usefulness and influence, but the Bible came forth conquering and to conquer: rejoicing as a giant to run his course, and like the sun, "there is nothing hid from the heat thereof."

3. The Bible only, of all the myriads of books the world has seen, is equally important and interesting to all mankind. Its tidings, whether of peace or of woe, are the same to the poor, the ignorant, and the weak, as to the rich, the wise, and the powerful.

4. Among the most remarkable of its attributes is justice, for it looks with impartial eyes on kings and on slaves, on the hero and the soldier, on philosophers and peasants, on the eloquent and the dumb. From all, it exacts the same obedience to its commandments. It promises to the good, the fruits of his labors; to the evil, the reward of his hands. Nor are the purity and holiness, the wisdom, the benevolence, and truth of the Scriptures less conspicuous than their justice.

5. In sublimity and beauty, in the descriptive and pathetic, in dignity and simplicity of narrative, in power and comprehensiveness, depth and variety of

thought, in purity and elevation of sentiment, the most enthusiastic admirers of the heathen classics have conceded their inferiority to the Scriptures.

6. The Bible, indeed, is the only universal classic, the classic of all mankind, of every age and country, of time and eternity, more humble and simple than the primer of the child, more grand and magnificent than the epic and the oration, the ode and the drama, when genius, with his chariot of fire, and his horses of fire, ascends in whirlwind, into the heaven of his own invention. It is the best classic the world has ever seen, the noblest that has ever honored and dignified the language of mortals!

7. If you boast that the Aristotles and the Platos and the Tullys, of the classic ages, "dipped their pens in intellect," the sacred authors dipped theirs in inspiration. If those were the "secretaries of nature," these were the secretaries of the very Author of nature.

8. If Greece and Rome have gathered into their cabinet of curiosities, the pearls of heathen poetry and eloquence, the diamonds of pagan history and philosophy, God himself has treasured up in the scriptures, the poetry and eloquence, the philosophy and history of sacred lawgivers, of prophets and apostles, of saints, evangelists and martyrs. In vain may you seek for the pure and simple light of universal truth in the Augustan ages of antiquity. In the Bible only is the poet's wish fulfilled,

"And, like the sun, be all one boundless eye."

QUESTIONS.—1. What does the word Bible mean? 2. How did the Bible come into the world? 3. Did God write the Bible? 4. If men wrote it, how can it be called God's book? 5. Was every part of the Bible written at the same time? 6. What is meant when it is said that the Bible contains the "records of eternity?" 7. How can you show it to be so? 8. Mention the six particulars in which the Bible differs from all other books?

ERRORS.—*Un-ly* for on-ly; *in-fin-nite* for in-fi-nite; *vol-um* for vol-ume; *in-floonce* for in-flu-ence; *in-trest-in'* for in-ter-es-ting; *ph'los-o-phers* for phil-los-o-phers; *con-spic-oo-ous* for con-spic-u-ous; *cu-ros'-ties* for cu-ri-os-i-ties; *re-cords* for rec-ords; *trans-cript* for tran-script; *ti-dins* for ti-dings.

SPELL AND DEFINE.—(1) transient, record, eternity; (2) transcript; (4) conspicuous; (5) comprehensiveness, enthusiastic, inferiority; (6) magnificent, classic; (8) curiosities, evangelists, martyrs.

LESSON LXIV.

RULE.—Be careful not to allow the voice to grow weaker and weaker as you approach the end of each sentence.

Tit for Tat.—MISS EDGEWORTH.

1. *Mrs. Bolingbroke.*—I wish I knew what was the matter with me this morning. Why do you keep the newspaper all to yourself, my dear?

2. *Mr. Bolingbroke.*—Here it is for you, my dear. I have finished it.

3. *Mrs. B.*—I humbly thank you for giving it to me when you have done with it. I hate stale news. Is there anything in the paper? I cannot be at the trouble of hunting it.

4. *Mr. B.*—Yes, my dear, there are the marriages of two of our friends.

5. *Mrs. B.*—Who? Who?

6. *Mr. B.*—Your friend, the widow Nettleby, to her cousin John Nettleby.

7. *Mrs. B.*—Mrs. Nettleby! Dear! But why did you tell me?

8. *Mr. B.*—*Because you asked me, my dear.*

9. *Mrs. B.*—Oh, but it is a hundred times pleasanter to read the paragraph one's self. One loses all the

pleasure of the surprise by being told. Well, whose was the other marriage?

10. *Mr. B.*—Oh, my dear, I will not tell you. I will leave you the pleasure of the surprise.

11. *Mrs. B.*—But you see I cannot find it. How provoking you are, my dear! Do pray tell me.

12. *Mr. B.*—Our friend, Mr. Granby.

13. *Mrs. B.*—Mr. Granby! Dear! Why did not you make me guess? I should have guessed him directly. But why do you call him *our* friend? I am sure he is no friend of mine, nor ever was. I took an aversion to him, as you remember, the very first day I saw him. I am sure he is no friend of mine.

14. *Mr. B.*—I am sorry for it, my dear, but I hope you will go and see Mrs. Granby.

15. *Mrs. B.*—Not I, indeed, my dear. Who was she?

16. *Mr. B.*—Miss Cooke.

17. *Mrs. B.*—Cooke! But there are so many Cookes—can't you distinguish her any way? Has she no Christian name?

18. *Mr. B.*—Emma, I think. Yes, Emma.

19. *Mrs. B.*—Emma Cooke!—No, it cannot be my friend Emma Cooke, for I am sure she was cut out for an old maid.

20. *Mr. B.*-This lady seems to me to be cut out for a good wife.

21. *Mrs. B.*—Maybe so—I am sure I'll never go to see her. Pray, my dear, how came you to see so much of her?

22. *Mr. B.*—I have seen very little of her, my dear. I only saw her two or three times before she was married.

23. *Mrs. B.*—Then, my dear, how could you decide that she was cut out for a good wife? I am sure you could not judge of her by seeing her only two or three times, and before she was married.

24. *Mr. B.*—Indeed, my love, that is a very just observation.

25. *Mrs. B.*—I understand that compliment perfectly, and thank you for it, my dear. I must own I can bear anything better than irony.

26. *Mr. B.*—Irony! my dear, I was perfectly in earnest.

27. *Mrs. B.*—Yes, yes, in earnest—so I perceive—I may naturally be dull of apprehension, but my feelings are quick enough. I comprehend too well. Yes, it is impossible to judge of a woman before marriage, or to guess what sort of a wife she will make. I presume you speak from experience. You have been disappointed yourself, and repent your choice.

28. *Mr. B.*—My dear, what did I say that was like this? Upon my word, I meant no such thing. I really was not thinking of you in the least.

29. *Mrs. B.*—No—you never think of me now. I can easily believe that you were not thinking of me in the least.

30. *Mr. B.*—But I said that only to prove to you that I could not be thinking ill of you, my dear.

31. *Mrs. B.*—But I would rather that you thought ill of me, than that you did not think of me at all.

32. *Mr. B.*—Well, my dear, I will even think ill of you, if that will please you.

33. *Mrs. B.*—Do you laugh at me? When it comes to this, I am wretched indeed. Never man laughed at the woman he loved. As long as you had the slightest remains of love for me, you could not make me an object of derision. Ridicule and love are incompatible—absolutely incompatible. Well, I have done my best, my very best, to make you happy, but in vain. I see I am not *cut out* to be a good wife. Happy, happy Mrs. Granby!

34. *Mr. B.*—Happy, I hope sincerely, that she will be with my friend, but my happiness must depend on

you, my love, so, for my sake, if not for your own,
be composed, and do not torment yourself with such
fancies.

35. *Mrs. B.*—I do wonder whether this Mrs.
Granby is really that Miss Emma Cooke. I'll go and
see her directly; see her I must.

36. *Mr. B.*—I am heartily glad of it, my dear; for
I am sure a visit to his wife will give my friend Granby
real pleasure.

37. *Mrs. B.*—I promise you, my dear, I do not go
to give him pleasure or you either, but to satisfy my
own *curiosity.*

QUESTIONS.—1. Does Mrs. B. evince much good sense by
the temper she displays?   2. May not people realize their own
fear by giving expression to their suspicions?   3. Is it wise for
a husband or a wife to speak in an unfriendly manner to each
other?

ERRORS.—*Um-bly* for hum-bly; *ra-ly* for re-al-ly; *whuth-er* for
wheth-er; *cu-ros-i-ty* for cu-ri-os-i-ty.

SPELL AND DEFINE.—(1) newspaper;   (2) finished;
(4) marriages; (9) paragraph; (11) provoking; (13) remember;
(17) distinguish;   (25) compliment, irony;   (27) apprehension,
experience, disappointed;   (33) incompatible;   (37) curiosity.

LESSON LXV.

RULE.—When similiar sounds come at the end of one word
and the beginning of the next word, they must not be blended
into one.

EXERCISES.—Mali*ce s*eeks to destroy.
The bree*ze s*ighs softly.
The *ice s*lowly melts.

Political Corruption.—McDUFFIE.

1. We are apt to treat the idea of our own corruptibility as utterly visionary, and to ask, with a grave

affectation of dignity—what! do you think a member of congress can be corrupted? Sir, I speak what I have long and deliberately considered, when I say, that since man was created, there never has been a political body on the face of the earth that would not be corrupted under the same circumstances. Corruption steals upon us in a thousand insidious forms when we are least aware of its approaches.

2. Of all the forms in which it can present itself, the bribery of office is the most dangerous because it assumes the guise of patriotism to accomplish its fatal sorcery. We are often asked, where is the evidence of corruption? Have you seen it? Sir, do you expect to see it? You might as well expect to see the embodied forms of pestilence and famine stalking before you, as to see the latent operations of this insidious power. We may walk amidst it and breathe its contagion, without being conscious of its presence.

3. All experience teaches us the irresistible power of temptation, when vice assumes the form of virtue. The great enemy of mankind could not have consummated his infernal scheme for the seduction of our first parents, but for the disguise in which he presented himself. Had he appeared as the devil, in his proper form, had the spear of Ithuriel disclosed the naked deformity of the fiend of hell, the inhabitants of paradise would have shrunk with horror from his presence.

4. But he came as the insinuating serpent, and presented a beautiful apple, the most delicious fruit in all the garden. He told his glowing story to the unsuspecting victim of his guile. "It can be no crime to taste of this delightful fruit. It will disclose to you the knowledge of good and evil. It will raise you to an equality with the angels."

5. Such, sir, was the process, and in this simple but impressive narrative, we have the most beautiful and

philosophical illustration of the frailty of man, and the power of temptation, that could possibly be exhibited. Mr. Chairman, I have been forcibly struck with the similarity between our present situation and that of Eve, after it was announced that Satan was on the borders of paradise. We, too, have been warned that the enemy are on our borders.

6. God forbid that the similitude should be carried any farther. Eve, conscious of her innocence, sought temptation and defied it. The catastrophe is too fatally known to us all. She went, "with the blessings of heaven on her head, and its purity in her heart," guarded by the ministry of angels—she returned, covered with shame, under the heavy denunciation of heaven's everlasting curse.

7. Sir, it is innocence that temptation conquers. If our first parent, pure as she came from the hand of God, was overcome by the seductive power, let us not imitate her fatal rashness, seeking temptation, when it is in our power to avoid it. Let us not vainly confide in our own infallibility. We are liable to be corrupted. To an ambitious man, an honorable office will appear as beautiful and fascinating as the apple of paradise.

8. I admit, sir, that ambition is a passion, at once the most powerful and the most useful. Without it, human affairs would become a mere stagnant pool. By means of his patronage, the president addresses himself in the most irresistible manner, to this, the noblest and strongest of our passions. All that the imagination can desire—honor, power, wealth, ease, are held out as the temptation. Man was not made to resist such temptation. It is impossible to conceive, Satan himself could not devise, a system which would more infallibly introduce corruption and death into our political Eden. Sir, the angels fell from heaven with less temptation.

QUESTIONS.—1. What is meant by the corruption of a political body? 2. What is the most dangerous form in which this can approach? 3. What is said of the passion of ambition? 4. By what is the progress of temptation in overcoming innocence illustrated?

ERRORS.—*C'rup-tion* for cor-rup-tion; *ov-fice* for office; *pu-er* and *peu-er* for pure.

SPELL AND DEFINE.—(1) corruptibility, visionary, affectation, deliberately, circumstances, insidious; (2) patriotism, accomplish, contagion; (3) irresistible, consummated, deformity; (4) insinuating, knowledge; (5) impressive, philosophical; (6) similitude, catastrophe, denunciation; (7) infallibility, ambitious, fascinating; (8) imagination, introduce.

LESSON LXVI.

RULE.—Be careful to observe the commas, and stop long enough to take breath.

The Blind Preacher.—WIRT.

1. As I traveled through the county of Orange, my eye was caught by a cluster of horses tied near a ruinous, old, wooden house in the forest, not far from the roadside. Having frequently seen such objects before, in traveling through these States, I had no difficulty in understanding that this was a place of religious worship.

2. Devotion alone should have stopped me, to join in the duties of the congregation, but I must confess, that curiosity to hear the preacher of such a wilderness was not the least of my motives. On enter-

ing, I was struck with his preternatural appearance. He was a tall and very spare old man. His head, which was covered with a white linen cap, his shriveled hands, and his voice, were all shaking under the influence of a palsy, and a few moments ascertained to me that he was perfectly blind.

3. The first emotions that touched my breast were those of mingled pity and veneration. How soon were all my feelings changed? The lips of Plato were never more worthy of a prognostic swarm of bees, than were the lips of this holy man! It was a day of the administration of the sacrament, and his subject was, of course, the passion of our Savior. I had heard the subject handled a thousand times. I had thought it exhausted long ago. Little did I suppose that in the wild woods of America, I was to meet with a man, whose eloquence would give to this topic a new and more sublime pathos than I had ever before witnessed.

4. As he descended from the pulpit to distribute the mystic symbols, there was a peculiar, a more than human solemnity in his air and manners, which made my blood run cold, and my whole frame shiver.

5. He then drew a picture of the sufferings of our Savior, his trial before Pilate, his ascent up Calvary, his crucifixion. I knew the whole history, but never until then had I ever heard the circumstances so selected, so arranged, so colored! It was all new. I seemed to have heard it for the first time in my life. His enunication was so deliberate that his voice trembled on every syllable, and every heart in the assembly trembled in unison.

6. His peculiar phrases had that force of description that the original scene appeared to be at that moment acting before our eyes. We saw the very faces of the Jews, the staring, frightful distortions of malice and rage. We saw the buffet. My soul kindled with

a flame of indignation, and my hands were involuntarily and convulsively clenched.

7. But when he came to touch on the patience, the
forgiving meekness of our Savior; when he drew, to
the life, his voice breathing to God a soft and gentle
prayer of pardon on his enemies, "Father, forgive
them, for they know not what they do,"—the voice
of the preacher, which had all along faltered, grew
fainter and fainter, until, his utterance being entirely obstructed by the force of his feelings, he raised
his handkerchief to his eyes, and burst into a loud and
irrepressible flood of grief. The effect is inconceivable.
The whole house resounded with the mingled groans,
and sobs, and shrieks of the congregation.

8. It was some time before the tumult had
subsided, so far as to permit him to proceed. Indeed,
judging by the usual, but fallacious standard of my
own weakness, I began to be very uneasy for the
situation of the preacher. For I could not conceive how
he would be able to let his audience down from the
height to which he had wound them, without impair-
ing the solemnity and dignity of his subject, or
perhaps shocking them by the abruptness of his fall.
But—no: the descent was as beautiful and sublime
as the elevation had been rapid and enthusiastic.

9. The first sentence, with which he broke the awful
silence, was a quotation from Rousseau: "Socrates
died like a philosopher, but Jesus Christ, like a God!"

10. I despair of giving you any idea of the effect
produced by this short sentence, unless you could
perfectly conceive the whole manner of the man, as
well as the peculiar crisis in the discourse. Never
before did I completely understand what
Demosthenes meant by laying such stress on delivery.

11. You are to bring before you the venerable figure
of the preacher; his blindness, constantly recalling to
your recollection old Homer, Ossian, and Milton, and

associating with his performance the melancholy grandeur of their geniuses. You are to imagine that you hear his slow, solemn, well-accented enunciation, and his voice of affecting trembling melody. You are to remember the pitch of passion and enthusiasm, to which the congregation was raised, and then the few moments of portentous, death-like silence, which reigned throughout the house. The preacher, removing his white handkerchief from his aged face, (even yet wet from the recent torrent of his tears,) and slowly stretching forth the palsied hand which held it, begins the sentence, "Socrates died like a philosopher"—then, pausing, raising his other, pressing them both, clasped together, with warmth and energy, to his breast, lifting his "sightless balls" to heaven, and pouring his whole soul into his tremulous voice—"but Jesus Christ—like a God!"

12. If he had been indeed and in truth an angel of light, the effect could scarcely have been more divine. Whatever I had been able to conceive of the sublimity of Massilon or the force of Bourdaloue, had fallen far short of the power which I felt from the delivery of this simple sentence.

13. If this description gives you the impression that this incomparable minister had anything of shallow, theatrical trick in his manner, it does him great injustice. I have never seen, in any other orator, such a union of simplicity and majesty. He has not a gesture, an attitude, or an accent, to which he does not seem forced by the sentiment he is expressing. His mind is too serious, too earnest, too solicitous, and, at the same time too dignified, to stoop to artifice.

14. Although as far removed from ostentation as a man can be, yet it is clear, from the train, the style and substance of his thoughts, that he is not only a polite scholar, but a man of extensive and profound

erudition. I was forcibly struck with a short yet beautiful character which he drew of your learned and amiable countryman, Sir Robert Boyle. He spoke of him, as if "his noble mind had, even before death, divested itself of all influence from his frail tabernacle of flesh;" and called him, in his peculiarly emphatic and impressive manner, "a pure intelligence; the link between men and angels."

15. This man has been before my imagination almost ever since. A thousand times, as I rode along, I dropped the reins of my bridle, stretched forth my hand, and tried to imitate his quotation from Rousseau. A thousand times I abandoned the attempt in despair, and felt persuaded, that his peculiar manner and power arose from an energy of soul, which nature could give, but which no human being could justly copy. As I recall, at this moment, several of his awfully striking attitudes, the chilling tide, with which my blood begins to pour along my arteries, reminds me of the emotions produced by the first sight of Gray's introductory picture of his Bard.

QUESTIONS.—1. Can you describe the personal appearance of the blind preacher?   2. What effect was produced by his manner?   3. What by his language?   4. When he described the character and conduct of Christ, what was the effect on the congregation?   5. What effect was produced by the circumstance of his blindness?   6. What was the secret of the preacher's great power?

ERRORS.—*Hos-ses* for hors-es; *jine* for join; *en-trin'* for en-ter-ing.

SPELL AND DEFINE.—(2) congregation, preternatural, shriveled, ascertained;   (3) veneration, administration;   (4) symbols;   (5) enunciation;   (6) distortions, indignation, involuntarily, convulsively;   (7) obstructed, handkerchief, inconceivable;   (8) fallacious, enthusiastic;   (11) melancholy, tremulous.

LESSON LXVII.

RULE.—Where two or more consonants come together, let the pupil be careful to sound everyone distinctly.

EXERCISES UNDER THE RULE.

Thou *indulged'st* thy appetite.

O wind! that *waft'st* us o'er the main.

Thou *tempted'st* him.

Thou *loved'st* him fondly.

Thou *credited'st* his story.

The *lists* are open.

Apostrophe to Light.—MILTON.

1. Hail! holy Light, offspring of Heaven first born,
   Or of the eternal co-eternal beam,
   May I express thee unblamed? Since God is light,
   And never but in unapproached light
5. Dwelt from eternity, dwelt then in thee,
   Bright effluence of bright essence increate,
   Or hear'st thou, rather, pure ethereal stream,
   Whose fountain who shall tell? Before the sun,
   Before the heavens, thou wert, and at the voice
10. Of God, as with a mantle, didst invest
    The rising world of waters dark and deep,
    Won from the void and formless infinite
    Thee I revisit now with bolder wing,
    Escaped the Stygian pool, though long detained
15. In that obscure sojourn, while in my flight,
    Through utter and through middle darkness
        borne
    With other notes than to the Orphean lyre
    I sung of chaos and eternal night.
    Taught by the heavenly muse to venture down
20. The dark descent, and up to reascend,
    Though hard and rare; Thee I revisit safe,
    And feel thy sovereign, vital lamp; but thou
    Revisit'st not these eyes, that roll in vain,
    To find thy piercing ray, and find no dawn;

25. So thick a drop serene hath quenched their orbs,
    Or dim suffusion veiled. Yet not the more
    Cease I to wander where the muses haunt,
    Clear spring or shady grove, or sunny hill,
    Smit with the love of sacred song; but chief

30. Thee, Sion, and the flowery brooks beneath,
    That wash thy hallowed feet, and warbling flow,
    Nightly I visit: nor sometimes forget
    Those other two, equaled with me in fate,
    So were I equaled with them in renown,

35. Blind Thamyris and blind Maeonides,
    And Tyresias and Phineas, prophets old:
    Then feed on thoughts that voluntary move
    Harmonious numbers; as the wakeful bird
    Sings darkling, and in shadiest covert hid,

40. Tunes her nocturnal note. Thus with the year,
    Seasons return, but not to me returns
    Day, or the sweet approach of even and morn;
    Or sight of vernal bloom, or summer's rose,
    Or flocks, or herds, or human face divine;

45. But cloud, instead, and ever-during dark
    Surrounds me, from the cheerful ways of men
    Cut off, and for the book of knowledge fair,
    Presented with a universal blank
    Of nature's works, to me expunged and razed,

50. And wisdom, at one entrance, quite shut out.
    So much the rather thou, celestial Light,
    Shine inward, and the mind through all her
        powers
    Irradiate: there plant eyes, all mist from thence
    Purge and disperse, that I may see and tell
    Of things invisible to mortal sight.

QUESTIONS.—1. Why does Milton mention light so reverently? 2. What was the Stygian pool? 3. Orphean lyre? 4. Was Milton blind? 5. What bird does he call the "wakeful bird?"

ERRORS.—*Fust* for first; *'spress* for ex-press; *up-proach* for ap-proach.

SPELL AND DEFINE.—(2) co-eternal; (6) increate; (7) ethereal; (12) infinite; (18) chaos; (20) reascend; (26) suffusion; (39) darkling; (40) nocturnal; (49) expunged; (53) irradiate.

LESSON LXVIII.

RULE.—Remember that the chief beauty and excellence of reading consists in a clear and smooth articulation of the words and letters.

Procrastination.—YOUNG.

1. Be wise today; 'tis madness to defer;
   Next day the fatal precedent will plead,
   Thus on, till wisdom is pushed out of life;
   Procrastination is the thief of time;
5. Year after year it steals, till all are fled,
   And to the mercies of a moment leaves
   The vast concerns of an eternal scene.
   If not so frequent, would not this be strange?
   That 'tis so frequent, this is stranger still.
10. Of man's miraculous mistakes, this bears
    The palm, that all men are about to live,
    Forever on the brink of being born.
    All pay themselves the compliment to think
    They one day shall not drivel; and their pride
15. On this reversion takes up ready praise,
    At least their own: their future selves applaud;
    How excellent that life they ne'er will lead!
    Time lodged in their own hands in folly's vails;
    That lodged in fate's, to wisdom they consign:

20. The thing they can't but purpose, they postpone;
    'Tis not in folly, not to scorn a fool;
    And scarce in human wisdom, to do more.
    All promise is poor dilatory man,
    And that through every stage: when young,
        indeed,
25. In full content we sometimes nobly rest
    Unanxious for ourselves; and only wish,
    As duteous sons, our fathers were more wise.
    At thirty man suspects himself a fool;
    Knows it at forty, and reforms his plan;
30. At fifty chides his infamous delay,
    Pushes his prudent purpose to resolve;
    In all the magnanimity of thought
    Resolves; and re-resolves; then dies the same.

QUESTIONS.—1. What is meant by procrastination?
2. Name some of the evils of procrastination.   3. What is the
meaning of lines 11 and 12?   4. What, of all things, are men most
disposed to defer?   5. What did the ancients regard as the best
kind of knowledge?

ERRORS.—*Pre-ce-dent* for prec-e-dent; *mir-ac'-lous* for
mir-ac-u-lous; *com-plum-munt* for com-pli-ment; *ex-ce-lent* for
ex-cel-lent.

SPELL AND DEFINE.—(1) defer;   (2) precedent;   (7) eternal,
scene;   (10) miraculous;   (13) compliment;   (14) drivel;
(15) reversion;   (16) applaud;   (19) consign;   (20) postpone;
(23) dilatory;   (26) unanxious;   (27) duteous;   (30) infamous;
(32) magnanimity;   (33) re-resolves.

LESSON LXIX.

RULE.—Let the pupil stand at as great a distance from the teacher as possible, and then try to read so loud and distinctly that the teacher may hear each syllable.

America.—PHILLIPS.

1. I appeal to History! Tell me, thou reverend chronicler of the grave, can all the illusions of ambition realized, can all the wealth of a universal commerce, can all the achievments of successful heroism, or all the establishments of this world's wisom, secure to empire the permanency of its possessions? Alas! Troy thought so once yet the land of Priam lives only in song!

2. Thebes thought so once, yet her hundred gates have crumbled, and her very tombs are as the dust they were vainly intended to commemorate! So thought Palmyra—yet where is she? So thought the countries of Demosthenes and the Spartan, yet Leonidas is trampled by the timid slave, and Athens insulted by the servile, mindless and enervate Ottoman!

3. In his hurried march, Time has but looked at their imagined immortality. All its vanities, from the palace to the tomb, have, with their ruins, erased the very impression of his footsteps! The days of their glory are as if they had never been, and the island, that was then a speck, rude and neglected in the barren ocean, now rivals the ubiquity of their commerce, they glory of their arms, the fame of their philosophy, the eloquence of their senate, and the inspiration of their bards!

4. Who shall say, then, contemplating the past, that England, proud and potent as she appears, may

not, one day, be what Athens is, and the young America yet soar to be what Athens was! Who shall say, that, when the European column shall have mouldered, and the night of barbarism obscured its very ruins, that mighty continent may not emerge from the horizon to rule, for its time, sovereign of the ascendant!

5. Sir, it matters very little what immediate spot may have been the birthplace of such a man as WASHINGTON. No people can claim, no country can appropriate him. The boon of Providence to the human race, his fame is eternity, and his residence creation. Though it was the defeat of our arms, and the disgrace of our policy, I almost bless the convulsion in which he had his origin.

6. If the heavens thundered, and the earth rocked, yet, when the storm had passed, how pure was the climate that it cleared! How bright, in the brow of the firmament, was the planet which it revealed to us! In the production of Washington, it does really appear as if Nature was endeavoring to improve upon herself, and that all the virtues of the ancient world were but so many studies preparatory to the patriot of the new.

7. Individual instances, no doubt, there were, splendid exemplifications, of some singular qualification. Caesar was merciful, Scipio was continent, Hannibal was patient; but it was reserved for Washington to blend them all in one, and, like the lovely masterpiece of the Grecian artist, to exhibit, in one glow of associated beauty, the pride of every model, and the perfection of every master.

8. As a general, he marshaled the peasant into a veteran, and supplied by discipline the absence of experience. As a statesman, he enlarged the policy of the cabinet into the most comprehensive system of general advantage, and such was the wisdom of

his views, and the philosophy of his counsels, that, to the soldier and the statesman, he almost added the character of the sage!

9. A conqueror, he was untainted with the crime of blood. A revolutionist, he was free from any stain of treason for aggression commenced the contest, and his country called him to the command. Liberty unsheathed his sword, necessity stained, victory returned it. If he had paused here, history might have doubted what station to assign him, whether at the head of her citizens, or her soldiers, her heroes, or her patriots. But the last glorious act crowns his career, and banishes all hesitation.

10. Who like Washington, after having emancipated a hemisphere, resigned its crown, and preferred the retirement of domestic life to the adoration of a land he might be said almost to have created!

11. Happy, proud America! The lightnings of heaven yield to your philosophy! The temptations of earth could not seduce your patriotism!

QUESTIONS.—1. What is the testimony of history on the permanence of national greatness? 2. What is said of the character of Washington? 3. How does he compare with Caesar, Scipio, Hannibal, Bonaparte?

ERRORS.—*His-try* for his-to-ry; *en'*-er-vate for en-er'-vate; *Le-on-a-das* for Le-on-i-das.

SPELL AND DEFINE.—(1) chronicler, achievements, establishments, permanency; (2) crumbled, commemorate, enervate; (3) immortality, impression; (4) contemplating, emerge, ascendant; (5) appropriate, convulsion; (6)firmament, endeavoring, preparatory; (8) marshaled, discipline, comprehensive; (9) revolutionist, aggression; (10) hemisphere; (11) patriotism.

LESSON LXX.

RULE.—Avoid reading in a monotonous way, as if you were not interested and did not understand what is read.

Thirsting after Righteousness.—BIBLE.

1. As the heart panteth after the water brooks,
   So panteth my soul after thee, O God!
   My soul thirsteth for God, for the living God:
   When shall I come and appear before God?
   My tears have been my meat day and night,
   While they continually say unto me, Where is thy
      God?
   When I remember these things, I pour out my soul
      in me:
   For I had gone with the multitude, I went with
      them to the house of God,
   With the voice of joy and praise,
   With a multitude that kept holy-day.

2. Why art thou cast down, O my soul?
   And why are thou disquieted within me?
   Hope thou in God:—for I shall yet praise him
   For the help of his countenance.

3. O my god! my soul is cast down within me:
   Therefore will I remember thee from the land of
      Jordan, and of the Hermonites,
   From the hill Mizar.
   Deep calleth unto deep, at the noise of thy water-
      spouts;
   All thy waves and thy billows are gone over me!
   Yet the Lord will command his loving kindness in
      the daytime,
   And in the night his song shall be with me,
   And my prayer unto the God of my life.

4. I will say unto God my rock, Why hast thou
    forgotten me?
  Why go I mourning, because of the oppression of
    the enemy?
  As with a sword in my bones, mine enemies
    reproach me;
  While they say daily unto me, Where is thy God?

5. Why art thou cast down, O my soul?
  And why art thou disquieted within me?
  Hope thou in God:—for I will yet praise him,
  Who is the health of my countenance, and my God.

QUESTIONS.—1. From 1st to 7th line, what feeling is
described. 2. To whom are the 2d and 4th verses addressed?
3. Under what circumstances was this psalm written?

ERRORS.—*Ar-ter* for af-ter; *con-tin-i-al-ly* for con-tin-u-al-ly;
sord for sword.

LESSON LXXI.

RULE.—Be careful not to read in a faint and low tone.

View from Mount Etna.—LONDON ENCYC.

1. The man who trends Mount Etna, seems like a
man above the world. He generally is advised to
ascend before daybreak. The stars now brighten, shining like so many gems of flames. Others appear which
were invisible below. The Milky Way seems like a pure
flake of light, lying across the firmament, and it is
the opinion of some that the satellites of Jupiter
might be discovered by the naked eye.

2. But when the sun arises, the prospect from the summit of Etna is beyond comparison the finest in nature. The eye rolls over it with astonishment and is lost. The diversity of objects, the extent of the horizon, the immense height, the country like a map at our feet, the ocean around, the heavens above, all conspire to overwhelm the mind, and affect it.

3. We must be allowed to extract Mr. Brydone's description of this scene. "There is not," he says, "on the surface of the globe, any one point that unites so many awful and sublime objects. The immense elevation from the surface of the earth, drawn as it were to a single point, without any neighboring mountain for the senses and imagination to rest upon and recover from their astonishment, in their way down to the world.

4. "This point or pinnacle, raised on the brink of a bottomless gulf, as old as the world, often discharges rivers of fire, and throws out burning rocks, with a noise that shakes the whole island. Add to this the unbounded extent of the prospect, comprehending the greatest diversity, and the most beautiful scenery in nature, with the rising sun advancing in the east, to illuminate the wondrous scene.

5. "The whole atmosphere by degrees kindles up, and shows dimly and faintly the boundless prospect around. Both sea and land appear dark and confused, as if only emerging from their original chaos, and light and darkness seem still undivided until the morning, by degrees advancing, completes the separation. The stars are extinguished, and the shades disappear.

6. "The forests, which but just now seemed black and bottomless gulfs, from whence no ray was reflected to show their form or colors, appear a new

creation rising to sight, catching life and beauty from every increasing beam. The scene still enlarges, and the horizon seems to widen and expand itself on all sides until the sun, like the great Creator, appears in the east, and with his plastic ray completes the mighty scene.

7. "All appears enchantment: and it is with difficulty we can believe we are still on earth. The senses, unaccustomed to the sublimity of such a scene, are bewildered and confounded. It is not until after some time that they are capable of separating and judging of the objects that compose it.

8. "The body of the sun is seen rising from the ocean, immense tracts both of sea and land intervening; the islands of Lipari, Panari, Alicudi, Strombolo, and Volcano, with their smoking summits, appear under your feet. You look down on the whole of Sicily as on a map, and can trace every river through all its windings, from its source to its mouth.

9. "The view is absolutely boundless on every side; nor is there any one object within the circle of vision to interrupt it, so that the sight is every where lost in the immensity; and I am persuaded, it is only from the imperfection of our organs, that the coasts of Africa, and even of Greece, are not discovered, as they are certainly above the horizon. The circumference of the visible horizon on the top of Etna, cannot be less than two thousand miles.

10. "At Malta, which is nearly two hundred miles distant they perceive all the eruptions from the second region and that island is often discovered from about one half the elevation of the mountain, so that, at the whole elevation the horizon must extend to nearly double that distance, or four hundred miles, which makes eight hundred miles for the diameter of the circle, and two thousand four hundred for the

circumference! But this is much too vast for our senses. They are not intended to grasp so boundless a scene.

11. "The most beautiful part of the scene is certainly the mountain itself, the island of Sicily, and the numerous islands lying round it. All these, by a kind of magic in vision, that I am at a loss to account for, seem as if they were brought close round the skirts of Etna, the distances appearing reduced to nothing.

12. "Perhaps this singular effect is produced by the rays of light passing from a rarer medium into a denser, which, (from a well-known law in optics,) to an observer in the rare medium, appears to lift up objects that are at the bottom of the dense one, as a piece of money placed in a basin appears lifted up as soon as the basin is filled with water.

13. "The Regione Deserta, of the frigid zone of Etna, is the first object that calls your attention. It is marked out by a circle of snow and ice, which extends on all sides to the distance of about eight miles. In the center of this circle, the great crater of the mountain rears its burning head, and the regions of intense cold, and of intense heat, seem forever to be united in the same point.

14. "The Regione Deserta is immediately succeeded by the Sylvosa, or the woody region, which forms a circle or girdle of the most beautiful green, which surrounds the mountain on all sides, and is certainly one of the most delightful spots on earth."

QUESTIONS.—1. Where is Mount Etna?   2. Describe the journey you would take to go to it.   3. What is Mount Etna? 4. What is a volcano?   5. Are there any volcanoes in the United States?   6. When are travelers advised to ascend Mount Etna? 7. Describe the appearance of things at that time, and afterwards till sunrise?   8. How far can you see from the summit of Mount

Etna? 9. Why cannot the shores of Africa and of Greece be seen from the top of Etna? 10. What is meant by saying (9) "as they are certainly above the horizon?" 11. How many miles does the circumference of vision embrace from the top of Etna? 12. Suppose you were at the top of the mountain, what different regions or kinds of country would you pass through before you would reach the bottom? 13. What islands are near Etna? 14. What cities? 15. If the country about Etna be so very delightful, would you not like to live there? 16. Why? [This question is intended to elicit a comparison of our own with foreign countries, both in point of natural scenery and civil institutions.]

ERRORS.—*Gen-er-ly* for gen-er-al-ly; *hor-ri-zon* for ho-ri-zon; *grand-er* for grand-eur; *Et-ny* for Et-na; *Si-pa-ri* pronounce See-pah-ree; *Pa-na-ri* pronounce Pah-nah-ree; *Al-i-cu-di* pronounce Ah-lee-coo-dee.

SPELL AND DEFINE.—(1) ascend, firmament, invisible, satellites; (2) diversity, horizon, grandeur; (3) astonishment; (4) pinnacle, comprehending, wondrous; (5) atmosphere, emerging, chaos, extinguished; (6) plastic; (7) unaccustomed, sublimity, bewildered; (8) intervening; (9) circumference; (10) diameter.

LESSON LXXII.

RULE.—Be careful to speak little words, such as *a, in, at, on, to, by,* etc., very distinctly, and yet not to dwell on them so long as on the more important words.

Sublime Virtues Inconsistent with Infidelity.—ROBERT HALL.

1. Infidelity is a soil as barren of great and sublime virtues as it is prolific in crimes. By great and sublime virtues are meant those which are called into action on great and trying occasions, which demand the

sacrifice of the dearest interests and prospects of human life, and sometimes life itself; the virtues, in a word, which, by their rarity and splendor, draw admiration, and have rendered illustrious the characters of patriots, martyrs, and confessors. It requires but little reflection to perceive, and whatever veils a future world, and contracts the limits of existence within the present life, must tend, in a proportionable degree, to diminish the grandeur and narrow the sphere of human agency.

2. As well might you expect exalted sentiments of justice from a professed gamester, as look for noble principles in the man whose hopes and fears are all suspended on the present moment, and who stakes the whole happiness of his being on the events of this vain and fleeting life.

3. If he be ever impelled to the performance of great achievements in a good cause, it must be solely by the hope of fame; a motive which, besides that it makes virtue the servant of opinion, usually grows weaker at the approach of death; and which, however it may surmount the love of existence in the heat of battle, or in the moment of public observation, can seldom be expected to operate with much force on the retired duties of a private station.

4. In affirming that infidelity is unfavorable to the higher class of virtues, we are supported as well by facts as by reason. We should be sorry to load our adversaries with unmerited reproach, but to what history, to what record will they appeal for the traits of moral greatness exhibited by their disciples? Where shall we look for the trophies of infidel magnanimity or atheistical virtue? Not that we mean to accuse them of inactivity. They have recently filled the world with the fame of their exploits—exploits of a different kind, indeed, but of imperishable memory and disastrous luster.

5. Though great and splendid actions are not the ordinary employments of life, but must from their nature, be reserved for high and eminent occasions, yet that system is essentially defective which leaves no room for their production. They are important, both from their immediate advantage and their remoter influence. They often save and always illustrate, the age and nation in which they appear. They raise the standard of morals. They arrest the progress of degeneracy. They diffuse a luster over the path of life.

6. Monuments of the greatness of the human soul, they present to the world the august image of virtue in her sublimest form, from which streams of light and glory issue to remote times and ages, while their commemoration, by the pen of historians and poets, awakens in distant bosoms the sparks of kindred excellence.

QUESTIONS.—1. What is meant by infidelity? 2. Are all infidels profane or immoral men? 3. Do they possess great and sublime virtues? 4. What is meant by great and sublime virtues? 5. To what is the infidel compared in paragraph 2? 6. Is the comparison just? 7. Do infidels possess no good qualities? 8. Perform no good actions? 9. What motive impels them ever to do good? 10. What is said of this motive? 11. What is the testimony of history on this point?

ERRORS.—*In-t'rests* for in-ter-ests; *gran-der* for grand-eur; *'u-man* for human; *il-lus-trous* for il-lus-tri-ous; *mon-i-ment* for mom-u-ment.

SPELL AND DEFINE.—(1) infidelity, prolific, illustrious, proportionable, grandeur; (2) sentiments, gamester, suspended; (3) achievements, approach; (4) unfavorable, adversaries, exhibited, disciples, magnanimity, atheistical, imperishable, disastrous; (5) employment, essentially, production, immediate, remoter, degeneracy; (6) monuments, august, commemoration.

LESSON LXXIII.

RULE.—In reading poetry, be careful to avoid the sing-song tone which is made by marking too strongly with the voice, all the accented syllables. In the example the fault will appear, if the words italicized are strongly accented.

EXAMPLE.—Sweet *is* my *work* my *God* and *King*
To *praise* the *name*, give *thanks* and *sing*.

The Alps.—W. Gaylord Clark.

1. Proud monuments of God! sublime ye stand
   Among the wonders of his mighty hand:
   With summits soaring in the upper sky,
   Where the broad day looks down with burning eye;
   Where gorgeous clouds in solemn pomp repose,
   Flinging rich shadows on eternal snows:
   Piles of triumphant dust, ye stand alone,
   And hold, in kingly state, a peerless throne!

2. Like olden conquerors, on high ye rear
   The regal ensign, and the glittering spear:
   Round icy spires the mists, in wreaths unrolled,
   Float ever near, in purple or in gold:
   And voiceful torrents, sternly rolling there,
   Fill with wild music the unpillared air:
   What garden, or what hall on earth beneath,
   Thrills to such tones, as o'er the mountains
           breathe?

3. There, though long ages past, those summits shone
   When morning radiance on their state was thrown;
   There, when the summer day's career was done,
   Played the last glory of the sinking sun;
   There, sprinkling luster o'er the cataract's shade,
   The chastened moon her glittering rainbow made;
   And blent with pictured stars, her luster lay,
   Where to still vales the free streams leaped away.

4. Where are the thronging hosts of other days,
Whose banners floated o'er the Alpine ways;
Who, through their high defiles, to battle, wound,
While deadly ordnance stirred the heights around?
Gone; like the dream that melts at early morn,
When the lark's anthem through the sky is borne:
Gone; like the wrecks that sink in ocean's spray,
And chill Oblivion murmurs, Where are they?

5. Yet "Alps on Alps" still rise; the lofty home
Of storms and eagles, where their pinions roam;
Still roam their peaks and magic colors lie,
Of morn and eve, imprinted on the sky;
And still, while kings and thrones shall fade and
  fall,
And empty crowns lie dim upon the pall;
Still shall their glaciers flash, their torrents roar,
Till kingdoms fail, and nations rise no more.

QUESTIONS.—1. In verse 1, what is the meaning of "piles of triumphant dust?" 2. What is an "anthem?" (verse 4) 3. And expecially what is a "lark's anthem?" 4. What hosts are referred to in verse 4, as crossing the Alps?

ERRORS.—*Gla-ziers* and *gla-shers* for gla-ci-ers (pronounced *gla-sherz*); *pic-ter'd* for pic-tur'd.

SPELL AND DEFINE.—(1) monuments, gorgeous, flinging, triumphant, peerless; (2) olden, ensign, voiceful, unpillared; (3) sprinkling, cataracts; (4) ordnance, oblivion, murmurs; (5) glaciers.

LESSON LXXIV.

RULE.—When two or more consonants come together, let the pupil be careful to *sound everyone distinctly.*

EXERCISES UNDER THE RULE.

He clenched his *fists.*

He *lifts* his awful form.

He makes his *payments.*

Thou *smoothed'st* his rugged path.

The *president's speech.*

Parallel between Pope and Dryden.

JOHNSON.

1. Pope professed to have learned his poetry from Dryden, whom, whenever an opportunity was presented, he praised through his whole life with unvaried liberality. Perhaps his character may receive some illustration, if he be compared with his master.

2. Integrity of understanding, the nicety of discernment were not allotted in a less proportion to Dryden than to Pope. The rectitude of Dryden's mind was sufficiently shown by the dismission of his poetical prejudices, and the rejection of unnatural thoughts and rugged numbers. But Dryden never desired to apply all the judgment that he had. He wrote and professed to write, merely for the people; and when he pleased others, he contented himself. He spent no time in struggles to rouse latent powers; he never attempted to make that better which was already good, nor often to mend what he must have known to be faulty. He wrote, as he tells us with very little consideration. When occasion or necessity called upon him, he poured out what the present moment happened to supply, and, when once it had passed the press, ejected it from his mind; for, when he had no pecuniary interest, he had no further solicitude.

3. Pope was not content to satisfy. He desired to excel, and therefore always endeavored to do his best. He did not court the candor, but dared the judgment of his reader, and, expecting no indulgence from others, he showed none to himself. He examined lines and words with minute and punctilious observation, and retouched every part with indefatigable diligence, till he had left nothing to be forgiven.

4. For this reason he kept his pieces very long in his hands, while he considered and reconsidered them. The only poems which can be supposed to have been written with such regard to the times as might hasten their publication, were the two satires of *Thirty-eight* of which Dodsley told me, that they were brought to him by the author, that they might be fairly copied. "Every line," said he, "was then written twice over. I gave him a clean transcript which he sent sometime afterwards to me for the press with every line written twice over a second time."

5. His declaration, that his care for his works ceased at their publication was not strictly true. His parental attention never abandoned them. What he found amiss in the first edition, he silently corrected in those that followed. He appears to have revised the *Iliad* and freed it from some of its imperfections. The *Essay on Criticism* received many improvements after its first appearance. It will seldom be found that he altered without adding clearness, elegance, or vigor. Pope had perhaps the judgment of Dryden, but Dryden certainty wanted the diligence of Pope.

6. In acquired knowledge, the superiority must be allowed to Dryden, whose education was more scholastic, and who, before he became an author, had been allowed more time for study with better means of information. His mind has a larger range, and he collects his images and illustrations from a more extensive circumference of science. Dryden knew

more of man in his general nature, and Pope in his local manners. The notions of Dryden were formed by comprehensive speculation, and those of Pope by minute attention. There is more dignity in the knowledge of Dryden, and more certainty in that of Pope.

7. Poetry was not the sole praise of either, for both excelled likewise in prose, but Pope did not borrow his prose from his predecessor. The style of Dryden is capricious and varied, that of Pope is cautious and uniform. Dryden obeys the motions of his own mind. Pope constrains his mind to his own rules of composition. Dryden is sometimes vehement and rapid. Pope is always smooth, uniform, and gentle. Dryden's page is a natural field, rising into inequalities, and diversified by the varied exuberance of abundant vegetation. Pope's is a velvet lawn, shaven by the scythe and leveled by the roller.

8. Of genius, that power which constitutes a poet, that quality without which judgment is cold, and knowledge is inert; the energy which collects, combines amplifies, and animates , the superiority must, with some hesitation, be allowed to Dryden. It must not be inferred that of this poetical vigor Pope had only a little, because Dryden had more, for every other writer since Milton must give place to Pope. Even of Dryden it must be said that if he has brighter paragraphs, he has not better poems.

9. Dryden's performances were always hasty, either excited by some external occasion or extorted by domestic necessity. He composed without consideration, and published without correction. What his mind could supply at call, or gather in one excursion, was all that he sought, and all that he gave. The dilatory caution of Pope enabled him to condense his sentiments, to multiply his images, and to accumulate all that study might produce, or chance might supply.

If the flights of Dryden, therefore, are higher, Pope continues longer on the wing. If the blaze of Dryden's fire is brighter, the heat of Pope's is more regular and constant. Dryden often surpasses expectation, and Pope never falls below it. Dryden is read with frequent astonishment, and Pope with perpetual delight.

10. This parallel will, I hope, when it is well considered, be found just, and if the reader should suspect me, as I suspect myself, of some partial fondness for the memory of Dryden, let him not too hastily condemn me: for meditation and inquiry may, perhaps, show him the reasonableness of my determination.

QUESTIONS.—1. During whose reigns did Pope and Dryden live? 2. Did Dryden labor his poems, as did Pope? 3. Which excelled in native genius? 4. Which in education? 5. Can you mention any of the poems of either author?

ERRORS.—*Lat-ent* for la-tent; *pow-er-ed* for pour-ed; *spec-e-la-tion* for spec-u-la-tion; *punc-til-ous* for punc-til-ious.

SPELL AND DEFINE.—(1) illustration;   (3) punctilious, indefatigable;   (4) transcript;   (7) exuberance;   (8) amplifies; (9) dilatory.

LESSON LXXV.

RULE.—When similar sounds come at the end of one word, and at the beginning of the next word, they must not be blended into one.

EXERCISES.—He sinks sorrowing to the tomb

Man loves society.

Time flies swiftly.

The birds sing.

Happy Consequences of American Independence.—MAXCY.

1. In a full persuasion of the excellency of our government, let us shun those vices which tend to its

subversion, and cultivate those virtues which will render it permanent, and transmit it in full vigor to all succeeding ages. Let not the haggard forms of intemperance and luxury ever lift up their destroying visages in this happy country. Let economy, frugality, moderation, and justice at home and abroad, mark the conduct of all our citizens. Let it be our constant care to diffuse knowledge and goodness through all ranks of society.

2. The poeple of this country will never be uneasy under its present form of government, provided they have sufficient information to judge of its excellency. No nation under heaven enjoys so much happiness as the Americans.

3. Convince them of this, and will they not shudder at the thought of subverting their political constitution, of suffering it to degenerate into aristocracy or monarchy? Let a sense of our happy situation awaken in us the warmest sensations of gratitude to the Supreme Being. Let us consider him as the author of all our blessings, acknowledging him as our beneficent parent, protector, and friend.

4. The predominant tendency of his providences towards us as a nation evinces his benevolent designs. Every part of his conduct speaks in a language plain and intelligible. Let us open our ears, let us attend, let us be wise.

5. While we celebrate the anniversary of our independence, let us not pass over in silence the defenders of our country. Where are those brave Americans whose lives were cloven down in the tempest of battle? Are they not bending from the bright abodes?

6. A voice from the altar cries, "these are they who loved their country, these are they who died for liberty." We now reap the fruit of their agony and toil. Let their memories be eternally embalmed in our

bosoms. Let the infants of all posterity prattle their fame, and drop tears of courage for their fate.

7. The consequences of American independence will soon reach to the extremities of the world. The shining car of freedom will soon roll over the necks of kings, and bear off the oppressed to scenes of liberty and peace. The clamors of war will cease under the whole heaven. The tree of liberty will shoot its top up to the sun. Its boughs will hang over the ends of the whole world, and wearied nations will lie down and rest under its shade.

8. Here in America stands the asylum for the distressed and persecuted of all nations. The vast temple of freedom rises majestically fair. Founded on a rock, it will remain unshaken by the force of tyrants, undiminished by the flight of time. Long streams of light emanate through its portals, and chase the darkness from distant nations. Its turrets will swell into the heavens, rising above every tempest, and the pillar of divine glory, descending from God, will rest forever on its summit.

QUESTIONS.—1. How does the form of government of the United States, compare with those of all other nations? 2. What is our happiness, compared with that of other nations? 3. What should we do to perpetuate our political institutions?

ERRORS.—*Ex'-lun-cy* for ex-cel-len-cy; *lux-e-ry* for lux-u-ry; *mod-e-ra-shin* for mod-e-ra-tion; *gov-e-munt* for gov-ern-ment; *con'-stu-tion* for con-sti-tu-tion.

SPELL AND DEFINE.—(1) Persuasion, excellency, government, subversion, permanent, succeeding, imtemperance, economy; (2) information; (3) political, constitution, degenerate, aristocracy, monarchy, acknowledging, beneficent; (4) predominant, providences, intelligible; (5) independence; (7) consequences, extremities; (8) asylum, majestically, undiminished, summit.

LESSON LXXVI.

RULE.—Let each pupil in the class observe and mention every syllable that is not correctly sounded as each one reads.

Satan and Death at the Gate of Hell.

MILTON.

1. Meanwhile the adversary of God and man,
  Satan, with thoughts inflamed of highest design,
  Puts on swift wings, and towards the gates of hell
  Explores his solitary flight! sometimes
5. He scours the right hand coast, sometimes the
    left,
  Now shaves with level wing the deep, then soars
  Up to the fiery concave towering high.
  As when far off at sea a fleet descried
  Hangs in the clouds, by equinoctial winds
10. Close sailing from Bengala, or the isles
  Of Ternate and Tidore, whence merchants bring
  Their spicy drugs; they, on the trading flood,
  Through the wide Ethiopian to the cape,
  Ply stemming nightly toward the pole: so
    seemed
15. Far off the flying fiend. At last appear
  Hell's bounds, high reaching to the horrid roof,
  And thrice three-fold the gates: three folds were
    brass,
  Three iron, three of adamantine rock
  Impenetrable, impaled with circling fire,
20. Yet unconsumed. Before the gates there sat
  On either side a formidable shape;
  The one seemed woman to the waist, and fair,
  But ended foul in many a scaly fold
  Voluminous and vast, a serpent armed

25. With mortal sting; about her middle round
    A cry of hell-hounds, never ceasing, barked
    With wide Cerberean mouths full loud, and rung
    A hideous peal. Far less abhorred than these
    Vexed Scylla, bathing in the sea that parts
30. Calabria from the hoarse Trinacrian shore:
    Nor uglier follow the night-hag, when, called
    In secret, riding through the air she comes,
    Lured with the smell of infant blood, to dance
    With Lapland witches, while the laboring moon
35. Eclipses at their charms. The other shape,
    If shape it might be called that shape had none
    Distinguishable in member, joint, or limb;
    Or substance might be called that shadow
      seemed;
    For each seemed either; black it stood as night,
40. Fierce as ten furies, terrible as hell,
    And shook a dreadful dart; what seemed his head
    The likeness of a kingly crown had on.
    Satan was now at hand; and from his seat
    The monster moving, onward came as fast
45. With horrid strides; hell trembled as he strode.
    The undaunted fiend what this might be admired,
    Admired, not feared; God and his Son except,
    Created thing nought valued he, nor shunned.
    And with disdainful look thus first began.
50. "Whence, and what art thou, execrable shape!
    That darest, though grim and terrible, advance
    Thy miscreated front across my way
    To yonder gates? Through them I mean to pass,
    That be assured, without leave asked of thee:
55. Retire or taste thy folly; and learn by proof,
    Hell-born! not to contend with spirits of heaven!"
    To whom the goblin, full of wrath, replied,
    Art thou that traitor angel, art thou he,
    Who first broke peace in heaven, and faith, till
      then

60. Unbroken, and in proud rebellious arms
    Drew after him the third part of heaven's sons
    Conjured against the highest, for which both thou
    And they, outcast from God, are here condemned
    To waste eternal days in woe and pain?
65. And reckonest thou thyself with spirits of heaven,
    Hell-doomed! and breathest defiance here and
       scorn,
    Where I reign king, and, to inflame thee more,
    Thy king and lord! Back to thy punishment,
    False fugitive! and to thy speed add wings,
70. Lest with a whip of scorpions I pursue
    Thy lingering, or with one stroke of this dart
    Strange horror seize thee, and pangs unfelt
       before."
    So spake the grisly terror, and in shape,
    So speaking and so threatening, grew ten-fold
75. More dreadful and deformed: on the other side,
    Incensed with indignation, Satan stood
    Unterrified, and like a comet burned,
    That fires the length of Ophiuchus huge
    In the arctic sky, and from his horrid hair
80. Shakes pestilence and war. Each at the head
    Leveled his deadly aim; their fatal hands
    No second stroke intend; and such a frown
    Each cast at the other, as when two black clouds
    With heaven's artillery fraught, come rattling on
85. Over the Caspian, then stand front to front
    Hovering a space, till winds the signal blow
    To join their dark encounter in mid air:
    So frowned the mighty combatants, that hell
    Grew darker at their frown; so matched they
       stood;
90. For never but once more was either like
    To meet so great a foe: and now great deeds
    Had been achieved, whereof all hell had rung,
    Had not the snaky sorceress, that sat

Fast by hell-gate, and kept the fatal key,
95. Risen, and with hideous outcry, rushed between.

QUESTIONS.—1. What beautiful comparison is there in the first fifteen lines? 2. Where are Bengala, Ternate, and Tidore? 3. What is meant by Cerberean mouths? 4. What is the fable to which allusion is made in line 32-36, &c. 5. Who was the snaky sorceress? 6. Why is Death represented as the son of Satan and Sin?

ERRORS.—*Find* for fiend (pronounced *feend*); *tur-ri-ble* for ter-ri-ble; *shuk* for shook; *un-don-ted* for un-daunt-ed (pronounced *un-dant-ed.)*

SPELL AND DEFINE.—(4) solitary;   (7) concave; (14) stemming;   (18) adamantine;   (19) impaled, impenetrable; (37) distinguishable; (52) miscreated; (73) grisly; (84) fraught; (93) sorceress.

LESSON LXXVII.

RULE.—While each pupil reads, let the rest observe, and then mention which syllables were pronounced wrong, and which were omitted or indistinctly sounded.

Evils of Dismemberment.—WEBSTER.

1. Gentlemen, the political prosperity which this country has attained, and which it now enjoys, it has acquired mainly through the instrumentality of the present government. While this agent continues, the capacity of attaining to still higher degrees of prosperity exists also.

2. We have, while this lasts, a political life capable of beneficial exertion, with power to resist or overcome misfortunes, to sustain us against the ordinary

accidents of human affairs, and to promote, by active efforts, every public interest.

3. But dismemberment strikes at the very being which preserves these faculties. It would lay its rude and ruthless hand on this great agent itself. It would sweep away, not only what we possess, but all power of regaining lost, or acquiring new, possessions.

4. It would leave the country, not only bereft of its prosperity and happiness, but without limbs, and organs, or faculties, by which to exert itself, hereafter, in the pursuit of that prosperity and happiness.

5. Other misfortunes may be borne, or their effects overcome. If disastrous war should sweep our commerce from the ocean, another generation may renew it. If it exhaust our treasury, future industry may replenish it. If it desolate and lay waste our fields, still, under a new cultivation, they will grow green again, and ripen to future harvests.

6. It were but a trifle, even if the walls of yonder capitol were to crumble, if its lofty pillars should fall, and its gorgeous decorations be all covered by the dust of the valley. All these might be rebuilt. But who shall reconstruct the fabric of demolished government? Who shall rear again the well-proportioned columns of constitutional liberty! Who shall frame together the skillful architecture which unites national sovereignty with State rights, individual security, and public prosperity?

7. No, gentlemen, if these columns fall, they will be raised not again. Like the Coliseum and the Parthenon, they will be destined to a mournful, a melancholy immortality. Bitterer tears, however, will flow over them, than were ever shed over the monuments of Roman or Grecian art, for they will be the remnants of a more glorious edifice than Greece or Rome ever saw—the edifice of constitutional American liberty.

8. But, gentlemen, let us hope for better things. Let us trust in that gracious Being who has hitherto held our country as in the hollow of his hand. Let us trust to the virtue and the intelligence of the people, and to the efficacy of religious obligation. Let us trust to the influence of Washington's example.

9. Let us hope that that fear of heaven, which expels all other fear, and that regard to duty, which transcends all other regard, may influence public men and private citizens, and lead our country still onward in her happy career. Full of these gratifying anticipations and hopes, let us look forward to the end of that century which is now commenced.

10. May the disciples of Washington then see, as we now see, the flag of the Union floating on the top of the capitol. Then, as now, may the sun in his course visit no land more free, more happy, more lovely, than this our own country!

QUESTIONS.—1. How was the political prosperity of our country obtained? 2. So long as this government lasts, what will be our situation? 3. What will be the effect of dismemberment?
4. Why would the destruction of our present form of government be an irretrievable loss of liberty? 5. In what is our chief hope for the permanency of our government to be placed?

ERRORS.—*Gen-tle-mun* for gen-tle-men; *in-ster-mun-tal-i-ty* for in-stru-men-tal-i-ty; *col-lumns* for col-umns; *ar-chi-tec-ture* should be pronounced ark-i-tec-ture.

SPELL AND DEFINE.—(1) instrumentality, government; (2) beneficial, misfortunes; (3) dismemberment, ruthless; (5) disastrous, replenish; (6) gorgeous, decorations, demolished, well-proportioned, constitutional, architecture, sovereignty; (7) Coliseum, Parthenon, melancholy, immortality constitutional; (9) transcends, anticipations.

LESSON LXXVIII.

RULE.—Be careful to pronounce the little words, like *a*, *the*, *and*, *in*, etc., distinctly, and not to join them to the next word.

No Excellence without Labor.—WIRT.

1. The education, moral and intellectual, of every individual, must be, chiefly, his own work. Rely upon it, that the ancients were right—both in morals and intellect—we give their final shape to our characters, and thus become, emphatically, the architects of our own fortune. How else could it happen that young men who have had precisely the same opportunities, should be continually presenting us with such different results, and rushing to such opposite destinies?

2. Difference of talent will not solve it, because that difference is very often in favor of the disappointed candidate. You shall see issuing from the walls of the same college—nay, sometimes from the bosom of the same family—two young men, of whom the one shall be admitted to be a genius of high order, the other, scarcely above the point of mediocrity. Yet you shall see the genius sinking and perishing in poverty, obscurity and wretchedness: while on the other hand, you shall observe the mediocre plodding his slow but sure way up the hill of life, gaining steadfast footing at every step, and mounting, at length, to eminence and distinction, an ornament to his family, a blessing to his country.

3. Now, whose work is this? Manifestly their own. They are the architects of their respective fortunes. The best seminary of learning that can open its portals to you can do no more than to afford you the opportunity of instruction. It must depend, at last on yourselves, whether you will be instructed or not, or to what point you will push your instruction.

4. Of this be assured—I speak, from observation, a certain truth: THERE IS NO EXCELLENCE WITHOUT GREAT LABOR. It is the fiat of fate from which no power of genius can absolve you.

5. Genius, unexerted, is like the poor moth that flutters around a candle till it scorches itself to death. If genius be desirable at all, it is only of that great and magnanimous kind, which, like the condor of South America, pitches from the summit of Chimborazo, above the clouds, and sustains itself, at pleasure, in that empyreal region, with an energy rather invigorated than weakened by the effort.

6. It is this capacity for high and long-continued exertion—this vigorous power of profound and searching investigation—this careering and widespreading comprehension of mind—and those long reaches of thought, that

"Pluck bright honor from the pale-faced moon,
Or dive into the bottom of the deep,
Where fathom line could never touch the ground,
And drag up drowned honor by the locks—"

7. This is the prowess, and these the hardy achievements, which are to enroll your names among the great men of the earth.

QUESTIONS.—1. What did the ancients say in respect to education? 2. How does it appear from facts, that it is labor rather than genius which gives eminence?

ERRORS.—*In-tel-lec-too-ul* and *in-tel-lec-chew-el* for in-tel-lect-u-al; *cun-tin-e-al-ly* for con-tin-u-al-ly; *'nor-na-munt* for an or-na-ment; *em-pir'-e-al* for em-py-re'-al.

SPELL AND DEFINE.—(1) intellectual, individual, ancients, emphatically, architects, continually; (2) disappointed, obscurity; wretchedness, mediocre; (3) manifestly, respective, opportunity, instruction; (4) excellence; (5) magnanimous, empyreal, invigorated; (6) investigation, comprehension, profound; (7) achievements.

LESSON LXXIX.

RULE.—In reading poetry that does not rhyme, there should be no pause at the end of a line, except when it terminates with an important word, or the sense requires it.

Thoughts in a Place of Public Worship.

HANNAH MORE.

1. And here we come and sit, time after time,
And call it social worship; Is it thus?
Oh thou! whose searching all pervading eye
Scans every secret movement of the heart,

5. And sees us as we are, why mourns my soul
On these occasions? Why so dead and cold
My best affections? I have found thee, oft
In my more secret seasons, in the field,
And in my chamber: even in the stir

10. Of outward occupations has my mind
Been drawn to thee, and found thy presence life:
But here I seek in vain, and rarely find
Thy ancient promise to the few that wait
In singleness upon thee, reach to us.

15. Most sweet it is to feel the unity
Of soul-cementing love, gathering in one,
Flowing from heart to heart, and like a cloud
Of mingled incense rising to the throne
Of love itself! then much of heaven is felt

20. By minds drawn thitherward, and closely linked
In the celestial union; 'tis in this
Sweet element alone, that we can live
To any purpose, or expect our minds
Clothed with that covering which alone prepares

25. For social worship. Therefore mourns my soul
In secret, and like one amidst the vast
And widely peopled earth would seek to hide
Myself and sorrows from the motley crowd
Of human observation. But Oh, thou

30. Whose bowels of compassion never fail
    Towards the creatures fashioned by thy hand,
    Reanimate the dead! and give to those
    Who never felt thy presence in their souls
    Nor saw thy beauty, both to see and feel
35. That thou art lovely, and thy presence life:
    Restore the wanderer, and support the weak
    With thy sustaining arm, for strength is thine.
    And Oh! preserve this tempest-beaten bark
    From sinking in the wave, whose swelling surge
40. Threatens to overwhelm; forsake her not
    But be her Pilot, though no sun nor star
    Appear amid the gloom; for if a ray
    From thy all cheering presence light her course,
    She rides the storm secure, and in due time
    Will reach her destined port, and be at peace.

QUESTIONS.—1. What is "blank verse?" 2. How many feet are there to a line in blank verse? 3. What is a foot? 4. What feeling is most necessary to social worship? 5. What is the petition offered in the last ten lines? 6. What is a "figure of speech?" 7. Is there one in this lesson? 8. Where?

ERRORS.—*Set* for sit; *wush-ip* for wor-ship; *ex-pict* and *ex-peck* for ex-pect.

SPELL AND DEFINE.—(14) singleness; (16) cementing; (21) celestial; (22) element; (24) prepares; (27) peopled; (29) observation; (30) compassion, bowels; (36) wanderer, restore; (37) sustaining; (39) surge; (41) pilot; (45) destined.

LESSON LXXX.

RULE.—Give a full and distinct sound to all the consonant sounds.

A Plea for Common Schools.

SAML. LEWIS.

1. In rising to address an assembly at the seat of government of the state of Ohio, on the subject of education, I cannot but recur to the times when I first heard of the beautiful rivers and plains of the West. My earliest recollections are associated with the glowing pictures that were drawn of the immense advantages that must result to all that would help to people this new state. When not more than eight years of age, and in the neighborhood of that spot, rendered almost sacred by the landing of the pilgrims nearly two hundred years before, I stood and listened, with all the curiosity of a child, to the questions of parents, grandparents and neighbors, put to those who pretended to know anything relating to this then almost heathen land.

2. You all recollect how highly this country was spoken of, and the most glowing panegyric was always finished by giving positive assurance that provision, the most ample, was made to educate the children of the rising state. I well recollect that this was considered one of its greatest advantages. Parents who proposed to emigrate were more particular in their inquiries on this than on any other subject.

3. I will add that nothing did more to secure an early sale and settlement of the lands of government than the appropriations for schools. I more than once heard the resolute but affectionate mother, when surrounded by friends dissuading her from emigration, assign it as a sufficient inducement to go to the far west, "*My* children will there be entitled to education

as well as the children of the *rich.*" With that ambition to see their children elevated, which only such
mothers feel, did many a young mother tear herself
from parents, brothers, sisters, and the home of her
youth, and with only her husband and weeping
children, throw herself into this valley, to realize those
hopes that had been inspired by government and the
agents of different land companies.

4. To what extent these hopes, so far as education
is concerned, have been realized, you all know. Here
let me contradict, in the most positive manner, the
assertion so often made by the older states, that the
general government has been liberal to this and the
other western states in educational endowments. Ohio
has never received the first farthing in money, nor
the first acre of land from this source, as a donation
for educational purposes. True, there was a vast tract
of uncultivated land owned by government, which she
desired to sell. To do this she had to devise some plan
that would allure men to the purchase. She accordingly assigned a certain portion for education—but
she did not give it—it was *a part of the consideration
paid*—the very same plan adopted by men who laid
out new towns— they gave away a part to secure a
sale of the residue, and no part of the immense public
domain has ever brought into the treasury so great
a return as that devoted to schools.

5. But the impression that ample provision was
made became so general and remained so long, that
for years our legislature omitted all action on the subject. To this cause alone do I attribute what would,
otherwise, seem to be an unpardonable neglect. Many
subjects, important in themselves, have claimed the
attention of those who have, from time to time, been
called to legislate for us, and where so much was to
be done, and in so short a time, it is not strange that
some things have been overlooked. It is indeed

wonderful that so much has been accomplished.

6. Our state, instead of requiring centuries to gain a standing among her elder sisters, has passed, almost by magic, from infancy to maturity. To maturity, did I say! Look at the gigantic plans of improvement just begun, and those in contemplation. Look at your immense facilities for agriculture, manufactures, and commerce; and, above all, look at the enterprise and public spirit manifested throughout your state. With all these in view, instead of saying that Ohio is at her maturity, must we not exclaim that she has just entered upon youth with all her energies—but that in her very youth she is greater than states and nations were wont to be in maturity?

7. We have not attained this exalted place without incurring corresponding responsibilities to the world and to posterity. Among these responsibilities, none rests with greater weight than our obligation to educate the rising generation. In this sentiment all will doubtless agree, and leaving to others to excuse themselves and hold back the general cause on the plea of hostility in the poeple—I venture to affirm that there is no subject which, if properly presented, would find greater favor with our citizens than the subject of general education.

8. After a residence of more than twenty years in this state, and observing public sentiment with some care, I affirm that I have never seen twenty men who would for themselves oppose a system of general instruction, adapted to the wants of the community. I have heard some professed friends of common schools express fears that others would not sustain an improvement of the system. I have heard those to whose care the schools were entrusted excuse themselves from taking measures to meet the demands of the community, by casting on that community the reproach of hostility, but I am much

mistaken if, on a direct appeal to the poeple, by cities and townships, there would be found one town in ten that would not sustain the most efficient measures.

9. Patronize education, establish common schools, and sustain them well, and you will, most assuredly, provide a place were all classes will, in childhood, become familiar, before the influence of pride, wealth, and family, can bias the mind. An acquaintance, thus formed, will last as long as life itself. Take fifty lads in a neighborhood, including rich and poor—send them in childhood to the same school—let them join in the same sports, read and spell in the same classes, until their different circumstances fix their business for life, some go to the field, some to the mechanic's shop, some to their merchandise: one becomes eminent at the bar, another in the pulpit: some become wealthy; the majority live on with a mere competency—a few are reduced to beggary!

10. But let the most eloquent orator that ever harangued a popular assembly, attempt to prejudice the minds of one part against the other—and so far from succeeding, the poorest of the whole world consider himself insulted, and from his own knowledge stand up in defence of his more fortunate schoolmate. I appeal to all who hear me, if the ties of friendship formed at school have not outlived every other, where relationship did not exist? Can the oldest man in this assembly meet the schoolmate of bygone days without feelings that almost hallow the greeting? These are the feelings that I would, by common schools, establish in the bosoms of every son and daughter of Ohio. Distinction will soon enough find its way into society from considerations of wealth and influence. It should be the duty of our legislature to provide an antidote against all its evil consequences. Now, you have the power. Now, your state is American in all its feelings. Wait not until those who

are hostile to such a measure are able to make head against you. We ought to remember that we occupy new ground in the world. We look to the past, but rather as a beacon than a guide.

11. No state before us has ever presented a spectacle so magnificent. Less than forty years ago and the state of Ohio was only in prospect. Since that time she has come into being. Behold her now the fourth state in the bright catalogue of all the states, with more than a million of people, intelligent and enterprising, with her four hundred miles of canals—her turnpikes, railroads constructing and projected. See her steamboats, her mills, her factories, her fields and her flocks! She sustains at the same time, the highest credit both at home and abroad. Does even ancient fable tell of anything like this! Add to all this that our government is of the most popular kind. Public will gives law, and enforces obedience: public sentiment, then, is the unlimited sovereign of this state. Other nations have hereditary sovereigns, and one of the most important duties of their governments is to take care of the education of the heir to the throne. *These children about your streets, some of whom cannot even speak your language, are to be your future sovereigns.* It is not important then that they should be well educated? Is it not important that they should understand the genius of your constitution and your laws? Should they not be able to read the daily issues from your different presses, civil and religious? Can you calculate highly on their judgment, either in governing themselves or selecting others for posts of honor, if they themselves are not intelligent?

12. All nations are looking on our experiment. Individuals bid us Godspeed. But every court in Europe would rejoice to see us do as they have long prophesied we must do, dissolve in anarchy. After having been, for a brief space, made the sport of

contending factions, and when our houses had been burned, our fields made desolate, and our families destroyed, hail as our deliverer the fortunate tyrant who had the address to seize the reins of government, hold them steadily enough to secure our lives and property, and trample upon our liberties.

13. From such a state all are ready to say, Good Lord deliver us! Many, perhaps, are disposed to say, the speaker dreams. But let me refer you to the history of other nations and other times. Did not France desire to be free? Did not she *deserve* to be *free*—if a sacrifice of blood and treasure could merit freedom? Nor was she without learning among the privileged orders. No court was ever so crowded with men of learning as that of the unfortunate Louis. But the great mass of the community were uneducated. Hence they were imposed upon by the few, and the people, after achieving all that patriotism, bravery, wealth, and numbers could do—and breasting the opposition of combined Europe with success—ultimately threw themselves into the arms of a Corsican soldier. Yes, they passed under the yoke of the most galling tyranny, to save themselves from the ravages of an outraged and ignorant mob!

QUESTIONS.—1. What high panegyric has been pronounced upon the State of Ohio?   2. What was one great cause of the early and rapid settlement of this state?   3. Is it true that the general government has made donations to the western states for educational purposes?   4. What did it do?   5. What has been the progress of this state in respect to education?   6. What obligations rest upon her in consequence of this?

ERRORS.—*P'tic-lar* for par-tic-u-lar; *in-que-ries* for in-qu'i-ries.

SPELL AND DEFINE.—(1) government, neighborhood; (2) panegyric;   (3) appropriations, dissuading, ambition; (4) realized, endowments, educational, uncultivated, consideration; (5) legislature, unpardonable, overlooked; (6) agriculture, manufactures, enterprise;   (7) responsibilities.

LESSON LXXXI.

RULE.—Avoid reading in a monotonous way, as if you were not interested and did not understand what is read.

Midnight Musings.—YOUNG.

1. The bell strikes One. We take no note of time
 But from its loss: to give it then a tongue
 Is wise in man. As if an angel spoke
 I feel the solemn sound. If heard aright,
5. It is the knell of my departed hours.
 Where are they? With the years beyond the flood.
 It is the signal that demands dispatch:
 How much is to be done? My hopes and fears
 Start up alarm'd, and o'er life's narrow verge
10. Look down—on what? A fathomless abyss.
 A dread eternity! how surely mine!
 And can eternity belong to me,
 Poor pensioner on the bounties of an hour?
 How poor, how rich, how abject, how august,
15. How complicate, how wonderful is man!
 How passing wonder He who made him such!
 Who center'd in our make such strange extremes,
 From different natures marvelously mix'd,
 Connection exquisite of distant worlds!
20. Distinguish'd link in being's endless chain!
 Midway from nothing to the Deity!
 A beam ethereal, sullied and absorpt!
 Though sullied and dishonor'd, still divine!
 Dim miniature of greatness absolute!
25. An heir of glory! a frail child of dust!
 Helpless immortal! insect infinite!
 A worm! a god!—I tremble at myself,
 And in myself am lost. At home a stranger,
 Thought wanders up and down, surpris'd, aghast,

30. And wondering at her own. How reason reels!
    O what a miracle to man is man!
    Triumphantly distress'd! what joy! what dread!
    Alternately transported and alarm'd;
    What can preserve my life! or what destroy!
35. An angel's arm can't snatch me from the grave;
    Legions of angels can't confine me there.
    'Tis past conjecture; all thing rise in proof.
    While o'er my limbs Sleep's soft dominion spread,
    What though my soul fantastic measures trod
40. O'er fairy fields, or mourn'd along the gloom
    Of pathless woods, or down the craggy steep
    Hurl'd headlong, swam with pain the mantled
        pool,
    Or scal'd the cliff, or danc'd on hollow winds
    With antic shapes, wild natives of the brain!
45. Her ceaseless flight, though devious, speaks her
        nature
    Of subtler essence than the trodden clod;
    Active, aerial, towering, unconfin'd,
    Unfetter'd with her gross companion's fall.
    Ev'n silent night proclaims my soul immortal;
50. Ev'n silent night proclaims eternal day!
    For human weal Heaven husbands all events:
    Dull sleep instructs, nor sport vain dreams in
        vain.

QUESTIONS.—1. What leads us to "take note of time?"
2. Repeat some of the epithets applied to man.   3. What conclusion is deduced from the activity of mind during sleep?

ERRORS.—*Mer-a-cle* for mir-a-cle; *an-gel* (pronounced ain-gel;)
con-jec-tur for con-jec-ture; *pens-ner* for pen-sion-er; *wun-ner-ful*
for won-der-ful; sub-tler, pronounced *sut-tler.*

SPELL AND DEFINE.—(9) verge;   (10) fathomless,
pensioner; (15) complicate; (19) exquisite; (32) triumphantly;
(36) legions; (39) fantastic; (41) craggy; (44) antic; (45) devious.

LESSON LXXXII.

RULE.—In reading such lessons as the following, be careful to read slowly, and with great deliberation and seriousness. When sentences are short, and yet contain a great deal of meaning, you must allow the hearer a little time to gather the sense and to dwell upon it.

Omnipresence of God.—BIBLE.

1. O Lord, thou hast searched me, and known me. Thou knowest my down sitting and mine up rising, thou understandest my thoughts afar off.

2. Thou compassest my path, and my lying down, and are acquainted with all my ways. For there is not a word in my tongue, but lo, O Lord thou knowest it altogether. Thou has beset me behind and before, and laid thine hand upon me.

3. Such knowledge is too wonderful for me: it is high, I cannot attain unto it.

4. Whither shall I go from thy spirit? or whither shall I flee from thy presence? If I ascend up into heaven, thou art there: if I make my bed in hell, behold, thou art there. If I take the wings of the morning and dwell in the uttermost parts of the sea: Even there shall thy hand lead me, and thy right hand shall hold me.

5. If I say, Surely the darkness shall cover me: even the night shall be light about me: Yea, the darkness hideth not from thee; but the night shineth as the day; the darkness and the light are both alike to thee.

QUESTIONS.—1. Can we do anything without God's seeing and knowing it? 2. Does he know what we speak and what we think, as well as what we do? 3. What is meant by (4) "If I make my bed in Hell, thou art there?" 4. How should the sentiments of this Psalm influence our conduct?

ERRORS.—*Sarch-ed* for search-ed; *set-ting* for sit-ting; *un-der-stand'st* for un-der-stand-est; *com'-sest* for com-pass-est; *thar'* for there; *kiv-er* for cov-er; *morn-in'* for morn-ing.

SPELL AND DEFINE.—(1) searched, understandest; (2) com-passest, acquainted; (3) attain; (4) ascend, uttermost.

LESSON LXXXIII.

RULE.—Be careful to give a full sound to the vowels. Regard to this rule will correct the common flat, clipping and uninteresting way in which many read.

EXERCISES in which the vowels italicised are to be prolonged.

H*ai*l! holy l*i*ght!

We pr*ai*se thee, *O* Lord God.

These names of the Deity are seldom pronounced with that full and solemn sound that is proper. *Lud* and *Law-ard* and *Gud* and *Gawd* are too frequently used instead of the proper sounds. If the pupil can learn to speak the three words, O—Lord—God, properly, it will be worth no little attention. Every pupil ought to be exercised on these words till they pronounce them properly, and in a full and solemn tone.

Henry Martyn and Lord Byron.

MISS BEECHER.

1. By reasoning from the known laws of mind, we gain the position that obedience to the Divine law is the surest mode of securing every species of happiness attainable in this state of existence.

2. The recorded experience of mankind does no less prove that obedience to the law of God is the true path to happiness. To exhibit this, some specific cases will be selected, and perhaps a fairer illustration cannot be presented than the constrasted records of two youthful personages who have made the most distinguished figure in the Christian, and the literary world: Henry Martyn, the missionary, and Lord Byron, the poet.

3. Martyn was richly endowed with ardent feelings, keen susceptibilities, and superior intellect. He was the object of many affections, and in the principal University of Great Britain, won the highest honors, both in classic literature and mathematical science. He was flattered, caressed, and admired. The road to fame and honor lay open before him, and the brightest hopes of youth seemed ready to be realized.

4. But the hour came when he looked upon a lost and guilty world, in the light of eternity, when he realized the full meaning of the sacrifice of our incarnate God; when he assumed his obligations to become a fellow worker in recovering a guilty world from the dominion of sin, and all its future woes.

5. "The love of God constrained him;" and without a murmur, for wretched beings, on a distant shore, whom he never saw, of whom he knew nothing but that they were miserable and guilty, he relinquished the wreath of fame, forsook the path of worldly honor, severed the ties of kindred, and gave up friends, country and home. With every nerve throbbing in anguish at the sacrifice, he went forth alone, to degraded heathen society, to solitude and privation, to weariness and painfulness, and to all the trials of missionary life.

6. He spent his days in teaching the guilty and degraded, the way of pardon and peace. He lived to write the law of his God in the wide spread character of the Persian nation, and to place a copy in the hands of its king. He lived to contend with the chief Moullahs of Mahomet in the mosques of Shiras, and to kindle a flame in Persia, more undying than its fabled fires.

7. He lived to endure rebuke and scorn, to toil and suffer in a fervid clime, to drag his weary steps over burning sands, with the daily dying hope that at last he might be laid to rest among his kindred, and on

his native shore. Yet even this last earthly hope was not attained, for after spending all his youth in ceaseless labors for the good of others, at the early age of thirty-two, he was laid in an unknown and foreign grave.

8. He died *alone*—a stranger in a strange land— with no friendly form around to sympathize and soothe him. Yet this was the last record of his dying hand: "I sat in the orchard, and thought with sweet comfort and peace of my God! In solitude, my company, my friend, my comforter!"

9. And in reviewing the record of his short, yet blessed life, even if we forget the exulting joy with which such a benevolent spirit must welcome to heaven the thousands he toiled to save; if we look only at his years of self-denying trial, where were accumulated all the sufferings he was ever to feel, we can find *more* evidence of *true happiness* than is to be found in the records of the youthful poet, who was gifted with every susceptibility of happiness, who spent his days in search of selfish enjoyment, who had every source of earthly bliss laid open, and drank to the very dregs.

10. We shall find that a mind that obeys the law of God, is happier when bereft of the chief joys of this world, than a worldly man can be when possessed of them all. The remains of Lord Byron present one of the most mournful exhibitions of a noble mind in all the wide chaos of ruin and disorder. He, also, was naturally endowed with overflowing affections, keen sensibilities, quick conceptions, and a sense of moral rectitude. He had all the constituents of a mind of first rate order. But he passed through existence amid the wildest disorder of a ruined spirit.

11. His mind seemed utterly unbalanced, teeming with rich thoughts and overbearing impulses, the sport of the strangest fancies, and the strongest

passions; bound down by no habit, restrained by no principle; a singular combination of great conceptions and fantastic caprices, of manly dignity and childish folly, of nobler feeling and babyish weakness.

12. The lord of Newstead Abbey—the heir of a boasted line of ancestry—a peer of the realm—the pride of the social circle—the leading star of poesy—the hero of Greece—the wonder of the gaping world, can now be followed to his secret haunts. There the veriest child of the nursery might be amused at some of his silly weaknesses and ridiculous conceits. Distressed about the cut of a collar, *fuming* at the color of his dress, intensely anxious about the whiteness of his hands, deeply engrossed with monkeys and dogs, and flying about from one whim to another with a reckless earnestness as ludicrous as it is disgusting.

13. At times this boasted hero and genius seemed nought but an overgrown child that had broken its leading strings and overmastered its nurses. At other times he is beheld in all the rounds of dissipation and the haunts of vice, occasionally filling up his leisure in recording and disseminating the disgusting minutiae of his weakness and shame, and with an effrontery and stupidity equalled only by that of the friend who retails them to the insulted world.

14. Again we behold him philosophizing like a sage, and moralizing like a Christian; while often from his bosom burst forth the repinings of a wounded spirit. He sometimes seemed to gaze upon his own mind with wonder, to watch its disordered powers with curious inquiry, to touch its complaining strings, and start at the response, while often with maddening sweep he shook every chord, and sent forth its deep wailings to entrance a wondering world.

15. Both Henry Martyn and Lord Byron shared the sorrows of life, and their records teach the dif-

ferent workings of the Christian and the worldly mind. Byron lost his mother, and when urged not to give way to sorrow, he burst into an agony of grief, saying, "I had but *one* friend in the world, and now she is gone!" On the death of some of his early friends, he thus writes: "My friends fall around me, and I shall be left a lonely tree before I am withered. I *have no resource but my own reflections,* and they present no prospect here or hereafter, except the selfish satisfaction of surviving my betters. I am indeed most wretched!"

16. And *thus* Henry Martyn mourns the loss of one most dear. "Can it be that she has been lying so many months in the cold grave? Would that I could always remember it, or always forget it; but to think a moment on other things, and then feel the remembrance of it come, as if for the first time, rends my heart asunder. O my gracious God, what should I do without Thee! But now thou art manifesting thyself as 'the God of all consolation.' Never was I so near thee. There is nothing in the world for which I could wish to live, except because it may please God to appoint me some work to do. O thou incomprehensibly glorious Savior, what hast thou done to alleviate the sorrows of life!"

17. It is recorded of Byron, that in society he generally appeared humorous and prankish, yet when rallied on his melancholy turn of writing, his constant answer was that though thus merry and full of laughter, he was at heart one of the most miserable wretches in existence.

18. Thus he writes: "Why, at the very height of desire and human pleasure, worldly, amorous, ambitious, or even avaricious, does there mingle a certain sense of doubt and sorrow—a fear of what is to come—a doubt of what is? If it were not for hope, what would the future be—a hell! As for the past,

what predominates in memory—hopes baffled! From whatever place we commence, we know *where it must all end.* And yet what good is there in knowing it? It does not make men wiser or better. If I were to live over again, I do not know what I would change in my life, unless it were for—*not to have lived at all.* All history, and experience, and the rest, teach us, that good and evil are pretty equally balanced in this existence, and that what is *most to* be desired is an *easy passage out of it.* What can it give us but years, and these have *little of good but their ending."*

19. And thus Martyn writes: "I am happier here in this remote land, where I seldom hear what happens in the world, than I was in England, where there are so many calls to look at things that are seen. The precious *Word* is now my only study, by means of translations. Time flows on with great rapidity. It seems as if life would all be gone before anything is done. I sometimes rejoice that I am but twenty-seven, and that unless God should ordain it otherwise, I may double this number in constant and successful labor. But I shall not cease from my happiness and scarely from my labor, by passing into the other world."

20. And thus they make their records at anniversaries, when the mind is called to review life and its labors. Thus Bryon writes: "At twelve o'clock I shall have completed thirty-three years! I go to my bed with a heaviness of heart at having lived so long and to so little purpose. It is now three minutes past twelve, and I am thirty-three!

"Alas, my friend, the years pass swiftly by."

But I do not regret them so much for what I have done, as for what I *might* have done."

21. And thus Martyn: "I like to find myself employed usefully, in a way I did not expect or foresee. The coming year is to be a perilous one, but

my life is of little consequence, whether I finish the
Persian New Testament or not. I look back with pity
on myself, when I attached so much importance to
my life and labors. The more I see of my own works,
the more I am ashamed of them, for coarseness and
clumsiness mar all the works of man. I am sick when
I look at the wisdom of man, but am relieved by reflecting, that we have a city whose builder and maker
is God. The least of *his* works is refreshing. A dried
leaf, or a straw, make me feel *in good company*, and
complacency and admiration take the place of disgust.
What a monentary duration is the life of man! "It
glides along, rolling onward forever," may be affirmed
of the river, but men pass away as soon as they begin
to exist. Well, let the moments pass!"

"They waft us sooner o'er
This life's tempestuous sea,
Soon we shall reach the blissful shore
Of blest eternity!"

22. Such was the experience of those who in youth
completed their course. The poet has well described
his own career:

"A wandering mass of shapeless flame,
A pathless comet and a curse,
The menace of the universe;
Still rolling on with innate force,
Without a sphere, without a course,
A bright deformity on high,
The monster of the upper sky!"

23. In holy writ we read of those who are "raging
waves of the sea, foaming out their own shame;
wandering stars to whom is reserved the blackness
of darkness forever." The lips of man may not apply
these terrific words to any whose doom is yet to be
disclosed, but there is a passage which none can fear

to apply. "Those that are wise shall shine as the brightness of the firmament, and they that turn many to righteousness, as stars forever and forever!"

QUESTIONS.—1. What truth have we gained by reasoning from the known laws of mind? 2. What else furnishes us with evidence of the same truth, and what two characters are given as examples? 3. What is said of Henry Martyn? 4. Why did he give up home, country, and the honors and pleasures of life? 5. Do you suppose he was happier in this world than he would have been if he had lived simply to seek pleasure for himself? 6. Will he be happier in heaven for the sacrifices he made on earth? 7. Who had the most of this world to enjoy— Martyn or Byron! 8. What is said of Byron? 9. Which had the most comfort in seasons of affliction? 10. How did Byron feel when he was enjoying himself the most? 11. How did Martyn feel when he was cut off from most of the pleasures that Bryon was seeking? 12. What was the difference in their feelings at their birthdays? 13. What two passages of Scripture indicate the future prospects of two such minds as Byron and Martyn?

ERRORS.—*Haunts* should be pronounced hants; *lei-sure* should be pronounced le-zhur; *sor-rers* for sor-rows; *ag-ur-ny* for ag-o-ny; *in-com-pra-hen-si-bly* for in-com-pre-hen-si-bly; *an-ner-ver-sa-ries* for an-ni-ver-sa-ries.

SPELL AND DEFINE.—(13) overmastered, disseminating; (14) entrance; (15) resource; (16) gracious; (17) melancholy; (18) predominates; (20) anniversaries; (21) perilous.

LESSON LXXXIV.

RULE.—Where two or more consonants come together, let the pupil be careful to sound every one distinctly.

EXERCISES UNDER THE RULE.

Thou *indulged'st* thy appetite.
O Wind! that waft'st us o'er the main.
Thou tempted'st him.
Thou loved'st him fondly.
Thou credited'st his story.
The *lists* are open.

Byron.—POLLOK.

1. He touched his harp, and nations heard,
   entranced.
   As some vast river of unfailing source,
   Rapid, exhaustless, deep, his numbers flowed,
   And oped new fountains in the human heart.
5. Where fancy halted, weary in her flight,
   In other men, his, fresh as morning rose,
   And soared untrodden heights, and seemed at
   home,
   Where angels bashful looked. Others, though
   great,
   Beneath their argument seemed struggling
   whiles;
10. He from above descending, stooped to touch
    The loftiest thought; and proudly stooped, as
    though
    It scarce deserved his verse. With nature's self
    He seemed an old acquaintance, free to jest
    At will with all her glorious majesty.
15. He laid his hand upon "the ocean's mane,"
    And played familiar with his hoary locks.
    Stood on the Alps, stood on the Apennines;
    And with the thunder talked, as friend to friend;
    And wove his garland of the lightning's wing,

20. In sportive twist—the lightning's fiery wing,
    Which, as the footsteps of the dreadful God,
    Marching upon the storm in vengeance seemed—
    Then turned, and with the grasshopper, who sung
    His evening song beneath his feet, conversed.
25. Suns, moons, and stars, and clouds his sisters
        were;
    Rocks, mountains, meteors, seas, and winds, and
        storms
    His brothers—younger brothers, whom he scarce
    As equals deemed.
    As some fierce comet of tremendous size,
30. To which the stars did reverence as it passed;
    So he through learning and through fancy took
    His flight sublime; and on the loftiest top
    Of fame's dread mountain sat; not soiled, and
        worn,
    As if he from the earth had labored up;
35. But as some bird of heavenly plumage fair,
    He looked, which down from higher regions came,
    And perched it there, to see what lay beneath.
    Great man! the nations gazed and wondered
        much,
    And praised: and many called his evil good.
40. Wits wrote in favor of his wickedness:
    And kings to do him honor took delight.
    Thus full of titles, flattery, honor, fame;
    Beyond desire, beyond ambition full,—
    He died—he died of what? Of wretchedness.
45. Drank every cup of joy, heard every trump
    Of fame; drank early, deeply drank; drank
        draughts
    That common millions might have quenched—
        then died
    Of thirst, because there was no more to drink.
    His goddess, nature, wooed, embraced, enjoyed,

50. Fell from his arms abhorred; his passions died;
    Died, all but dreary, solitary pride;
    And all his sympathies in being died.
    As some ill-guided bark, well built and tall,
    Which angry tides cast on our desert shore,
55. And then retiring, leave it there to rot
    And moulder in the winds and rains of heaven;
    So he, cut from the sympathies of life,
    And cast ashore from pleasure's boisterous surge,
    A wandering, weary, worn and wretched thing,
60. Scorched, and desolate, and blasted soul,
    A gloomy wilderness of dying thought,—
    Repined and groaned, and withered from the
    earth.

QUESTIONS.—1. Who was Byron? 2. Where did he die?
3. Why is he compared to a comet? 4. What was his character?
5. Are talents a blessing or curse to such a man as Byron?

ERRORS.—*Drort* for draught (pronounced *draft*); *mor-nin'* for
morn-ing; *fur-mil-i-ar* for fa-mil-i-ar; *wretch-id-ness* for wretch-ed-
ness; *tre-men-jis* for tre-men-dous (pronounced *tre-men-dus*);
me-tors for me-te-ors.

SPELL AND DEFINE.—(1) entranced; (3) exhaustless;
(9) struggling; (12) nature; (16) familiar; (17) Apennines;
(19) garland; (26) meteors; (29) tremendous; (31) fancy;
(32) sublime; (33) soiled; (40) wits; (42) flattery; (49) goddess;
(52) sympathies; (54) tides; (58) boisterous; (61) wilderness.

LESSON LXXXV.

RULE.—Speak every syllable distinctly, and do not slip over the little words, nor pronounce them incorrectly.

Chesterfield and Paul.—MISS BEECHER.

1. To these youthful witnesses* whose remains show the difference between the happiness of those who obey or disobey the law of God, may be added the testimony of two who had fulfilled their years. The first was the polished, the witty, the elegant and admired Earl of Chesterfield, who tried every source of earthly enjoyment, and at the end makes this acknowledgment.

2. "I have seen," says he, "the silly rounds of business and of pleasure, and have done with them all. I have enjoyed all the pleasures of the world, and consequently know their futility, and do not regret their loss. I appraise them at their real value, which is, in truth, very low. Whereas those that have not experienced, always overrate them. They only see their gay outside, and are dazzled at the glare.

3. "I have been behind the scenes. I have seen all the coarse pulleys and dirty ropes which exhibit and move the gaudy machines. I have seen and smelt the tallow candles which illuminate the whole decoration, to the astonishment and admiration of the ignorant audience.

4. "When I reflect on what I have seen, what I have heard, and what I have done, I can hardly persuade myself that all that frivolous hurry of bustle and pleasure of the world had any reality, but I look upon all that is passing as one of those romantic dreams, which opium commonly occasions. I do by no means desire to repeat the nauseous dose, for the sake of the fugitive dream.

---

* Martyn and Byron.

5. "Shall I tell you that I bear this melancholy situation with that meritorious constancy and resignation, which most people boast of? No, for I really cannot help it. I bear it, because I *must* bear it, whether I will or no! I think of nothing but killing time the best way I can, now that he is become my enemy. It is my resolution to *sleep in the carriage* during the remainder of the journey of life."

6. The other personage was Paul, the Aged. For Christ and the salvation of those for whom Christ died, Paul "suffered the loss of all things;" and this is the record of his course; "in labors abundant, in stripes above measure, in prisons more frequent, in deaths, oft; in journeyings often, in perils of waters, in perils of robbers, in perils by the heathen, in perils in the wilderness, in perils among false brethren. In weariness and painfulness, in watchings often, in hunger and thirst, in fastings often, in cold and nakedness,—and that which cometh daily upon me, the care of all the churches.

7. "We are troubled on every side, yet not distressed; we are perplexed, yet not in despair; persecuted, but not forsaken; cast down, but not destroyed. For though our outward man perish, yet the inward man is renewed day by day. For our *light* affliction, which is but for a moment, worketh for us a far more exceeding and eternal weight of glory."

8. And as the time drew near when he was to be "offered up," and he looked back on the past course of his life, these are his words of triumphant exultation: "I have fought a *good* fight! I have finished my course! I have kept the faith! Henceforth there is laid up for me a crown of righteousness, which Christ, the righteous judge shall give!"

9. To this testimony of the experience of mankind, may be added that of Scripture. "Whoso trusteth in the Lord, happy is he! The fear of the Lord, *that is*

wisdom, and to depart from evil is understanding. Wisdom is better than rubies, and all the things that may be desired are not to be compared to her. Her ways are ways of pleasantness, and all her paths are peace. Keep sound wisdom, so shall it be life to thy soul. Then shalt thou walk in thy way safely, and when thou liest down thou shalt not be afraid, yea, thou shalt lie down, and thy sleep shall be sweet."

10. And thus the Redeemer invites to his service: "Come unto me all ye that labor and are heavy laden, and I will give you rest. Take my yoke upon you, and learn of me, for I am meek and lowly in heart, and ye shall find rest unto your souls!"

QUESTIONS.—1. What two persons who lived to be old, have left their testimony in regard to the way to be happy? 2. What is said of Lord Chesterfield? 3. How did he look on past life? 4. What did he resolve to do? 5. What is said of Paul? 6. Which was the happier man of the two? 7. What does the Bible say respecting the way of happiness?

ERRORS.—*El-e-gunt* for el-e-gant; *con-ser-quent-ly* for con-se-quent-ly; *'cause* for be-cause; *per-son-ige* for per-son-age.

SPELL AND DEFINE.— (1) acknowledgment; (2) consequently; (3) illuminate; (4) nauseous; (5) resignation; (7) persecuted; (8) triumphant; (9) compared; (10) Redeemer.

LESSON LXXXVI.

RULE.—Let each pupil in the class observe and mention every syllable that is not sounded as each one reads.

Henry First after the Death of his Son.

HEMANS.

1. The bark that held the prince went down,
　　The sweeping waves rolled on;
　　And what was England's glorious crown

To him that wept a son?
He lived—for life may long be borne,
    Ere sorrow breaks its chain;
Still comes not death to those who mourn;
    He never smiled again!

2. There stood proud forms before his throne,
    The stately and the brave;
But which could fill the place of one,
    That one beneath the wave?
Before him passed the young and fair,
    In pleasure's reckless train?
But seas dashed o'er his son's bright hair—
    He never smiled again!

3. He sat where festal bowls went round;
    He heard the minstrel sing;
He saw the tourney's victor crowned
    Amid the mighty ring;—
A murmur of the restless deep
    Mingled with every strain,
A voice of winds that would not sleep:
    He never smiled again!

4. Hearts in that time, closed o'er the trace
    Of vows once fondly poured;
And strangers took the kinsman's place
    At many a joyous board;
Graves, which true love had bathed with tears.
    Were left to heaven's bright rain;
Fresh hopes were born for other years:
    He never smiled again!

QUESTIONS.—1. Relate the historical event upon which this poem is founded. 2. Is there anything in earthly splendor that can soothe the suffering heart? 3. What is the allusion in the third verse?

SPELL AND DEFINE.—(1) bark; (2) reckless; (3) festal, tourney; (4) vows, kinsman, joyous.

LESSON LXXXVII.

RULE.—Be careful to give a full sound to the vowels. Regard to this rule will correct the common flat, clipping and uninteresting way in which many read.

Effects of Gambling.—TIMOTHY FLINT.

1. I am a father. I live in a region where gambling is the common and crying sin. I witness its demoralizing and ruinous consequences on every side. The village in which I write could furnish from its annals a hundred warning examples of hopeless misery and ruin—consequences of the indulgence of this sin. My heart as a parent, my feelings as a man, my conscience as professing to be a Christian, have prompted me to address a word of warning to the community of which I am a member against this sin. There is not another, against which I have more earnestly prayed God to guard my children. In attempting to warn them, and my young readers, and the community in general, against it, so many images of desolation and ruin crowd upon my mind, that I find it difficult to select those most calculated to breathe abhorrence.

2. In many parts of our country, this vice is little practised and less tolerated. In other and very extensive regions of our country, it is a sweeping epidemic. It pollutes the city, and, associated with drunkenness, blasphemy and murder, stalks abroad in the community, shameless and triumphant. High and low, rich and poor, suspend their money on the turn of the cards. Even females, who lead the fashions and give tone to public sentiment are seen alternately blenching with terror and flashing with rage, around the gambling table.

3. The serious, and even professors of religion, see it so universally practised, or tolerated, that they lose

something of just abhorrence, and catch something of the contagious indifference. The savages on our borders gamble like the whites, and when they have lost all, commit suicide. The free negroes gamble, and go on wallowing down the descending slough of debauchery and crime. The poor slaves, when they have accumulated a little by the labors of one holiday, when the next returns, sit down to imitate the pernicious example of their superiors.

4. In short, in these regions, the mania of gambling is a sweeping pestilence, infecting in its course, the magistrate, the planter, the professional man, and the young aspirant after fame and honor, just commencing life; spreading its contagion around the fashionable card table, making its way into the dark cells of groceries and taverns, carrying misery and ruin in its course, and adding to the sins of blasphemy, drunkenness, and cheating, the last sickly finish of despair.

5. No eloquence can reach, no pen adequately describe its withering influence in unnerving all honest exertion, in searing all moral feeling, and in adding to the squalidness of poverty, the recklessness of guilt, and the ultimate prospect of temporal and eternal ruin. Ye, who are yet free from the contagion, if ye have not made an immutable covenant with death and with hell. "watch and pray, that ye enter not into temptation."

6. In tracing the enormity of this sin, compared with others, there is little danger of assigning it too forward a place in the black catalogue. The avaricious "love of money," when operating even upon honest pursuits, "is the root of all evil." But when the unbridled appetite for accumulation gets scope in the direction of gambling, sharpening it, as the gambling table ordinarily does, by all that can tempt the eye or inflame the blood, then it is that we see avarice

becoming the most seducing and ruinous passion of human nature.

7. Then it is that we sometimes see men and women, sustaining the highest rank in society, struggling to suppress the visible manifestations on their countenance of what is passing within, and laboring to seem calm when a vulture is preying upon their bosoms. Then it is that we sometimes hear the impious ejaculation, the loathsome curse, proceeding even from the lips of beauty. Who could have witnessed such scenes, and not have felt, as we have felt, for the degradation of our race?

8. It steals, perhaps more often than any other sin, with an imperceptible influence on its victim. Its first pretext is inconsiderable, and falsely termed innocent play, with no more than the gentle excitement necessary to amusement. This plea, once indulged, is but too often "as the letting out of water." The interest imperceptibly grows. Pride of superior skill, opportunity, avarice, and all the over whelming passions of depraved nature, ally themselves with the incipient and growing fondness. Dam and dyke are swept away. The victim struggles in vain, and is borne down by the uncontrolled current.

9. Thousands have given scope to the latent guilty avarice, unconscious of the guest they harbored in their bosoms. Thousands have exulted over the avails of gambling, without comprehending the baseness of using the money of another, won without honest industry, obtained without an equivalent, and perhaps from the simplicity, rashness, and inexperience of youth. Multitudes have commenced gambling, thinking only to win a small sum, and prove their superior skill and dexterity, and there pause.

10. But it is the teaching of all time, it is the experience of human nature, that effectual resistance to powerful propensities, if made at all, is usually

made before the commission of the first sin. My dear reader, let me implore you, by the mercies of God and the worth of your soul, to contemplate this enormous evil only from a distance. Stand firmly against the first temptation, under whatsoever specious forms it may assail you. "Touch not." "Handle not." "Enter not into temptation."

11. It is the melancholy and well known character of this sin, that, where once an appetite for it has gained possession of the breast, the common motives, the gentle excitements, and the ordinary inducements to business or amusement, are no longer felt. It incorporates itself with the whole body of thought, and fills with its fascination all the desires of the heart. Nothing can henceforward arouse the spell-bound victim to a pleasurable consciousness of existence, but the destructive stimulus of gambling.

QUESTIONS.—What does the writer say of himself by way of introduction to the subject? 2. How is it in different portions of our country in respect to the prevalence of the vice of gambling? 3. What rank does this vice hold in comparison with others? 4. How does it usually acquire power over an individual? 5. What is the only safe course to pursue in respect to this vice?

ERRORS.—*Gamb-lin'* for gamb-ling; *de-mor-ul-i-zin'* for de-mor-al-i-zing; *cal-c'la-ted* for cal-cu-la-ted; *ab-hor-runce* for ab-hor-rence.

SPELL AND DEFINE.—(1) demoralizing, consequences, community; (2) extensive, epidemic, drunkenness, blasphemy, triumphant; (3) contagious, indifference; (4) mania, pestilence, magistrate, professional, commencing; (5) eloquence, adequately, squalidness, immutable; (6) enormity, catalogue, accumulation, ordinarily; (7) manifestations, ejaculation, loathsome; (8) inconsiderable, imperceptible; (9) unconscious, equivalent, inexperience; (10) propensities, contemplate; (11) melancholy, fascination.

LESSON LXXXVIII.

RULE.—Be careful to give a full sound to the vowels. Regard to this rule will correct the common flat, clipping and uninteresting way in which many read.

Effects of Gambling.—CONTINUED.

1. Another appalling view of gambling is, that it is *the prolific stem, the fruitful parent, of all other vices*. Blasphemy, falsehood, cheating, drunkeness, quarrel and murder are all naturally connected with gambling. What has been said, with so much power and truth, of another sin, may, with equal emphasis and truth, be asserted of this: "Allow yourself to become a confirmed gambler; and detestable as this practice is, it will soon be only one among many gross sins of which you will be guilty." Giving yourself up to the indulgence of another sinful course, might prove your ruin; but then you might perish only under the guilt of the indulgence of a single gross sin.

2. But, should you become a gambler, you will in all probability, descend to destruction with the added infamy of having been the slave of all kinds of iniquity, and "led captive by Satan at his will." Gambling seizes hold of all the passions, allies itself with all the appetites, and compels every propensity to pay tribute. The subject, however plausible in his external deportment, becomes avaricious, greedy, insatiable. Meditations upon the card table occupy all the day and night dreams. Had he the power, he would annihilate all the hours of this our short life, that necessarily intervene between the periods of his favorite pursuit.

3. *Cheating* is a sure and inseparable attendant upon a continued course of gambling. We well know with what horror the canons of the card table repel this charge. It pains us to assert our deep and deliberate conviction of its truth. There must be pro-

stration of moral principle, and silence of conscience, even to begin with it. Surely a man who regards the natural sense of right, laying the obligations of Christianity out of the question, cannot sit down with the purpose to win the money of another in this way.

4. He must be aware, in doing it, that avarice and dishonest thoughts, it may be almost unconsciously to himself, mingle with his motives. Having once closed his eyes upon the unworthiness of his motives, and deceived himself, he begins to study how he may deceive others. Every moralist has remarked upon the delicacy of conscience, and that, from the first violation, it becomes more and more callous, until finally it sleeps a sleep as of death, and ceases to remonstrate. The gambler is less and less scrupulous about the modes of winning, so that he can win. No person will be long near the gambling table of high stakes, be the standing of the players what it may, without hearing the charge of CHEATING bandied back and forwards, or reading the indignant expression of it in their countenances. One half of our fatal duels have their immediate or remote origin in insinuations of this sort.

5. The altercations of loss and gain, the preternatural excitement of the mind, and consequent depression when that excitement has passed away, the bacchanalian merriment of guilty associates; the loss of natural rest; in short, the very atmosphere of the gambling table, foster the temperament of *hard drinking*. A keen sense of interest may, indeed, and often does restrain the gambler, while actually engaged in his employment, that he may possess the requisite coolness to watch his antagonist, and avail himself of every passing advantage.

6. But the moment the high excitement of play is intermitted—the moment the passions vibrate back to the state of repose, what shall sustain the sinking

spirits. What shall renerve the relaxed physical nature; what shall fortify the mind against the tortures of conscience, and the thoughts of "a judgment to come," but intoxication? It is the experience of all time, that a person is seldom a gambler for any considerable period without being also a drunkard.

7. *Blasphemy* follows, as a thing of course and is, indeed, the well known and universal dialect of the gambler. How often has my heart sunk within me, as I have passed the dark and dire receptacles of the gambler, and seen the red and bloated faces, and inhaled the mingled smells of tobacco and potent drink and heard the loud, strange, and horrid curses of the players; realizing the while, that these beings so occupied were candidates for eternity, and now on the course which, if not speedily forsaken, would fix them forever in hell.

8. We have already said that gambling naturally leads to *quarrelling and murder*. How often have we retired to our berth in the steamboat and heard charges of dishonesty, accents of reviling and recrimination, and hints that these charges must be met and settled at another time and place, ring in our ears, as we have been attempting to commune with God and settle in a right frame to repose! Many corpses of young men, who met a violent death from this cause, have we seen carried to their long home! Every gambler, in the region where we write, is always armed to the teeth, and goes to his horrid pursuit, as the gladiator formerly presented himself on the arena of combat.

9. The picture receives deeper shades, if we take into the grouping the *wife*, or the *daughter*, or the *mother*, who lies sleepless, and ruminating through the long night, trembling lest her midnight retirement shall be invaded by those who bring back the husband

and the father wounded, or slain, in one of those sudden frays which the card table, its accompaniments, and the passions it excites, so frequently generate. Suppose these forebodings should not be realized, and that he should steal home alive in the morning, with beggary and drunkenness, guilt and despair written on his haggard countenance, and accents of sullenness and ill-temper falling from his tongue, how insupportably gloomy must be the prospects of the future to that family!

10. These are but feeble and general sketches of the misery and ruin to individuals and to society from the indulgence of this vice, during the present life. If the wishes of unbelief were true, and there were no life after this, what perverse and miserable calculations would be those of the gambler, taking into view only the present world! But, in any view of the character and consequences of gambling, who shall dare close his eyes upon its *future bearing* on the interest and the eternal welfare of his soul? Who shall dare lay out of the calculation the *retributions of eternity*?

11. Each of the sins that enters into this deadly compound of them all, must incur the threatened displeasure and punishment of the Almighty. If there be degrees in the misery and despair of the tenants of that region, "where the worm dieth not, and the fire is not quenched," how must the persevering and impenitent gambler sink, as if "a millstone were hung about his neck, and he cast into the sea!" Say thou, my youthful reader, I implore thee, looking up to the Lord for firm and unalterable purpose, "I will hold fast my integrity and not let it go!"

12. We scarcely remember an instance in which a confirmed and persevering gambler did not end his career in poverty. But, even, if cases could be cited, as no doubt there might be, in which gamblers were

ultimately sucessful, and transmitted their ill-gotten gains to posterity, vitiated as moral feeling is in the regions where gambling prevails, there is no region so depraved, as that the inhabitants would not indignantly point out these men, as they passed, and say, "There is the man who won his money by gambling!"

13. There is another punishment inficted by public feeling, which, to a man who has a heart, is more terrible still. Though we have no coat of arms for descent of honorable deeds, there is one for those of infamy. The third and fourth generation will remember how you acquired your wealth, and will bring it up in derision and scorn to your posterity.

14. Even as respects fashionable gambling, it has too often been our lot to be required, by circumstances, to be present where fashionable gambling was practiced. We have seen it poorly and thinly veiled under the forms of politeness. We have seen it steadily advance from the small stake, put down as a counter, to deep play. We have seen the suppressed emotion, the bitter smile, and have heard the half uttered curse, and the indirect and implied charge of dishonesty. We have seen the thing, in short, commence in the spirit of apparent kindness and good will, and for mere amusement, and soon end in its own unveiled and undisguised deformity. Show me those who now play fashionably and for amusement, and, in a short time, I will show you the same persons transformed into confirmed gamblers.

15. We cannot persuade ourselves to dismiss a subject which lies so deeply on our heart, without citing a recent case of the results of gambling. We would be glad, if our limits allowed us, to hang up a thousand beacons of this sort in the dark and dreary history of gamblers, that they might stand recorded as solemn warnings to deter others.

16. It is given me by a friend, as having occurred in this vicinity. A young man immigrated here from the north, and was engaged as an overseer. His cheek was fresh with the healthy blood which had been fanned by the northern breeze. He had a fine person, was well educated, and what was better than all, he sustained an unblemished moral character. He had been reared in a virtuous family, under that religious discipline which was formerly the glory of that portion of the country.

17. But he wanted, as too many interesting young men, who come among us from that region, want, that deep and settled principle, that unyielding purpose, which will make no compromise with what is wrong. He married an amiable and distinguished young lady, who brought him an ample fortune. For a couple of years nothing seemed wanting to his prosperity and enjoyment. He had the entire affection of his wife and friends, and was growing in the esteem of the country. As is too often the case, he gradually imbibed the infection of the general example.

18. Everybody about him gambled. He, of course, had his daily temptations. He at first regarded cards with abhorrence. Some kind of thorn rankles in almost every bosom and, amidst all his seeming prosperity, he had his. He was stung with the charge of an enemy that he was a needy adventurer, a fortune-hunter, who brought his wife nothing. He sometimes played cards, merely as a trial of skill, and was generally triumphant.

19. It occurred to him, that success at cards, which seemed so much at his command, might redeem him from the reproach of having been a needy fortune-hunter. He was gradually seduced to the gambling table; often, however, stating to the narrator his mental unbraidings, and the compunctious visitings of his conscience. As is an unvarying circumstance

in the annals of a gambler, he went deeper and deeper, and was for a long time successful. He had bargained for a plantation, which he intended as an affectionate present of surprise to his wife and, in the view of others, to redeem him from the stigma of having brought her nothing. I need not follow him in his downward course. He had nearly realized what would enable him to complete his purchase.

20. The fiend that had tempted him thus far, at length deserted him. He doubled stake upon stake, until he had lost all his winnings, and all that the affection of his wife had enabled him to lose. Her own fortune, much as he professed to love her, would have been equally sacrificed, but for the stern and yet just and benevolent providence of the laws among us. He even put up, at a certain value, the ultimate chance of reversion, in case of her decease before him and lost it. His eyes opened at last, but he had not the courage to return to her to whom report would soon carry the whole transaction. He fled.

21. He was traced on shipboard, a self-despising outcast from a happy and peaceful home, an affectionate wife, and an infant babe. The community which cherished him, in despising him, cruelly threw the stigma on the country of his birth. She pines still for his return and fondly thinks that the next steamboat will bring him back. He probably wanders, if he lives, a vagabond on the sea. May we not hope, that the influence of an early, pious education will be as an invisible tie about his neck, to bring him, a prodigal, penitent and reformed, to his wife, his babe, his country, and his God?

QUESTIONS.—1. What appalling view of gambling is presented in this chapter? 2. What vice is the first sure attendant upon gambling? 3. What is the evidence supporting this assertion? 4. What vice next follows? 5. How is it brought on? 6. What follows next to hard drinking? 7. What is the ultimate result? 8. What effect is produced by considering the wife, mother, etc.? 9. What is the future bearing of this vice? 10. What punishment is inflicted by public sentiment on this vice? 11. Narrate the case of the young man here mentioned.

ERRORS.—*Quar-rul* for quar-rel; *pur-ish* for per-ish; *med-'ta-tions* for med-i-ta-tions.

SPELL AND DEFINE.—(1) prolific; (3) card table; (7) candidates; (8) recrimination; (9) haggard, insupportably; (11) compound; (12) confirmed, vitiated; (14) practiced; (16) immigrated; (17) compromised, infection; (18) temptations, adventurer, rankles; (19) command, plantation, compunctious, unvarying; (20) fiend; (21) community, penitent, reformed, prodigal.

LESSON LXXXIX.

RULE.—Observe the commas, and stop at each long enough to take breath.

The Miser.—POLLOK.

1. Gold many hunted, sweat and bled for gold;
   Waked all the night, and labored all the day;
   And what was this allurement, dost thou ask?
   A dust dug from the bowels of the earth,
5. Which, being cast into the fire, came out
   A shining thing that fools admired, and called
   A god: and in devout and humble plight
   Before it kneeled, the greater to the less.
   And on its altar, sacrificed ease, peace,
10. Truth, faith, integrity; good conscience, friends,
    Love, charity, benevolence, and all
    The sweet and tender sympathies of life;
    And to complete the horrid murderous rite,
    And signalize their folly, offered up
15. Their souls, and an eternity of bliss,
    To gain them; what? an hour of dreaming joy,

A feverish hour that hasted to be done,
And ended in the bitterness of woe.
Most, for the luxuries it bought, the pomp,
20. The praise, the glitter, fashion, and renown,
This yellow phantom followed and adored.
But there was one in folly, farther gone,
With eye awry, incurable, and wild,
The laughing-stock of devils and of men,
25. And by his guardian angel quite given up,
The miser, who with dust inanimate
Held wedded intercourse.
Ill-guided wretch!
Thou mightst have seen him at the midnight
     hour,
30. When good men slept, and in light-winged dreams
Ascended up to God, in wasteful hall,
With vigilance and fasting worn to skin
And bone, and wrapped in most debasing rags,
Thou mightst have seen him bending o'er his
     heaps,
35. And holding strange communion with his gold;
And as his thievish fancy seemed to hear
The night-man's foot approach, starting alarmed,
And in his old, decrepit, withered hand,
That palsy shook, grasping the yellow earth
40. To make it sure.
Of all God made upright,
And in their nostrils breathed a living soul,
Most fallen, most prone, most earthy, most
     debased;
Of all that sold Eternity for Time,
45. None bargained on so easy terms with death.
Illustrious fool! Nay, most inhuman wretch!
He sat among his bags, and, with a look
Which hell might be ashamed of, drove the poor
Away unalmsed, and midst abundance died,
Sorest of evils! died of utter want.

QUESTIONS.—1. What is the subject of this extract? 2. What are some of the evil consequences of the love of money? 3. What good can wealth bestow on its votaries? 4. What are some of the marks of a miserly character? 5. What are the effects of avarice upon body and mind? 6. What is the miser's fate?

ERRORS.—*Bowles* for bow-els; *'arth* for earth; *in-teg-er-ty* for in-teg-ri-ty; *fol-ler-ed* for fol-low-ed.

SPELL AND DEFINE.—(3) allurement; (4) bowels; (6) admired; (10) integrity, conscience; (11) benevolence; (12) sympathies; (13) murderous; (14) signalize; (21) phantom; (23) awry, incurable; (24) laughingstock; (26) inanimate; (32) vigilance; (38) decrepit; (46) illustrious; (49) unalmsed.

LESSON XC.

RULE.—Read slowly and distinctly, and pronounce every syllable.!

True Wisdom.—BIBLE.

1. But where shall wisdom be found?
   And where is the place of understanding?
   Man knoweth not the price thereof;
   Nor can it be found in the land of the living.
5. The deep saith, It is not with me;
   And the sea saith, It is not with me.
   It cannot be gotten for gold,
   Nor shall silver be weighed out as the price
       thereof.
   It cannot be purchased with the gold of Ophir,
10. With the precious onyx, or the sapphire.
   Gold and crystal are not to be compared with it;
   Nor can it be purchased with jewels of fine gold.
   No mention shall be made of coral, or of crystal,
   For wisdom is more precious than pearls.

15. The topaz of Ethiopia cannot equal it,
    Nor can it be purchased with the purest gold.
    Whence then cometh wisdom?
    And where is the place of understanding?
    Since it is hidden from the eyes of all the living,
20. And kept close from the fowls of the air.
    Destruction and Death say,
    We have heard of its fame with our ears.
    God only knoweth the way to it;
    He only knoweth its dwelling-place.
25. For he seeth to the ends of the earth,
    And surveyeth all things under the whole heaven.
    When he gave the winds their weight,
    And adjusted the waters by measure;
    When he prescribed laws to the rain,
30. And a path to the glittering thunderbolt;
    Then did he see it, and make it known;
    He established it, and searched it out;
    But he said unto man,
    Behold! the fear of the Lord, that is thy wisdom,
35. And to depart from evil, thy understanding.

QUESTIONS.—1. What are onyx and sapphire?   2. What is
true wisdom?

ERRORS.—*Pree-cious* for pre-cious; *arth* for earth, *per-scri-bed*
for pre-scr-ibed.

SPELL AND DEFINE.—(1) wisdom;   (2) understanding;
(10) onyx, sapphire;   (11) crystal;   (15) topaz;   (21) destruction;
(28) adjusted;   (29) prescribed;   (30) glittering;   (32) established.

LESSON XCI.

RULE.—Be careful to speak such little words as *the*, *of*, *a*, *in*, *from*, *at*, *by*, etc., very distinctly, and yet not to dwell on them so long as on the other more important words.

The Wife.—W. IRVING.

1. I have often had occasion to remark the fortitude with which women sustain the most overwhelming reverses of fortune. Those disasters which break down the spirit of a man, and prostrate him in the dust, seem to call forth all the energies of the softer sex, and give such intrepidity and elevation to their character, that at times it approaches to sublimity.

2. Nothing can be more touching than to behold a soft and tender female, who had been all weakness and dependence, and alive to every trivial roughness, while treading the prosperous paths of life, suddenly rising in mental force to be the comforter and supporter of her husband under misfortune, and abiding, with unshrinking firmness, the most bitter blasts of adversity.

3. As the vine, which has long twined its graceful foliage about the oak, and been lifted by it into sunshine, will, when the hardy plant is rifted by the thunderbolt, cling around it with its caressing tendrils, and bind up its shattered boughs; so is it beautifully ordered by Providence, that woman, who is the mere dependent and ornament of man in his happier hours, should be his stay and solace when smitten with sudden calamity; winding herself into the rugged recesses of his nature, tenderly supporting the drooping head, and binding up the broken heart.

4. I was once congratulating a friend who had around him a blooming family, knit together in the strongest affection. "I can wish you no better lot," said he, with enthusiasm, "than to have a wife and children. If you are prosperous, there they are to share your prosperity; if otherwise, there they are to comfort you."

5. And, indeed, I have observed, that a married man, falling into misfortune, is more apt to retrieve his situation in the world than a single one. Partly, because he is more stimulated to exertion by the necessities of the helpless and beloved beings who depend upon him for subsistence, but chiefly, because his spirits are soothed and relieved by domestic endearments, and his self-respect kept alive by finding that though all abroad is darkness and humiliation, yet there is still a little world of love at home, of which he is the monarch.

6. Whereas, a single man is apt to run to waste and self-neglect, to fancy himself lonely and abandoned, and his heart to fall to ruin, like some deserted mansion, for want of an inhabitant.

QUESTIONS.—1. What is said of the fortitude of the female sex? 2. What effect is produced on the mind by the view of this trait? 3. To what natural object is it beautifully compared? 4. Why should man have a family? 5. What is apt to be the case with the single man, as to character and comfort? 6. Do married persons generally *live longer* than unmarried?

ERRORS.—*Of'n for* often; *o-ver-wel-min'* for o-ver-whelm-ing; *for-tin* and *for-chune* for fort-une.

SPELL AND DEFINE.—(1) fortitude, overwhelming, disasters, intrepidity, sublimity; (2) dependence, roughness, unshrinking, adversity; (3) foliage, thunderbolt, rifted, shattered, beautifully, solace, recesses, rugged, tendrils; (4) congratulating, enthusiasm, prosperous; (5) stimulated, retrieve, necessities, subsistence, domestic; (6) abandoned.

LESSON XCII.

RULE.—Be careful to give all the consonants their full sound in each word.

Duty of the American Orator.—GRIMKE.

1. One theme of duty still remains, and I have placed it alone because of its peculiar dignity, sacredness and importance. Need I tell you that I speak of the union of the states? Let the American orator discharge all other duties but this, if indeed it be not impossible, with the energy and eloquence of John Rutledge, and the disinterested fidelity of Robert Morris, yet shall he be counted a traitor, if he attempt to dissolve the union.

2. His name, illustrious as it may have been, shall then be gibbeted on every hilltop throughout the land, a monument of his crime and punishment, and of the shame and grief of his country. If indeed he believe, and doubtless there may be such, that wisdom demands the dissolution of the union, that the south should be severed from the north, the west be independent of the east, let him cherish the sentiment, for his own sake, in the solitude of his breast, or breathe it only in the confidence of friendship.

3. Let him rest assured, that as his country tolerates the monarchist and the aristocrat of the old world, she tolerates him, but should he plot the dismemberment of the union, the same trial, judgment, and execution await him as would await them, should they attempt to establish the aristocracy of Venice, or the monarchy of Austria on the ruins of our confederacy. To him as to them she leaves freedom of speech, and the very licentiousness of the press and permits them to write, even in the spirit of scorn, and hatred, and unfairness.

4. She trembles not at such effort, reckless and hostile as they may be. She smiles at their impotence, while she mourns over their infatuation. But let them lift the hand of parricide, in the insolence of pride, or the madness of power, to strike their country, and her countenance, in all the severity and terrors of a parent's wrath shall smite them with amazement and horror. Let them strike, and the voices of millions of freemen from the city and hamlet, from the college and the farmhouse, from the cabins amid the western wilds, and our ships scattered around the world, shall utter the stern irrevocable judgment, self banishment for life, or ignominious death.

5. Be it then among the noblest offices of American eloquence to cultivate, in the people of every state, a deep and fervent attachment to the union. The union is to us the marriage bond of states; indissoluble in life, to be dissolved, we trust, only on that day when nations shall die in a moment, never to rise again. Let the American orator discountenance, then, all the arts of intrigue and corruption, which not only pollute the people and dishonor republican institutions, but prepare the way for the ruin of both—how secretly, how surely, let history declare. Let him banish from his thoughts, and his lips, the hypocrisy of the demagogue, equally deceitful and degraded,

"With smooth dissimulation, skill'd to grace
A devil's purpose, with an angel's face."

6. Let that demagogue and those arts, his instruments of power, be regarded as pretended friends, but secret and dangerous enemies of the people. Let it never be forgotten that to him and to them we owe all the licentiousness and violence, all the unprincipled and unfeeling persecution of party spirit. Let the American orator labor then, with all the solemnity of a religious duty, with all the inten-

sity of filial love, to convince his countrymen that the danger to liberty in this country is to be traced to those sources. Let the European tremble for his institutions, in the presence of military power and for the warrior's ambition.

7. Let the American dread, as the archenemy of republican institutions, the shock of exasperated parties, and the implacable revenge of demagogues. The discipline of standing armies, is the terror of freedom in Europe, but the tactics of parties, the standing armies of America, are still more formidable to liberty with us.

8. Let the American orator frown, then, on that ambition, which, pursuing its own aggrandizement and gratification, perils the harmony and integrity of the union, and counts the grief, anxiety, and expostulations of millions, as the small dust of the balance. Let him remember that ambition, like the Amruta cup of Indian fable, gives to the virtuous an immortality of glory and happiness, but to the corrupt an immortality of ruin, shame and misery.

9. Let not the American orator, in the great questions on which he is to speak or write, appeal to the mean and groveling qualities of human nature. Let him love the people, and respect himself too much to dishonor them, and degrade himself by an appeal to selfishness and prejudice, to jealousy, fear, and contempt. The greater the interests, and the more sacred the rights which may be at stake, the more resolutely should he appeal to the generous feelings, the noble sentiments, the calm considerate wisdom, which become a free, educated, peaceful Christian people. Even if he battle against criminal ambition and base intrigue, let his weapons be a logic, manly, intrepid, honorable, and an eloquence magnanimous, disinterested, and spotless.

10. What a contrast between his duties and those of Athenian eloquence where the prince of orators was but the prince of demagogues. How could it be otherwise! with a religion that commanded no virtue, and prohibited no vice; with deities, the model of every crime and folly, which deform and pollute even man; with a social system, in which refinement, benevolence, forbearance, found no place. How could it be otherwise! With a political system, in which war was the chief element of power and honor in the individual, and of strength, security, and glory in the state, while the ambition or resentment of rulers found a cheerful response in the love of conquest, plunder, or revenge on the part of the people.

11. How could it be otherwise! With such domestic relations between the republics as made it the duty of the ancient orator to aggrandize his own at the expense of all the rest, to set state against state, to foment jealousies and bickerings among them, to deceive and weaken the strong, to oppress and seize on the feeble. How could it be otherwise! When such were the domestic and foreign relations, viewed as a whole, that the duty of the ancient orator was to cultivate the union of the states, not as a matter of deep and lasting importance at home, not as the very life of peace and harmony there, but only as an expedient against foreign invasion, while partial and hostile combinations, headed by Athens, or Thebes, or Sparta, were the current events of their domestic policy.

12. Compared to such duties and such scenes, who can turn to the obligations and field of American eloquence, without a thrill of spirit-stirring admiration and gratitude? His office in our union, how full of benignity and peace, of justice, majesty, and truth! Where, except in the Christian pulpit, shall we find its parallel? Why do we find it there—but that the

Christian ministry are, like him, the advocates of purity, forbearance and love. How delightful, how honorable the task, to calm the angry passions, to dissipate error, to reconcile prejudice, to banish jealousy, and silence the voice of selfishness!

13. American eloquence must likewise cultivate a fixed, unalterable devotion to the union, a frank, generous, ardent attachment of section to section, of state to state, and in the citizen, liberal sentiments towards his rulers, and cordial love for his countrymen. Nor is this all. Let the American orator comprehend, and live up to the grand conception, that the union is the property of the world, no less than of ourselves; that it is a part of the divine scheme for the moral government of the earth, as the solar system is a part of the mechanism of the heavens; that it is destined, whilst traveling from the Atlantic to the Pacific, like the ascending sun, to shed its glorious influence backward on the states of Europe, and forward on the empires of Asia.

14. Let him comprehend its sublime relations to time and eternity, to God and man, to the most precious hopes, the most solemn obligations, and the highest happiness of human kind. What an eloquence must that be whose source of power and wisdom are God himself, the objects of whose influence are all the nations of the earth; whose sphere of duty is coextensive with all that is sublime in religion, beautiful in morals, commanding in intellect, and touching in humanity. How comprehensive, and therefore how wise and benevolent, must then be the genius of American eloquence, compared to the narrow-minded, narrow-hearted, and therefore selfish, eloquence of Greece and Rome.

15. How striking is the contrast between the universal social spirit of the former, and the individual, exclusive character of the latter. The

ECLECTIC FOURTH READER.

boundary of this is the horizon of a plain; the circle
of that the horizon of a mountain summit. Be it then
the duty of American eloquence to speak, to write,
to act, in the cause of Christianity, patriotism, and
literature; in the cause of justice, humanity, virtue,
and truth; in the cause of the people, of the union,
of the whole human race, and of the unborn of every
clime and age. Then shall American eloquence, the
personification of truth, beauty, and love,

> "—walk the earth, that she may hear her name
> Still hymn'd and honor'd by the grateful voice
> Of human kind, and in her fame rejoice."

QUESTION.—1. How shall the orator be regarded who
attempts to dissolve the union? 2. Suppose he believe a separation desirable, what shall he do with his opinion? 3. Why is
freedom of speech and the press allowed both to bad and
good? 4. What feeling towards the union must be cherished in
every American bosom? 5. How should the American regard
party spirit, and the arts of demagogues? 6. To what,
sentiments of the human mind should he always appeal, and to
what others never? 7. Contrast the American with the Athenian
orator, 10-13. 8. While the orator cherishes union of state to
state, of section to section, how shall he regard the country in
respect to the world? 9. To time—eternity? 10. Sum up the contrast contained in the close of this lesson, between what ancient
eloquence was, and what American eloquence ought to be.

ERRORS.—*Gib-bet-ed* ought to be pronounced jib-bet-ted;
'lus-tra-ous for il-lus-tri-ous; *mon-er-ment* for mon-u-ment;
ir-re-vo'-ca-ble for ir-rev'-o-ca-ble; *for-got* for for-got-ten;
zas-per-ate for ex-as-per-ate.

SPELL AND DEFINE.—(1) disinterested; (2) gibbeted,
independent, dissolution; (3) monarchist, aristocrat, confederacy;
(4) irrevocable; (5) indissoluble, dissimulation; (10) demagogues;
(11) combinations; (14) comprehend.

LESSON XCIII.

RULE.—Be careful to give the vowels their proper sound.

The Patriotism of Western Literature.

DR. DRAKE.

1. Our literature cannot fail to be patriotic. Its patriotism will be American, composed of a love of country mingled with an admiration for our political institutions.

2. The slave, whose very mind has passed under the yoke, and the senseless ox whom he goads onward in the furrow are attached to the spot of their animal companionship, and may even fight for the cabin and the field where they came into existence, but this affection, considered as an ingredient of patriotism, although the most universal, is the lowest. To rise into a virtue it must be discriminating and comprehensive, involving a varied association of ideas, and embracing the beautiful of the natural and moral world, as they appear around us.

3. To feel in his heart, and infuse into his writings, the inspiration of such a patriotism, the scholar must feast his taste on the delicacies of our scenery, and dwell with enthusism on the genius of our constitution and laws. Thus sanctified in its character, this sentiment becomes a principle of moral and intellectual dignity—an element of fire, purifying and subliming the mass in which it glows.

4. As a guiding star to the will, its light is inferior only to that of Christianity. Heroic in its philanthropy, untiring in its enterprises, and sublime in the martyrdoms it willingly suffers, it justly occupies a high place among the virtues which ennoble the human character. A literature animated with this

patriotism is a national blessing, and such will be the literature of the West.

5. The literature of the whole Union must be richly endowed with this spirit, but a double portion will be the lot of the interior, because the foreign influences which dilute and vitiate this virtue in the extremities, cannot reach the heart of the continent, where all that lives and moves is American.

6. Hence a native of the West may be confided in as his country's hope. Compare him with the native of a great maritime city, on the verge of the nation, his birthplace the fourth story of a house, hemmed in by surrounding edifices, his playground a pavement, the scene of his juvenile rambles an arcade of shops, his young eyes feasted on the flags of a hundred alien governments, the streets in which he wanders crowded with foreigners, and the ocean, common to all nations, forever expanding to his view.

7. Estimate *his* love of country, as far as it depends on local and early attachments, and then contrast him with the young backwoodsman, born and reared amidst objects, scenes, and events, which you can all bring to mind;—the jutting rocks in the great road, half alive with organic remains, or sparkling with crystals; the quiet old walnut tree, dropping its nuts upon the yellow leaves, as the morning sun melts the October frost; the grapevine swing; the chase after the cowardly black snake, till it creeps under the rotten log; the sitting down to rest upon the crumbling trunk, and an idle examination of the mushrooms and mosses which grow from its ruins.

8. Then the wading in the shallow stream, and upturning of the flat stones, to find bait with which to fish in the deeper waters. There is the beech tree with its smooth body, on which he cuts the initials of her name interlocked with his own; finally, the great hollow stump, by the path that leads up the valley

to the log schoolhouse, its dry bark peeled off, and the stately polk-weed growing from its center, and bending with crimson berries which invite him to sit down and write upon its polished wood. How much pleasanter it is to extract ground squirrels from beneath its roots, than to extract the square root, under that labor-saving machine, the ferule of a teacher!

9. The affections of one who is blest with such reminiscences, like the branches of our beautiful trumpet flower, strike their roots into every surrounding object, and derive support from all which stand within their reach. The love of country is with him a constitutional and governing principle. If he be a mechanic, the wood and iron which he moulds into form are dear to his heart because they remind him of his own hills and forests. If a husbandman, he holds companionship with growing corn, as the offspring of his native soil. If a legislator, his dreams are filled with sights of national prosperity to flow from his beneficent enactments. If a scholar, devoted to the interests of literature, in his lone and excited hours of midnight study, while the winds are hushed and all animated nature sleeps, when the silence is so profound, that the stroke of his own pen grates, loud and harsh, upon his ear, and fancy, from the great deep of his luminous intellect, draws up new forms of smiling beauty and solemn grandeur. The genius of his country hovers nigh, and sheds over its pages an essence of patriotism, sweeter than the honey-dew which the summer night distils upon the leaves of our forest trees.

QUESTIONS.—1. What is American patriotism? 2. Where is this kind of patriotism most likely to be found? in the cities of the seashore, or in the West? 3. What are the causes which make it greater in the West?

ERRORS.—*Cum-po-sed* for com-po-sed; *com-pra-hen-sive* for com-pre-hen-sive; *dil-ute* for di-lute; *na-tyve* for na-tive.

SPELL AND DEFINE.—(1) patriotism;   (2) discriminating; (3) intellectual;   (6) arcade;   (7) backwoods;   (8) initials; (9) reminiscences, constitutional.

LESSON XCIV.

RULE.—In poetry that does not rhyme, no pause need be made at the end of such lines as terminate with unimportant words, except when the sense requires it.

Rome.—BYRON.

1. Oh Rome! my country! city of the soul!
   The orphans of the heart must turn to thee,
   Lone mother of dead empires! and control
   In their shut breasts their petty misery,
   What are our woes and sufferance? Come and see
   The cypress, hear the owl, and plod your way
   O'er steps of broken thrones, and temples, ye!
   Whose agonies are evils of a day—
   A world is at our feet, as fragile as our clay.

2. The Niobe of nations! there she stands,
   Childless, and crownless, in her voiceless woe;
   An empty urn within her withered hands,
   Whose holy dust was scattered long ago;
   The Scipios' tomb contains no ashes now;
   The very sepulchers are tenantless
   Of their heroic dwellers; dost thou flow,
   Old Tiber! through a marble wilderness?
   Rise, with thy yellow waves, and mantle her
      distress!

3. The Goth, the Christian, Time, War, Flood, and
     Fire,
   Have dealt upon the seven hilled city's pride;
   She saw her glories star by star expire,
   And up the steep, barbarian monarchs ride,
   Where the car climbed the Capitol; far and wide
   Temple and tower went down, nor left a site:
   Chaos of ruins! who shall trace the void,
   O'er the dim fragments cast a lunar light,
   And say here "was, or is" where all is doubly
     night.

4. The double night of ages, and of her
   Night's daughter, ignorance, hath wrapt and
     wrap
   All round us; we but feel our way to err,
   The ocean hath his chart, the stars their map,
   And knowledge spreads them on her ample lap;
   But Rome is as the desert, where we steer
   Stumbling o'er recollections; now we clap
   Our hands, and cry, "Eureka!" it is clear—
   When but some false mirage of ruin rises near.

5. Alas! the lofty city! and alas!
   The trebly hundred triumphs! and the day
   When Brutus made the dagger's edge surpass
   The conqueror's sword in bearing fame away!
   Alas, for Tully's voice, and Virgil's lay,
   And Livy's pictured page! but these shall be
   Her resurrection; all beside—decay.
   Alas, for earth, for never shall we see
   That brightness in her eye she bore, when Rome
     was free.

6. Oh, thou, whose chariot rolled on fortune's wheel,
   Triumphant Sylla! thou, who did'st subdue
   Thy country's foes, ere thou would'st pause to
     feel

The wrath of thy own wrongs, or reap the due
Of hoarded vengeance, till thine eagles flew
O'er prostrate Asia; thou who with thy frown
Annihilatedst senates; Roman, too,
With all thy vices, for thou did'st lay down,
With an atoning smile, a more than earthly crown

7. The dictatorial wreath—could'st thou divine
To what would one day dwindle that which made
Thee more than mortal? and that so supine
By aught than Romans, Rome should thus be
    laid?
She who was named eternal, and arrayed
Her warriors but to conquer—she who veiled
Earth with her haughty shadow, and displayed,
Until the o'ercanopied horizon failed,
Her rushing wings.   *   *   *

8. Yes! let the winds howl on! their harmony
Shall henceforth be my music, and the night
The sound shall temper with the owlet's cry,
As now I hear them, in the fading light
Dim o'er the bird of darkness' native site,
Answering each other on the Palatine,
With their large eyes, all glistening gray and
    bright,
And sailing pinions. Upon such a shrine
What are our petty griefs? Let me not number
mine.

9. Cypress and ivy, weed and wall-flower grown
Matted and massed together, hillocks heaped
On what were chambers, arch crushed, column
    strown
In fragments, choked up vaults, and frescos
    steeped
In subterranean damps, where the owl peeped
Deeming it midnight'—temples, baths, or halls?
Pronounce who can; for all that learning reaped

From her research hath been, that these are
  walls—
Behold the Imperial Mount!—'tis thus the
  mighty falls.

10. There is a moral of all human tales;
    'Tis but the same rehearsal of the past,
    First Freedom, and then Glory—when that fails,
    Wealth, vice, corruption,—barbarism at last,
    And History with all her volumes vast,
    Hath but one page,—'tis better written here,
    Where gorgeous tyranny had thus amassed
    All treasures, all delights, that eye or ear,
    Heart, soul could seek, tongue ask—Away with
      words! draw near,

11. Admire, exult—despise—laugh—weep—for here
    There is much matter for all feeling;—Man!
    Thou pendulum betwixt a smile and tear,
    Ages and realms, are crowded in this span,
    This mountain, whose obliterated plan
    The pyramid of empires pinnacled,
    Of glory's gew-gaws shining in the van,
    Till the sun's rays with added flame were filled!
    Where are its golden roofs? where those who
      dared to build?

12. Tully was not so eloquent as thou,
    Thou nameless column, with the buried base!
    What are the laurels of the Caesar's brow?
    Crown me with ivy, from his dwelling place.
    Whose arch or pillar meets me in the face,
    Titus' or Trajan's? No! 'tis that of time;
    Triumph, arch, pillar, all he doth displace,
    Scoffing; and apostolic statues climb
    To crush the imperial urn,* whose ashes slept
      sublime.

---

* Trajan's.

13. Where is the rock of triumph, the high place
Where Rome embraced her heroes? Where the steep
Tarpeian? fittest goal of treason's race,
The promontory, whence the traitor's leap
Cured all ambition; did the conquerors heap
Their spoils here? Yes! and in yon field below,
A thousand years of silenced factions sleep—
The Forum, where immortal accents glow,
And still the eloquent air breathes—burns with Cicero!

QUESTIONS.—1. Why does Byron call Rome "my country?" 2. Who was Niobe, and what her story? 3. How is Rome the Niobe of nations? 4. Upon what site was Rome built? 5. What "double night" rests upon Rome? 6. What ancient Grecian exclaimed "Eureka," and why? 7. What great men of Rome are mentioned in verse 5? 8. What is narrated of Sylla in verses 6 and 7? 9. Is Rome a mere mass of ruins? or are these, descriptions of parts of the city? 10. In verse 10 what moral is drawn from the rehearsal of the past? 11. What beautiful metaphor in verse 11? 12. What is said of the imperial urn, and what fact referred to? 13. What is said of the Forum? 14. What was the forum? 15. What was the Tarpeian?

ERRORS.—*Ni-obe* for Ni-o-be; *chile-less* for child-less; *Skip-i-o* for Scip-i-o; *chris-chin* for chris-tian (christ-yan.)

SPELL AND DEFINE.—(1) cypress, fragile; (2) crownless, voiceless, sepulchers; (3) barbarian, fragments, lunar; (4) stumbling, recollections, (5) hundred, triumphs; (6) triumphant, annihilatedst; (7) dictatorial, o'ercanopied; (8) harmony, palatine; (9) subterranean; (10) rehearsal; (11) pyramid; (13)Tarpeian.

LESSON XCV.

RULE.—Be careful not to slip over or mispronounce the small words.

Rebellion in Massachusetts State Prison.
BUCKINGHAM.

1. A more impressive exhibition of moral courage, opposed to the wildest ferocity, under the most appalling circumstances, was never seen, than that which was witnessed, by the officers of our State Prison, in the rebellion which occurred about five years ago.

2. Three convicts had been sentenced under the rules of the prison to be whipped in the yard, and by some effort of one of the other prisoners, a door had been opened at midday, leading to the large dining hall, and through the warden's lodge out into the street.

3. The dining hall is long, dark and damp, from its situation near the surface of the ground; and in this all the prisoners assembled, with clubs and such tools as they could seize in passing through the workshops.

4. Knives, hammers, and chisels, with every variety of such weapons, were in the hands of the ferocious spirits, who are drawn away from their encroachments on society, forming a congregation of strength, vileness, and talent, that can hardly be equaled on earth, even among the famed brigands of Italy.

5. Men of all ages and characters, guilty of every variety of infamous crime, dressed in the motley and peculiar garb of the institution, and displaying the wild and demoniac appearance that always pertains to imprisoned wretches, were gathered together for the single purpose of preventing the punishment

which was to be inflicted on the morrow, upon their comrades.

6. The warden, the surgeon, and some other officers of the prison, were there at the time, and were alarmed at the consequences likely to ensue from the conflict necessary to restore order. They huddled together, and could scarcely be said to be calm, as the stoutest among them lost all presence of mind in overwhelming fear. The news rapidly spread through the town, and a subordinate officer, of most mild and kind disposition, hurried to the scene, and came calm and collected into the midst of the officers. The most equable tempered and the mildest man in the government was in this hour of peril the firmest.

7. He instantly dispatched a request to Major Wainwright, commander of the marines stationed at the navy yard, for assistance, and declared his purpose to enter into the hall and try the force of firm demeanor and persuasion upon the enraged multitude.

8. All his brethren exclaimed against an attempt so full of hazard, but in vain. They offered him arms, a sword and pistols, but he refused them, and said, that he had no fear, and in case of danger, arms would do him no service. Alone, with only a little rattan, which was his usual walking stick, he advanced into the hall, to hold parley with the selected, congregated, and enraged villains of the whole commonwealth.

9. He demanded their purpose, in thus coming together with arms, in violation of the prison laws. They replied, that they were determined to obtain the remission of the punishment of their three comrades. He said, it was impossible; the rules of the prison must be obeyed, and they must submit.

10. At the hint of submission, they drew a little nearer together, prepared their weapons for service.

As they were dimly seen in the farther end of the hall, by those who observed, from the gratings that opened up to the day, a more appalling sight cannot be conceived, nor one of more moral grandeur, than that of the single man, standing within their grasp, and exposed to be torn limb from limb instantly, if a word or look should add to the already intense excitement.

11. That excitement, too, was of a most dangerous kind. It broke not forth in noise and imprecations, but was seen only in the dark looks and the strained nerves, that showed a deep determination. The officer expostulated. He reminded them of the hopelessness of escape, that the town was alarmed, and that the government of the prison would submit to nothing but unconditional surrender. He said, that all those who would go quietly away, should be forgiven for this offense; but that, if every prisoner was killed in the contest, power enough would be obtained to enforce the regulations of the prison.

12. They replied, that they expected that some would be killed, that death would be better than such imprisonment, and with that look and tone, which bespeaks an indomitable purpose, they declared, that not a man should leave the hall alive, till the flogging was remitted. At this period of the discussion, their evil passions seemed to be more inflamed, and one or two offered to destroy the officer, who still stood firmer, and with a more temperate pulse, than did his friends who saw from above, but could not avert the danger that threatened him.

13. Just at this moment, and in about fifteen minutes from the commencement of the tumult, the officer saw the feet of the marines, whose presence alone he relied on for succor, filing by the small upper lights. Without any apparent anxiety he had repeatedly turned his attention to their approach, and now he

knew that it was his only time to escape, before a conflict for life became, as was expected, one of the most dark and dreadful in the world.

14. He stepped slowly backwards, still urging them to depart, before the officers were driven to use the last resort of firearms. When within three or four feet of the door, it was opened, and closed instantly again, as he sprang through, and was thus unexpectedly restored to his friends.

15. Major Wainwright was requested to order his men to fire down upon the convicts through the little windows, first with powder and then with ball, till they were willing to retreat, but he took a wiser as well as a bolder course, relying upon the effect which firm determination would have upon men so critically situated. He ordered the door to be again opened, and marched in at the head of twenty or thirty men, who filed through the passage and formed at the end of the hall, opposite to the crowd of criminals huddled together at the other.

16. He stated that he was empowered to quell the rebellion, that he wished to avoid shedding blood, but that he should not quit that hall alive, till every convict had returned to his duty. They seemed balancing the strength of the two parties, and replied, that some of them were ready to die, and only waited for an attack to see which was the most powerful, swearing that they would fight to the last, unless the punishment was remitted, for they would not submit to any such punishment in the prison. Major Wainwright ordered his marines to load their pieces, and, that they might not be suspected of trifling, each man was made to hold up to view the bullet which he afterwards put in his gun.

17. This only caused a growl of determination, and no one blenched or seemed disposed to shrink from the foremost exposure. They knew that their number

would enable them to bear down and destroy the handful of marines, after the first discharge, and before their pieces could be reloaded. Again they were ordered to retire, but they answered with more ferocity than ever. The marines were ordered to take their aim so as to be sure and kill as many as possible—their guns were presented—but not a prisoner stirred, except to grasp more firmly his weapon.

18. Still desirous to avoid such a tremendous slaughter, as must have followed the discharge of a single gun, Major Wainwright advanced a step or two, and spoke even more firmly than before, urging them to depart. Again, and while looking directly into the muzzles of the guns, which they had seen loaded with ball, they declared their intention "to fight it out." This intrepid officer then took out his watch, and told his men to hold their pieces aimed at the convicts, but not to fire till they had orders; then turning to the prisoners, he said, "You must leave this hall—I give you three minutes to decide—if at the end of that time a man remains, he shall be shot dead."

19. No situation of greater interest than this can be conceived. At one end of the hall a fearful multitude of the most desperate and powerful men in existence, waiting for the assault—at the other, a little band of disciplined men, waiting with arms presented, and ready, upon the least motion or sign, to begin the carnage, and their tall and imposing commander, holding up his watch to count the lapse of three minutes, given as the reprieve to the lives of hundreds. No poet or painter can conceive of a spectacle of more dark and terrible sublimity—no human heart can conceive a situation of more appalling suspense.

20. For two minutes not a person nor a muscle was moved, not a sound was heard in the unwonted stillness of the prison, except the labored breathings

of the infuriated wretches, as they began to pant, between fear and revenge—at the expiration of two minutes, during which they had faced the ministers of death, with unblenching eyes, two or three of those in the rear and nearest the further entrance, went slowly out—a few more followed the example, dropping out quietly and deliberately, and before half of the last minute had gone, every man was struck by the panic, and crowded for an exit. The hall was cleared as if by magic. Thus the steady firmness of moral force, and the strong effect of determination, acting deliberately, awed the most savage men, and suppressed a scene of carnage, which would have instantly followed the least precipitancy or exertion of physical force.

QUESTIONS.—1. What is the use of the State Prison? 2. Where is the Penitentiary of this State? 3. What accounts for the conduct of the subordinate officer, who, though ordinarily the mildest, was on this occasion the firmest? 4. Suppose Major Wainwright had fired through the windows, as he was advised, what would have been, in all probability, the result? 5. Narrate the substance of the 19th and 20th paragraphs. 6. What gained this bloodless victory?

ERRORS.—*Ap-pal-ing* for ap-pall-ing; *sence* for since; *con-vics* for con-victs; *sit-oo-a-tion* for sit-u-a-tion; *weep-on* for weap-on (pronounced *wep-on*); *strenth* for strength; *geth-er-ed* for gath-er-ed; *temp'-rit* for tem-pe-rate; *jist* and *jest* for just.

SPELL AND DEFINE.—(1) impressive, ferocity, appalling, rebellion; (4) encroachment, brigands; (5) motley, demoniac; (6) warden, subordinate; (7) demeanor; (11) expostulated; (12) indomitable; (16) empowered; (17) blenched; (19) sublimity; (20) precipitancy.

LESSON XCVI.

RULE:—When two or more consonants come together, let the pupil be careful to *sound every one distinctly*.
EXERCISES UNDER THE RULE.

He clenched his *fists*.
He *lifts* his awful form.
He makes his *payments*.
Thou *smoothed'st* his rugged path.
The *president's speech*.

Prince Arthur.—SHAKSPEARE.

Hubert. Heat me these irons hot; and, look thou stand
Within the arras; when I strike my foot
Upon the bosom of the ground, rush forth,
And bind the boy, which you shall find with me,
Fast to the chair: be heedful: hence, and watch.

First Attendant, I hope your warrant will bear out the deed.

Hub. Uncleanly scruples! Fear not you: look to it—
(Exit Attendants.)
Young lad, come forth; I have to say with you.
(Enter Arthur.)

Arthur. Good-morrow, Hubert.

Hub. Good-morrow, little prince.

Arth. As little prince (having so great a title
To be more prince) as may be;—You are sad.

Hub. Indeed, I have been merrier.

Arth. Mercy on me!
Methinks no person should be sad but I:
Yet I remember, when I was in France,
Young gentlemen would be as sad as night,
Only for wantonness. By my christendom,
So I were out of prison, and kept sheep,
I should be merry as the day is long;
And so I would be here, but that I doubt
My uncle practises more harm to me:

He is afraid of me, and I of him:
Is it my fault that I were Goeffrey's son?
No, indeed, is't not; and I would to heaven
I were your son, so you would love me, Hubert.

Hub. If I talk to him, with his innocent prate
He will awake my mercy, which lies dead:
Therefore I will be sudden, and dispatch. *(Aside.)*

Arth. Are you sick, Hubert? You look pale to-day.
In sooth, I would you were a little sick;
That I might sit all night, and watch with you.
I warrant I love you more than you do me.

Hub. His words do take possession of my bosom.—
Read here, young Arthur. *(Showing a paper.)* How
now, foolish rheum! *(Aside.)*
Turning dispiteous torture out the door!
I must be brief; lest resolution drop
Out at mine eyes, in tender womanish tears.—
Can you not read it? Is it not fair writ?

Arth. Too fairly, Hubert, for so foul effect:
Must you with hot irons burn out both mine eyes?

Hub. Young boy, I must.

Arth. And will you?

Hub. And I will.

Arth. Have you the heart? When your head did but
ache,
I knit my handkerchief about your brows,
(The best I had, a princess wrought it me,)
And I did never ask it you again:
And with my hand at midnight held your head,
And like the watchful minutes to the hour,
Still and anon cheered up the heavy time;
Saying, What lack you? and, Where lies your grief?
Or, What good love may I perform for you?
Many a poor man's son would have lain still,
And ne'er have spoke a loving word to you;
But you at your sick service had a prince.
Nay, you may think my love was crafty love,

And call it cunning: do, and if you will:
If heaven be pleased that you should use me ill,
Why, then you must.—Will you put out mine eyes?
These eyes, that never did, nor never shall,
So much as frown on you?
    Hub. I have sworn to do it;
And with hot irons must I burn them out.
    Arth. Ah, none but in this iron age would do it:
The iron of itself, though heat red-hot,
Approaching near these eyes, would drink my tears,
And quench its fiery indignation,
Even in the matter of mine innocence:
Nay, after that, consume away in rust,
But for containing fire to harm mine eye.
Are you more stubborn-hard than hammered iron?
And if an angel should have come to me,
And told me Hubert should put out mine eyes,
I would have believed no tongue but Hubert's
    Hub. Come forth. *(Stamps.)*
    (Re-enter Attendants, with cord, irons, & c.)
Do as I bid you.
    Arth. Oh, save me, Hubert, save me! My eyes
are cut,
Even with the fierce looks of the bloody men.
    Hub. Give me the iron, I say, and bind him here.
    Arth. Alas! what need you be so boisterous-rough?
I will not struggle, I will stand stone-still.
For heaven's sake, Hubert! let me not be bound!
Nay, hear me, Hubert! drive these men away,
And I will sit as quiet as a lamb:
I will not stir, nor wince, nor speak a word,
Nor look upon the irons angrily;
Thrust but these men away, and I'll forgive you,
Whatever torment you do put me to.
    Hub. Go stand within; let me alone with him.
    First Attend. I am best pleased to be from such a
deed.

(Exit Attendants.)

Arth. Alas! I then have chid away my friend:
He hath a stern look, but a gentle heart:—
Let him come back, that his compassion may
Give life to yours.

Hub. Come, boy, prepare yourself.

Arth. Is there no remedy?

Hub. None, but to lose your eyes.

Arth. Oh heaven! that there were but a mote
in yours,
A grain, a dust, a gnat, a wandering hair,
Any annoyance in that precious sense!
Then, feeling what small things are boisterous there,
Your vile intent must needs seem horrible.

Hub. Is this your promise? Go to, hold your
tongue.

Arth. Hubert, the utterance of a brace of tongues
Must needs want pleading for a pair of eyes:
Let me not hold my tongue; let me not, Hubert!
Or, Hubert, if you will, cut out my tongue,
So I may keep mine eyes; Oh, spare mine eyes,
Though to no use, but still to look on you!
Lo, by my troth, the instrument is cold,
And would not harm me.

Hub. I can heat it, boy.

Arth. No, in good sooth, the fire is dead with grief—
Being create for comfort—to be used.
In undeserved extremes: See else yourself:
There is no malice in this burning coal;
The breath of heaven hath blown its spirit out,
And strewed repentant ashes on his head.

Hub. But with my breath I can revive it; boy.

Arth. And if you do, you will but make it blush
And glow with shame of your proceedings, Hubert;
Nay, it perchance will sparkle in your eyes,
And, like a dog, that is compelled to fight,

Snatch at his master that does tarre* him on.
All things, that you should use to do me wrong,
Deny their office; only you do lack
That mercy, which fierce fire, and iron extends,—
Creatures of note, for mercy-lacking uses.

Hub. Well, see to live; I will not touch thine eyes
For all the treasure that thy uncle owns;
Yet I am sworn, and I did purpose, boy,
With this same very iron to burn them out.

Arth. Oh, now you look like Hubert! all this while
You were disguised.

Hub. Peace: no more: Adieu!—
Your uncle must not know but you are dead:
I'll fill these dogged spies with false reports.
And, pretty child, sleep doubtless, and secure
That Hubert, for the wealth of all the world,
Will not offend thee.

Arth. Oh heaven!—I thank you, Hubert.

Hub. Silence: no more. Go closely in with me:
Much danger do I undergo for thee.

QUESTIONS.—1. Who was Prince Arthur? 2. Where did he live? 3. Who was Hubert? 4. Who had instigated Hubert to perpetrate such cruelty? 5. What does Hubert mean in saying, "How now foolish rheum?" 6. Enumerate the motives by which the prince induces Hubert to spare him.

ERRORS.—*Fers* for fierce; *an-gel* for a'n-gel; *sper-it* for spir-it; *dan-ger* for da"n-ger.

SPELL AND DEFINE.—arras, exit, wantonness, dispiteous, indignation, boisterous, wince, angrily.

---

* set.

LESSON XCVII.

RULE.—In reading peotry, be careful to avoid the sing-song tone which is made by marking too strongly with the voice, all the accented syllables. In the example the fault will appear, if the words italicized are strongly accented.

EXAMPLE.—Sweet *is* the *work* my *God* and *King*
　　　　　　To praise thy *name,* give *thanks* and *sing.*

The Child's Inquiry.—DOANE.

1. What is that, mother?
   The lark, my child.
   The morn has just looked out, and smiled,
   When he starts from his humble grassy nest,
   And is up and away with the dew on his breast,
   And a hymn in his heart, to yon pure bright sphere
   To warble it out in his Maker's ear.
   Ever, my child, be thy morn's first lays,
   Tuned, like the lark's, to thy Maker's praise.

2. What is that, mother?
   The dove, my son.—
   And that low sweet voice, like a widow's moan,
   Is flowing out from her gentle breast,
   Constant and pure by that lonely nest,
   As the wave is poured from some crystal urn,
   For her distant dear one's quick return.
   Ever, my son, be thou like the dove;
   In friendship as faithful, as constant in love.

3. What is that, mother?
   The eagle, my boy,
   Proudly careering his course of joy,
   Firm, in his own mountain vigor relying;
   Breasting the dark storm; the red bolt defying;
   His wing on the wind, and his eye on the sun,
   He swerves not a hair, but bears onward, right on.
   Boy, may the eagle's flight ever by thine;
   Onward, and upward, and true to the line.

4. What is that, mother?
   The swan, my love.
   He is floating down from his native grove,
   No loved one now, no nestling nigh;
   He is floating down by himself, to die.
   Death darkens his eye, and unplumes his wings,
   Yet his sweetest song is the last he sings.
   Live so, my love, that when death shall come,
   Swanlike and sweet it may waft thee home.

QUESTIONS.—1. May we not often derive useful instruction from observation of nature? 2. What lesson is drawn from the lark? 3. What from the dove? 4. The eagle? 5. the swan? 6. What beautiful figure in verse second?

ERRORS.—*Hime* for hymn (pronounced *him*); *pow-er-ed* for pour-ed.

SPELL AND DEFINE.—(1) sphere, warble; (2) friendship; (3) careering, swerves; (4) nestling, unplumes.

LESSON XCVIII.

RULE.—In reading poetry that rhymes, there should be a slight pause after the words that rhyme, even when the sense does not require it.

Christian Hymn of Triumph; from "The Martyr of Antioch."—MILMAN.

1. Sing to the Lord! let harp, and lute, and voice,
   Up to the expanding gates of heaven rejoice,
   While the bright martyrs to their rest are borne!
   Sing to the Lord! their blood-stained course is run,
   And every head its diadem hath won,
   Rich as the purple of the summer morn—
   Sing the triumphant champions of their God,
   While burn their mounting feet along their sky-
       ward road.

2. Sing to the Lord! for her, in beauty's prime,
Snatched from this wintry earth's ungenial clime,
In the eternal spring of paradise to bloom;
For her the world displayed its brightest treasure,
And the airs panted with the songs of pleasure.
Before earth's throne she chose the lowly tomb,
The vale of tears with willing footsteps trod,
Bearing her cross with thee, incarnate Son of God.

3. Sing to the Lord! it is not shed in vain,
The blood of martyrs! from its freshening rain
High springs the church like some fount-
   shadowing palm:
The nations crowd beneath its branching shade,
Of its green leaves are kingly diadems made,
And wrapt within its deep, embosoming calm,
Earth shrinks to slumber like the breezeless deep,
And war's tempestuous vultures fold their wings
   and sleep.

4. Sing to the Lord! no more the angels fly—
Far in the bosom of the stainless sky—
The sound of fierce, licentious sacrifice.
From shrin'd alcove and stately pedestal,
The marble gods in cumbrous ruin fall;
Headless, in dust, the awe of nations lies;
Jove's thunder crumbles in his mouldering hand,
And mute as sepulchers the hymnless temples
   stand.

QUESTIONS.—Explain the last line of the first stanza.
2. Explain the last line of the second.　3. With what propriety
can vultures be called "tempestuous?"　4. Who is "Jove?"

ERRORS.—*Tem-pes-ti-ous* and *tem-pes-too-ous* for tem-pest-
u-ous; *vul-ters* for vul-tures; *fare* for far; *se-pul-chers* for
sep-ul-chers.

SPELL AND DEFINE.—(1) triumphant, champion, skyward;
(2) ungenial, incarnate;　(3) diadem, tempestuous, vultures;
(4) licentious, alcove, pedestal, cumbrous, sepulchers.

LESSON XCIX.

RULE.—When similar sounds come at the end of one word and the beginning of the next word, they must not be blended into one.

EXERCISES.—Mali*ce s*eeks to destroy.

The bree*ze s*ighs softly.

The i*ce s*lowly melts.

Charles de Moor's Remorse.—SCHILLER.

1. I must rest here. My joints are shaken asunder. My tongue cleaves to my mouth. It is dry as a potsherd. I would beg of some of you, to fetch me a little water, in the hollow of your hand, from yonder brook, but all of you are weary to death.

2. How glorious, how majestic, yonder setting sun! 'Tis thus the hero falls, 'tis thus he dies—in godlike majesty! When I was a boy—a mere child—it was my favorite thought, to live and die like that sun.

3. 'Twas an idle thought, a boy's conceit. There was a time—leave me, my friends, alone—there was a time, when I could not sleep, if I had forgot my prayers! Oh that I were a child once more!

4. What a lovely evening! What a pleasing landscape! That scene is noble! This world is beautiful! The earth is grand! But I am hideous in this world of beauty—a monster on this magnificent earth—the prodigal son:—My innocence! Oh, my innocence!— All nature expands at the sweet breath of spring; but, Oh God, this paradise—this heaven is a hell to me!— All is happiness around me, all in the sweet spirit of peace; the world is one family—but its father there above is not my father.

5. I am an outcast—the prodigal son! I'm the companion of murderers, of viperous fiends! I'm bound down enchained to guilt and horror!—Oh, that I could

return once more to peace and innocence, that I hung an infant on the breast, that I were born a beggar—the meanest kind—a peasant of the field.

6. I would toil, till the sweat of blood dropt from my brow, to purchase the luxury of one sound sleep, the rapture of a single tear!—There was a time when I could weep with ease. Oh, days of bliss! Oh, mansion of my fathers! Scenes of my infant years, enjoyed by fond enthusiasm, will you no more return? No more exhale your sweets to cool this burning bosom?

7. Oh, never, never shall they return! No more refresh this bosom with the breath of peace. They are gone! gone forever!

QUESTIONS.—1. Who was Schiller? 2. Can you conceive of a being so wretched as here represented?

ERRORS.—*Pots-herd* for pot-sherd; *yer* for your; *yan-der*, *yun-der*, and *yen-der* for yon-der; *fur-got* for for-got; *hij-jus* for hid-e-ous; *ex-zale* for ex-hale.

SPELL AND DEFINE.—(1) potsherd; (2) majestic, favorite; (4) landscape, hideous, magnificent, innocence; (5) outcast, viperous, enchained; (6) luxury, rapture, mansion, enthusiasm; (7) refresh.

LESSON C.

RULE.—Be careful to give the right sound to the vowel sounds.

Value of Mathematics.—E. D. MANSFIELD.

1. Man may construct his works by irregular and uncertain rules, but God has made an unerring law for his whole creation, and made it too in respect to the physical system, upon principles, which, as far as we now know, can never be understood without the aid of mathematics.

2. Let us suppose a youth who despises, as many do, these *cold* and *passionless abstractions of the mathematics.* Yet, he is intellectual. He loves knowledge. He would explore nature, and know the reason of things, but he would do it, without aid from this *rigid, syllogistic, measuring, calculating science.* He seeks indeed, no "royal road to geometry," but he seeks one not less difficult to find in which geometry is not needed.

3. He begins with the mechanical powers. He takes the lever and readily understands that a weight will move it. But the principle upon which *different* weights, at *different* distances move it he is forbidden to know for *they* depend upon *ratios* and *proportions.* He passes to the inclined plane, but quits it in disgust when he finds its action depends upon the relations of angles and triangles. The screw is still worse, and when he comes to the wheel and axle, he gives them up forever. They are *all mathematical!*

4. He would investigate the laws of falling bodies, and moving fluids, and would know why their motion is *accelerated* at different periods, and upon what their momentum depends. But roots and squares, lines, angles and curves float before him in the mazy dance

of a disturbed intellect. The very first proposition is a *mystery*, and he soon discovers that mechanical philosophy is little better than mathematics itself.

5. He still has his *senses*. He will, at least, not be indebted to diagrams and equations for their enjoyment. He gazes with admiration upon the phenomena of light, the many-colored rainbow upon the bosom of the clouds, the clouds themselves reflected with all their changing shades from the surface of the quiet waters. Whence comes this beautiful imagery? He investigates and finds that every hue in the rainbow is made by a different *angle of refractions*, and that each ray reflected from the mirror, has its angle of incidence equal to its angle of reflection. As he pursues the subject further, in the construction of lenses and telescopes, the whole family of triangles, ratios, proportions and conclusions arise to alarm his excited vision.

6. He turns to the heavens, and is charmed with its shining host, moving in solemn procession, "through the halls of the sky," each star, as it rises and sets marking time on the records of nature. He would know the structure of this beautiful system, and search out, if possible, the laws which regulate those distant lights. But astronomy forever banishes him from her presence. She will have none near her to whom mathematics is not a *familiar friend*. What can *he* know of her parallaxes, anomalies, and precessions, who has never studied the conic sections, or the higher orders of analysis? She sends him to some wooden orrery, from which he may gather as much knowledge of the heavenly bodies, as a child does of armies from the gilded troopers of the toy shop.

7. But if he can have no companionship with optics nor astronomy, nor mechanical philosophy, there *are* sciences, he thinks, which have better taste and less austerity of manners. He flies to chemistry, and her

garments float loosely around him. For a while, he goes gloriously on, illuminated by the *red lights* and *blue lights* of crucibles and retorts. But, soon he comes to compound bodies, to the composition of the elements around him, and finds them all in fixed relations. He finds that gases and fluids will combine with each other, and with solids only in a certain *ratio*, and that all possible compounds are formed by nature in *immutable proportion*. Then starts up the whole doctrine of chemical equivalents, and mathematics again stares him in the face.

8. Affrighted he flies to mineralogy. Stones he may pick up, jewels he may draw from the bosom of the earth and be no longer alarmed at the stern visage of this terrible science. But, even here, he is not safe. The first stone that he finds—quartz, contains a *crystal*, and that crystal assumes the dreaded form of geometry. Crystallization allures him on; but, as he goes, cubes and hexagons, pyramids and dodecagons arise before him in beautiful array. He would understand more about them, but, must *wait* at the portal of the temple, till introduced within, by that honored of time and science, our friendly *Euclid*.

9. Now, where shall this student of nature without the aid of mathematics, go for his knowledge, or his enjoyments? Is it to natural history? The very *birds* cleave the air in the form of the cycloid, and mathematics prove it the *best*. Their feathers are formed upon calculated mechanical principles; the muscles of their frame are moved by them; the little bee has constructed his cell in the very geometrical figure, and with the precise angles, which mathematicians, after ages of investigation, have demonstrated to be that which contains the greatest *economy of space and strength.*—Yes!—he who would shun mathematics must fly the bounds of "flaming space,"

and in the realms of chaos, that,

"_____ dark,
Illimitable ocean, _____"

where Milton's Satan wandered from the wrath of
heaven, he may *possibly* find some spot visited by
no figure of geometry, and no harmony of proportion.
But nature, this beautiful creation of God, has no
resting place for him. All its construction is
mathematical; all its uses *reasonable*; all its ends *har-
monious*. It has no elements mixed without regulated
law; no broken chord to make a false note in the music
of the spheres.

QUESTIONS.—1. How is it illustrated, that without
mathematics, it is impossible for the student to understand the
principles of the physical system? 2. Suppose he turns to
mechanics? 3. Suppose he trusts to the senses? 4. Turns to
chemistry? 5. To mineralogy? 6. To natural history?

ERRORS.—*Er-reg'-lar* for ir-reg-u-lar; *syl-li-gis-tic* for
syl-lo-gis-tic.

SPELL AND DEFINE.—(1) mathematics;   (2) syllogistic,
abstractions, geometry: (3) mechanical, proportions;
(4) momentum, philosophy; (5) diagrams, equations, phenomena,
imagery, refraction, telescopes; (6) parallaxes, anomalies,
precessions; (7) companionship, composition, immutably;
(8) cycloid, illimitable.

LESSON CI.

RULE.—Do not slide over the little words, nor omit any
syllable of any word.

Value of Mathematics.—CONTINUED.

1. Let us take another student, with whom
mathematics is neither despised nor neglected. He
sees in it the means of *past success* to others. He reads

in its history the *progress of universal improvement*; and he belives that what has contributed so much to the civilization of the world, what is even now contributing so much to all that humanizes society, and what the experience of all mankind has sanctioned, *may* perchance, be useful to his own intellectual development,

2. He opens a volume of geometry, and steadily pursues its abstractions from the definition of a right line, through the elegant properties of the right angled triangle, the relations of similar figures, and the laws of curved surfaces. He finds a chain of *unbroken* and *impregnable* reasoning; and is at once possessed of all the knowledge of postulates, syllogisms and conclusions, which the most accomplished school of rhetoric could have taught him.

3. He looks upon society, and wherever he turns, arts, sciences, and their *results*, from carpentry to civil engineering; from architecture to hydraulics; from the ingenious lock upon a canal, to the useful mill upon its sides, disclose their operations, no longer mysterious to his enlightened understanding. Many an interesting repository of knowledge this key has opened to his vision, and as he thus walks through the *vestibule* of science, he longs to penetrate those deep aisles and ascend that magnificent stairway, which lead up to the structure of the universe.

4. With the properties of the ellipsis, the laws of motion demonstrated by mathematics, and two facts drawn from observation, the one that bodies fall towards the earth, and the other, the regular motion of the planets, he demonstrates beyond the power of refutation, the laws of the celestial system. He traces star after star, however eccentric their course, through the unseen immensity of space, and calculates with *unfailing certainty*, the hour of its return, after ages have passed away.

5. He does more. He weighs matter in the balances of creation, and finds that to complete the harmony of the system, a planet is wanting in some distant corner of its wide domain, no mortal eye has ever seen it, no tradition tells of its existence. Yet, with the confidence and zeal of prophecy, he announces that it *must exist*, for *demonstration has proved it*. The prediction is recorded in the volume of science.

6. Long after, astronomy, by the aid of mathematics, discovers the long lost tenant of the skies. Fractured though it be, while its members perform their revolution, no living soul can be permitted to doubt the *worth of mathematics*, or the powers of his own immortal mind.

7. And what were the glorious contemplations of that pupil of mathematical philosophy, as he passed behind the clouds of earth to investigate the machinery of celestial spheres! Alone, yet not solitary, amidst the glowing lights of heaven, he sends his spirit forth through the works of God. He has risen by the force of cultivated intellect to heights which mortal fancy had never reached.

8. He has taken line and figure and measure, and from proposition to proposition, and from conclusion to conclusion, *riveting* link after link, he has bound the universe to the throne of its creator, by that.

> "_____ golden, everlasting chain,
> Whose strong embrace holds heaven and
> earth and main."

9. And is there no *moral* instruction in this? Does he learn no lesson of wisdom? Do no strong emotions of love and gratitude arise towards that being who thus delights him with the charms of intellectual enjoyment, and blesses him with the multiplied means of happiness? *Harder* than the adamant of his own reasoning—*colder* than the abstractions in which he

is *falsely* supposed to move, must be he who *thus* conducted by the handmaid of the arts and sciences, through whatever humanizes man, through whatever is sublime in his progress to a higher state, through all the vast machinery, which the Almighty has made tributary to his comfort, and its happiness, yet feels no livelier sentiment of duty towards him, no kinder or more peaceful spirit towards his fellow man.

QUESTIONS.—1. In what light does the student regard mathematics?   2. Can you sketch his career?   3. What is the moral instruction to be derived from this?

ERRORS.—*Pro-gress* for prog-ress; *div-el-up-munt* for de-vel-op-ment; *suf-fa-ses* for sur-fa-ces.

SPELL AND DEFINE.—(1) civilization, humanizes; (2) impregnable, postulates, accomplished;   (3) engineering, architecture, hydraulics, vestibule;   (4) ellipsis, demonstrated; (5) prophecy;   (8) universe;   (9) adamant.

LESSON CII.

RULE.—In reading poetry that does not rhyme, there should be no pause at the end of a line, except when it terminates with an important word, or the sense requires it.

Washing Day.—MRS. HERMANS.

1. The Muses are turned gossips; they have lost
   The buskined step, and clear high-sounding
      phrase,
   Language of Gods. Come then, domestic Muse,
   In slipshod measure loosely prattling on
5. Of farm or orchard, pleasant curds and cream,
   Or drowning flies, or shoe lost in the mire
   By little whimpering boy, with rueful face;

Come, Muse, and sing the dreaded Washing Day.
Ye who beneath the yoke of wedlock bend,
10. With bowed soul, full well ye know the day
Which week, smooth sliding after week, brings on
Too soon;—for to that day nor peace belongs
Nor comfort;—ere the first gray streak of dawn,
The red-armed washers come and chase repose.
15. Nor pleasant smile, nor quaint device of mirth,
E'er visited that day: the very cat,
From the wet kitchen scared, and reeking hearth,
Visits the parlor,—an unwonted guest.
The silent breakfast meal is soon dispatched;
20. Uninterrupted, save by anxious looks
Cast at the lowering sky, if sky should lower.
From that last evil, O preserve us, heavens!
For should the skies pour down, adieu to all
Remains of quiet: then expect to hear
25. Of sad disasters,—dirt and gravel stains
Hard to efface, and loaded lines at once
Snapped short,—and linen-horse by dog thrown
    down,
And all the petty miseries of life.
Saints have been calm while stretched upon the
    rack,
30. And Guatimozin smiled on burning coals;
But never yet did housewife notable
Greet with a smile a rainy washing-day.
—But grant the welkin fair, require not thou
Who call'st thyself perchance the master there,
35. Or study swept, or nicely dusted coat,
Or usual 'tendance;—ask not, indiscreet,
Thy stockings mended, though the yawning rents
Gape wide as Erebus; nor hope to find
Some snug recess impervious: shouldst thou try
40. The 'customed garden walks, thine eye shall rue
The budding fragrance of thy tender shrubs,
Myrtle or rose, all crushed beneath the weight

Of coarse checked apron,—with impatient hand
Twitched off when showers impend: or crossing
    lines
45. Shall mar thy musings, as the wet cold sheet
Flaps in thy face abrupt. Woe to the friend
Whose evil stars have urged him forth to claim
On such a day the hospitable rites!
Looks, blank at best, and stinted courtesy,
50. Shall he receive. Vainly he feeds his hopes
With dinner of roast chickens, savory pie,
Or tart or pudding:—pudding he nor tart
That day shall eat: nor, though the husband try,
Mending what can't be helped, to kindle mirth
55. From cheer deficient, shall his consort's brow
Clear up propitious:—the unlucky guest
In silence dines, and early slinks away.
I well remember when a child, the awe
This day struck into me; for then the maids,
60. I scarce knew why, looked cross, and drove me
    from them:
Nor soft caress could I obtain, nor hope
Usual indulgences; jelly or creams,
Relic of costly suppers, and set by
For me their petted one; or buttered toast,
65. When butter was forbid; or thrilling tale
Of ghost or witch, or murder—so I went
And sheltered me beside the parlor fire:
There my dear grandmother, eldest of forms,
Tended the little ones, and watched from harm,
70. Anxiously fond, though oft her spectacles
With elfin cunning hid, and oft the pins
Drawn from her raveled stockings, might have
    soured
One less indulgent.—
At intervals my mother's voice was heard,
75. Urging dispatch: briskly the work went on,
All hands employed to wash, to rinse, to wring,

To fold, and starch, and clap, and iron, and plait.
Then would I sit me down and ponder much
Why washings were. Sometimes through hollow
    bowl
80. Of pipe amused we blew, and sent aloft
The floating bubbles; little dreaming then
To see, Mongolfier, thy silken ball
Ride buoyant through the clouds—so near
    approach
The sports of children and the toils of men.

QUESTIONS.—1. What is meant by "buskined step?"
2. Who was Guatimozin and what was his history? 3. What was
Erebus? 4. Who was Mongolfier?

ERRORS.—*Cruds* for curds; *hurth* for hearth; *scurs* for scarce;
rinch for rinse.

SPELL AND DEFINE.—(1) muses, gossips; (7) whimpering;
(15) quaint, device; (17) reeking; (19) dispatched;
(20) uninterrupted; (26) efface; (31) housewife; (33) welkin;
(39) impervious; (45) musings; (56) propitious; (62) indulgences;
(71) elfin; (83) buoyant.

LESSON CIII.

RULE.—When similar sounds come at the end of one word,
and at the beginning of the next word, they must not be blended
into one
EXERCISES.—He sink*s* *s*orrowing to the tomb.
            Man love*s* *s*ociety.
            Time flie*s* *s*wiftly.
            The bird*s* *s*ing.

Capturing the Wild Horse.—W. IRVING.

1. We left the buffalo camp about eight o'clock, and had a toilsome and harassing march of two hours, over ridges of hills, covered with a ragged forest of scrub oaks, and broken by deep gullies.

2. About ten o'clock in the morning, we came to where this line of rugged hills swept down into a valley, through which flowed the north fork of Red River. A beautiful meadow, about half a mile wide, enameled with yellow autumnal flowers, stretched for two or three miles along the foot of the hills, bordered on the opposite side by the river whose banks were fringed with cottonwood trees, the bright foliage of which refreshed and delighted the eye, after being wearied by the contemplation of monotonous wastes of brown forest.

3. The meadow was finely diversified by groves and clumps of trees, so happily disposed, that they seemed as if set out by the hand of art. As we cast our eyes over this fresh and delightful valley, we beheld a troop of wild horses, quietly grazing on a green lawn, about a mile distant, to our right, while to our left, at nearly the same distance, were several buffaloes; some feeding, others reposing, and ruminating among the high, rich herbage, under the shade of a clump of cottonwood trees. The whole had the appearance of a broad beautiful tract of pasture land, on the highly ornamented estate of some gentleman farmer, with his cattle grazing about the lawns and meadows.

4. A council of war was now held, and it was determined to profit by the present favorable opportunity, and try our hand at the grand hunting maneuver, which is called "ringing the wild horse," This requires a large party of horsemen, well mounted.

5. They extend themselves in each direction, at certain distances apart, and gradually form a ring of two

or three miles in circumference, so as to surround the game. This must be done with extreme care, for the wild horse is the most readily alarmed inhabitant of the prairie, and can scent a hunter at a great distance, if to windward.

6. The ring being formed, two or three ride towards the horses, which start off in an opposite direction. Whenever they approach the bounds of the ring, however, a huntsman presents himself, and turns them from their course. In this way, they are checked, and driven back at every point, and kept galloping round and round this magic circle, until being completely tired down, it is easy for the hunters to ride up beside them, and throw the *lariat** over their heads. The prime horses of the most speed, courage, and bottom, however, are apt to break through, and escape, so that, in general, it is the second rate horses that are taken.

7. Preparations were now made for a hunt of this kind. The pack horses were now taken into the woods, and firmly tied to trees, lest in a rush of wild horses, they should break away.

8. Twenty-five men were then sent under the command of a lieutenant, to steal along the edge of the valley within the strip of wood that skirted the hills. They were to station themselves about fifty yards apart, within the edge of the woods, and not advance or show themselves until the horses dashed in that direction. Twenty-five men were sent across the valley, to steal in like manner along the river bank that bordered the opposite side, and to station themselves among the trees.

9. A third party of about the same number was to form a line, stretching across the lower part of the valley, so as to connect the two wings. Beatte and

---

* The lariat is a noose of rope, fastened to the saddle-bow.

our other half-breed Antoine, together with the ever officious Tonish, were to make a circuit through the woods, so as to get to the upper part of the valley, in the rear of the horses, and drive them forward, into the kind of sack that we had formed, while the two wings should join behind them, and make a complete circle.

10 The flanking parties were quietly extending themselves out of sight, on each side of the valley, and the residue were stretching themselves like the links of a chain across it, when the wild horses gave signs that they scented an enemy: snuffing the air, snorting, and looking about. At length they pranced off slowly toward the river, and disappeared behind a green bank.

11. Here, had the regulations of the chase been observed, they would have been quietly checked and turned back by the advance of a hunter from among the trees. Unluckily, however, we had our wildfire, Jack-o'lantern little Frenchman to deal with.

12. Instead of keeping quietly up the right side of the valley to get above the horses, the moment he saw them move toward the river, he broke out of the covert of woods and dashed furiously across the plain in pursuit of them. This put an end to all system. The half-breeds, and a half a score of rangers, joined in the chase.

13 Away they all went over the green bank. In a moment or two, the wild horses reappeared, and came thundering down the valley, with Frenchman, half-breeds and rangers, galloping and bellowing behind them. It was in vain and the line drawn across the valley, attempted to check, and turn back the fugitives. They were too hotly pressed by their pursuers. In their panic they dashed through the line, and clattered down the plain.

14. The whole troop joined in the headlong chase, some of the rangers without hats or caps, their hair flying about their ears, and others with handkerchiefs tied round their heads. The buffaloes, which had been calmly ruminating among the herbage, heaved up their huge forms, gazed for moment at the tempest that came scouring down the meadow, then turned and took to heavy rolling flight. They were soon overtaken. The promiscuous throng were pressed together by the contracting sides of the valley, and away they went, pell-mell, hurry-scurry, wild buffalo, wild horse, wild huntsman, with clang and clatter, and whoop and halloo, that made the forests ring.

15. At length the buffaloes turned into a green brake, on the river bank, while the horses dashed up a narrow defile of the hills, with their pursuers close at their heels. Beatte passed several of them, having fixed his eye upon a fine Pawnee horse that had his ears slit, and saddle marks upon his back.

16. He pressed him gallantly, but lost him in the woods. Among the wild horses, was a fine black mare, which in scrambling up the defile, tripped and fell. A young ranger sprang from his horse, and seized her by the mane, and muzzle. Another ranger dismounted, and came to his assistance. The mare struggled fiercely, kicking and biting, and striking with her fore feet, but a noose was slipped over her head, and her struggles were in vain.

17. It was some time, however, before she gave over rearing and plunging, and lashing out with her feet on every side. The two rangers then led her along the valley, by two strong lariats, which enabled them to keep at a sufficient distance on each side, to be out of the reach of her hoofs, and whenever she struck out in one direction, she was jerked in the other. In this way her spirit was gradually subdued.

18. As to Tonish, who had marred the whole scheme by his precipitancy, he had been more successful than he deserved, having managed to catch a beautiful cream colored colt about seven months old that had not strength to keep up with its companions. The mercurial little Frenchman was beside himself with exultation. It was amusing to see him with his prize. The colt would rear and kick, and struggle to get free, when Tonish would take him about the neck, wrestle with him, jump on his back, and cut as many antics as a monkey with a kitten.

19 Nothing surprised me more, however, than to witness how soon these poor animals thus taken from the unbounded freedom of the prairie, yielded to the dominion of man. In the course of two or three days, the mare and colt went with the lead horses and became quite docile.

QUESTIONS.—1. Near what river did this expedition commence? 2. Where is that river? 3. Describe the country, scenery, etc. 4. What animated objects presented themselves to view upon the right and the left? 5. To what is the whole scene compared? 6. What hunting maneuver was commenced? describe it. 7. What is the lariat? 8. Describe the proceedings of the party in this maneuver. 9. What interrupted its successful completion? 10. Give the striking contrast between the flight of the wild horses and that of the buffaloes. 11. Describe the capture of the black mare. 12 What was the conduct of the captured animals in respect to being tamed? 13. Was not this cruel sport?

ERRORS.—*Nuth-in'* for noth-ing; *med-ers* for mead-ows; *hosses* for hors-es; *per-a-ra* for prai-rie; *Beat-te* pronounced By-at.

SPELL AND DEFINE.—(1) buffalo, harassing; (2) enameled, autumnal, contemplation, monotonous; (3) ruminating; (4) maneuver; (5) circumference, windward; (6) huntsman; (7) preparations; (10) flanking; (11) regulations, wildfire, jack-o'lantern; (13) reappeared; (14) handkerchief; (16) scrambling; (18) mercurial, exultation; (19) unbounded, prairie.

LESSON CIV.

RULE.—Be careful and give a full sound to the vowels. Regard to this rule will correct the commom flat, clipping and uninteresting way in which many read.

EXERCISES in which the vowels italicized are to be prolonged.

H*ai*l! holy l*i*ght.

We pr*ai*se thee, *O* Lord God.

These names of the Deity are seldom pronounced with that full and solemn sound that is proper. *Lud* and *Law-ard* and *Gud* and *Gawd* are too frequently used instead of the proper sounds. If the pupil can learn to speak the three words, O—Lord—God, properly, it will be worth no little attention. Every pupil ought to be exercised on these words till they pronounce them properly and in a full and solemn tone.

The Gods of the Heathen.

BIBLE.

1. Not unto us, O Lord! not unto us,
   But unto thy name give glory,
   For thy mercy, and for thy truth's sake.
   Wherefore should the heathen say,
   Where is now their God?
   But our God is in the heavens:
   He hath done whatsoever he hath pleased.

2. Their idols are silver and gold,
   The work of men's hands.
   They have mouths—but they speak not:
   Eyes have they—but they see not:
   They have ears—but they hear not:
   Noses have they—but they smell not:
   They have hands—but they handle not.
   Feet have they—but they walk not:
   Neither speak they through their throat.
   They that make them are like unto them;
   So is everyone that trusteth in them.

3. O Israel! trust thou in the Lord:
He is their help and their shield.
O house of Aaron! trust in the Lord:
He is their help and their shield.
Ye that fear the Lord, trust in the Lord:
He is their help and their shield.

4. The Lord hath been mindful of us: he will bless us;
He will bless the house of Israel:
He will bless the house of Aaron.
He will bless them that fear the Lord,
Both small and great.
The Lord shall increase you more and more,
You and your children.
Ye are blessed of the Lord
Which made heaven and earth.

5. The heaven, even the heavens are the Lord's:
But the earth hath he given to the children of men.
The dead praise not the Lord,
Neither any that go down into silence.
But we will bless the Lord
From this time forth and for evermore,
Praise the Lord!

QUESTIONS.—1. What is the general sentiment intended to be inspired by this Psalm? 2. What is the contrast made between the true God, and the idols of the heathen?

ERRORS.—*Unter* for un-to; *mear-cy* for mer-cy; *ni-ther* for neith-er.

SPELL AND DEFINE.—(1) heathen, whatsoever; (2) trusteth; (4) increase; (5) evermore.

LESSON CV.

RULE.—In reading anything solemn, a full, slow and distinct manner should be preserved, and particular attention paid to the stops.

The Fall of Babylon.—JEBB'S SACRED LIT.

1. And after these things, I saw another angel
    descending from heaven,
    Having great power: and the earth was
    enlightened with his glory:
    And he cried mightily with a loud voice: saying
    She is fallen! she is fallen!
5. Babylon the great!
    And is become the habitation of demons
    And the hold of every impure spirit;
    And the cage of every impure and hateful bird;
    For in the wine of the wrath of her lewdness hath
    she pledged all nations;
10. And the kings of the earth have with her
    committed lewdness.
    And the merchants of the earth, from the excess
    of her wanton luxury, have waxed rich;
    And I heard another voice from heaven, saying:
    Come out of her, my people;
    That ye be not partakers of her sins,
15. And of her plagues that ye may not receive:
    For her sins have reached up unto heaven,
    And God hath remembered her iniquities:
    Repay to her as she also hath repaid,
    And double to her double, according to her works.
20. In the cup which she hath mingled, mingle to her
    double;
    As much as she hath glorified herself and played
    the luxurious wanton,

So much give to her torment and sorrow:
For in her heart she saith,
"I sit a queen
25. And a widow am not I:
And sorrow I shall not see;"—
Therefore, in one day shall come her plagues;
Death, and mourning, and famine,
And with fire shall she be consumed;
30. For strong is the Lord God, who hath passed
    sentence upon her.
Then shall bewail her, and smite the breast for
    her,
The kings of the earth who have committed
Lewdness with her, and lived in wanton luxury,
When they shall see the smoke of her burning,
35. Standing afar off, because of the fear of her
    torment; saying,
"Woe! Woe! the great city, Babylon the strong
    city!
In one hour thy judgment is come!"
And the merchants of the earth shall weep and
    mourn over her,
For their merchandise no man buyeth any more:
40. Merchandise of gold and silver:
Of precious stones and pearls;
And of fine linen and of purple:
And of silk and scarlet;
And every odorous wood and every vessel of
    ivory;
45. And every vessel of most precious wood:
And of brass and iron and marble;
And cinnamon and amomum:
And perfumes, and myrrh, and incense;
And wine and oil;
50. And fine flour and wheat;
And cattle and sheep:
And horses and chariots and slaves;

And the souls of men:

And the autumnal fruits of thy soul's desire are
  gone from thee:

55. And all delicacies and splendors have vanished
  from thee.

And thou shalt never find them any more!

The merchants of these things, who were enriched
  by her,

Shall stand afar off because of the fear of her
  torment:

Weeping and mourning: saying,

60. "Woe! Woe! the great city!

She who was clothed in fine linen, and purple, and
  scarlet.

, And was decked with gold, and precious stones,
  and pearls!

For in one hour is brought to desolation this so
  great wealth!"

And every shipmaster, and every supercargo,

65. And mariners, and all who labor on the sea,

Stood afar off, and cried aloud,

When they saw the smoke of her burning; saying:

"What city, like the great city!"

And they cast dust upon their heads

70. And cried aloud, weeping and mourning; saying:

"Woe! Woe! the great city!

Wherein all who had ships upon the sea waxed
  rich

By her costliness;

For in one hour has she been made desolate!"

75. Rejoice over her thou heaven!

And ye saints! and ye apostles! and ye prophets!

For God hath for her crimes against you passed
  sentence upon her!

And a mighty angel took up a stone like a huge
  millstone, and cast it into the sea; saying:

"Thus with violence shall be thrown down

Babylon the great city, and shall be found no
    more;
80. And the voice of harpers, and musicians and flute
    players, and trumpeters shall be heard in thee
    no more
    And any artificer of any ingenious art shall be
    found in thee no more:
    And the sound of a millstone shall be heard in
    thee
    no more:
    And the light of a lamp shall be seen in thee no
    more:
    And the voice of the bridegroom, and of the bride,
    shall be heard in thee no more,
85. For thy merchants were the great ones of the
    earth;
    For by thy sorceries were deceived all the nations,
    And in her the blood of prophets and saints hath
    been found:
    And of all those who were slain upon the earth.''
    And after these things I heard as it were the voice
    of a great multitude in heaven, saying,
    "HALLELUJAH!
90. Salvation, and glory, and honor
    And power, be unto the Lord our God!
    For true and righteous are his judgments;
    For he hath judged the great harlot
    Who corrupted the earth with her lewdness;
95. And he hath avenged the blood of his servants at
    her hand.''
    And, a second time they said, "HALLELUJAH!''
    And her smoke ascendeth forever and ever!

QUESTIONS.—1. By whom were the Revelations written?
2. Where?   3. What city is designated by the name "Babylon?''
4. Why is this supposed?   5. Are these prophecies yet accomplished?

ERRORS.——*Per-ta-kers* for par-ta-kers; *in-ik-i-ties* for in-iq-ui-ties.

SPELL AND DEFINE.—(6) demons; (8) hateful; (11) merchants; (17) iniquities, (31) bewail; (39) merchandise; (47) cinnamon, amomum; (48) perfumes, myrrh, incense; (63) desolation; (89) hallelujah.

LESSON CVI.

RULE.—When similar sounds come at the end of one word, and at the beginning of the next word, they must not be blended into one.

EXERCISES.—He sink*s* *s*orrowing to the tomb.

Man love*s* *s*ociety,

Time flie*s* *s*wiftly.

The bird*s* *s*ing.

Antony's Oration over Caesar's Dead Body.

SHAKSPEARE.

1. Friends, Romans, countrymen! Lend me your
      ears
   I come to bury Caesar, not to praise him.
   The evil that men do, lives after them;
   The good is oft interred with their bones:
   So let it be with Caesar! Noble Brutus
   Hath told you, that Caesar was ambitious.
   If it were so, it was a grievous fault;
   And grievously hath Caesar answered it.
   Here, under leave of Brutus and the rest,

(For Brutus is an honorable man;
So are they all, all honorable men,)
Come I to speak in Caesar's funeral.

2. He was my friend, faithful and just to me:
But Brutus says, he was ambitious;
And Brutus is an honorable man.
He hath brought many captives home to Rome,
Whose ransoms did the general coffers fill:
Did this in Caesar seem ambitious?
When that the poor have cried, Caesar hath wept.
Ambition should be made of sterner stuff.
Yet Brutus says he was ambitious;
And Brutus is an honorable man.
You all did see, that, on the Lupercal,
I thrice presented him a kingly crown;
Which he did thrice refuse: Was this ambition?
Yet Brutus says he was ambitious;
And, sure, he is an honorable man.
I speak not to disprove what Brutus spoke;
But here I am, to speak what I do know.
You all did love him once; not without cause;—
What cause withholds you then to mourn for him?
O judgment! thou art fled to brutish beasts,
And men have lost their reason.—Bear with me:
My heart is in the coffin there with Caesar;
And I must pause till it come back to me.

3. But yesterday the word, Caesar, might
Have stood against the world! Now lies he there,
And none so poor to do him reverence.
O Masters! if I were disposed to stir
Your hearts and minds to mutiny and rage,
I should do Brutus wrong, and Cassius wrong,
Who, you all know, are honorable men.
I will not do them wrong—I rather choose
To wrong the dead, to wrong myself and you,
Than I will wrong such honorable men.

But here's a parchment, with the seal of Caesar.
I found it in his closet: 'tis his will.
Let but the commons hear his testament,
(Which, pardon me, I do not mean to read,)
And they would go and kiss dead Caesar's wounds,
And dip their napkins in his sacred blood;
Yea, beg a hair of him for memory,
And, dying, mention it within their wills,
Bequeathing it, as a rich legacy,
Unto their issue.

4. If you have tears, prepare to shed them now.
You all do know this mantle: I remember
The first time ever Caesar put it on;
'Twas on a summer's evening in his tent:
That day he overcame the Nervii—
Look! In this place ran Cassius' dagger through—
See what a rent the envious Casca made—
Through this the well-beloved Brutus stabbed;
And, as he plucked his cursed steel away,
Mark how the blood of Caesar followed it!
This, this was the unkindest cut of all!
For when the noble Caesar saw him stab,
Ingratitude, more strong than traitor's arms,
Quite vanquished him! Then burst his mighty
    heart,
And in his mantle muffling up his face,
Even at the base of Pompey's statue,
(Which all the while ran blood,) great Caesar fell.
O, what a fall was there, my countrymen!
Then I, and you, and all of us, fell down,
Whilst bloody treason flourished over us.
O, now you weep; and I perceive you feel
The dint of pity! These are gracious drops.
Kind souls! What, weep you when you but behold
Our Caesar's vesture wounded? Look ye here!
Here is himself—marred, as you see, by traitors.

5. Good friends! Sweet friends! Let me not stir you
   up
To any sudden flood of mutiny.
They that have done this deed, are honorable.
What private griefs they have, alas! I know not,
That made them do it. They are wise and
   honorable,
And will, no doubt, with reason answer you.
I come not, friends, to steal away your hearts!
I am no orator, as Brutus is;
But, as you know me all, a plain, blunt man,
That love my friend—and that they know full well,
That gave me public leave to speak of him!
For I have neither wit, nor words, nor worth,
Action, nor utterance, nor power of speech,
To stir men's blood—I only speak right on.
I tell you that which you yourselves do know—
Show you sweet Caesar's wounds, poor, poor,
   dumb mouths,
And bid them speak for me. But, were I Brutus,
And Brutus Antony, there were an Antony
Would ruffle up your spirits, and put a tongue
In every wound of Caesar, that should move
The stones of Rome to rise and mutiny.

QUESTIONS.—1. Who was Casca?   2. Where was Pompey's
statue situated?   3. Was Antony sincere in disavowing an
intention to "stir the Romans up to mutiny?"   4. Why does he
express such respect for Brutus?   5. Relate the story of Caesar's
death.

ERRORS.—*Griev-yus* for griev-ous (pronounced *griev-us*);
coff'n for cof-fin.

SPELL AND DEFINE.—(1) interred, grievously; (2) ambitious,
captives, judgment; (3) disposed, mutiny, parchment, testament;
(4) envious, vanquished, ingratitude, gracious, vesture, marred;
(5) utterance, ruffle.

LESSON CVII.

RULE.—Pronounce the consonant sounds very distinctly.

EXAMPLE.—Prolong the consonant sounds that are itali-cized,—*b*-old, *d*-eign, *f*-ather, *g*-ather, *j*-oy, *l*-ight, *m*-an, *n*-o, *q*-ueer, p-*r*-ay, *v*-ale, *w*-oe, *y*-ours, *z*-one, *h*-ang.

Egyptian Mummies, Tombs, and Manners.—BELZONI.

1. Gournou is a tract of rocks about two miles in length, at the foot of the Lybian mountains, on the west of Thebes, and was the burial-place of the great city of a hundred gates. Every part of these rocks is cut out by art, in the form of large and of small chambers, each of which has its separate entrance. Though they are very close to each other, it is seldom that there is any interior communication from one to another. I can truly say it is impossible to give any description sufficient to convey the smallest idea of those subterranean abodes and their inhabitants. There are no sepulchers in any part of the world like them. There are no excavations, or mines, that can be compared to these truly astonishing places, and no exact description can be given of their interior, owing to the difficulty of visiting these recesses. The inconvenience of entering into them is such that it is not everyone who can support the exertion.

2. A traveler is generally satisfied when he has seen the large hall, the gallery, the staircase, and as far as he can conveniently go. Besides, he is taken up with the strange works he observes cut in various places, and painted on each side of the walls, so that when he comes to a narrow and difficult passage, or a de-scent to the bottom of a well or cavity, he declines taking such trouble, naturally supposing that he can-not see in these abysses anything so magnificent as

what he sees above, and consequently deeming it useless to proceed any farther.

3. Of some of these tombs many persons could not withstand the suffocating air, which often causes fainting. A vast quantity of dust rises, so fine that it enters into the throat and nostrils, and chokes the nose and mouth to such a degree, that it requires great power of lungs to resist it, and the strong effluvia of the mummies. This is not all. The entry or passage where the bodies are, is roughly cut in the rocks, and the falling of the sand from the upper part or ceiling of the passage causes it to be nearly filled up. In some places there is not more than a vacancy of a foot left, which you must contrive to pass through in a creeping posture like a snail, on pointed and keen stones, that cut like glass.

4. After getting through these passages, some of them two or three hundred yards long, you generally find a more commodious place, perhaps high enough to sit. But what a place of rest! surrounded by bodies, by heaps of mummies in all directions, which, previous to my being accustomed to the sight, impressed me with horror. The blackness of the wall, the faint light given by the candles or torches for want of air, the different objects that surrounded me, seeming to converse with each other, and the Arabs with the candles or torches in their hands, naked and covered with dust, themselves resembling living mummies, absolutely formed a scene that cannot be described. In such a situaton I found myself several times, and often returned exhausted and fainting, till at last I became inured to it, and indifferent to what I suffered, except from the dust, which never failed to choke my throat and nose. Fortunately, I am destitute of the sense of smelling, but I could taste that the mummies were rather unpleasant to swallow.

5. After the exertion of entering into such a place, through a passage of fifty, a hundred, three hundred, or perhaps six hundred yards, nearly overcome, I sought a resting-place, found one, and contrived to sit, but when my weight bore on the body of an Egyptian, it crushed like a bandbox. I naturally had recourse to my hands to sustain my weight, but they found no better support, so that I sank altogether among the broken mummies, with a crash of bones, rags, and wooden cases, which raised such a dust as kept me motionless for a quarter of an hour, waiting till it subsided again. I could not remove from the place, however, without increasing it, and every step I took I crushed a mummy in some part or other.

6. Once I was conducted from such a place to another resembling it, through a passage of about twenty feet in length, and no wider than what a body could be forced through. It was choked with mummies, and I could not pass without putting my face in contact with that of some decayed Egyptian, but as the passage inclined downwards, my own weight helped me on. I could not avoid being covered with bones, legs, arms, and heads, rolling from above. Thus I proceeded from one cave to another, all full of mummies piled up in various ways, some standing, some lying, and some on their heads.

7. The purpose of my researches was to rob the Egyptians of their papyri, of which I found a few hidden in their breasts under their arms, in the space above the knees, or on the legs, and covered by the numerous folds of cloth that envelop the mummy. The people of Gournou, who make a trade of antiquities of this sort, are very jealous of strangers, and keep them as secret as possible, deceiving travelers, by pretending that they have arrived at the end of the pits, when they are scarcely at the entrance. * * *

8. I must not omit, that among these tombs we saw

some which contained the mummies of animals inter-mixed with human bodies. There were bulls, cows, sheep, monkeys, foxes, bats, crocodiles, fishes, and birds in them. Idols often occur; and one tomb was filled with nothing but cats, carefully folded in red and white linen, the head covered by a mask repre-senting the cat, and made of the same linen. I have opened all these sorts of animals. Of the bull, the calf, and the sheep, there is no part but the head which is covered with linen, and the horns project out of the cloth; the rest of the body being represented by two pieces of wood, eighteen inches wide, and three feet long, in a horizontal direction, at the end of which was another, placed perpendicularly, two feet high, to form the breast of the animal.

9. The calves and sheep are of the same structure, and large in proportion to the bulls. The monkey is in its full form, in a sitting posture. The fox is squeezed up by the bandages, but in some measure the shape of the head is kept perfect. The crocodile is left in its own shape, and after being well bound round with linen, the eyes and mouth are painted on this covering. The birds are squeezed together, and lose their shape, except the ibis, which is found like a fowl ready to be cooked, and bound round with linen like all the rest. * * *

10. The next sort of mummy that drew my atten-tion, I believe I may with reason conclude to have been appropriated to the priests. They are folded in a manner totally different from the others, and so carefully executed, as to show the great respect paid to those personages. The bandages are stripes of red and white linen intermixed, covering the whole body, and producing a curious effect from the two colors. The arms and legs are not enclosed in the same envelope with the body, as in the common mode, but are bandaged separately, even the fingers and toes

being preserved distinct. They have sandals of painted leather on their feet, and bracelets on their arms and wrists. They are always found with the arms across the breast, but not pressing it, and though the body is bound with such a quantity of linen, the shape of the person is carefully preserved in every limb. The cases in which mummies of this sort are found, are somewhat better executed, and I have seen one that had the eyes and eyebrows of enamel, beautifully executed in imitation of nature. * * *

11. The dwelling place of the natives is generally in the passages, between the first and second entrance into a tomb. The walls and the roof are as black as any chimney. The inner door is closed up with mud, except a small aperture sufficient for a man to crawl through. Within this place the sheep are kept at night, and occasionally accompany their masters in their vocal concert. Over the doorway there are always some half-broken Egyptian figures, and the two foxes, the usual guardians of burial-places. A small lamp, kept alive by fat from the sheep, or rancid oil, is placed in a niche in the wall, and a mat is spread on the ground. This formed the grand divan wherever I was.

12 There the people assembled round me, their conversation turning wholly on antiquities. Such a one had found such a thing, and another had discovered a tomb. Various articles were brought to sell to me, and sometimes I had reason to rejoice at having stayed there. I was sure of a supper of milk and bread served in a wooden bowl, but whenever they supposed I should stay all night, they always killed a couple of fowls for me, which were baked in a small oven heated with pieces of mummy cases, and sometimes with the bones and rags of the mummies themselves. It is no uncommon thing to sit down near fragments of bones: hands, feet, or skulls, are often in the way, for these people are so accustomed to be among the

mummies, that they think no more of sitting on them than on the skins of their dear calves. I also became indifferent about them at last, and would have slept in a mummy pit as readily as out of it.

13. Here they appear to be contented. The laborer comes home in the evening, seats himself near his cave, smokes his pipe with his companions, and talks of the last inundation of the Nile, its products, and what the ensuing season is likely to be. His old wife brings him the usual bowl of lentils and bread moistened with water and salt, and (when she can add a little butter) it is a feast. Knowing nothing beyond this, he is happy. The young man's chief business is to accumulate the amazing sum of a hundred piastres (eleven dollars and ten cents,) to buy himself a wife, and to make a feast on the wedding day.

14. If he has any children, they want no clothing. He leaves them to themselves till mother Nature pleases to teach them to work, to gain money enough to buy a shirt or some other rag to cover themselves, for while they are children they are generally naked or covered with rags. The parents are roguishly cunning, and the children are schooled by their example, so that it becomes a matter of course to cheat strangers. Would anyone believe that, in such a state of life, luxury and ambition exist? If any woman be destitute of jewels, she is poor, and looks with envy on one more fortunate than herself, who perhaps has the worth of half a crown round her neck, and she who has a few glass beads, or some sort of coarse coral, a couple of silver brooches, or rings on her arms and legs, is considered as truly rich and great. Some of them are as complete coquettes, in their way, as any to be seen in the capitals of Europe.

15. When a young man wants to marry, he goes to the father of the intended bride, and agrees with him what he is to pay for her. This being settled, so

much money is to be spent on the wedding day feast. To set up housekeeping, nothing is requisite but two or three earthen pots, a stone to grind meal, and a mat which is the bed. The spouse has a gown and jewels of her own, and if the bridegroom presents her with a pair of bracelets of silver, ivory, or glass, she is happy and fortunate indeed.

16. The house is ready, without rent or taxes. No rain can pass through the roof; and there is no door, for there is no want of one, as there is nothing to lose. They make a kind of box of clay and straw, which, after two or three days' exposure to the sun, becomes quite hard. It is fixed on a stand, an aperture is left to put all their precious things into it, and a piece of mummy case forms the door. If the house does not please them, they walk out and enter another, as there are several hundreds at their command. I might say several thousands, but they are not all fit to receive inhabitants.

QUESTIONS.—1. Where are the Lybian mountains?   2. Do you know anything of the history of Thebes?   3. Why do so few travelers succed in penetrating to the bottom of the tombs? 4. Mention some of the sources of annoyance in exploring them.   5. What was the result when Belzoni attempted to rest upon a mummy?   6. Are there any animals found embalmed? 7. What was Belzoni's object in exploring these tombs?   8. Why did he value the bits of Papyrus?   9. Describe the furniture of the dwelling places of the natives.

ERRORS.—*Bel-zo-ni* to be pronounced Belt-zo-nee; *swal-ler* for swal-low; *set* for sit; *pos-ter* for pos-ture; *per-pen-dic'-lar-ly* for per-pen-dic-u-lar-ly; *brass-let* for brace-let; *pa-pur-us* for pa-py-rus.

SPELL AND DEFINE.—(1) Lybian, subterranean, inconvenience, sepulchers;   (2) cavity, abysses, magnificent; (3) suffocating, effluvia;   (4) commodious, torches, exhausted; (6) contact;   (7) papyri, antiquities;   (8) horizontal, perpendicularly;   (10) appropriated, intermixed.

LESSON CVIII.

RULE.—Be careful to speak little words, such as *a*, *in*, *at*, *on*, *to*, *by*, etc., very distinctly, and yet not to dwell on them so long as on the more important words.

Address to the Mummy
in Belzoni's Exhibition, London.

NEW MONTHLY MAG.

1. And thou hast walk'd about (how strange a
      story!)
   In Thebes' streets three thousand years ago,
   When the Memnonium was in all its glory,
   And time had not begun to overthrow
   Those temples, palaces, and piles stupendous,
   Of which the very ruins are tremendous.

2. Speak! for thou long enough hast acted Dummy,
   Thou hast a tongue—come, let us hear its tune;
   Thou'rt standing on thy legs, above ground,
      Mummy!
   Revisiting the glimpses of the moon,
   Not like thin ghosts or disembodied creatures,
   But with thy bones and flesh, and limbs and
      features.

3. Tell us—for doubtless thou canst recollect,
   To whom should we assign the sphinx's fame?
   Was Cheops or Cephrenes architect
   Of either Pyramid that bears his name?
   Is Pompey's pillar really a misnomer?
   Had Thebes a hundred gates as sung by Homer?

4. Perhaps thou wert a Mason, and forbidden
   By oath to tell the mysteries of thy trade,
   Then say what secret melody was hidden
   In Memnon's statue that at sunrise played?

Perhaps thou wert a Priest—if so, my struggles
Are vain;—Egyptian priests ne'er owned their
    juggles

5. Perchance that very hand, now pinioned flat,
  Has hobb-a-nobb'd with Pharoah glass to glass;
  Or dropped a halfpenny in Homer's hat,
  Or doffed thine own to let Queen Dido pass,
  Or held, by Solomon's own invitation,
  A torch at the great Temple's dedication.

6. I need not ask thee if that hand, when armed,
  Has any Roman soldier mauled and knuckled,
  For thou wert dead, and buried, and embalmed,
  Ere Romulus and Remus had been suckled:—
  Antiquity appears to have begun
  Long after thy primeval race was run.

7. Since first thy form was in this box extended,
  We have, above ground, seen some strange
    mutations;
  The Roman empire has begun and ended;
  New worlds have risen—we have lost old nations,
  And countless kings have into dust been
    humbled,
  While not a fragment of thy flesh has crumbled.

8. Didst thou not hear the pother o'er thy head,
  When the great Persian conqueror, Cambyses,
  March'd armies o'er thy tomb with thundering
    tread,
  O'erthrew Osiris, Orus, Apis, Isis,
  And shook the Pyramids with fear and wonder,
  When the gignatic Memnon fell asunder?

9. If the tomb's secrets may not be confessed,
  The nature of thy private life unfold:—
  A heart has throbb'd beneath that leathern
    breast,

And tears adown that dusky cheek have rolled:—
Have children climb'd those knees, and kissed
   that face?
What was thy name and station, age and race?

10. Statue of flesh—immortal of the dead!
Imperishable type of evanescence!
Posthumous man, who quitt'st thy narrow bed,
And standest undecayed within our presence,
Thou wilt hear nothing till the Judgment
   morning
When the great trump shall thrill thee with its
   warning.

11. Why should this worthless tegument endure,
If its undying guest be lost forever?
O let us keep the soul embalmed and pure
In living virtue; that when both must sever,
Although corruption may our frame consume,
Th' immortal spirit in the skies may bloom.

QUESTIONS.—1. What was the Memnonium?   2. Relate the
fable of Memnon's statue. 3. Who were Romulus and Remus?
4. Osiris?   5. Apis?   6. Isis?   7. What moral lesson is deduced?

ERRORS.—*Ar-che-tect* for ar-chi-tect (pronouned ar-ke-tect);
The-bes for Thebes; *spir-ut* for spir-it.

SPELL AND DEFINE.—(1) memnonium, stupendous;
(2) revisiting; (3) pyramid, misnomer; (4) mysteries, juggles;
(5) pinioned;   (6) mauled, primeval;   (7) mutations;
(10) evanescence, posthumous;   (11) tegument.

LESSON CIX.

RULE.—When two or more consonants come together, let the pupil be careful to sound every one distinctly.

EXERCISES UNDER THE RULE.

He clenched his *fists*.
He *lifts* his awful form.
He makes his *payments*.
Thou *smoothed'st* his rugged path.
The *president's speech*.

On the Value of Studies.—LORD BACON.

1. Studies serve for delight, for ornament, and for ability. Their chief use for delight, is in retired privacy; for ornament, in discourse; and for ability, in the arrangement and disposition of business. Expert men can execute, and, perhaps, judge of particulars, one by one; but general councils, and the plots and marshaling of affairs, come best from the learned. To spend too much time in studies is slothfulness. To use them too much for ornament is affectation. To form one's judgment wholly by their rules is the humor of a scholar. They perfect nature, and are perfected by experience. Natural abilities are like natural plants, and need pruning by study. Studies themselves give forth directions too much at large, unless they are hedged in by experience.

2. Crafty men condemn studies. Simple men admire, and wise men use them, for they teach not their own use, but that is a wisdom without them and above them, won by observation. Read not to contradict and confute, nor to believe or take for granted, nor to find matter merely for conversation, but to weigh and consider. Some books are to be tasted; others, to be swallowed; and some few, to be chewed and digested; that is, some books are to be only glanced at; others are to be read, but not critically; and some few are to be read wholly, and with diligence and attention. Some books, also may be read by

deputy, and extracts received from them which are made by others. They should be only the meaner sort of books, and the less important arguments of those which are better. Otherwise, distilled books are, like common, distilled waters, flashy things.

3. Reading makes a full man; conversation, a ready man; and writing, an exact man. Therefore, if a man writes little, he needs a great memory. If he converses little, he wants a present wit, and, if he reads little, he ought to have much cunning, that he may seem to know what he does not. History makes men wise; poetry makes them witty; mathematics, subtle; natural philosophy, deep; moral philosophy, grave; logic and rhetoric, able to contend: nay, there is no obstruction to the human faculties but what may be overcome by proper studies. Obstacles to learning, like the diseases of the body, are removed by appropriate exercises.

4. Thus, bowling is good for a weakness in the back; gunning, for the lungs and breast; walking, for the stomach; riding for the head, and the like; so, if one's thoughts are wandering, let him study mathematics; for, in demonstrating, if his attention be called away ever so little, he must begin again. If his faculties be not disciplined to distinguish and discriminate, let him study the schoolmen, for they are (*cymini sectores*) the cutters of cummin. If he is not accustomed to con over matters, and call up one fact with which to prove and illustrate another, let him study the lawyers' cases. Hence, every defect of the mind may have its special receipt.

5. There are three chief vanities in studies, by which learning has been most traduced, for we deem those things vain which are either false or frivolous— which have no truth, or are of no use. Those persons are considered vain, who are either credulous or curious. Judging, then, either from reason or

experience, there prove to be three distempers of learning: the first is fantastical learning, the second, contentious learning, and the last, affected learning —vain imaginations, vain altercations, and vain affections.

QUESTIONS.—1. What is said of the influence of study upon the natural abilities? 2. For what purpose should we read? 3. Are all books to be read in the same manner? 4. What is said of abridgments? 5. What influence has the reading of history upon the mind? 6. Poetry? 7. Mathematics? 8. Logic and rhetoric? 9. Who are "the schoolmen?"

ERRORS.—*Per-tic-'lars* for par-tic-u-lars; *nat-ter-al* for nat-u-ral; *ar-gy-ment* for ar-gu-ment; *po-'try* for po-e-try; *dem'-en-tra-ting* for de-mon'-stra-ting.

SPELL AND DEFINE.—(1) ornament, ability, arrangement, councils, affectation; (2) condemn, conversation; (4) mathematics, demonstrating; (5) frivolous, imaginations.

LESSON CX.

RULE.—Be careful to pronounce every syllable distinctly.

Natural Ties among the Western States.

DR. DRAKE.

1. Let us leave the history and resume the physical and political geography of the West for the purpose of considering the relations of its different regions— not to the *Atlantic States,* but to *each other.* In reviewing their boundaries and connections, we find much to excite reflection and inspire us with deep emotion. The geography of the interior, in truth, ad-

monishes us to live in harmony, cherish uniform plans of education, and found similar institutions. The relations between the upper and lower Mississippi States, established by the collective waters of the whole Valley, must forever continue unchanged. What the towering oak is to our climbling winter grape, the "Father of Waters" must ever be to the communities along its trunk and countless tributary streams—an imperishable support, an exhaustless power of union. What is the composition of its lower coasts and alluvial plains, but the soil of all the upper states and territories, transported, commingled, and deposited by its waters?

2. Within her own limits, Louisiana has indeed, the rich mould of ten sister states, which have thus contributed to the fertility of her plantations. It might almost be said that for ages this region has sent thither a portion of its soil, where, in a milder climate, it might produce the cotton, oranges and sugar, which, through the same channel, we receive in exchange for the products of our corn fields, work shops, and mines. Facts which prepare the way, and invite to perpetual union between the West and South.

3. The state of Tennessee, separated from Alabama and Mississippi on the south, and Kentucky on the north, by no natural barrier, has its southern fields overspread with floating cotton, wafted from the two first by every autumnal breeze, while the shade of its northern woods, lies for half the summer day on the borders of the last. The songs and uproar of a Kentucky *husking* are answered from Tennessee, and the midnight racoon-hunt that follows, beginning in one state, is concluded in the other.

4. The Cumberland, on whose rocky banks the capital of Tennessee rises in beauty, begins and terminates in Kentucky—thus bearing on its bosom at the same moment, the products of the two states

descending to a common market. Still further, the fine river Tennessee drains the eastern half of that state, dips into Alabama, recrosses the state in which it arose, and traverses Kentucky to reach the Ohio river, thus uniting the three into one natural and enduring commercial compact.

5. Further north, the cotton trees which fringe the borders of Missouri and Illinois, throw their images toward each other in the waters of the Mississippi—the toiling emigrant's axe, in the depths of the leafless woods, and the crash of the falling rail-tree on the frozen earth, resound equally among the hills of both states—the clouds of smoke from their burning prairies, mingle in the air above, and crimson the setting sun of Kentucky, Indiana and Ohio.

6. The pecan tree sheds its fruit at the same moment among the people of Indiana and Illinois, and the boys of the two states paddle their canoes and fish together in the Wabash, or hail each other from opposite banks. Even villages belong equally to Indiana and Ohio, and the children of the two commonwealths trundle their hoops together in the same street.

7. But the Ohio river forms the most interesting boundary among the republics of the West. For a thousand miles its fertile bottoms are cultivated by farmers who belong to the different states, while they visit each other as friends or neighbors. As the school boy trips or loiters along its shores, he greets his playmates across the stream, or they sport away an idle hour in its summer waters. These are to be among the future, perhaps the opposing statesmen of the different commonwealths.

8. When, at low water, we examine the rocks of the channel, we find them the same on both sides. The plants which grow above, drop their seeds into the common current, which lodges them indiscriminately

on either shore. Thus the very trees and flowers emigrate from one republic to another. When the bee tree sends out its swarms, they as often seek a habitation beyond the stream, as in their woods.

9 Throughout its whole extent, the hills of Western Virginia and Kentucky, cast their morning shadows on the plains of Ohio, Indiana, Illinois, and Missouri. The thunder cloud pours down its showers on different commonwealths, and the rainbow resting its extremities on two sister states, presents a beautiful arch, on which the spirits of peace may pass and repass in harmony and love.

10. Thus connected by nature in the great valley, we must live in the bonds of companionship, or imbrue our hands in each other's blood. We have no middle destiny. To secure the former to our posterity, we should begin while society is still tender and pliable. The saplings of the woods, if intertwined, will adapt themselves to each other and grow together. The little bird may hang its nest on the twigs of different trees, and the dewdrops fall successively on leaves which are nourished by distinct trunks. The tornado strikes harmlessly on such a bower, for the various parts sustain each other, but the grown tree, sturdy and set in its way, will not bend to its fellow, and when uprooted by the tempest, is dashed with violence against all within its reach.

11. Communities, like forests grow rigid by time. To be properly trained they must be molded while young. Our duty, then, is quite obvious. All who have moral power, should exert it in concert. The germs of harmony must be nourished, and the roots of present contrariety or future discord, torn up and cast into the fire. Measures should be taken to mold an uniform system of manners and customs, out of the diversified elements which are scattered over the West.

12. Literary meetings should be held in the different states, and occasional conventions in the central cities of the great valley, be made to bring into friendly consultation, our enlightened and zealous teachers, professors, lawyers, physicians, divines, and men of letters, from its remotest sections. In their deliberations, the literary and moral wants of the various regions might be made known, and the means of supplying them devised.

13. The whole should successively lend a helping hand to all the parts, on the great subject of education, from the primary school to the University. Statistical facts, bearing on this absorbing interest, should be brought forward and collected; the systems of common school instruction should be compared, and the merits of different school books, foreign and domestic, freely canvassed.

14. Plans of education, adapted to the natural, commercial, and social condition of the interior, should be invented, a correspondence instituted, among all our higher seminaries of learning, and an interchange established of all local publications on the subject of education. In short, we should foster western genius, encourage western writers, patronize western publishers, augment the number of western readers, and create a western heart.

15. When these great objects shall come seriously to occupy our minds, the union will be secure, for its center will be sound, and its attraction on the surrounding parts irresistible. Then will our state governments emulate each other in works for the common good; the people of remote places begin to feel as the members of one family, and our whole intelligent and virtuous population unite, heart and hand, in one long, concentrated, untiring effort, to raise still higher the social character, and perpetuate forever, the political harmony of the green and growing WEST.

QUESTIONS.—1. What river establishes a commercial and social connection between Missouri and Louisiana? 2. What states are bound together by the Tennessee river? 3. What states does the Ohio river bind together? 4. In what manner will harmony among the western states perpetuate the Union?

ERRORS.—*Ruz-zume* for re-sume; *trib-er-ta-ry* for trib-u-ta-ry; *trav-us-ses* for trav-ers-es; *ex-treme-i-ties* for ex-trem-i-ties; *ub-sorb* for ab-sorb.

SPELL AND DEFINE.—(1) physical, connections; (3) barrier; (4) terminates; (5) emigrants; (7) cultivated, commonwealth; (8) habitation; (11) diversified; (14) commercial, correspondence; (15) concentrated.

LESSON CXI.

RULE.—Let the pupil stand at as great a distance from the teacher as possible, and then try to read so loud and distinctly that the teacher may hear each syllable.

The Venomous Worm.—JOHN RUSSELL.

—"Outvenoms all the worms of Nile."—
Shakespeare.

1. Who has not heard of the rattlesnake or copperhead? An unexpected sight of either of these reptiles will make even the lords of creation recoil, but there is a species of worm, found in various parts of this state, which conveys a poison of a nature so deadly, that, compared with it, even the venom of the rattlesnake is harmless. To guard our readers against this foe of human kind is the object of this lesson.

2. This worm varies much in size. It is frequently an inch in diameter, but, as it is rarely seen, except

when coiled, its length can hardly be conjectured. It is of a dull lead color, and generally lives near a spring or small stream of water, and bites the unfortunate people who are in the *habit of going there to drink.* The brute creation it never molests. They avoid it with the same instinct that teaches the animals of Peru to shun the deadly coya.

3.　Several of these reptiles have long infested our settlements, to the misery and destruction of many of our fellow citizens. I have, therefore, had frequent opportunities of being the melancholy spectator of the effects produced by the subtle poison which this worm infuses.

4.　The symptoms of its bite are terrible. The eyes of the patient become red and fiery, his tongue swells to an immoderate size, and obstructs his utterance, and delirium of the most horrid character quickly follows. Sometimes, in his madness he attempts the destruction of his nearest friends.

5.　If the sufferer has a family, his weeping wife and helpless infants are not unfrequently the objects of his frantic fury. In a word, he exhibits, to the life, all the detestable passions that rankle in the bosom of a savage. Such is the spell in which his senses are locked, that, no sooner has the unhappy patient recovered from the paroxysm of insanity, occasioned by the bite, than he seeks out the *destroyer* for the sole purpose of being *bitten again.*

6.　I have seen a good old father, his locks as white as snow, his steps slow and trembling, beg in vain of his only *son* to quit the lurking place of the worm. My heart bled when he turned away, for I knew the fond hope that his son would be the "staff of his declining years," had supported him through many a sorrow.

7.　Youths of America, would you know the name of this reptile? It is called the *Worm of the Still.*

QUESTIONS.—1. Why is intemperance worse than the bite of the most venomous serpent? 2. What is the coya?

ERRORS.—*Re-kile* for re-coil; *'genst* for a-gainst; *sub-tle* pronounced sut-tle.

SPELL AND DEFINE.—(1) copperhead, reptiles, recoil, venom; (2) unfortunate, molest; (3) infested, infuses; (5) rankle; (6) declining.

LESSON CXII.

RULE.—In reading poetry, be careful not to join the final consonant of one word to the vowel of the next word.

EXAMPLE.—Loud as his thunder shout his praise
And sound it lofty as his throne.

The following way of reading it, shows the fault to be remedied, by observing the rule.

Loud as his thunder shout his praise
And soun dit lofty as his throne.

The Better Land.— MRS. HEMANS.

1. "I hear thee speak of the better land;
   Thou call'st its children a happy band;
   Mother! oh, where is that radiant shore?
   Shall we not seek it, and weep no more?
   Is it where the flower of the orange blows,
   And the fireflies dance through the myrtle
       boughs?"
               —"Not there, not there, my child!"

2. "Is it where the feathery palm trees rise,
   And the date grows ripe under sunny skies?
   Or midst the green islands of glittering seas,
   Where fragrant forests perfume the breeze,
   And strange bright birds, on their starry wings,
   Bear the rich hues of all glorious things?"
               —"Not there, not there, my child!"

3. "Is it far away, in some region old,
Where the rivers wander o'er sands of gold,
Where the burning rays of the ruby shine,
And the diamond lights up the secret mine,
And the pearl gleams forth from the coral strand?
Is it there, sweet mother! that better land?"
— "Not there, not there, my child!

4. "Eye hath not seen it, my gentle boy!
Ear hath not heard its deep sounds of joy;
Dreams cannot picture a world so fair;
Sorrow and death may not enter there;
Time doth not breathe on its fadeless bloom,
Beyond the clouds, and beyond the tomb;
—It is there, it is there, my child!"

QUESTIONS.—What climate produces the myrtle, palm. and date? 2. Why is the palm tree called feathery?

SPELL AND DEFINE.—(1) radiant; (2) glittering, fragrant; (3) gleams, diamond, coral, region.

LESSON CXIII.

RULE.—When similar sounds come at the end of one word, and at the beginning of the next word, they must not be blended into one.

EXERCISES.—He sink*s s*orrowing to the tomb.
Man love*s s*ociety.
Time flie*s s*wiftly.
The bird*s s*ing.

Benefits of Literature.—LORD LYTTLETON.

1. *Hercules.* Do you pretend to sit as high on Olympus as Hercules? Did you kill the Nemaean lion, the Erymanthian boar, the Lernean serpent, and Stymphalian birds? Did you destroy tyrants and robbers?

You value yourself greatly on subduing one serpent. I did as much as that while I lay in my cradle.

2. *Cadmus.* It is not on account of the serpent that I boast myself a greater benefactor to Greece than you. Actions should be valued by their utility, rather than their splendor. I taught Greece the art of writing, to which laws owe their precision and permanency. You subdued monsters. I civilized men. It is from untamed passions, not from wild beasts, that the greatest evils arise to human society. By wisdom, by art, by the united strength of a civil community, men have been enabled to subdue the whole race of lions, bears, and serpents; and, what is more, to bind by laws and wholesome regulation, the ferocious violence and dangerous treachery of the human disposition. Had lions been destroyed only in single combat, men had had but a bad time of it, and what, but laws, could awe the men who killed the lions? The genuine glory, the proper distinction of the rational species, arises from the perfection of the mental powers. Courage is apt to be fierce, and strength is often exerted in acts of oppression, but wisdom is the associate of justice. It assists her to form equal laws, to pursue right measures, to correct power, protect weakness, and to unite individuals in a common interest and general welfare. Heroes may kill tyrants, but it is wisdom and laws that prevent tyranny and oppression. The operations of policy far surpass the labors of Hercules, preventing many evils which valor and might cannot even redress. You heroes regard nothing but glory and scarcely consider whether the conquests, which raise your fame, are really beneficial to your country. Unhappy are the people who are governed by valor not directed by prudence, and not mitigated by the gentle arts!

3. *Hercules.* I do not expect to find an admirer of my strenuous life, in the man who taught his coun-

trymen to sit still and read, and to lose the hours of youth and action in idle speculation and the sport of words.

4. *Cadmus*. An ambition to have a place in the registers of fame is the Eurystheus which imposes heroic labors on mankind. The Muses incite to action, as well as entertain the hours of repose, and I think you should honor them for presenting to heroes so noble a recreation, as may prevent their taking up the distaff when they lay down the club.

5. *Hercules*. Wits as well as heroes can take up the distaff. What think you of their thin-spun systems of philosophy, or lascivious poems, or Milesian fables? Nay, what is still worse, are there not panegyrics on tyrants, and books that blaspheme the gods, and perplex the natural sense of right and wrong? I believe if Eurystheus were to set me to work again, he would find me a worse task than any he imposed. He would make me read over a great library, and I would serve it as I did the Hydra, I would burn it as I went on, that one chimera might not rise from another, to plague mankind. I should have valued myself more on clearing the library, than on cleansing the Augean stables.

6. *Cadmus*. It is in those libraries only that the memory of your labor exists. The heroes of Marathon, the patriots of Thermoplyae, owe their fame to me. All the wise institutions of lawgivers, and all the doctrines of sages, had perished in the ear, like a dream related, if letters had not preserved them. O Hercules! It is not for the man who preferred Virtue to Pleasure, to be an enemy to the Muses. Let Sardanapalus and the silken sons of luxury, who have wasted life in inglorious ease, despise the records of action, which bear no honorable testimony to their lives, but true merit, heroic virtue, should respect the sacred source of lasting honor.

7. *Hercules.* Indeed, if writers employed themselves only in recording the acts of great men, much might be said in their favor. Why do they trouble people with their meditations? Can it be of any consequence to the world what an idle man has been thinking?

8. *Cadmus.* Yes it may. The most important and extensive advantages mankind enjoy, are greatly owing to men who have never quitted their closets. To them mankind are obliged for the facility and security of navigation. The invention of the compass has opened to them new worlds. The knowledge of the mechancial powers has enabled them to construct such wonderful machines, as perform what the united labor of millions, by the severest drudgery, could not accomplish. Agriculture too, the most useful of arts, has received its share of improvement from the same source. Poetry, likewise, is of excellent use, to enable the memory to retain with more ease, and to imprint with more energy upon the heart, precepts and examples of virtue. From the little root of a few letters, science has spread its branches over all nature, and raised its head to the heavens. Some philosophers have entered so far into the counsels of Divine Wisdom, as to explain much of the great operations of nature. The dimensions and distances of the planets, the causes of their revolutions, the path of comets, and the ebbing and flowing of tides, are understood and explained.

9. Can any thing raise the glory of the human species more, than to see a little creature, inhabiting a small spot, amidst innumerable worlds, taking a survey of the universe, comprehending its arrangement, and entering into the scheme of that wonderful connection and correspondence of things so remote, and which it seems a great exertion of Omnipotence to have established? What a volume of

wisdom, what a noble theology, do these discoveries open to us? While some superior geniuses have soared to these sublime subjects, other sagacious and diligent minds have been inquiring into the most minute works of the Infinite Artificer. The same care, the same providence, is exerted through the whole, and we should learn from it, that, to true wisdom, utility and fitness appear perfection, and whatever is beneficial is noble.

10. *Hercules*. I approve of science as far as it is an assistant to action. I like the improvement of navigation, and the discovery of the greater part of the globe, because it opens a wider field for the master spirits of the world to bustle in.

11. *Cadmus*. There spoke the soul of Hercules. But if learned men are to be esteemed for the assistance they give to active minds in their schemes, they are not less to be valued for their endeavors to give them a right direction, and moderate their too great ardor. The study of history will teach the legislature by what means states have become powerful, and in the private citizen, they will inculcate the love of liberty and order. The writings of sages point out a private path of virtue, and show that the best empire is self-government, and that subduing our passions is the noblest of conquests.

12. *Hercules*. The true spirit of patriotism acts by a generous impulse, and wants neither the experience of history, nor the doctrines of philosophers to direct it. But do not arts and science render men effeminate, luxurious, and inactive? Can you deny that wit and learning are often made subservient to very bad purposes?

13. *Cadmus*. I will own that there are some natures so happily formed, they scarcely want the assistance of a master, and the rules of art, to give them force or grace in every thing they do. But these favored

geniuses are few. Learning flourishes only where ease, plenty, and mild government subsists. In so rich a soil, and under so soft a climate, the weeds of luxury will spring up among the flowers of art, but the spontaneous weeds would grow more rank if they were allowed the undisturbed possession of the field. Letters keep a frugal, temperate nation from growing ferocious, a rich one from becoming entirely sensual and debauched. Every gift of heaven is sometimes abused, but good sense and fine talents, by a natural law, gravitate towards virtue. Accidents may drive them out of their proper direction, but such accidents are an alarming omen, and of dire portent to the times. For if virtue cannot keep to her allegiance those men, who in their hearts confess her divine right, and know the value of her laws, on whose fidelity and obedience can she depend? May such geniuses never descend to flatter vice, encourage folly, or propagate irreligion, but exert all their powers in the service of Virtue, and celebrate the noble choice of those, who, like Hercules, preferred her to Pleasure!

QUESTIONS.—1. Who was Hercules?   2. Can you enumerate some of the principal exploits of Hercules? 3. What is the difference between the character of the exploits of Hercules, and those of Cadmus?   4. Who was Cadmus?   5. What did Cadmus do?   6. How should actions be valued?   7. From what must the genuine glory of rational beings arise?   8. To which of his labors does Hercules compare the reading of a modern library? (the cleansing of it?)   9. Since so much trash and folly is written, what is the use of writers?   10. What does Hercules think of science?   11. What is patriotism?

ERRORS.—*Pur-tend* for pre-tend; *Her-cules* for Her-cu-les.

SPELL AND DEFINE.—(1) Olympus, Stymphalian; (2) wholesome, tyranny;   (3) strenuous;   (4) Eurystheus; (5) panegyrics, Augean;   (6) Marathon;   (8) philosophers; (9) omnipotence, infinite;   (13) ferocious.

LESSON CXIV.

RULE.—In reading poetry that does not rhyme, there should be no pause at the end of a line, except when it terminates with an important word, or the sense requires it.

Thalaba among the Ruins of Babylon.

SOUTHEY.

1. The many-colored domes*
   Yet wore one dusky hue;
   The cranes upon the mosque
   Kept their night clatter still;
   When through the gate the early traveler pass'd.
   And when, at evening, o'er the swampy plain
   The bittern's boom came far,
   Distinct in darkness seen,
   Above the low horizon's lingering light,
   Rose the near ruins of old Babylon.

2. Once, from her lofty walls the charioteer
   Look'd down on swarming myriads; once she flung
   Her arches o'er Euphrates' conquered tide,
   And, through her brazen portals when she poured
   Her armies forth, the distant nations looked
   As men who watch the thunder-cloud in fear,
   Lest it should burst above them.—She was
       fallen!
   The queen of cities, Babylon was fallen!
   Low lay her bulwarks; the black scorpion basked
   In palace courts: within the sanctuary
   The she-wolf hid her whelps.

3. Is yonder huge and shapeless heap, what once
   Hath been the aerial gardens, height on height
   Rising, like Media's mountains, crowned with
       wood,
   Work of imperial dotage? Where the fane

---

* Of Bagdad.

Of Belus? Where the golden image now,
Which, at the sound of dulcimer and lute,
Cornet and sackbut, harp and psaltery,
The Assyrian slaves adored?
A labyrinth of ruins, Babylon
Spreads o'er the blasted plain.
The wandering Arab never sets his tent
Within her walls. the shepherd eyes afar
Her evil towers, and devious drives his flock.
Alone unchanged, a free and bridgeless tide,
Euphrates rolls along,
Eternal nature's work.

4. Through the broken portal,
Over weedy fragments,
Thalaba went his way.
Cautious he trod, and felt
The dangerous ground before him with his bow.
The jackal started at his steps;
The stork, alarmed at sound of man,
From her broad nest upon the old pillar top,
Affrighted fled on flapping wings:
The adder, in her haunts disturbed,
Lanced at the intruding staff her arrowy tongue.

5. Twilight and moonshine, dimly mingling, gave
An awful light obscure:
Evening not wholly closed—
The moon still pale and faint,—
An awful light obscure,
Broken by many a mass of blackest shade;
Long columns stretching dark through weeds and
    moss;
Broad length of lofty wall,
Whose windows lay in light,
And of their former shape, low-arched or square,
Rude outline on the earth
Figured with long grass fringed.

6. Reclined against a column's broken shaft,
   Unknowing whitherward to bend his way,
   He stood and gazed around.
   The ruins closed him in:
   It seemed as if no foot of man
   For ages had intruded there.
   He stood and gazed awhile,
   Musing on Babel's pride, and Babel's fall;
   Then, through the ruined street,
   And through the farther gate,
   He passed in silence on.

QUESTIONS.—1. Where was Babylon situated, and of what the capital? 2. How could a charioteer look down from the walls? 3. Describe the "aerial gardens." 4. What were the dimensions of the temple of Belus? 5. Do you know anything relative to the golden image mentioned in this lesson? 6. From what book do you learn this story?

ERRORS.—*Eve-nin'* for e-ven-ing; *welps* for whelps; *dul-cer-mur* for dul-ci-mer; *with-er-ward* for whith-er-ward.

SPELL AND DEFINE.—(1) mosque; (2) charioteer, myriads, bulwarks; (3) imperial, dotage, dulcimer, psaltery, labyrinth; (4) portal, haunts; (6) column.

LESSON CXV.

RULE.—Be careful not to join the last part of one word to the beginning of the next word.

William Tell.—KNOWLES.

SCENE 1.—*A mountain with mist. Gesler seen descending with a hunting pole.*

Gesler. Alone—Alone! And every step the mist
Thickens around me! On these mountain tracks
To lose one's way, they say, is sometimes death!
What, Ho! Holloa! No tongue replies to me!
What thunder hath the horror of this silence!
Cursed slaves, to let me wander from them!
    Ho—Holloa!
My voice sounds weaker to mine ear; I've not
The strength to call I had; and through my limbs
Cold tremor runs—and sickening faintness seizes
On my heart. O, heaven, have mercy! Do not see
The color of the hands I lift to thee!
Look only on the strait wherein I stand,
And pity it! Let me not sink—Uphold!
Support me! Mercy! Mercy! (*He falls with faintness.*
    Albert enters, almost breathless with the fury of
    storm.)
Albert. I'll breathe upon this level, if the wind
Will let me. Ha! A rock to shelter me!
Thanks to it—a man! And fainting. Courage, friend!
Courage.—A stranger that has lost his way—
Take heart—take heart: you are safe. How feel you
    now?
Ges. Better.
Alb. You have lost your way upon the hills?
Ges. I have.
Alb. And whither would you go?
Ges. To Altorf.
Alb. I'll guide you thither.

Ges. You are a child.

Alb. I know the way; the track I've come
Is harder far to find.

Ges. The track you have come!—What mean you?
Sure You have not been still farther in the mountains?

Alb. I have traveled from Mount Faigel.

Ges. No one with thee?

Alb. No one but Him.

Ges. Do you not fear these storms?

Alb. He's in the storm.

Ges. And there are torrents, too,
That must be crossed?

Alb. He's by the torrent too.

Ges. You are but a child.

Alb. He will be with a child.

Ges. You are sure you know the way?

Alb. 'Tis but to keep the side of yonder stream.

Ges. But guide me safe, I'll give thee gold.

Alb. I'll guide thee safe without.

Ges. Here's earnest for thee. Here—I'll double that,
Yea, treble it—but let me see the gate of Altorf.
Why do you refuse the gold? Take it

Alb. No.

Ges. You shall.

Alb. I will not.

Ges. Why?

Alb. Because
I do not covet it;—and though I did,
It would be wrong to take it as the price
Of doing one a kindness.

Ges. Ha!—Who taught thee that?

Alb. My father.

Ges. Does he live in Altorf?

Alb. No; in the mountains.

Ges. How—a mountaineer?
He should become a tenant of the city:
He would gain by it.

Alb. Not so much as he might lose by it
Ges. What might he lose by it?
Alb. Liberty.
Ges. Indeed! He also taught thee that?
Alb. He did.
Ges. His name?
Alb. This is the way to Altorf, sir.
Ges. I would know thy father's name.
Alb. The day is wasting—we have far to go.
Ges. Thy father's name, I say?
Alb. I will not tell it thee.
Ges. Not tell it me! Why?
Alb. You may be an enemy of his.
Ges. May be a friend.
Alb. May be; but should you be
An enemy—although I would not tell you
My father's name—I would guide you safe to Altorf.
Will you follow me?
Ges. Never mind thy father's name;
What would it profit me to know it? Thy hand;
We are not enemies.
Alb. I never had an enemy.
Ges. Lead on.
Alb. Advance your staff
As you descend, and fix it well. Come on.
Ges. What! Must we take that steep?
Alb. 'Tis nothing! Come,
I'll go before. Never fear—come on! come on! (*Exit.*)

SCENE 2.—*The Gate of Altorf. Enter Gesler and Albert.*

Alb. You are at the gate of Altorf. (*Is returning.*)
Ges. Tarry, boy!
Alb. I would be gone; I am waited for.
Ges. Come back!
Who waits for thee? Come, tell me; I am rich
And powerful, and can reward.

Alb. 'Tis close
On evening; I have far to go; I'm late.

Ges. Stay! I can punish, too.
Boy, do you know me?

Alb. No.

Ges. Why fear you, then
To trust me with your father's name?—Speak.

Alb. Why do you desire to know it?

Ges. You have served me,
And I would thank him, if I chanced to pass
His dwelling.

Alb. 'Twould not please him that a service
So trifling should be made so much of.

Ges. Trifling! You have saved my life.

Alb. Then do not question me,
But let me go.

Ges. When I have learned from thee
Thy father's name. What, ho! (*Knocks.*)

Sentinel. (*Within.*) Who's there?

Ges. Gesler. (*Soldiers enter.*)

Alb. Ha, Gesler!

Ges. (*To the soldiers.*) Seize him. Wilt thou tell me
Thy father's name?

Alb. No.

Ges. I can bid them cast thee
Into a dungeon! Wilt thou tell it now?

Alb. No.

Ges. I can bid them strangle thee! Wilt tell it?

Alb. Never.

Ges. Away with him! Send Sarnem to me.
(*Soldiers take Albert off.*)
Behind that boy I see the shadow of
A hand must wear my fetters, or 'twill try
To strip me of my power. How I loathed the free
And fearless air with which he trod the hills!
I wished some way
To find the parent nest of this fine eaglet,

And harrow it! I'd like to clip the broad
And full grown wing that taught his tender pinion
So bold a flight. (*Enter Sarnem.*)
Ha, Sarnem! Have the slaves
Attended me returned?

   Sarnem. They have.

   Ges. You'll see
That every one of them be laid in fetters.

   Sar. I will.

   Ges. Did'st see that boy just now?

   Sar. That passed me?

   Ges. Yes.

   Sar. A mountaineer.

   Ges. You'd say so, saw you him
Upon the hills; he walks them like their lord!
I tell thee, Sarnem, looking on that boy,
I felt I was not master of those hills,
He has a father. Neither promises
Nor threats could draw from him his name—a father
Who talks to him of liberty. I fear that man.

   Sar. He may be found.

   Ges. He must—and soon
As found disposed of. I live
In danger till I find that man. Send parties
Into the mountains, to explore them far
And wide; and if they chance to light upon
A father, who expects his child, command them
To drag him straight before us. Sarnem, see it done.

                     (*Exit.*)

QUESTIONS.—1. Why does Gesler allude to the color of his
hands in line 11?   2. To what purpose is a hunting pole applied?
3. What is meant by, "Here's earnest for thee?"

ERRORS.—*Air-nest* for ear-nest (pronounced *er-nest*); *strangl'*
for stran-gle.

SPELL AND DEFINE.—tremor, breathe, mountaineer,
dungeon, eaglet, threats, straight.

LESSON CXVI.

RULE.—Be careful to pronounce the little words, like *a*, *the*, *and*, *in*, etc., distinctly, and not to join them to the next word.

William Tell.—CONTINUED.

SCENE 3.—*A chamber in the Castle. Enter Gesler, Officers, and Sarnem, with Tell in chains and guarded.*

Sar. Down, slave! Behold the governor.
Down! down! and beg for mercy.
　　Ges. (*Seated.*) Does he hear?
　　Sar. He does, but braves thy power.
　　Officer. Why don't you smite him for that look?
　　Ges. Can I believe
My eyes?—He smiles! Nay, grasps
His chains as he would make a weapon of them
To lay the smiter dead. (*To Tell.*)
Why speakest thou not?
　　Tell. For wonder
　　Ges. Wonder?
　　Tell. Yes, that thou should'st seem a man.
　　Ges. What should I seem?
　　Tell. A monster!
　　Ges. Ha! Beware—think on thy chains.
　　Tell. Though they were doubled, and did weigh me
　　　　down
Prostrate to earth, methinks I could rise up—
Erect, with nothing but the honest pride
Of telling thee, unsurper, to thy teeth,
Thou art a monster! Think upon my chains!
How came they on me?
　　Ges. Darest thou question me?
　　Tell. Darest thou not answer?
　　Ges. Do I hear?
　　Tell. Thou dost.
　　Ges. Beware my vengeance.
　　Tell. Can it more than kill?

Ges. Enough—it can do that.

Tell. No; not enough:
It cannot take away the grace of life—
Its comeliness of look that virtue gives—
Its port erect with consciousness of truth—
Its rich attire of honorable deeds—
Its fair report that's rife on good men's tongues:
It cannot lay its hands on these, no more
Than it can pluck the brightness from the sun,
Or with polluted finger tarnish it.

Ges. But it can make thee writhe.

Tell. It may.

Ges. And groan.

Tell. It may; and I may cry,
Go on, though it should make me groan again.

Ges. Whence comest thou?

Tell. From the mountains. Wouldst thou learn
What news from them?

Ges. Canst tell me any?

Tell. Ay; they watch no more the avalanche.

Ges. Why so?

Tell. Because they look for thee. The hurricane
Comes unawares upon them; from its bed,
The torrent breaks, and finds them in its track.

Ges. What do they then?

Tell. Thank heaven, it is not thou!
Thou hast perverted nature in them.
There's not a blessing heaven vouchsafes them, but
The thought of thee—doth wither to a curse.

Ges. That's right! I'd have them like their hills
That never smile, though wanton summer tempt
Them ever so much

Tell. But they do sometimes smile.

Ges. Ay!—When is that?

Tell. When they do talk of vengeance.

Ges. Vengeance! Dare they talk of that?

Tell. Ay, and expect it too.

Ges. From whence?

Tell. From heaven!

Ges. From heaven?

Tell. And their true hands
Are lifted up to it on every hill
For justice on thee.

Ges. Where's thy abode?

Tell. I told thee on the mountains,

Ges. Art married?

Tell. Yes.

Ges. And hast a family?

Tell. A son.

Ges. A son! Sarnem!

Sar. My lord, the boy.—(*Gesler signs to Sarnem to
    keep silence, and, whispering, sends him off.*)

Tell. The boy!—What boy?
Is't mine?—and have they netted my young
fledgeling?
Now heaven support me, if they have! He'll own me,
And share his father's ruin! But a look
Would put him on his guard—yet how to give it!
Now, heart, thy nerve; forget thou art flesh, be rock.
They come—they come.
That step—that step—that little step, so light
Upon the ground, how heavy does it fall
Unon my heart! I feel my child!—(*Enter Sarnem with
    Albert, whose eyes are riveted on Tell's bow,
    which Sarnem carries.*)
'Tis he!—We can but perish.

Sar. See!

Alb. What?

Sar. Look there!

Alb. I do, what would you have me see?

Sar. Thy father.

Alb. Who? That—that my father!

Tell. My boy—my boy!—My own brave boy!
He's safe! (*Aside.*)

Sar. (*Aside to Gesler.*) They're like each other.

Ges. Yet I see no sign
Or recognition to betray the link
Unites a father and his child.

Sar. My lord,
I am sure it is his father. Look at them.
It may be
A preconcerted thing 'gainst such a chance,
That they survey each other coldly thus.

Ges. We shall try. Lead forth the caitiff.

Sar. To a dungeon?

Ges. No; into the court.

Sar. The court, my lord?

Ges. And send
To tell the headsman to make ready. Quick!
The slave shall die! You marked the boy?

Sar. I did. He started—'tis his father.

Ges. We shall see. Away with him!

Tell. Stop!—Stop!

Ges. What would you?

Tell. Time! A little time to call my thoughts
together.

Ges. Thou shalt not have a minute.

Tell. Some one, then, to speak with.

Ges. Hence with him!

Tell. A moment!—Stop!
Let me speak to the boy.

Ges. Is he thy son?

Tell. And if
He were, art thou so lost to nature, as
To send me forth to die before his face?

Ges. Well! speak with him.
Now, Sarnem, mark them well.

Tell. Thou dost not know me, boy—and well for
thee
Thou dost not. I'm the father of a son
About thy age. Thou,

I see, wast born like him upon the hills;
If thou should'st 'scape thy present thraldom, he
May chance to cross thee; if he should, I pray thee
Relate to him what has been passing here,
And say I laid my hand upon thy head,
And said to thee—if he were here, as thou art,
Thus would I bless him. Mayest thou live, my boy!
To see thy country free, or die for her,
As I do! (*Albert weeps.*)

   Sar. Mark! he weeps.

   Tell. Were he my son,
He would not shed a tear! He would remember
The cliff where he was bred, and learned to scan
A thousand fathoms' depth of nether air;
Where he was trained to hear the thunder talk,
And meet the lightning eye to eye—where last
We spoke together—when I told him death
Bestowed the brightest gem that graces life—
Embraced for virtue's sake—he shed a tear!
Now were he by I'd talk to him, and his cheek
Should never blanch, nor moisture dim his eye—
I'd talk to him—

   Sar. He falters!

   Tell. 'Tis too much!
And yet it must be done! I'd talk to him—

   Ges. Of what?

   Tell. The mother, tyrant, thou dost make
A widow of!—I'd talk to him of her.
I'd bid him tell her, next to liberty,
Her name was the last word my lips pronounced.
And I would charge him never to forget
To love and cherish her, as he would have
His father's dying blessing rest upon him!

   Sar. You see, as he doth prompt the other acts.

   Tell. So well he bears it, he doth vanquish me.
My boy—my boy! O for the hills, the hills,
To see him bound along their tops again,

With liberty.

Sar. Was there not all the father in that look?

Ges. Yet 'tis 'gainst nature.

Sar. Not if he believes
To own the son would be to make him share
The father's death.

Ges. I did not think of that! 'Tis well
The boy is not thy son—I've destined him
To die along with thee.

Tell. To die?—For what?

Ges. For having braved my power, as thou hast.
Lead
Them forth.

Tell. He's but a child.

Ges. Away with them!

Tell. Perhaps an only child.

Ges. No matter.

Tell. He may have a mother.

Ges. So the viper hath;
And yet, who spares it for the mother's sake?

Tell. I talk to stone! I talk to it as though
'Twere flesh; and know 'tis none. I'll talk to it
No more. Come, my boy—
I taught thee how to live—I'll show thee how to die.

Ges. He is thy child?

Tell. He is my child.

Ges. I've wrung a tear from him! Thy name?

Tell. My name?
It matters not to keep it from thee now;
My name is Tell.

Ges. Tell!—William Tell?

Tell. The same.

Ges. What! he, so famed 'bove all his countrymen
For guiding o'er the stormy lake the boat?
And such a master of his bow, 'tis said
His arrows never miss!—Indeed—I'll take
Exquisite vengeance!—Mark! I'll spare thy life—

Thy boy's too—both of you are free—on one
Condition.

Tell. Name it.

Ges. I would see you make
A trial of your skill with that same bow
You shoot so well with.

Tell. Name the trial you
Would have me make.

Ges. You look upon your boy
As though instinctively you guessed it.

Tell. Look upon my boy!—What mean you? Look
    upon
My boy as though I guessed it?—Guessed the trial
You'd have me make!—Guessed it
Instinctively! You do not mean—No—no—
You would not have me make a trial of
My skill upon my child!—Impossible!
I do not guess your meaning.

Ges. I would see
Thee hit an apple at the distance of
A hundred paces.

Tell. Is my boy to hold it?

Ges. No.

Tell. No!—I'll send the arrow through the core'

Ges. It is to rest upon his head.

Tell. Great heaven, you hear him!

Ges. Thou dost hear the choice I give—
Such trial of the skill thou art master of,
Or death to both of you; not otherwise
To be escaped.

Tell. O, monster!

Ges. Wilt thou do it?

Alb. He will! he will!

Tell. Ferocious monster!—Make
A father murder his own child.

Ges. Take off
His chains if he consent.

Tell. With his own hand!

Ges. Does he consent?

Alb. He does (*Gesler signs to his officers, who proceed to take off Tell's chains; Tell all the time unconscious what they do.*)

Tell. With his own hand!
Murder his child with his own hand—This hand!
The hand I've led him, when an infant, by!—
'Tis beyond horror—'tis most horrible.
Amazement! (*His chains fall off.*) What's that you've
    done to me?
Villains! put on my chains again. My hands
Are free from blood, and have no gust for it,
That they should drink my child's! Here! here! I'll not
Murder my boy for Gesler.

Alb. Father—Father!—
You will not hit me, father!—

Tell. Hit thee! Send
The arrow through thy brain—or, missing that,
Shoot out an eye—or, if thine eye escape,
Mangle the cheek I've seen thy mother's lips
Cover with kisses!—Hit thee—hit a hair
Of thee, and cleave thy mother's heart—

Ges. Dost thou consent?

Tell. Give me my bow and quiver.

Ges. For what?

Tell. —To shoot my boy!

Alb. No—father—no!
To save me!—You'll be sure to hit the apple—
Will you not save me, father?

Tell. Lead me forth—
I'll make the trial!

Alb. Thank you!

Tell. Thank me? do
You know for what?—I will not make the trial,
To take him to his mother in my arms,
And lay him down a corpse before her!

Ges. Then he dies this moment—and you certainly
Do murder him whose life you have a chance
To save, and will not use it.
  Tell. Well—I'll do it: I'll make the trial.
  Alb. Father—
  Tell. Speak not to me:
Let me not hear thy voice—Thou must be dumb;
And so should all things be—Earth should be dumb;
And heaven—unless its thunders muttered at
The deed, and sent a bolt to stop it!—Give me
My bow and quiver!
  Ges. When all's ready.
  Tell. Well—Lead on!

QUESTIONS.—1. Why does Gesler express joy that his subjects are unhappy? 2. Why does Albert appear not to recognize his father? 3. Why does Tell at last acknowledge Albert?

ERRORS.—*Weep-on* for weap-on (pronounced *wep-on*); *a-gin* for a-gain (pronounced a-gen); *na-tur* for na-ture.

SPELL AND DEFINE.—avalanche, hurricane, vouchsafe, fledgeling; thraldom, instinctively, amazement, quiver, consciousness, rife, tarnish.

LESSON CXVII.

RULE.—When two or more consonants come together, let the pupil be careful to *sound every one distinctly.*

William Tell.—CONTINUED.

SCENE 4.—*Enter slowly, people in evident distress—Officers, Sarnem, Gesler, Tell, Albert, and soldiers— one bearing Tell's bow and quiver—another with a basket of apples.*

Ges. That is your ground. Now shall they measure thence a hundred paces. Take the distance.

Tell. Is the line a true one?

Ges. True or not, what is't to thee?

Tell. What is't to me?—A little thing,
A very little thing—a yard or two
Is nothing here or there—were it a wolf
I shot at!—Never mind.

Ges. Be thankful, slave,
Our grace accords thee life on any terms.

Tell. I will be thankful, Gesler!—Villain, stop!
You measure to the sun.

Ges. And what of that?
What matter whether to or from the sun?

Tell. I'd have it at my back—the sun should shine
Upon the mark, and not on him that shoots.
I cannot see to shoot against the sun—
I will not shoot against the sun!

Ges. Give him his way! Thou hast cause to bless
  my mercy

Tell. I shall remember it. I'd like to see
The apple I'm to shoot at.

Ges. Stay! Show me the basket!—There—

Tell. You've picked the smallest one.

Ges. I know I have.

Tell. O! do you?—But you see
The color on't is dark—I'd have it light,
To see it better.

Ges. Take it as it is:
Thy Skill will be the greater if thou hitt'st it.

Tell. True—true!—I did not think of that—I
wonder
I did not think of that—give me some chance
To save my boy! (*Throws away the apple with all his
  force.*)
                   I will not murder him,
If I can help it—for the honor of
The form thou wearest, if all the heart is gone.

Ges. Well: choose thyself.

Tell. Have I a friend among the lookers on?

Verner. (*Rushing forward.*) Here, Tell!

Tell. I thank thee, Verner!

He is a friend runs out into a storm

To shake a hand with us. I must be brief.

When once the bow is bent, we cannot take

The shot too soon. Verner, whatever be

The issue of this hour, the common cause

Must not stand still. Let not tomorrow's sun

Set on the tyrant's banner! Verner! Verner!

The boy!—The boy—thinkest thou he hath the courage

To stand it?

Ver. Yes.

Tell. Does he tremble?

Ver. No.

Tell. Art sure?

Ver. I am.

Tell. How looks he?

Ver. Clear and smilingly.

If you doubt it—look yourself

Tell. No—no—my friend;

To hear it is enough.

Ver. He bears himself so much above his years—

Tell. I know!—I know.

Ver. With constancy so modest—

Tell. I was sure he would—

Ver. And looks with such relying love

And reverence upon you—

Tell. Man!—Man!—Man!

No more! Already I'm too much the father

To act the man!—Verner, no more, my friend!

I would be flint—flint—flint. Don't make me feel

I'm not—do not mind me! Take the boy

And set him, Verner, with his back to me.

Set him upon his knees—and place this apple

Upon his head, so that the stem may front me,

Thus, Verner; charge him to keep steady—tell him
I 'll hit the apple!—Verner, do all this
More briefly than I tell it thee.

    Ver. Come, Albert! (*Leading him out.*)
    Alb. May I not speak with him before I go?
    Ver. No.
    Alb. I would only kiss his hand.
    Ver. You must not.
    Alb. I must!—I cannot go from him without.
    Ver. It is his will you should.
    Alb. His will is it?
I am content then—come.
    Tell. My boy! (*Holding out his arms to him.*)
    Alb. My father! (*Rushing into Tell's arms.*)
    Tell. If thou canst bear it, should not I?—Go now,
My son—and keep in mind that I can shoot—
Go boy—be thou but steady, I will hit
The apple—go!—God bless thee—go.—My bow!
                    (*The bow is handed to him.*)
Thou wilt not fail thy master, wilt thou?—Thou
Hast never failed him yet, old servant—no,
I 'm sure of thee—I know thy honesty,
Thou art staunch—staunch.—Let me see my quiver.
    Ges. Give him a single arrow.
    Tell. Do you shoot?
    Soldier. I do.
    Tell. Is it so you pick an arrow, friend?
The point you see is bent; the feather jagged—(*Breaks
it.*)
That's all the use 'tis fit for.
    Ges. Let him have another.
    Tell. Why 'tis better than the first,
But yet not good enough for such an aim
As I'm to take—'tis heavy in the shaft;
I'll not shoot with it! (*Throws it away.*) Let me see my
    quiver.
Bring it!—'Tis not one arrow in a dozen

I'd take to shoot with at a dove, much less
A dove like that.—

    Ges. It matters not.

Show him the quiver.

    Tell. See if the boy is ready.

            (*Tell here hides an arrow under his vest.*)

    Ver. He is.

    Tell. I'm ready too! Keep silent for
Heav'n's sake, and do not stir—and let me have
Your prayers—your prayers—and be my witnesses
That if his life's in peril from my hand.
'Tis only for the chance of saving it. (*To the people.*)

    Ges. Go on.

    Tell. I will.

O friends, for mercy's sake, keep motionless
And silent. (*Tell shoots—a shout of exultation bursts
from the crowd. Tell's head drops on his bosom; he
with difficulty supports himself upon his bow.*)

    Ver. (*Rushing in with Albert.*) Thy boy is safe, no
hair of him is touched.

    Alb. Father, I'm safe—your Albert's safe, dear
father,—
Speak to me! Speak to me!

    Ver. He cannot. boy!

    Alb. You grant him life?

    Ges. I do.

    Alb. And we are free?

    Ges. You are. (*Crossing angrily behind.*)

    Alb. Thank heaven!—Thank heaven!

    Ver. Open his vest,
And give him air. (*Albert opens his father's vest, and
the arrow drops. Tell starts—fixes his eye on Albert,
and clasps him to his breast.*)

    Tell. My boy!—My boy!

    Ges. For what
Hid you that arrow in your breast?—Speak, slave!

    Tell. To kill thee, tyrant, had I slain my boy!

QUESTIONS.—1. In what kind of tone should you read, "True, I did not think of that," line 31? 2. Why! 3. Relate the whole story in your own language. 4. What was the fate of Gesler?

ERRORS.—*Stid-dy* for steady-y; *pint* for point; *bo-som* for bosom. pronounced boze-um.

SPELL AND DEFINE.—reverence, staunch, briefly, constancy, vest, peril, issue, tyrant, banner, jagged, motionless.

LESSON CXVIII.

RULE.—When similar sounds come at the end of one word, and at the beginning of the next word, they must not be blended into one.

EXAMPLE.—Flower*s s*oon fade.
He addresse*th th*e understanding.
Presumptuou*s s*ins.
Time flie*s s*ilently.
A parent'*s s*orrow.

The Vision of Mirza.—ADDISON.

1. On the fifth day of the moon, which according to the custom of my forefathers, I always kept holy, after having washed myself, and offered up my morning devotions, I ascended the high hills of Bagdat, in order to pass the rest of the day in meditation and prayer. As I was here airing myself on the tops of the mountains, I fell into a profound contemplation on the vanity of human life. Passing from one thought to another, "Surely," said I, "man is but a shadow, and life a dream."

2. While I was thus musing, I cast my eyes towards the summit of a rock, that was not far from me, where I discovered one, in the habit of a shepherd, with a

musical instrument in his hand. As I looked upon him he applied it to his lips, and began to play upon it. The sound of it was exceeding sweet, and wrought into a variety of tunes that were inexpressibly melodious, and altogether different from anything I had ever heard. They put me in mind of those heavenly airs that are played to the departed souls of good men upon their first arrival in paradise, to wear out the impressions of the last agonies and qualify them for the pleasures of that happy place.

3. My heart melted away in secret raptures. I had been often told that the rock before me was the haunt of a Genius, and that several had been entertained with music, who had passed by it, but never heard that the musician had before made himself visible. When he had raised my thoughts, by those transporting airs which he played, to taste the pleasure of his conversation, as I looked upon him, like one astonished, he beckoned to me, and, by the waving of his hand, directed me to approach the place where he sat.

4. I drew near, with that reverence which is due to a superior nature, and, as my heart was entirely subdued by the captivating strains I had heard, I fell down at his feet, and wept. The Genius smiled upon me with a look of compassion and affability that familiarized him to my imagination, and, at once, dispelled all the fears and apprehensions with which I approached him. He lefted me from the ground, and taking me by the hand, "Mirza," said he, "I have heard thee in thy soliloquies: follow me,"

5. He then led me to the highest pinnacle of the rock, and, placing me on the top of it, "Cast thy eyes eastward," said he, "and tell me what thou seest." "I see," said I, "A huge valley, and a prodigious tide of water rolling through it." "The valley that thou seest," said he, "is the valley of misery, and the tide of water that thou seest is part of the great tide of

eternity." "What is the reason," said I, "that the tide I see rises out of a thick mist at one end, and again loses itself in a thick mist at the other?"

6. "What thou seest," said he, "is that portion of eternity which is called time, measured out by the sun, and reaching from the beginning of the world to its consummation. Examine now," said he, "this sea, that is thus bounded with darkness at both ends, and tell me what thou discoverest in it." "I see a bridge," said I, "standing in the midst of the tide." "The bridge thou seest," said he, "is human life: consider it attentively." Upon a more leisurely survey of it, I found that it consisted of three-score and ten entire arches, with several broken arches, which, added to those that were entire, made up the number about a hundred.

7. As I was counting the arches, the Genius told me that the bridge consisted, at first, of a thousand arches, but that a great flood swept away the rest, and left the bridge in the ruinous condition I now beheld it. "But tell me further," said he. "what thou discoverest on it." "I see multitudes of people passing over it," said I, "and a black cloud hanging on each end of it."

8. As I looked more attentively, I saw several of the passengers dropping through the bridge into the great tide that flowed underneath it, and, upon further examination, perceived there were innumerable trapdoors that lay concealed in the bridge, which the passengers no sooner trod upon, but they fell through them into the tide, and immediately disappeared. These hidden pitfalls were set very thick at the entrance of the bridge, so that throngs of people no sooner broke through the cloud than many of them fell into them. They grew thinner towards the middle, but multiplied and lay closer together towards the end of the arches that were entire.

9. There were indeed some persons, but their number was very small, that continued a kind of hobbling march on the broken arches, but fell through, one after another, being quite tired and spent with so long a walk. I passed some time in the contemplation of this wonderful structure, and the great variety of objects which it presented.

10. My heart was filled with a deep melancholy to see several dropping, unexpectedly, in the midst of mirth and jollity, and catching by every thing that stood by them to save themselves. Some were looking up towards the heavens in a thoughtful posture, and, in the midst of a speculation, stumbled and fell out of sight. Multitudes were very busy in the pursuit of bubbles that glittered in their eyes and danced before them. Often, when they thought themselves within the reach of them, their footing failed, and down they sank.

11. In this confusion of objects, I observed some with cimeters in their hands, and others with lancets, who ran to and fro upon the bridge, thrusting several persons on trapdoors which did not seem to lie in their way, and which they might have escaped, had they not been thus forced upon them.

12. The Genius, seeing me indulge myself in this melancholy prospect, told me I had dwelt long enough upon it. "Take thine eyes off the bridge," said he, "and tell me if thou yet seest any thing thou dost not comprehend." Upon looking up, "What mean," said I, "those great flights of birds that are perpetually hovering about the bridge, and settling upon it from time to time? I see vultures, harpies, ravens, cormorants, and, among many other feathered creatures, several little winged boys, that perch, in great numbers, upon the middle arches."

13. "These," said the Genius, "are Envy, Avarice, Superstition, Despair, Love, with the like cares and

passions that infest human life." I here fetched a deep sigh. "Alas!" said I, "man was made in vain! how is he given away to misery and mortality! tortured in life, and swallowed up in death!" The Genius, being moved with compassion towards me, bid me quit so uncomfortable a prospect. "Look no more," said he, "on man, in the first stage of his existence, in his setting out for eternity, but cast thine eye on that thick mist, into which the tide bears the several generations of mortals that fall into it."

14. I directed my sight as I was ordered, and whether or no the good Genius strengthened it with any supernatural force, or dissipated part of the mist, that was before too thick for the eye to penetrate, I saw the valley opening at the farther end, and spreading forth into an immense ocean, that had a huge rock of adamant running through the midst of it, and dividing it into two equal parts. The clouds still rested on one half of it, insomuch that I could discover nothing in it, but the other appeared to me a vast ocean, planted with innumerable islands, that were covered with fruits and flowers, and interwoven with a thousand little shining seas, that ran among them.

15. I could see persons dressed in glorious habits, with garlands upon their heads, passing among the trees, lying down by the sides of fountains, or resting on beds of flowers and could hear a confused harmony of singing birds, falling waters, human voices, and musical instruments. Gladness grew in me upon the discovery of so delightful a scene. I wished for the wings of an eagle, that I might fly away to those happy seats, but the Genius told me there was no passage to them, except through the gates of death, that I saw opening every moment upon the bridge.

16. "The islands," said he, "that lie so fresh and green before thee, and with which the whole face of

the ocean appears spotted, as far as thou canst see, are more in number than the sands on the sea shore. There are myriads of islands behind those which thou here discoverest, reaching farther than thine eye, or even thine imagination, can extend itself. These are the mansions of good men after death, who, according to the degrees and kinds of virtue in which they excelled, are distributed among these several islands, which abound with pleasures of different kinds and degrees, suitable to the relishes and perfections of those who are settled in them. Every island is a paradise accommodated to its respective inhabitants.

17. "Are not these, O Mirza, habitations worth contending for? Does life appear miserable, that gives thee opportunities of earning such a reward? Is death to be feared, that will convey thee to so happy an existence? Think not man was made in vain, who has such an eternity reserved for him." I gazed with inexpressible pleasure on those happy islands. At length, said I, "Show me now, I beseech thee, the secrets that lie under those dark clouds, that cover the ocean on the other side of the rock of adamant."

18. The Genius making me no answer, I turned about to address myself to him a second time, but I found that he had left me. I then turned again to the vision which I had been so long contemplating, but instead of the rolling tide, the arched bridge, and the happy islands, I saw nothing but the long, hollow valley of Bagdat, with oxen, sheep, and camels grazing upon the sides of it.

QUESTIONS.—1. What is this kind of fiction called?   2. Why is the scene of almost all allegories laid in the East?   3. Why is instruction conveyed by parable or allegory, more likely to be remembered than that communicated by any other method? 5. What by the pitfalls?   6. Who are the persons with cimeters?

ERRORS.—'*Cor-ding* for ac-cord-ing; *in-strur-ment* for in-stru-ment; *'ston-ish-ed* for as-ton-ish-ed

SPELL AND DEFINE.—(1) ascended, contemplation; (2) impressions; (3) entertained, transporting; (4) captivating, dispelled, apprehensions; (5) pinnacle; (6) consummation; (7) arches; (8) concealed; (10) posture; (14) strengthened, supernatural, interwoven; (16) myriads, imagination; (17) inexpressible.

LESSON CXIX.

RULE.—While each pupil reads, let the rest observe, and then mention which syllables were pronounced wrong, and which were omitted or indistinctly sounded.

A Dirge.—CROLY

1. "Earth to earth, and dust to dust!"
   Here the evil and the just,
   Here the youthful and the old,
   Here the fearful and the bold,
   Here the matron and the maid,
   In one silent bed are laid;
   Here the vassal and the king,
   Side by side, lie withering:
   Here the sword and scepter rust:
   "Earth to earth, and dust to dust!"

2. Age on age shall roll along,
   O'er this pale and mighty throng;
   Those that wept them, those that weep,
   All shall with these sleepers sleep:
   Brothers, sisters of the worm,
   Summer's sun, or winter's storm,
   Song of peace, or battle's roar,
   Ne'er shall break their slumbers more;
   Death shall keep his sullen trust,
   "Earth to earth, and dust to dust!"

3. But a day is coming fast,
    Earth, thy mightiest and thy last!
    It shall come in fear and wonder,
    Heralded by trump and thunder:
    It shall come in strife and toil;
    It shall come in blood and spoil;
    It shall come in empires' groans,
    Burning temples, trampled thrones:
    Then, ambition, rue thy lust!
    "Earth to earth, and dust to dust!"

4. Then shall come the judgment sign;
    In the east, the king shall shine;
    Flashing from heav'n's golden gate,
    Thousands, thousands round his state;
    Spirits with the crown and plume;
    Tremble, then, thou solemn tomb;
    Heav'n shall open on our sight;
    Earth be turned to living light,
    Kingdom of the ransomed just!
    "Earth to earth, and dust to dust!"

5. Then thy mount, Jerusalem,
    Shall be gorgeous as a gem:
    Then shall in the desert rise
    Fruits of more than Paradise,
    Earth by angel feet be trod,
    One great garden of her God!
    Till are dried the martyr's tears
    Through a thousand glorious years:
    Now in hope of him we trust,
    "Earth to earth, and dust to dust!"

QUESTIONS.—1. For what occasion is a "Dirge" used?
2. What is inculcated in the first verse? 3. What is taught in
the second verse? 4. What in the fourth? 5. What in the
fifth? 6. What is the argument of the whole?

ERRORS.—*Spile* for spoil; *thou-suns* for thousands; *sper-ets* for spir-its; *mat-ron* for ma-tron; *trim-ble* for trem-ble.

SPELL AND DEFINE.—(1) vassal; (3) heralded, ambition; (4) ransomed; (5) gorgeous, paradise, martyr.

LESSON CXX.

RULE.—Be careful and give a full sound to the vowels. Regard to this rule will correct the common flat, clipping and uninteresting way in which many read.

EXERCISES in which the vowels italicized are to be prolonged.

H*ai*l! holy l*i*ght.

We pr*ai*se thee, O Lord God.

These names of the Deity are seldom pronounced with that full and solemn sound that if proper. *Lud* and *Law-ard* and *Gud* and Gawd are too frequently used instead of the proper sounds. If the pupil can learn to speak the three words, *"O—Lord—God,"* properly, it will be worth no little attention. Every pupil ought to be exercised on these words till they pronounce them properly and in a full and solemn tone.

Ladies' Headdresses.—SPECTATOR.

1. There is not so variable a thing in nature as a lady's headdress. Within my own memory, I have known it rise and fall above thirty degrees. About ten years ago, it shot up to a very great height, insomuch that the female part of our species were much taller than the men. The women were of such an enormous stature that we appeared as grasshoppers before them. At present the whole sex is in a manner dwarfed and shrunk into a race of beauties that seem almost another species.

2. I remember several ladies who were once very near seven feet high that at present want some inches

of five. How they came to be thus curtailed, I cannot learn. Whether the whole sex be at present under any penance, which we know nothing of, or whether they have cast their headdresses in order to surprise us with something of that kind which shall be entirely new, or whether some of the tallest of the sex, being too cunning for the rest, have contrived this method to make themselves appear sizeable, is still a secret: though I find some are of opinion, they are at present like trees new lopped and pruned, that will certainly sprout up and flourish with greater heads than before.

3. For my own part, as I do not love to be insulted by women who are taller than myself. I admire the sex much more in their present humiliation, which has reduced them to their natural dimensions, than when they had extended their persons, and lengthened themselves out into formidable and gigantic figures. I am not for adding to the beautiful edifices of nature, not for raising any whimsical superstructure upon her plans. I must therefore repeat it, that I am highly pleased with the coiffure now in fashion, and think it shows the good sense which at present very much reigns among the valuable part of the sex. One may observe that women in all ages have taken more pains than men to adorn the outside of their heads, and indeed I very much admire, that those architects, who raise such wonderful structures out of ribbons, lace, and wire, have not been recorded for their respective inventions. It is certain that there have been as many orders in these kinds of buildings, as in those which have been made of marble. Sometimes they rise in the shape of a pyramid, sometimes like a tower, and sometimes like a steeple.

4. In Juvenal's time, the building grew by several orders and stories, as he has very humoroutly described it.

With curls on curls they build her head before,
And mount it with a formidable tower.

But I do not remember, in any part of my reading,
that the headdress aspired to such an extravagance
as in the fourteenth century when it was built up in
a couple of cones or spires which stood so excessively
high on each side of the head, that a woman who was
but a pigmy without her headdress appeared like a
colossus upon putting it on. Monsieur Paradin says,
"That these old-fashioned fontanges rose one ell above
the head; that they were pointed like steeples, and
had long loose pieces of crape fastened to the tops
of them, which were curiously fringed, and hung down
their backs like streamers."

5. The women might possibly have carried this
Gothic building much higher, had not a famous monk,
Thomas Connecte by name, attacked it with great zeal
and resolution. This holy man traveled from place to
place to preach down this monstrous commode, and
succeeded so well in it, that, as the magicians sacrificed their books to the flames upon the preaching
of an apostle, many of the women threw down their
headdresses in the middle of his sermon, and made
a bonfire of them within sight of the pulpit. He was
so renowned, as well for sanctity of his life, as his
manner of preaching, that he had often a congregation of twenty thousand people; the men placing
themselves on the one side of the pulpit, and the
women on the other, they appeared, to use the
similitude of an ingenious writer, like a forest of
cedars with their heads reaching to the clouds.

6. He so warmed and animated the people against
this monstrous ornament, that it lay under a kind of
persecution, and whenever it appeared in public, was
pelted down by the rabble, who flung stones at the
persons that wore it. Notwithstanding this prodigy
vanished while the preacher was among them, it

began to appear again some months after his departure, or, to tell it in Monsieur Paradin's own words,
"The women, that, like snails in a fright, had drawn
in their horns, shot them out again as soon as the
danger was over."

7. It is usually observed that a good reign is the
only proper time for the making of laws against the
exorbitance of power. In the same manner an ex-
cessive headdress may be attacked the most effectually when the fashion is against it. I do therefore
recommend this paper to my female readers by way
of prevention.

8. I would desire the fair sex to consider how impossible it is for them to add anything that can be
ornamental to what is already the masterpiece of
nature. The head has the most beautiful appearance,
as well as the highest station, in the human figure.
Nature has laid out all her art in beautifying the face.
She has touched it with vermilion, planted in it a
double row of ivory, made it the seat of smiles and
blushes, lighted it up and enlivened it with the
brightness of the eyes, hung it on each side with
curious organs of sense, given it airs and graces that
cannot be described, and surrounded it with such a
flowing shade of hair, as sets all its beauties in the
most agreeable light. In short, she seems to have
designed the head as the cupola to the most glorious
of her works, and when we load it with such a pile
of supernumerary ornaments, we destroy the symmetry of the human figure, and foolishly contrive to
call off the eye from great and real beauties, to
childish gewgaws, ribbons, and bone-lace.

QUESTIONS.—1. Do you know any of the authors who
contributed to the Spectator? 2. In whose reign was it
published? 3. May not the remarks in this lesson be with
propriety applied to fashions in general? 4. Are we at liberty
to disregard fashion entirely?

ERRORS.—*Ar-che-tects* for ar-chi-tects (pronounced *ar-ke-tecks*); *gi-jan-tic* for gi-gan-tic.

SPELL AND DEFINE.—(1) degrees, enormous;   (2) curtailed; (3) humiliation, edifices, coiffure;   (4) century, colossus; (5) commode, similitude; (8) masterpiece.

LESSON CXXI.

RULE.—Pronounce the consonant sounds very distinctly.

EXAMPLE.—Prolong the consonant sounds that are italicized.—*b*-old, *d*-eign, *f*-ather, *g*-ather, *j*-oy, *l*-ight, *m*-an, *n*-o, *q*-ueer. p-*r*ay, *v*-ale, *w*-oe, *y*-ours, *z*-one, *h*-ang.

Apostrophe to the Ocean.—BYRON.

1. There is a pleasure in the pathless woods,
   There is a rapture on the lonely shore,
   There is society where none intrudes
   By the deep sea, and music in its roar.
   I love not man the less, but Nature more,
   From these our interviews, in which I steal
   From all I may be, or have been before,
   To mingle with the universe and feel
   What I can ne'er express, yet cannot all conceal.

2. Roll on, thou deep and dark blue ocean—roll!
   Ten thousand fleets sweep over thee in vain,
   Man marks the earth with ruin—his control
   Stops with the shore:—upon the watery plain
   The wrecks are all thy deed, nor doth remain
   A shadow of man's ravage, save his own,
   When for a moment, like a drop of rain,
   He sinks into thy depths with bubbling groan,
   Without a grave, unknelled, uncoffined, and
      unknown.

3. The armaments which thunderstrike the walls
   Of rock-built cities, bidding nations quake,
   And monarchs tremble in their capitals;
   The oak leviathans, whose huge ribs make
   Their clay creator the vain title take
   Of lord of thee, and arbiter of war;
   These are thy toys, and, as the snowy flake,
   They melt into thy yeast of waves, which mar
   Alike the Armada's pride, or spoils of Trafalgar.

4. Thy shores are empires, changed in all save thee—
   Assyria, Greece, Rome, Carthage,—what are they?
   Thy waters wasted them while they were free,
   And many a tyrant since; their shores obey
   The stranger, slave, or savage; their decay
   Has dried up realms to deserts:—not so thou,
   Unchangeable save to thy wild waves' play—
   Time writes no wrinkles on thine azure brow—
   Such as creation's dawn beheld, thou rollest now.

5. Thou glorious mirror, where the Almighty's form
   Glasses itself in tempests; in all time,
   Calm or convulsed—in breeze, or gale, or storm,
   Icing the pole, or in the torrid clime
   Dark heaving;—boundless, endless, and sublime—
   The image of Eternity—the throne
   Of the Invisible; even from out thy slime
   The monsters of the deep are made; each zone
   Obeys thee—thou goest forth, dread, fathomless,
   alone.

QUESTIONS.—1. What is the society which exists where none intrudes? 2. What is meant by "oak leviathans?" 3. How is the ocean the image of eternity?

ERRORS.—*Rap-tor* for rap-ture; *'spress* for ex-press; *mo-munt* for mo-ment; *ar-mum-ments* for ar-ma-ments.

SPELL AND DEFINE.—(1) interviews; (2) unknelled; (3) thunderstrike, leviathans, arbiter; (4) realms, azure.

LESSON CXXII.

RULE.—Be careful to speak little words, such as *a*, *in*, *at*, *on*, *to*, *by*, etc., very distinctly, and yet not to dwell on them so long as on the more important words.

Reflections in Westminster Abbey.

ADDISON.

1. When I am in a serious humor, I very often walk by myself in Westminster Abbey, where the gloominess of the place, and the use to which it is applied, with the solemnity of the building, and the condition of the people who lie in it, are apt to fill the mind with a kind of melancholy, or rather thoughtfulness, that is not disagreeable. I yesterday passed a whole afternoon in the churchyard, the cloisters, and the church, amusing myself with the tombstones and inscriptions which I met with in those several regions of the dead.

2. Most of them recorded nothing else of the buried person, but that he was born upon one day, and died upon another. The whole history of his life being comprehended in these two circumstances that are common to all mankind. I could not but look upon those registers of existence, whether of brass or marble, as a kind of satire upon the departed persons, who had left no other memorial of themselves, but that they were born, and that they died.

3. Upon my going into the church, I entertained myself with the digging of a grave and saw, in every shovelful of it that was thrown up, the fragment of a bone or skull, intermixed with a kind of fresh mouldering earth, that, some time or other, had a place in the composition of a human body. Upon this, I began to consider with myself, what innumerable multitudes of people lay confused together under the

pavements of that ancient cathedral. How men and women, friends and enemies, priests and soldiers, monks and prebendaries, were crumbled amongst one another, and blended together in the same common mass. How beauty, strength, and youth, with old age, weakness, and deformity, lay undistinguished in the same promiscuous heap of matter.

4. After having thus surveyed this great magazine of mortality as it were in the lump, I examined it more particularly by the accounts which I found on several of the monuments which are raised in every quarter of that ancient fabric. Some of them were covered with such extravagant epitaphs, that, if it were possible for the dead person to be acquainted with them, he would blush at the praises which his friends have bestowed upon him. There are others so excessively modest that they deliver the character of the person departed in Greek or Hebrew, and by that means are not understood once in a twelvemonth. In the poetical quarter, I found that there were poets who had no monuments, and monuments which had no poets. I observed, indeed. that the present war had filled the church with many of those uninhabited monuments, which had been erected to the memory of persons whose bodies were perhaps buried in the plains of Blenheim, or in the bosom of the ocean.

5. I could not but be very much delighted with several modern epitaphs, which are written with great elegance of expression and justness of thought, and which therefore do honor to the living as well as the dead. As a foreigner is very apt to conceive an idea of the ignorance or politeness of a nation from the turn of their public monuments and inscriptions, they should be submitted to the perusal of men of learning and genius, before they are put into execution. Sir Cloudesley Shovel's monument has very often given me great offence. Instead of the brave rough

English admiral which was the distinguishing character of that plain gallant man, he is represented on his tomb by the figure of a beau, dressed in a long periwig, and reposing himself upon velvet cushions under a canopy of state.

6. The inscription is answerable to the monument, for, instead of celebrating the many remarkable actions he had performed in the service of his country, it acquaints us only with the manner of his death, in which it was impossible for him to reap any honor. The Dutch, whom we are apt to despise for want of genius, show an infinitely greater taste in their buildings and works of this nature than we meet with in those of our own country. The monuments of their admirals, which have been erected at the public expense, represent them like themselves, and are adorned with rostral crowns and naval ornaments, with beautiful festoons of seaweed, shells, and coral.

7. I know that entertainments of this nature are apt to raise dark and dismal thoughts in timorous minds and gloomy imaginations; but for my own part, though I am always serious, I do not know what it is to be melancholy; and can therefore take a view of nature in her deep and solemn scenes, with the same pleasure as in her most gay and delightful ones. By these means I can improve myself with objects which others consider with terror.

8. When I look upon the tombs of the great, every emotion of envy dies in me. When I read the epitaphs of the beautiful, every inordinate desire goes out. When I meet with the grief of parents upon a tombstone, my heart melts with compassion. When I see the tomb of parents themselves, I consider the vanity of grieving for those whom we must quickly follow. When I see kings lying by those who deposed them, when I consider rival wits placed side by side, or the holy men that divided the world with their contests

and disputes, I reflect with sorrow and astonishment on the little competitions, factions, and debates of mankind. When I read the several dates of the tombs, of some that died yesterday, and some six hundred years ago, I consider that great day when we shall all of us be contemporaries, and make our appearance together.

QUESTIONS.—1. To what use is Westminster Abbey applied? 2. What reflections are apt to arise in the mind on visiting such a place? 3. Are such reflections salutary?

ERRORS.—*Fur-reign-er* for for-eign-er; *Blen-heem* for Blen-heim (pronounced *Blen-hime*); *an-cient* pronounced ane-shent; *sa-tire* for sat-ire.

SPELL AND DEFINE.—(1) inscriptions, cloisters; (4) fabric, epitaphs; (6) genius, rostral; (8) contemporaries.

LESSON CXXIII.

RULE.—Let the pupil stand at as great a distance from the teacher as possible, and then try to read so loud and distinctly that the teacher may hear each syllable.

The Journey of a Day: A Picture of Human Life.—DR. JOHNSON.

1. Obidah, the son of Abensina, left the caravansary early in the morning, and pursued his journey through the plains of Hindustan. He was fresh and vigorous with rest; he was animated with hope; he was incited by desire. He walked swiftly forward over the valleys, and saw the hills gradually rising before him.

2. As he passed along his ears were delighted with the morning song of the bird of paradise. He was

fanned by the last flutters of the sinking breeze, and sprinkled with dew by groves of spices. He sometimes contemplated the towering height of the oak, monarch of the hills, and sometimes caught the gentle fragrance of the primrose, eldest daughter of the spring. All his senses were gratified, and all care was banished from his heart.

3. Thus he went on till the sun approached his meridian, and the increasing heat preyed upon his strength. He then looked round about him for some more commodious path. He saw, on his right hand, a grove that seemed to wave its shades as a sign of invitation. He entered it, and found the coolness and verdure irresistibly pleasant. He did not, however, forget whither he was traveling, but found a narrow way, bordered with flowers, which appeared to have the same direction with the main road, and was pleased, that, by this happy experiment, he had found means to unite pleasure with business, and to gain the rewards of diligence without suffering its fatigues.

4. He, therefore, still continued to walk for a time, without the last remission of his ardor, except that he was sometimes tempted to stop by the music of the birds, whom the heat had assembled in the shade, and sometimes amused himself with plucking the flowers that covered the banks on either side, or the fruits that hung upon the branches. At last, the green path began to decline from its first tendency, and to wind among the hills and thickets, cooled with fountains, and murmuring with waterfalls.

5. Here Obidah paused for a time, and began to consider, whether it were longer safe to forsake the known and common track, but, remembering that the heat was now in its greatest violence, and that the plain was dusty and uneven, he resolved to pursue the new path, which he supposed only to make a few

meanders, in compliance with the varieties of the ground, and to end at last in the common road.

6. Having thus calmed his solicitude, he renewed his pace, though he suspected he was not gaining ground. This uneasiness of his mind inclined him to lay hold on every new object, and give way to every sensation that might soothe or divert him. He listened to every echo, he mounted every hill for a fresh prospect, he turned aside to every cascade, and pleased himself with tracing the course of a gentle river that rolled among the trees, and watered a large region, with innumerable circumvolutions.

7. In these amusements, the hours passed away unaccounted. His deviations had perplexed his memory, and he knew not towards what point to travel. He stood pensive and confused, afraid to go forward lest he should go wrong, yet conscious that the time of loitering was now past. While he was thus tortured with uncertainty, the sky was overspread with clouds, the day vanished from before him, and a sudden tempest gathered round his head.

8. He was now roused by his danger, to a quick and painful remembrance of his folly. He now saw how happiness is lost when ease is consulted. He lamented the unmanly impatience that prompted him to seek shelter in the grove, and despised the petty curiosity that led him on from trifle to trifle. While he was thus reflecting, the air grew blacker, and a clap of thunder broke his meditation.

9. He now resolved to do what remained yet in his power,—to tread back the ground which he had passed, and try to find some issue, where the wood might open into the plain. He prostrated himself upon the ground, and commended his life to the Lord of nature. He rose with confidence and tranquility, and pressed on with his saber in his hand, for the beasts of the desert were in motion, and on every hand were

heard the mingled howls of rage, and fear, and ravage, and expiration. All the horrors of darkness and solitude surrounded him; the winds roared in the woods, and the torrents tumbled from the hills.

10. Thus, forlorn and distressed, he wandered through the wild, without knowing whither he was going, or whether he was every moment drawing nearer to safety or to destruction. At length, not fear, but labor, began to overcome him. His breath grew short, and his knees trembled, and he was on the point of lying down, in resignation to his fate, when he beheld, through the brambles, the glimmer of a taper. He advanced towards the light, and finding that it proceeded from the cottage of a hermit, he called humbly at the door, and obtained admission. The old man set before him such provisions as he had collected for himself, on which Obidah fed with eagerness and gratitude.

11. When the repast was over, "Tell me," said the hermit, "by what chance thou hast been brought hither. I have been now twenty years an inhabitant of this wilderness, in which I never saw a man before." Obidah then related the occurrences of his journey, without any concealment or palliation.

12. "Son," said the hermit, "let the errors and follies, the dangers and escapes, of this day, sink deep into thy heart. Remember, my son, that human life is the journey of a day. We rise in the morning of youth, full of vigor, and full of expectation; we set forward with spirit and hope, with gaiety and with diligence, and travel on a while in the straight road of piety, towards the mansions of rest. In a short time we remit our fervor, and endeavor to find some mitigation of our duty, and some more easy means of obtaining the same end.

13. "We then relax our vigor, and resolve no longer to be terrified with crimes at a distance, but rely upon

our own constancy, and venture to approach what we
resolve never to touch. We thus enter the bowers of
ease, and respose in the shades of security. Here the
heart softens, and vigilance subsides. We are then
willing to inquire whether another advance cannot be
made, and whether we may not, at least, turn our eyes
upon the gardens of pleasure. We approach them with
scruple and hesitation. We enter them, but enter
timorous and trembling, and always hope to pass
through them without losing the road of virtue, which
we, for awhile, keep in our sight, and to which we pro-
pose to return.

14. "But temptation succeeds temptation, and one
compliance prepares us for another. We, in time, lose
the happiness of innocence, and solace our disquiet
with sensual gratifications. By degrees we let fall the
remembrance of our original intention, and quit the
only adequate object of rational desire. We entangle
ourselves in business, immerge ourselves in luxury,
and rove through the labyrinths of inconstancy, till
the darkness of old age begins to invade us, and
disease and anxiety obstruct our way. We then look
back upon our lives with horror, with sorrow, and with
repentance; and wish, but too often vainly wish, that
we had not forsaken the paths of virtue.

15. "Happy are they, my son, who shall learn, from
thy example, not to despair, but shall remember, that,
though the day is past, and their strength is wasted,
there yet remains one effort to be made; that reformation is never hopeless, nor sincere endeavors ever
unassisted; that the wanderer may at length return,
after all his errors: and that he, who implores strength
and courage from above, shall find danger and difficulty give way before him. Go now, my son, to thy
repose; commit thyself to the care of Omnipotence;
and, when the morning calls again to toil, begin anew
thy journey and thy life."

QUESTIONS.—1. What species of composition is this lesson? 2. Repeat the chief incidents of the story, with their appropriate moral. 3. Is it because we have but few men who are *capable* of becoming great, that so few distinguish themselves?

ERRORS.—*Ar-ly* for ear-ly; *'muse-ments* for a-muse-ments; *lam-ent-ed* for la-ment-ed.

SPELL AND DEFINE.—(1) caravansary, animated; (7) deviations, loitering; (9) tranquility; (10) resignation; (13) timorous; (14) labyrinths, gratifications.

LESSON CXXIV.

RULE.—In reading poetry that does not rhyme, there need be no pause at the end of lines terminating with unimportant words, except when the sense requires it.

Morning.—ANONYMOUS.

1. How lovely is the morn!
    Earth wakes like a young maiden from her sleep,
    And smiles. The playful breeze, that all night long
    Has sported with thy flowers, and sipped at will
5. Their balmy breath, shakes freshness from its
        wings,
    And greets alike the fevered brow of care,
    Roused from his broken slumbers, and the cheek
    Of cherub youth, which, sleeping, smiles as
        though
    It dreamed of paradise. It visits e'en
10. The crowded city, and breaks in upon
    The miser, gloating o'er his thrice-told heap
    Of dross, a visitor unwelcome, for
    Its purity reproves his heart *impure*.
    Then perchance it greets the fading cheek.

15. And wasted form, of one whose step was once
    As light and joyous as the fairies' trip
    In moonlit dance. In her ear it whispers
    Hopes of happier days, and as it leaves her,
    Sighs in sorrow for her fate, whose hopes
20. Before its next return, may all decay,
    And nought be left behind, but the sad wreck
    Of all that once was lovely.
    Now the sun
    Appears, and with his golden beams illumes
25. The mountain's brow with hues of heaven, and
       wakes
    The bustling earth from dull inaction. Now
    The haunts of men, once more are seen teeming
    With life; and birds and beasts once more rejoice
    In their renewed existence. *These* again
30. With joyous twitter, seem to chirp their praise;
    Those, in their various ways, their gratitude
    Express, while thankless man, with eye scarce
       turned
    To heaven, once more renews his toil, nor thinks
    Of Him to whom he owes his life renewed,
35. His health preserved, his friends still true,
       and all
    The countless blessings which have made this
       earth
    A paradise.

QUESTIONS.—1. What is the character of a miser?   2. What does "told" signify, in the 11th line? 3. Who were the "fairies?"   4. What does "*these*" refer to in line 29? 5. "*Those*," in line 31?

ERRORS.—*Pure-ty* for pu-ri-ty; *par'-dise* for par-a-dise; *honts* for haunts; *a-gin* for a-gain.

SPELL AND DEFINE.—(9) paradise;   (11) gloating; (14) perchance; (24) illumes; (27) teeming; (30) twitter.

LESSON CXXV.

Woe to Ariel.—BIBLE.

1. Woe to Ariel! to Ariel!
   The city where David dwelt:
   Add ye year to year;
   Let them kill sacrifices.
5. Yet I will distress Ariel!
   And there shall be heaviness and sorrow:
   And it shall be unto me as Ariel.
   And I will camp against thee round about,
   And I will lay siege against thee with a mount,
10. And I will raise forts against thee.
    And thou shalt be brought down, and shalt speak
       out of the ground,
    And thy speech shall be low out of the dust,
    And thy voice shall be, as of one that hath a
       familiar spirit, out of the ground,
    And thy speech shall whisper out of the dust.
15. Moreover the multitude of thy strangers shall be
       like small dust.
    And the multitude of the terrible ones shall be as
       chaff that passeth away:
    Yea, it shall be at an instant suddenly.
    Thou shalt be visited of the Lord of hosts
    With thunder, and with earthquake, and great
       noise,
20. With storm and tempest,
    And the flame of devouring fire.
    And the multitude of all the nations
    That fight against Ariel,
    (Even all that fight against her and her munition,
       and that distress her,)
25. Shall be as a dream of a night vision.
    It shall even be

As when an hungry man dreameth, and, behold!
   he eateth;
But he awaketh! and his soul is empty:
Or, as when a thirsty man dreameth, and, behold!
   he drinketh;
30. But he awaketh—and, behold! he is faint, and his
   soul hath appetite:
So shall the multitude of all the nations be,
That fight against Mount Zion.
Stay yourselves, and wonder!
Cry ye out, and cry!
35. They are drunken—but not with wine;
They stagger—but not with strong drink.
For the Lord hath poured out upon you the spirit
   of deep sleep,
And hath closed your eyes:
The prophets, and your rulers, the seers hath he
   covered
40. And the vision of all is become unto you
As the words of a book that is sealed,
Which men deliver to one that is learned
Saying, Read this, I pray thee:
And he saith, I cannot; for it is sealed:
45. And the book is delivered to him that is not
   learned,
Saying, Read this, I pray thee:
And he saith, I am not learned.
Wherefore the Lord said,
Forasmuch as this people draw near me with their
   mouth,
And with their lips do honor me,
50. But have removed their heart far from me,
And their fear toward me is taught by the precept
   of men:
Therefore, behold! I will proceed to do a
   marvelous work among this people,
Even a marvelous work and a wonder:

For the wisdom of their wise men shall perish,
55. And the understanding of their prudent men shall
 be hid.

LESSON CXXVI.
The Proverbs of Solomon.—BIBLE.

1. A wise son maketh a glad father:
 But a foolish son is the heaviness of his mother.
 Treasures of wickedness profit nothing:
 But righteousness delivereth from death.
 The Lord will not suffer the soul of the righteous to
  famish:
 But he casteth away the substance of the wicked.
 He becometh poor that dealeth with a slack hand:
 But the hand of the diligent maketh rich.

2. He that gathereth in summer is a wise son:
 But he that sleepeth in harvest is a son that
  causeth shame.
 Blessings are upon the head of the just:
 But violence covereth the mouth of the wicked.
 The memory of the just is blessed:
 But the name of the wicked shall rot.
 The wise in heart will receive commandments:
 But a prating fool shall fall.

3. He that walketh uprightly walketh surely:
 But he that perverteth his ways shall be known.
 He that winketh with the eye causeth sorrow:
 But a prating fool shall fall.
 The mouth of a righteous man is a well of life:
 But violence covereth the mouth of the wicked.
 Hatred stirreth up strifes:
 But love covereth all sins.

4. In the lips of him that hath understanding wisdom
    is found:
  But a rod is for the back of him that is void of
    understanding.
  Wise men lay up knowledge:
  But the mouth of the foolish is near destruction.
  The rich man's wealth is his strong city:
  The destruction of the poor is their poverty.
  The labor of the righteous tendeth to life:
  The fruit of the wicked to sin.

5. He is in the way of life that keepeth instruction:
  But he that refuseth reproof erreth.
  He that hideth hatred with lying lips,
  And he that uttereth a slander, is a fool.
  In the multitude of words there wanteth not sin:
  But he that refraineth his lips is wise.
  The tongue of the just is as choice silver:
  The heart of the wicked is little worth.

6. The lips of the righteous feed many:
  But fools die for want of wisdom.
  The blessing of the Lord, it maketh rich,
  And he addeth no sorrow with it.
  It is as sport to a fool to do mischief:
  But a man of understanding hath wisdom.
  The fear of the wicked, it shall come upon him:
  But the desire of the righteous shall be granted.

7. As the whirlwind passeth, so is the wicked no
    more:
  But the righteous is an everlasting foundation.
  As vinegar to the teeth, and as smoke to the eyes,
  So is the sluggard to them that send him.
  The fear of the Lord prolongeth days:
  But the years of the wicked shall be shortened.
  The hope of the righteous shall be gladness:
  But the expectation of the wicked shall perish.

8. The way of the Lord is strength to the upright:
   But destruction shall be to the workers of iniquity.
   The righteous shall never be removed:
   But the wicked shall not inhabit the earth.
   The mouth of the just bringeth forth wisdom:
   But the froward tongue shall be cut out.
   The lips of the righteous know what is acceptable:
   But the mouth of the wicked speaketh
     frowardness.

LESSON CXXVII.

Comfort ye my People.—BIBLE.

1. Comfort ye, comfort ye my people!
   Saith your God.
   Speak ye comfortably to Jerusalem, and cry
     unto her,
   That her warfare is accomplished,
5. That her iniquity is pardoned:
   For she hath received of her Lord's hand
   Double for all her sins.
   The voice of him that crieth in the wilderness,
   Prepare ye the way of the Lord;
10. Make straight in the desert a highway for our
      God!
    Every valley shall be exalted,
    And every mountain and hill shall be made low:
    And the crooked shall be made straight,
    And the rough places plain:
15. And the glory of the Lord shall be revealed,

And all flesh shall see it together:

For the mouth of the Lord hath spoken it.—

The voice said, Cry! And he said, What shall
    I cry?

All flesh is grass,

20. And all the goodliness thereof is as the flower
    of the field:

The grass withereth, the flower fadeth:

Because the spirit of the Lord bloweth upon it:

Surely the people is grass.

The grass withereth, the flower fadeth:

25. But the word of our God shall stand forever.

O Zion, that bringest good tidings! get thee up
    into the high mountain;

O Jerusalem, that bringest good tidings!

Lift up thy voice with strength;

Lift it up, be not afraid;

30. Say unto the cities of Judah, Behold your
    God!

Behold! the Lord your God will come with
    strong hand,

And his arm shall rule for him:

Behold! his reward is with him,

And his work before him.

35. He shall feed his flock like a shepherd:

He shall gather the lambs with his arm,

And carry them in his bosom,

And shall gently lead those that are with young.

Who hath measured the waters in the hollow of
    his hand,

40. And meted out heaven with the span,

And comprehended the dust of the earth in a
    measure,

And weighed the mountains in scales,

And the hills in a balance?

Who hath directed the Spirit of the Lord,

45. Or, being his counselor, hath taught him?

With whom took He counsel, and who
    instructed him,
And taught him in the path of judgment,
And taught him knowledge,
And showed to him the way of understanding?
50. Behold! the nations are as a drop of a bucket,
And are counted as the small dust of the
    balance:
Behold! he taketh up the isles as a very little
    thing.
And Lebanon is not sufficient to burn,
Nor the beasts thereof sufficient for a burnt
    offering.
55. All nations before him are as nothing;
And they are counted to him less than nothing,
    and vanity.
To whom then will ye liken God?
Or what likeness will ye compare unto him?
The workman melteth a graven image
60. And the goldsmith spreadeth it over with gold,
And casteth silver chains.
He that is so impoverished that he hath no
    oblation
Chooseth a tree that will not rot;
He seeketh unto him a cunning workman to
    prepare a graven image, that shall not be
moved.
65. Have ye not known? have ye not heard?
Hath it not been told you from the beginning?
Have ye not understood from the foundations of
    the earth?
It is He that sitteth upon the circle of the earth,
And the inhabitants thereof are as
    grasshoppers;
70. That stretcheth out the heavens as a curtain,
And spreadeth them out as a tent to dwell in:
That bringeth the princes to nothing;

He maketh the judges of the earth as vanity.

Yea—they shall not be planted;

75. Yea—they shall not be sown:

Yea—their stock shall not take root in the earth:

And He shall also blow upon them, and they
shall wither,

And the whirlwind shall take them away as
stubble.

To whom then will ye liken Me,

80. Or shall I be equal?

Saith the Holy One.

Lift up your eyes on high, and behold!

Who hath created these things?

That bringeth out their host by number:

85. He calleth them all by names: by the greatness
of his might, (for that he is strong in power)

Not one faileth.

Why sayest thou, O Jacob! and speakest, O
Israel!

My way is hid from the Lord,

And my judgement is passed over from my
God?

90. Hast thou not known? hast thou not heard,

That the everlasting God, the Lord,

The Creator of the ends of the earth,

Fainteth not, neither is weary?

There is no searching of his understanding.

95. He giveth power to the faint;

And to them that have no might he increaseth
strength.

Even the youths shall faint and be weary,

And the young men shall utterly fall;

But they that wait upon the Lord shall renew
their strength;

100. They shall mount up with wings as eagles;

They shall run, and not be weary;

And they shall walk, and not faint.

LESSON CXXVIII.
The Celestial City.—BIBLE.

1. And I saw heaven opened, and, behold, a white horse; and He that sat upon him was called Faithful and True, and in righteousness He doth judge and make war. His eyes were as a flame of fire, and on His head were many crowns; and He had a name written, that no man knew, but He himself. And He was clothed with a vesture dipped in blood: and His name is called, The Word of God. And the armies which were in heaven followed Him upon white horses, clothed in fine linen, white and clean. And out of His mouth goeth a sharp sword, that with it He should smite the nations: and He shall rule them with a rod of iron: and He treadeth the winepress of the fierceness and wrath of Almighty God. He hath on His vesture and on His thigh a name written, KING OF KINGS, AND LORD OF LORDS.

2. I saw an angel standing in the sun; and he cried with a loud voice, saying to all the fowls that fly in the midst of heaven, Come and gather yourselves together unto the supper of the great God, that ye may eat the flesh of kings, and the flesh of captains, and the flesh of mighty men, and the flesh of horses, and of them that sit on them, and the flesh of all men, both free and bond, both small and great!

3. I saw the beast, and the kings of the earth, and their armies, gathered together to make war against Him that sat on the horse, and against His army. And the beast was taken, and with him the false prophet that wrought miracles before him, with which he deceived them that had received the mark of the beast, and them that worshiped His image. These both were cast alive into a lake of fire burning with brimstone. And the remnant were slain by the sword

of Him that sat upon the horse, which sword proceeded out of his mouth: and all the fowls were filled with their flesh.

4. I saw an angel come down from heaven, having the key of the bottomless pit and a great chain in his hand. And he laid hold on the Dragon, that old Serpent, which is the Devil, and Satan, and bound him a thousand years, and cast him into the bottomless pit, and shut him up, and set a seal upon him, that he should deceive the nations no more, till the thousand years should be fulfilled: and after that he must be loosed a little season.

5. I saw thrones, and they that sat upon them, and judgment was given unto them: and I saw the souls of them that were beheaded for the witness of Jesus, and for the word of God, and which had not worshiped the beast, neither his image, neither had received his mark upon their foreheads, or in their hands; and they lived and reigned with Christ a thousand years. But the rest of the dead lived not again until the thousand years were finished. This is the first resurrection. Blessed and holy is he that hath part in the first resurrection, on such the second death hath no power, but they shall be priests of God and of Christ, and shall reign with him a thousand years.

6. When the thousand years are expired, Satan shall be loosed out of his prison, and shall go out to deceive the nations which are in the four quarters of the earth, Gog and Magog, to gather them together to battle: the number of whom is as the sand of the sea. They went up on the breadth of the earth, and compassed the camp of the saints about, and the beloved city: and fire came down from God out of heaven, and devoured them. The Devil that deceived them was cast into the lake of fire and brimstone, where the beast and the false prophet are, and shall be tormented day and night for ever and ever.

7. I saw a great white throne, and Him that sat on it, from whose face the earth and the heaven fled away; and there was found no place for them. I saw the dead, small and great, stand before God; and the books were opened: and another book was opened, which is the book of life: and the dead were judged out of those things which were written in the books, according to their works. And the sea gave up the dead which were in it; and Death and Hell delivered up the dead which were in them: and they were judged every man according to their works. And Death and Hell were cast into the lake of fire. This is the second death. And whoseever was not found written in the book of life was cast into the lake of fire.

8. I saw a new heaven and a new earth: for the first heaven and the first earth were passed away; and there was no more sea. I John saw the Holy City, New Jerusalem, coming down from God out of heaven, prepared as a bride adorned for her husband. I heard a great voice out of heaven saying, Behold! The tabernacle of God is with men, and he will dwell with them, and they shall be his people, and God himself shall be with them, and be their God. God shall wipe away all tears from their eyes; and there shall be no more death, neither sorrow, nor crying, neither shall there be any more pain: for the former things are passed away.

9. He that sat upon the throne said, Behold! I make all things new. He said unto me, Write: for these words are true and faithful. He said unto me, It is done! I am Alpha and Omega, the Beginning and the End. I will give unto him that is athirst of the fountain of the water of life freely. He that overcometh shall inherit all things; and I will be his God, and he shall be my son. But the fearful, and unbelieving, and the abominable, and murderers, and whoremongers, and sorcerers, and idolaters, and all liars, shall have

their part in the lake which burneth with fire and
brimstone: which is the Second death.

10. There came unto me one of the seven angels
which had the seven vials full of the seven last
plagues, and talked with me, saying, Come hither, I
will show thee the Bride, the Lamb's wife. He carried
me away in the spirit to a great and high mountain,
and showed me that great city, the Holy Jerusalem,
descending out of heaven from God, having the glory
of God.—And her light was like unto a stone most
precious, even like a jasper stone, clear as crystal; and
had a wall great and high, and had twelve gates, and
at the gates twelve angels, and names written
thereon, which are the names of the twelve tribes of
the children of Israel: on the east three gates; on the
north three gates; on the south three gates; and on
the west three gates. The wall of the city had twelve
foundations, and in them the names of the twelve
apostles of the Lamb.

11. He that talked with me had a golden reed to
measure the city, and the gates thereof, and the wall
thereof. The city lieth foursquare, and the length is
as large as the breadth: and he measured the city with
the reed, twelve thousand furlongs. The length and
the breadth and the height of it are equal. He
measured the wall thereof, an hundred and forty and
four cubits, according to the measure of a man, that
is, of the angel.—And the building of the wall of it
was of jasper: and the city was pure gold, like unto
clear glass. The foundations of the wall of the city
were garnished with all manner of precious stones.
The first foundation was jasper; the second, sapphire;
the third, a chalcedony; the fourth, an emerald; the
fifth, sardonyx; the sixth, sardius; the seventh,
chrysolite; the eighth, beryl; the ninth, a topaz; the
tenth, a chrysoprasus; the eleventh, a jacinth; the
twelfth, an amethyst. The twelve gates were twelve

pearls; every several gate was of one pearl; and the street of the city was pure gold, as it were transparent glass.

12. I saw no temple therein: for the Lord God Almighty and the Lamb are the temple of it. The city had no need of the sun, neither of the moon, to shine in it: for the glory of God did lighten it, and the Lamb is the light thereof.—And the nations of them which are saved shall walk in the light of it: and the kings of the earth do bring their glory and honor into it. And the gates of it shall not be shut at all by day (for there shall be no night there;) and they shall bring the glory and honor of the nations into it. There shall in nowise enter into it anything that defileth, neither whatsoever worketh abomination, or maketh a lie: but they which are written in the Lamb's book of life.

13. He showed me a pure river of water of life, clear as crystal, proceeding out of the throne of God and of the Lamb. In the midst of the street of it, and on either side of the river, was there the tree of life, which bare twelve manner of fruits, and yielded her fruit every month: and the leaves of the tree were for the healing of the nations. And there shall be no more curse: but the throne of God and of the Lamb shall be in it; and his servants shall serve him: and they shall see his face; and his name shall be in their foreheads. There shall be no night there; and they need no candle, neither light of the sun; for the Lord giveth them light: and they shall reign for ever and ever.

LESSON CXXIX.

*America.—National Hymn.**—MASON'S
SACRED HARP.

1. My country! 'tis of thee,
   Sweet land of liberty,
   Of thee I sing;
   Land, where my fathers died;
   Land of the pilgrims' pride;
   From every mountain side,
   Let freedom ring.

2. My native country! thee,
   Land of the noble free,
   Thy name I love:
   I love thy rocks and rills,
   Thy woods and templed hills;
   My heart with rapture thrills,
   Like that above.

3. Let music swell the breeze,
   And ring from all the trees,
   Sweet freedom's song;
   Let mortal tongues awake,
   Let all that breathe partake,
   Let rocks their silence break,
   The sound prolong.

4. Our fathers' God! to thee,
   Author of liberty!
   To thee we sing;
   Long may our land be bright,
   With freedom's holy light,
   Protect us by thy might,
   Great God, our King!

---

*This beautiful lesson is found, set to music, in "Mason's Sacred Harp," a new collection of hymn tunes, sacred songs and anthems.

Stalin's desire for "the Baltic States . . . but also . . . expansion to the west, presumably by advancing the Lithuanian borders into East Prussia" and obtaining "naval and air bases in Finland . . ."[8]

No wonder Roosevelt was tired and cranky.

He also received a detailed memo from the office of the legal advisor at the State Department explaining how, while the Constitution was clear on declaring war, it was silent on declaring peace. "The Constitution itself contains no specific grant of power to any branch of the Government to make peace." It had been discussed at the Constitutional Convention in August of 1787 "to give Congress the power to declare both war and peace. The motion was unanimously rejected." This power had been in the Articles of Confederation. Any conclusion of hostilities required a treaty, and that required the approval of the U.S. Senate. However, the fabled document gave the president broad powers. According to constitutional experts, "It is the right of the president, and not of Congress, to determine whether the terms [of peace] are advantageous, and if he refuses to make peace, the war must go on." Even Woodrow Wilson said only the Senate could ratify peace.[9]

A House special investigating committee also released a report that said "thousands of Nazis, Fascists, Japs are active there" in South America. In Argentina alone, it was charged that over 2,000 Gestapo agents were operating, and there "was reason to believe that a large contingent of Storm Troopers has 1been organized and that secret drilling is now in progress." Also, the committee report claimed that there were 90,000 Nazis in the Buenos Aires area alone.[10] The German embassy in that city was little more than a printing press for propaganda.

The German embassy had taken the speeches of Charles Lindbergh, put them in a brochure, and distributed them widely throughout Argentina.[11] Lindbergh, erstwhile American hero, would suffer a permanent blow to his reputation and prestige because of his previous pro-German, isolationist stance. The congressional report on these matters was comprehensive and had been assembled in a short period of time. Senator Harry Truman's steadfast work rooting out corruption was also impressive.

Whether one agreed or disagreed with all the actions of Congress, those actions were nonetheless impressive in speed and scope.

It was time for the editors of the United Press to poll their editors and rank the top ten stories of 1941. The attack at Pearl Harbor was the lead-pipe cinch for first place. Of the succeeding nine, all were war related, from Lend-Lease to the Atlantic Charter to the pitched sea battle between the *Bismarck* and the *Hood* in the Atlantic. Not even Joe Louis's epic title defenses or Joe DiMaggio's fifty-six game hitting streak or Ted Williams' phenomenal season hitting over .400 made the top ten stories.[12]

In Washington, a former silent screen star, Corrine Griffith, and her husband, "wealthy Washington (D.C.) laundry operator Clark Griffith" were granted full custody in the adoption of two young girls. Buried at the bottom of the small newspaper item, it was also noted that Griffith was the owner of the "Washington professional football Redskins."[13]

The national debt was announced at $57 billion dollars.[14]

Initially, the War Department had put out a call for skilled welders and steel-workers needed to help build ships at Pearl Harbor, but it was revealed several days later that, in fact, the workers were needed to "help repair the damage" at the war-torn island. "Those needed include mechanics, laborers and helpers. Among the journeyman trades the pay will vary from $1.02 an hour to $1.30 an hour, depending on the type of work. One hundred laborers at 62 cents an hour and 100 helpers at 74 cents an hour are needed. Single men are preferred . . . all applicants will be subjected to . . . [a] Federal Bureau of Investigation fingerprint test."[15]

The war industry continued to ramp up speedily as the president set higher and higher production quotas. Exhibiting his usual knack for the inspirational phrase, FDR called America's massive manufacturing might the Arsenal of Democracy. At first, business leaders as well as Congress (which had to come up with the astronomical funding) balked at some of his ambitious demands. Soon, though, the war economy was firing on all cylinders and producing weaponry and materiel at levels previously deemed utterly impossible. Germany and its Axis partners were about to get a taste of America's will. At a plant in Johnsville, Pennsylvania, new dive bombers were near to being turned out only weeks after the factory opened. Without revealing any details, the designers of the new plane promised it would fly circles around the German Stuka. The new American plane's initial name was "Buccaneer."[16]

To build planes, trains, automobiles, tanks, ships, guns, ,etc., raw materials were needed—and lots of them. So the government's requisitioning of privately owned material accelerated. "OPM Priorities Director Donald M. Nelson yesterday announced the seizure by the Navy of more than one million dollars worth of critical scarce materials being held in warehouses and railroad terminals for shipment to foreign countries. The requisitioning, first under new powers granted to the Office of Production Management by Executive Order, included more than 13 million pounds of steel, 3½ million pounds of copper, 34,000 pounds of tin and 70,000 feet of teakwood. The steel had been located by OPM research and statistics bureau's survey of lost, hidden and frozen inventories . . . . The owners of the property taken . . . will be compensated for the value of the materials."[17] The navy also helped itself to "four of [the] Gulf's finest yachts" in Mobile, Alabama.[18]

With astonishing speed, the U.S. government had not only identified privately held metals, woods, and other materials but had also taken them for the war effort. Government was all-pervasive by the twentieth. Not since the special powers that President Lincoln had appropriated for himself during the Civil War had the centralized authority of the U.S. government moved with such alacrity and such trampling of private property, if not of the Constitution for that matter. During the existential crisis of the Civil War, Lincoln used his war powers to suspend the writ of habeas corpus, proclaim a blockade, and spend funds without congressional authorization. Most of his actions were subsequently upheld by Congress and the courts. Now, America faced another existential crisis, and FDR had precedent for dispensing with a few inconvenient democratic niceties.

The *Wall Street Journal* fretted about the new war powers granted FDR by Congress. "President Roosevelt now holds greater powers over life and property than any President before him. Legislation to give him still more power already is being planned. Two additional legislative grants of power are to be asked soon, government officials disclose. Also, it is anticipated that the President will soon ask Congress to eliminate the Tabor amendment to the Property Requisitioning Bill." If eliminated, it would allow outright seizure of factory equipment by the government for the war effort.[19] Unlike some editors in the Civil War who had been ordered imprisoned by Lincoln because their opposition had displeased him, Roosevelt made no such move against newspapers that opposed him, including the *Journal*.

The Office of Production Management was being reorganized. This, for the few defenders of an unfettered free market, was cause for concern. The OPM regulated just about everything already, from rubber to salad oil. Now it was poised to directly manage all of industry and the entire workforce, including "the curtailment of production for civilian use." It was also preparing to take over the "pulp and paper; printing and publishing; lumber and building materials; plumbing and heating; electrical appliances; automobiles; transportation and farm equipment; industrial and office machinery." The list just continued on and on.[20]

Because of the rapid expansion of the federal war bureaucracy, some government functions were actually suggested to be outsourced to other locations around the country to make room for the war effort in Washington. All in all, twelve federal agencies including the Patent Office, the Rural Electrification Administration, the Fish and Wildlife Service, and others were proposed to be moved to New York City, St. Louis, and Chicago, among other locations. For the 10,000 federal workers potentially being displaced, the government promised to pay their moving costs and help them find adequate housing, or, if they could not move, the government promised to help them find comparable jobs.[21] The forced private-sector layoffs came with no such guarantees.

America's medical schools on the East Coast announced that becoming a board certified physician would now take only three years, as opposed to the usual four-year plan because of the desperate need for doctors in military hospitals. A "Victory Book" campaign was organized nationally to get people to send works of fiction and nonfiction to servicemen for their reading pleasure. The Girl Scouts organized a "Senior Scout" program to train their elder girls "in emergency feeding, messenger service, care of children, preparation of emergency shelters and packing of emergency rations and equipment."[22] A contingent of members of the Canadian Air Cadets came through New York on a publicity tour, with the idea of starting a similar program for American boys. The ages of the air cadets were fourteen to eighteen, and they were described as the "kindergarten of the Royal Air Force."[23]

Perhaps because of the Christmas season, the city of Washington was displaying a pubic spiritedness not normally associated with the Capitol of Cynicism. Dupont Circle and Glover Park organized air-raid watching groups, as did Takoma Park in Maryland. A "D.C. Committee of 70" was set up to collect scrap paper, rubber, metal, and old rags.[24]

Blind Americans were also doing their part for the war effort. At "fifty-four workshops for the blind in twenty-seven states," they were churning out for the military "brooms, mops, deck swabs, mattresses, cocoa mats, pillowcases, whisk brooms, mailing bags, mop handles and similar articles."[25]

Because skilled labor was needed, some of the new vocational and academic teaching programs for the blind came as a direct result of the war effort, because skilled labor was needed. Over 2,000 patriotic sightless citizens working in these various plants wanted to kick the stuffing out of the Axis thugs too.

Even Fido was being recruited for the war effort. The commander of the Los Angeles harbor, Colonel W. W. Hicks, put out an all-points bulletin for "canine recruits." He "said the dogs could be of all sizes or breeds, but must be in good health and sufficiently intelligent to pass the canine equivalent of the Stanford universal achievement test." What the lucky dogs would be engaged in was termed a "military secret." It was recalled that "in the last war, they were used at the front to carry messages."[26]

It may have been the holiday season that brought people together, but marriages still ended and some badly. In order to secure a divorce, a public notice ran in the New York Times: "My wife, Phyllis Zenerino, having left my bed and board . . . [I] will not be responsible for her debts. Frank Zenerino, 608 9th Avenue, New York."[27]

The spirit of Christmas and esprit de corps and sacrifice were almost everywhere else though. In the Philippines, the 6,000 criminals of the penitentiary offered to donate blood for the Allied cause and to fight the Japanese if released. "The prisoners reaffirmed their faith in the United States and the Philippines."[28] A group of thirteen criminals, most of them serving life sentences, went one better and offered themselves to FDR as a "suicide squad." They wrote a letter to Roosevelt, which the warden allowed to go to the White House and in which they proposed "to serve as human torpedoes to help crush the Japanese. It is far better to sacrifice one life than to lose thousands," the missive said.[29] Sacrifice for a higher calling, even among crooks, was deep in the American creed.

Across America, religious and seasonal Christmas songs burst forth in department stores, on city sidewalks, in government buildings, in public schools, on radios, and all across the country. Everybody wished everybody else "Merry Christmas!" and no one was offended. Bibles were everywhere, as were crèches—scenes of the manger where Christ was born. Big write-ups in all the papers detailed planned church festivities, and there were extensive stories in the Washington papers of the planned activities of the Roosevelt clan on Christmas Eve. Christmas lighting had been kept to a minimum, but the sacrifices of war made the American people all the more resolute and, indeed, righteous in wanting to celebrate the birthday of Jesus Christ. The fact that America was fighting for its life made the Christmas of 1941 deeply meaningful because it represented, to most people, the very thing that made fighting worthwhile. Understandably then, beneath the Christmas joy was a seriousness of purpose among the American people.

So much so, that many factories were humming and operating on December 25. "To supply steel for war, many plants in the industry, will operate on Christmas Day for the first time in 24 years, or since the first World War." Some of the plants that would be open included Carnegie-Illinois Steel Corporation, Republic Steel, and, appropriately, Bethlehem Steel. All workers would receive time-and-a-half, and the president of Carnegie, J. L. Perry, remarked, "It is not longer a question of how much steel can be provided to industry but how quickly. Delay in the production of steel means delay in the production of material vital to national welfare."[30]

Christmas was being celebrated in Hawaii, albeit it in a truncated manner.

Blackouts were still in effect, but during the day, Navy enlistees in their white uniforms were spotted carrying packages on the streets of Honolulu. "Nobody seems downhearted. Nevertheless, the territorial office of civilian defense has established a public morale section to promote loyalty to the United States and interracial harmony . . . This section is headed by an American, with one Chinese assistant and another of Japanese-American ancestry."[31]

But what was on everybody's mind in Hawaii was when the bars and nightclubs and liquor stores would open back up.[32]

Even with the massive disruption in the national economy, consumer spending was projected to increase greatly in 1942 "despite higher taxes and rising prices."[33] After years of grim deprivation during the Depression, there was a huge pent up demand for consumer goods and a better life. Anticipating the upswing in the economy, the Spiegel Company of Chicago, a department store and mail-order house, announced it was for the first time offering a credit plan for mail orders, with no interest charges, only a small "carrying charge."[34] Adding to the holiday spirit was the release of a new Shirley Temple movie, *Kathleen*, after a two-year hiatus for the hugely popular young movie actress.[35]

Reality was always deeply woven into the fabric, however. There were ongoing discussions about cancelling the annual New Year's Eve festivities in Times Square in New York City. Boston's archbishop, William Cardinal O'Connell, canceled the traditional midnight Mass for Christmas Eve because of the fear of what could happen to a large group of unsuspecting churchgoers. "The action was taken in a move to co-operate with defense authorities by eliminating the possibility of congestion of hundreds of persons after dark in the event of an emergency."[36] A letter had gone out to every Catholic church in America to be read at Mass on Sunday, the twenty-first, asking all parishioners to get involved in war work.

The Jews of Europe were also grounded in reality, a monstrously horrible one: "the Paris municipal government ordered new measures against Jews in the German-occupied capital and surrounding Seine department." Jews were required to notify Gestapo officials of any change in their addresses. "For the last week, the Gestapo has been rounding up Jews and sending them to concentration camps. Travelers arriving at Vichy said several thousand had been arrested."[37]

Navy sources also revealed that German U-boats had been sighted off the Eastern Seaboard, sometimes within eyesight of land. The main Philippine island of Luzon was under increased assault by Japanese forces, which had made yet another successful beachhead on the island.[38] American and Filipino soldiers and flyers were doing their best under impossible circumstances.

Just a few weeks earlier, most Americans could probably not find Luzon on a map. Now they were learning about faraway places they had never before heard of, with odd and even funny names, but which were quickly becoming very important to them and their country. Just that day, they learned that American forces on Mindanao near the town of Davao were engaged in "some of the most serious battling of the war," where the Japanese had opened yet a new front in the fight for the Philippines. Meanwhile, the British had taken Derna and El Mekili in North Africa.[39]

From the Russian Front, "Tarussa, sixty-five miles northeast of Kaluga, and the town of Kanino, southeast of Kaluga, also were reported captured. Kaluga is an important rail junction on the line running south to Bryansk and Kiev."[40] They also learned that American fighter planes had downed four Japanese bomber planes over Chungking.[41] However, twenty-four Japanese planes bombed, again, this time hitting the U.S. base at Cavite near Manila Bay.

The situation in Hong Kong worsened for the British. Giant fires were seen in the area, and there were reports of hand-to-hand fighting in the streets. Wake Island was enduring its thirteenth day of attack. They'd been undergoing an underreported story of "long hammering by bombs and shells, of endless hours without rest or sleep, of the dogged spirit which has turned aside attack after attack in more than 300 hours of almost constant attack."[42] The island was no more than 2,600 acres, and "the highest point above sea level is 15 feet."[43] The tough marines and navy seamen on the island repelled another two attempts by the Japanese to take the little atoll.

The leaders of the Marine Corps were getting ready to roll out their new recruiting poster for billboards across the country. It featured a "rough and ready marine, against a background of the sea and ships, holding his hand out to greet prospective enlistees." The caption read, "Want Action? Join the United States Marine Corps."[44] The battle for Wake Island certainly served as an inspiration for the poster and for the American people. The Japanese had, at the outset of the war, claimed they had captured Wake Island, but the marines and the navy said "nuts".

Enlisting was one thing. That only began the process. Young enlistees only had a few days to settle their civilian affairs; break the news to alternatively angry, scared, and proud parents; tell their friends and employers, maybe a girlfriend or at least the girl next door; pass the physical and then report to a recruiting office to swear their loyalty to the Constitution of the United States and to follow the orders of the president of the United States and their superior officers. A recruiting doctor observed that Northern boys had "good feet and bad teeth," while Southern boys had just the opposite. His theory was boys in the South liked to go barefoot while boys in the North ate "too much candy and soft foods."[45] Ironically, both bad teeth and flat fleet could earn a young man a 4-F designation, though other restrictions against serving, including hernias, hay fever, or a "nasal deformity," had been lowered.[46]

Often, towns would hold parades for the young men with good teeth and good feet, cheering and watching them march off even as they were still in "civvies," with bands, and crowds, and fanfare, before they boarded a bus or a train and headed for six weeks of hell in boot camp. It was all rough going, learning how to kill other men, eat lousy food, and live in drafty barracks with no air conditioning and poor heating, and drill instructors yelling at them all the time. One "boot" at Fort Dix swore the breakfast sausages were stuffed with sawdust. At no time did any "boot" have any privacy. They marched together, ate together, showered together, and slept together. They went into the military as little more than boys but came out as men, forever changed. The marines had the roughest boot camps of all, complete with hazing and harassing. Of the first twenty-eight days in camp, nine were spent learning how to shoot and handle a rifle.[47]

There had never been a military man in the history of the nation who did not say service in uniform did not change his life forever. Friendships also sprang up, some that lasted a lifetime—however short that might now be.

The day had been relatively quiet on the Malayan Peninsula, but most thought the Japanese were regrouping for a massive assault on Singapore. American and British troops were earning their combat pay. American military leaders told reporters that, despite all the problems, they believed MacArthur would hold on to the Philippines with his 130,000 troops, despite the fact that supplies were running perilously low. MacArthur also had maintained the warm support of Philippine president Manuel Quezon.[48] It would be difficult. The Philippines all told had over 300 separate islands and atolls that, combined, made up more shoreline than that of the entire continental United States.[49]

It was not known if the island redoubt of Corregidor had yet been attacked, but the telltale smoke associated with antiaircraft gunfire was seen over the island. Also, the Philippines were overrun with Japanese sympathizers. At one location, American servicemen discovered a mirror in a tree, obviously put there as a signal to Japanese bomber pilots.[50]

One of the cushiest U.S. Army assignments of the war may have been to the new garrison on the island of Bermuda. The closest the island came to war was having the British name one of their bomber planes after it, or maybe a visit from the occasional German submarine. True, it was out of harm's way, away from the action, but if eating cold K-rations in a wintry fox-hole in Europe was not your cup of tea or if sweating out the war in the engine room of a warship in the Pacific was not up your alley, then pulling easy duty on a balmy island while still getting a ribbon on your chest was a good way to go. And to top it off, there were regular Pam Am Clipper fights between the island and Miami.

Meeting the press the day before, FDR was in a lousy mood, "his face graven and serious, his manner brusque and preoccupied. Mr. Roosevelt started talking without preamble, without a trace of a smile. As somber as his heavy black suit and the lines bracketing his mouth, the President paced off his conference quickly." After a long day, he slipped out for a "pre-dinner swim and an evening of work." The president's health was markedly deteriorating, but this fact was kept hidden from an anxious nation that needed confidence in its leaders. The White House staff also was burning the midnight oil.[51]

A mini-crisis developed over the weekend when Secretary of State Cordell Hull had to angrily knock down a rumor that the State Department had "asked the Navy to suspend patrolling activities west of Hawaii during his pre-war negotiations with Japanese diplomats here." He blamed Fifth Columnists who were "spreading the foulest reports that the most mendacious mind can conceive."[52] The accusation was that Hull wanted to create a peaceful atmosphere by having the navy stand down, as it would send a signal to the Japanese that the United States did not suspect them of possible dirty pool. It would have been the ultimate white flag.

The issue over a congressional investigation into the events at Pearl Harbor was slipping once again out of its box, having already been scotched twice by the White House. Senator Robert Taft, Republican of Ohio, spoke out and said that just because Roosevelt had created his own blue ribbon committee, it should not preclude a Capitol Hill inquiry from going forward.[53]

Another mini-crisis coming out of FDR's Business-Labor meeting was that unions were balking now at abiding by a no-strike pledge if they could not protect their "closed shops." As more and more men and women were coming into the war industries, it was not clear that they had to be compelled to join unions as they had for years. The goal had been to get unions to agree to no strikes for the duration of the war, but when this became a sticky wicket, Congress threatened more legislation expanding the no-strike laws.

The next day, Sunday the twenty-first, was the championship game for the NFL. The game, to be played in Chicago, would feature the "Monsters of the Midway," the Bears, against the New York Giants. The Bears, the defending champions, were heavily favored, and were coached by the legendary George Halas, aka "Papa Bear." But with everything going Chicago's way in advance of the game, ticket sales were way off, and game officials were not expecting anything close to a sellout.

Fans could be forgiven for having other things on their minds.

CHAPTER 21

THE TWENTY-FIRST
OF DECEMBER

Report Sub Attacks Off U.S.

Chicago Sunday Tribune

Son Is Not Dead, Navy Apologies, Gloom Vanishes

Boston Sunday Globe

Arab Cheers Greet British at Derna

Washington Post

I f Saturday the twentieth had been a day of big little news, Sunday the twenty-first was a day of little big news. Under giant black headlines: "The Navy said ... it had received unconfirmed reports that two oil tankers had been attacked by submarines ... and that one had sent out an S.O.S." The two ships were the 6,912-ton ship *Emidio* and the 6,771-ton *Agriworld*.[1]

The *Agriworld* had been only a hundred miles from San Francisco, en route to Los Angeles.[2] The crew of the *Agriworld* put on their life belts, fearful of being sunk. Despite being fired upon repeatedly by the submarine's deck gun, rolling seas threw off the aim of the gun crew, and she survived. The attack on the Emidio, less lucky, was off of Blunts Reef, near the tiny California town of Eureka, only fifteen miles off shore. The ship had "sustained a torpedo attack." The navy later sighted the crippled ship and radioed that it was riding "low in the water." Both ships escaped, despite the *Emidio* being hit repeatedly by shells from the unidentified submarine. The crews for both ships clearly identified submarines, however no markings.[3]

Navy and army planes searched for the attacking warships, but to no avail. Several days earlier, an unidentified submarine had been sighted off of Puget Sound and military planes had engaged the vessel, firing on it, but this was only revealed several days later.[4] Some officials suspected the Japanese had a secret, hidden sub base in Latin America. One man claimed he'd seen Japanese fishing boats hauling cement there for years.[5]

These attacks on the oil tankers, plus the new sightings of German U-boats off the East Coast, brought the war much closer than it had been before. After two weeks of unremitting war news and emergency announcements, the American people could be forgiven if they'd become a bit disconsolate. Telltale signs emerged of flagging morale. Still, "news of the submarine actions of San Francisco did not disturb the outward calm of Los Angeles. Church bells echoed all the morning and the roads were clogged with the usual Sunday traffic."[6]

It was also confirmed that an American commercial vessel, the *Cynthia Olson*, with a cargo of lumber, some 700 miles from the West Coast, had been fired upon and hit by a Japanese submarine on the day of December 7th.[7] The *Cynthia Olson* had been sunk with all hands lost.

More bad news came from the Far East when it was learned that communications with the city of Davao on the island of Mindanao had been cut off. The Japanese had made landfall the day before and now General MacArthur could not get any information out of that battle zone.[8] "No word has been received from there since yesterday afternoon." It was reported the Japanese had come ashore "in fairly substantial forces . . . [T]he Davao campaign may develop into the most important land battle yet in the Philippines archipelago."[9] The goal of the Japanese was to quickly build airfields on conquered territories and establish air supremacy as soon as possible.

The situation was also deteriorating in Manila. Douglas MacArthur warned that looters would face the death penalty. Before the blackout came, reports got out that the Moro tribe, a tough bunch of bolo-swinging native warriors, joined the fight against the Japanese on Mindanao.[10]

MacArthur then discovered, to his dismay, that twenty Japanese ships including destroyers and submarines were engaged in the battle for the Philippines: more than he'd previously known about.[11] The odds were stacking up against the optimistic general.

Underestimating the Japanese was proving costly. The Japanese were thorough and had well-developed plans. Several months before the attack on Hawaii and other military installations—including Guam—it turned out that a Japanese ship suffered a deliberate wreck at Guam just so the officers and crew could get a close good look at the island's defenses—defenses they later overcame.[12]

Hong Kong was teetering. "The Japanese say they have the city of Victoria and that lorries flying the scarlet ball of the rising sun are roaring through the streets, packed with disarmed British soldiers; the remnants of the British garrison are encircled on the peak of the island, Mount Victoria."[13] The Japanese had already captured or destroyed large quantities of oil, rice, vehicles, medicines, and much of the colony was aflame. The slim hope was for relief by Free Chinese forces. No relief for the gutsy British troops hiding and fighting a last-gasp guerilla battle was contemplated by London.

While the loss of Hong Kong to the Japanese would be devastating, the loss of the strategically located Singapore would be cataclysmic. Singapore had deep sea anchorages, docks for repairing large ships, "workshops for machinery and guns, one of the most powerfully transmitting stations in the world, and huge underground oil and armament depots." But Britain's "crown jewel" was even more than that. "The vital significance of Singapore is not simply because it lies athwart trade routes supplying both the United Kingdom and the United States; it is the one spot in that part of the world able to accommodate large fleets in an emergency."[14] From Singapore, attacks could be launched against Sumatra, Borneo, and Australia. For the U.S. fleet to have a port in the Far East from which to wage war, it had to be Singapore. The facilities at Guam were unfinished and had been lost to the Japanese; the facilities at the Philippines were inadequate. If the navy lost Singapore, it would push the United States back thousands of miles.

For all of these reasons and many others, the Allies were fighting hard to hold on to Singapore. "British units fighting along the 400-mile Malaya penin-sula leading to Singapore include English infantrymen, Scottish Highlanders, Australians, Sikhs, Moslem riflemen, Gurkhas and Malayans."[15]

Not all the news was bad. Wake Island was still holding on. "Three days after the Japanese had claimed the island, two days after the President had warned the nation to expect its loss, the isolated band of heroes sent out one of the most astounding communiqués of the war. They still held Wake. They had repulsed four landing attacks. They had succeeded in sinking a Japanese cruiser and a Japanese destroyer. Whether they held the island indefinitely depended upon reinforcements and supplies but already they had taught Nippon that what looked like a pushover on paper can be hell on earth when it is defended by the United States Marines. It was in the tradition ... of the Argonne, Chateau Thierry, and Belleau Wood, where Marine marksmanship and Marine bayo-nets literally exterminated the pride of the German Army," boasted the *Boston Sunday Globe*.[16] Now, of course, there was a new German army to defeat.

The *Saturday Evening Post* ran a long story which detailed that the Third Reich was planning for a five-year war against the Allied Powers. Like the citi-zens of England, Japan, and America, their government was not only asking for sacrifices from the citizenry, they were demanding it. Propaganda Minister Joseph Goebbels went on state radio to call on the German people to donate blankets to their soldiers on the Russian front.[17] The Germans meanwhile were embarking on a massive shipbuilding program. Their shipyards were operating twenty-four hours a day.

War was not only all hell, it was also vile. As the German troops fell back from their thrusts into Russia, they desperately needed transportation of any kind. As a rouse, they announced in Russian towns that free salt was available. Peasants came from everywhere via horse and sleigh when the word spread of the free salt. Except there was no free salt. The Germans took the horses, the sleighs, and shot any Russians who protested the theft.

For Hitler and Nazi Germany, there were no longer civilians, women or children. Any human being, in any circumstance, was fair game. The German people themselves would eventually learn the terrible consequences of total war on their own soil, but that would come later, when the tables had turned against them. In 1941, at the apex of their power, the German conquerors cut a murderous swath through every invaded country, with no compunction and with complete impunity. They were particularly savage toward the Russians, whom they considered *untermenschen*, subhuman.[18]

The War Department, concerned about the nation's morale, began churning out stories of heroes and of American successes. The tale of Captain Colin P. Kelly, Jr. who had sacrificed his life to sink a Japanese war ship had been in the paper for days. It was later learned Captain Kelly had ordered six of the crew in his plane to parachute to safety, leaving him and two others to finish the mission in their shot up and battered plane. After his demise, he was posthumously awarded the Distinguished Service Cross by Douglas MacArthur.[19]

Yet another daring pilot was thrilling Americans with his exploits, Colonel Claire Chennault, of the now-famous "Flying Tigers." Chennault had volunteered to fight with the Chinese against the Japanese like so many other young American adventurers, however, to do so, he had to "resign" from the Army Air Corps. That was before December 7 changed everything. Chennault was a ruggedly handsome Texan and natural leader who shot down numerous Japanese planes, flew the "Hump" over Burma, was a virulent anti-communist and graced the covers of *Look* and *Time* magazine.[20]

Roosevelt was pushing hard to organize a Supreme War Council and the name of Wendell Willkie was floated to either chair or at least serve on the committee. "The Council members would be given broad policy-making powers and authority over all segments of the Nation's wartime life—from civilian activities to actual naval and military operations. They would be responsible only to Mr. Roosevelt." The council was described by one White House insider as "embryonic." On the surface, the White House seemed in command and organized but if the surface was scratched, human beings would be found who were just as disorganized and panicky as anyone else in the country. He was also still trying to get a planning operation going that would involve the British, American, Russian, Chinese, Dutch, "and other governments allied in the world-wide war against the Axis."[21]

Joe Stalin was being a pain in the ass, as per usual. The British Foreign Minister, Anthony Eden, had been in Moscow for days, holding the Soviet Dictator's hand, trying to get him to play nice with everybody else. In a confidential telegram to Secretary of State Cordell Hull, a British official wrote it became "apparent at the most recent meetings between Eden and Stalin that it would be impossible to reconcile the British and Soviet drafts of the proposed pacts on the joint war effort and European post-war problems, in view of the Soviet attitude with respect to the recognition of the 1941 frontiers." Stalin was also delusional as he told Eden "he had expressed the belief that Germany will be defeated within one year and Japan possibly within six months."[22]

All told, FDR had five big items on his "to do" list including "reorganization of the machinery of the United States and British governments to integrate and expedite the war tasks of the two nations."[23] He met that Sunday with the British Ambassador, Lord Halifax, to begin the work on an agenda for a planned meeting that week of the Allies. Though the Russians still hadn't declared war on Japan, they wanted in on the talks.[24]

Curiously, even as of two weeks after the beginning of the war, it was still not commonly being referred to as "World War II" or the "Second World War." Nor was the "Great War" being commonly referred to as "World War I." These appellations appeared here and there in one form or another but would take time to take root in the common lexicon.

Willkie had been on the radio just the evening before, giving the American people what for, telling them they were not sacrificing enough and that they had to get used to a future of "Spartan simplicity and hard work."[25] If his 1940 GOP presidential opponent was willing to play bad cop, FDR was more than happy to play good cop.

In his 1940 effort, hundreds of "Associated Willkie Clubs of America" had sprung up. By 1941, they had become the "Independent Clubs of America." By December 1941, they had become nothing, disbanding to concentrate on the war effort.[26] The Chairman of the Republican National Committee, Joe Martin, sent a letter to all GOP state chairmen informing them of his decision to cancel the party's annual meeting in Washington in January. However, Martin did suggest that countrywide "Lincoln Day dinners" be held on the anniversary of the sixteenth president's birthday as "patriotic demonstrations."

He continued, "Let us publicly proclaim our support of the Administration in an irresistible effort to win the war."[27]

FDR already had a "War Cabinet" working on solving the problems facing the American military and he'd met with them on Saturday, in the Cabinet Room of the White House. It was an amalgamation of White House staff like Harry Hopkins and Cabinet officials like Attorney General Francis Biddle and Labor Secretary Francis Perkins.[28] A bit of good news greeted the War Cabinet in Washington and Winston Churchill's war planners in London, when the British army scored another breakthrough in Libya against the German tank corps. As the Brits rolled into Derna, Libya, they were greeted by "cheering and smiling Arab tribesmen."[29]

Just days before, the government was assuring the American people that food was plentiful and would be so for the foreseeable future, and nothing like the last war. Then Paul McNutt, Federal Security Administrator, told the National Defense Gardening Conference that Americans needed to conserve food and that the "meatless Mondays" of the last war were not inconceivable.[30] Fearing a run on sugar would drive up prices, the government stepped in and froze the cost.[31]

Whereas several days earlier American flags sales were only up modestly, near the end of the month, they had increased sharply—at least for the thirty flag manufacturers in the greater Chicago area. "Orders by the thousands are pouring into the some 30 companies which manufacturer the 'Star-Spangled Banner' and other patriotic insignia. It's the war, of course."[32] Washington was encouraging all Americans to display the stars and bars.

The American Institute of Public Opinion, headed by the up and coming pollster, George Gallup, took a survey of the American people and asked if they would be willing to work an extra eight hours a week in order to help the war effort. An astonishing 88 percent said yes and only 12 percent said no. "Despite long working hours in many war plants, the overwhelming majority of defense workers interviewed indicated their willingness to work an extra eight hours a week in order to speed production."[33]

Washington was moving ahead with what it hoped would be a streamlining of labor, bringing the state and local governments effectively under the control of the national government. The plan was to have a workforce that responded "rapidly" to the needs of the war effort. "President Roosevelt, acting to utilize the man power and woman power of the country for armament production to the fullest extent, ordered creation of a national industrial recruiting agency, which would merge the State and territorial affiliates of the United Sates Employment Services." The plan included "more effective use of those already employed through transfer of needed workers from less essential jobs to war production."[34]

Private property was being confiscated left and right, especially in Washington. One example was a picture-frame shop across from the White House. It had been there for years, filling the orders of presidents as far back as Teddy Roosevelt. It was taken for the war effort and the old building raised. "The land, it seems, is needed for construction of a Government building. Spared were the historic Decatur and Blair houses."[35]

While the government was seizing private property for the war effort, it was also taking control of some twenty foreign-owned plants in the Philadelphia area. The Axis-owned factories were taken over by Treasury officials, after the FBI identified their ownership. "Treasury agents, following a pre-arranged plan, moved in quietly to prevent sabotage and insure maximum production of defense products."[36]

Like their German counterparts, American shipbuilders were also working overtime and ten navy ships slid into the water in one day. "Destroyers, submarine chasers, cargo ships and tankers were represented in the launchings, many of them going into the water far ahead of schedule." Ships were launched in Charleston, South Carolina, New York, and Chester, Pennsylvania.[37] In Charleston, two ships "splashed" within ten minutes of each other. Of course, it had already been determined that these shipyards would be fully operational on Christmas Day.[38]

Three Republican senators came forward to say they would not be "gagged" by the war, despite FDR's power and popularity. This ran contrary to a proclamation the Republican National Committee had issued some days earlier.

The chairman of the RNC and the chairman of the Democratic National Committee, issued a joint communiqué and sent a telegram to FDR pledging to set aside partisanship for the duration of the emergency. The pledge lasted nearly two weeks—pretty impressive, considering politicians made the promise.

The three who decided to battle the headwinds of near-unconditional national support for Roosevelt were Wayland "Curly" Brooks of Illinois, Styles Bridges of New Hampshire, and "Mr. Republican" himself, the redoubtable Robert Taft of Ohio and the leader of conservatives in America, such as they were in 1941.

The three represented three differing viewpoints of the GOP which may have explained their apparent permanent minority status since 1932. Brooks was an out-and-out isolationist, bitterly opposing FDR, Bridges was an out-and-out internationalist, supporting FDR, and Taft was somewhere in the middle. He told the Associated Press that he did not believe that all of FDR's "recommendations . . . must be accepted blindly." Elaborating, he said "Certainly in all fiscal matters we must exercise our own judgment." The three said they planned on critiquing civilian decisions but not those by the military, and they promised not to try to "run the war in Congress."[39]

Others joined the flow with enthusiasm. The publisher of the *Chicago Tribune*, Colonel Robert R. McCormick, a fierce opponent of Roosevelt's for years, and a champion of the America First movement, significantly announced from his own radio station, WGN, that America would someday rule the waves and that America would someday have "command of the sea" and "command of the air."[40] Heads must have shaken in the White House when they heard of the internationalist address by McCormick.

McCormick wasn't anything if he wasn't a patriot, though. Two weeks after the attack, American newspapers were still filled with angry editorials and tough cartoons attacking the Germans, the Italians, but most especially, the Japanese. McCormick's *Tribune* was no exception. One of his reporters had an unusually salient point. At the 1932 Olympics, the Japanese swimmers had done surprisingly well, especially in the shorter competition. It was later learned that the swimmers had been pumped full of fresh oxygen. The *Tribune's* point was that if the Japanese cheated then, and had cheated two weeks earlier at Pearl, they could be counted on to continue cheating.[41]

As it was the weekend before Christmas, Americans were engaged in last-minute shopping. There were only three shopping days left. For women, jewelry, slippers, quilted robes, lounge pajamas, house coats and gowns were suggested, while smoking jackets, pajamas, White Owl cigars, a Palmolive Shaving Kit and shirts were offered for men. Portable radios were also suggested by retailers as good gifts—for war news of course—as were albums of Nelson Eddy and Rise Stevens, Kate Smith, and the "Dorsey Brothers Favorites."[42]

For girls, baby buggies, rag dolls and tricycles were dancing in their heads, while for boys, BB guns and bicycles were what kept them mostly nice and not naughty.

It was an especially busy season as shopping, cooking, wrapping, church services, caroling, decorating, and school plays, intermingled with meetings and lectures on incendiary bombs and the ethics of leaving children in school during air raids as opposed to parents taking them home. The *Post* took note of "Gay Caroling Ushers in Christmas Week."[43]

As always, Americans were flocking to their favorite movie theatres to see their favorite actors and actresses. One new film had no actors though. It was a documentary entitled *Target for Tonight*, and the newspapers ads for it shouted, "How Would You Like To Bomb Germany Tonight?" The film was a feature-length depiction of an RAF squadron from takeoff to dropping bombs over Germany, dodging harrowing anti-aircraft fire and attempting to return safely to England.[44] Still, the Motion Picture Board that represented women's and civic clubs selected *Citizen Kane* as the best picture of the year, followed by *How Green Was My Valley*. Also appearing on the list were *Dumbo* and *Meet John Doe*.[45]

War Bonds were also popular Christmas gifts, especially Series E. They sold in denominations of $25, $50, $100, $500 and $1,000, but this was their value at maturity after ten years. Their purchase price, respectively, was $18.75, $37.50, $75, $375 and $750. They paid a respectable 2.9 percent interest annually and could be cashed in for their full face amount after 10 years. Of course, the full faith and credit of the U.S. government backed up the principle and the interest of every bond. For the small patriotic investor including tykes, war stamps were available at 10 cents, 25 cents, 50 cents, $1 and $5 dollars. Bonds were also available in Series F, but these were large amounts, beyond the reach of nearly all Americans, going as high as $10,000.[46]

Americans—at least those of a marriageable age—also had something on the minds, namely matrimony. The Cook County Clerk said a new record was set for marriage licenses, 350 in one day, December 19. "The spurt was attributed to the presence in Chicago of many soldiers, sailors and marines on Christmas leave." Conversely, the county also reported that the number of divorces had plunged since December 7.[47] The Post Office reported voluminous mail[48] and crime was reportedly down across the nation.

An early Christmas present came for the family of navy man Oscar Thompson, 21, of Geneva, Illinois, whose family had received a telegram ten days earlier that their son was missing and presumed dead. Then his father, Fred, received a telegram saying that Oscar "was among the survivors, and there were apologies about the previous report being untrue."[49]

For the first time since December 7, navy recruiting offices would close from 4 p.m. on Christmas Eve to 8 a.m. on the twenty-sixth. The navy also announced that all recruits, both active duty and on reserve, could go home for Christmas if they could make it. It was generous, as they would have off the twenty-second until the twenty-seventh.[50]

Before December 7, many servicemen and officers wore their civilian clothing as much as possible, as a military career was not held in high regard by many Americans. Now, everybody held them in high regard, especially those in the services themselves, who wore their uniforms with unbridled pride.

Most civilians had a tough time telling a staff sergeant from a seaman or a colonel from a corporal. To help American distinguish ranks and services, many of the papers helpfully displayed the stripes and stars of shoulder boards for generals and admirals as well as the insignias of lesser ranks.

Army servicemen wore khakis and a black tie, tucked neatly into their shirt between the second and third button with the "overseas" cap that looked like a large, #10 envelope when laid on a table. The army was updating its officers' uniforms, dropping the great looking Sam Browne belt that for years featured the across the chest from right shoulder to the left hip supporting leather strap over their suit coat.

Some thought the navy had the best uniforms, both officers and swabs.

The officers wore dress whites in summer, dress blues in winter, and for day-time dress, wore khaki suits. For the summer, they also had the option of white shorts, short sleeve shirts, stretch white socks, and white bucks. Some of their formal uniforms were eye-catching. The seamen also had dress white and blue uniforms for going ashore and got to wear dungaree pants and denim shirts when shipboard. The round "gob's" cap was classic, as were the buttoned-not-zippered pants with bellbottoms and the flap on the back of their pull-over tunics. The flap was popularized by the British navy to keep uniforms from being soiled by greasy pigtails (not an issue for American sailors in 1941.)

For many, the marines had the others beat hands down, both for the officers and the lowly privates. The mix of light blue, dark blue, red trim, and white officer cap for their formal dress uniform was smashing. That the most important general in the marines wore the same dress uniform as the men in the ranks told of a singleness of purpose which screamed "always faithful."

Two Admirals who had new braid added to their uniforms were Admiral Ernest J. King, whom Roosevelt promoted to commander-in-chief of the United States Naval Fleet, replacing Admiral Husband Kimmel; and Rear Admiral Royal E. Ingersoll, who was appointed commander of the Atlantic Fleet. The replacement of Kimmel was pro forma, as he'd already been relieved of command of the Pacific Fleet.[51] King was unique among the elder gentlemen of the navy in that he knew how to fly an airplane and had served aboard submarines, as well as ships during the Spanish-American War. He was one of the most rounded and experienced men in the navy.[52] Because King outranked Chief of Navy Operations Admiral Harold Stark, he only had to report to the Secretary of the Navy Frank Knox and the president of the United States. King was tall, no nonsense, described as "a pleasant gentleman ashore but a tough hombre at sea."[53] King's nickname at Annapolis had been "Old Eagle Eye."[54]

At train stations and bus depots, volunteers for the Red Cross and the Salvation Army, often pretty girls, were there to hand out free coffee and doughnuts as well as pencils and writing papers.

Restaurants and coffee shops in those terminals were jammed with travelers. At some of those restaurants and at others across the country, they were in the process of changing their menus and "rechristening Italian spaghetti" as "Liberty Noodles."[55]

CHAPTER 22

THE TWENTY-SECOND
OF DECEMBER

Major Battle Is Raging in Phillipines

Birmingham News

GOP Chiefs Agree Party Must Keep Eye on New Deal Actions

Birmingham News

Holiday Mail Breaks Record

Los Angeles Times

Three More Attacks On U.S. Ships by Jap Submarines Revealed

Evening Star

U.S. Attorney General Francis Biddle began creating seventy "Alien Enemy Hearing Boards" situated around the country to determine the fate of the thousands of Japanese, Germans, and Italians being held by the government at various detention centers. "The quasi-judicial panels, which start functioning as soon as they are appointed, will hear the cases of all enemy aliens brought before them individually and will make recommendations to the attorney general, who will render the final decisions."[1]

Like the local Draft Boards, the Enemy Hearing Boards would be comprised of civic leaders, businessmen, local politicians, and clerics. Each board, after reviewing each case, could recommend to Biddle the "unconditional release" of the incarcerated individual, their parole, or that they be "interned for the duration of the war." Further, "the alien enemy may be accompanied by a relative, friend or adviser, but will not be permitted to be represented by anyone in the capacity of an attorney."[2]

Among the 35,000 reported Japanese nationals living on the various Hawaiian islands, 272 were being held as accused Fifth Columnists. (The number of Japanese in both America and the Hawaiian islands swung wildly around.) All known subversives were imprisoned, but the search continued for others.[3]

The treatment of Germans, Italians, and especially Japanese living in the United States was on the minds of many. The *Washington Post* generally supported the internment policy but also urged caution. "How necessary is the roundup, how strict must be the security, needs no emphasis after the revelation of what the Fifth Column did in Hawaii. We must give the benefit of doubt to our own security." However the paper also noted the need to not jump to conclusions over "inoffensive, loyal aliens. The best way to create disaffection among an otherwise loyal alien population would be to treat them as enemies in our midst."[4] The *New York Times* also addressed the matter in an editorial entitled, "The Slanting Eye."[5]

Americans were worried though. Over the weekend, civilian guards and Santa Barbara police at the Miguelito Canyon Reservoir had gotten into a gun fight with unknown saboteurs, suspected of wanting to destroy the water supply for the city and nearby Camp Cooke. It was the second attempt, and though they were chased off, "a dozen leaders in colonies of Japanese vegetable workers in the vicinity were rounded up . . . and sent off to Midwest concentration camps."[6] There was also the occasional violence against Japanese in America. In Los Angeles, unidentified assailants had shot a Japanese man in the back.[7]

Roosevelt received yet another in a interminable and unceasing line of memos on "Dealing with the West Coast Japanese Problem," authored again by his secret operative, John Franklin Carter. The document complained about overblown comments by Navy Secretary Frank Knox about "Fifth Columnists. This term is loose and has been widely abused." Yet it also went into great detail about saboteurs, but mostly doubting the danger they posed.

The document counseled caution for FDR. "The loyal Japanese citizens should be encouraged by a statement from high government authority . . . Their offers of assistance should be accepted . . ." Other documents that day making their way to the president covered North Africa, food supplies, the Supreme War Council, and more British memoranda.[8]

Roosevelt also met that day with his cousin, Theodore Roosevelt, Jr. That afternoon, he and Eleanor had cocktails in the Red Room and several hours later, hosted a dinner with seventeen guests including Churchill, Lord Beaverbrook, Hull, Hopkins, and others. Roosevelt turned in just before 1:00 a.m.[9]

Henry Luce, publisher of *Life* magazine and *Time*—both hugely influential publications—had been all for going to war in the guise of Charles Foster Kane, beating the war drums for months. Luce's magazines had also been cruelly dismissive of any point of view other than total internationalism.

Luce also had his own ideas on how to treat "aliens." Now that America was at war with Japan, both of his publications ran side-by-side photos of Chinese and Japanese, complete with diagrams and charts, explaining how Americans could tell the difference between the two races. Explaining the reason for the full page depictions, *Life* magazine explained, "U.S. citizens have been demonstrating a distressing ignorance on the delicate question of how to tell a Chinese from a Jap."[10] For the Japanese subject, Luce picked a photo of General Tojo—not the most popular man in America as of late December, 1941. For the Chinese subject, he chose a low-level "Chinese public servant." Whereas the Chinese subject had "lighter facial bones" and a "higher bridge" the Japanese had a "flatter nose" and "earthy yellow complexion" and a "broader, shorter face" the publication patiently explained.[11]

The Chinese had received better press in America than had the Japanese for a number of years, thanks in part to Pearl Buck's hugely popular novel, *The Good Earth*, about American missionaries in China, which won a Pulitzer in 1932, Frank Capra's movie *Lost Horizon*, and Charlie Chan, the popular B-movie detective.

Biddle's efforts were proving more successful than others in the administration, who were running into bureaucratic resistance over moving the Patent Office out of Washington. Patent lawyers deluged the White House with letters and protests and the staff of 1,400 complained over the moving of 20,000,000 files. They estimated those files weighed 4,717 tons and the cabinets they were stored in weighed another 3,325 tons. Through all the previous wars, the Patent Office had stayed put, even during the War of 1812, when their records were stored in the only government building not burned by the British.[12]

The Roosevelt White House held the hand of the Patent Office employees and reassured them that they would only have to move to New York for the duration of the war. The government had agreed to pay for the cost of moving the employees and their household items, but not the cost of moving their families. The bureaucrats spent the better part of December thumbing "through law books . . . trying to find a law under which transportation costs of an employee's dependents could be paid. They found none."[13]

The Federal City had other problems. They had conducted their first air raid alarm which on the surface seemed successful. Lights flashed, radio bulletins went out, and phone calls were hurriedly made. Buses, trains, and cabs stopped. The police stopped traffic. "But the defense establishment in the Wardman Park Hotel heard no whistle. . . ." Off in the far distance, people in the city heard a whistle or a siren but only if they strained to listen. "The Willard Hotel wardens" from five blocks away "heard faintly a whistle in the distance."[14] Compared to those of other locales, D.C.'s drill, with the exception of the mute sirens, was a smashing success, though one local paper called the whole thing a "fiasco."[15]

Byron Price had already been sworn in as head of the Censorship Bureau. His oath of office included the part where he promised to defend the Constitution against all enemies, foreign and domestic. Very few pointed out the incongruity of his job and his oath. A columnist, Blair Bolles of the *Evening Standard* was one of the few. "One day last week President Roosevelt made a speech about the glories of the Bill of Rights. Two days later he appointed a national censor, whose business it is to infringe on the Bill of Rights' guarantee of freedom of the press. Nobody protested. War is paradoxical, and we accept the idea that even in a war fought to protect the system of which the Bill of Rights is a part, free publication of information must be restricted."[16]

The paradox went unaddressed as Price's mission was to stop all information that could aid the Axis Powers—very often a subjective determination. Who was to determine what really aided the enemy and what the American people had a right to know? This was no debate over how many Founding Fathers could dance on the head of a pin: it went to the core of the very existence of the American Republic. Was it necessary to sublimate the Constitution in order to save it?

The matter had been fought between Jefferson and Hamilton; over the Sedition Acts of the early 1800s; over the actions of Abraham Lincoln during the Civil War when he imprisoned, without due process, newspaper editors who wrote articles that displeased him; or over the powers granted Woodrow Wilson during the Great War and what some thought was his low regard for the Constitution, seeing it as an impediment to executive progress.

Without even flinching, the National Association of Broadcasters had gone right along with the new state of censorship in America and in many ways, took the policy one step further, on its own and without government coercion. The NAB issued their own new guidelines against "sensationalism, carelessness and second-guessing in news broadcasts—as well as 'ad lib' broadcasts on the street or in the studio. . . . Other 'do nots' included the second guessing of military officers, over-estimating American military power or under-estimating enemy strength: broadcasting unformed reports, and the use of sponsors of news as a springboard for advertising 'commercials.'"[17]

Radio had already been banned from broadcasting weather reports and now the NAB said broadcasts designed to "increase tension" were "do nots." The guide also stated, "An open microphone accessible to the general public constitutes a very real hazard in times of war. Any question regarding the war or war production might make trouble."[18]

Anxious over a surprise attack by the enemy during Christmas week, civil defense units asked their thousands of volunteer spotters all over America—

but especially on the East Coast—to organize platoon systems and be on the watch for enemy planes, twenty-four hours a day for the duration of Christmas Week. In Neshaminy, Pennsylvania, O. P. Titus, a seventy-seven-year-old widow walked her post every day from 11 a.m. to 1 p.m., surely convinced her town was of vital importance to the enemy.[19]

On the West Coast, all private planes within 150 miles of the coastline were abruptly ordered grounded until further notice.[20]

Americans who had already signed up for civil defense were more than happy to do so and did so, but if the photos that were guiding them on Japanese planes were anything like those running in *Life* magazine, they were woefully out of date, by five to ten years at least. *Life* published photos as a guide for Americans, but they were of biplanes and open cockpit planes, neither of which was in use by either side for combat, especially the Japanese, for years.[21]

Eyes toward the sky were helpful, but it paid to be watchful of the waves as well. The Pacific Ocean, including along the California coastline, now resembled a shooting gallery. After the shock that two oil tankers had been attacked so close to the California coast, the U.S. Navy announced that enemy submarines had several days earlier attacked other American vessels close to the Golden State. Both the steamships *Samoa* and *Lahaina* were attacked and the latter sunk en route to San Francisco.[22]

The tanker *L. P. St. Clair* reported that torpedoes had been fired on her and the Coast Guard said another tanker, *H.M. Storey*, owned by the Standard Oil Company, had been fired upon off the coast of Santa Barbara.[23] A coast guardsman saw the whole thing from the shore, including the *Storey*'s on-deck gun firing and missing the sub as it slipped beneath the surface.[24] Navy patrol boats dropped depth charges after responding to the attack. Other captains fought back as well. The skipper of the *Agriworld*—previously fired upon—actually attempted to ram the unidentified sub assailing his tanker.[25]

New details emerged about the attack on the Emidio, including the atrocious actions of the unknown sub on defenseless seamen. After being torpedoed, the crew abandoned ship and hunkered down in three lifeboats alongside. The enemy submarine then turned its deck gun on the unarmed and helpless civilian seamen, blasting repeatedly. The first reports indicated no casualties, but followup reports said all twenty-two seamen were believed dead. The ship had issued an S.O.S. and American planes responded within ten minutes, dropping depth charges, but it was unknown if the sub had been hit.[26]

The Atlantic was also a shooting gallery, but this time it was favoring the United States. Secretary of the Navy Frank Knox announced that fourteen German U-boats had either been hit or sunk, though it was not said when the actual fighting took place. FDR had, in fact, issued his "shoot on sight" order several months before.

Knox had a meeting the day before with the president, and upon its completion, immediately issued his statement to refute "any thought in the public mind that 'the Navy has done nothing about' the daring approach of Axis sea 'rattlesnakes' to United States shores . . . [giving] assurance that 'appropriate counter measures' have been taken."[27] Americans indeed had been wondering, since December 7, about the U.S. Navy.

Citizens had heard about the exploits of the army and the marines and the daring deeds of Army Air Corps pilots and the American volunteers with the RAF and the Chinese, but little about the navy. Indeed, this announcement by the navy was the first official acknowledgement of any sea action whatsoever against "sub-surface fight craft."[28] The storyline was that FDR wanted to keep the Germans guessing, since they were still sinking American commercial ships with impunity, but now it seemed clear the greater worry was the morale of the American people. Of course, no details involving ships or compliments were released. Knox hinted also that the "silent service" was engaged in the battle for the Philippines and that navy was taking steps to deal with the enemy subs running amuck on the West Coast. But they would have their hands full.

"Activity of Jap undersea boats near the Pacific coast, coupled with a stepped up assault on the Philippine Islands, led to the belief the enemy in the West has thrown out a submarine screen to prevent reinforcement of hard-pressed United States forces in the Pacific."[29]

The Japanese claimed they had sunk nine Allied submarines and had taken prisoner an untold number of Dutch, American, and British officers.[30]

The War Department estimated that Tokyo had as many as forty submarines that could reach the West Coast of America from their home waters. At least half the Japanese submariner fleet, Congress was told, was capable of distances in the neighborhood of 14,000 to 18,000 miles, without refueling. The distance from Seattle to Yokohama Bay was just over four thousand miles. This gave the Japanese navy a considerable cushion to do the maximum damage along the American West Coast. And if they refueled along the way in the Marshall or Caroline Islands, they could patrol the West Coast even longer.[31]

Some were also capable of laying up to sixty floating mines. The Japanese sub fleet was brand new, with not one submersible older than three years. On the surface, they made twenty knots, giving them plenty of speed to catch up to tankers and cargo ships.[32]

The situation in the Philippines was desperate. Douglas MacArthur was now facing an all-out invasion of the main island of Luzon. The Japanese were all in, committing somewhere between 80–100,000 troops to the invasion. At least eighty troop transports were landing on the island, only 150 miles from Manila. Whereas MacArthur had once been confident of fighting off the invading Japanese, a spokesman could only say the American and Filipino soldiers were "behaving well."[33] The *Washington Post* put the best light on the situation saying, "General Douglas MacArthur's headquarters has anticipated an attempted landing in force there and preparations have long been completed to meet just such an eventuality."[34]

The Japanese bombed the hometown of Philippine president Manual Quezon, which was bad enough. His town of Baler was obscure, inland, was considered an "open city," and the only reason to bomb it would be to undermine Filipino morale. But Japanese troops also encountered a busload of young girls and boys who were students at the University of Manila trying to get to their home province of Batangas. The bus driver and the boys rushed forward to defend the girls and were machine-gunned down. The Japanese soldiers then "mistreated" the girls. "The whole community . . . relatives of the students, is reported to be infuriated while word of the outrage is spreading throughout the province."[35]

A *Time* correspondent on the scene filed this report. "Manila this evening was very tense ... smoldering fires started in the noontime raid ... Civilians are assuming wartime posts of censorships, patrols, evacuating, bandage-making ... Talking to already stubble-bearded, grimy Yanks soldiers at undisclosed posts: 'I'd like another crack at those low-flying bastards. Write my mother I'm a hero. I'll stay here. I'll stick it out' ... Night sounds: howling dogs, shouts from sentries, douse that cigarette, turn off those lights, shrill police whistles ... the babble of Filipino and American voices. . . ."[36]

In Hong Kong, the British "Tommies" were holding on by the skin of their teeth. The Japanese were carrying out a furious campaign to destroy what was left of the British garrison, and the Allies' only hope was relief from the Chinese. The battle "raged across Happy Valley," ran one report with no obvious sense of irony. Artillery, aided by naval guns, shelled British shore batteries and fortifications. Japanese accounts said one after another British strong point was being reduced on the rock-bound island and that complete control was only a matter of time."[37] The Japanese had also bottled in 100 ships and that as many as half had been sunk including destroyers, gunboats, tankers and transports. King George VI sent a message to his men telling them "thoughts of all at home [are] with you." A radio message crackled back, "organized resistance continues ... heavy fighting." The Union Jack was still flying over parts of Hong Kong but "the defenders" were "doomed" to a "certain death or war-long captivity."[38]

The story was somewhat better in Singapore, where the British were mounting a counteroffensive after first retreating forty-five miles to regroup. "British forces, drawn up on a new line across the Malay peninsula about 300 miles north of Singapore, were reported today to have smashed heavily at Japanese forces gathering. . . ."[39] The Allies needed to hold onto Singapore and were throwing everything into the fight.

For their part, the U.S. Marines were still holding onto Wake Island, still repelling the Japanese. U.S. relief ships had been repelled by the Japanese, but the marines kept fighting. "The valiant chapter in the history of warfare being written by a handful of United States marines on Wake Island in the Pacific yesterday gained another few lines. Isolated and alone, beyond the possibility of immediate help, dependant on what food and ammunition they have with them, this little force yesterday still held out after two weeks of constant attack."[40]

The day before, Wake had been hit two more times by bombing planes. And still it held on. So too was Midway, apparently.

A small Associated Press story moved on the wires, though many papers chose not to run it. But the *Birmingham News* did print it under the headline, "Nazis Execute 5 Jews in Occupied France." The story, as picked up from Vichy Radio, said the executions were punishment for "renewed attacks" on German military.[41]

There was an air of desperation blowing in Berlin. For the first time in years, there would be no Christmas furloughs for the German army. Every man was ordered to stay at his post. They were also dealing with a huge outbreak of typhus among their troops in Russia, as well as their faltering military campaigns in Libya and Russia.

Illustrating how tenuous their positions had become on the Eastern Front and in North Africa, Berlin began pulling troops out of Norway and reassigning them to the two battle zones. Norway had been occupied by Germany, though they were a courageous people with an active underground working to trip up the Germans. Crown Prince Olav was a thorn in the side of the Germans but they dared not execute him. He was hugely popular, in part because of his frank way of speaking. He wanted to join the Allies and declare war on Japan but lamented, "We can't get a parliament together to do it."[42]

Hitler fired his top military commander and took over direction of the German army personally, after telling the German people he did so because of an "inner call."[43] In light of his stunning early successes, Hitler fancied himself a military genius. However, even though his bold gambles had paid off in the beginning of the war, he was a mediocre military strategist whose stubbornness paved the way for many colossal blunders, as would soon become apparent. But he was riding high in 1941, and no German officer dared oppose him, yet.

The Monor family of Ft. Myers, Florida got an unexpected Christmas gift. Previously notified by the War Department that their son, Kenneth, had been killed at Pearl Harbor, they received another notice—this one saying that the telegram was in error and their boy was alive after all.[44]

The news was not so welcome in other homes. In Humboldt, Tennessee, Mr. and Mrs. V. A. Kennington learned of their double loss at Pearl Harbor, sons Cecil, 21, and Milton, 20. When informed by the navy, Mr. Kennington said, "I have four more sons. I will give them all and I, too, would fight to put down such sneaking and deadly enemies as the Japs, Hitler and Mussolini." The family had already lost their eldest son fighting "in the first World War."[45]

The Barber family in New London, Wisconsin, received the terrible news in triplicate. The three eldest sons, Malcolm, 22, LeRoy, 21 and Randolph, 19, had all been aboard the Oklahoma, serving as firemen. Just hours before attending services at the Most Precious Blood Catholic Church, Mrs. and Mrs. Peter Barber received the horrible report. All three of their boys died in the attack. The family priest, Fr. Raymond Fox, announced the news to the stunned congregation. "I am glad they died like men and could give their lives for their country," said Peter, their dad. The parents told of how their sons had asked the navy to serve together and how in Hawaii they had met the actor and singer, Gene Autry, who then hosted the three in his home in California when the Barber boys had received a furlough. Mr. and Mrs. Barber still had two sons left at home, aged 16 and 9 and the father said, "When their brothers are old enough, I am sure they will avenge their deaths."[46]

Their church planned a requiem high mass for the lost sons of New London.

Revenge was also on the mind of Fletcher Lindsay, 20, of Alabama. His big brother James, 23, had been killed on the Arizona. The young man walked into a Navy recruiting office in Mobile and signed up only twelve hours after finding out his brother was dead. Fletcher's mother signed his papers without hesitation. Bereaved and angry brothers all over America were swearing revenge.[47]

Lou Boudreau received an early Christmas gift when he was appointed manager of the Cleveland Indians. This made the shortstop the youngest manager in the history of major league baseball.

The day also marked the sixty-second birthday of Josef Stalin. Two years earlier, when they were uneasy allies, Hitler had sent "Uncle Joe" a birthday greeting. "Accept my most sincere congratulations on your sixtieth birthday, my best wishes for your personal wellbeing and a happy future for the Soviet people."[48] That was before Hitler invaded his country, an act which tended to put a damper on friendships of convenience and strategic alliances. The strange fact was, the incessantly suspicious Stalin had actually trusted the German dictator. Stalin was genuinely shocked when Hitler violated their nonaggression pact and sent his Panzers rolling toward Moscow. The rest of the world was less surprised.

Not everybody in America was interested in home and hearth for the holidays. Many liked to travel and though cruises to South America were still available, the seas seemed uncertain to many and travel and touring closer to home was becoming more attractive by the minute. The state of Alabama took out big ads in the *New York Times* "inviting Winter tourists to visit Alabama on the trips South. The ad advised travelers to take time to see Alabama's giant power dams, huge defense industries, army camps, surging cities, stately antebellum homes, cotton fields, fine herds of cattle, historic scenes of the Civil War and glorious azaleas of Mobile."[49]

Congress was looking at a national sales tax as a means of raising even more revenue for the war. It was proposed as an alternative to the "so-called withholding tax which the Treasury suggested for consideration a few weeks ago and which employers would be required to deduct from workers' pay checks."[50]

A national sales tax was seen as a "less painful" way to collect new revenue. A Republican member of the House, Bertrand Gearhart of California, touted the sales tax and believed it "would lose much of its 'bugaboo' when contrast with such proposals as the 15 percent withholding tax being proposed by Secretary of the Treasury Morganthau." Others fretted that the sales tax would adversely affect those "least able to pay" while others argued for increasing the excess profits tax on corporations.[51]

More and more evidence of the effects of the war appeared in the daily lives of the American people. At first they were told there would be plenty of food, then that story changed, and then it changed again. Now the government advised exactly what foods they should stock in their pantries. Government nutritionists recommended the following: Sixteen cans of evaporated milk, cans of beans, cans of corn, cans of "meat or fish," cans of peas, cans of tomatoes, cans of sauerkraut, cans of luncheon meat, cans of salmon, cans of sardines, cans of tomato juice, cans of grapefruit juice, soda crackers, whole wheat crackers, sixteen bars of chocolate, chocolate syrup, sugar, jam, coffee, peanut butter, tea, and "one pound of prunes."[52]

Women were advised that while there was not a foreseeable shortage of gloves, they should engage in "wise buying."[53] Doctors were advising Americans of the healthfulness of whole milk. "For the adult, whole milk alone and without fortification can serve for complete nutrition for a long time," said Professor E.B. Hart of the University of Wisconsin. Of course, he advocated that if one tried to live by milk alone—for, say, six months—they might try "fortifying their diet with copper, iron and manganese."[54]

Just as the government warned people not to hoard sugar, Americans did precisely that, cleaning out stores in many parts of the nation. There appeared to be no shortage of booze however. All sorts and manner were recommended to help with the holiday cheer. "What every woman wants to know about a man.... That he is adept in mixing holiday cheer ... and equally considerate in choosing the whiskey he gives and serves his friends. Old Schenley."[55]

To get to the supermarket or department store or liquor store and stock up on groceries and milk and gloves and whiskey, the Goodyear Tire and Rubber Co. came out with the "War Tire." It was made from regenerated rubber. The idea behind it was to keep "the civilian wheel of America from coming to a stop."[56] The contrivance was flimsy and unreliable.

Goodyear was in danger of losing its rubber plantations in Sumatra, just across from Malaya, where the fierce fight for Singapore was raging on. The president of the Goodyear Company, P. W. Litchfield, told the American consumer his company could keep rolling out War Tires indefinitely as long as automobile operators did not drive "over 35 miles per hour."[57]

CHAPTER 23

THE TWENTY-THIRD
OF DECEMBER

Churchill In Unity Talks At White House

New York Times

U.S. Ship Fired On Only Six Miles Off Pacific Coast

The Birmingham News

Japs Land on Luzon

Evening Star

Japs Land on Wake Island

Lethbridge Herald

In the low, backwater country around Orlando, Florida, a "cracker" hurried into a Navy recruiting office, demanding an immediate haircut and shave for his excessively long locks and beard. The chief machinist mate who was in charge of recruiting, inquired why he wanted it so badly and why now. "Well, I'll tell you. I been out huntin' and fishin' down on the St. Johns—kinda away from things. An' by doggo, I just found out them danged Japs is a-fighin' us."[1]

The people pushing into the ranks of the U.S. military came from all walks and ways: oldsters, youngsters, blue collar, white collar, Sun Belt, Farm

413

Belt, Bible Belt, Mid-West, Mid-Atlantic, West Coast, East Coast, Gulf Coast, Confederates, Yankees, city slickers, country boys, black men, white men, Hispanic men, Asian men, fathers, sons, grandfathers, and even a few elected officials. The army said over 28,000 men had enlisted in the first two weeks after December 7.[2] Truth be told, some women wanted to go and fight too.

"Although the Army has called most of the lieutenants, captains and majors in the . . . Field Artillery Reserves to active duty, for the present at least it does not need its commanding officer, Col. Harry S. Truman, junior Senator from Missouri, and his confidential aide, Lieut. Harry Vaughan, it was learned yesterday." As it turned out, Truman and Vaughan had been berating the War Department for days to put them into active duty. "They volunteered to serve as soon as this war was declared, but were told that they have a more useful function to fulfill as Senator and Senator's aide."[3] Truman was then fifty-seven years old, only two years younger than FDR.

With all the men pouring into the lists, they were draining the work pool. The male labor shortage was such that the owner of a large cab company in San Diego complained that with all the men either going into war industries or enlisting, he might be forced to hire women to drive his taxis. He "petitioned the City Council for 'chauffeurette' licenses."[4] A New York legislator was advocating the full use of the thousands of prisoners in the state penitentiaries to be mobilized to make up the country's labor shortage.[5]

The day after the NFL championship, the most poorly attended in league history, the annual college draft began. Because of their records, the Pittsburgh Steelers and the Washington Redskins went first. The Redskins drafted Bill DeCorrevont of Northwestern and the Steelers took Bill Dudley of Virginia. Dudley went on to a Hall of Fame career as a star running back in the forties and fifties. DeCorrevont—in four seasons for the Redskins, Chicago Cardinals, Chicago Bears, and Detroit Lions—rushed 75 times for 233 yards and a 3.1 yard-per-carry average, fumbling on eight occasions, which meant he gave up the ball over 10 percent of the time. At quarterback, he threw for 155 yards, tossing ten interceptions and only three touchdown passes, completing just 42 percent of his passes. DeCorrevont went into the rug cleaning business in Chicago after his less-than-illustrious pro-football career. At the end of his career and with little left to give the game, Dudley finished his remaining days with the Redskins.[6]

FDR was more astute in his draft choices than the Redskins. He nominated, for U.S. attorney for Northern Ohio, Don Miller, who in a previous incarnation had been one of the famous "Four Horsemen" of the great Notre Dame teams coached by Knute Rockne.[7] At 5:00 p.m., FDR again had cocktails in the Red Room with Eleanor and some guests.[8]

In the battle of wills, the U.S. Patent Office stared down the FDR White House, so rather than moving to New York, a frantic search was on to find suitable office space elsewhere in Washington or even in suburban Virginia, or at last resort, as far south as Richmond.

The government agency, like all the others, came to the battle well-armed and well-flacked. Of the 153 government bureaucracies in Washington, all told they had nearly 35,000 "press agents" all ready to do battle to trumpet their good works, protect their fiefdoms and live and die by their code: the first rule of the bureaucracy is to protect the bureaucracy. "They agree on one point—the value of the work they describe and the indispensability of the agency engaged in it," sniffed the *Birmingham News*.[9]

Roosevelt's Labor-Business conference was still deadlocked over the issue of the closed shop and a war-long no-strike pledge. The union and corporate bureaucracies had been at loggerheads for days with no resolution in sight.

Gossip columnist and Roosevelt acolyte Walter Winchell was still pushing the rumor that Charles Lindbergh and his wife, Anne Morrow Lindbergh were headed for a divorce. Why? Because she'd been spotted dining with her mother, sans husband Lindbergh. In his characteristically snide manner, Winchell referred to the aviator as "the Lone Dodo."[10] In Winchell's mind, anyone who ran afoul of him wasn't merely an opponent—they were an enemy who had to be destroyed. Winchell was a supporter of FDR and his policies; after the war, the hugely influential opinion-maker would sing a different and considerably darker tune, embracing the McCarthyism of the day to smear many of his former Democratic friends as communists, homosexuals, and spies. Winchell always trimmed his sails to the prevailing winds. In 1941, he tacked toward the winds of war.

The heroine of the South, Margaret Mitchell, authoress of *Gone with the Wind*, journeyed above the Mason-Dixon Line to attend the launching of the *USS Atlanta*, a new cruiser. Garbed in a Red Cross uniform, photographed at the Brookwood station, she looked happy for the entire world to see, though she was painfully shy.[11]

Incredibly, yet another American tanker was fired upon—and sunk—off the California coast. The 400-foot-long *Montebello* went to the bottom, though four life boats did make it to shore, but not before they too were fired upon by the submarine. The seamen cursed and yelled at the sub, wishing for their own weapons. "Sherriff Murray C. Hathaway said longboats and fishing craft trying to rescued (sic) survivors from the *Montebello* were [also] shelled and fired on by machine guns from the attacking craft."[12]

Another America ship, the *Larry Doheny*, was fired upon as well, though not sunk. "It was the eighth submarine attack on American freighters and tankers in nearby Pacific waters since opening of the war with Japan."[13] Overnight, people along the coast around Morro Bay and Estero Bay heard loud gunfire and explosions.[14]

Americans were getting jumpy and rightly so. An American freighter was making for San Diego under full steam, bellowing a thick trail of black smoke out of her stack. Thinking a naval battle was underway, nervous residents along the West Coast called the police and other officials.[15]

The dribble of announcements of the dead or missing from Pearl and other battle scenes became a torrent. In San Diego, four young men, all city natives, were revealed to have been killed.[16] In Alabama, a seaman in his forties who had been called back to active duty in August of 1940 was missing in action.[17] In Los Angeles, the first of many of the sons of the city, Lieutenant Commander Charles Michael, who'd been lost on the *Utah*, was announced as among the dead.[18] Then two sons of an employee of the *Los Angeles Times*, Wesley Heidt, 24, and Edward J. (Bud) Heidt, 25, both firemen–first class on the *Arizona*, were both reported missing.[19]

As part of a campaign to buck up American morale, the War Department made available some of the survivors of the attack on Pearl to give their first-hand accounts of what happened. "Graphic first-hand narratives of what happened at Pearl Harbor December 7 [were] told with dramatic coolness today by three naval officers who had leading parts in the titanic defense of giant warships against a sky full of Japanese planes that pounced on them suddenly 'from out of nowhere.'" They told of the attacks, heroism, and tragedy. "During the early morning attack a marine said to an officer, 'Pull this piece of metal out of my back.' It was a bomb splinter so hot the officer had to use a rag to remove it. The wounded marine returned to his machine gun and remained on duty until late that afternoon."[20] There were hundreds of such tales of can-do Americanism. This was the first of such revelations about the attack, though Washington officials were still guarded about the extent of the damage.[21]

Another story from CBS radio told the story of Lt. Walter Cross, an Army Air Corps pilot whose aircraft had been hit by enemy planes. Cross bailed and hit the silk, as Japanese planes buzzed around him, taking turns shooting at him as he floated helplessly to earth. Miraculously, they failed to hit him, "and his only injury was a pair of blistered feet in an eight-day hike back to Manila through mountainous terrain inhabited only savage tribesmen."[22]

Another pilot found himself in a similar situation. As he floated to the ground, natives waited. They were going to tear him to shreds. Their village had already been bombed by the Japanese, and to them all airplanes and pilots were alike. That's when the American flyer doffed his airman's cap. "This intruder definitely was not a Japanese—he had a shock of flaming red hair."[23]

By now America thought it was immune to surprise. Who should show up for breakfast the morning of the twenty-third, but British Prime Minister Winston Churchill!

Only a handful knew of his and FDR's plans to meet in Washington and nary a word of it leaked out. Some reporters intimated that they knew in advance but knew such reporting was now verboten and writing about it before the prime minister completed his sojourn could get them into a lot of hot water. He'd actually arrived late Monday and went directly to the White House, getting there around 5:40 p.m.[24]

A brief statement was issued: "The British prime minister has arrived in the United States to discuss with the president all questions relevant to the concerted war effort. Mr. Churchill is accompanied by Lord Beaverbrook and a technical staff."[25] They had many things to discuss, large and small, from the size of the Allied army to how to handle Ireland and how to convince the Irish to allow Allied sub bases there. They would be later joined by Canadian Prime Minister Macenzie King. The Nazis believed Churchill had left London and suspected he was headed for conferences in the Middle East, but did not rule out Moscow or Washington.[26]

White House press secretary Steve Early knew, of course, but could not tell the press or confirm or deny that the historic meeting was forthcoming. Only until an announcement was made in Great Britain could he go ahead and tell the press corps. "Early's desk will never look the same. In the scramble for mimeographed statements a lamp was knocked over, a porcelain donkey was broken, gadgets and knickknacks were jumbled." The *Boston Globe* noted, "Three days before the birth anniversary of the Prince of Peace two great leaders were deep in discussion of war."[27]

It was the second time in six months that Roosevelt and Churchill had met, but this time he was already in the White House, deep in conversation over drinks and dinner with Roosevelt before the Americans knew "Winnie" was in the country. Their first meeting was about the *HMS Prince of Wales* in August of 1941, when they devised the Atlantic Charter. Churchill's mother, Jennie Jerome, had been an American, and had visited the U.S. four times before; the first in 1890, the second at the invitation of Mark Twain in 1900, and again in 1929 and 1931 on lecture tours.

FDR set an "all hands" conference for the next day at 6:00 p.m. On Tuesday, top brass and civilian leadership were to meet with the Prime Minister and the eighty political and military experts who had accompanied him on his boat trip across the Atlantic. Churchill's presence in the United States was a tonic to the country's morale and to FDR's morale.

Roosevelt so looked forward to seeing Churchill, he went by car to an unidentified nearby airport to meet his friend as he flew into Washington. Churchill arrived in a blue navy "pea jacket" and "dark yachting cap." The uniform was that of the Trinity House Lighthouse Service, "a semi-governmental organization concerned with life-saving and the operation of lighthouses."[28] In his hand, he carried a cane, equipped with a flashlight for blackouts. Roosevelt was in a gray double breasted business suit whose pant legs, while cuffed, appeared too long. The snap brim of his fedora was turned up, befitting the style of the obliging nobles of the era. "The car slipped in through the gates of the southgrounds, then rolled up at the entrance looking out across the still-green lawn and to the towering Washington monument in the distance."[29]

Churchill's trip—which had been his idea—had been risky to say the least, boarding a blacked out train in London, then a crossing over the war-torn Atlantic to Massachusetts, and then a flight into Washington. It took a number of days to complete and rumors floated around London and Washington as to his whereabouts. "The White House would neither confirm nor deny the reports, but issued warnings of the possible grave consequences of speculation or mention of the subject in any way."[30] Despite the arduous journey, Churchill looked in good health.

Upon arrival at the White House, they posed briefly for photographs and Churchill hid his cigar for a moment. FDR was using his leg braces, a cane in his right hand and his left hand was gripped on the arm of White House naval attaché Captain John R. Beardall.[31] "The sheer drama of the meeting on American soil . . . should have salutary psychological reactions. . . ."[32] Just over their heads were parts of the White House that had been painted over to cover the scorch marks made by the fire the British had set to the White House in the War of 1812, nearly burning it to the ground. Then they were bitter enemies. Now the two countries were allies "forged" by a fire set in a different century.[33]

While waiting for Churchill to arrive, FDR had met that day with his fifth cousin, Teddy Roosevelt Jr., who was a brigadier general.[34] Most of the day, he spent in the Oval Office, in one-on-one and small meetings with foreign dignitaries accompanied by Vice President Henry Wallace.

FDR also went through paperwork including sending a memo to John Franklin Carter, responding to an obliquely circuitous memo in which "Jack" (which FDR called him) discussed at length their concerns about security in New York. Carter, between the lines, was suggesting the creation of an independent security force comprised of individuals "now debarred by reason of age, formal education . . . ." He had already identified some willing to help and said they did not lack for "funds or facilities. The individuals . . . seem to be able, intelligent and know what they are doing." He suggested to Roosevelt that in recruiting a certain kind of help in the New York area, that what was needed was "a relaxation of red tape, especially at the moment when rapid expansion of functions and activities is essential."[35]

After darkness had covered Washington, he went to the south portico entrance and got into a car and went to meet Mr. Churchill.[36] That evening, FDR and the British Prime Minister stayed up talking until 1 a.m.[37]

The next morning, the two world leaders, exhausted, slept in. "Both rose long after the White House staff was bustling with its duties of the day."[38]

The rest of that Tuesday brought more unwanted news. Japanese forces had finally made a landing on Wake Island after a dozen or more strikes against the marines and navy seamen. But there was no word from the G.I.s that they'd surrendered or that they were still fighting. "The invaders landed Tuesday morning, the navy said. Information was not immediately forthcoming whether the 'leatherneck' defenders were still resisting."[39]

The Japanese had also made yet another landing on Luzon where the American forces were attempting to throw them back into the sea, and though the battered British garrison was holding on in Hong Kong, two top Canadian officers were killed there. Worse, the Japanese claimed they had taken over a thousand prisoners in Hong Kong. Many news reports on the situation in Hong Kong took note of the hour of the day, so as to keep a running story in perspective. It was reported that on Monday alone, "about 100 bombs fell on the island." The tenacious Brits, Indians, and Canadians had destroyed a bridge and two enemy ships.[40] If they were going down, they were going down fighting.

The Japanese had landed and taken Borneo, but found only burnt offerings left behind by the British. "Three men of the Royal Engineers said they began putting the torch to wells, pipe lines, pumping stations and refineries a few days after war broke out."[41]

The fighting on Luzon was described as "intense." Douglas MacArthur was issuing hopeful statements, still saying he had things "well in hand" but his tanks and artillery were more useful in fighting off the enemy surge.[42] Commanding the troops in the field under MacArthur was a capable man, Major General Jonathan M. Wainwright.[43] U.S. forces had reportedly sunk "47 Nipponese Troop Transports" which was welcomed news. But Japanese planes had also bombed a civilian center on Luzon where many Filipino government officials were being housed. The Japanese had also landed a strong contingent at the Lingayen coast, some 150 miles north of Luzon, an apparent "pincer" move.[44]

In spite of his brave public statements, MacArthur was sending fraught telegrams to the War Department, pleading for reinforcements. "PURSUIT AND DIVE BOMBER REINFORCEMENT BY MEANS OF AIR-CRAFT CARRIER STOP PRESENT ENEMY ENCIRCLEMENT PERMITS INTERRUPTION OF FERRY ROUTE TO SOUTH DUE TO DAY BOMBARDMENT MINDANAO FIELDS STOP EARLY REINFORCEMENT BY CARRIER WOULD SOLVE PROBLEM STOP CAN I EXPECT ANYTHING ALONG THAT LINE ... IN THIS GENERAL CONNECTION CAN YOU GIVE ME ANY INKLING OF STRATEGIC PLANS PACIFIC FLEET ... MACARTHUR."[45]

Time magazine wryly observed, "The U. S. had been reacting to 'other peoples' war. It was now in its own war."[46] Between Hawaii, Guam, Wake Island, the Philippines, the waters of the West Coast and Midway, America knew all too well. Guam hadn't been heard from since the tenth. The last message from the navy said, "Last attack centered at Agana. Civilians machine-gunned in streets. Two native wards of hospital and hospital compound machine-gunned. Building in which Japanese nationals are confined bombed."[47]

Curiously, even with all the action in the Pacific occupying the American forces and with so little action against Germany so far, the Gallup Polling organization surveyed the American people and found that, by a whopping margin of 64 percent to 15 percent, they considered Germany to be the greater threat to America than Japan.[48] The poll results presaged what would become a continual source of tension and debate among American and British military leaders: which theater of war deserved the most attention, Europe or the Pacific? From the beginning of the global conflict until V-E day, the effort in Europe would take precedence. Despite the desperate lobbying of generals such as MacArthur, who wanted ever-more resources to combat the Japanese, the Nazis were always perceived by FDR and Churchill as the greater menace. Hitler would have to be dealt with, first and foremost. As early as December 1941, American opinion in this regard was influenced by the news of yet another sinking by the Germans, this time of the British carrier *Formidable*. The loss of the 23,000-ton ship had a devastating effect on the war effort and on public opinion.[49]

In Hong Kong, some of the fiercest fighting was taking place on the "broad playing fields of the Happy Valley recreation areas east of Victoria."[50] News reports of Hong Kong noted the upbeat tones of the British forces, even as the reports also called the soldiers there "beleaguered."[51] Some 20,000 British soldiers were fighting on, standing their ground while also defending "3,000 white women and children who remained [and] are now living in caves. . . ."[52] The Japanese had been blasting away at Hong Kong by plane and warship for days and now their troops were closing in on the desperately outnumbered Brits.

Some observers said the fall of Hong Kong would not be as devastating as the loss of Singapore. But in point of fact, Hong Kong was an excellent, natural harbor, strategically important. "Japan gains a fine naval anchorage behind the fortified rocky island, a good airfield only 600 miles from Manila, and some shipbuilding facilities and three dry docks. . . . Hong Kong was the Gibraltar of the East and well named that."[53] From Hong Kong, the Japanese could intensify the fight south. Australia knew that if the Philippines fell and Malaya fell, it would only be a matter of time before the Japanese landed on their northern shores.

Churchill was becoming a beloved figure in America—described by the *Atlanta Constitution* as a "rotund little fighting premier"[54]—perhaps more popular in the land of his mother's birth than the land of his father's birth. Indeed, some of his political adversaries held his mother's country of birth against him.[55] "Britain's ruling class still considers him brilliant, erratic, unsafe."[56]

His arrival in America was reported on widely and enthusiastically. He was an extrovert and a character, again like his mother, with a knack for tossing off the perfect bon mot. Once at a dinner party, he told his seat mate, "We are all worms. But I do believe that I am a glow-worm."[57]

He'd been up and down in British politics, and had changed parties several times; it was sometimes difficult to keep track of the state of his career. But beginning in the early 1930s, he saw the German military buildup and began to loudly protest it, despite the claims of the status quo in Parliament that he was wrong and that Hitler would abide by the Treaty of Versailles. Even as Hitler moved into other European countries, the British pooh-poohed it. They simply had no more stomach for war. After the Germans invaded Poland—with whom England had a mutual defense agreement—in September of 1939, the die was cast.

Churchill was a Renaissance Man. A soldier, a statesman, writer, and many other guises, he'd seen battles, both military and otherwise, many political battles he'd started himself. After losing a seat in Parliament in 1923, he packed his troubles and his brushes and went to Egypt to paint scenery. He'd won medals in 1895, 1897, and in 1916 for helping the Cubans fight the Spanish; for his bravery in India; and for action in the Nile, in the Boer Wars, and service on the Western Front. "Soldier, newspaper man, adventurer, lecturer, artist, bricklayer, politician and statesman, Churchill has served in more wars, held more offices and practiced more arts than any man of his time in the British Empire. In the middle of the last war, Churchill was a colonel in charge of a regiment. In a foxhole being shelled, he was urged to move on by a superior officer saying, "I tell you, this is a very dangerous place." Churchill replied, "Yes sir, but after all this is a very dangerous world."[58]

The day before, Sunday, December 21, Roosevelt asked Americans to pray and declared that January 1st, 1942 would be a national day of prayer. "We are confident in our devotion to country, in our love of freedom, in our inheritance of strength. But our strength, as the strength of all men everywhere, is of greater avail as God upholds us." He declared January 1 "a day of . . . asking forgiveness for our shortcoming of the past, of consecration to the tasks of the present, of asking God's help in days to come."[59] The proclamation was widely reported in the press without cynicism or rancor or question.

Unlike Woodrow Wilson, who cancelled all his press conferences during the Great War, FDR was holding them on an almost daily basis now. From the night of the eighth, when he'd broadcast a national radio message to the country from the basement of the White House, already partially blacked out—where he'd invited reporters and photographers in—right up through the coming of Christmas and beyond, Roosevelt courted the press, seeing them as an important ally, unlike Wilson, whom the press turned on. "Mr. Roosevelt met the press, lectured them on what they might and might not print. He looked calm, rested, cheery and buoyant."[60]

Archbishop Francis J. Spellman was the military vicar of the United States. He gave a radio broadcast over the CBS radio network and in front of a live audience of three hundred military and civic leaders in New York at the National Catholic Community Service clubhouse. In this, his first speech as the military vicar, he asked the American people not to go on strike, but the speech went much, much further. It was a testament to the high moral plane upon which he believed America operated and the direness of the world situation. "What will it profit us, however, to emerge victorious over attacks from abroad if at the same time we do not preserve the ideals of democracy at home and their indispensable supports of religion and morality."[61]

Spellman had worked on the address for hours, pouring over news clippings. At one point he quoted publisher Henry Luce. "The high resolve is yet to come . . . it would be better to leave America in a heap of smoking stones than surrender it to the mechanized medievalism which is the Mikado, or to the Antichrist which is Hitler."[62] The speech was a magnificent testament to the "American Century" of the country's charity and selflessness, of its moral bearings, but also a warning to not lose its moral compass. Luce had coined the phrase, "American Century."[63]

Even with the surprise visit of Churchill and his huge entourage and all the comings and goings in the White House because of the war, it still promised to be a quiet Christmas for the Roosevelts. All four sons were now on active duty. "For the first time since the Roosevelts moved into the White House, there won't be a child or a grandchild home for Christmas."[64] Mrs. Roosevelt was busy though. Because of her duties as assistant civilian defense director, she had meetings to attend and speeches to give. She also attended a "slum clearance project" where Christmas carols were sung. There, "a tiny Negro woman edged up to her . . . very elderly but very pert." She was introduced to Mrs. Roosevelt as "Betty Queen Anne." When her age of ninety-seven was mentioned to the first lady, the elderly woman replied, "Lordy, I'm more dan dat." Betty claimed she had been a slave near Fredericksburg, Virginia.[65]

When Eleanor Roosevelt arrived back at the White House, a dinner had to be prepared for Churchill and his aides. She also hung a stocking in the Oval Office containing a bone for "Fala," the family pooch.[66]

Before the meeting of the "War Council," Churchill and FDR sat together behind the president's untidy desk cluttered with keepsakes in the Oval Office and faced the journalists in an historic press conference which lasted about half an hour.[67] The setting was described as "electric."[68]

Churchill pulled on his customary cigar, and the president smoked several Camel cigarettes, as always attached to his ivory cigarette holder clamped between his teeth. Roosevelt was in gray suit and was still wearing the mourning band on his left arm for his mother. Churchill was in "formal striped trousers and a dark blue coat. He was wearing polka-dot blue and white bow tie."[69] The New York Times said he stared "unperturbedly into space" as he waited for things to begin.[70] As always, Harry Hopkins was standing off to the side.

The reporters in the back could not see the two men, so Roosevelt asked Churchill to stand for a moment "while those in the crowded back rows could get a glimpse of him." Churchill, 67, immediately jumped to his feet but still, he could not be seen, so he clambered onto his chair "grinning broadly and waving his cigar."[71] The reporters applauded and cheered.

During the course of the press conference, the leaders said "the key to the whole conflict is the resolute manner in which the American and British democracies are going to throw themselves into this war." The Evening Star reported, "Pulling on his cigar from his mouth, [Churchill] smiled wryly then as he remarked that someday the Allied nations might wake up and find themselves short of Huns."[72] Asked about how long the war might take, the prime minister remarked that it would take twice as long if it were managed "badly." FDR and the reporters laughed. "The reporters hurled a barrage for questions—and soon found the prime minister adept in swift replies."[73] The prime minister was eloquent, and "displayed his marked gift for turning phrases—a gift which has made his speeches and writings literary achievements."[74]

Churchill also announced he would broadcast a Christmas Eve message to the American people the next day and said there was much to thank God for. Prior, they'd met with State Department officials.[75] Roosevelt announced yet another new bureaucracy, this one the new Office of Defense Transportation.[76]

Following the press conference, reporters filed out and political and military aides filed in for a two-hour meeting. No real details were made public at the time but the two men wanted to address "all questions related to the concerted war effort."[77]

What Roosevelt and Churchill had in mind was a "Victory Program" to create an Allied Force of such magnitude it would simply roll over Axis opposition. They were talking in terms of producing 1,500 four-engine bombers a month, a Supreme Commander in the Far East (MacArthur was the popular and logical choice) as well as a Supreme Commander in Europe and a standing army of 20,000,000 men among all the Allied Powers. They also divided the world into four war zones; "Europe, the Middle East and North Africa, The North Atlantic and The Pacific and Far East."[78]

Speculation was rife that Hitler would mount a renewed offensive against Russia, or would invade England, or would invade Spain. There were also rumors of discord within his military command. The fact was that little was really known of what the next plans were for the Third Reich. Churchill had told war planners, "That he looked for a new German offensive in some theatre to counter-balance the humiliating reverses in Russia. He mentioned a thrust towards the Mediterranean and an invasion of Britain . . . but said frankly that he did not know where it would come."[79]

Attending the "War Council" meeting were all the top administration officials including the Secretary of War Henry Stimson, Secretary of State Cordell Hull, the Chief of Naval Operations Harold Stark, Secretary of the Navy Frank Knox, the new commander in chief of the fleet, Admiral Ernest King, and as always, FDR's friend and confidant, Hopkins. Attending for the British were Sir Dudley Pound, Admiral of the fleet; Sir Charles Portal, Air Chief Marshal; and Sir John Dill, Field Marshal.[80] The goal was straightforward: The eradication of Hitlerism from the world, as Roosevelt said. They saw Japan as an extension of Germany. "The matter of immediate urgency is, of course, the Battle of the Pacific. . . ."[81] This was untrue.

A plan was coming together to accomplish total victory though: "Worldwide strategy and worldwide supply leading to worldwide victory."[82]

FDR and Churchill had mutually decided that nothing less than unconditional surrender of the Axis scourge would be acceptable.

CHAPTER 24

THE TWENTY-FOURTH
OF DECEMBER

Californians See Sub Attack U.S. Ship

Evening Star

Wake Marines, Fighting to End, Sink Two Ships

Washington Post

Fall of Philippine Isles Inevitable Japanese Boast

Birmingham News

W inston Churchill, FDR's guest in the White House, was surprised to find he was served not one but two eggs with his breakfast. All of Great Britain had been on a ration of one egg per day and to set an example, Churchill followed suit. "Mrs. Franklin D. Roosevelt confided today that the White House's distinguished guest had interrupted war conferences with President Roosevelt to eulogize his breakfasts—breakfasts of fruit juice, eggs, bacon, toast and coffee that are just routine in many American homes this side of the Atlantic." In addition to his solitary egg, the prime minister normally had only toast and tea. This was a gustatory moment, and he enthused about it "with boyish glee."[1]

The reviews were coming in for their performance the day before from the press and they were all favorable. "Two great statesmen-showmen, sharing the star parts in a world drama that will be read and studied for centuries to come, played a sparkling and unique scene at the White House yesterday. There were President Roosevelt, debonair and facile as usual, and Britain's Prime Minister Churchill, jaunty and ruddy. Their audience was composed of 200 hand-picked Washington correspondents, described by Mr. Roosevelt as the 'wolves' of the American press, and including a score of foreign journalists."[2] It was a surreal scene, reporters milling about, letting their cigarette ashes fall to the floor.

Still, both men made it abundantly clear that the Allies were on the defensive and would be for a long time before they could engage in offensive operations and begin rolling back the Axis. "Mr. Churchill promised the utmost in defensive operations until such time as favorable conditions permit the beginning of a general offensive."[3]

His appearance was of some fascination to the media and the American public. As was often then case when someone meets a person whom they had only known through photos and newsreels. "He has a pinkish complexion, blue eyes and a wisp of reddish-gray hair remaining on his nearly bald head. These features, plus a roundish countenance, give him a look that has been described as cherubic. There are times when he assumes an expression that has led his countrymen to hail him as the personification of Britain's bulldog courage. His mouth tightens into a straight line, his jaw hardened and his blue eyes flash." A reporter used the American slang "lick" which Churchill was not familiar with, but otherwise it had been a smashing performance.[4]

Christmas Eve promised to be a busy day for the president and the first lady and their extraordinary guest, as well as all of official (and some of unofficial) Washington. It was also, as all knew, the busiest day of the year for a flying wonder of the world whose permanent home was someplace north of the Arctic Circle.

The good-natured Santa Claus planned to make a visit to Sing Sing, the notorious maximum-security prison in Ossining, New York, to give its hardened inmates talcum powder, safety razors, candy, clean white shirts, shaving cream, and tobacco. "The 29 men in the death house awaiting execution would receive the same gifts—except for the razors."[5]

The navy suspended its annual custom of inviting poor children on board their ships because of the war but would still host parties for the children of its various posts.[6]

Mrs. Roosevelt's itinerary was crammed. In the morning there was the Central Union Mission where twelve hundred children would be "entertained." At 12:30 p.m. she would speak to the Volunteers of America party where some five hundred baskets would be distributed to the needy of Washington. Then there was the Salvation Army at 1:30; she was to hand out the first of the toys for poor children. Following that, she would participate in the lighting of the tree on the South Lawn at 4:30 p.m., after which Christmas carols would be sung. There was also the White House Christmas party to attend to as well as her own family with a new grandbaby boy, courtesy of their son, Franklin Delano Roosevelt Jr.[7]

Roosevelt spent the day in meetings with Churchill. Much of the discussion centered on how to best allocate the resources of the other members of the Allied Powers in combating the Axis. "The American and British experts in strategy working here together on the master-plan for the war against the Axis are fitting Russia and the other allies closely into their world-wide battle scheme...."[8]

They also went over a detailed memo analyzing the political state of the world, including relations between the Third Reich and the Arab World. "The Führer has always supported the Arab cause and deplored the vicissitudes suffered by the Arabs at the hands of the British and the Jews." The memo noted the "Mufti" had been given a place of honor on the occasion of the delivery of Hitler's speech of December 11."[9] From an intercepted Arab news report: "The Tripartite powers are fighting against the Anglo-Saxon plutocrats, the Jews and the Bolsheviks and are therefore fighting for the Arab cause."[10] This was temporary expediency on the part of the Nazis, of course. Little did the Arabs fathom Hitler's true contempt for what he regarded as their unclean, inferior race. In his mind, a German "solution" would come to the swarthy tribes of the Middle East, in good time.

FDR also reviewed piles of paperwork, including a memo from John Franklin "Jack" Carter, Roosevelt's personal aide, whose job it was to snoop around government bureaus and Washington and report exclusively back to the president. Carter generated a mound of confidential memos, all for Roosevelt's eyes alone. On the twenty-fourth, Carter asked FDR to give him a letter which he could present to government bureaucrats which would explain his "authority . . . to avoid embarrassment."[11] He also gave FDR a memo on security problems in the "Long Beach Naval Defensive Sea Area."[12]

Earlier that day, the White House announced that Churchill and Roosevelt would attend church together the next day at the Foundry Methodist Church for the 11:00 a.m. service. Security would be tight. Unless someone were a regular congregant or a member of the prime minister's entourage or the White House staff, or they held a special ticket, there was little chance of getting in. Special tickets were printed and had to be shown to get into the building. "Even cabinet members who have not obtained tickets will be barred by secret service men who will direct admission."[13]

Mrs. Roosevelt had sympathized earlier that day with Churchill that it was too bad he was "so far away from home on Christmas." He replied, "Holidays and work days are just the same. Until this war is over, there is nothing else but work that can be in our minds."[14]

As far as the rest of the city, "The glad tidings of Christmas will be sung in the half-darkened streets of Washington this week, but the upsurge of the season's spirit already is expressed in excited announcements of events to be both gay and religious."[15] Charity seemed to be everywhere with no one high-hatting, at least for one day. Except of course for Hollywood.

Warner Brothers studios gave itself a gift as only the moguls of Tinsel Town knew how. Assuming it was a prime target for high-level enemy bombers, the studio built itself a bomb shelter to outdo all other bomb shelters. It was actually four cavernous underground havens, large enough to house thirty-five hundred employees. "The completed shelters are concrete basements, reinforced with sandbags, and equipped with hospital units, beds, water in gas-proof containers, kitchens and gas protection."[16] They also had access to ambulances and "field telephones have been installed all over the lot."[17]

Whether champagne and bartenders were available in the plush shelters is uncertain. But one thing was certain: the immigrant Jews who invented the motion picture business and founded Hollywood saw World War II as their biggest chance yet to gain long-coveted legitimacy in American society. The war was an opportunity to banish their sense of being outsiders and to prove that they were loyal Americans. For their part, the Warners wired President Roosevelt that "personally we would like to do all in our power within the motion picture industry and by use of the talking screen to show the American people the worthiness of the cause for which the free peoples of Europe are making such tremendous sacrifices."[18] Patriotic pictures also were good box office.

In the nation's capital—as in the rest of the country—movie attendance, gift giving and other forms of consumer activity were up over the previous year. The department stores—especially in Washington—were jammed with last-minute shoppers. Nationwide, public school and parochial school kids were already out for Christmas break.

Even the "Ambassador Extraordinary and Plenipotentiary of His Majesty the Son of Heaven" Admiral Kichisaburo Nomura put his pants on leg at a time. This was also true with his underwear which is why an attaché still at the Japanese Embassy in Washington went shopping for "drawers" for Nomura. The attaché was surrounded by a "brace of FBI agents." The day before, a Christmas tree had been spotted being delivered to the Embassy.[19] FDR had received a letter that very day from Generalissimo Chiang Kai-shek, expressing his gratitude to Roosevelt and explaining his idea for a "Supreme War Council" to effectively fight the Axis and, especially, the Japanese.[20]

The Germans were less celebratory of the Christmas season. In the town of Folkestone, England, in the Kentish Coastal District, as children sang Christmas carols in some of the towns that dotted the White Cliffs of Dover, huge explosions punctuated the tranquil evening. The Germans, with their big guns in France, were lobbing shells at the civilian targets, all the way to the South of England, some twenty-two miles across the English Channel. "The children's voices trembled, but they sang on while the explosions echoed along the cliffs of Dover."[21]

The RAF, possessed of more Christmas spirit than the Germans, suspended their bombings for Christmas Eve and Christmas Day.[22]

British radio intercepted a German message in which they announced completion of "intensive fortification works along the Atlantic coast of Europe" after eighteen months of labor. Miles and miles of reinforced batteries and "bombproof shelters for submarines [were] built and camouflage shelters erected for land troops." Ideally, they could be used for "a complete base and support for offensive operations against Britain." Also, the Germans noted the emplacements would not only give them an offensive capability but also "security against invasion of Europe."[23]

Two more commercial ships were attacked along the West Coast, one American and one Canadian. The *Absaroka* and the *Rosebank*—both freighters—had been torpedoed within an hour of each other. The *Absaroka* was apparently sinking, and all hands had abandoned ship. The attack was in the morning and spectators on the shore could clearly see the attacking submarine on the surface. "Onlookers on shore watched as a crew of approximately 35 took to lifeboats."[24] The *Rosebank* had been thought to have been sunk but it was later learned it had limped back to a harbor.

The *President Harrison* had been in "Far East waters" when the war broke out and while many civilians liners made it through safely, the Japanese did capture this ship.[25] Packet boat service between Los Angeles and Catalina Island was suspended because of the repeated attacks.[26]

Another commercial ship, the *Lahaina*, had been torpedoed repeatedly by a Japanese sub on December 11, hitting the huge freighter as many as twelve times before it sank. Thirty of the crew made it into a lifeboat designed for seventeen men and then drifted for over twenty days—armed with only a makeshift sail and a single compass. They finally washed up on the shore at Maui, where they were first mistaken for invaders. A couple of the men had died at sea from exposure, though their tiny boat was well-supplied with vegetables and fruits.[27] For these men to wash up on a speck of an island in the middle of the enormous Pacific had to be considered a Christmas miracle.

Navy officials had not heard from Wake Island for more than a day and conceded it had probably been lost to the Japanese. The navy would only say that "an enemy force effected a landing on Wake Island the morning of the 23rd."[28] The fourteen-day battle by the U.S. Marines was the stuff of legends. Commanded by Major James P. S. Devereux, the garrison had no more than 385 men on three little islands not much bigger than the campus of a small university. Together, the three totaled some 2,600 acres. Devereux only had twelve fighter planes at his disposal and a "small quantity of weapons."[29] He had some anti-aircraft guns also, but that was about it.

One of the last reports from Wake was they had managed to sink two more Japanese ships before apparently succumbing to the invaders. The enemy had already claimed they had conquered the territory and conceded that they'd lost two ships.[30] The Japanese may have been aided by the cover of a dark and stormy Monday evening.

All knew the garrison could not hold on indefinitely but still, the loss was yet another blow. A small amount of solace could be taken in the moral victory that the marines had held on so long and that they had taken so many Japanese men and so much materiel down with them, but the United States already had plenty of moral victories. It was time for some real victories.

The navy issued a one-sentence statement: "Radio communication with Wake Island has been severed."[31] The Japanese had also restarted their shelling of Palmyra Island and Johnston Island.

The British were in no better shape in Hong Kong but were fighting just as valiantly as the American marines. The attempts by the Chinese to relieve the British troops had not come. As far as London knew, the Chinese contingent was too small and too far away to be of much good to the struggling and dug-in Brits, Indians, and Canadians in the "crown colony." They were given "little chance of holding out unless aid could be gotten through to them."[32] "The hopelessly outnumbered defenders . . . were losing heavily, and the situation was acknowledged to be critical."[33]

On the Malayan Peninsula, the British seemed to have regrouped and had, it appeared, slowed the Japanese drive toward Singapore.

The Dutch in the Western Pacific knew something about real victories. So far, they had averaged sinking one Japanese ship per day with their fighter and bomber planes. The Netherland government announced that "the Japanese, in retaliation, had bombed and machine-gunned outlying Netherland islands, inflicting civilian casualties."[34]

In the Philippines, the situation was worsening quickly. Overnight, the Japanese had landed more men "in heavy numbers." They were also bringing tanks ashore now. General MacArthur's forces were now outnumbered, and in at least four areas on Luzon murderous fighting was going on. "Enemy airplanes have been particularly active in supporting landing and shore operations."[35] Air raids had become a commonplace occurrence and the Japanese bombing campaigns had created numerous fires near Ft. McKinley. "The enemy is exerting 'great pressure' an army spokesman said of the Lingayen battle."[36]

The islands were impossible to defend, especially with the relatively small army MacArthur had at his disposal. He'd estimated that he needed at least 500,000 men to adequately defend the country, and he had far less than that, even including the Filipino troops at his disposal. "With the Philippine defenders said to be outnumbered and hard pressed north and south of the capital, the War Department announced the appearance of enemy troop ships off Batangas on the southern tip of Luzon Island, about 65 miles southwest of Manila."[37] The Japanese propagandists claimed they had complete dominion over all aspects of the Battle for the Philippines.

The Department also announced the first seventy-five recipients of the Distinguished Flying Cross, some awarded posthumously including Captain Colin P. Kelly, whose saga of his heroic actions against a Japanese ship, and who died in the line of duty had, like the marines on Wake, become the stuff of folklore. Possibly one pilot who deserved the DFC was Lt. Hewitt Wheless, whose B-17 bomber was attacked by no less than eighteen Japanese Zeros, hitting the plane fifteen hundred times yet not bringing it down! "When we got back, the plane looked like a sieve," the calm Lt. said. "But the holes just gave us more fresh air inside. These babies (the Flying Fortress) sure live up to their reputations."[38]

The award, which had been authorized by Congress in 1926, was for anybody in the Air Corps who had "distinguished himself by heroism or extraordinary achievement in an aerial flight." The seventy-five recipients were not just those who piloted the planes, but those who attended to them as well.[39] Master sergeants, staff sergeants, corporals, and privates were among the awardees.

The sports writers of the Associated Press voted the Cleveland Indians the biggest disappointment of 1941. The year before, they'd missed the American League pennant by the skin of their teeth, just one game, and the Yankees took it. In 1941, the Indians finished twenty-six games out of first place. The best fight of the year was voted the Joe Louis and Billy Conn fight. The worst fight of the year was voted the Joe Louis and Lou Nova fight.[40]

Box office hot Mickey Rooney, 21, and the unknown aspiring secretary, Ava Gardner, 17, announced their commitment to life-long fidelity and matrimony.[41] The film industry was working with the government to ensure the government did not censor the film industry. "President Roosevelt has appointed Lowell Mellett, Director of the Office of Government Reports, as coordinator of Government films during the war emergency with the statement that he wants no censorship of motion pictures."[42]

The Southern Bell Telephone and Telegraph Company took out large newspaper ads pleading with readers not to make any long distance phone calls on Christmas Day and New Year's Day and possibly jam the lines, when the government needed them.[43]

For the first time since December 7, the War Department had allowed journalists and photographers to inspect the damage done at Hickam Field. "Tattered skeletons of huge hangars at the army's Hickam Field stood Wednesday as gaunt evidence of the surprise Japanese attack on this placid pleasure spot, and in them lay . . . the twisted and charred wreckage of the many once-mighty guardians of Hawaiian skies . . . The baseball field was covered with bomb craters."[44] Most of the casualties at the field had occurred while men were still in their barracks, many still in bed. Some, as at Wheeler Field, never got off the ground. "American pilot casualties at Wheeler were . . .

two killed by strafers as they were taking off, and one as he was boarding his plane to attack."[45] They never had a chance.

The lion and the lamb settled down together and gave FDR and the country an unexpected Christmas gift. The business and labor conference, which just the day before had seemed at an impossible impasse, came to a historic agreement. Labor would agree to no strikes for the duration of the war if business agreed to no lockouts. Jaws dropped all over the country when the two old antagonists, labor and business, further agreed to settle all disputes by "peaceful means," including the matter of closed shops.[46] America was united in purpose; patriotism trumped even economic self-interest.

Congress had mostly fled the city for their home districts and home states but a few still remained, including some members of the House Ways and Means Committee, who were trying to determine how to raise the massive funds needed to fund the war effort. Some members "predicted the bill might bite huge chunks out of individual and corporation incomes...."[47] An "unlimited tax" was under advisement. Setting an income cap for all Americans, after which the government would take everything, was bandied about. Other radical plans were also discussed including collecting tax in the actual tax year. But some members thought "it was premature to discuss suggestions that the 1942 tax bill be collected immediately on 1942 incomes. Federal taxes normally are collected in the year after which income is received."[48]

Marshal Petain broadcast a gloomy Christmas message to the people of France, telling his conquered countrymen that peace was a long way off and that many families in France had already been separated by the Germans, due to imprisonment.[49] Rumors were thick in political and diplomatic circles that the Germans were getting ready to push Petain out of his feeble and emasculated position as head of the French Vichy government. The plan was to replace him with a new figurehead who was out-and-out pro-Nazi.[50]

Meanwhile, the pope issued his annual Christmas Eve message from

Vatican City in which he issued a Five Point Plan for a post-war world. In a broadcast on Vatican Radio, Pope Pius XII called for the elimination of aggression, "oppression of minorities," against future wars and armaments and "persecution directed against religious sects or churches because faith 'is one of the rights of mankind.'"[51] His remarks were carried live in the U.S. on the Mutual Radio Network.[52]

That afternoon, as the sun dipped over the horizon, Churchill and FDR both addressed a crowd of twenty thousand on the South Lawn of the White House (attendance estimates varied widely) and the nation by radio, as the president flipped the switch to light the big Christmas tree. It was the first time the White House Christmas tree had ever actually been placed on the White House grounds. Previously, it had been on the Ellipse, Lafayette Park, and Sherman Square. The Marine Band played and the crowd sang Christmas songs just before the lights of the cedar tree were turned on. The songs included, "Joy to the World" and "Silent Night." The Band had played "God Save the King" and "The Star Spangled Banner," which, of course, commemorated the American success over Churchill's forebearers at the battle of Ft. McHenry in the War of 1812. The invocation was given by Father Joseph Corrigan of Catholic University.[53]

It was noted that some in the crowd had waited as much as a whole hour before being admitted through the Southwest and Southeast gates which opened at just after 4:00 p.m. and where army tents had been erected to check individuals. Because no packages or cameras were allowed on the grounds, they were lined up along the fencing to wait until their owners returned to claim them. Some women—called by the *Washington Post* the "indomitable species"—asked soldiers on duty to hold their packages but the men in uniforms refused, albeit politely.[54] After a time, the gates were closed and no one inside would be allowed out until the proceeding had been completed.

The weather had been unseasonably warm with daytime temperatures in the low sixties. "The sunset gun at Fort Myer boomed just before the two men walked onto the portico. A crescent moon hung overhead. To the southward loomed the Washington Monument, a red light burning in its lofty window."[55]

FDR and Churchill appeared on the south portico and both stood to give their remarks. "Over the traditional ceremony hung the pall of war, but there were signs of merriment and good cheer." At 5:00 p.m., their remarks

were carried live across the nation on all radio networks. In his plummy aris-
tocratic baritone, the Englishman opened by saying, "I have the honor to add
an appendix to the message of Christmas goodwill and kindness with which
my illustrious friend the President has encircled the homes and families of
the United States. . . ." He spoke eloquently of his home, of his mother's "ties
of blood" to America and the commanding sentiment of comradeship in the
common cause of great races who speak the same language and to a very large
extent worship at the same altar and pursue the same ideas . . . This is a strange
Christmas Eve. Almost the whole world is locked in deadly struggle." He also
spoke of the "terrible weapons which science can devise."[56] There was a marvelous rhythm to his remarks and his cadence was mesmerizing. Churchill
was a strong leader, but he also was a gifted writer and speaker.

Continuing, he said, "I cannot feel myself a stranger here in the center of
the summit of these United States. I feel a sense of unity and fraternal association, which through all your kindness, convinces me that I have a right to
sit at your fireside and share your Christmas joys."[57]

Churchill said to the gathering that the young across the globe "shall not
be robbed of their inheritance or denied their right to live in a free and decent
world." Concluding with a climactic poetic grace, in a way that only Churchill
could, he intoned, "Here then, for one night only, each home throughout
the English-speaking world should be a brightly lit island of happiness and
peace . . . And so, in God's mercy, a Happy Christmas to you all."[58]

Roosevelt had spoken first and then introduced the British prime minister
as one of the "great leaders" in the world. A newspaper noted that it may
have been the only time FDR had "played second fiddle" to a superior public
speaker. It was noted that the crowds were silent as Churchill spoke and "restless" when FDR addressed them.[59]

In his "Yule Message," Roosevelt's remarks were sprinkled heavily with
reference to the war and sacrifice but also of hope and the Christian philosophy of love and charity. "The year 1941 has brought upon our Nation a war
of aggression by powers dominated by arrogant rulers whose selfish purpose
is to destroy free institutions . . . Our strongest weapon in this war is that

conviction of the dignity and brotherhood of man which Christmas signifies—more than any other day or any other symbol."[60]

In his gracious and eloquent comments, he never mentioned Germany or Japan by name, but made clear that the forces of the Allies represented the forces of light and the Axis Powers represented the forces of darkness. "The new year of 1942 calls for the courage and the resolution of old and young to help win a world struggle in order that we may preserve all we hold dear."[61]

Their remarks were broadcast live on radio, coast-to-coast. The Reverend Oscar Blackwelder of the Washington Federation of Churches gave the Benediction. The whole program, from the lighting of the tree which had been placed near the fence bordering the South Lawn through the playing of the Bands and the speeches and remarks lasted but thirty-five minutes, just as stars in the sky began to twinkle. Yet those in attendance knew they had seen something special.

Roosevelt had also sent a Christmas message to the Armed Forces of America and if there was anyone who needed prayers at the time, it was the boys and girls in blue and khaki:

> To the Army and Navy: In the crisis which confronts the Nation, our people have full faith in the steadfastness and the high devotion to duty demonstrated by the men of all ranks of our Army and Navy. You are setting an inspiring example for all the people, as you have done so often in the past. In sending my personal Christmas greeting to you I feel that I should add a special measure of gratitude to the admiration and affection which I have always felt and have expressed in other years. I am confident that during the year which lies before us you will triumph on all fronts against the forces of evil which are arrayed against us.
>
> Franklin D. Roosevelt, Commander in Chief.[62]

That evening, Churchill joined the Roosevelts for Christmas Eve dinner, where instead of the British favorite of goose, he dined on turkey and cranberries.[63]

CHAPTER 25

THE TWENTY-FIFTH
OF DECEMBER

Government and U.S. Forces May Leave Manila;
200,000 Japanese Estimated Landed on Luzon
Washington Post

Japs Claim Capture of Hong Kong
Birmingham News

Submarines Attack More U.S. Vessels
Evening Star

War Cast Shadow Over Christmas Joy Throughout Land
New York Times

The enemy was closing in on Douglas MacArthur from what seemed to be all sides. Enemy troops were coming ashore at Lamon Bay and Cavite, both near Manila, and a half dozen other hard-to-pronounce but easy-to-understand locations. Ferocious ground fighting was everywhere and large armadas of transports filled with fresh Japanese troops ready to come ashore were reported south of Manila. No one in the American military had anticipated or prepared for this avalanche of enemy soldiers. They certainly hadn't been sighted.

Japanese planes had swarmed over Luzon most of the day and were deliberately bombing the business and civilian areas of the island. Discussions were held to consider declaring Manila an "open city" so as to halt the bombing. Brussels, Paris, Belgrade, and other cities had been declared in such a manner so as to save the lives of civilians while preserving the culture and architecture of those cities. The Quezon government fled the city.[1]

MacArthur was now facing possibly 200,000 Japanese fighting men who had landed on the island since the beginning of hostilities, and they were advancing quickly on American and Filipino strongholds. "Japanese hordes swarmed toward Manila from all directions today and this city was thrown into a supreme battle for its freedom on Christmas Day. . . ." A message the night before "told of heavy Japanese reinforcements lying off Luzon; at least 100 enemy transports accompanied by strong naval and air escort. . . ."[2]

The War Department issued a brutally frank statement. "Though American and Philippine troops are greatly outnumbered, they are offering stiff resistance to the Japanese forces in a series of delaying actions."[3] Delaying actions only meant to delay the inevitable. The number of War Department communiqués was going up, but American morale was going down.

Given the situation on the ground, the U.S. announced that it might have to withdraw its forces from the Philippines. That made it one of the lousiest Christmases for Franklin Roosevelt and the American citizenry in recent memory, certainly since 1777 and Valley Forge, in which the embers of a newborn nation were nearly snuffed out, or the Christmases of 1812 and 1813 or 1861 through 1863, again when those embers almost died.

There was an additional sense of loss and distress because of Wake Island. Post-mortems were filed in many papers, speculating on what happened to the surviving marines. "What became of the little garrison is not known."[4] The Japanese were not known for their charity toward prisoners of war. Profiles of the fearless commander, Major James Devereaux, along with his wife and ten children began appearing in the press. Devereaux was a career Marine and hailed from a family of military men.

Military leaders had wanted a base on Wake because it had a protected cove which they were dredging of coral heads and, once constructed and outfitted with oil tankers, runways, buildings, docks and the like, would be an excellent forward base of operations against the Japanese in the Pacific. It was a link in a chain from the West Coast to Hawaii to Midway to Wake to Guam to Manila. Now the chain was broken.

Just a few days earlier, no one in America knew Wake Island from Treasure Island. It was a dot in the middle of the vast Pacific and only became more widely known after Pan Am had erected a seaplane operation there a few years earlier. Human footprints were rarely found on the island. It was a strategic defeat in a young war in which America had yet to win anything. In relation to its small size, the island's loss was an outsized psychological blow to the morale of Americans, who knew the flag of the Rising Sun now flew over former U.S. territory. The defenders of Wake had held out two days longer than the defenders of the Alamo, a fact which the marines noted with solemn if disconsolate pride.

The tattered British garrison at Hong Kong finally succumbed to the Japanese as well, making this Christmas lousy for Winston Churchill and the British too. The Japanese government made the announcement of the British capitulation, and London did not deny the claim. Tokyo's propagandists twisted the knife when they announced on state radio that the island was a "Christmas gift" from the military to the Japanese people.[5] Of course the Japanese were not Christian but rather Shinto and Buddhist.

"The last-ditch defense of Hong Kong has broken under relentless assault by land, sea and air and the crown colony which for a century has been a British bastion off the southeast China coast has fallen to the Japanese. So ends a great fight against overwhelming odds," the British Colonial Office said.[6] By the early evening of the twenty-fifth, Japanese officials were meeting with the British governor of Hong Kong, Sir Mark Young, to discuss the terms of surrender and the disposition of civilians and combatants.[7]

A confidential memo from British Ambassador Lord Halifax to Franklin Roosevelt spelled out the problems in Hong Kong. "During previous 24 hours enemy kept up incessant attacks and local raids accompanied by intensive bombardment by artillery mortars and dive bombers. Troops very tired." Halifax told FDR that water had been cut off, "food supplies greatly reduced by enemy action." The memo went on to review the world, in the eyes of the British, and with the exception of Libya, and it wasn't very pretty.[8]

Churchill was quickly becoming a popular boarder in the White House. He often got up early as he was still on London time—five hours ahead—but he worked diligently and quietly, armed with an endless supply of Cuban cigars. Around 4:00 p.m., he would take a break and retire for a nap that would last an hour or two and then go back to work, often by transatlantic telephone or cable, until 1:00 a.m. "He has endeared himself to the White House staff with his sense of humor, his entertaining quips, and an amazing vitality and capacity for work."[9]

He was also without shame. As Jon Meacham noted in "Franklin and Winston," "Churchill, fresh from his bath, was in his guest room at the White House, pacing about naked—'completely starkers,' recalled Patrick Kinna, a Churchill assistant who was taking dictation from the dripping prime minister. There was a tap at the door, and Churchill said, 'Come in.' Roosevelt then appeared and, seeing the nude Churchill, apologized and began to retreat. Stopping him, Churchill said, 'You see Mr. President, I have nothing to hide from you.' Roosevelt loved it.

'Chuckling like a school boy, he told me about it later,' said presidential secretary Grace Tully. 'You know Grace . . . I just happened to think of it now. He's pink and white all over.'"[10]

Churchill went to church in the same car as Eleanor and Franklin Roosevelt. The prime minister was in "dark blue topcoat" and carried a cane for the 11:00 a.m. service. Security was extremely tight and government agents and police were everywhere; only a few of the onlookers caught a glimpse of the two men. Many regular congregants had to stand outside of their own place of worship, the Foundry Methodist Church, unable to get in. FDR walked in holding a cane in one hand and the arm of his ever-present naval aide, Captain John Beardall on the other. While in church, they were spotted singing out the carols, Churchill wearing his reading glasses and FDR with his trademark pince-nez eyewear.[11]

After the service, Churchill and Roosevelt spent much of the day in war planning. The White House let it leak out that Roosevelt was "too busy" to open his Christmas gifts but even the most ardent Rooseveltians had to roll their eyes at this too obvious public relations ploy. "Although a day behind schedule, aides said he expected to find a spot during today's heavy engagement calendar to call Fala, his Scotty, and open their presents."[12]

The White House looked surreal that evening. Most windows had been shrouded in blackout fabric as seen from the south. No other lights appeared except those on the Christmas tree on the South Lawn and some ground lights that illuminated the South Portico.

Given the news of the day, Christmas dinner was somber, though the meal itself was sumptuous enough. The menu included oysters on the half shell, soup with sherry, roast turkey with chestnut dressing, giblet gravy, venison sausage, olives and fresh vegetables, sweet potato casserole, grapefruit salad, cheese crescents, plum pudding, cake and ice cream, and even bon bons.[13]

Churchill and the Roosevelts were joined by Harry Hopkins and his daughter, Diane, for the dinner, along with 60 guests according to his schedule. It was followed by "movies and carols." That night, he and Churchill met alone in the Prime Minister's room for over and hour, past 1:00 a.m.[14] Hopkins' wife, Barbara, had died of cancer in 1937, and he and his daughter now lived in a suite in the private residence of the White House. Hopkins had three older sons, all of whom served, including Stephen, a Marine, who was killed in the Pacific.

Following dinner the plan was to call friends and family members separated by the war. The Roosevelts were keen to speak with their far-flung sons. Via a transatlantic phone call, the prime minister's wife, Clementine, and their daughters "sent their greetings" to their father and husband.[15] Roosevelt also sent "Mrs. Churchill" a cablegram wishing her a Merry Christmas. "It is a joy to have Winston. He seems very well and I want you to know how grateful I am to you for letting him come. Franklin D. Roosevelt."[16] Clementine Churchill responded two days later, thanking the Roosevelts for their kindnesses, mentioning "how good you both have been" to her husband.[17] Roosevelt received a note from Lord Halifax conveying the Christmas wishes of "His Royal Highness the Duke of Kent: 'My very best wishes for Christmas and the New Year—George.'"[18]

Even with a world at war, Christmas was celebrated around the globe in some fashion or another, even as in many war zones and battle fields no truces had been called. The Philippines were, it was noted, "the only Christian Nation in [the] Orient."[19] A little girl there asked her mother if the Japanese would allow Santa Claus through. No packages for servicemen had made it through the Japanese blockade. Of course, no lights were allowed on to celebrate the day of enlightenment.[20]

"Lack of food and materials, the separation of families, the blackouts, and other restrictions reduced festivities in many lands."[21] Even so, pilgrims streamed into Bethlehem as bells pealed "amid the crags of the Judean Hills" to attend services at the Church of the Nativity, praying for peace on an earth that, as of December 25, had virtually no peace. "Hundreds of pilgrims, among them uniformed Czechs, Polish, Greek, Yugloslav, Free French and British soldiers, stood outside the adjacent church of the Covenant of St. Catherine where the Latin patriarch, Msgr. Louis Barlassina, intoned the pontifical high mass accompanied by a Franciscan choir."[22] Bethlehem was celebrating a Christmas for those who prayed for peace more than anyone else, the soldier.

The atheistic Soviets saw the propaganda value in Christmas. They distributed cards with the caption "Tannenbaum, Tannenbaum" complete with a "dead German soldier under a lighted, snow-laden Christmas tree." The newspaper of the Russian Army, the *Red Star*, "published its own Christmas card. It portrayed Santa Claus giving Hitler a calendar opened at the date December 22. It said 'Congratulations Herr Führer! Today is just six months since the start of your six-week march on Moscow.'"[23]

In England, Brits went back to London to attend religious services in many bombed-out places of worship. They were warned that the Germans may attack at any time but returned nonetheless to their "shell-bruised churches." Worldwide, British subjects were celebrating Christmas Day as best they could. "In Africa the British troops who were pursuing the Axis legions westward in Libya had no time for Christmas celebrations, except for a hasty gulp of plundered Italian and German wines which they found on the way. Hundreds of cases of beer and other luxuries, however, were flown from Egypt to British units in the rear."[24]

Charity and kindness were rampant. Women made blankets for elderly women in nursing homes, gift packages were delivered to orphanages, and the vacant house of Oliver Wendell Holmes, a justice of the Supreme Court, was opened as a home for girls who had come to Washington, desperate for work. "If a girl arrives in town without any place at all to go—as is often the case these days—she can find lodging" at the large house. Holmes had died in 1935, leaving his entire estate to the federal government. The house had been empty since his death, but found a new purpose in giving safety and refuge to hundreds of homeless girls. At one point, the house on I Street NW had almost been a victim of the wrecking ball to make room for a parking lot.[25]

The Evening Star, NBC, and Warner Brothers studios gave out hundreds of gifts and meals for poor children but as a matter of fact, all the newspapers across the country engaged in many forms of charity and not just at Christmas but many, such as the "Jimmy Fund" in Boston, were boosted throughout the year.[26] CBS, the army, and the navy arranged for some children in America to talk with their fathers who were stationed in England.[27] In Baltimore, "65 negro children patients" had a Christmas party with ice cream, cake, presents, and a visit from Santa Claus.[28]

At Long Beach, the navy put on a Christmas party for some 2,500 navy children, including some who had lost fathers at Pearl Harbor. It was "heart-rending," according to the Los Angeles Times.[29] The climax of the party was the appearance of the omnipresent Santa Claus. Indeed, St. Nick had made so many appearances so quickly and efficiently around the country, one might be forgiven for suspecting that there was more than one jolly fat man.

The Treasury Secretary, Henry Morganthau and his wife threw a party for the 125 soldiers who had permanently billeted at the Treasury Department since the beginning of the war. "The soldiers were given packs of gum, cigarettes, handkerchiefs, razors, candy and toiletries," recounted one report. But there were more festivities to come. "This afternoon, Treasury girl employees will dance with the soldiers in the corridors to the music of an orchestra provided by the Red Cross."[30]

In preparation for Christmas Day, the War Department ordered 1,500,000 pounds of turkey for the men who had not been granted a leave for Christmas. The Quartermaster Corps was preparing a lavish spread for the twelve thousand cafeterias and mess halls around the country.[31] Crowding their serving of turkey, the men had sage dressing, mashed potatoes and

Hubbard squash, buttered peas, soups, fruits, nuts, mince pie, ice cream, mints, and candy.[32]

It could be a sad and lonely time for those young men with loved ones and sweethearts far away and the military wanted to do what it could to help keep morale and spirits up. The halls were seasonably decked with holly, poinsettias, crepe paper, ribbons, and decorated Christmas trees. After dinner the boys were treated to "'an informal entertainment session' . . . with army songs and Christmas carols." To meet the spiritual needs of the men, army chapels featured special Christmas services.[33] All told, "[a] long list of dances, church services, carol 'sings,' open house programs and musicals are available to service men on Christmas leave. . . ."[34]

Christmas in Honolulu took on a serious and sober air of its own. Several days after the 7th, things had loosened a bit but now officials tightened things up, even more. On guard to the point of paranoia about another surprise attack, the strictest possible blackout measures were imposed and martial law was strictly enforced including a prohibition of all hard liquor. "Service men were not allowed to leave their posts and stations. Honolulu remained on the alert, not to be caught off guard again." Purchases of gas were restricted to 10 gallons per month and stores had to close by 3:30 so workers could be home by 4:00 p.m. Sightseeing was banned. A year before, Christmas in Hawaii had been a rollicking movable feast of fun, but this year, "many men were spending Christmas digging bomb shelters."[35]

The contents of the few Japanese planes shot down on December 7 were released for the first time to the American people. There was the usual propaganda material, as expected, including bad drawings of FDR. Yet also, "the planes were stocked with well-aged whisky, concentrated foodstuffs, cider, soda pop, candy, chocolate paste impregnated with whisky, hardtack, tooth powder and chopsticks."[36]

More importantly, the first causalities from Pearl Harbor who could be moved appeared by ship in San Francisco Bay on Christmas Day. "Ambulances moved away through the barricades while mothers stood in a steady rain, watching with hopeful eyes as the passengers emerged."[37] The name of the ship was not released for security reasons, but from Hawaii to California, it had to pursue a "zig zag" course to avoid possible torpedoes from enemy submarines. The Army Nursing Service put out an all points bulletin asking for volunteer women to step forward and help with the wounded.[38] All of the men had stories of bravery and death. They were, the *New York Times* noted, "Filled with cold anger at the Japanese...."[39]

Because of the new restrictions on tin and the limitations on paper, Americans were asked to save their wrapping paper and take them to recycling centers. The Rogers Peet Company of New York, a men's clothier, suggested as Christmas gifts officers uniforms for the Army, Navy, and Marine Corps.[40] Sealtest Ice Cream hosted a Christmas special radio show that featured the great actor Lionel Barrymore, reading *A Christmas Carol* to millions of listeners.[41]

The *Los Angeles Times* held their annual Christmas party for their more than 750 paperboys, complete with entertainment by Bob Hope.[42] The new movie, *The Maltese Falcon* starring Humphrey Bogart and Mary Astor had opened to favorable reviews, and the top box office draw for 1941 was Mickey Rooney, followed by Clark Gable, Judy Garland, and Spencer Tracy.[43] Another new movie debuted, *You're in the Army Now*, starring Phil Silvers, Jimmy Durante, and an up-and-coming comedic actress, Jane Wyman.[44] In 1941, every studio started churning out service comedies. In this offering from Warner Bros., Silvers and Durante play hapless vacuum-cleaner salesmen mistakenly inducted into the army; zany antics predictably and humorously ensue.

A memo was posted in the navy's headquarters in New York, warning the men to be careful of women spies. "Women are being employed by the enemy to secure information from navy men, on the theory they are less liable to be suspected than male spies. Beware of inquisitive women as well as prying men. See everything, hear everything, say nothing."[45]

The war dominated everything. Even as children had gone to bed the night before, thinking and hoping for gifts under the tree, "titanic world events cast their shadow over the spirit of the holiday throughout the land."[46]

For the first time, members of Congress were required to carry photo identification for security reasons to enter the U.S. Capitol, because, while the

Capitol Police recognized the members, the new soldiers guarding Capitol Hill did not.[47] The business of government went on despite the holiday. The Office of Price Administration announced price controls on shoes and many other leather products. The Office of Production Management put out a call for old flashlights, urging Americans find their old ones before purchasing new ones. "Stubbed toes during blackouts can be averted," a Washington official averred.[48]

Yet another commercial freighter, the *Dorothy Phillips*, was torpedoed close to the California coastline. This time however, American planes responded quickly and it appeared they nailed the enemy submarine. The army said a debris field had been spotted floating in the water.[49] The whole country was on a high state of alert, thinking the enemy would enjoy nothing more than to hit America again hard on December 25. "Extra precautions were taken throughout the country in all vital industries and installations lest there be a concerted enemy attempt to sabotage important facilities. On the Pacific Coast, the navy declared a 'double alert' against surprise attacks."[50] The army warned the governors of the Western states to be on the alert for "Fifth Columnist" activities.

The prime minister of Ireland, Eamon De Valera, gave a national radio broadcast in which he announced his decision to stay neutral and keep the Irish out of the war. "It is our duty to Ireland to try to keep out of war. And with God's help, we hope to succeed." He offered the Americans his "sympathies," but nothing more. He offered the British nothing.[51]

King George VI made a brilliant and moving Christmas radio broadcast speaking of the sacrifices of the British people and exhorting them on to great efforts. "I am glad to think millions of people in all parts of the world are listening to me now ... if skies before us are still dark and threatening there are stars to guide us on our way. Never did heroism shine more brightly than it does now, nor fortitude, nor sacrifice, nor sympathy, nor neighborly kindness. And with them, the brightest of all stars is our faith in God. These stars will we follow with his help until light shall shine and darkness shall collapse."[52]

Seventy-seven years earlier, Henry Wadsworth Longfellow penned, "

> I HEARD the bells on Christmas Day
> Their old, familiar carols play,
> And wild and sweet
> The words repeat
> Of peace on earth, good-will to men![53]

That poem, *Christmas Bells*, was written as America was hurtling through a war with itself, over what kind of country—or countries—it would be. Three quarters of a century later, many of the old internal debates in America still existed, but a larger debate had taken over: Would the world allow itself to be enslaved by the Axis forces or live free? The factionalism inside America had mostly been set aside. At least for the time being, the story was not a Farewell to Arms but a Call to Arms.

Eloquence was at its best on this day, and many of the newspapers had superb and moving commentaries on the meaning of Christmas in the context of a world at war.

The greatest miracle of all time is celebrated today by all Christendom. Two thousand years ago a child was born in a humble crib in the little town of Bethlehem, and the event brought a unity to mankind and an impulse. . . .

It is sometimes said we are entering upon a new Dark Ages. All the outwards signs, to be sure, point to it. The Dark Ages were ushered in by the scourges which assailed mankind in the early centuries of the Christian era. The scourge was the irruption of the Germanic barbarians, who overran the Roman Empire, under the aegis of which Christian civilization grew up. It was Christian England, and England alone of all the Roman provinces, that escaped being overwhelmed and kept the flame alight . . . No Christian order can be recaptured, no Christian civilization can be saved, till the Christian world rediscovers its integrity. . . . It is easy under the pressure of danger to develop a common front for fighting a common enemy. It is less easy to develop an common front for living together . . . Our main hope that a Christian shape will be given to tomorrow's life is that the star is shining—the same star that shone on the shepherds as they watched their flocks on the Bethlehem hillside and in the morning led the wise men of their East to the inn in the town. Thither our wise men must also repair.[54]

Yet another concluded, "The American people recognize in Christmas the symbol of the purpose for which they toil and fight. With firm reliance upon a Merciful God, they anticipate the happier Christmases yet to dawn."[55]

The love manifest in the celebration of Christmas threw all of these great global issues into sharp relief. However, regardless of their particular religion—whether it was Christian, Jewish, Muslim, Hindu, or any of the myriad forms of worship—civilized people the world over knew that the Axis represented unadulterated evil.

"I don't see much future for the Americans. It is a decayed country. My feelings against Americanism are feelings of hatred and deep repugnance . . . . Everything about the behavior of American society reveals that it's half Judanized and the other half Negrified."[56] So proclaimed the Prince of Evil, Adolf Hitler.

Rarely had all of the races and creeds of humanity faced such a stark choice between civilization and barbarism, between decent society and a thousand years of darkness.

CHAPTER 26

THE TWENTY-SIXTH
OF DECEMBER

Manila Declared "Open City"

Chicago Daily Tribune

War Tide to Turn by 1943, Churchill Says

Evening Star

Enemy Submarine Sunk Off California

Hartford Courant

Winston Churchill's historic address to a joint session of Congress was decided upon only at the last minute and took place in the Senate chamber rather than the House chamber, where nearly all such Capitol Hill addresses occurred, for the simple reason the lower chamber had more seating space than the upper. But Congress was out of session and most members had gone home and, as such, had not received sufficient notice to get back in time for the momentous remarks. Even House Speaker Sam Rayburn was out of town. "Despite the fact that many Senators and Representatives had gone home for Christmas, both houses had unexpectedly large delegations present."[1]

The smaller Senate chamber also had better acoustics. After the representatives, first dibs for seats went to the diplomatic corps and government

453

bureaucrats. "Chairs for House members, the Supreme Court Justices and the President's cabinet will be placed among the 96 desks of the Senators."[2] The Russian ambassador, Maxim Litvinoff, was seated next to Lord Halifax, the British ambassador. The envoys for other countries including Belgium, Luxembourg, South Africa, Denmark, Poland, Greece, and others were present while astonishingly the representatives for Canada and Australia—both part of the greater British Commonwealth—were "not in evidence."[3] And nearly as surprising, both Secretary of State Hull and Secretary of War Stimson were also absent.

But the public was barred "from the history-making ceremonies because of the limited accommodations. Only people with access cards could get in, and the only people who could get access cards were congressional members, government officials, and those in the diplomatic corps."[4] These restrictions did not stop hundreds of Americans from queuing in a long snaking line in a vain attempt to get into the U.S. Capitol.

All indications were that the prime minister was just as eager. The legislature opened for business at noon, and Churchill rose to speak at exactly 12:30 p.m. to an overflowing crowd. The attendees had their cameras taken away but, for the first time in the history of the Senate, a live broadcast was allowed and, again for the first time, movie cameras were also allowed in. Procedurally, the body was actually in recess though "unanimous consent was granted by the Senate to have the proceedings printed in the Congressional Record...."[5] It was an unusual method for accommodating an invited speaker who was not a member of the Senate. The Marquis de Lafayette had addressed the Senate in such a fashion during his farewell tour in 1824, yet another rare speaker to that body had been, ironically, the King of Hawaii, Kalahaua, in December of 1874.[6]

In the well of the Senate and surrounded by a forest of microphones in front of the prime minister—CBS, NBC, MBS, and others—and a handful of politicians seated behind him including Vice President Henry Wallace and Majority Leader Alben Barkley of Kentucky, sound cameras could be heard whirling in the balcony. In front of Churchill were many though not all of the members of Congress, nearly all men. But, curiously enough, "women predominated" in the galleries which surrounded the room on three sides.[7] Sentries were everywhere. Churchill was sporting a dark bow tie and three-piece Oxford gray suit, his left hand often gripping his lapel, his right index finger slashing the air for effect. Other times, his hands were on his hips, thumbs forwards, or used to grip both lapels. He was a master showman and like many showmen, more at ease in front of big crowds than in small settings.

He was introduced by the president of the Senate, Vice President Henry Wallace, simply as "The Prime Minister of Great Britain!"[8] Churchill then took a bronze green case out of his pocket and removed a pair of spectacles which he settled on his nose and ears.

The air was electric and it was simply one more thrilling moment in a town that should have become used to thrilling moments long ago. He began with a joke. "I can't help but reflect if my father had been American and my mother British, instead of the other way around, I might have gotten here on my own."[9] The appreciative Americans roared with laughter.

Churchill made a fleeting reference to his own long and "not . . . uneventful" life as well as making the kind and gracious remarks any Englishman was known for, including a self-deprecating wit. Had he made it to Congress on his own, he joshed, "I would not have needed any invitation, but if I had it is hardly likely that it would have been unanimous."[10] A human quote machine in the best British traditions of Shakespeare, Wilde, Dickens, and Disraeli, Churchill was such a profoundly literate and quotable man that a term already was being coined in the American press to describe his style: *Churchillian*. He said America had "drawn the sword for freedom and cast away the shadow."[11] And, "Now we are the masters of our fate."[12]

Gesturing for emphasis, Churchill didn't pull any punches, in the character of the British government under his rule. Since he had ascended to the prime ministership, Churchill had quite deliberately rejected the "gloss it over" happy talk, ignore the threat tenures, of Stanley Baldwin and Neville Chamberlin. Part of his falling out with Baldwin was over Churchill warning the British people of the military buildup by Nazi Germany and Adolf Hitler. Baldwin and the status quo he led in London wanted to appease Hitler or simply ignore him. Churchill felt this was irresponsible, but most did not agree with him until September 1, 1939, when Germany invaded Poland. Churchill was proven right but because the Poles had a mutual defense treaty with the British; it meant a new war for England. Churchill had little regard for his fellow Tory, Baldwin. "Stanley occasionally stumbles over the truth, but he always hastily picks himself up and hurries on as if nothing had happened."[13]

This Conservative Member of Parliament from Epping and relatively new prime minister hit the British subjects right between the eyes with the truth.

Now he did the same with Congress and the American people.

Early in his political career, he started out as a conservative, left to become a liberal, and then later in life, returned to the conservative fold. As Churchill put it: "Anyone can rat, but it takes a certain amount of ingenuity to re-rat."[14] He was a conservative like Baldwin and Chamberlain, but a far different kind, similar in many ways to the American conservatism of the Founders, which was essentially an anti-status quo movement of ideas. Churchill never feared or looked down on the citizenry, again like the American Founding Fathers. "I am a child of the House of Commons. I was brought up . . . to believe in democracy; trust the people."[15] He embraced his predecessor, the great Benjamin Disraeli, when Disraeli lamented that the world in his time was "for the few and for the very few."[16]

While never mentioning Lincoln, he scored impressively by taking a populist position against "privilege and monopoly," saying, "I have always steered confidently toward the Gettysburg ideal of government of the people, by the people, for the people." He gave the inner looking Americans a quick thumbnail sketch of his life and career in Parliament where members were "servants of the state, and would be ashamed to be its masters."[17]

In his half hour speech, he said that while 1942 would start off badly for the Allies, the year—or maybe not until 1943—would finish much better as the full industrial and political might of America would become felt in the war. "He predicted that in a year or 16 months the flow of munitions in the United States and Britain will produce results in war power 'beyond anything that has been seen of foreseen in the dictatorial states.'" Expanding, he said it was reasonable to "hope that end of 1942 will find us quite definitely in a better position than now and the year 1943 will find us able to take the initiative on an ample scale."[18] It took a lot of courage to tell the citizens of the Allied Powers they might not taste victory for another year or more. And yet he also saw hope.

"But here in Washington, in these memorable days, I have found an

Olympian fortitude which, far from being based upon complacency, is only the mark of an inflexible purpose and the proof of a sure, well-grounded confidence in the final outcome." He was interrupted repeatedly with applause and huzzahs. He spoke of the common bonds and common mission of Great Britain and the United States. "Now that we are together, now that we are linked in a righteous comradeship of arms, now that our two nations, each in perfect unity, have joined all the life energies in a common resolve, you will see milestones upon which a steady light will glow and brighten."[19]

He concluded by telling the American legislators of his faith and mission. "I will say that he must indeed have a blind soul who cannot see that some great purpose and design is being worked out here below, for which we have the honor to be the faithful servant. It is not given to us to peer into the mysteries of the future; yet, in the days to come, the British and American peoples will, for their own safety and for the good of all, walk together in majesty, in justice and in peace."[20]

When he finally sat down, he was showered with several minutes of applause. The Senate chamber hadn't heard such eloquence and oratory since the "Great Triumvirate" of Daniel Webster, Henry Clay, and John C. Calhoun. As he left, Churchill raised his right hand and with his index and middle fingers, formed the "V" for victory sign. The audience went wild again and he left to the sound of thunderous approbation.

With characteristic irony, he once said that history would be kind to him because he intended to write it. With this extraordinary speech to Congress, he wrote a big chapter in that history of his life and times. On Capitol Hill, they called it "Churchill Day." One of those attending, Senator Ernest McFarland of Arizona, mentioned to Churchill that his wife missed the event because she was ill and in the hospital. With that, Churchill telephoned the woman to say he "hoped she would have a speedy recovery."[21]

Roosevelt listened on radio, along with millions of Americans and Brits. Afterwards, the precise articulation of Churchill was uniformly praised by the often tongue-tied and inarticulate politicians of Washington.

After a lunch with the congressional leadership, the British prime minister left the Capitol but spotting a group of fans and supporters, "he strolled across the Capitol Plaza until he was within a few feet of the cheering crowd of spectators gathered there. Bowing and smiling and waving his black hat at the crowd which was dotted with sight-seeing American soldiers, he bade them farewell with the 'V' sign."[22]

That day, Churchill also met with FDR to discuss the economics of war. They had already covered the military aspects and the diplomatic. Now they had to figure out how to pay for it and how much it would cost to win the world by winning a war. They met with economists and budget experts from their respective governments, both civilian and military. Estimates of the cost to the Allies for 1942 alone totaled $40 billion.[23] The cost alone for three indoor shooting ranges at Ft. Dix, New Jersey, was over $100,000.[24]

In the Senate, a national lottery was proposed as a means of raising needed revenue.[25] The plan behind the lottery was also to put the government in direct competition with illegal gaming in the country. Its goal would be to "kill the numbers racket, slot machines, pinball nickel grabbers and bookie establishments." Prizes would range from $100 to $1,000 dollars.[26]

Churchill and Roosevelt were guided in their discussions by a detailed memo on the "Victory Program" authored in abstruse bureaucratese by Henry Stimson. The cost of ginning up a worldwide machine to wage war and destroy the enemy would be put to paper in black and white. Everything from "Planes, Spare Engines and Parts" to "Small Arms and Automatic Weapons and AC Cannon" were covered in a budget of $33,347,460,905 for 1942 but this was just for the Army and the Air Corps. Stimson was still reviewing the navy's and the Maritime Commission's budget needs.[27] President Roosevelt also reviewed a memo authored by Army Chief of Staff George Marshall making recommendations on the Africa campaign and putting troops in Casablanca.[28]

Before Pearl Harbor, the president tended to be cautious in his projections of public spending, reluctant to antagonize a frugal-minded Congress. On December 7, all of that changed—irrevocably. The very same Congress that had almost voted against the draft was now, after Pearl Harbor, endorsing new and colossal funding requests from FDR that previously were unthinkable. Roosevelt was setting ostensibly far-fetched production goals and in response, a newly quiescent Congress simply opened the spending floodgates. The mobilization for war was releasing sweeping political and economic forces that would forever transform American society. Washington would never again be a relatively small, southern town.

Even though Congress was out of session, in recognition of the holidays, congressional committees kept meeting to go over the financing of the war and slash projected or hoped for billions from domestic programs to help pay for the military. To win the war, the New Deal would have to be shelved. Progressive senator Robert La Follette of Wisconsin pitched a fit, denouncing the suggested elimination or cutbacks of the Farm Security Administration, the National Youth Administration, and the Civilian Conservation Corps, saying this would "knock some of the major props of Federal support out from under our social structure in the lower income levels."[29]

More motivational posters were coming out now, definitely better than the first ones of the war. The Red Cross released one of a downright sexy brunette nurse, shapely with full lips, in white nurse's garb and blue cape, with Uncle Sam standing behind her, his left hand gently on her shoulder.[30] Others told civilians "DON'T 1) Talk Loosely to Strangers 2) Spread Rumors." This poster, it was reported "was designed for taverns . . . to warn drinkers against inadvertently passing on valuable military information or causing trouble by spreading rumors. Loose talk is dangerous in wartime!"[31] Another encouraged buying (what else?) war bonds.

It would take more than posters and bonds to see the U.S. through the days ahead. Churchill was right in preparing the American and the British people for more bad news because it was coming hour by hour and day after day. After all, the Allies were up against "wicked men," but in the end, they "would be called to terrible account."[32] Some of that bad news included word from Wake Island that the Japanese captured almost four hundred marines and another thousand civilians, mostly construction workers on the island.[33]

News from Europe was grave as well. The Russian counteroffensive against the German invasion appeared to have slowed and the Germans were digging in, resisting harder. Even the Soviet propaganda tabloid *Izvestia* reported that "the Germans had heavily fortified this place and exerted every effort to stop our offensive. Stubborn street engagements ensued. . . ."[34] The *New York Tribune* reported that "German resistance is increasing all along the front."[35] And the German war industry was turned up even higher, as more and more of their women went to work in the factories. The Germans also had another brutal advantage: slave labor from the occupied territories.

The Germans claimed they had sunk twenty-seven British ships in the month of December alone. The Japanese claimed they'd destroyed forty British planes in the air and another eight on the ground in a new assault on Rangoon, Burma.[36] The Japanese were occupying Thailand and had, since the first hours of the war, with nary a squeak from the Allies, who were too busy holding on by their fingernails to other territories in the Western Pacific.

New reports were coming from Hong Kong that suggested civilian riots had broken out there in the last days as the Japanese had cut off the water supply. The outpost had been bombed forty-five times in eight days by planes not including the constant shelling from the sea.[37]

There was good news from Midway. For the first time in days, Allies received communications from its embattled forces there, and amazingly it appeared as if the marines had successfully held the island. "We are still here," flashed one message.[38] "The Navy said today its force of Marines on Midway Island is still holding out. The Midway garrison was in communication with headquarters here yesterday but the Navy would not discuss the messages nor how the Marines were faring on the mid-Pacific isle."[39]

The really bad news was rolling in from Manila. The Japanese forces were advancing on the city from two directions, laying waste to everything in their path, military and civilian. They "intensified a two-way assault on Manila, with an artillery fight northwest of the capital and a tank battle to the southeast, where Japanese pressure has been increased an Army communiqué declared late today. Casualties were reported heavy in the tank battle."[40] The Japanese trickle of tanks put ashore had rapidly become a caravan. Tokyo made public claims that they had destroyed the entire American fleet operating in the waters around the islands of the Philippines.

The threat to the civilian population of 600,000 had forced the decision on Douglas MacArthur to declare Manila an "open city," meaning it would be neutral and that all warring parties would agree to not conduct any battles there. He did so, he declared, "to spare the metropolitan area from the possible ravages of attack. . . ."[41] Japanese planes flew over the city, but stopped dropping bombs and American anti-aircraft guns stopped firing on those planes when over the city. Under the rules of engagement, all belligerents were supposed to steer clear of such designated areas. Douglas MacArthur had already departed his headquarters in Manila to take personal command of the army in the field.

The Roosevelt administration was faced with the very real possibility of losing the Philippines to the Japanese. "Washington reports conceded that eventual loss of the Philippines archipelago was distinctly possible as Japanese hordes poured onto Luzon, and Manila was threatened from several sides simultaneously."[42]

All through history, military battles were planned by old men, but executed by young men. This war was no different. The American army and navy were comprised of downy-faced boys, not much removed from being tucked into feather beds by their mothers; but if possible, the Japanese troops were even younger, some as young as fifteen years of age, sweating it out and struggling and fighting in the jungles of the Philippines, whose people were also putting what were essentially little more than boys into the life-and-death struggle of the fight.

In the background of the national debate of late December 1941 were the beginnings of a small pushback against the "First War Powers Act of 1941," as it had become known, and all the power granted President Roosevelt over most forms of private or privately owned communications in America as of December 18, 1941.

The Espionage Act of 1917 had never been repealed. The more radically restrictive Sedition Act of 1918 had been repealed by 1921. Essentially, one had the freedom of expression in America, but only up to a point. Among the verboten verbiage were "false statements to interfere with the success of the United States," which was so open to interpretation as to cause a chilling effect on the ability of anybody and everybody to express their own opinion. Only the overt act of treason was a constitutional offense. That standard was a bit more fixed; an individual had to act to topple the government by "levying war" against the U.S. or "give aid and comfort to the enemy," as specified in Article Three, Section Three.[43]

Perhaps Churchill and his government's bluntness, as opposed to the often less than forthcoming U.S. government, led a small but hardy band of civil libertarians to wonder how many public facts of the war the government should be left in control of. After all, it was December 26, and Americans still had not been told all the facts of Pearl Harbor or the other battles raging in the Pacific. The Roosevelt government often confused the facts of the war with the secrets of the war.

The U.S. Supreme Court expressed its own opinions on censorship when it ruled seven to zero that corporations and businesses had the right to speak out against labor unions and labor problems without it being considered a violation of the Wagner Act. Organized labor considered the 1935 Wagner Act to be the Holy Grail of the labor movement, as it severely restricted what businesses could do in the face of labor organizing and activities. By overturning this key portion of the Wagner Act, the high court gave the American people a moment to pause and reflect on the power of government to censor and just how much power it should really have.

Previously, Woodrow Wilson had made it clear that he felt the Constitution and the Bill of Rights was an impediment to progressive society and proved it shortly after the beginning of the First World War by asking Congress for broad powers to censor. His bill called for imprisonment for life, of anybody who distributed in wartime, any information deemed to interfere with U.S. war policies. The goal was to shut down political opposition to Wilson. The bill passed the Senate but died in the House. Yet another bill offered by Wilson after America's entry into that war would have made it a crime for anyone to publish anything the chief executive deemed to be of use to the enemy. American newspapers rose up in opposition, lead by the Hearst newspaper chain and the bill was heavily amended.[44]

It was the simple nature of some men to want to control the knowledge and freedom of other men, and the debate had been at the core of the American experiment since before the days of the Founding Fathers.

Government bureaucrats were not only capable of dumb mistakes and over-reaching, they were also often guilty of dumb overreacting. Deep in the heartland of Pennsylvania, the eternal flame at Gettysburg, signifying a great victory for the United States, was doused by the National Park Service, fearful that the light would be an attractant for enemy bombing of the ancient battlefield and cemetery.[45]

Other inanities were mercifully reversed. The "Flying Santa" of New England, a pilot who flew gifts each year to lonely lighthouse keepers and their families, had been initially grounded by military officials. At the last minute they relented, realizing they had gone too far, and the Flying Santa was airborne again, spreading good will and cheer, up and down the coast.

The bountiful nature of Washington was such that nearly five thousand more meals were prepared for Christmas Day than there were soldiers to eat them. The best laid plans of the District Defense Committee were to arrange for dinners to be prepared in five thousand homes where families had volunteered to take in soldiers for the day. The meals all arrived and everything had been carried out except for one thing; they were missing soldiers because at the last minute, Washington had been declared a war emergency zone and all leaves were cancelled. Servicemen and officers had to stay on base or on their ships for Christmas Day. No one had bothered to tell the organizers, who had expended thousands of hours in an attempt to provide for a home cooked meal for serviceman away from home. Finally, a call was placed to a local post and the officer who answered haughtily replied, "You people in Washington don't seem to realize that a war emergency does exist."[46]

Actually, the civilian population was all too familiar with the issues of life and death, of sacrifice and charity, and of peace and war. In just a two day period, over 400 people including many children had died in America because of accidents. "Death stalked the highways . . . but also struck 97 times in other forms—fire, guns, lightening, planes."[47] A group of ten in St. Louis had attended midnight Mass, boarded a bus, got into an accident and the ensuing fire killed them on Christmas Day.[48]

In New York, a former school teacher, Isabelle Hallin, 32, was found dead by her own hand on Christmas Day, the unlit gas pilots in her stove open. Four years earlier, she'd been falsely accused of serving alcohol to members of the Saugus, Massachusetts, drama club by the town harpy, who a wire story said was a "prominent Saugus clubwoman."[49] The *Boston Daily Globe* said her accuser was the wife of a local minister.[50] Hallin, who was described as a "pretty blonde" lost her job, sued for libel, won the case, and left town to take a job as a copywriter in New York but the false accusations crushed her spirit and she finally took her life. She left no suicide note.[51] Massachusetts had a long and cherished history of smearing and ruining people in the name of righteous mean-spirited busybodies.

Of all the sad stories of December of 1941, the death of Howard Lusk was one of the saddest. He'd been an orphan in Michigan, not knowing anything about any member of his family. He ran away from orphanages continuously until, at age sixteen, he was discovered on the mean streets of Baltimore in the darkest and deepest days of the Great Depression. He was penniless, disheveled and hungry and was taken in by the Travelers' Aid Society. Eventually, an unknown sister was discovered, who had also been abandoned as a child, like Howard. He'd travelled on the rails for years, North and South, East and West, in a vain attempt to find his parents.

Eventually, Howard found a home in the army and then as a private in Pearl Harbor on December 7, 1941, found death at the age of 25.[52]

CHAPTER 27

THE TWENTY-SEVENTH
OF DECEMBER

Japs Blast Undefended Manila

Birmingham News

Papers in U.S. Hit New Peak in Circulation

Atlanta Constitution

Ban Tires for Family Cars

Chicago Daily Tribune

O n Christmas Day in Rhode Island, Henry "Daddy" Johnson celebrated his 107th birthday. Henry was a former slave, who had met
Abraham Lincoln after the Emancipation Proclamation and was
in remarkably good health, perhaps because he chose to never marry so he
could "stay out of trouble." Until the prior year, he'd lived unaided in a rough
cabin in the woods of the tiny state.[1] Andrew Jackson was president when
Johnson was born.

In Missouri, General John M. Claypool, 95, of the former Confederate
Army of the Confederate States of America and, by 1941, the national commander of the United Confederate Veterans, was photographed signing
up for civil defense work in St. Louis.[2] James K. Polk was president when
Claypool was born.

Meanwhile in Georgia, William Jones, 105, led more than three dozen former slaves in prayer "that this country may be victorious, as the Atlanta Ex-Slave Association held its annual Christmas party. . . ."[3] Martin Van Buren was president when Jones, a former slave himself, was born.

In 1941, the grandsons of slaves and grandsons of Confederate generals took up arms together, united to fight a common enemy which had embraced a perverted aim of elevating a "Master Race" over the rest of humanity. Ironically, the U.S. Armed Forces were, at the time, racially segregated, mirroring the color barrier throughout the rest of American society. This great paradox would be tackled with full force, but not until after the war.

Just then the Democratic political machine in Chicago was having its own problems with race, as the chief justice of the Windy City's Municipal Court, Edward Scheffler, refused to recognize the appointment of a black attorney, Patrick B. Prescott Jr., as an associate justice on the same bench. The appointment of Prescott was made by the Illinois' Republican governor, Dwight Green.[4]

There was a bond growing between Churchill and Roosevelt. Philosophically, they disagreed on much, one the liberal the other the conservative, but they liked each other personally and respected each other's political skills. They also shared the same basic worldview, particularly against the backdrop of Nazism. Certainly their love of the sea was an important bond as well. During the First World War, Roosevelt had been assistant secretary of the navy, the same time that Churchill had been First Lord of the Admiralty in Britain.

They both had suffered political reversals and rejections and had come through those trials as hardened and tougher men. They'd first met in 1918, when they were far younger, somewhat callow, and neither carried a cane. Both were the children of rank and privilege, though Americans would sometimes complain they had no royalty. The Roosevelts, the Vanderbilts, the Rockefellers, the Whitneys, the Cabots, and the Lodges defied that hollow protest. Classless society, indeed. A mordant ditty made the rounds, among high society and hoi polloi alike: "New England, land of the bean and the cod, where the Lodges talk only to the Cabots, and the Cabots talk only to God."

The next time they met wasn't until, fittingly, on a ship in the middle of the Atlantic, the *Augusta*, in August 1941 to produce the Atlantic Charter. The document was not a mutual defense treaty but a framework for how democracies should conduct themselves in relation to other democracies. Churchill had sailed to Newfoundland to confer Roosevelt on the *Prince of Wales*, the very same battleship sunk later by the Japanese.

While both men were known for their humor, Churchill's was more intellectual; he could be devastating but was also self-depreciating. At his lunch with the congressional leadership the day before, Senator Josiah Bailey of North Carolina told him that ever since the Boer War, "I have always believed that you would be Prime Minister of Great Britain" to which Churchill replied, "Senator you are wrong. My future is behind me."[5]

The after-action reports continued to roll in for his landmark speech to Congress and they were 100 percent favorable. Everybody knew when the *Atlanta Constitution* editorialized, "It was a great speech. It was moving, inspiring and full of power" and then singled out his reference to Gettysburg for accolades that the world had indeed changed in those twenty days since December 7, that America was a changed country. Factionalism—at least for the moment—had been set aside.[6]

The only countries where it had been predictably, badly reviewed were Germany and Italy. The German "view is that the catastrophic situation in Anglo-American conduct of war has led to this meeting." The Italian press said it was one more "step by England along path of political submission to United States."[7] In one other regard were Roosevelt and Churchill similar; they were supreme egotists, obsessed with praises but also brickbats.

Some saw it in a broader context that Congress, even with the bombing of Pearl Harbor and with America losing the war for the Pacific, still needed to hear from Churchill to gain a greater perspective on what was at stake in the war for the world. Churchill had to remind his American audience they his people also "had the same feeling in our darkest days."[8]

Said syndicated columnist David Lawrence, "He brought with him a tonic of reassurance and confidence that makes long range planning for victory seem comprehensible in spite of the setbacks and defeats of the immediate future. Nothing compares with it. . . ."[9]

That Saturday, FDR had eight separate meetings, all dealing with the war, and Churchill attended six of them. Some of the meetings dealt with better communications and co-ordination among not just Great Britain, Russia, and America but also Australia, Norway, and Belgium, the latter [two] having "refugee governments." They also met with Soviet Ambassador Maxim Litvinoff who, like all the Russians it seemed, had to be handled with kid gloves.[10]

The war planners were also still trying to decipher the Third Reich's next move. Some thought a renewed effort in North Africa, where the British had finally gained the upper hand, or an invasion of Turkey or an invasion of Spain. Hitler's surprise moves of the past seven years had kept his enemies guessing and had not changed.

Meanwhile, another man of the sea, Admiral Chester Nimitz, reported to Pearl Harbor to assume his new command as head of the Pacific fleet.

The Japanese agreement with General MacArthur to treat Manila as an "open city" and thus not to be touched by either's military, lasted exactly one day. By the twenty-seventh, the Japanese renewed their heavy bombing campaign, apparently only waiting for MacArthur to move his anti-aircraft guns out of the city so they could attack with impunity. In all the destruction falling from the sky, not one shot was fired from the ground in retaliation to the silvery and glistening twin engine bombers.[11]

Attacking an unarmed city filled with innocent civilians offended sensibilities, no less so than if a country attacked another and then declared war after the attack. War, according to the Geneva Conventions, was supposed to be conducted civilly and that meant not making unnecessary war on noncombatants. "Rivaling if not surpassing the stab-in-the-back assault on Pearl Harbor, the raiders visited terror upon the helpless metropolis . . ."[12] They sank one and badly damaged another ocean-going liner at anchor in the Manila harbor while also damaging two American war ships. While bulletins and news reports on the battle for the Philippines were readily available, very few photos of the carnage and destruction were appearing in any of the nation's broadsheets. Many of the stories were angry and graphic though, including the strafing of civilians in the Intramuros district of the old city.

Even the normally unruffled and fact-based Associated Press wire service hotly reported, "Japan treacherously violated the laws of human decency anew Saturday when Japanese bombers savagely attacked Manila, killing many and setting fires, 24 hours after the Philippine capital had been declared an open, undefended city." Much of the bombing campaign had focused on the area around a large hotel "where several hundred Americans and Britons were sheltered."[13] Dozens of planes over many hours pounded the city and the first estimates were of fifty killed and many wounded but the count of the dead multiplied as the day went on.

A 350-year-old church, Santo Domingo, was hit by Japanese bombing planes and caught fire. Much of the old walled portions of the city built hundreds of years earlier by the Spanish were leveled. A radio report said the church had been "smashed by one direct hit."[14] Japanese ground troops were even closer to the city now, just over sixty miles away. Americans and Filipino forces were falling back, again and again, to fight and fall back yet again. The bombing campaign by the Japanese had pretty much wiped out what was left of MacArthur air corps and air fields. Oil fires were everywhere, the Manila port was a bombed-out wreak and the U.S. naval base at Cavite had been spewing black smoke for over two days. Explosions of gas and ammo dumps were frequently heard.

Cordell Hull, Roosevelt's Secretary of State, was asked his opinion of the Japanese regard for the international law and the civility of war. The normally understated elderly man let loose comparing the behavior of the Japanese to those of Nazi Germany, saying they were "practicing the barbaric methods of cruelty and inhumanity that Hitler had been using in Europe." He noted the cruelty also of the Japanese when they invaded China in 1937. Senator Burton K. Wheeler, Democrat of Montana and noted isolationist before December 7, said of the Japanese, "we face only a half-civilized race and in the future they have to be treated as such."[15] Then he could not resist a shot at FDR and Lend–Lease saying how much he regretted not having the bombs to "bomb the hell out of" Japanese cities because "we have given them away!"[16]

Bert Silen, an NBC broadcaster in Luzon said over the air, "The cry is for help—help from America. And if this does not come soon, all of us have resigned ourselves to the inevitable."[17] The Japanese were reportedly dropping bombs all over the island and while Tokyo said nothing about violating the rules dealing with open cities, Berlin radio ridiculously said the Japanese did not recognize it as such because MacArthur had not consulted with the civilian population before announcing his decision. The Berlin broadcast was picked up by NBC short-wave radio.

Late in the evening of the twenty-sixth, the War Department issued a communiqué on the crisis in the Philippines. "Philippine theatre. Fighting in the Lingayen Gulf area north of Manila, is of desultory character. Combat operations in the southeast, in the general vicinity of Lamon Bay, are very heavy. The enemy is being continually reinforced from fleets of troopships in Lingayen Gulf and off Atimonan. Enemy air activity continued heavy over all fronts. There is nothing to report from other areas."[18] Lamon Bay was on the east coast of the Philippines and Lingayen was on the west coast of the Philippines and Manila was right in between.

The Japanese navy minister Shigetaro Shimada went before the Diet and claimed that the Japanese had nearly destroyed the British and the American navies and air forces operating in the Western Pacific. "He asserted British and American naval losses included seven battleships sunk, three heavily damaged and one less seriously damaged; two cruisers sunk and six damaged; a destroyer sunk and four damaged; nine submarines, nine gunboats, seven torpedo boats and sixteen merchant [ships] sunk and fifty captured." He also said they had destroyed 338 American planes in the Philippines and together, including British planes lost, had destroyed 803."[19] Again, the Allies did not dispute the enormous and impressive claims and again, all this was widely printed in the Western newspapers, and there was little the U.S. government could do to censor the stories or gloss them over. The word "retreat" appeared in a number of those stories.[20]

Bulletins appeared of how friends and associates of General MacArthur feared for his life. In the "world war" he was known to take risks—some which were thought to be reckless—and his capture by the Japanese would be a huge propaganda victory for Tokyo and equally disheartening for Americans. "MacArthur's headquarters staff in Manila went to an air raid shelter each time Japanese planes approached, but the general remained in his office, smoking and studying war maps."[21] Of great concern too was the safety of his wife Jean and their son, Arthur. Of the fight for the Philippines, the American High Commissioner, Francis B. Sayre summed it up in one short sentence: "We will fight to the last man."[22]

The Japanese were not only destroying, they were also restoring. In Borneo, retreating British engineers had laid waste to some 150 oil wells, in the hopes of denying or delaying the precious liquid for the enemy. The ploy failed as the Japanese, within days, brought seventy of them back on line, producing by their estimate some 700 tons of oil a day.[23] The Japanese alacrity in restoring the oil wells underscored the degree to which their conquest of East Asia was in large part predicated on their strategic need to capture rich oil resources, once controlled by the British. The Japanese knew full well that without sufficient oil to power their war machine, their aspirations for greater Empire would be futile.

In capturing the area of Sarawak from the British, the Japanese, had fall into their lap, tons of precious tin, rubber, guns, "armors cars" and other spoils of war.[24] Additionally, a report from the British colonial office said the Japanese were now "operating" in the Gilbert Islands which were approximately halfway between the Hawaiian Islands and Australia. "The announcement expressed fears that some European residents of the little chain of 16 coral atoll islands might have been taken prisoners."[25]

Americans were following the news of their country and the news of the world as newspaper circulation reached an all-time high, according to *Editor and Publisher*.[26] Morning papers were up, afternoon papers were up, and Sunday papers were up. Most papers cost 2 to 3 cents.

For weeks, women had been warned that the days of silk stockings—at least during the war effort—were probably over and now it appeared they were, as many department stores had pushed their purchase hard for the Christmas buying season. The National Association of Hosiery expected inventories to run out, as there had been a run on them since December 7. Silk would be needed to fill more important roles including parachutes and the powder bags for the large guns on warships if the Allies were going to get a leg up over the Axis Powers.

Washington finally got its policy together on civilian purchase of new tires during the war and the course of action was essentially "Hit the road, Jack." Plain, everyday citizens had no hope (at least legally) of getting new tires but neither did cabbies or those who lived in rural areas. Tires in 1941 were not steel-belted or vulcanized or pneumatic or nylon-belted and did not last for thousands of miles. They were essentially a thin rubber balloon inside a hard circle of rubber that wrapped around a steel rim, and the contraption did not last long. A board with nails, glass in the road, were daggers at the throat of these poorly made tires. Even if they did not meet their demise due to puncture, they wore out very quickly as did the tread. Getting stuck in snow, ice, and mud was an everyday occurrence and the solution for many was to place chains around their tires which also destroyed the soft tar of city streets. An outright ban on tires was essentially a ban on driving. This was not an inconsequential decision by the government. The cessation of the sale of new tires had a broad and potentially devastating ramification for the economy. As many people drove their cars to work each day or took cabs, it would definitely have an effect on employment. Goodyear pitched their flimsy contrivances saying, "You can safely run your tire until the non-skid tread design practically disappears. Then you can have them safely regrooved. Later, if your tire carcasses are sound, you can safely have them retreaded and drive them nearly as far again."[27]

"The nation's 32,000,000-odd motor car owners today face an almost complete tire famine," said one story.[28] Local rationing boards were set up with three members from each community, like the Draft Boards and the Enemy Alien Boards. The members would be appointed by each state's governor and would be empowered to issue certificates for purchase "to those few operators that come under the classifications outlined by Washington and all law enforcement agencies have been asked to aid in enforcing the rationing rules."[29]

The rubber shortage was such that people were advised against going for Sunday drives, to walk more, and to only drive for essential reasons and when one did, combine all your errands together. Comedian Bob Hope was in newspaper ads astride a Schwinn bicycle.[30]

New tire sales were limited to police and fire departments, doctors, nurses, veterinarians, trucks that delivered oil, farm tractors and other equipment needed for the production of food, and delivery trucks for scrap metals and trucks for "garbage removal."[31] For delivery vehicles like milk trucks, it was no go. The Office of Production Management later amended their rules to allow for the manufacture of fire hoses.[32] American farmers were urged to plant a Russian imported dandelion as some scientists saw the weed as being able to produce a modicum of rubber to replace at least some of the shortage, according to the National Chemurgic Council.[33] One side effect of the new rule: "Stores were quickly cleaned out of golf balls."[34]

City fathers in Detroit of all places made plans to bring out of retirement over a hundred streetcars to fill the need for public transportation created by the tire shortage.[35] The shortage was so severe in Great Britain, the Minister of Supply issued an outright ban on anything made out of the now-rare substance including "corsets . . . golf tees and garden hoses."[36]

With all the seriousness and seriousness of purpose in America, it was sometimes difficult to remember that the country also still had a seedy underside, fueled by easy money, notoriety, and booze. Young millionaire heiress Gloria Vanderbilt was so often in the news it was reasonable to assume she employed an army of publicists. But she was also a "Jonah," bringing trouble and bad luck to everybody around her it seemed. At her engagement party, two men who claimed to be princes got into a fistfight and this made the newspapers, even as war was raging all around and even as young American boys were fighting and dying.[37]

Just as American families were getting over the weeklong food festival of Christmas week, they were staring down the barrel of yet another festival of food and fun during New Year's Week. Still, with the new regulations on tires, Americans would have plenty of opportunity to walk off the extra poundage they gained over the holiday season. Ralph's, a chain supermarket in the Los Angeles area, was touting all sorts of meats, fruits, vegetables, and staples for customers to restock their shelves. Interestingly, of all the staples listed, including salt and pepper, Maxwell House coffee (1 pound was just 31 cents), and potatoes (10 pounds for 27 cents), sugar was nowhere to be found in their print ads. They also now carried the new disclaimer at the bottom, "We Reserve the Right to Limit Quantities."[38]

They would also have plenty of jobs in manual labor to sweat over, building the arsenal of democracy. Government planners in a myriad of agencies, including the National Youth Administration, were conceiving new job training programs for men and women, as there was a "skilled labor gap." The effort involved "federal, state and local agencies" who were "cooperating in an all-out program to provide skilled workers to fill the wide gaps in industrial plant rosters growing out of the acceleration of production to meet war needs." The plans included moving workers around the country to meet the needs of various industries. Also, women would be "encouraged" to join the work force. "As a first big step, the big-scale employment of women looms, hence they are now being trained for jobs now reserved for male workers. Women soon will dominate in many machine shops, drafting rooms, engineering departments, light assembly divisions, light riveting and spot welding."[39]

The American government continued its crackdown on "enemy aliens" in the country. In Alabama, fruit orchards owned by Japanese nationals were seized by the Department of the Interior, while the Justice Department issued a terse statement that all "Japanese, German and Italian nationals in seven Pacific coast states" had until 11 a.m. on Monday, the twenty-ninth to surrender to authorities any radio-transmitting equipment, especially short-wave radios, as well as any cameras they owned. Those states the edict applied to were Washington, California, Utah, Montana, Oregon, Idaho, and Nevada.[40] A second group of twenty-three enemy aliens was trucked from San Francisco to "a Missoula internment camp. . . . About 100 local aliens previously have been sent to Montana. Several carloads of Southern California aliens were scheduled to be placed aboard the same train at Sacramento."[41]

If possible, security measures were becoming even tighter in America three weeks after the outbreak of war. Additional cordons were thrown up around defense plants, identification cards for workers were being issued, and tightly controlled and law enforcement officials often pulled over drivers for no apparent reason. Washington tightened even further the border with Mexico, not allowing anyone to carry any form of correspondence across the boundaries. All letters would be confiscated.[42]

While nobody used the phrase "Police State," a blanket of state-sponsored security—along with the acquiescence of most Americans—was settling over the country. The Santa Anita thoroughbred racing meeting was canceled for the first time ever. Public officials were debating banning any gathering of more than 10,000 people. To enter the Los Angeles harbor—as with others around the country—specially issued photo identification was needed but they also contained "fingerprint, status of citizenship and physical description of the holder."[43]

The harbor had already been designated a "Navy sea defense district" by presidential order. "Photographing in the area is prohibited and no one can divulge movements of shipping or naval activities under penalty of violation of the Espionage Act or other Federal or state laws. . . ."[44]

The costs for civil defense had gone up exponentially. As a result, money available for other municipal programs was severely restricted. The lead editorial in the *Los Angeles Times* read, "Where to Cut to Save Money for War." Editorials in the *New York Times*, the *New York Herald-Tribune*, the *Indianapolis News*, and others applauded the new restrictions and offered advice to citizens on how to stay out of trouble.[45]

If anybody did complain about all the censorship, shortages, rationing, checkpoints, blackout drills, ubiquitous guards, and any number of other infringements and inconveniences, the Pavlovian response was, "Don't you know there's a war on?" as if the questioning party was somehow unpatriotic.

The matter of the Japanese, German, and Italian legations was still to be resolved, though the United States pledged to abide by the international conventions. The German staff and ambassador had been removed from Washington and were comfortably ensconced at the Greenbrier hotel in West Virginia, mostly eating and drinking too much. They were awaiting their deportation which was delayed because of the niceties of diplomats, the intermediary Swiss, and foot-dragging bureaucrats.[46] The Germans though weren't in any hurry to leave.

Further, the Roosevelt administration pledged that in the matter of Japanese prisoners of war, here it too would abide by the 1929 articles of Geneva endorsed and ratified at the time by forty-seven countries. Ominously, Japan never ratified the conventions. "The United States has informed the Japanese government that all Japanese prisoners captured by American armed forces will be treated in accordance with the prisoner-of-war convention. . . ." The Americans expected the Japanese to reciprocate and "grant all American prisoners of war reciprocal fair and humane treatment."[47] It was asking a lot.

The Japanese already had a sizable number of American POW's including the marines taken at Wake Island, in China, and at Guam, plus the sailors taken off a gunboat captured in Shanghai. The Americans only had a handful including several pilots shot down in Pearl and the crew of one of the "midget" submarines captured in that battle. According to the 1929 document as created by the International Red Cross, prisoner exchanges had to be arranged and POW camps opened for international inspection.

Representatives of the World Alliance of the Young Men Christian's Association, including Dr. Darius Davis, had gone on an inspection tour of the Russian, German, French, and English POW camps and found that each was generally abiding by the Geneva Convention, although the Germans fed their Russian prisoners less than prisoners "of other nationalities. "Each day, the Russians were given "a cooked turnip 'with a little codfish thrown in.'"[48] Many governments sent "supplementary" food to their captive men: Davis was asked if prisoners could survive without supplementary food and he remarked that the Serbs and the Poles got nothing from home, "And they are still able to live."[49] No inspections had yet been made of Japanese POW camps and, of course, there was no mention of the German concentration camps where the extermination of millions of human beings was just getting underway.

As abruptly as the torpedo attacks along the California coast had begun, they by and large ceased. No doubt the increased surveillance by civilians and the law enforcement along the shore, as well as vastly increased over flights by the military and the additional precautions taken by ship captains, combined to have a positive effect. However, it could also have been that the subs—presumably Japanese—had run low on fuel and supplies and were thus forced to withdraw to safer waters to re-provision. Still, fishing on the West Coast was severely restricted because boat insurance had jumped up and with it, the cost of sardines.[50]

The American people had digested the situation with more than some aplomb. There was never a general panic among the populace and given what submarines were capable of doing to defenseless ships and shore emplacements, they would have been justified in panicking more. Shipping along the coast was vitally important to the local economy at the time. There were few roads up and down the West Coast.

Airplanes were not big enough to haul sufficient quantities of food and other goods, so it was up to ships and trains to carry the load. The very thought of commercial ships being sunk at random could have set off a panic, sending food prices spiraling upwards with runs on grocery stores and yet, those Americans along the West Coast had taken the whole matter in stride, perhaps inured a bit to the new vicissitudes of war.

For them, war and sacrifice already had become a way of life. Little could Americans realize, in those heady first days of rekindled patriotism, just how long and costly this global conflict would prove to be.

CHAPTER 28

THE TWENTY-EIGHTH
OF DECEMBER

Japanese Bombs Fire Open City of Manila;
Roosevelt and Churchill Fix War Strategy

New York Times

Japs Demand Filipinos "Cease All Resistance"

Atlanta Constitution

Night Shifts for Women in Plane Plants Seen

Los Angeles Times

The twenty-eighth marked the third week after Pearl Harbor. It was also the last Sunday of the year, and the churches of America were packed with congregants and parishioners listening to ministers and priests asking them to pray for their president, for Winston Churchill, for their elected leaders, but most importantly for the people on the front lines fighting for America.[1] The Archbishop of Chicago, Father Samuel Stritch, asked his parishioners to pray for Roosevelt and against the "Godless … fury."[2] The day before, in a synagogue in New York, Rabbi Elias Solomon spoke to his flock of FDR and Churchill, "Like Joseph of old, they seem to have been chosen to preserve life and liberty for all men and nations."[3]

It would be nice to imagine that the national emergency and the holiday season might cool the partisanship and mean-spiritedness in America, but not so. In addition to getting on Roosevelt's nerves over his mismanagement of the Office of Civil Defense, Fiorello La Guardia, as mayor, ordered the head of the Office of Commissioner of Markets in New York City, William Morgan Jr., to fire Mrs. Preston Davie, whom newspaper accounts said was a "blue blooded leader in Republican women circles."[4]

La Guardia was a Republican in only the most casual and tissue-thin interpretation. In 1941, the Republican Party was home to many moderates and liberals, especially in the Northeast. La Guardia was a New Dealer through and through and had campaigned for Roosevelt in 1936 and 1940. La Guardia won Gracie Mansion by running against corruption and then ran the city like a little dictator rather than a "Little Flower." He also ran for mayor on the ticket of the American Labor Party, an ultra-liberal organization. Mrs. Roosevelt had been installed by her husband as the assistant director of the Office of Civil Defense to keep an eye on La Guardia for FDR, and because she herself had been mildly critical of his stewardship of the OCD.[5]

When Morgan refused to fire Mrs. Davie, La Guardia got tough and one of his lackeys referred publicly to Mrs. Davie as Morgan's "girlfriend."[6] Morgan threw up his hands and resigned.

Candor was the Western watchword in the waning days of December. Australian Prime Minister John Curtin gave a speech before his parliament in Canberra in which he warned of more and more reversals for the Allied Powers. The leaders of the Allied Powers had little choice but to tell people this as the news each day seemed to become gloomier and gloomier. The best they could do against Japan, Curtin said, was to "slow the enemy down."[7]

Curtin also understood what he and the Allies were up against. "We face an enemy nurtured in the tradition that to die for the nation is the highest virtue."[8] Not everyone was convinced that the Allies felt that defeating the Japanese carried the same weight as defeating Nazi Germany, including many, not surprisingly, in the Pacific. Indeed, in the war conferences in Washington, on at least one occasion, Allied representatives suggested that the war in the

Pacific could wait. "Diplomatic circles reported . . . that one of the prem-
ises basic to the conference was that Hitler's Germany was the chief and, at
present, perhaps the most vulnerable enemy and that Japan, if she could be
checked at Singapore and its approaches including the Philippines, could be
taken care of later."[9] The premise was dangerous and foolish because even a
cursory look at the broadsheets of the days made clear that the battles for
Singapore and the Philippines were not going at all well for the Allies. There
might not be much, later.

Another harsh critic of the "Europe First" policy, Sir Keith Murdoch,
publisher of the *Melbourne Herald*, took Churchill to task, denouncing him
for being "Atlantic-minded" and said in no uncertain terms that if Singapore
fell, then the Churchill government would fall. "Some of those in office
are ready to say we can finish the Japanese after beating the Germans," he
stormed.[10] Australia was not a member of FDR's "War Council," but many
thought she should be, including Murdoch. The *New York Times* editorially
called for "Anglo-American Unity."[11] Sir Keith eventually sired a son named
Rupert, who inherited his father's publishing empire, greatly expanded it, and
went on to display the same pugnacious streak.

To Murdoch's point, it was announced that the Japanese had seized two
of the Gilbert Islands, Makin and Abalang. The islands were a part of the
British Commonwealth and only 2,000 miles from Hawaii.[12]

FDR had his own problems with publishers, one in particular. Basil
Brewer, the publisher of the *New Bedford Standard-Times* went hard after
the Roosevelt administration over the Philippines, the lack of adequate
defenses there, and Douglas MacArthur's decision to declare Manila an open
city. "The stupidity of removing defenses from Manila and declaring it an
open city with the expectation that Japan would respect its civil population
finds its expected answer in the death and destruction wrought there today."
Brewer ripped FDR even further, saying his decisions contained a "profound
lack of realism."[13]

With the Japanese rapidly moving down the Asian coastline, gobbling up
one country after another, one colony after another, one outpost after another,
the Australians' impatience was understandable. They were nervous about
the Japanese and had recent history on their side to point to. At some point,
having taken everything else, the Japanese could be counted on to invade

Australia and while the Aussies had a standing army of about 300,000 men, their equipment and training was considered poor. They had a small navy and virtually no air force.[14] With no significant prior threats, Australia had never seen the need to invest in their military and was now looking to the United States and Great Britain.

But the British had their point of view as well and they considered it valid. From where Churchill sat, Hitler was more of a threat to the bulk of the British people than Japan. The British Empire may have had 500 million people—factoring in India and other parts of the Commonwealth—but not all of them voted and not all of them had been bombed day and night by the German Luftwaffe. The British in private sometimes shook their heads about the American reaction to the bombing of Pearl Harbor. During their blitz, it wasn't unusual for London to be hit hundreds of times in a single day by thousands of bombs.

Plus, the war with Germany was over two years old. The war with Japan was only three weeks old. First things first.

Out of those war conferences arranged in Washington by President Roosevelt came a consensus for the conduct of the war against the Axis. Speaking for the nearly three dozen countries arrayed against the Axis— all now members of the Allied Powers—"President Roosevelt and Prime Minister Churchill [assumed] dramatic leadership of the ... war against Axis aggression, spread before the accredited representatives of 33 nations yesterday the advanced blueprints for marshaling every economic and fighting resource of this globe-encircling front."[15] No details were of course revealed but the mere fact that so many countries could agree on anything was in and of itself a miracle. Even America's allies, the Russians and the Chinese, were in agreement. Other countries sending representatives included Mexico, Costa Rica, Honduras, Cuba, and, Paraguay and in fact, nearly all the countries of Central and South America were on hand. Roosevelt said they had made "excellent progress."[16]

White House press secretary Stephen Early handed out a statement from FDR which read, in part:

As a result of all these meetings, I know tonight that the position of the United States and of all the nations aligned with us has been strengthened immeasurably. We have advanced far along the road toward achievement of the ultimate objective—the crushing defeat of those forces that have attacked and made war upon us. The present overall objective is the marshaling of all resources, military and economic, of the world-wide from opposing the Axis.[17]

A surprisingly happy addition to the Allied efforts was the Netherlands as a result of their victories in the Far East against Japanese ships and planes. Truth be told, their military successes in the early days of the Pacific war were greater than those of either America or Great Britain. Just the day before, the Dutch had sunk two Japanese warships. The minister for the Netherlands, Dr. Alexander Loudon, was granted a private audience with Roosevelt and Churchill.[18] The Free French were not prevalent at the meeting and it may have been because both Washington and London were miffed at Charles De Gaulle for taking two tiny islands off the coast of Newfoundland without first checking with them. The French then banned any ship from any country to make port in either St. Pierre or Miquelon.[19]

Some of the representatives simply had to step out of their embassies and hail a cab to take them to the White House for these meetings, but others had more harrowing journeys, including the representatives of eight refugee governments who had been "driven from their homelands or have bowed to the exigencies of war to transfer their principal activities to new centers."[20] Some of them were included in the final meeting of the day: Poland, Denmark, Luxembourg, Greece, Czechoslovakia and others. One more meeting was postponed until the next day because Churchill and Roosevelt had been going non-stop and needed a break after the long Saturday. Churchill would be leaving the next day.

On Sunday, Churchill departed via train for Ottawa where he was to give a speech before the Canadian Parliament. He climbed aboard a private car at Union Station in Washington at 2:15 p.m. and headed north through Baltimore and Philadelphia before stopping in New York at 6:10 p.m. It took three hours to get to Springfield, Massachusetts, where he arrived at 9:40 p.m. In and out of White River Junction, Vermont after 1:00 a.m., he did not arrive in Ottawa until 9:00 a.m. the next morning.[21]

Cigarettes and the tobacco industry were hugely important to the civilian population and military government, and it was big news when a new brand came out or, heaven forbid, manufacturers raised the price on a pack of cigarettes. The Office of Price Administration raised a stink when American Tobacco wanted to raise its prices by 57 cents on every 1,000 cigarettes. The increase to the consumer would be about one penny for a pack of 20 cigarettes and the OPM pressured nine other tobacco companies not to follow suit.[22] The cost of a pack of cigarettes was, depending on where you lived, around 20 cents per pack and over sixty percent of all smokers smoked filterless Lucky Strikes, filterless Camels, or filterless Chesterfields.

Big advertisements filled the magazines of America featuring soldiers and sailors and marines in uniform with cigarettes dangling from their mouths with the screaming headline, WE WANT CAMELS![23] Other ads featured kindly looking doctors with silver-haired temples, dressed in white lab coats, assuring smokers of the healthful benefits of certain cigarette brands. To preempt growing anxieties about the bad physical effects of smoking, tobacco companies increasingly featured bogus "medical evidence" that their brands were actually good for you. They also actively curried favor with physicians and physician groups, leveraging the enormous respect and authority that the medical profession enjoyed in society.

Now, with America at war, cigarette advertisements were starting to feature heroic doctors in battle, supplying fighting men with the medical attention—and cigarettes—that they so desperately needed. As one advertisement had it: "[The medical man] well knows the comfort and cheer there is in a few moments' relaxation with a good cigarette . . . like Camel . . . the favorite cigarette with men in all the services."[24]

Meanwhile, another government entity, the Office of Production Management, issued new orders of its own to makers of farm equipment. The companies were told to "curtail" the manufacturing of new equipment while stepping up the "output of repair parts." "The purpose is to conserve scarce metals while assuring that farmers will be able to keep presently-owned machinery in good working condition." The order, it was said, affected everything "from windmills to wheelbarrows." At the time, some fifty thousand Americans were employed in the farm manufacturing industry, in which there were approximately a thousand companies churning out milk cans, tractors, combines, harrows, hoes, shovels, pickaxes, spades, and spade shovels; the tools for the men and women who had wrought miracles out of the American wilderness and with those tools, their hands, and their fortitude had fed millions of Americans with high-quality and low-cost food.[25]

In the cities, where the sophisticates sometimes looked down their noses at their country cousins, they were getting ready for New Year's Eve. To most farmers, it was simply another day but to the city slickers, it was an excuse to get dolled up, men in black tie, women in furs and flowing fur coats. A dinner jacket at Raleigh's Haberdasher in Washington was going for $55, enough to feed a family of four for a month. For the police and fire departments of New York, New Year's Eve would be spent patrolling the Great White Way, looking for saboteurs on the ground and bombers in the air. Big crowds were expected as with each New Year's Eve and officials thought the throngs would be a tempting target to the enemy. The city had been under pressure to cancel the reverie on December 31, but they went ahead and made sure seven hundred of New York's finest were out and about to ensure no harm befell the partiers.

For the women, before going out, print ads reminded them—sometimes in the bluntest terms—to take care of their hygiene. "Go to bed, Mary," said one ad for Mum deodorant. "That phone won't ring tonight. No one ever calls Mary anymore. No one ever calls on any girl who is careless about underarm odour (sic). You need Mum to prevent odour to come." Other ads advised women that if they had any chance at all for a man, they'd better use Lux Soap, or Palmolive Soap, or Cashmere Bouquet Soap. "That exquisite, lingering scent is the success secret of your romantic rival. . . ."[26] Ivory Snow laundry detergent was recommended for women's increasingly rare silk stockings because "perspiration is acid."[27]

Print ads in Los Angeles newspapers urged people to make their reservations now for the Hollywood Palladium where Tommy Dorsey "and his trombone and orchestra" would perform for the revelers on the Palladium's opening night.[28] On the bill for that evening was a wafer-thin twenty-four-year-old kid from Hoboken, New Jersey, named Frank Sinatra.

For those who wanted to party New Year's Eve in Hawaii, "intoxicating liquor" was still not available by order of the military governor. The only way to obtain beer, liquor, or wine was with a prescription written by a physician. If the "sick" individual was in the military, then their liquor prescription could only be filled by a military pharmacist. If the "sick" individual was a civilian, well, this one gave new meaning to bureaucracy. "Prescriptions written by civilian physicians, dentists and veterinarians must be submitted in duplicate form to the pharmacist who is required to note on the duplicate the action he takes. Then the pharmacist must forward daily the copy with his notation to the controller of civilian medical supplies. . . ."[29] The runaround to getting a drink was enough to drive a man to drink.

J. B. Poindexter, the military governor, was cracking down in other ways. Beginning on December 31, all residents of Hawaii over the age of six years old would have to be registered and fingerprinted. Only military personnel were exempted. The entire "Hawaiian Defense Act" took up a full page in mouse type in the December 28 *Honolulu Advertiser*. Anything and everything in the islands from gasoline consumption to residences to curfews had rules and regulations. The paper also was running classified ads selling bomb shelters. "Can be installed immediately."[30]

Irony was a part of war. It was reported that "several" of the Japanese pilots who had been shot down on December 7 were wearing class rings issued by the University of Hawaii and McKinley High School.[31]

Local radio stations in Honolulu came on no earlier than 6:30 a.m. and their broadcasting day ended at just after 10 p.m. No longer would an enemy use the overnight broadcasting of a radio station as a homing beacon as the Japanese had done early in the morning of December 7. The first show on KGMB was, appropriately, "Dawn Patrol."[32]

The number of Japanese, Germans, and Italians deported from the West Coast and shipped to Montana was increasing. Prisoners who had been held in the Terminal Island Federal jail in the Los Angeles area were cleaned out "and moved to an internment camp." Further, "This was disclosed yesterday with reports that more than 100 Japanese and German nationals had been transported to the internment camp together with a group from San Francisco."[33] Also, all the Japanese-owned shops in the Terminal Island "settlement" were closed.[34]

Across the country, rumors went around that employers were dismissing workers of Italian, German, and Japanese descent, even though they were either American citizens or legal aliens and loyal to their adopted country. Attorney General Francis Biddle cautioned Americans against racism and xenophobia. "Among those who died fighting off the treacherous attacks upon Manila and Pearl Harbor were men named Wagner and Petersen and Monzo and Bossini and Mueller and Rasmussen. To bar aliens from employment is both short-sighted and wasteful."[35] The government then made a high profile arrest of a "Bund Leader" in Los Angeles, Herman Max Schwinn, "one-time alleged West Coast chieftain of the German-American Bund and many other Nazis and Italians have been arrested for investigation by G-men in a surprise and sensational roundup of aliens in Southern California."[36] Biddle would be an unsung hero of the era, successfully arguing to FDR that the mass internment of Japanese, favored by the military and others, was wrong.

F.B.I. Director J. Edgar Hoover took the credit for busting a German spy ring operating in the U.S. long before the war started. Thirty-three were arrested, and by mid-December fourteen had been convicted in federal court and the remaining nineteen had pleaded guilty. The spies used invisible writing and a "complicated code based on pages from the novel *All This and Heaven, Too.*"[37] Hoover was a master at promoting himself and for taking credit for the hard work of subordinates; this was no exception.

Possibly to make amends to Roosevelt, La Guardia's Office of Civil Defense announced its new operating hours which was all the time. Employees would, for the duration of the war, work twelve-hour shifts. *Time* magazine described La Guardia's operations there as "confused and unprepared" and he as "hen-shaped."[38]

Adjustments in work schedules were also being considered in airplane plants on the West Coast. Though operating on a twenty-four hour basis, the regulations prevented women from working the "graveyard" shifts unless they were paid overtime, even as the men who worked those hours, were paid at the normal rate. It was recommended that this rule be amended or changed because of the national emergency "and because the airplane plants already pay far above the legal minimum wage for women."[39]

The Office of Production Management also "requested" of defense plants, nationwide, that they put in a regular work schedule on New Year's Day. "Since the men at the front, are not taking time off to celebrate New Year's Day, we feel that this should not be considered a holiday for defense plants."[40]

Sub attacks on American vessels had declined dramatically; in part because of increased surveillance by the military and decreased provisions for the subs. Navy officials also credited the decline to quiet citizens. Two phrases popped up, "A slip of the lip may sink a ship" and "That friendly chap may tell a Jap." The Office of War Information and the navy launched a public relations campaign to ask Americans not to talk about "disclosure of . . . ship movements." One official said, "Much of this information is undoubtedly obtained by enemy agents and fifth columnists from conversations which they initiate or overhear in public places." He then put an edge on it with the threat. The "federal Espionage Act . . . carries a maximum penalty of 20 years imprisonment for communicating, either directly or indirectly, information relating to national defense."[41] Mum's the word.

In its lead editorial the *Los Angeles Times* took up the military's lament against so-called Monday morning quarterbacks, "arm-chair generals, table-cloth admirals and all-round amateur runners-of-the-war." The long editorial berated readers for all real or imagined complaints against the conduct of the war and defended the War Department. "Our military and naval leaders are among the ablest of their professions in the world."[42] Most of the complaining came from editorialists and columnists. To wit, an editorial the same day criticized the U.S. military for being taken in by the Japanese, for being foolish enough to believe they would abide by the rules of engagement pertaining to open cities—in this case, Manila—after the Japanese surprise attack. "We should have known that a government capable of such a monstrous crime as was perpetrated at Honolulu would not hesitate at the mere bombing of an open city in defiance of the international code of war. . . ."[43] This hard-hitting editorial ran second to the lead in the *Los Angeles Times*. Few have successfully made a charge of consistency stick to the American press.

The siege of Manila and the Philippines now dominated much of the news and with it, the utter and complete denunciation of the Japanese for their bombing of innocent civilians. Inexorably, Japanese troops were driving toward Manila, and Senator Burton K. Wheeler of Montana declared the enemy "an inhuman and half-civilized race."[44]

The death toll overnight had risen and part of Manila seemed to have more bomb craters than standing buildings. One bomb reportedly hit a church killing eighty people and wounding twenty more. Several nuns were killed.[45] The famed Santo Domingo Church, built by the Dominicans in 1590, had been destroyed in the bombings according to reports.[46] Despite the fires and the carnage and the danger, many of the residents of the heavily Catholic city attended Mass on the 28th.

The citizenry begged MacArthur to return with the American army in tow to defend the city. But the notion was taking hold that America was going along with Churchill's plan to put the main emphasis of the Allies in Europe. "Despite the Manila news and a steady Japanese advance northward and southward through Luzon, it was reported in Washington that Britain and the United States had agreed, in the interests of a wider strategy, to concentrate on Germany."[47] The Japanese broadcast a message over Tokyo radio which was tantamount to an ultimatum to the Filipino people: lay down your arms and we will stop bombing Manila. A CBS listening post picked up the broadcast. The Japanese demand "was greeted with scorn and derision."[48] A town only 55 miles from Manila, Lucena, now flew the Japanese flag of the rising sun and up to 15,000 ground troops were estimated just in this one area.[49] Despite the threat, the Filipino people refused, in part because they believed, as did MacArthur, that American aid was forthcoming. There was no aid coming.

Fortunately, the monument to Ferdinand Magellan, who brought Christianity and western civilization after he discovered the islands in 1521, was untouched amid the destruction.[50] A small victory. Meanwhile the streets were strewn with bodies, body parts, blood, and "tattered school books and examination papers from the bombed Intramuros Catholic elementary school. . . ."[51]

The Japanese attack of the day before was enraging to all. They bombed at almost a leisurely pace, wave after wave after wave of planes, doing so in almost three hours, knowing there was no danger from anti-aircraft guns.

They also bombed Kuala Lumpur on Saturday and destroyed an ancient mosque, described as one of Malaya's "oldest and finest."[52] The bombing had taken place when many Muslims there were praying.

Washington politicians were lamenting how America had been "twice burnt" and many thundered for direct retaliation against Japan's cities. Senator Alben Barkley was practically offering to carry the bombs to Tokyo on his back. He accused the Japanese of "sadistic cruelty."[53] Problem was, those cities were too far off for American land bombers to make the round trip from any airfields controlled by the Allies. And America had no available planes in the area at the time and no secret airfields.

CHAPTER 29

THE TWENTY-NINTH
OF DECEMBER

Our Fleet "Is Not Idle," the Navy Declares
New York Times

Russia, England Agree on Method of War Conduct
Birmingham News

Positive Aid Pledged by Roosevelt and Navy in Philippine Fighting
The Sun

The Japanese bombed Manila again around noon, on the twenty-ninth. The city had done everything possible to make it clear it was open for peace, short of taking out ads in the Tokyo newspapers. Any remaining ships in Manila Harbor were towed out—so not to be confused by the Japanese with naval warships—and blown up and sunk.[1]

"The second day of savage, unopposed air-raids left Manila an inferno of burning churches and office buildings. Many persons lay dead among the debris."[2] The second attack of the day also involved repeated strafing of Ft. Murphy, which General MacArthur had already evacuated. The most famous Catholic statue in Manila, "Our Lady of the Rosary," was fortunately saved from the bombing campaign "by priests and church servants who braved the flames and entered the church shortly after bombs had wrecked the bell tower and roof" of the Santo Domingo cathedral, first built in 1588.[3] But tragically, a priceless library at the church went up in smoke, destroying 200,000 folios and books. In that library was a complete record of every Filipino dialect spoken over the past 300 years in the islands. "Ironically, the library also contained original manuscripts from Dominican missions in China and Indo-China. They were brought to Manila a few months ago to save them from the ravages of war on the Asiatic mainland."[4]

The Japanese state media, *Domei*, announced that the government intended to have the Philippines conquered and catalogued by New Year's Day, which was a big holiday in Japan.[5]

President Roosevelt, under pressure to do something, pledged aid to the beleaguered country, and to one of his favorite generals, MacArthur. Late the day before, he went on short wave radio and proclaimed his "solemn pledge that their freedom will be redeemed and their independence established and protected. The entire resources of the United States, in men and materiel, stand behind that pledge, the President's message assured."[6] Almost immediately, the navy issued a statement claiming, "The Fleet is not idle. The United States Navy is following an intensive and well-planned campaign against the Japanese forces which will result in positive assistance to the defense of the Philippine Islands."[7] It was bluster. Or disinformation. Other than submarines, there was no attempt or planned attempt involving American surface ships to come to the defense of the Philippines.[8]

Even if Washington had the ability to send anything, a Japanese blockade of the Philippines was forming up to keep anything from getting in. Some wondered about the whereabouts of the American Pacific fleet, such as it was, and a knowledgeable source said, "Be patient." Strategic reasons necessitated silence, but the nation was reassured that the navy would strike when the time was right.[9]

The navy as much as admitted that there had been no military contact between U.S. ships and the Japanese since the beginning of the war. "Naval strategists believe that major contact between the Japanese and United States navies will not occur for some time, maybe months—perhaps a year or more."[10] Of course, without naval "contact," there would be no re-provisioning of the Philippines. The Japanese had complete air superiority over Luzon so that option was out for the American forces. The Japanese saturation bombing of Clark Field and Nichols Field had obliterated hundreds of planes on the ground, and those that escaped were eventually shot down or were grounded for a lack of replacement parts.

Navy Secretary Frank Knox claimed the fleet was at sea and that "the main body of the fleet with its battleships, cruisers, aircraft carriers and submarines was '. . . seeking contact with the enemy.'"[11] The contradictory information coming from naval sources—other than announcing their submarines successes—was the first real information of any kind since the week after Pearl Harbor. The navy may have been engaged in a disinformation campaign so as to not reveal to the Japanese the true location of the fleet. "The Japanese government is circulating rumors for the obvious purpose of persuading the United States to disclose the location and intentions of the American Pacific fleet. It is obvious that these rumors are intended for and directed at the Philippine Islands."[12]

Among all the services, the navy was in the worst shape when it came to men and materiel. The Air Corps had lost hundreds of planes at Hickam but airplanes were easier to replace than destroyed or damaged warships, which tended to take longer to refloat.

Despite the rush at recruitment offices, large ads continued to run looking for "College Men . . . to be Naval Officers." No sugar-coating, the ads practically begged that "the Navy needs 7000 Seniors now in college or college graduates as prospective officers. In addition, the Navy needs 5000 men now in their Junior year in college as prospective officers." Upon completion of training, "you will be commissioned as an Ensign, U.S.N.R., at $125 a month and allowances." However, the Navy also needed "15,000 men now in their Senior, Junior or Sophomore years . . . as prospective Naval aviators. As full-fledged Naval Aviators their pay will be $205 per month plus allowances."[13]

But as far as the final word on the disposition of the Pacific Fleet, columnist Paul Mallon who wrote the "News Behind the News" syndicated column said, "The truth probably is that our naval command has decided not to risk heavy ships in waters where the enemy has air superiority, especially after what happened to the *Prince of Wales* and the *Repulse*. It is also probable a third of the fleet was in the Atlantic when the blow fell. A redistribution of naval forces is obviously necessary. The British should have enough of their own capital ships to take care of the Atlantic. . . ."[14] Mallon was an unusually trenchant columnist.

Japanese parachutists were spotted floating down over Manila, a prelude to invasion and occupation. "Filipino police, sole-remaining defenders of Manila, rushed through the bomb-ravaged and burning city early this morning hunting Japanese parachutists who were said to have been seen swooping down during the night, apparently attempting to prepare the way for invading armies."[15] The Japanese War Office broadcast a statement in which they refused to recognize Manila as an open city. "The Japanese will not consider their action at all limited by such 'arbitrary and unilateral announcements' and will proceed to carry out their war objectives," they said.[16]

American anti-aircraft guns—what few there were outside the city—scored a couple of hits and brought down three Japanese planes, but the bombings and the invasion continued. The Japanese advised the remaining civilians in the city to evacuate, via air dropped pamphlets. They were told to go to two refugee centers, Antipolo and Montalban. It wasn't that the Filipino and American troops weren't up to the challenge. They were; they fought bravely and tirelessly and by all accounts their equipment was better, but they were now facing overwhelming numbers of Japanese troops. "Outnumbered American and Philippine troops dug in among the coconut groves fringing the Tiaong River . . . for a stand against 10,000 to 15,000 Japanese invaders pushing up the Tabayas Isthmus. Their stand was costing the Japanese ten men for every fallen defender."[17]

MacArthur had been training these troops for several years, and it had paid off in a superior fighting soldier but as a substitution for victory, he would have gladly accepted more tanks, planes, and men, had they been forthcoming from Washington. One American anti-tank gun was, on average, taking out three Japanese tanks along with field guns.[18] "This question of reinforcement is difficult because the Philippines lie 7,000 miles from the United States and are amid Japanese island positions that hold a constant threat to reinforcement by air or sea." The best Washington could realistically offer MacArthur was "Hopeful."[19]

The Japanese storm continued to rage across the entire Pacific. They had finally gained a toe-hold in the mineral rich Dutch East Indies. The move was a strategic one, aimed at possessing bases near Singapore to stop re-supply and aid from getting to the battered British garrison there.[20] Inhabitants of the East Indies were warned not to run out of their homes when the Japanese dropped leaflets, as it was a ploy.

In Penang, on the Malaya Peninsula, leaflets had been dropped and then Japanese planes strafed the individuals who came out to read the paper which said the Japanese wanted peace.[21]

The Japanese were also dropping paratroopers onto the Malaya Peninsula and claimed they now controlled one third of the isthmus. Singapore announced it had received assurance from both London and Washington that help was on the way, and the Australian Expeditionary Force was mounting a resilient and valiant effort against the Japanese invaders.[22] British leaders were already vowing to take back Hong Kong, but that was so much blue sky over the Pacific as they didn't have the manpower to stop the Japanese advance, much less actually defeat them in open battle. That very day, the Japanese held a triumphal troop review in Hong Kong while announcing they had captured six thousand British troops and fifteen thousand Indian troops.[23]

The final chapter of the American presence in China was written when the Japanese seized the consul there and with it, some sixty noncombatants were taken into custody including Kenneth Yearns, the U.S. Consul.[24] It was an open question whether it would also be the final chapter in the American presence in the Western Pacific if the Philippines fell. At this point, Japanese troops had closed to within forty miles of Manila.

A mound of paper crossed President Roosevelt's desk that day but none of it apparently dealing with the Philippines. FDR's inbox was especially heavy, the twenty-ninth. Memos from Secretary of State Cordell Hull on Borneo,[25] copies of British diplomatic memoranda, to the State Department including a memo defining "Security," and another on the organizational problems in localities where various agencies were crowding and stepping on each other's toes.[26]

As often the case, there was a confidential memorandum from John Franklin Carter, a writer (and covert White House operative) who worked out of the National Press Club building in Washington. His memos went directly to FDR, and no one else, and it seemed as if he was a free agent on the outside, outside any chain of command, working exclusively and directly for the president. His memos littered Roosevelt's desk.

A new one, dated the twenty-seventh, dealt with "Intelligence Problems in the New York Area."[27] "After discussions with F.B.I., O.N.I. [Office of Naval Intelligence] . . . I am convinced . . . Civil Service should be asked to waive or modify some of its rules on recruiting civilian personal for intelligence services." In so many words, Carter was advocating the creation of a network of private individuals, including Mafiosi and wise guys, to act as covert operatives in behalf of the U.S. government. "There is a need for greater pooling of intelligence reports and services on the New York Area at least."[28] Roosevelt wrote back and advised Carter to take the matter up with William H. McReynolds and Vincent Astor.[29] McReynolds was a White House aide who carried a portfolio with a wide latitude and extensive contacts in the agencies, and Astor was a New York socialite who, because of his connections to horse racing, presumably had contacts in Gotham's underworld.

He also received a copy of a classified British memo on how Great Britain was dealing with their Alien problem. "The initial policy was to impose on enemy aliens restrictions graduated according to their estimated potential danger. . . . the Executive advised a policy of general internment . . ."[30] Roosevelt also sent a note on White House stationary to "H.H." saying, "Will you read this over and I will talk with you about it later? F.D.R."[31] The H.H. was Harry Hopkins, and widespread internment of Japanese was for once on the horizon.

The survivors of yet another previous Japanese attack on a civilian American ship in the Pacific washed ashore at Hawaii. But there were only thirteen men out of a compliment of thirty-four aboard the *Prusa*, a 7,000-ton freighter.[32]

Life magazine published the most comprehensive set of photos of the carnage of Pearl Harbor, but the bulk dealt with the damage done to civilian targets and not the military in the Harbor or at Hickam Field. "First pictures of Jap onslaught show death & destruction at American base."[33] Still, few military targets were shown and no images of torpedoed ships were printed. Only the photo of a blasted out hangar and a B-17 that had been forced to belly land were published along with those of some destroyed P-40s that never got off the ground. One surprisingly gruesome photo was of seven dead civilians in the morgue: "[S]even corpses—three men, three women and one child—lie sheeted in an emergency morgue." The publication claimed, "Now for the first time they [readers] may look on the bodies of their own dead."[34]

To end on a happier note, this being the Christmas season, *Life* ran a montage of boys in uniforms saying good bye to loved ones. At an undisclosed location, up to four troop trains stopped daily.

"As each arrives, volunteer agents of the local Red Cross, the Knights of Columbus or the U.S.O. quickly appears with baskets of books, magazines and jig-saw puzzles which they give away, cartons of cigarets [sic] which they sell at any cost." Because of the short stay, the young men were not allowed to get off. "As trains vanish into the night the soldiers shout goodbye to the girls on the platform 'See you again,' they cry 'We'll bring you a necklace of Jap ears.'"[35]

Henry Luce's *Life* magazine seemed to have a direct pipeline into the War Department. In this pre-television era, government publicists saw the splashy, picture-intensive magazine as an important tool in telling the story of the American military and to boost civilian and military morale. Features ran the gamut, from the "Anatomy of Bombs"[36] and the personal story of "Buzz" Wagoner and how he bagged two Japanese Zeros in the Philippines,[37] to the story of the marines and "parachutists,"[38] to "How Nazi Planes May Bomb New York."[39] The thick, visually compelling weekly was filled with the stories and tales of the American fighting man, including full-sized photos of handsome young G.I.s in uniform.

One feature profiled Ensign George T. Weems, a handsome, six-foot tall specimen of American manhood with everything going for him. Humorously, *Life* also mentioned his one weak spot. The young navy man whose career goal was to become an admiral suffered from "seasickness."[40]

That same week, Luce's *Time* magazine sported a flattering profile of MacArthur in the Pacific with a quote from the general saying, "When George Dewey sailed into Manila Bay on May 1, 1898, it was Manifest Destiny working itself out. By God, it was Destiny that brought me here. It was Destiny." MacArthur smoked a cigarette as he watched Japanese bombs drop from the sky.[41] The lengthy and gushy two-page profile reviewed his career, that of his father's, his devotion to the Philippines, and his physical courage, as proved in Europe beginning in 1917.

Interestingly, the magazine opened by opining, "For the first time in nearly 10 years of publication, *Time* finds itself unable to tell its readers freely and frankly of all the things it [knows]."[42] While this may have been true, the Luce publishing empire found itself in a position to tell Americans a lot more than what they were getting from other publications and broadsheets, even down to Admiral Chester Nimitz's nickname, "Cottonhead."[43] Indeed, the periodical had dozens of stories about the war and the men conducting the war in great detail, practically swimming in facts.

The magazine that week also had the complete insider dope on how poorly Fiorello La Guardia was running the Office of Civil Defense. The story and the extensive details could have only come from sources close to a White House very down on the mayor's stewardship. "Indications were that Mr. Roosevelt . . . was getting ready to pluck the Little Flower from OCD."[44]

As FDR and Churchill were wrapping up their historic meeting outlining a plan for defeating the Axis Powers, it was revealed that Anthony Eden, Foreign Secretary in the Churchill government, had made a secret trip to Moscow to meet with Marshall Josef Stalin and his generals to work out the plans to defeat the Axis as it pertained to Russia. It was a "momentous" development, "paralleling the Roosevelt-Churchill meetings in Washington," said the Associated Press.[45] Discussions between the British and the Russians were also held on a post-war world and a "communiqué [outlined] the Anglo-Soviet exchange of views regarding [a] post-war organization of peace 'provide much useful material which will facilitate further elaboration of concrete proposals on the subject.'"[46] The Eden-Stalin meetings were termed "friendly."[47]

Several names had been devised to identify what the Roosevelt administration called the "War Council" but the press also called it the "Supreme War Council," the "Allied Command," and the "World G.H.Q." Roosevelt was also exploring a sort of "National War Council" whose composition and purpose was "to consist of a few top military men and civilians; with broad executive powers to order coordination of the domestic war effort on the military, industrial, civilian and labor fronts . . . Meanwhile through the government men snapped orders and made decisions that changed or would change the lives of millions . . ." According to sources, as many as six thousand new government employees were headed to Washington each and every month to join the war effort.[48]

The Allied plan didn't explicitly dwell on what was obvious at the time: the Allies were on the defensive. The Axis Powers had been chopping up the world piecemeal, taking one territory at a time—and at quick clip. Japan followed this tack in the Pacific, and the Third Reich had perfected this strategy in Europe, taking nation after nation. Though the invasion of Russia was of questionable efficacy, in December 1941, the German army still had a huge if embattled presence inside the country. For all the recent ballyhoo about Soviet pushback, they were fighting on their own soil. However, the Germans were withdrawing from Yugoslavia, where a ragtag guerrilla army of Serbs had beat the stuffing out of Reich soldiers. Three times the Germans had launched offensive operations to root out the tough Serb nationals and neutralize the country and three times, they were forced to withdraw.

The idea of a united front—an "Allied High Command"—did not originate with FDR or with Winston Churchill but interestingly, with Generalissimo Chaing Kai-shek, leader of the Free Chinese forces in Asia. Immediately, Churchill ordered "General Sir Archibald Wavell to further British cooperation with China" and directed Eden to Moscow to hold the paranoid hand of Joe Stalin and on him the plan.[49] Roosevelt immediately sent a classified letter to Chiang suggesting an immediate meeting of the representatives of all the nations warring against the Axis Powers.

"It is our thought that, in order to make such command effective, a joint planning staff should at once be organized consisting of representatives of the British, American and Chinese governments. If you consider it practicable, and Russia agrees, a Russian representative might be included. This staff should function under your supreme command. Your views in this matter will be greatly appreciated by me. ROOSEVELT."[50]

The Allies knew they needed to defend their six strongest naval positions; England, Gibraltar, Singapore, Pearl Harbor, Suez, and the Panama Canal. Despite Roosevelt's public pronouncements to the contrary, the Philippines were not on the list. Each of these was an important chokepoint and from each of these assaults could be launched against the Axis. And each of these was in the crosshairs of the Axis Powers as they knew exactly what the Allies knew. "These fortresses are the key points in the Allies mobility, vitally necessary if the Allies are to continue helping each other fight on farflung battlefields. By breaking any two of those key points, the Axis could virtually cut hemisphere from hemisphere." Gibraltar was a concern because the British "suspected Spain and were not sure of Portugal." Germany had invaded North Africa in the hopes of controlling the Mediterranean and still had a strong force there and the Japanese were making progress in their drive down the Malayan peninsula towards their goal of capturing Singapore. The "Allied High Command" was beginning "the battle of the world" very much on the defensive.[51]

Stitching together another part of the Allied High Command, Winston Churchill arrived in Ottawa on schedule, to the wild cheers of the Canadians. As he stepped off the train, with cigar stuck in his mouth, he doffed his hat with one hand and gave the "V" sign with his other hand. He'd arrived in Roosevelt's own special Pullman car, "with the crew of porters and secret service men who normally look after the president's safety and comfort."[52]

The Ottawa station was jammed with admirers, and the Royal Canadian Mounted Police and Boy Scouts tried to maintain control. Even in the deep of the Canadian winter, clerks and secretaries in the nearby office building flung open their windows to get a glimpse of one of the most famous men in the world.[53]

The wire story noted that Churchill had left Washington in "wartime secrecy" and then proceeded to relay every detail of the trip including his department time from Washington and the stops in New York and Springfield where the local police cleared the platforms of all people. He'd made the trip with Canadian Prime Minister MacKenzie King and spent much of the trip, which carried them through a Massachusetts snow storm, in deep conversation with his parliamentary counterpart. He also worked late into the night on the speech he would deliver on Tuesday to the Canadian Parliament.

On the trip, he slipped into his favorite "Teddy Bear" coveralls. During the London Blitz, on cold evenings, it became uncomfortable and inconvenient to try to switch from pajamas to suits so Churchill took to wearing the zippered garment. "The gray ... coveralls gave the Prime Minister the appearance of a jovial Kewpie puffing on a cigar as he lounged and worked. He has both lights and heavies, and the red flannel weather of Vermont and Quebec called for the heavies."[54]

With Churchill gone, Washington got back to the business of running a wartime economy. Since rubber usage has been so severely restricted, gasoline consumption was now under study as well. Gas was plentiful, oil stocks were high, and ever since Great Britain had returned some tankers she'd borrowed the year before, the East Coast restrictions had been lifted. Also, it was noted that "Petroleum supply in the United States, which possess great resources of oil, is principally a matter of transportation." Still, the "petroleum coordinator," who reported to Secretary of the Interior Harold Ickes, was ordered by Ickes to make a feasibility study of a gas rationing plan. The initial figure bandied about was a 35 percent reduction in gas usage for 1942.[55]

The citizens of Manila were astonished to wake up and hear over station KGEI that Japanese planes were bombing San Francisco and it was already in flames. It was a hoax; officials suspected that the Japanese had used a more powerful transmitter to interrupt the regular broadcast by an "English speaking announcer" reading "Flash" bulletins several times. "The interference obviously came from a powerful Japanese station deliberately intruding on the KGEI wave[length]."[56] A government official said, "This was the first evidence of an apparent new propaganda technique by the Japanese—an effort to create panic by means of the direct lie."[57]

Government officials began a public awareness campaign aimed at curbing venereal diseases especially, they said, around industrial plants and among the military. "The American Social Hygiene Association, at the urgent request of the army [and] navy ... is playing an indispensible role in the nation's all-out effort to protect soldier, sailor and marine from syphilis and gonorrhea." An editorial in the *Birmingham News* said "The problem, however, remains to be solved, and in wartime, naturally, it becomes more acute. This is true not only with respect to our armed forces, but also with regard to industrial workers, particularly those in the war industries."[58]

At the same time, ill-mannered women were the target of a new, "anti-profanity campaign." Arthur S. Colborne was on a one man mission to wipe out swearing in America. Not just the garden-variety four lettered words either, but also "hell" and "gee-wizz" and doggone" and "dad burn it" because as far as he was concerned, these were "leader on words," (gateway drugs, as some might later think of them). He said women in bars were the worst offenders. They, in turn, thought he was full of . . . well, it's better left unsaid. Curiously, Colborne was also the founder of the "Safe and Sane Fourth of July Movement."[59]

A young ill-mannered German woman in New Jersey, Helga Schlueter, was arrested and convicted on the charge of "defiling" the American flag. During a fire fighter's parade in Lakewood in 1940, in full view she tore up a flag and threw it on the ground. She was in the custody of the FBI, although she had already been sentenced to two years in a reformatory for women. The New Jersey state Supreme Court had already upheld her conviction by an Ocean County court.[60]

Another woman of ill fame, "heiress Gloria Vanderbilt" as she was commonly known, finally got married in Santa Barbara after day upon day of stories about her, her money, her much older fiancé, her family, her controversial young life—all printed ad nauseum in the country's newspapers.[61] There were also plenty of photos in the papers of the pretty young heiress. The righteous were also quite prurient at times.

The Reverend Samuel Shoemaker of the Calvary Episcopal Church thought he knew what was ailing America. It lacked, he said, a "national philosophy. The strength of the enemy countries lies in their unity, and their unity comes from the way they as nations look upon life. I believe that Christianity is the forgotten ideology of America...."[62] The Reverend Dr. Norman Vincent Peale said what was needed in America was a "Spiritual Army."[63]

A woman of no fame, just good spiritual character, was volunteering in New Jersey to spot for enemy planes. Lavina Mount Minton was no stranger to war, having once nursed injured Civil War soldiers. Lavina was 97-years-old and going strong. "I've lived through three horrible wars and I'll see the finish of this one."[64]

At an army base in Illinois, a young lonely private, Joseph Dee Everingham, sent a letter to the *Chicago Tribune*, announcing: "I am certainly the loneliest private this side of the Mississippi." Within days, his barracks were deluged with cards, letters, cakes and "lots of lonely girls sent along their pictures. Even a Lonely Hearts club sent a list of wealthy widows." He received cookies, lobsters, candy, sweaters, socks. "He got enough Sunday dinner invitations to last him through the emergency."[65]

As was now an everyday occurrence, another young man thought dead in the Pacific turned up alive. Carl Frank Stewart, 19, had been mistakenly thought to have been killed and the navy notified his mother, who for three weeks through her grief could not bring herself to believe it was true. She took to her bed, dreaming of her boy. She refused to accept the proceeds from an insurance policy on young Carl's life. Then she got another missive from the navy, advising her that Carl was not dead but had been wounded "seriously, but will recover."[66] Perhaps it was mothers' intuition.

Without any fanfare, a gentleman by the name of George Herman Ruth Jr. walked into the Manhattan Bond office and quietly ordered $100,000 worth of War Bonds. Told that the restrictions only allowed for the purchase of $50,000 per year, the man who went by the nickname of "Babe" bought $50,000 and left an order for another $50,000 to be picked up on January 2, 1942.[67] War Bonds and Defense Stamps had become so interwoven in society, appliance stores offered them for free with the purchase of washers, dryers, and ranges.[68]

The Archbishop of New York, Francis Joseph Spellman, donated $1,000 to the Red Cross for the war fund and "disclosed that he had contributed one pint of ecclesiastical blood for the blood bank."[69]

And the Archbishop of Canterbury, following Franklin Roosevelt's suit, called for the British to be in church on New Year's Eve and New Year's Day. "Throughout this country members of the various religious faiths will join with their co-religionists in the United States in observing a day of prayer...."

The Anglican Archbishop fired a rhetorical shot across the bow of his church's old adversary saying, "We recommend that in all Catholic churches there be prayers."[70] Lambs did not always play well together.

A former associate of Mr. Ruth, Louis Gehrig, had died several years earlier but Hollywood thought so much of him, his life, and his courage in facing death, it decided to make a movie about him and announced Gary Cooper would portray the "Iron Man." Hollywood also announced the beginning of filming of a new Tarzan movie starring Johnny Weissmuller, who was, for a generation, the only and the best Ape Man.

Japanese, German, and Italian "Axis Aliens" began showing up at police stations all over the West to surrender thousands of cameras and massive amounts of radio equipment, per the directive of the federal government. For each item, a receipt was given "if Federal authorities release it at some future date."[71]

More war songs were pouring forth, but not the type found in church. The popular band leader Sammy Kaye penned, "Remember Pearl Harbor." The lyrics revealed Kaye's Catholicism: "We'll always remember Pearl Harbor, Brightest jewel of the blue southern sea, Our lips will be saying 'Pearl Harbor', On each bead of our rosary."[72] As many as 260 patriotic songs were submitted to Tin Pan Alley, slang for the group of music publishers clustered in New York City who dominated songwriting in America at the time. The very first song about the war they rushed out was "We Did It Before and We Can Do It Again," by Dinah Shore and Eddie Cantor. Other song titles by various artists included: "You're a Sap, Mr. Jap," and this particularly blunt tune: "We're Going to Find a Fellow Who is Yellow and Beat Him Red, White and Blue."[73]

In accordance with the new restrictions in Hawaii, all 215 buses of the Honolulu Rapid Transit Company had their roofs painted black.[74] All movie theatres in Hawaii stopped showing films at 4 p.m. including the Roosevelt, Waikiki, Kaimuki, Kapahulu, Kewalo, Kalihi, and Wahiawa theatres.[75]

New information and tales kept coming out about the attack.

A young wife, Margaret Bickell, 20, was in Oahu on December 7 with her husband, First Lieutenant George Bickell, 25, eating breakfast when they heard the first attack. Lt. Bickell reported immediately to his base and got up and flew against the Japanese until being shot down and crashing in the ocean, right in front of his wife. She then saw her husband swim to shore, get another plane, take off, and resume the fight.[76]

Mrs. Bickell also told of "sullen Japanese servants" in Oahu who, after December 7, had turned on lights during blackouts and smoked cigarettes out of doors when the general order was to not light anything for fear the enemy would spot it.[77]

CHAPTER 30

THE THIRTIETH
OF DECEMBER

Britain Bombed Heaviest in Weeks

The Sun

F.D.R. "Pushed Europe into War Against Me," Nazi Leader Complains

International News Service

Red Men Bury Hatchet to Aid War on Axis

Associated Press

As a means of helping Germany with their war effort, a committee of Frenchmen appointed by Vichy French President Marshal Petain seriously considered demolishing the Eiffel Tower and salvaging the 1,000 tons of steel in the edifice worth at the time some $1,000,000. "Paris' 984-foot Eiffel Tower, known to millions since it was built 52 years ago, may be scrapped by a national metal collection committee working under Marshal Petain...."[1]

The committee's stated purpose was to identify buildings that lacked any real artistic or historical value. Surprising as it might seem, the tower didn't make the cut. One member of the French Academy, writer Henry Bordeaux, deemed Alexander Eiffel's 1889 creation for the World's Fair "an insult to aesthetic taste."[2] However, although controversial when it was first erected, the pioneering steel tower soon became an object of affection and veneration for Parisians—and a symbol of France itself.

After June 1940, the French Tricolor no longer flew from the Eiffel Tower but rather the flag with the menacing black spider of the Third Reich, as German troops had marched into what had been known as the City of Light with near impunity, save the tears of a few old Frenchmen pining for the days of lost Napoleonic glory.

The news of the tower's intended destruction arrived to the world by a circuitous path. "Tokyo radio tonight carried a *Domei* agency dispatch from Lisbon quoting a dispatch from New York based on a British broadcast heard by American short wave listeners." It had originated on Berlin radio coming from an official announcement from Vichy.[3]

Small wonder Winston Churchill had little respect for the men of the Seine. In his speech to the Canadian Parliament he acidly said,

> The British Empire and the United States . . . are going to fight out this new war against Japan together. We have suffered together and we shall conquer together. But the men of Bordeaux, the men of Vichy they would do nothing like this. They lay prostrate at the foot of the conqueror. They fawned upon him.
>
> What have they got out of it?
>
> This fragment of France which was left to them is just as powerless, just as hungry as, and even more miserable, because more divided, than the occupied regions themselves. Hitler plays from day to day . . . with these tormented men.[4]

There was still a huge debate raging in Washington over sources of new revenues for the national emergency. In the month of December alone, the war effort had cost nearly $2.2 billion dollars.[5]

War Bonds, stamps, and the current tax structure wouldn't suffice, according to many of the bureaucrats responsible for having opinions on such matters. Funding for the war was already consuming some 23 percent of the national income, but it would shortly rocket up from there.[6] Henry Morgenthau, Secretary of the Treasury, hired a new tax aide, Randolph Paul, who had some interesting notions on tax policy. "Prime obstacle to an effective tax structure . . . is the fact that taxpayers (at least in peacetime) have an insufficient 'sense of debt to society and little intelligent interest in the continuation of the conditions which enable satisfactory living.'"[7] Paul did not stop there. He made fun of companies for wanting to keep "surplus accumulations." Expanding, he continued that "the primary function of consumption taxes should be to control production, not raise revenue." Paul had helped Congress write the "Excess Profits Tax" which the government slapped on businesses in 1940 which the rate of earnings—weighted—of "not more than 10%."[8]

One thing was for sure. War was not only hell, it was expensive. As Roosevelt and his advisors tallied things, to effectively prosecute the war would take roughly half the national economy by midyear 1943; that was about fifty billion dollars. Yet another name was coined for the effort. It would be called, imaginatively, "The War Program." Even as the president told the press about such enormous sums, he pooh-poohed the money owed the U.S. by Britain under Lend-Lease. "Bookkeeping and questions of repayment . . . are almost a thing of the past," he breezily asserted.[9]

He also announced that the government was seriously considering going on "Daylight Savings" for 1942. "Mr. Roosevelt recalled that estimates were made that as much as 500,000 kilowatt hours of electric energy would be saved each day by a country-wide program extended from the spring to the fall. That, he added, is an awful lot of power."[10]

Funding had already gone forth though for a massive building program of Liberty Ships, which would become famous as the backbone of the Maritime navy. The very first Liberty ship, the *Patrick Henry*, had been completed in September of 1941 but was commissioned in December. The initial plan of the Maritime Commission was to build 312 of these workhorse boats, which were used for all manner of transporting goods and troops. The *Patrick Henry* was quickly followed by the *John Randolph* and the *American Mariner* and shortly, hundreds more would be splashed with little fanfare, but much admiration.[11]

Bond sales had exploded in the month of December as Americans bought more than $400 million worth of the paper notes signifying their loan to the U.S. government, but Treasury officials said, when all is said and done, the total haul could go as high as $500 million. Many banks and Bond offices had actually run out, because of the run on Bonds. November saw less than half that number, around $220 million. "War probably was the big stimulus," the Associated Press dryly noted.[12]

Congressman W. Disney, Democrat of Oklahoma, was not fantasizing when he proposed a massive $11 billion dollar tax increase to pay for the national emergency.[13] Morganthau said in no uncertain terms that to conduct the war successfully meant a "considerable rearrangement of people's finances."[14]

Part of the cost of the new war would go for the proposed new women's volunteer army. A supplementary to the regular army, "Women volunteers in khaki uniforms would be enrolled as privates and officers of the U.S. Army under a plan approved . . . by the War Department and now awaiting congressional action."[15] The plan for voluntary women to back up the men was the brainchild of Congresswoman Edith Nourse Rodgers, a Republican from Massachusetts. The inspiration had come from the auxiliary organizations of women in Great Britain who worked in uniform in the front office to support the men in uniform at the front. Secretary of War Henry Stimson was all for it.

The women, it was proposed, would be stationed right along with the men at military bases around the globe and the pay would be similar to that of the men. These women, it was envisioned, would practice close-order drilling and the officers and noncommissioned officers would be picked by merit. "They would live in barracks and be subject to military discipline. Outside of several drill hours weekly they would do clerical and secretarial jobs and work as teleprinter operators, cooks, bakers, dieticians, pharmacists, telephone operators and hospital and laboratory technicians."[16] Stimson also envisioned they could take over the entire air warning system in the country, replacing the voluntary hodgepodge set up by the Office of Civil Defense.

Cigarettes would not go up in cost after all, at least for the foreseeable future. The millions of smokers in America, from the president down to the neighborhood paperboy, heaved a smoky sigh of relief when the government stepped in to prevent the hike. The American Tobacco Company had refused the request to hold the line on a price increase by the Office of Price Administration so the OPM changed the request to an edict that no tobacco companies could raise the price of a pack of cigarettes. Americans were free to smoke abundantly and cheaply.[17]

Washington also ordered that manufacturers of soap and paint were barred from hoarding eighteen hundred different kinds of fats and oils. Everything from cottonseed to "lemon, camphor, clove, wintergreen and citronella" was covered by the directive from the OPM.[18] The OPM was also displeased with the allocation of all raw materials to the war effort and one official called for the control of all such supplies from the "bottom up."[19]

The nation's capital was laying in the final plans for the mandated tire-rationing program to begin January 5, 1942. "The ordinary civilian motorist probably has bought his last new tire for a long time to come." The administration of much of the program would be laid off on the state governments to administer. One governor when told his state would handle the bureaucracy responded, "Where's the money coming from?"[20] Companies such as the Firestone Tire and Rubber Co. took out full-page ads in publications explaining essentially why they could no longer sell new tires. They also produced a booklet entitled, "How to Get More Mileage from Your Tires."[21]

Some saw the silver lining in the rubber rationing. According to a Gallup survey, a majority of Americans did nothing for exercise, and that the walking that came with the new realities was a benefit because "health authorities [urged] Americans to take more exercise." The survey noted that among those Americans who did walk, "the medium average distance walked in any one day is only about one and one half miles."[22] These paternalistic assertions must have come as a surprise to the many Americans who hoed fields, worked with their hands, operated heavy equipment, lifted dirty laundry, shoveled snow off their sidewalks, raked yards, threw newspapers while they pedaled bicycles, carried groceries out of the store and into the kitchen, lifted barges, and toted bales.

Meanwhile, officials of the National Stockyards reported a "marked increase" in purchases of horses and mules.[23]

As New Year's Eve was fast-approaching, women were buying out the remaining stocks of silk stockings for those under-exercised legs. The previous August, the government had mandated that no more silk stockings be manufactured but retailers could sell out their inventories, though "promotion of Nylon and new constructions of other fibers are expected to expand to cushion exhausting of the all-silk product."[24]

Rumors were going around military circles that Adolf Hitler would be ousted in a military coup in 1942 and replaced by a military junta. Rumors were also cirulating that German generals had secretly flown to Ireland for God knows what. A German plane had made a forced landing in Ireland recently, but there was no one above the rank of a sergeant in the plane. German planes were however over London in large waves for the first time in a long time as it was the first anniversary of the giant firebombing of the old city by the Luftwaffe. This bombing lacked the punch of earlier German over-flights and the stiff-upper-lipped Brits brushed off the attack, as they would a buzzing mosquito." [D]amage nowhere was serious and the number of casualties were small," ran one report.[25]

Rumors were rampant in the Dutch East Indies "that Allied reinforcements were on their way to the Pacific and that a general offensive against Japan could be expected soon."[26] There were no reinforcements coming.

Great Britain retaliated to the renewed shelling of London, by bombing Nazi-held installations along the coast of France all the way to Norway; a thousand-mile front. The British hit munitions plants, synthetic rubber plants, sunk eight ships, blew up oil stores, ammunition dumps, and hit other assorted targets.[27] The British attack had more sting with their Mosquito bombers than did the Germans with their Junkers.

Adolf Hitler sat down for an interview with the famed war correspondent Pierre J. Huss, British correspondent for the International News Service. When asked who was the cause of the war, the Führer said, "Ja, Herr Roosevelt—and his Jews." He also dismissed the rumor that he "chews rugs" when irate. The setting could have been that of a pleasant grandfather—roaring fire, rain pelting at the window, a dog—with a "swastika collar strolled lazily up to Hitler and nuzzled his hand. He stroked the head. . . ." His paranoia of FDR was evident though. "He wants to run the world and rob us all of a place in the sun. He says he wants to save England but he means he wants to be ruler and heir of the British Empire. I first saw this some years ago when Roosevelt began his undeclared war on me through speeches, boycotts and political intriguing in all chancelleries of Europe. Every time I reached forth my hand he slapped it down. When I began to show him that meddling in European affairs was not so easy and might be dangerous, he lost all control of himself and began his campaign of vilification." He also made reference to the "sabotage of Munich" and how this too was Roosevelt's fault. He also made an anti-Semitic allusion to "Roosevelt and his golden calf."[28]

Huss knew otherwise, of course. Being there with this monster, he said, "[gives] you the uncomfortable feeling that none but the führer should be heard or seen, lest perhaps a blitz of unrestrained temper and authority hit the man nearest this volcano." Huss referred to Hitler's aides as "flunkies with booted black pants . . . ."[29]

This portion of the historic interview concluded with the führer ranting that Roosevelt had broken political tradition in America by seeking a third term but even so, he could outwait FDR because, "I am young and healthy. Roosevelt is not."[30]

The circle was closing on Manila and Singapore. Overnight, Japanese planes had raided Singapore four times, bombing it heavily. Since Christmas Eve, bombs had fallen on Manila, but then they went silent. However, no one thought for a minute that the Japanese had changed their minds and withdrawn their forces. They just had a new target to go after: Corregidor.

The Japanese began bombing Corregidor Island, only thirty miles from Manila. For three hours, they blasted at the island with a "very large force of enemy aircraft."[31] The tactic was designed to weaken the fortification strength of the Allied military there as a possible prelude to the Japanese navy steaming into Manila Harbor. "Corregidor is of natural rock formation and is about 6½ miles long. It is five miles from the northern mainland shore, about midway at the bay's mouth." The island was surrounded by several smaller islands, also fortified. Corregidor was honeycombed with caves where supplies had been stored "for any siege and where its defenders could shelter from air-raids and artillery barrages from the mainland."[32] Bristling with big guns, no navy commander in his right mind would attempt to enter Manila Bay without first neutralizing Corregidor.

But Douglas MacArthur did have a new ally in the war for the Philippines. The Balugas, a pigmy tribe whose men stood no taller than five feet, announced their opposition to the Empire of Japan, led by "King Alfanso."[33] They lived in the mountains on the island of Luzon and as tribute to the Allies, turned over to the Americans three Japanese soldiers who had parachuted into their domain.

The Japanese propagandists had tried to divide the Filipinos from the Americans, but there was a bond and a history between the two that ran deep. MacArthur, who had a long and warm history with the Philippines, including his own father, Arthur MacArthur's service there as Civilian Governor, had raged and denounced the Japanese for the bombings of Manila, which he himself had declared an open city, but there was little other than that which he could do against the surging tide of the Japanese invasion.

MacArthur noted what seemed to be a deliberate attempt by the Japanese to obliterate the religious culture of Manila. "The great Cathedral of the immaculate Conception was a special target of Japanese bombs. It was sought out and attacked on three successive days. The College of San Juan Lateran, with its irreplaceable library of original manuscripts, was likewise attacked. Repeated attacks on successive days were made on Santa Rosa Convent and Santa Catalina Convent. The San Juan Dedios Hospital was also the object of vicious attacks."[34]

Things were faring better for the Americans who had volunteered to fly and fight with the Chinese air force. The American Volunteer Squadron had, on December 26th alone, shot down 26 Japanese planes in dog fights over Rangoon. The Americans, led by the legendary Col. Claire Chennault, meanwhile had lost only two planes.[35]

As soon as Winston Churchill returned to Washington from Ottawa, Franklin Roosevelt planned on convening another "war council" meeting. "Military and naval . . . experts have been laboring on a master strategy plan for the past week."[36] Churchill, while in Ottawa, gave a sterling speech to the Canadian Parliament. It was there where he assured Australia, another parliamentary government, and member of the Commonwealth, and their nervous if also steely prime minister, John Curtin, that the Allies would not leave their friends down under, to the mercy of the merciless Japanese. But his speech was also vague and news reports only said that "Churchill and President Roosevelt have decided on definite measures of defense for both British and American interests in the Pacific."[37]

Churchill had hailed the Canadian contribution to the war and mocked the Axis Powers, interrupted often by the applauding audience in the House of Commons. He said the war "must be an assault on the citadel and homeland of the guilty powers, both in Europe and Asia." The British Prime Minister said the goal was straightforward: "the total extirpation of Hitler tyranny, Japanese frenzy and the Mussolini flop." Churchill loved tormenting Benito Mussolini. The Italian dictator was a preening and vain egomaniac, obsessed with his own machismo. These qualities made Il Duce an easy target of ridicule; even his ally Hitler considered him to be an embarrassment. "[Churchill's] speech was filled with jibes and taunts at the Axis partners which moved the crowded chamber to cheers and laughter, but most of it was a calm, confident review of the road already travelled and the road still left to travel."[38]

His praise of Roosevelt was fulsome and heartfelt. "I have been all this week with the President of the United States, that great man whom destiny has marked for this climax of human fortune."[39] The crowds inside and outside Parliament Hill went wild. Loudspeakers broadcast his speech to the thousands standing in the cold and snow. "Hitler and his Nazi gang have sown the wind—let them reap the whirlwind."[40]

For Winston Churchill and the people of Great Britain, it had been a long and lonely quest as they had been the only major power opposing Nazism. At one point, observers felt there was a real chance England could fall to the Third Reich. No sane person wished for war but the only way to end this new conflict was for more countries to declare war and by the end of December 1941, 90 percent of the countries of the world were at war with someone. Though his headcount clashed with that of the U.S. State Department, Churchill told the Canadians "more than 30 States and nations" were arrayed against the Axis but the striped pants set of Foggy Bottom, ever cautious, low-balled it to 29.[41]

He concluded his peroration, as only the old master could: "The power of the enemy is upon us," he said. "Let us then, sir, address ourselves to our task, not in any way underrating its tremendous difficulties and perils; but in good heart and sober confidence, resolved that whatever the cost, whatever the sufferings, we shall stand by one another, true and faithful comrades, and do out duty, God helping us to the end."[42]

As with all his wartime speeches, Churchill's remarks were a pleasure to read and a joy to hear. The words and phrases cascaded over his listeners, convincing them of Churchill's righteousness and why they needed to join in his cause. There is no doubt that he saved England from Hitlerism and by extension, saved the world from a new dark age. At few times in history had a man been so clearly and perfectly thrust forward to fulfill his destiny.

Other volunteers were springing forth. Under one of the most awful headlines of the month, the Associated Press moved a story: "Red Men Bury Hatchet to Aid War on Axis." It detailed how California's Indian tribes, having been at odds with Washington since 1850, "patched up their differences and will support the United States in its war against the Axis. The Mission Indian Foundation, with 3,000 . . . members, telegraphed President Roosevelt . . . 'a message of loyalty and readiness to serve our great nation.'"[43]

A reclusive college professor ensconced in Princeton, a sleepy college town in New Jersey, gave a rare interview just before he was to address the American Physical Society. The organization was dedicated to the pleasure of knowledge, not the flesh. "Dr. Albert Einstein, renowned German Jewish refugee scientist and once a militant pacifist, said tonight the democracies eventually would win over the totalitarian powers but that 'we must strike hard and leave the breaking to the other sides.'" The interview with the sixty-two-year-old mathematician "with the great shock of unruly white hair" was conducted in his modest, green-shuttered home, as he smoked a pipe and pondered the often inane questions of his journalistic inquisitors. When asked about conditions in Nazi Germany—3,000 miles away—he replied, "I have no methods of observation" there.[44] His books had been banned for years in the Third Reich. The brilliant Einstein, whose groundbreaking Theory of Relatively had forever changed humankind's basic notions of the physical universe, had been hounded by the Nazis for practicing what they mocked as "Jew science." Like many of his talented colleagues, Einstein had seen the writing on the wall in Hitler's Germany and fled to the United States before the outbreak of war. Luckily for the civilized world, the Nazis had chased from their midst the very geniuses who could have given Hitler the atomic bomb.

Other scientists were also pondering the practical application of science to killing the enemy. Naturally, they met in Cleveland.[45] "Astronomy is turning practical for wartime to increase the range and accuracy of guns and to advance aerial photography, the American Astronomical Society heard tonight. Scores of astronomers now are applying their knowledge of mathematics and telescopes to ballistics . . . The problem of an astronomical body moving peacefully through the ether is much the same mathematically as that involving a bullet moving through the air."[46]

Yet another obscure scientist said the theory of the expanding universe was all wet. After six years of staring each night through the largest telescope in the world at Mt. Wilson in California, Dr. Edwin P. Hubble, stated his belief that the universe was static, not dynamic, filled with approximately one hundred million Milky Way galaxies.[47]

And in a startling announcement, scientists said that there was absolutely no doubt about it, water existed on Mars! They weren't sure though if oxygen existed on the "Red Planet."[48]

The territorial civilian governor of Hawaii, Joseph Poindexter, had already announced the mandatory finger-printing of all island residents but other new strictures were announced in the *Honolulu Advertiser* and other papers. Long forms were printed in the broadsheets for everybody to fill out including the number of radios owned, and questions about their make, were they long wave, short wave, did the individual have either a receiver or transmitter? Number of beds in place of residences, and were the beds doubles, singles or three quarter? The government also wanted to know the number of bathrooms in one's domicile. Would the renter or owner be willing to take in evacuees? With all the questions about fingerprints, nationality, "Racial Extraction," etc., the curiosity of the government seemed limitless.[49]

Poindexter was also granted executive authority over all bakery goods under the "M-Day Act." It said, "Bakery products may be offered for sale as long as they are fit for human consumption. . . ."[50] Something no doubt rarely considered before his administration.

The paper also had a long list of civilian residents of Hawaii whom friends and loved ones on the "mainland" had not been able to get a hold of since December 7. Worried individuals had been contacting the Red Cross asking for their assistance and got the cooperation of the newspaper to do so. "It will be appreciated if anyone whose name appears below will call the local American Red Cross office . . . and notify their present status, in order that a reply might be cabled to the National Headquarters in Washington as soon as possible."[51]

Residents of the islands, who had served in the military of any other country other than the United States, had to turn themselves in to the local police station immediately. Regulations were also issued for fishing boats including all boats had to be painted white, fish only in designated areas and in designated hours and only American citizens were allowed to own fishing licenses.[52]

An elaborate air-raid system was being constructed on the various islands of Oahau, Kauai, Maui, and Hawaii so hopefully all the residents could know at the same time if another attack was forthcoming. "The new system will be ready for operation in the very near future and installation is now contingent only upon the arrival of equipment."[53]

Fantastic stories of the overt operations of "Fifth Columnists" operating in Hawaii were emerging including a United Press story, published in the *New York Times* in which the navy secretary said huge arrows were cut in the "sugar fields pointing to hangars, munitions" and that some Japanese routinely strolled around the Schofield barracks. He detailed the "general espionage and sabotage network," including shopkeepers, a "host of spies, chiefly proprietors of small stores, restaurants, cafes . . . Japanese naval intelligence, which ran a much more extensive organization . . . its agents included fishermen and seamen." After saying such, came the clarification that this was not "an indictment of all Japanese in Honolulu. On the whole, they were industrious, dependable and well behaved. But enough of them were fifth columnists to make the attack successful."[54]

The order by the attorney general to "enemy aliens" to turn over camera equipment and radio broadcasting equipment was, by all accounts, enthusiastically obeyed. Francis Biddle's directive was originally aimed at seven states in the West but then was extended to the rest of the country. In the Los Angeles area alone, some four thousand now-contraband items had been surrendered to the local police, including "several hundred [firearms], mostly rifles and shotguns. . . ." The Los Angeles Board of Equalization also revoked the liquor licenses of all German, Italian, and Japanese aliens, affecting several hundred businesses.[55]

Roosevelt's secret operative, John Franklin Carter, got the go-ahead to start hiring civilian operatives in the New York area who were not part of civil service. Per FDR's directive, Carter had taken the matter up with others and they advised him under "Executive Order No. 8564" that the Office of Naval Intelligence and Army Intelligence could recruit their own civilian operatives. Euphemistically, Carter made reference to the "pooling of certain Intelligence functions in the New York Area." He also indicated that some of the more stuffy individuals in government intelligence including Bill Donovan (the head of the Office of Strategic Services, the precursor to the CIA) thought his idea was nuts. "I am doubtful that any of the services will be co-operative," he said.[56] And again, while Carter never put it in writing, it seemed clear his intention was to recruit underworld figures to help the U.S. government defeat a bigger set of criminals.

Gloria Vanderbilt was back in the news. In Beverly Hills, she and her sister were held up and had $4,000 worth of jewelry stolen by a gunman "at their palatial Beverly Hills home."[57] She also received an "extra" allowance from her estate now that she was married. The robber—who had posed as a chauffeur—had second thoughts as one of the pins he'd stolen was a diamond encrusted "V" for victory brooch, valued at $1,000. The robber returned to the scene of the crime and, knocking on the door, pushed a package into the hands of a maid. Inside was the "V" pin along with a note from the Captivating Crook. "Mon Dieu et mon droit"—"My God and My Right."[58] Hollywood often had some of the most charming crooks in America.

Americans along the West Coast had been skittish for days now, after so many submarine attacks, and at Ft. MacArthur, servicemen thought they spotted more. "The guns were trained on the two shadowy objects in the water but before the command to fire was given, another observer flashed the signal: "Whales."[59]

The war in the Pacific had gone badly for America and it was getting worse. Between December 23 and 27, the Japanese had sunk at least sixteen American submarines and damaged an indeterminate number of others, or so *Domei* claimed.[60] The War Department did not dispute the braggadocio of Tokyo. Again, MacArthur was forced to withdraw his lines of defense as more Japanese troops came ashore. "In the last few days the enemy has been heavily reinforced by several infantry divisions, tank regiments and horse cavalry. Japanese units are composed of veteran soldiers with modern equipment."[61] He also had to concern himself with up to four thousand American civilians scattered throughout the Philippines.

On the Malaya Peninsula in both the east and the west, Japanese troops had broken through the defensive lines and were marching along some excellent roads, right into the city of Singapore. Despite the fact that the Dutch seemed the only Allied nation who knew how to fight the Japanese, even their own East Indies were threatened. Again, proximity and easier supply lines were contributing to their problems. If the Japanese gained this strategically important stretch of islands, they could launch strikes all over the areas including at Singapore and Australia. "The Japanese now threaten the Netherlands Indies from bases in North Borneo, from Mindanao in the Philippines and from Penang, which is only 200 miles across the Strait of Malacca from the well-developed and wealthy region of Northeast Sumatra."[62]

The Atlantic was no better. Not only was the U.S. Navy not scoring there, a German submarine sunk the freighter *Sagadahoc* as she steamed for South Africa.[63] Nor was the Russian Front looking good; Germans were effectively attacking the Russian counter-attacks. But the Axis had troubles of its own: Hitler had asked Benito Mussolini "for ten more Italian divisions for Russia, but Il Duce refused on the grounds that Italian soldiers were not inured to the Russian climate."[64]

Charles Lindbergh was trying to re-enlist in the Army Air Corps, but was getting the run around from a government that mostly despised him. At his press conference, FDR was asked about the application of the "Lone Eagle" to be reinstated in the Air Corps Reserves so he could go on active duty but he brushed aside the question, saying he had "no information" on the matter.[65]

General "Hap" Arnold, chief of the Air Corps, was anxious to have Lindbergh rejoin. "Lindbergh's act indicates a definite change from his former isolationist stand."[66] Others around the White House were less enthused about the reinstatement of their old antagonist.[67]

American morale could reach no lower than when it was learned that the Statue of Liberty, in following police blackout orders, would not be brilliantly illuminated. "Instead of being a blaze of glory, the Statue of Liberty will throw just enough light to indicate her presence in the bay." Before the beginning of the war, plans had been made to "install three new 3,000-watt-mercury-vapor lamps, to replace the thirteen 1,000-watt incandescent bulbs" but now that had been junked. The lamp beside the Golden Door was darkened.[68]

The entire Statue of Liberty—great symbol of American Exceptionalism—all 151 feet, one inch of her, and in the middle of New York Harbor—was to be lighted with just two measly 100 watt bulbs.[69]

Nonetheless, Lady Liberty's gaze remained steady, in confident anticipation of brighter days ahead.

CHAPTER 31

THE THIRTY-FIRST
OF DECEMBER

Manila Radio Falls Silent as Japan Attackers Near

Honolulu Advertiser

50 Billion a Year is Set by President as Our War Outlay

New York Times

Churchill Thinks Japs Are In For Surprises Before War Ends

Birmingham News

As the year ends, the Grand Alliance looming upon the horizon is perhaps the most astonishing in history."[1] So wrote the great Anne O'Hare McCormick, Pulitzer Prize winning columnist for the *New York Times*. Indeed, recent events had been astonishing. The world had changed radically—it was aflame with war, but prayers for peace were prevalent too. The United States had also changed greatly and was aflame with a unity never seen before. A "National Will" was afoot in the land.

Even in England, on New Year's Day, there was a "religious festival at Albert Hall [for] the national day of prayer. The Archbishop of Canterbury and Cardinal Arthur Hinsley will give short addresses."[2] If the Church of England and the Church of Rome could get along in their own Grand Alliance, then anything was possible.

They knew however, what it was they were fighting for. "The object of the meeting is to emphasize the fact to those here and elsewhere that the Allies are fighting for the restoration and preservation of Christendom."[3] Nearly the entire British government, clergy, and royal family were on hand, save Winston Churchill.

On the desks of many professionals in 1941 was a calendar, one page for each day of the year, usually placed in a cheap plastic holder with two rings in which to insert the pages. When all three hundred and sixty-five pages had been turned, a new year was placed in the desk calendar and the process began once again. This last day of 1941 was turned on desks across the country and with it a page of history.

It was New Year's Eve in America and Benny Goodman was entertaining in the Terrace Room of the Hotel New Yorker. The hotel hit handsomely dressed patrons with a $10 cover charge to listen to the "King of Swing" and his magical clarinet. Yet as McCormick noted, "We are at the end of our careless, easy years. . . ."[4]

Six thousand miles away, another man who often wore a formal white jacket, Admiral Chester Nimitz, was due to assume command of the crippled Pacific fleet the next day, January 1. The decision by President Roosevelt to replace Admiral Husband Kimmel with Nimitz would prove to be monumental but this ceremony, in white day uniforms would be a formality, with Kimmel actually replacing Vice-Admiral William Pye who had temporarily replaced Kimmel.

Also scheduled in New York for the big night was Broadway star Kitty Carlisle singing with Dick Gasparre and his orchestra, in the Persian Room at The Plaza which had a $15 cover charge. Meanwhile, at Billy Rose's Diamond Horseshoe in the Hotel Paramount, the minimum was only a dollar. Around the world, from Los Angeles to New York to Sydney, New Year's Eve celebrants were warned about excessive rejoicing. "Don't congregate. Keep moving outside. Celebrate—mildly, please—indoors."[5] Fiorello La Guardia asked New Yorkers not to blow horns. The Little Flower was still under severe disapproval. "I have suffered too much during the last six months absorbing the criticism, the abuse, the smears and jeers of people including some of the press, who wouldn't cooperate when we were seeking to train people for just this emergency," he whimpered.[6] The barrel-chested, staccato-speaking Italian was a character right out of the newspaper movie, *His Girl Friday*.

The city of Boston imposed a midnight tariff on food, and the *Globe* noted that "despite taxes and the Axis, capacity crowds will welcome the New Year here."[7] CBS, NBC, and Mutual radio planned to broadcast an evening of big band and orchestra music. They would intersperse local "pickups" around the country with radio men interviewing citizens on the street, asking them about New Year's, their resolutions, and how they were enjoying the evening.

In London, because of heavy Christmas consumption, it was unknown if there would be enough wine and whiskey for the New Year's festivities.[8] Of course, liquor had already been banned in Hawaii and the police were cracking down heavily on bootleggers. The big radio station, KGMB was due to end its broadcasting day at 10:30 p.m. after the news and fifteen minutes of popular swing music. Because of the island-wide curfew, there would be no nightclubbing around Honolulu or any other part of the territory on December 31. Fireworks were of course banned in Oahu. The provost judge, Lt. Colonel Neal D. Franklin, had already handed out fines for blackout violations.[9]

Hawaiians could take comfort though, knowing that they had an oversupply of bananas which they could consume "for health and as a means of saving money."[10] The next day, the Daughters of Hawaii planned on placing leis and flowers on the graves of the men killed on December 7.[11] "At noon, there will be a Hawaiian chant, and a group of Hawaiians will sing 'Aloha On.'"[12]

Besides the Hotel New Yorker, in Baltimore, the Caribbean Tea Room, Twenty-One, Nates & Leons, and Marty's all planned bashes for New Year's.[13] Tommy Dorsey and his trombone were set to ring in the New Year at the Palladium in Los Angeles with special guests Frank Sinatra and the drummer Buddy Rich. Sinatra and Rich, two of the most talented (and headstrong) men in the jazz world, despised each other. Dorsey's band only had room for one breakout star, and they each vied for that honor. The personal enmity between Sinatra and Rich would one day erupt into fisticuffs. In the meantime, for the New Year's soiree they headlined, a $5.00 cover charge got the patron a private table, dinner, and party favors.[14] Still, "The World War which engulfed the United States in 1941 cast a dark shadow over ... efforts to celebrate the arrival of the New Year with a rollicking fling."[15]

One hundred and ninety-nine years had passed since George Frederick Handel's "Messiah" had first been heard in Dublin and now, many churches throughout the West were planning on bringing in the New Year with a choral rendition of the oratorio. Many Americans had opted this night to celebrate the ringing in of the New Year on their knees, but sober.

Factories were working at full steam, 24/7, including New Year's Eve, while government doctors were spewing forth about American diets and American marriages. For Rosie the Riveter and her husband Walt the Welder, a diet that included the daily consumption of "eggs, leafy vegetables, fresh fruit, milk, cheese, meat and bread" was recommended as the way to go.[16] Bananas were not specifically mentioned. The American marriage was thought, because of the war, to be in better health than at anytime recently.

But the workers at the Ford Motor Company, where employees worked ten hour shifts to make machines for the Willow Run airplane factory, had a problem. First, the men wanted some time off during those ten hours to "rest and wash up."[17] To make matters worse, management opposed the men smoking cigarettes, pipes, and cigars while they operated heavy equipment. The paternalistic Henry Ford, known for his abstemious nature, expected the same of his workers. Fighter planes and bombers were already "rolling off the production lines of U.S. manufacturers at the rate of 2,000 a month." Tanks were being built at the rate of almost 3,000 per month.[18]

The reality of war was all around. It was announced Mt. Palomar, the site of the famed giant telescope in San Diego, was closed for the duration of the war.[19] On campuses, opinion was divided over whether sports programs should be cut back or participation made mandatory, as means of preparing the young men for combat. Government officials estimated there was a ready supply of some 25 million American males qualified for combat duty.

Thursday the First was officially a holiday but many of the 200,000 federal workers had been "asked" by the various agencies to "contribute their holiday in the interests of an 'all out'—war effort and work New Year's Day."[20]

A new campaign by the government, "Salvage for Victory!" also reminded Americans that even on this night the war was never very far from their doorstep. "Save waste paper, rags, old skates, bicycle tires, rubber boots, children's toys . . ."[21] One government official puffed out his chest and proclaimed, "in a shooting war our planes, tanks, ships and guns have enormous appetites for metal. Mr. and Mrs. America have already made sacrifices. They must be prepared to make still more sacrifices."[22] The Office of Production Management came up with another slogan, "Get in the Scrap!" extolling Americans to save and salvage, as a way to join the war effort.[23]

As investors predicted, railroad stocks climbed sharply. With the new restrictions on rubber, people would turn back the pages of time and traverse the country as before, on the B&O and the Lehigh Valley, the Reading and the Erie Lackawanna. Among the various railroad companies, a hundred thousand new boxcars were ordered to accommodate the war effort and the shift by the civilian population from cars and trucks, to trains. While not taking Americans "back to horse and buggy days," the ban did push the railroads again "to the forefront as movers of passengers and freight."[24] The president of the Association of American Railroads, J. J. Pelley, wrote the presidents of colleges and universities asking that their football teams not travel by train "and keep student travel to a minimum so that we can devote our passenger facilities to troop movements."[25] Stocks in tire companies had plummeted though and theft became widespread.

Some worried that American women's style would falter in the face of the war, but right there on the fashion pages was a shapely model posing in what was sure to be popular haute couture for 1942. "Today's defense worker (or shall we call them war workers?) are going about their jobs efficiently in sturdy denim fashions adapted from men's work clothes. This mechanic's suit is styled for comfort."[26]

Ted Williams was voted baseball's "Man of the Year" by the *Sporting News*, making up for the fact that he'd lost out to Joe DiMaggio for MVP.[27] He was the first ballplayer to bat over .400 since 1923. The Chicago Bears, winner of the NFL championship, were on their way to New York for the annual All-Star game pitting the defending champs against a team made up of the best players from the rest of the league.

Baseball in January of 1942 was declared essential by the president personally, but even so, so many ballplayers left to join the fight, that the quality of the game fell precipitously. It stumbled through using has-beens, never-weres, old men, young men, and in St. Louis, the joke of the league Browns, used a one-armed ballplayer, Pete Gray, in the outfield because he could not serve in the military. The Browns won the American League pennant in 1944.

Citizen Kane was chosen as picture of the year by the New York Film Critics, and the annual list of the ten best dressed women in the world was released.[28] Topping it for 1941 was the Duchess of Windsor, the twice-divorced and many-loved Wallis Simpson, for whom a man gave up a throne, a crown and an Empire and in so doing, changed the course of history for Great Britain and the world. Sentimentalized in the press as the "Love Story of the Century," the reality behind Simpson and Edward was actually quite tawdry. Unknown to the public at the time, Simpson remained promiscuous, even while married to Edward. For his part, the weak-willed Edward showed Nazi sympathies and proved such a security risk that an angry Churchill demanded that the erstwhile king be isolated from any secrets of state. The public saw the Duke of Windsor as a romantic figure, when, in fact, he would prove a royal embarrassment for many years to come.

After one last transmission from General MacArthur's command, all official communication stopped from Manila as of 3:35 a.m. (EST) the morning of December 31. "The enemy is driving in great force from both north and south. His dive-bombers practically control the roads from the air. The Japanese are using great quantities of tanks and armored units. Our lines are being pushed back," was the last message heard.[29]

A Tokyo broadcast was monitored calling on the American forces to cease all resistance in the Philippines "to assure the safety and protection of lives and property in Manila."[30] The Netherland press reported that Allied relief was just over the horizon. "Allied reinforcements were reported by Dutch newspapers tonight to be en route to the Pacific war theatre. . . ."[31] No such luck. It was also reported that Winston Churchill had cabled Australian Prime Mister John Curtin with assurances that resources would be made available to defend his country. But there was, again, no mention of the Philippines. The Philippines eventually fell and MacArthur was forced for a time onto the tiny island of Corregidor and then, ordered off that island fortress by FDR and sent to Australia. Meanwhile, thousands of American, British, Australian, and Filipino troops fell into the hands of the murderous Japanese and faced a long death march in Bataan.

Things continued to go badly for the Americans in the Western and Central Pacific in 1942 with ships such as the *Langley*, the *Edsall*, and the *Peary* and many others sunk by the Japanese until Chester Nimitz, with three aircraft carriers and a hell of a lot of luck, sank four of the Japanese fire line carriers at the Battle of Midway in June of 1942. All four of the carriers had been used in the attack on Pearl and everybody marinated themselves in the joy of revenge. Still, some members of congress called for Nimitz's impeachment because he did not—they felt—more aggressively pursue the badly damaged and limping Japanese armada.

His predecessor knew something about being unfairly hounded. Admiral Husband Edward Kimmel, broken and bitter, took an early retirement in 1942 and spent most of the rest of his life trying to pick up the pieces of his shattered reputation, even as his son Manning was killed aboard a navy sub in 1944.

Twenty years after his command was destroyed before his very eyes, he wrote a book simply called *Admiral Kimmel's Story*, attempting to exonerate himself, but the book was filled with bitter recriminations against Roosevelt. The forward to the book could only muster this defense of Kimmel: "It must be remembered that Admiral Kimmel was never formally charged with dereliction of duty . . . ."[32] Admiral Husband Kimmel, in his book, went so far as to call Roosevelt a "criminal."[33]

General Walter Short also retired from the military in early 1942. He moved to Dallas and seemed less obsessed with restoring his name than Kimmel. Short died in 1949 of heart disease.[34]

Kimmel and Short were exonerated on several occasions in later years, through studies, papers, and reports but as a result, rather than being scape-goats, they morphed into victims and no real fighting man wanted to be regarded as either.

An act of congress in 1947 allowed every man in uniform to receive the lifetime benefits of his highest rank in the war, except for two: Kimmel and Short.

Singapore had been hit again in late December of 1941 four times by Japanese bombers and looting broke out as the social structure began to break down. The pattern that was playing out in the Philippines and had played out in Hong Kong and Guam and Wake Island was now playing out in the Malaya city. Blitzkrieg bombing night and day to neutralize the enemy planes and ground batteries while unnerving the civilian populations, were followed by a massive, quick striking invasion, all supported by a naval bombardment. Martial law was declared in Singapore to help stabilize the state of affairs. Spain, while officially neutral, was unofficially acting as a leader in the cheering section for Japan when the state radio in Madrid said the Japanese, in bombing Manila, had only hit military targets. Madrid said it had Tokyo's word on that.[35]

Douglas MacArthur and other American officials had assured and reassured the people of the Philippines that a relief effort was on the way; in fact Washington had ordered most of the American navy to withdraw to Australia to save what ships it had left, operating in the Western Pacific. Only a number of U.S. subs remained. "The little Asiatic Fleet, based in the Philippines, was never intended as anything other than a harassing and delaying fleet . . . it was never expected to prevent Japanese landings."[36] This, plus the fact that the only reliable port was in Singapore, also crippled the navy's operations in the South China Sea, and the U.S. subs that were operating got poor reviews. In fact, the navy would not take any significant action until February of 1942 when the *Yorktown* and the *Enterprise* attacked the Japanese in the Marshall and Gilbert Islands.[37]

In one of his final communiqués before evacuating his command post, MacArthur promised to mete out revenge for the bombing of Manila.

Eventually, he moved his family and forces to the Bataan section of Luzon and then, onto the island of Corregidor for one last stand before he could return.[38]

Word was spreading that MacArthur's position was tenuous, faltering. "Private advices received in New York indicate that the fall of Manila is imminent." MacArthur had attempted to evacuate three hundred wounded by ship.[39] "Yankee and Filipino soldiers fought desperately to block the assault, but the sheer weight of Jap numbers and equipment forced our men slowly back towards the capital."[40]

The Japanese were crowing about their successes in the Pacific, claiming to have destroyed over 540 American, British, and Dutch aircraft, and to have sunk or badly damaged 33 large warships and four smaller vessels. They also claimed to have killed over 3,000 Allied troops while capturing 7,000 POWs.[41]

One sailor they did not kill, but whose own government thought they had, was Clifford Kickbush, 19, who "saw a grave marked as his own and talked to a friend who thought he had helped bury him in the Hawaiian Islands informed his parents he was very much alive." He contacted his very relieved parents and assured his startled shipmate that he had not seen a ghost. "What the devil! I helped bury you yesterday."[42] The story only became public three weeks after the attack.

Most Americans had assumed that the Burma Road was a vital link to China and the Free Chinese Forces, along which munitions, medicine, and materiel passed from the Allies; in truth, the road was a highway of pirates, privateers, con men, crooks and murderers. "It has been, and still remains both a national scandal and a national disgrace. Because the Burma Road has for years been dominated by racketeers and war profiteers ... 10,000 Chinese soldiers have gone without rifles, hand grenades or munitions."[43] Thousands of tons of materiel destined for the Free Chinese never made it, left alongside the long road, stolen, destroyed, or which ended up on the black market, ever since its opening in 1938.

Mohandas Gandhi, the "Little Leader" stepped down as the head of the All-India Nationalist Congress because of his commitment to nonviolence. India, where opposition to British colonial rule was brewing, conditionally supported England. Some there wanted to leverage support for England in exchange for independence, but Gandhi would have none of it. "I could not identify myself with opposition to war efforts on the ground of ill-will against Britain." In essence, he would not support violence in exchange for peace. "If such were my view and I believed in the use of violence for gaining independence . . . I would consider myself guilty of unpatriotic conduct."[44] The decision by the Indian government was a practical one though. The Japanese were threatening to bomb Calcutta. They were also suspected by the navy of having opened up submarine operations in the waters off Alaska.

Closer to home, the U.S. Congress wrapped up a rather eventful first session. In the 77th Congress, all they did was declare war on three countries, pass a huge new defense budget, give the president extraordinary authority under the War Powers Act, including the ability to censor just about anybody and any entity, pass a huge tax increase, pass the Lend-Lease Act, undo most of the Neutrality Acts of the 1930s, pass a new Selective Service Act, and conduct numerous investigations including corruption and fraud in defense lobbying.

Legislation they did not get around to passing included anti-lynching laws, stopped by a ferocious filibuster in the Senate. Proponents of the law thought that 1941 would be their year to finally get federal laws against lynching moved through Congress, but it was not to be so. The *Birmingham News*, while opposing a federal law against lynching, said hopefully, that in all of 1941 there had only been four in the country, according to the Tuskegee Institute. This was down from thirty-nine lynchings in the years 1936 to 1941, and over three hundred from 1922 to 1936. "Almost any year now the nation may be able to go through an entire 12-month period without a lynching. This would be about the best answer to those who persist in agitating for a federal anti-lynching law."[45]

They also did not get the planned investigation into war propaganda in the movies, but by December, it was a moot point. With the government's complicity, Hollywood had helped manufacture a consensus in favor of war.

Then "the Senate passed resolutions for sine die adjournment Jan. 2 and convening of the new Congress Jan. 5," at which time, they would consider legislation, to allow FDR the executive authority, to direct the country to abide by daylight savings. The House did likewise. One of the first bills they

would take up in 1942 was the "establishment of a separate air force. . . ."[46]
The 77th Congress began 1941 riddled with factionalism and petty bick-
ering, Democrats versus Republicans and Democrats versus Democrats.
There simply weren't enough Republicans to fight amongst themselves. They
also began the year arguing over a $17 billion dollar federal budget. Twelve
months later, they were in near unanimous agreement that the country
needed a $61.5 billion dollar budget, all of it save $8 billion slated for national
defense.[47] Capitol Hill in January of 1941 was dominated by isolationists. In
December of 1941, it was dominated by internationalists.

The city of Washington finally staged a successful blackout drill, after
numerous failed attempts to do so. All it took was twelve thousand air raid
wardens bellowing throughout the city for residents to get off the streets and
turn off their lights. "By intent, it was only a partial blackout. Street lights
were extinguished only in the downtown section and even there lights continued to glow . . . for the order in such cases were simply to use as little light
as possible."[48]

Via his odious Propaganda Minister, Joseph Goebbels, Adolf Hitler
addressed the German people on New Year's Eve. So, too, did Marshal Petain
address the French people on that day. Hitler claimed to have been behind the
Japanese attack on Pearl Harbor but a confidential memo to FDR from Rome
refuted that. There, Hermann Goering had a conversation with an undercover
British operative in which the German signaled his interest and approval of
the Japanese operations in the Pacific. Although out of favor with Hitler for
the recent failures of his Luftwaffe, Goering probably would have known if
there had been any coordination between Berlin and Tokyo on December 7.
Goering said, "I should consider it a great pleasure if Japan would be so kind
as to instruct me in their method of conducting these operations. I feel that I
have made a great mistake in not giving more study to the matter of launching
aerial torpedoes."[49]

In the continuation of his exclusive interview with Pierre Huss of the
International News Service, it was clear Hitler was still paranoid, ill-informed,
insecure, and delusional. "He may have heard that astrologers are saying in

the eighth year of his favorable sign in the heaven is the last. It is a worrisome thing." One thing was for sure. Adolf Hitler was absolutely obsessed with Franklin Roosevelt.[50]

The rumor was still going around that Hitler would be overthrown by his generals in 1942 and they would immediately sue for peace. A memo from the Office of Naval Intelligence laid it out, saying the German military was divided between "two factions, the first—Extremist, the second—Conservative. The Extremists are strong adherents of Hitler . . . Marshal Goering is now inclined toward the Conservative group, which is the real reason for his present alienation from Hitler. He and other members of the Conservative faction are under close surveillance of the Gestapo." The memo continued, "The Conservatives aim at final liquidation of the Nazi party at the earliest opportunity . . . ."[51]

In an earlier broadcast, he'd referred to President Roosevelt as "Frau Roosevelt."[52] British astrologers also forecast a bad 1942 for Adolf Hitler.

Still ringing in the ears of the Allies were the immortal words of Churchill "There will be no halting or half measures. There will be no compromise or parley. These gangs of bandits have sought to darken the light of the world . . . and thence march forward into their inheritance. They shall themselves be cast into the pit of death and shame, and only when the earth has been cleansed and purged of their crime and of their villiany will we turn from the task which they have forced upon us . . . The enemies have asked for total war. Let us make sure they get it."[53]

Mr. Churchill was due back in Washington on January 1st and few men fired up the American people like the British Prime Minister.

The first time Churchill and Roosevelt met in London in 1918, they did not like each other though they did share a fondness for "tobacco, strong drink, history, the sea, battleships, hymns, pageantry, patriotic poetry, high office and hearing themselves talk." But they grew to respect each other, and on Churchill's part, there was a genuine fondness. He once said that FDR was like opening a new bottle of champagne and FDR once said to Churchill, I am glad we live in the same decade.[54]

At the stroke of midnight on January 1st, 1942, America had technically been at war ___days ___hours ___minutes since the attack on Pearl Harbor. On December 8, President Roosevelt had made it official and then he did so again on December 11. America was thrust into a new world war; one in which she had vowed never to be involved; one that polling established the vast majority of the American people opposed, and one that had been forced upon a reluctant nation and indolent capital. "A languid Southern town with a pace so slow that much of it simply closed down for the summer grew almost overnight into a crowded, harried, almost frantic metropolis struggling desperately to assume the mantle of global power, moving haltingly and haphazardly and only partially successfully to change itself into the capital of the free world."[55]

Once forced into battle, the American people quickly rallied to the cause of patriotic grace, passion, desire, commitment, fear, revenge, love, hate, anger—all the emotions one would expect when one's country is unfairly and maliciously and sneakily attacked. Especially if that country was America in 1941, with its particularly strong streak of patriotism and sense of fair play.

The events of December 7, 1941, changed America and changed America forever. It sent the country careening off on a wildly different path of history than the one it had traveled in the days before that fateful day. In the two hours of the attack, the Navy lost more men than in World War I and the Spanish-America War combined. However, the nearly 3,000 dead did not come close to representing or reflecting the dimensions of the radical changes to America.

On December 6, 1941, America was an old body at rest. By the afternoon of December 7, it was a young body in motion. Action had been initiated and now America was obliged to engage in reaction. Yet it was more than just mere physics.

On December 6, 1941, America was in many ways, a tired and run down country and many thought she had seen her best days. The cloud of the Great Depression hung over the country despite the best (and some said harebrained) efforts of the New Dealers. The "Brain Trust" around FDR, who had come into power in 1933 full of promise and full of themselves had, by 1941, drifted away, frustrated with their failures. FDR was essentially alone with only his last New Deal companion, Harry Hopkins, still at his side, still believing that government could prime the pump.

In joining the Allied effort against the Huns, as they had in 1917, America took the lead but also learned from the mistakes at the Treaty of Versailles; the French insisted on humiliating the German people, giving rise to Adolf Hitler, giving rise to a new world war. No one in America really knew why the world went to war in August of 1914, except Barbara Tuchman. The assassination of the Archduke Ferdinand by Gavrilo Princip is cited as the flashpoint which triggered a series of mutual defense treaties, but European countries had battled each other for hundreds of years and it was often difficult to tell the good guys from the bad.

The war had revived a dying, wandering, and meandering America, without national purpose. And it changed the country forever. Never at any point in American history had the country been as united as it had been following December 7. Not on July 4, 1776, not on September 17, 1787, not for the War of 1812, certainly not in April 1861, not for the Spanish-American War, and not for the War to End All Wars. Indeed, in 1917 Congress debated for days before voting to support Woodrow Wilson and even then, dozens of members voted against the War Resolution. After 1919, Americans asked themselves, "What did we get out of the first world war but death, debt, and George M. Cohan?"[56] It was a good question.

Never again would America be an isolationist country as it had been after 1919, refusing to join the League of Nations. After this war, America took the lead in creating the United Nations. Rather than turning its back on the Empire of Japan and Nazi Germany, America chose instead to rebuild those war-torn countries and, going even further, implement the Marshall Plan as a means of rebuilding other countries in Europe, to protect them and America from Soviet advances, even as an Iron Curtin fell across Europe. It changed the Soviet Union, too, leading to a Cold War, in turn, leading to America's victory over the Soviets.

It forever changed the culture of America, kicking off a new realization of human rights for women and blacks.

It forever changed the economy as a heretofore unknown "Middle Class" sprung into being. It changed education, as the G.I. Bill, one of the greatest and kindest pieces of legislation ever passed by a grateful country, gave access to the academy to millions of G.I.s. It changed labor in America and the view towards government. The gentility of the past melted away. A brutality was evident at the end of the war that was not there at the beginning. For months after Pearl Harbor, American publications did not print photos of dead American soldiers. The subject was confined to private memos that ended up on Roosevelt's desk, as on December 11, when "Cincpac" Fleet Surgeon Elphege A.M. Gendreua wrote, "The dead were fingerprinted, where possible, identification marks and teeth charted, bodies marked with attached wooden tag, and wrapped in canvas."[57]

It changed the airplane from a marginally important player in economics and warfare to a central role in the world. Roosevelt's first Secretary of War, George H. Dern, dismissed the airplane in war as "the fantasy of a dreamer."[58] Airplanes fought during World War II as the Army Air Corps, making a decisive difference on the battlefield. In the end, the war would hinge on who controlled the skies. The U.S. Air Force became its own service in 1947, marking the undisputed primacy of air power in warfare. After the war, the country was awash in commercial airlines and had plenty of experienced pilots to fly for them. It changed science, as rockets, once thought of as kids' stuff, became a reality in war and then in peace, leading to satellites, men in space, and walking on the moon.

This war, beginning in 1939, was easier to comprehend and it was easier to tell the good guys from the bad guys. It was *The Good War* as Studs Terkel so memorably dubbed it.[59]

Newspapers across the country contained full-page ecumenical ads entreating Americans to go to the church of their choice for "A Universal Day of Prayer" as called for by President Roosevelt just a few days earlier.[60] New Year's Day was celebrated in the Catholic Church as the Feast of Circumcision but all churches throughout America would be open from early the morning of January 1, 1942, until well into the evening for prayer, communion, and supplication.

This prayer—recited in America and across the globe—had been marked "Triple Priority" for the American Embassy because it was to be read in London as well:

The year 1941 had brought upon our nation, as the past two years have brought upon other nations, a war of aggression by powers dominated by arrogant rulers whose selfish purpose is to destroy free institutions. They would thereby take from the freedom-loving peoples of the earth the hard-won liberties gained over many centuries.

The new year of 1942 calls for the courage and the resolution of old and young to help win a world struggle in order that we may preserve all we hold dear.

We are confident in our devotion to country, in our love of freedom, in our inheritance of courage. But our strength, as the strength of all men everywhere, is of greater avail as God upholds us.

In making this first day of the year 1942 a day of prayer, we ask forgiveness for our shortcomings of the past, consecration to the tasks of the present, and God's help in days to come.

We need His guidance that this people may be humble in spirit but strong in the conviction of the right; steadfast to endure sacrifices and brave to achieve a victory of liberty and peace.[61]

Franklin Delano Roosevelt

America had the will to succeed; this much was certain. To do so would require the necessary "blood, toil, tears and sweat."

EPILOGUE

"A failure of imagination . . ."

After the devastating fire of 1967 in which *Apollo One* astronauts Gus Grissom, Ed White, and Roger Chafee were burned alive on the ground in a seemingly routine drill. Another astronaut, Frank Borman, was ordered to head up the NASA investigation.

He was hauled before a hostile congressional committee and towards the end was asked, "How could this have happened? How are three men killed in a ground test of the *Apollo* capsule?" Borman, a taciturn man, thought for a moment and replied to New Mexico Senator Clinton Anderson, "Senator, it was a failure of imagination. . . ." Elaborating, Borman said, "No one ever imagined . . . [we] just didn't think that such a thing could happen."

So it was with the attack by the Japanese on December 7, 1941. Sure, memos had been written and hypotheticals discussed, but when it got down to cases, no one—until it was too late—really ever thought the Japanese could sail thousands of miles undetected and attack Pearl Harbor.

No one in America imagined that the Japanese would have the cunning and tenacity to attempt such a feat, and yet they succeeded because of a failure of imagination on the part of those in power in Washington, both civilian and in the military. It had been speculated, war-gamed, theorized, but nobody really thought it could happen.

There is not one shred of evidence that President Roosevelt somehow manipulated events to get America into the war. At the most, the War

Department believed, as of November 28, "Japanese future action unpredictable, but hostile action possible at any moment."[1] FDR had also been given several severe warnings about the Japanese in confidential memos, some of which specifically mentioned Hawaii, yet even still, the idea was so farfetched so as to be dismissed by nearly all. Everybody believed the next Japanese move would be an invasion of Thailand.

Carl Jung, the great Swiss philosopher fashioned the notion of "synchronicity," which he called "a causal connection of two or more psycho-physic phenomena. . . ." Events, he said, were not only grouped by cause but by meaning as well. What might seem coincidental was, in fact, often part of a larger interconnectivity of unfolding events according to Jung.[2]

Few things in American and world history illustrate synchronicity better than the attack on Pearl Harbor. Events conspired to help the Japanese, and hurt America and the world in the short run, but ironically hurt Japan and help America and the world in the long run.

"December 7, 1941 . . . will live as one of the most brilliant military performances of all time. Superbly planned and superbly executed. . . ." And that was the analysis of the American military. The question why was answered by Admiral Isoroku Yamamoto with his directive of November 5, 1941. The Japanese desired to "drive Britain and America from Greater East Asia," a long cherished goal.[3] Consider that Franklin Roosevelt runs for an unprecedented third term and wins, breaking the "no third term" rule which had governed all previous second term presidents. This liberates him and begins a seemingly unrelated chain reaction of events that winds its way through history, from December 7, 1941, right up until today. He initiates both Lend-Lease and the Atlantic Charter, both revolutionary developments, and neither of which might have gone forward, either the year before, or if Wendell Willkie were elected president in 1940. Willkie made staying out of Europe the centerpiece of his campaign.

In the fall of 1941, Congress decided by one vote to preserve a standing army, by maintaining a draft. At the time, there were few enlistees and those who wanted to join up were by and large, poor physical specimens.

A beautiful American spy living in Europe, Amy Thorpe Pack, had been recruited by the British Security Coordination to make use of her red hair, flashing green eyes, and feminine wiles to steal the German decoding technology called "Enigma" which eventually ended up as the contraption nicknamed "Magic" by the American military men who operated it in 1941. The revolutionary machine decodes the secret messages between Tokyo and the Japanese Embassy in Washington. The technology was called "the greatest secret and most spectacular intelligence achievement of the war."[4]

The Americans thought themselves safe because of the discovery, assuming that they would know as soon as the Japanese diplomats knew of any military actions by the war-like Axis Power. War warnings were sent to Kimmel and Short, but with no amplifying details, and while the Philippines and other locations were mentioned, Hawaii was not.[5] The headline of the *Hilo Tribune Herald* on November 30, 1941, shouted, "JAPAN MAY STRIKE OVER WEEKEND."[6] The premature warning cooled enthusiasm a tad for the stolen technology. Meanwhile, analysts were unduly and increasingly confident about their own ability to interpret the subtle and "enigmatic" oriental mind.

Just months earlier, FDR angered some navy admirals, including James Richardson, who happened to be the head of the Pacific Fleet at the time, by ordering the fleet to move from San Diego to Honolulu. This set off a chain of events with the Japanese, who saw the move as provocative and a challenge. Roosevelt, angered at Richardson, removed him and replaced him with Admiral Husband E. Kimmel, whose stewardship of the Fleet in Hawaii became an important part of this storyline.

Plans went forward in Tokyo to destroy the fleet and secure the Western and Central Pacific, the main target being the American carriers. The whole idea of the bombing came from the astonishing successful aerial strike by the British on the Italian navy at Taranto.

To Jung's point, all wars of the time seemed to begin on a Sunday. The Archduke Franz Ferdinand was shot on a Sunday, and his assassination kicked off World War I. Germany invaded Belgium and France on a Sunday, some weeks later. Great Britain and France both declared war on Germany on a Sunday in September of 1939 after the German invasion of Poland. Greece was invaded by Italy on a Sunday in World War II and Germany invaded Russia on a Sunday in June of 1941. How surprising was it that Japan attacked America on a Sunday?

The attack was not as successful as the Japanese had hoped. The American carriers were not present at Pearl, and the Japanese failed to destroy the fuel dumps and the dry docks, which allowed the Americans to rebuild quickly.

The attack triggered the Germany declaration of war on America and thereby pushed the reluctant country into the European conflict, signaling the eventual demise of the Nazis and the rise of the Soviet state. Had America not entered, it is possible that an armistice might have been signed by Great Britain and Nazi Germany with London allowing Chancellor Hitler to keep his new territories. Had the Japanese not attacked Pearl Harbor, the Americans would have most likely never entered the Pacific War or the European conflict.

If Germany started her invasion of Russia in April or maybe even as late as May, the invasion of Russia would have become another spectacular success for Hitler and, with a new Eastern Border, he could have devoted more men and materiel to North Africa, defeating the British there and thus devoted more men and material to an invasion of Great Britain. To the end, Hitler had blamed "international Jewry" for the war and managed to exterminate over 6 million Jews, giving rise just a few years later to the creation of the modern nation-state of Israel.

The world was changed in great earth-shattering ways and small painful ways, too. The attack was a pebble dropped in a pool and the concentric circles moved outward, forever.

Ellsworth Westbook Shirley had to quit his thriving life insurance business because it included delivering checks to the parents of boys who had died in the war, just as his oldest son, "Barney" had. When the parents to whom he brought the checks began crying, he did, too, and finally could not take it anymore. He sold the business and went into another line of work. His wife, Georgia's hair went white in a matter of weeks after hearing about the death of her eldest son. Ellsworth's mother, Cora Shirley, was never the same again, nor were Barney's aunts, Lola and Maude, nor were Barney's two brothers, Eddie and Ronnie.

The departed was our uncle Ellsworth Abbott "Barney" Shirley, who was killed by Japanese troops in French Indo-China in January of 1945. He'd dropped out of high school in 1943 and enlisted in the navy at the age of eighteen with his parents' permission. He became a radio operator on a TBF-1 Avenger plane on board the *Essex*.

On his twentieth birthday on January 10, 1945, Airman Second Class Shirley volunteered for a mission to bomb Japanese docks in Indo China. He needed the air hours to be promoted to Airman 1C. He must have had an omen that day though because, before taking off, he gave away all his priceless possessions in his footlocker while telling his bunkmates he didn't think he was coming back. The plane took off the morning of December 10, 1945.

After acquiring their target and dropping their bomb, the pilot, Donald Henry of Drummond, Idaho, radioed the squadron leader that he still had one bomb left and circled back to make a second pass at the docks.

Instead, the plane was shot down by Japanese anti-aircraft fire and crashed in a park in Saigon. Japanese troops discovered the badly wounded Airman Shirley in the wreckage of the plane and killed him. Henry survived the crash and was secreted away by the French Underground, but was later discovered by the Japanese and killed too.

He was called Barney because when he was born, a grandfather exclaimed, "Why he's got great big eyes, just like Barney Google!" Google was a character in the popular comic strip, "Barney Google and Snuffy Smith."

Like millions of others, the lives of the Shirley family were forever altered by the events of December 7, 1941.

The world was also changed for American blacks because of December 7. In that battle, a new hero emerged. Doris "Dorrie" Miller, mess attendant, was picking up laundry onboard the *West Virginia* when the attack began. He was initially ordered to help move wounded men and then told to man a 50 caliber anti-aircraft gun. Miller stayed at his post, firing repeatedly at Japanese planes, as torpedoes hit his ship, bullets whizzed by, and men died around him. Miller never flinched and only left his duty station when ordered after the situation had become hopeless.

For his bravery Miller was awarded the Navy Cross in early 1942 by another Texan, Admiral Chester Nimitz. In presenting the award to Cook Third Class Miller, Nimitz said, "This marks the first time in this conflict that such high tribute had been made in the Pacific Fleet to a member of his race and I'm sure that the future will see others similarly honored for brave acts."[7] Two years later, Miller was killed with 646 other seamen aboard the escort carrier *Liscome Bay*.

Miller received the Purple Heart, the American Defense Service Medal, the Asiatic-Pacific Campaign Medal, a Fleet Clasp and the Victory Medal. In 1973, the ship USS *Miller*, a frigate, was commissioned.

Dorie Miller's body was never recovered.

Douglas MacArthur, who could have been another scapegoat except for his war-zone command, his savvy skills, his rapport with the American people, and his close relationship with Roosevelt, went to Australia, became the Supreme Commander of the Southwest Pacific forces, and with little resources and men, mounted one of the most brilliant counter offensives in military history. As his troops were closing in on invading Japan, atomic bombs detonated over Hiroshima and Nagasaki, killing tens of thousands of civilians as per the order of the new president, Harry Truman. Roosevelt died before seeing the successful victory in the world war which he, more than any other man on the face of the earth, was responsible for winning.

MacArthur's brilliant occupation of the defeated country should have earned him the Nobel Peace prize. Several years later, duty called the old general once again and he went to Korea where he once again mounted a dazzling counter offensive. After America was lied to by the new Red Chinese government and watched them invade Korea, the general tried to take control of the mess. In so doing he ran afoul of President Truman and was fired from his post.

MacArthur came home to a hero's welcome, revered and beloved by the American people. Truman, who sought another term in 1952, was badly embarrassed in the New Hampshire primary, saw his approval rating fall to the mid-20s, and finally withdrew from the race. His departure opened the door for yet another general, Dwight D. Eisenhower, to serve two underappreciated presidential terms, while the country enjoyed peace and prosperity and saw unprecedented growth and development in civil rights, technology, education, transportation, and medicine. Truman went home to Independence, Missouri, and though he lived to be eighty-eight, he never saw the resurrection of his reputation and presidency. By the mid-1970s, historians had finally come to appreciate the accomplishments and wisdom that characterized the seven years the failed haberdasher was in the White House. Truman would have never been president if Roosevelt had not run again in 1940.

America emerged from the Second World War as the only unchallenged superpower, but that status didn't last long. Another Evil Empire rose up to replace the Third Reich and enslaved the very same Eastern European countries the Germans had ground under their boots. This new empire proved even more vicious and immoral than the Third Reich, if that were possible.

In one of the great historical ironies, Japan and Germany emerged as American allies against Moscow, rebuilt as prosperous democracies by the United States. An organization to settle international disputes—once rejected by the United States—was created with American leadership. English emerged as the international language of all pilots, as the only planes flying after World War II were American and British.

A Cold War took hold. Moscow and Washington, the unchallenged superpowers, eyed each other carefully, and their competition led to an unprecedented arms race only outpaced by a science race with an American eventually walking on the moon, a direct result of America's entry into World War II.

In 1961, another man ascended to the presidency. Had he not been a hero in the Pacific and skillfully used that heroism in his congressional and presidential campaigns, John Kennedy would have likely been dismissed as a rich, philandering playboy, and history would have been drastically altered yet again. It was he who committed the United States to landing a man on the Moon before the end of 1970. He was soon assassinated by a loyal follower of Soviet communism. Before his assassination, he committed U.S. troops in a ground war on the Asian continent and years later, and after the loss of more than 57,000 American troops, America lost her first war and with it, for a time, her sense of national purpose, and of national destiny.

The country stumbled through the 1970s, an embarrassing shell of its former greatness until another man was elected and summonned forth the greatness of the country one again, scaring the hell out of the elites but beloved by the uncommon men and women of his country. He called Soviet Communism what it was: An Evil Empire. He rejected the containment and détente policies of the past 35 years and embarked on a campaign to destroy the Soviet Union and win the Cold War.

That new Evil Empire eventually collapsed as America and the West defeated it both economically and militarily, setting millions free who had once been imprisoned by the Soviet State and whose parents and grandparents had been threatened and imprisoned and murdered by Hitler and Stalin.

The city of Washington changed radically because of the war and became, because of the attack, the headquarters for the Free World. A city that once had been little more than a bumpkin byway became an awkward player on the world stage, even as it accumulated along the way all the trappings of power including corruption, greed, and one of the highest rates of venereal disease in the country, perhaps confirming that power is the ultimate aphrodisiac.

Because of Pearl Harbor, the culture of America changed radically. Women only partially retreated from the factory floor back to the kitchen floor. More and more women, men, and blacks who never thought about college began attending, especially the returning G.I.s under one of the greatest pieces of legislation ever conceived: the G.I. Bill.

America never again retreated from the world stage, as it did in the early 1800s, as it did after the Spanish-American War, and as it did in 1919 after the end of the First World War. After World War II, the philosophy changed from "America First" to "America First In."

Another president, Ronald Reagan, a former New Dealer, whose movie career unraveled because of Pearl Harbor, unraveled the agreements of Yalta, made by FDR and Churchill in which whole chunks of Eastern Europe and the Baltics were handed over to the evil and monstrous thug Josef Stalin.

A wall went up. A wall came down. What had been free and independent was free and independent again after 1991, as the periods of servitude first under Hitler and then under Stalin were finally ended.

The world changed over many times, but the attack on Pearl Harbor was the lynchpin that set off a global synchronicity, whose effects are still being felt today.

NOTES

PREFACE

1. Franklin Delano Roosevelt Presidential Library and Museum, "Japanese Intelligence and Propaganda in the United States During 1941," December 4, 1941, Hyde Park, NY, 2.
2. Franklin Delano Roosevelt Presidential Library and Museum, "Japanese Intelligence and Propaganda in the United States During 1941," December 4, 1941, Hyde Park, NY, 4.
3. Franklin Delano Roosevelt Presidential Library and Museum, "Japanese Intelligence and Propaganda in the United States During 1941," December 4, 1941, Hyde Park, NY, 12-13.
4. Bill Henry, "By the Way," *Los Angeles Times*, December 9, 1941, A1.
5. Jack Shafer, "Who Said It First? Journalism Is the 'First Rough Draft of History," *Slate Magazine*: Posted August 30, 2010, http://www.slate.com/id/2265540/.
6. *Boston Globe*, "388 to 1," December 9, 1941, 18.

CHAPTER 1: THE FIRST OF DECEMBER

1. *New York Times*, "Daily Newspapers Sell 42,385,807 a Day," February 18, 1942, 17.
2. *Dunkirk (NY) Evening Observer*, "Petain Ready to Give Rest of His Nation to Nazis," December 1, 1941, 1.
3. *Time*, "Army: Battle of the Carolinas," December 1, 1941, 32.
4. Associated Press, "U.S. Army Will Use Live Ammunition in 1942 Maneuvers," *Washington Evening Star*, December 1, 1941, A7.
5. *Time*, "Navy: World's Mightiest," December 1, 1941, 34.
6. *Time*, "Huck's New Boat," December 1, 1941, 76.
7. *Life*, "Japanese Bow and Grin for the Camera But Get Nowhere in Washington," December 1, 1941, 36.
8. F. Tillman Durdin, "Singapore Doubts Japanese Threats," *New York Times*, December 4, 1941, 5.
9. Associated Press, *Baltimore Sun*, December 1, 1941, 1.
10. Associated Press, "FR, Hull Confer; No Final Answer Filed from Tokyo," *Bismarck (ND) Tribune*, December 1, 1941, 1.
11. *Emporia (KS) Daily Gazette*, December 1, 1941, 5.
12. *Emporia (KS) Daily Gazette*, December 1, 1941, 5.
13. Edward E. Bomar, Associated Press, "String of Military Bases," *Ironwood (MI) Daily Globe*, December 1, 1941, 1.
14. United Press, "British Navy Reinforced in Pacific," *Coshocton (OH) Tribune*, December 1, 1941, 1.
15. International News Service, "Tojo Statement Ends Vacation for Executive," *Charleston (SC) Gazette*, December 1, 1941, 1.

16. Dewitt Mackenzie, "Nazi Setbacks Stop the Japs," *Emporia (KS) Daily Gazette*, December 1, 1941, 1.

17. Constantine Brown, "This Changing World," *Washington Evening Star*, December 1, 1941, A11.

18. Constantine Brown, "This Changing World," *Washington Evening Star*, December 1, 1941, A11.

19. *Time*, "National Affairs: Advice to Japan," December 1, 1941, 14.

20. Associated Press, "R.A.F. Drops 150 Tons of Bombs on Hamburg," *Bakersfield Californian*, December 1, 1941, 3.

21. Associated Press, "Flashes," *Bakersfield Californian*, December 1, 1941, 1.

22. *Coshocton (OH) Tribune*, "Home From Russia," December 1, 1941, 4.

23. United Press, "Goebbels Says U.S. Can't Save England," *Dunkirk (NY) Evening Observer*, December 1, 1941, 1.

24. Associated Press, "Brett's Plane Fired Upon by Axis Warship," *Greeley (CO) Daily Tribune*, December 1, 1941, 2.

25. Associated Press, "F. D. R. Envisioned Nazi Effort at World Dominance in 1939," *Birmingham (AL) News*, December 1, 1941, 1.

26. *Life*, "The Pursuits Fly from Any Level Meadow," December 1, 1941, 92.

27. *Life*, "Even the Bombers Operate Out of Dispersion Fields," December 1, 1941, 96.

28. *Bakersfield Californian*, "Air School," December 1, 1941, 6.

29. Hanson W. Baldwin, "Sees Big Losses for Army in War," *New York Times*, December 1, 1941, 10.

30. William A. Baker, "1,400 Conscientious Objectors Toil in 20 Camps at Own Expense, Without Pay," *Tucson (AZ) Daily Citizen*, December 1, 1941, 12.

31. Associated Press, "1800 'Over Age' Men of 29th Division Soon to Be Released," *Cumberland (MD) Evening Times*, December 1, 1941, 1.

32. Paul Mallon, "News Behind the News," *Bakersfield Californian*, December 1, 1941, 15.

33. Associated Press, "Call of the Sea Brings 'Pop' Back to Navy," *Birmingham (AL) News*, December 1, 1941, 3.

34. U.S. Census Bureau, *Historical Statistics of the United States: Colonial Times to 1970* (Washington, D.C., 1960), 70.

35. *New York Times*, "Powerful New Gun Developed By U.S.," December 4, 1941, 13.

36. *Bakersfield Californian*, "A Future Problem," December 1, 1941, 15.

37. Alexander D. Noyes, "Stock Market Averages Go to Lowest Since 1938—Strike Troubles and Japanese Deadlock," *New York Times*, December 1, 1941, 27.

38. *New York Times*, "Stock Market Averages," December 1, 1941, 28.

39. Associated Press, "Pay Roll Tax Can Finance Pensions, Downey Claims," *Bakersfield Californian*, December 1, 1941, 6.

40. *Time*, "Public Opinion: Fear, But Not of Entanglement," December 1, 1941, 18.

41. David Brinkley, *Washington Goes to War* (New York: Alfred A. Knopf, 1988), 17.

42. *Life*, "Army Fires Businessman," December 1, 1941, 30.

43. Thomas Wolfe, *The Complete Short Stories of Thomas Wolfe*, ed. Francis E. Skipp (New York: Simon and Schuster, 1989), 192.

44. *Life*, "Parker," December 1, 1941, 1.

45. *Time*, "Delivering the Goods for Uncle Sam," December 1, 1941, 1.

46. *Time*, "Soap Suds That Turn Into Rubber," December 1, 1941, 1.

47. *Life*, "Plymouth: The Low-Priced Car Most Like High-Priced Cars," December 1, 1941, 1.

48. *Life*, "Columbia," December 1, 1941, 16.

49. *Life*, "Schwinn-Built Bicycles," December 1, 1941, 88.

50. *Coshocton (OH) Tribune*, "Defense Expected to Limit New Car Buyers' Choice," December 1, 1941, 1.

51. *Albuquerque Journal*, December 1, 1941, 8.

52. *Life*, December 1, 1941, 7.

53. *Life*, December 1, 1941, 8.

54. *Life*, "Stromberg—Carlson," December 1, 1941, 86.

55. *Time*, "Radio: From Washington," December 1, 1941, 50.
56. Richard Kluger, *Ashes to Ashes: America's Hundred-Year Cigarette War, the Public Health, and the Unabashed Triumph of Philip Morris* (New York: Random House, 1997), 192.
57. *Washington Evening Star*, "Camel—the Cigarette of Costlier Tobaccos," December 1, 1941, B10.
58. *Boston Daily Globe*, "Something New Has Been Added," December 1, 1941, 11.
59. *Life*, "Call for Phillip Morris," December 1, 1941, 113.
60. *Life*, "Grandpa Goes Modern," December 1, 1941, 54.
61. United Press, "Oregon State and Duke to Play in Famed Rose Bowl," *Brainerd (MN) Daily Dispatch*, December 1, 1941, 8.
62. *Brainerd (MN) Daily Dispatch*, "Meet Joe DiMaggio III," December 1, 1941, 8.
63. *Fitchburg (MA) Sentinel*, "Leaving Fenway?" December 1, 1941, 8.
64. *Beatrice (NE) Daily Sun*, "Mountaineer and Child Bride," December 1, 1941, 2.
65. *Portsmouth (NH) Herald*, "Parents Protest New York Crime Wave," December 1, 1941, 5.
66. United Press, "Gov. Talmadge Refuses to Pardon Six Floggers," *Fitchburg (MA) Sentinel*, December 1, 1941, 3.
67. *Life*, "The Governor of Georgia Remembers That He Was Once a Flogger Himself," December 8, 1941, 40.
68. *Coshocton (OH) Tribune*, "Communist Hires Willkie as Counsel," December 1, 1941, 1.
69. *Life*, "Latin-American Black Is New," December 8, 1941, 99.
70. *Kingsport (TN) Times*, "Social Calendar," December 1, 1941, 3.
71. *Greeley (CO) Daily Tribune*, "Modest Maidens," December 1, 1941, 6.
72. *New York Times*, "The Robin Moor, Reportedly Torpedoed, May Be First U.S. Victim of a Nazi Attack," June 10, 1941, 1.
73. Charles Herd, "Reuben James Hit," *New York Times*, November 1, 1941, 1.
74. Associated Press, "Tale of Heroism Aboard the Kearny After Torpedo Hit Told by Ensign," *New York Times*, November 4, 1941, 4.
75. United Press, "Kearny Fought U-Boat Pack," *New York Times*, December 4, 1941, 3.
76. Associated Press, "Seven Americans Lost," *New York Times*, December 4, 1941, 3; Associated Press, "Navy to Man Guns on Ships If Armed," *New York Times*, October 12, 1941, 5.
77. Associated Press, "Tells Boston Audience Aid Bolsters RAF," *Hartford Courant*, October 31, 1940, 1.
78. Associated Press, "Far Eastern Crisis Grows More Acute," *Hartford Courant*, December 1, 1941, 1.
79. Associated Press, "Far Eastern Crisis Grows More Acute," *Hartford Courant*, December 1, 1941, 1.
80. Associated Press, "FR, Hull Confer; No Final Answer Filed from Tokyo," *Bismarck (ND) Tribune*, December 1, 1941, 1.
81. Associated Press, "F.D.R Speeds Back to Capital," *Bakersfield Californian*, December 1, 1941, 1.
82. *Time*, "National Affairs: Advice to Japan," December 1, 1941, 13.
83. International News Service, "Tojo Statement Ends Vacation for Executive," *Charleston (SC) Gazette*, December 1, 1941, 1; Associated Press, "FR, Hull Confer; No Final Answer Filed from Tokyo," *Bismarck (ND) Tribune*, December 1, 1941, 1.
84. Associated Press, "Americans Advised to Leave Shanghai," *Atlanta Constitution*, December 1, 1941, 1; International News Service, "Yanks Put on Alert," *Charleston (SC) Gazette*, December 1, 1941, 1.
85. International News Service, "British Reinforce East," *Charleston (SC) Gazette*, December 1, 1941, 1.
86. International News Service, "British Reinforce East," *Charleston (SC) Gazette*, December 1, 1941, 1
87. Richard C. Wilson, United Press, "Far East Waits War Outburst," *Bakersfield Californian*, December 1, 1941, 1.
88. Associated Press, "F.D.R Speeds Back to Capital," *Bakersfield Californian*, December 1, 1941, 1; Associated Press, "Japan to 'Redouble Efforts' with U.S.," *Bakersfield Californian*, December 1, 1941, 1.

89. James B. Reston, "4 Powers Ready, Washington Says," *New York Times*, December 1, 1941, 1; United Press, "President and War Chiefs Confer on Oriental Crisis," *Los Angeles Times*, November 26, 1941, 1; Associated Press, "Americans Again Urged to Quit Japan," *Washington Post*, November 26, 1941, 1; John O'Donnell, "F.D. Arrives Today; To See War Cabinet," *Washington Times Herald*, December 1, 1941, 1.

90. Paul W. Ward, "Japan Crisis Ends Vacation of Roosevelt," *Baltimore Sun*, December 1, 1941, 1.

91. *Middlesboro (KY) Daily News*, "President Roosevelt Carves Again," December 1, 1941, 1.

92. *Time*, "The Presidency: Battle Stations," December 1, 1941, 15.

93. Frank L. Kluckhohn, "President Is Grim," *New York Times*, December 1, 1941, 1; Associated Press, "F.D.R. Cancels Georgia Vacation," *Atlanta Constitution*, December 1, 1941, 1.

94. *Life*, "Japanese Bow and Grin for the Camera But Get Nowhere in Washington," December 1, 1941, 36.

95. Associated Press, "FR, Hull Confer; No Final Answer Filed from Tokyo," *Bismarck (ND) Tribune*, December 1, 1941, 1; James B. Reston, "4 Powers Ready, Washington Says," *New York Times*, December 1, 1941, 1.

96. *Time*, "The Presidency: Battle Stations," December 1, 1941, 15; Associated Press, "F.D.R. Cancels Georgia Vacation," *Atlanta Constitution*, December 1, 1941, 1.

97. Frank L. Kluckhohn, "President Is Grim," *New York Times*, December 1, 1941, 1.

98. Frank L. Kluckhohn, "President Is Grim," *New York Times*, December 1, 1941, 1.

99. *Washington Evening Star*, "Fala 'Announces' President's Return to White House," December 1, 1941, A2.

100. Julius C. Edelstein, "Parley Requested By Jap Emissaries; May Reject Terms," *Washington Times Herald*, December 1, 1941, 1.

101. Otto D. Tolischus, "U.S. Principles Rejected By Japanese as 'Fantastic,'" *New York Times*, December 1, 1941, 1.

102. John Franklin Carter, "Memorandum on Mexican Border Situation (Eastern Portion)," December 1, 1941, Franklin Delano Roosevelt Presidential Library and Museum, Hyde Park, NY.

103. *New York Times*, "Japan's Imports Cut 75% by War," December 2, 1941, 6.

104. Chicago Tribune Press Service, "War's Pinch to Be Widely Felt; Japan to Suffer More Than U. S.," *Chicago Daily Tribune*, December 9, 1941, 31.

105. Associated Press, "FR, Hull Confer; No Final Answer Filed from Tokyo," *Bismarck (ND) Tribune*, December 1, 1941, 1.

106. Franklin Delano Roosevelt Presidential Library and Museum, "FDR: Day by Day—The Pare Lorentz Chronology," December 1, 1941.

107. Associated Press, "Both Sides Admit Situation Is Grave," *Portsmouth (NH) Herald*, December 1, 1941, 1.

108. *Salt Lake Tribune*, "Summary of Day's News From Europe, Far East," December 1, 1941, 2.

109. Associated Press, "Nazi Reversals Cause Japs to Ask More Time," *Panama City News-Herald*, December 1, 1941, 1.

110. United Press, "Strategic Areas Are Ordered on War-Time Basis," *Idaho Evening Times*, December 1, 1941, 1.

CHAPTER 2: THE SECOND OF DECEMBER

1. *Birmingham (AL) News*, "55 Minutes to Atlanta 4 Flights Daily $6.50," December 1, 1941, 11.

2. *Washington Evening Star*, "Fast Non-Stop Commuter Service to New York," December 2, 1941, A7.

3. *New York Times*, "Subway Smokers Beware," December 1, 1941, 21.

4. Associated Press, "Those Service Men on Leave: 'Give Them a Lift,'" *San Francisco Chronicle*, December 1, 1941, 4.

5. Floyd Healey, "'Secession' Movement Is Backed," *San Francisco Chronicle*, December 1, 1941, 1.

6. *Washington Evening Star*, "Yerela, Calif.—Thursday 'Rebels' Show Determination," December 2, 1941, A4.

7. Associated Press, "11 Per Cent Gain Seen in U.S. Use of Gasoline," *Washington Evening Star*, December 1, 1941, A3.

8. *Washington Evening Star*, "Traffic Report," December 1, 1941, A12.

9. *Time*, "Missouri: Scientifically Drunken Drivers," December 1, 1941, 18.

10. *Washington Evening Star*, "Nation's Auto Dealers Told U.S. Will Stop Inflation in Prices," December 1, 1941, A12.

11. Gordon William Prange, Donald M. Goldstein, and Katherine V. Dillon, *At Dawn We Slept: The Untold Story of Pearl Harbor* (New York: McGraw-Hill, 1981), 154.

12. *Time*, "A Few More Billions," December 1, 1941, 32.

13. Associated Press, "Buffalo Sets Stamp Sale Record," *New York Times*, December 3, 1941, 10.

14. *Time*, "Building: More Dirt," December 1, 1941, 72.

15. Associated Press, "House Groups to Air Role of Lobbying in Defense Contracts," *Washington Evening Star*, December 1, 1941, A1.

16. *Washington Evening Star*, "Two Hearings to Open Tomorrow on Defense Contract Lobbying," December 2, 1941 A3.

17. *New York Times*, "Permanence in Workers' Areas Seen by Miss Gladys Miller, Consultant—Number of New Units Equals Slam Razings," December 1, 1941, 16.

18. Associated Press, "Pro Football Title Game Will Be Played December 21," *Washington Evening Star*, December 1, 1941, A1.

19. Associated Press, "American Football Meets to Plan Expansion," *Washington Evening Star*, December 6, 1941, 1A.

20. *Time*, "The Real Thing," December 1, 1941, 49.

21. *Time*, "Words, Words," December 1, 1941, 49.

22. *Boston Daily Globe*, "Lodge Says U.S. Needs a Standing Army of 750,000," December 2, 1941, 2.

23. *Boston Daily Globe*, "R.H. White's Basement," December 2, 1941, 2.

24. *Boston Daily Globe*, "Jordan Marsh Company," December 2, 1941, 3.

25. *Boston Daily Globe*, "Jordan Marsh Company," December 2, 1941, 7.

26. *Boston Daily Globe*, "Conrad's," December 2, 1941, 11.

27. *Washington Post*, "Woodward and Lathrop," December 2, 1941, 4.

28. Associated Press, "O. P. M. Asks Public to Economize on Yule Wrappings," *Washington Evening Star*, December 1, 1941, A12.

29. Associated Press, "Don't Be Too Practical in Yule Buying, Mrs. Roosevelt Urges," *Atlanta Constitution*, December 2, 1941, 4.

30. *Washington Post*, "Indians Here to Demand Fire Water," December 2, 1941, 15.

31. *Time*, "Words, Words," December 1, 1941, 49.

32. *Time*, "Casualties," December 1, 1941, 49.

33. Tallulah Bankhead, *Tallulah: My Autobiography* (New York: Harper, 1952), 101.

34. Eugene S. Duffield, "How'll They Pay? Mr. L, Income $30,000, Adjusts His Savings Plan to Meet Higher Taxes," *Wall Street Journal*, December 1, 1941, 1.

35. *Time*, "The Presidency: The Old Master," December 1, 1941, 13.

36. *Time*, "National Affairs: Advice to Japan," December 1, 1941, 14.

37. *Time*, "Foreign Relations: Aid to Iceland," December 1, 1941, 14.

38. *Time*, "Foreign Relations: How to Beat Rationing," December 1, 1941, 24.

39. *Time*, "Medicine: War & Sanity," December 1, 1941, 54.

40. *Time*, "Medicine: War & Sanity," December 1, 1941, 54.

41. *Time*, "Welcome Stranger!" December 1, 1941, 31.

42. *Washington Evening Star*, "Sugar-Control Bill Passes House Despite Opposition by Hull," December 2, 1941, A3.

43. *Time*, "Music: Juke-Box Divas," December 1, 1941, 36.

44. *Time*, "Art: Artists' Rations," December 1, 1941, 39.

45. *Time*, "Education: First Two R's," December 1, 1941, 57.

46. *Time*, "Education: History Lesson," December 1, 1941, 57.

47. *Atlanta Constitution*, "Today's Radio, Tuesday's Local Programs," December 2, 1941, 17.

48. *Time*, "Cinema: Baghdad-on-the-Pacific," December 1, 1941, 82.

49. *Los Angeles Times*, "Day for Soviet Aid Proclaimed," December 1, 1941, 12.

50. *Birmingham (AL) News*, "'Citizen Kane' Will Be Shown Next at Empire," December 1, 1941, 25.

51. *Time*, "Cinema: Baghdad-on-the-Pacific," December 1, 1941, 82.

52. *Time*, "Books: Great Improbabilities," December 1, 1941, 88.

53. *Time*, "Books: Murder in November," December 1, 1941, 92.

54. *Christian Science Monitor*, "U.S.-Tokyo Talks Resumed; Nazi's Face New Soviet Peril; British Push Ahead in Libya," December 1, 1941, 1.

55. Associated Press, "Nazis Fleeing From Rostov Facing Trap," *Washington Evening Star*, December 2, 1941, 1.

56. United Press, "Din of Moscow Battle Heard on Air in London," *New York Times*, December 1, 1941, 2.

57. Franklin Delano Roosevelt Presidential Library and Museum, "Informal Remarks of the President to State Chairmen of Birthday Ball Committees December 2, 1941—5:00 P.M.," December 2, 1941, Hyde Park, NY.

58. Associated Press, "America First Reveals Plan for Role in 1942 Election," *Baltimore Sun*, December 2, 1941, 9.

59. *Look*, "Colgate Dental Cream," December 2, 1941, 25.

60. *Look*, "Chesterfield," December 2, 1941, 68.

61. *Boston Daily Globe*, "Lux Toilet Soap," December 2, 1941, 19.

62. Raymond Clapper, "What Roosevelt Is Not Telling Us," *Look*, December 2, 1941, 11.

63. *New York Times*, "288 Men, 1 Woman Listed in Dollar-a-Year Class," December 4, 1941, 11.

64. Carlisle Bargeron, "'Wall Street Wolf' Protects the Little Businessman," *Look*, December 2, 1941, 18.

65. *Look*, "Café Society Holds a Board Meeting," December 2, 1941, 22.

66. *Look*, "Meet The People: Meet the Men and Women of Russia, Whom Hitler Will Never Enslave," December 2, 1941, 28.

67. Samuel Spewack, "What's Happening to the Rich in England," *Look*, December 2, 1941, 30.

68. *Look*, "Vice-President Wallace Sets a Hollywood Fashion," December 2, 1941, 36.

69. John C. Henry, "76 and 80 Cent Pay Raises Won By Rail Unions," *Washington Evening Star*, December 2, 1941, A1.

70. Associated Press, "18 Convicted of Plot Against Army Face Terms of 10 Years," *Washington Evening Star*, December 2, 1941, A2.

71. Associated Press, "British Report Sinking Italian Destroyer, Two Supply Ships," *Washington Evening Star*, December 2, 1941, A1.

72. Associated Press, "Nazi's Cut Through British Ring to Rescue Force in East Libya; Capture Rezegh in Fierce Battle," *Washington Evening Star*, December 2, 1941, 1X.

73. Matthew Halton, "Libyan Sand Wastes Strewn With Litter of 'Dead' Axis Tanks," *Boston Daily Globe*, December 2, 1941, 21.

74. British Embassy, Washington, D. C., Memo to The Honorable Franklin D. Roosevelt President of the United States of America, December 2, 1941, Franklin Delano Roosevelt Presidential Library and Museum, Hyde Park, NY.

75. Associated Press, "Churchill Proposes Extending Draft to Men 18 to 50," *Washington Evening Star*, December 2, 1941, 1X.

76. Otto D. Tolischus, "U.S. Principles Rejected By Japanese as 'Fantastic,'" *New York Times*, December 1, 1941, 1.

77. Garnett D. Horner, "U.S. Asks Japan to Explain Troop Moves: Prompt Reply Is Requested By President," *Washington Evening Star*, December 2, 1941, A1.

78. Associated Press, "Japanese Troops Drill With Parachutes," *Boston Evening Globe*, December 2, 1941, 19.

79. United Press, "Japan Seizing Private Shipping for Transport Duty," *Boston Evening Globe*, December 2, 1941, 19.

80. Garnett D. Horner, "U.S. Asks Japan to Explain Troop Moves: Prompt Reply Is Requested By President," *Washington Evening Star*, December 2, 1941, A1.

81. Associated Press, "Roosevelt Is Reported Taking Personal Role In Washington Talks," *Birmingham (AL) News*, December 2, 1941, 29.

82. Frank L. Kluckhohn, "Roosevelt Calls In Navy Adviser to Hear Hull Report on Orient," *Washington Post*, December 2, 1941, 1.

83. Frank L. Kluckhohn, "A Test for Tokyo." *New York Times*, December 3, 1941, 1.

84. Garnett D. Horner, "U.S. Asks Japan to Explain Troop Moves: Prompt Reply Is Requested By President," *Washington Evening Star*, December 2, 1941, A1.

85. Franklin Delano Roosevelt Presidential Library and Museum, "FDR: Day by Day—The Pare Lorentz Chronology," December 1, 1941.

86. Frank L. Kluckhohn, "Japan Sees Hull." *New York Times*, December 2, 1941, 1.

87. Associated Press, "Roosevelt, Stark Confer Knox Says Fleet Is Ready Tokyo Continues Talks," *Hartford Courant*, December 2, 1941, 1.

88. Associated Press, "F.D.R. Calls Navy Aide in Asia Crisis," *Los Angeles Times*, December 2, 1941, 1.

89. Constantine Brown, "This Changing World," *Washington Evening Star*, December 2, 1941, A9.

90. Garnett D. Horner, "U.S. Asks Japan to Explain Troop Moves: Prompt Reply Is Requested By President," *Washington Evening Star*, December 2, 1941, A1.

91. Associated Press, "Battleship Leads British Flotilla into Singapore," *Washington Evening Star*, December 2, 1941, 1X.

92. Associated Press, "Battleship Leads British Flotilla into Singapore," *Washington Evening Star*, December 2, 1941, 1X.

93. Associated Press, "Japanese Are Not Told," *New York Times*, December 4, 1941, 4.

94. Associated Press, "All Marines Out of Shanghai; Will Remain in Philippines," *Washington Evening Star*, December 2, 1941, 1X.

95. Garnett D. Horner, "U.S. Asks Japan to Explain Troop Moves: Prompt Reply Is Requested By President," *Washington Evening Star*, December 2, 1941, A1.

96. Royal Arch Gunnison, "Philippines Maintain Ceaseless 'War Alert' Against Japanese," *Washington Evening Star*, December 2, 1941, A3.

97. Associated Press, "Just Like '76, Tokyo Says," *Baltimore Sun*, December 2, 1941, 2.

98. Associated Press, "U.S. Revenue Collections Only Third of Spending," *Washington Evening Star*, December 2, 1941, 1X.

99. *Washington Evening Star*, "Knox Plan to Change Navy Cafeteria Setup Brings Controversy," December 2, 1941, 2X.

100. *Washington Evening Star*, "Knox Plan to Change Navy Cafeteria Setup Brings Controversy," December 2, 1941, 2X.

101. The White House, Washington, "Memorandum for the President" by J.R. Beardal, December 6, 1941, Franklin Delano Roosevelt Presidential Library and Museum, Hyde Park, NY.

102. Franklin Delano Roosevelt Presidential Library and Museum, "Memorandum on Poles in U.S.S.R.," December 6, 1941, Hyde Park, NY.

103. Associated Press, "Navy Is Ready for Anything, Knox Asserts," *Atlanta Constitution*, December 2, 1941, 1.

104. *Atlanta Constitution*, "Patrolling the Sea," December 2, 1941, 1.

105. *Washington Evening Star*, "Exit From the Ark Royal," December 2, 1941, A1.

106. Associated Press, "Cruiser May Have Been Sunk By Pocket Battleship," *Washington Evening Star*, December 2, 1941, A3.

107. Associated Press, "48 Merchant Vessels, 11 Naval Craft Sunk in Month, Nazis Say," *Washington Evening Star*, December 2, 1941, A6.

108. Associated Press, "Baltimore Yards Will Launch Six Ships This Month," *Washington Post*, December 2, 1941, 8.

109. Walter Lippmann, "Today and Tomorrow: The Turning Point at Home," *Los Angeles Times*, December 2, 1941, 4.

110. *Washington Post*, "House Asked to Have Pegler Explain Epithets," December 2, 1941, 6.

111. Matthew Frye Jacobson and Gaspar González, *What Have They Built You To Do? The Manchurian Candidate and Cold War America* (Minneapolis, MN: University of Minnesota Press, 2006), 6.

112. Kenneth Goff, *Red Betrayal of Youth* (Enterprise Print, 1946), 29.

113. *Washington Post*, "Parking Fee Control Here Is Proposed," December 2, 1941, 13.

114. Dewey L. Fleming, "One Hostile Tokyo Act May Mean Conflict at Once, Washington Hears," *Baltimore Sun*, December 2, 1941, 1.

115. Franklin Delano Roosevelt Presidential Library and Museum, "FDR: Day by Day—The Pare Lorentz Chronology," December 1, 1941.

116. David Lawrence, "Formula Yet May Save Pacific Peace," *Washington Evening Star*, December 2, 1941, A9.

CHAPTER 3: THE THIRD OF DECEMBER

1. *Washington Evening Star*, "Bureaucrats Blamed for Blocking Plans for Army of Jews," December 3, 1941, A4.

2. John Barry, "War Diary (823d Day—Dec. 3, 1941)," *Boston Evening Globe*, December 3, 1941, 2.

3. *Boston Evening Globe*, "New Zealanders Await With Bayonets," December 3, 1941, 2.

4. John C. Henry, "Roosevelt Pledges Lease-Lend Defense Supplies to Turkey: Move Is Viewed As U.S. Attempts to Thwart Axis," *Washington Evening Star*, December 3, 1941, A1.

5. *Washington Evening Star*, "Aid-to-Russia Policy Stands, White House Replies to Critics," December 3, 1941, A5.

6. *New York Times*, "India Is Reported Getting U.S. Aid," December 3, 1941, 11.

7. Associated Press, "America First Reveals Plan for Role in 1942 Elections," *Baltimore Sun*, December 2, 1941, 9.

8. *New York Times*, "Murrow Sees End of War in Our Hands," December 3, 1941, 9.

9. British Embassy, Washington, D. C., Memo to The Honorable Franklin D. Roosevelt President of the United States of America, December 3, 1941, Franklin Delano Roosevelt Presidential Library and Museum, Hyde Park, NY.

10. H. Ford Wilkins, "Quezon Avows His Loyalty to Roosevelt," *Washington Post*, December 2, 1941, 24.

11. Associated Press, "New U.S. Arctic Base in Far North Atlantic to Check Nazis Asked," *Birmingham (AL) News*, December 3, 1941, 2.

12. Associated Press, "Germans Driven 12 to 24 Miles, Russians Claim," *Washington Evening Star*, December 3, 1941, 1X.

13. Associated Press, "Nazis Threaten Moscow Anew; Rout From Rostov Continues," *Atlanta Constitution*, December 3, 1941, 11.

14. Associated Press, "British Re-form Lines for New Battle in Libya," *Birmingham (AL) News*, December 3, 1941, 1.

15. Edward Kennedy, Associated Press, "British in Libya Established on Strong Offensive Line," *Washington Evening Star*, December 3, 1941, 2X.

16. *Washington Evening Star*, "Examples Are Cited," December 3, 1941, A6.

17. United Press, "Hull Pessimistic About Far East," *Boston Evening Globe*, December 3, 1941, 1.

18. *Washington Evening Star*, "Wheeler Criticizes Policy," December 3, 1941, A6.

19. *Christian Science Monitor*, "The Isolationists Put on a Show," September 10, 1941, 24.

20. Associated Press, "Lewis Indorses Sen. Wheeler For Presidency," *Washington Post*, July 3, 1940, 3.

21. Associated Press, "All Thumbs Real or In Films," *Washington Evening Star*, December 3, 1941, A15.

22. Dorothy Thompson, "On the Record: America First Committee's Attitude Called Hindrance to U.S. in Japanese Negotiations," *Washington Evening Star*, December 3, 1941, A11.

23. J.A. O'Leary, "Far-Reaching Measure Passed 252 to 136," *Washington Evening Star*, December 3, 1941, A1.

24. *San Francisco Chronicle*, "State Farmers: Laws to Curb Sabotage of Defense Program Urged," December 3, 1941, 9.

25. George Gallup, "Big Majority Would Forbid All Defense Strikes By Law," *Tucson (AZ) Daily Citizen*, December 3, 1941, 5.

26. Associated Press, "NLRB Benefits Denied Unions With Bundists, Reds in House Move," *Birmingham (AL) News*, December 3, 1941, 1.

27. Editorial, "Where There Is No 'Right to Strike,'" *Los Angeles Times*, December 3, 1941, 4.

28. Associated Press, "20 C.I.O. Aides Cited as Having Police Records," *Washington Post*, December 3, 1941, 1.

29. *New York Times*, "Red Activities Laid to City Students; Coudert Committee Sees Real 'Peril,'" December 3, 1941, 1.

30. Dale Harrison, "Everybody's New York," *Birmingham (AL) News*, December 3, 1941, 9.

31. *New York Times*, "Dentistry to Cut Army Rejections," December 2, 1941, 18.

32. *Hartford Courant*, "5 Negroes Among 197 Given Tests," December 2, 1941, 5.

33. *Portsmouth (NH) Herald*, "30 to Take Selective Service Exam Tomorrow," December 2, 1941, 1.

34. *Atlanta Constitution*, "State Receives Draft Order for 707 More Men," December 3, 1941, 24.

35. *Atlanta Constitution*, "Alleged Draft Evader Pleads for Chance 'To Serve Country,'" December 3, 1941, 24.

36. Associated Press, "Draft-Age Mexicans Need Entry Permits," *Washington Evening Star*, December 3, 1941, A16.

37. *Atlanta Constitution*, "Defense Program Causes Rush for Birth Certificates," December 3, 1941, 5.

38. Frank Bristol, "Globe Exclusive: Nazis Train Mexican Youth for 'Foreign Legion' Service," *Boston Daily Globe*, December 3, 1941, 24.

39. Dale Harrison, "Everybody's New York," *Birmingham (AL) News*, December 3, 1941, 9.

40. Tom Treanor, "The Home Front," *Los Angeles Times*, December 3, 1941, 1A.

41. *San Francisco Chronicle*, "Inland Shipyard: Denver to Share Work," December 3, 1941, 5.

42. Associated Press, "Prison Labor Shares in Wage Bonuses," *Christian Science Monitor*, December 3, 1941, 3.

43. Blair Bolles, "$5,503 Fee for Arms Contracts Totaling $16,572 Revealed," *Washington Evening Star*, December 3, 1941, 1X.

44. *Washington Evening Star*, "560 Are Disqualified for Federal Jobs by Loyalty Tests," December 3, 1941, A1.

45. Associated Press, "Pacifist Duke of Bedford Takes Seat With Lords," *Washington Evening Star*, December 3, 1941, A1.

46. Associated Press, "Lady Astor Charges Churchill Draft of Women Is Too Weak," *Washington Evening Star*, December 3, 1941, 1X.

47. *Atlanta Constitution*, "Poll Reveals Britain Approves Defense Conscription of Women," December 3, 1941, 2.

48. Dan E. Clark II, "Angelenos Vote Against Draft Law for Women," *Los Angeles Times*, December 3, 1941, 9.

49. Dorothy Dix, "Be a Square Shooter and Hold Your Husband," *Boston Daily Globe*, December 3, 1941, 27.

50. *New York Times*, "Japan's Imports Cut 75% by War," December 2, 1941, 6.

51. Associated Press, "Episode Considered Effort to Determine Tokyo's Good Faith," *Atlanta Constitution*, December 3, 1941, 1.

52. Associated Press, "Japan Asked to Explain War Moves," *Los Angeles Times*, December 3, 1941, 1.

53. Associated Press, "F. D. Pushes Tokyo Showdown; Demands Japan State Aims in Indo-China," *Boston Daily Globe*, December 3, 1941, 1.

54. Frank L. Kluckhohn, "A Test for Tokyo," *New York Times*, December 3, 1941, 1.

55. Garnett D. Horner, "Showdown in Pacific Hinges on Tokyo's Reply to U.S.," *Washington Evening Star*, December 3, 1941, 1X.

56. Lloyd Lehrbas, Associated Press, "F.D.R.'s Jap Query May Hurry Nippon to Take Her Choice," *Birmingham (AL) News*, December 3, 1941, 1.

57. Associated Press, "Washington Awaiting Japan's Answer," *Birmingham (AL) News*, December 3, 1941, 8.

58. Frank L. Kluckhohn, "A Test For Tokyo," *New York Times*, December 3, 1941, 1.

59. Frank L. Kluckhohn, "A Test For Tokyo," *New York Times*, December 3, 1941, 1.

60. Dewey L. Fleming, "Roosevelt Asks Tokyo Just What Its Plans Are," *Baltimore Sun*, December 3, 1941, 1.

61. Wilfrid Fleisher, "Japanese Deny Tojo Made 'Purge' Speech," *Washington Post*, December 3, 1941, 2.

62. Claude A. Mahoney, "Situation in Pacific Prompts Naval Speed, Bard Declares," *Washington Evening Star*, December 3, 1941, B24.

63. Associated Press, "Navy Aware of Japanese Naval Power, Bard Says," *Baltimore Sun*, December 3, 1941, 4.

64. Hedley Donovan, "Reply on Troops in Indo-China May Settle Issue of Peace or War," *Washington Post*, December 3, 1941, 1.

65. *Washington Post*, "Tokyo Must Explain Actions," December 3, 1941, 1.

66. Hedley Donovan, "Reply on Troops in Indo-China May Settle Issue of Peace or War," *Washington Post*, December 3, 1941, 1.

67. United Press, "Japan to Exhaust All Peace Avenues; Tokyo Reported Reconsidering Points in Reply to Hull," *Washington Post*, December 3, 1941, 2.

68. Hedley Donovan, "Reply on Troops in Indo-China May Settle Issue of Peace or War," *Washington Post*, December 3, 1941, 1.

69. Lloyd Lehrbas, Associated Press, "F.D.R.'s Jap Query May Hurry Nippon To Take Her Choice," *Birmingham (AL) News*, December 3, 1941, 1.

70. Clark Lee, "Japanese Reported Massing Huge Forces in South Indo-China," *Washington Evening Star*, December 3, 1941, 1X.

71. Office of Naval Intelligence, "Bulletin," December 3, 1941, Franklin Delano Roosevelt Presidential Library and Museum, Hyde Park, NY.

72. Larry Rue, "London Papers See U. S. Action if Japs Attack," *Chicago Daily Tribune*, December 2, 1941, 5.

73. Royal Arch Gunnison, "Dutch Are Reported Pressing British to Move Into Thailand," *Washington Evening Star*, December 3, 1941, A8.

74. Editorial, "Eating His Own Words," *Chicago Daily Tribune*, December 2, 1941, 14.

75. *Chicago Daily Tribune*, "The Tribune's Platform: Save Our Republic," December 2, 1941, 14.

76. Frank L. Kluckhohn, "Japanese See Hull," *New York Times*, December 2, 1941, 1.

77. Associated Press, "U.S. Navy Can Shoot Straight, Connally Warns Japanese," *Washington Evening Star*, December 3, 1941, 2X.

78. *Baltimore Sun*, "Japan Decides to Continue Her Discussions With Us," December 2, 1941, 12.

79. *Atlanta Constitution*, "War Imminent in Vast Orient," December 3, 1941, 11.

80. *New York Times*, "Saks Fifth Avenue," December 2, 1941, 11.

81. Associated Press, "Soldiers Are Polled on Gift Desires, and Money Leads," *Washington Evening Star*, December 3, 1941, A6.

82. *New York Times*, "Tell Macy's Where He Is," December 3, 1941, 9.

83. *Washington Evening Star*, "George's Radio Co.," December 3, 1941, A16.

84. *Washington Evening Star*, "Radio Program, Wednesday, December 3, 1941," December 3, 1941, B22.

85. *Atlanta Constitution*, "Next Friday Night Will Be 'Shirley Temple Time,'" December 3, 1941, 21.

86. *Washington Evening Star*, "Coal: High Quality—Low Prices," December 3, 1941, B24.

87. *Washington Evening Star*, "Furloughs Forecast Record Travel for Holiday Season," December 3, 1941, A7.

88. *Atlanta Constitution*, "Camel," December 3, 1941, 11.

89. Ralph McGill, "Soldier Stretches 10-Day Pass Into 22 Years, But Comes Back," *Atlanta Constitution*, December 3, 1941, 1.

90. *Baltimore Sun*, "U.S. $5 Auto Tax May Be Repealed," December 2, 1941, 13.

91. Associated Press, "Taxes Have Reached Near-Peak Levels, Senator George Says," *Washington Evening Star*, December 3, 1941, A2.

92. *Washington Post*, "Treasury Spends $3 for Every $1 Revenue," December 3, 1941, 29.

93. Associated Press, "Senators Discuss Special Treatment for Small Firms," *Washington Evening Star*, December 3, 1941, A3.

94. Walter W. Ruch, "Says Reich's Debt Is Near 18 Total," *New York Times*, December 3, 1941, 7.

95. Associated Press, "U.S. Purchases Chile's Secondary Metal Output," *Washington Evening Star*, December 3, 1941, A4.

96. Associated Press, "Use Statues for Bullets, Congressman Proposes," *Atlanta Constitution*, December 3, 1941, 7.

97. *Chicago Daily Tribune*, "U. S. Lets Huge Aluminum Pile Go to Waste," December 2, 1941, 1.

98. Stephen Trumbull, "Puerto Rico Called U. S. Headache," *Hartford Daily Courant*, December 3, 1941, 9.

99. Stephen Trumbull, "Poverty and Disease Make Puerto Rico Problem for Army," *Washington Evening Star*, December 3, 1941, A5.

100. E.M. Castro, "U.S. Navy Is on Patrol Duty as Brazil Bolsters Defenses," *Washington Evening Star*, December 3, 1941, B6.

101. *Los Angeles Times*, "Irish Expect Attacks at Sea," December 3, 1941, 7.

102. *Los Angeles Times*, "Axis Planes Stranded Liner," December 3, 1941, 7.

103. *Washington Evening Star*, "Decrease in Atlantic Sinking 'Good Story' Knox Tells Press," December 3, 1941, A3.

104. *Los Angeles Times*, "America Turning Out Ship a Day," December 3, 1941, 9.

105. United Press, "Warships Launched Daily by the Navy," *New York Times*, December 3, 1941, 1.

106. *Los Angeles Times*, "Shipping News," December 3, 1941, 26.

107. *Los Angeles Times*, "Air Mail Schedule," December 3, 1941, 26.

108. Judson Bailey, Associated Press, "Mel Ott Named Playing Manager of Giants, Succeeding Terry; Bill 'Promoted' Into General Manager Role," *Atlanta Constitution*, December 3, 1941, 16.

109. Associated Press, "Boudreau Picks Aides," *Atlanta Constitution*, December 3, 1941, 16.

110. Ron Kaplan, "From Pike to Hirsch: Jews on First (and Second, and . . .)," *Jewish News*, December 21, 2006, 10.

111. Jack Troy, "All in the Game," *Atlanta Constitution*, December 2, 1941, 17.

112. Associated Press, "Griffith Joins Nats," *Atlanta Constitution*, December 3, 1941, 16.

113. Associated Press, "Morris Brown Can Win Negro Title Saturday," *Atlanta Constitution*, December 3, 1941, 17.

114. *Los Angeles Times*, "Slave's Son, 100, to Wed," December 3, 1941, A1.

115. *Washington Evening Star*, "Airport Coffee Shop Refuses to Serve Colored Quartet," December 3, 1941, A6.

116. Associated Press, "Jury Convicts Ex-Warden in Negro's Death," *Atlanta Constitution*, December 3, 1941, 1.

117. Associated Press, "Georgia Negro Troops Seize Tampa Air Field in Blackout," *Atlanta Constitution*, December 3, 1941, 7.

118. Otto D. Tolischus, "Japan Still Says U.S. Must Give In," *New York Times*, December 3, 1941, 4.

119. Associated Press, "Nazi Peace Move Seen," *New York Times*, December 3, 1941, 4.

CHAPTER 4: THE FOURTH OF DECEMBER

1. Franklin Delano Roosevelt Presidential Library and Museum, "Japanese Intelligence and

Propaganda in the United States During 1941," December 4, 1941, Hyde Park, NY.

2. Franklin Delano Roosevelt Presidential Library and Museum, "Japanese Intelligence and Propaganda in the United States During 1941," December 4, 1941, Hyde Park, NY.

3. *Washington Evening Star*, "Randolph Protests Moving U.S. Bureaus to Crowded Cities," December 4, 1941, A-2. United Press, "Jap Evacuates Ship Sails After Mail Is Ordered Taken Off," *Tucson (AZ) Daily Citizen*, December 3, 1941, 2.

4. *Washington Evening Star*, "Leaders to Tell Plans for War Office Roads," December 4, 1941, B1.

5. Associated Press, "Army Plans to Add 38,728 Acres to Site of Hill Reservation," *Washington Evening Star*, December 4, 1941, B13.

6. *Washington Evening Star*, "Fingerprints to Be Required of Many D.C. Licensees," December 4, 1941, 1X.

7. *Washington Evening Star*, "Defense Units Study Means to Protect Girls Hired by U.S.," December 3, 1941, A2.

8. *Washington Evening Star*, "Roomers in 'A' Zones," December 5, 1941, A-12. *Washington* 1941, B1.

9. *Washington Evening Star*, "Defense Units Study Means to Protect Girls Hired by U.S.," December 3, 1941, A2.

10. Wyona Daswood, "To Change the Subject: The Other Side of the Picture," *Christian Science Monitor*, December 6, 1941, 13.

11. *Washington Post*, "D.C. Rent Czar Will Be Chosen By Weekend," December 3, 1941, 3.

12. *Washington Post*, "Bundles for U.S. Bluejackets to Warm Them on Patrol," December 3, 1941, 9.

13. *Washington Post*, "Government Girl, 19 Years Old, Reported Missing," December 3, 1941, 1.

14. *Washington Post*, "Capitol's First Woman Air Raid Warden Enrolled," December 3, 1941, 21.

15. *Birmingham (AL) News*, "No Man's Land: Lulu Tells Betty What's Going On in Washington," December 7, 1941, B1.

16. *Washington Post*, "2,000 Cars of Troops Move Through Capital," December 4, 1941, A3.

17. Associated Press, "Slow Drivers' War Continues," *Los Angeles Times*, December 4, 1941. I16.

18. *Washington Evening Star*, "Densest Fog in Years Hits Traffic in D.C., East and Midwest," December 4, 1941, A8.

19. *Boston Globe*, "The War's to Blame as Banshee Wails Rend Boston's Fog," December 4, 1941.

20. *Washington Evening Star*, "Senator Complains Uniform Is 'Unwelcome' in District," December 4, 1941, 2X.

21. *Washington Evening Star*, "Randolph Says He Won't Drop Suffrage Fight," December 4, 1941, B12.

22. *Washington Evening Star*, "If You Have Cold Stay Home, Say Health Chiefs," December 4, 1941, B18.

23. Associated Press, "Industrialists Urge Ban on Antidefense Strikes," *Los Angeles Times*, December 4, 1941, A1.

24. Franklin R. Kent, "The Great Game of Politics," *Los Angeles Times*, December 4, 1941, B1.

25. Associated Press, "Ford Making Munitions, but He Still Hates War," *Los Angeles Times*, December 4, 1941, 7.

26. *Washington Post*, "Men Trailer Redcaps to Check Upon Their Tips Hearing Told," December 3, 1941, 11.

27. *Washington Post*, "Air Attaché and Mrs. Kenny Honored at Informal Party Given by Canadian Minister," December 4, 1941, B3.

28. *Washington Post*, "Nelson Rockefellers Are Dinner Hosts," December 4, 1941, B3.

29. Hope Ridings Miller, "Capital Whirl," *Washington Post*, December 3, 1941, 19.

30. *Washington Evening Star*, "Army Orders," December 3, 1941, B15.

31. *Washington Evening Star*, "Radio Program; Short-Wave Programs," December 4, 1941, D8.

32. Devon Francis, "Plant Is Dedicated as 'Breeding Nest' for Dive Bombers," *Evening Star*, December 4, 1941, A2

33. *New York Times*, "War Victims to Be Aided," December 3, 1941, 11.

34. *New York Times*, "President of Cuba Asks Extra Powers," December 3, 1941, 11.

35. *New York Times*, "Argentina Seeking to Thaw U.S. Credits," December 3, 1941, 11.

36. K.W.B. Middleton, *Britain and Russia*, England, U. K., Hutchinson, 1947, 177.

37. Royal Arch Cunnison, "'War Alert': The Entire Far East Is on a War Footing—The Next Move Is Up to Japan," *San Francisco Chronicle*, December 3, 1941, 3.

38. Daniel T. Brightham, "Russians Smash to Taganrog; Turks Get Lease-Lend Help; Hull Not Hopeful on Japan," *New York Times*, December 4, 1941, 1.

39. H. O. Thompson, Associated Press, "Solon Predicts Pincer Move By French and Japs," *Idaho Evening Times*, December 3, 1941, 1.

40. H. O. Thompson, Associated Press, "Solon Predicts Pincer Move By French and Japs," *Idaho Evening Times*, December 3, 1941, 1.

41. Jay G. Hayden, "Peace Means Revolution for Japan," *Washington Evening Star*, December 4, 1941, A13.

42. Jay G. Hayden, "Peace Means Revolution for Japan," *Washington Evening Star*, December 4, 1941, A13.

43. Associated Press, "Envoys Deliver Note Contents Undisclosed; Sees Chief of Army," *Washington Evening Star*, December 5, 1X.

44. Associated Press, "Japanese Diplomats in Mexico Speed Up Plans to Go Home," *Washington Evening Star*, December 4, 1941, A1.

45. Associated Press, "Tokio Agency Calls Hull Plan Unacceptable," *Washington Evening Star*, December 4, 1941, A1.

46. National Geographic Society, "Where Are They Fighting," *Washington Evening Star*, December 4, 1941, A19.

47. Associated Press, "Tokio Agency Calls Hull Plan Unacceptable," *Washington Evening Star*, December 4, 1941, A1.

48. United Press, "Collapse of Pacific Parleys Expected," *Los Angeles Times*, December 4, 1941, 1.

49. *Washington Evening Star*, "Japan's Intentions," December 4, 1941, A12.

50. *Washington Evening Star*, "Japan's Intentions," December 4, 1941, A12.

51. Associated Press, "Roosevelt Sees Congress Chiefs on Far East," *Washington Evening Star*, December 4, 1941, 1X.

52. INS News Agency, "Hopes of Japanese-American Agreement Fading Hourly: Secretary Hull Is Pessimistic on Main Issues," *Atlanta Constitution*, December 4, 1941, 15.

53. Associated Press, "Germans Are Caustic on U.S. Extending Aid to Turkey," *Washington Evening Star*, December 4, 1941, A3.

54. Associated Press, "Germans Are Caustic On U.S. Extending Aid to Turkey," *Washington Evening Star*, December 4, 1941, A3.

55. Associated Press, "Sees Japan Joining U.S.," *New York Times*, December 4, 1941, 5.

56. Associated Press, "Japan's Privy Council Discusses Crisis at 2-Hour Meeting," *Washington Evening Star*, December 4, 1941, A2.

57. INS News Agency, "Hopes of Japanese-American Agreement Fading Hourly; Secretary Hull Is Pessimistic on Main Issues," December 4, 1941, 15.

58. Associated Press, "Tokyo Reply Awaited in Washington," *The Hartford Courant*, December 4, 1941, 1.

59. Royal Arch Gunnison, "Fleet at Singapore to Curb Japanese and Halt Nazi Raids," *Washington Evening Star*, December 4, 1941, A9.

60. Associated Press, "Australian Cruiser Sunk After Destroying Raider," *Daily Boston Globe*, December 3, 1941, 16.

61. Associated Press, "Reuben James Survivor Wants to Get Back to Sea," *Washington Evening Star*, December 4, 1941, A7.

62. Associated Press, "U.S. Would Take Cash for Sinking," *Tucson Daily Citizen*, November 3, 1941, 1.

63. Associated Press, "Article 3," *New York Times*, December 4, 1941, 11.

64. Associated Press, "German Parachutist Arrested in Dublin," *Washington Evening Star*, December 4, 1941, A4.

65. Associated Press, "Nephew of Churchill, Canadian War Pilot, Missing in Action," *Washington Evening Star*, December 4, 1941, A6.
66. *Washington Post*, "Navy Launching a Ship a Day," December 3, 1941, 8.
67. Chicago Tribune Press Service, "U.S. Navy Bares 'Possible' Hit in Battling U-Boat," December 5, 1941, 5.
68. Associated Press, "Sub Apparently Was Damaged, Navy Is Told," *Washington Evening Star*, December 4, 1941, A1.
69. *Los Angeles Times*, "Japan Sends Ships to Indo-China Base," December 5, 1941, 6.
70. United Press, "Japan to Exhaust All Peace Avenues," *Washington Post*, December 3, 1941, 2.
71. *Washington Evening Star*, "Speedup in Delivery of Liberty Ships Sought," December 4, 1941, A5.
72. Associated Press, "Three Axis Divisions Are Locked in Battle With Serb Guerillas," *Washington Evening Star*, December 4, 1941, 1X.
73. United Press, "Siege of Belgrade By Serbs Reported; Ankara," *New York Times*, December 3, 1941, 7.
74. Associated Press, "36 Nazi Prisoners Killed as German Plane Bombs Them," *Daily Boston Globe*, December 4, 1941, 23.
75. Associated Press, "189 More Firms Put on U.S. Blacklist," *Washington Evening Star*, December 4, 1941, 1X.
76. Associated Press, "189 More Firms Put on U.S. Blacklist," *Washington Evening Star*, December 4, 1941, 1X.
77. Associated Press, "189 More Firms Put on U.S. Blacklist," *Washington Evening Star*, December 4, 1941, 1X.
78. Associated Press, "Nazis Set Deadline for Surrender of French Terrorists," *Washington Evening Star*, December 4, 1941, A18.
79. Associated Press, "Nazis Set Deadline for Surrender of French Terrorists," *Washington Evening Star*, December 4, 1941, A18.
80. United Press, "Inquiry Turns to Remington," *Telegraph-Herald*, December 5, 1941, 11.
81. Associated Press, "Workers at Bell Warplane Plants Vote to Strike," *Daily Boston Globe*, December 1, 1941, 8.
82. *Atlanta Constitution*, "Nobody Can Argue With a Paid Check," December, 4, 1941, 5.
83. *Atlanta Constitution*, "Nobody Can Argue With a Paid Check," December, 4, 1941, 5.
84. Chesly Manly, "F.D.R.'s War Plans," *Chicago Daily Tribune*, December 4, 1941, 1.
85. *Washington Evening Star*, "Source of War Plans Story to Be Probed, Early Says," December 4, 1941, A2.
86. *Washington Evening Star*, "Source of War Plans Story to Be Probed, Early Says," December 4, 1941, A2.
87. Associated Press, "Roosevelt Sees Congress Chiefs on Far East," *Evening Star*, December 4, 1941, 1X.
88. *Washington Evening Star*, "Source of War Plans Story to Be Probed, Early Says," December 4, 1941, A2.
89. E *Washington Evening Star*, "Source of War Plans Story to Be Probed, Early Says," December 4, 1941, A2.
90. *Washington Evening Star*, "Source of War Plans Story to Be Probed, Early Says," December 4, 1941, A2.
91. Dorothy Thompson, "America-Firsters Japan's Ace in Hole, Thompson Charges," *Atlanta Constitution*, December 4, 1941, 1.
92. *Washington Evening Star*, "Give Sports the Lasting Gift," December 4, 1941, A4.
93. *Washington Evening Star*, "Her Husband Was a Stranger," December 4, 1941, B13.
94. *Washington Evening Star*, "Roger Smith Hotel," December 4, 1941, B14.
95. *Washington Evening Star*, "The Pall Mall Room," December 4, 1941, B14.
96. *Washington Evening Star*, "Cocktails—Dancing—Entertainment," December 4, 1941, B14.

97. Associated Press, "Juke Box Mardi Gras Hits Carolina Towns as 29th Says Adieu," *Washington Evening Star*, December 4, 1941 B16.

98. "For Maximum Defense Economy, The New 1942 Crossley," December 4, 1941, A20.

99. *Washington Post*, "Tops For Breakfast; These Cool Mornings," December 2, 1941, 7.

100. *Daily Boston Globe*, "Baldness Can Be Prevented," December 4, 1941, 5.

101. *Boston Evening Globe*, "Wake Up Clearheaded," December 4, 1941, 6.

102. Associated Press, "Baer to Be Welcomed Back to Native State," *Sarasota Herald-Tribune*, December 4, 1941, 7.

103. *Atlanta Constitution*, "Dickens 'The Life of Our Lord' Will Appear in Constitution," December 4, 1941, 1.

104. Associated Press, "Anti-Nazi Offices Raided," *Washington Evening Star*, December 4, 1941, A6.

105. Associated Press, "Moore Draws $500 Fine for Striking Auld," *Atlanta Constitution*, December 4, 1941, 3.

106. *Los Angeles Times*, "Car Hop Shoots Herself; Draft Feared for Boy Friend," December 4, 1941, 4.

107. *Daily Boston Globe*, "Our Army," December 4, 1941, 12.

108. *Daily Boston Globe*, "OK if Mistaken for Southerners,' Says Y-D Officer," December 4, 1941, 13.

109. *Los Angeles Times*, "U.S. Not 'Bluffing' LaGuardia Says," December 4, 1941, 16.

110. *Daily Boston Globe*, "U.S. Sub Halibut Launched at Yard in Portsmouth," December 4, 1941, 16.

111. Associated Press, "Output of 50,000 Planes for 1942 Now Held Likely," *Boston Evening Globe*, December 4, 1941, 5.

112. Frederick R. Barkley, "New Defense Bill Brings Total Near 68 Billions," *New York Times*, December 4, 1941, 1.

113. Associated Press, "Troops for Air Raid Defense Maneuvers to Arrive Today," *Los Angeles Times*, December 4, 1941, 6.

114. Associated Press, "Troops for Air Raid Defense Maneuvers to Arrive Today," *Los Angeles Times*, December 4, 1941, 6.

115. Celestine Sibley, "1941 World's Champion Typist Shows Atlanta How It's Done," *Atlanta Constitution*, December 4, 1941, 4.

116. *Atlanta Constitution*, "Auto Takes Dip," December 4, 1941, 30.

117. *Los Angeles Times*, "Down the Decades with Los Angeles," December 4, 1941, 22.

118. *Los Angeles Times*, "Down the Decades with Los Angeles," December 4, 1941, 22.

119. *Los Angeles Times*, "Down the Decades with Los Angeles," December 4, 1941, 22.

120. Associated Press, "Too Much Radio Grounds for Divorce," *Los Angeles Times*, December 4, 1941.

121. *New York Times*, "The Siege of Japan," December 4, 1941, 24.

122. *New York Times*, "The Siege of Japan," December 4, 1941, 24.

123. Dewey L. Fleming, "U.S. and England Ready for Blockade of Japan if Tokyo Provokes War," *Baltimore Sun*, December 4, 1941, 1.

124. *Atlanta Constitution*, "Mrs. Roosevelt Speaks on 'Town Meeting' Show," December 4, 1941, 27.

125. Associated Press, "Mrs. Roosevelt Assures Fairness to Aliens," *Evening Star*, December, 4, 1941, A18.

CHAPTER 5: THE FIFTH OF DECEMBER

1. Thomas R. Henry, "Of Stars, Men and Atoms," *Washington Evening Star*, December 4, 1941, A12.

2. Frank Carey, "British and Nazi Astronomers Exchange Views Despite War," *Birmingham (AL) News*, December 8, 1941, 4.

3. Associated Press, "Amateur Operator Develops New Radio Which Quiets Static," *Washington Evening Star*, December 4, 1941, B18.

4. Associated Press, "Boom in Plastics Industry May Avert Post-War Slump," *Washington Evening Star*, December 4, 1941, B19.

5. *Washington Evening Star*, "Wild Hedges Found Rich in Vitamins," December 5, 1941, A5.

6. Thomas R. Henry, "Of Stars, Men And Atoms," December 6, 1941, A10.

7. *New York Times*, "Powerful New Gun Developed By U.S.," December 4, 1941, 13.

8. Associated Press, "70-Ton Flying Boat Catches Fire During Tests at Baltimore," *Washington Evening Star*, December 5, 1941, A1.

9. *Washington Evening Star*, "Rain Here Last Night Totaled More Than in All of November," December 5, 1941, 1X.

10. *Atlanta Constitution*, "Sanitary Precautions Seen as Major Factor in Prolonging Life," December 5, 1941, 3A.

11. George Gallup, "Gallup Poll Reveals: U. S. Public Is Food Conscious," *Atlanta Constitution*, December 5, 1941, 7A.

12. Uncle Dudley, "Why Thailand?" *Boston Daily Globe*, December 4, 1941, 18.

13. Pertinax, "Vichy Assent Hinted In Japanese Move into Indo-China," *Washington Evening Star*, December 5, 1941, A6.

14. Walter Lippmann, "U. S. Declared to Be on Verge of All-Out War," *Boston Daily Globe*, December 4, 1941, 18.

15. *Baltimore Sun*, "Realities in the Pacific as Mr. Hull Loses Hope," December 5, 1941, 16.

16. F. Tillman Durdin, "Singapore Doubts Japanese Threats," *New York Times*, December 4, 1941, 5.

17. Associated Press, "Russians Admit Nazi Big Guns Shell Moscow," *Washington Evening Star*, December 5, 1941, A1.

18. Associated Press, "Red Drive Futile Germans Insist," *New York Times*, December 6, 1941, 5.

19. Associated Press, "British Repulse 3 Axis Attacks Near Tobruk," *Washington Evening Star*, December 5, 1941, 1X.

20. Associated Press, "Pepper and McNary Clash Over Defense Support," *Washington Evening Star*, December 5, 1941, A5.

21. *Washington Evening Star*, "Representative Fish Testifies Before Jury Probing Propaganda," December 5, 1941, 1X.

22. *Washington Evening Star*, "Stimson Denounces Publication of Story on U.S. 'War Plans,'" December 5, 1941, 1X.

23. Associated Press, "Nipponese Army Reported in Skirmish With Reds on Border," *Washington Evening Star*, December 5, 1941, 1X.

24. Associated Press, "Night Clubs Bar Uniformed Men, Senator and General Charge," *Washington Evening Star*, December 5, 1941, 2X.

25. *Washington Evening Star*, "On Week-End Leave?" December 5, 1941, A17.

26. *Washington Post*, "Yule Spirit to Greet Service Men," December 6, 1941, 18.

27. *Washington Evening Star*, "On Week-End Leave?" December 5, 1941, A17.

28. *Washington Evening Star*, "On Weekend Leave?" December 5, 1941, A16; *Washington Post*, "Clubs Offering Fun for Service Men," December 6, 1941, 18.

29. Associated Press, "Army Plans to Train 10,000 Bombardiers Within Next Year," *Washington Evening Star*, December 5, 1941, A2.

30. *Washington Post*, "War Department Building Takes Shape," December 4, 1941, 14; *Washington Evening Star*, December 5, 1941, A3.

31. Associated Press, "Export Violation Case Indictment," *Christian Science Monitor*, December 5, 1941, 9.

32. Associated Press, "South American Presidents May Meet on War," *Washington Evening Star*, December 5, 1941, A1.

33. *Washington Evening Star*, "Restricted Covenants in Land Sales Upheld," December 5, 1941, 2X.

34. Associated Press, "Court in New Jersey Reverses Bund Case, Voids Race Hatred Law," *Washington Evening Star*, December 5, 1941, A2.

35. Associated Press, "Bergdoll Is Denied Parole for Christmas Homecoming," *Washington Evening Star*, December 5, 1941, A1.

36. Associated Press, "Americans in France to Broadcast to U.S.," *Washington Evening Star*, December 5, 1941, A1.

37. Associated Press, "German Major Wounded in New Paris Attack," *Washington Evening Star*, December 5, 1941, 1X.

38. Associated Press, "Serb Flanking Movements Against Nazis, Reported," *Washington Evening Star*, December 5, 1941, 1X.

39. Overseas News Agency, "King Michael Reported Nazi Prisoner as Plot Leader," *Boston Daily Globe*, December 5, 1941, 1.

40. Associated Press, "'V' Army Ordered to Become Active," *Washington Evening Star*, December 5, 1941, A1.

41. *Washington Evening Star*, "Far East Reported Preparing for Early U.S. Tokyo Break," December 5, 1941, 1X.

42. *Washington Post*, "President's Day," December 6, 1941, 2.

43. *Washington Post*, "President's Day," December 6, 1941, 2.

44. John C. Henry, "Reply to U.S. Cites Vichy's O.K. on Army," *Washington Evening Star*, December 5, 1941, A1.

45. John C. Henry, "Reply to U.S. Cites Vichy's O.K. on Army," *Washington Evening Star*, December 5, 1941, A1.

46. *Washington Evening Star*, "Far East Reported Preparing for Early U.S. Tokyo Break," December 5, 1941, 1X.

47. Associated Press, "Nipponese Army Reported in Skirmish With Reds on Border," *Washington Evening Star*, December 5, 1941, 1X.

48. Associated Press, "Nipponese Army Reported in Skirmish With Reds on Border," *Washington Evening Star*, December 5, 1941, 1X.

49. Associated Press, "Japan 'Cannot Accept' Terms, Tokyo Is Told," *Atlanta Constitution*, December 5, 1941, 1A.

50. Associated Press, "Tokyo Hedges on War; Britain in New Warning," *Christian Science Monitor*, December 5, 1941, 1.

51. Associated Press, "Japan 'Cannot Accept' Terms, Tokyo Is Told," *Atlanta Constitution*, December 5, 1941, 1A.

52. *Boston Daily Globe*, "Hull Under Fire in Japan for Baring U. S. Terms," December 5, 1941, 1.

53. Associated Press, "Nipponese Army Reported in Skirmish With Reds on Border," *Washington Evening Star*, December 5, 1941, 1X.

54. Associated Press, "Alexander Warns Japan Aggression Won't Pay," *Washington Evening Star*, December 5, 1941, A9.

55. Paul Mallon, "News Behind the News," *Birmingham (AL) News*, December 5, 1941, 1.

56. Associated Press, "Faster Draft Rate Expected to Keep Up Strength of Army," *Washington Evening Star*, December 5, 1941, A4.

57. Oliver Wendell Holmes and Richard A. Posner, *The Essential Holmes: Selections From the Letters, Speeches, Judicial Opinions, and Other Writings of Oliver Wendell Holmes, Jr.* (Chicago: University of Chicago Press, 1997), XIV–XV.

58. Jonas Klein, *Beloved Island: Franklin & Eleanor and the Legacy of Campobello* (Forest Dale, VT: Paul S. Eriksson, 2000), 228.

59. *Washington Evening Star*, "Hard to Determine When Subs Are Sunk, President Says," December 5, 1941, A10.

60. Uncle Dudley, "Sea Battle," *Boston Daily Globe*, December 5, 1941, 26.

61. "Bulletin," December 5, 1941, Franklin Delano Roosevelt Presidential Library and Museum, Hyde Park, NY.

62. "Report on Talk With Vincent Astor," December 5, 1941, Franklin Delano Roosevelt Presidential Library and Museum, Hyde Park, NY.

63. *Washington Evening Star*, "Bill Signed to Pay Man $830 for Capitol Injury," December 5, 1941, A14.

64. Frank I. Weller, "Shift From China Cuts Fabulous Pay of U.S. Marines," *Washington Evening Star*, December 5, 1941, C10.

65. *Birmingham (AL) News*, "Americans Itching: To Get After Japs," December 5, 1941, 1.

66. Pertinax, "Vichy Assent Hinted in Japanese Move Into Indo-China," *Washington Evening Star*, December 5, 1941, A6.

67. Constantine Brown, "The Changing World: Diplomats Giving 100-to-1 Odds That War Will Break Out Involving Japan," *Washington Evening Star*, December 5, 1941, A13.

68. Constantine Brown, "The Changing World: Diplomats Giving 100-to-1 Odds That War Will Break Out Involving Japan," *Washington Evening Star*, December 5, 1941, A13.

69. Associated Press, "Karl Decker, Famous War Correspondent, Dies in New York," *Washington Evening Star*, December 5, 1941, A14.

70. Associated Press, "Martin and Landon Plead for Return to Two-Party System," *Washington Evening Star*, December 5, 1941, A18.

71. Associated Press, "Mrs. Roosevelt Buys Bedroom Sleepers For 22 Children," *Washington Evening Star*, December 5, 1941, A18.

72. *Washington Evening Star*, "Activities of Interest to Diplomatic and Official Circles Here," December 5, 1941, B3.

73. Associated Press, "W.C.T.U. Puts Liquor Cost Since Repeal at 50 Billions," *Washington Evening Star*, December 5, 1941, B6.

74. *Washington Evening Star*, "Hershey Milk Chocolate," December 5, 1941, C6; *Washington Evening Star*, "Super Specials: Anacin Tablets," December 5, 1941, C6.

75. Associated Press, "13 Recommendations Made by N.A.M. on Post-War Economy," *Washington Evening Star*, December 5, 1941, A20.

76. Sheilah Graham, "Bruno Walter Defends Playing of Music of German Masters," *Washington Evening Star*, December 5, 1941, B18.

77. Sheilah Graham, "Bruno Walter Defends Playing of Music of German Masters," *Washington Evening Star*, December 5, 1941, B18.

78. *Washington Evening Star*, "U.S. Movies Continue to Hold Popularity in Unconquered Europe," December 5, 1941, C4.

79. Harold Heffernan, "Actresses' Worst Enemy Is Nervous Breakdown," *Washington Evening Star*, December 5, 1941, D5.

80. Eleanor Roosevelt, "My Day: The President's Dog Misses Georgia Visit," *Atlanta Constitution*, December 5, 1941, 8A.

81. United Press, "Sport Just Won't Be Downed by Mere Train or Automobile," *Birmingham (AL) News*, December 5, 1941, 17.

82. Associated Press, "Cat Rescued After 3 Days in Well," *Boston Daily Globe*, December 5, 1941, 14.

83. *Washington Evening Star*, "Radio Program: Friday, December 5, 1941," December 5, 1941, D10.

84. *Atlanta Constitution*, "Shirley Temple Bows Tonight on Radio Hour," December 5, 1941, 7F.

85. Associated Press, "Ten Georgia Colleges Suspended From Southern Accredited List Because of 'Political Interference': Suspension to Take Effect in September," *Atlanta Constitution*, December 5, 1941, 1A.

86. Sam Clarke, "Georgia Farmers Have Folding Money This Holiday Season," *Atlanta Constitution*, December 5, 1941, 7A; United Press, "New Holiday Sales Record Predicted," *Washington Post*, December 5, 1941, 19; Paul Gesner and John Beckley, "Families Are Urged to Readjust Spending to Offset High Prices," *Birmingham (AL) News*, December 5, 1941, 2.

87. *Wall Street Journal*, "Treasury Offering Today $1 Billion 2s, $500 Million 2s; Subscription Rules Tightened to Cut Speculation," December 4, 1941, 8.

88. *Birmingham (AL) News*, "Alabama Power Company: Restriction of Power Use Lifted," December 5, 1941, 3.

89. *Atlanta Constitution*, "Georgia Power Company: Blackout Lifted," December 6, 1941, 7.

90. *Birmingham (AL) News*, "Parisian's Christmas Sale," December 5, 1941, 25.

91. *Boston Daily Globe*, "Rogers Jewelers: 5 Tube Radio," December 5, 1941, 20.

92. *Saturday Evening Post*, "General Electric," December 6, 1941, 7.

93. Associated Press, "Loot From 1852 Mail Robbery Found in Philadelphia Attic," *Washington Evening Star*, December 5, 1941, A2.

94.   *Birmingham (AL) News*, "Americans Itching: To Get After Japs," December 5, 1941, 1.
95.   Editorial, "On All Fronts, Including the American," *Los Angeles Times*, December 5, 1941, A4.
96.   Associated Press, "Tokyo Envoy to Mexico Ordered Home as U.S.-Japan Crisis Grows: Many Others, Fearing War, Plan to Leave," *Baltimore Sun*, December 5, 1941, 1.

CHAPTER 6: THE SIXTH OF DECEMBER

1.   Associated Press, "Feller to Enlist in Service, But hopes To Pitch on Weekends," *Atlanta Constitution*, December 6, 1941, 17.
2.   Associated Press, "Feller Will Reveal His Plans Next Week," *Washington Post*, December 6, 1941, 20.
3.   Walter Winchell, "Walter Winchell on Broadway; Things I Never Knew and Still Dunno," *St. Petersburg (FL) Times*, December 8, 1941, 7.
4.   *Calgary (Alberta Canada) Herald*, "Japs Can't Equal U.S. Naval Power," December 8, 1941, 5.
5.   Naval History and Heritage Command, "Ships Present at Pearl Harbor, 0800 7 December 1941," http://www.history.navy.mil/faqs/faq66-2.htm.
6.   Robert Cressman, *"The Official Chronology of the U.S. Navy in World War II,"* (Annapolis, MD, Naval Institute Press, 2000,) 57.
7.   Robert Cressman, *"The Official Chronology of the U.S. Navy in World War II"* (Annapolis, MD, Naval Institute Press, 2000), 57.
8.   Robert Cressman, *"The Official Chronology of the U.S. Navy in World War II"* (Annapolis, MD, Naval Institute Press, 2000), 59.
9.   John B. Lundstrom, *"The First Team: Pacific Naval Air Combat From Pearl Harbor to Midway"* (Annapolis, MD, Naval Institute Press, 2005), 27.
10.   Marc T. Greene, "U.S. Air Force Grows in Pacific," *Baltimore Sun*, December 7, 1941, 17.
11.   *Washington Evening Star*, "Surrounded by Fog, Stimson Gets a Lift Home," December 7, 1941, A4.
12.   *Christian Science Monitor; Weekly Magazine Section*, "Battle of Fifth Avenue," December 6, 1941, 12.
13.   *Baltimore Sun*, "Hitler & The US; Manifesto By 16 Pastors," December 6, 1941, 11.
14.   Associated Press, "Japanese Accuse U.S. of Trying to 'Pass Buck,'" *Hartford (CT) Courant*, December 6, 1941, 3.
15.   Associated Press, "Japan Justifies Troop Movements into Indo-China," *Hartford (CT) Courant*, December 6, 1941, 1.
16.   Richard L. Strout, "Tokyo Reply Keeps Door Open," *Christian Science Monitor*, December 6, 1941, 1.
17.   *Christian Science Monitor*, "Göttliche Führung," December 6, 1941, 12.
18.   Joseph G. Harrison, "Intimate Message: Washington," *Christian Science Monitor*, December 6, 1941, 13.
19.   Otto D. Tolisch, "Japan Confident Talks Will Go On," *New York Times*, December 6, 1941, 2.
20.   *Los Angeles Times*, "Where Silence Seems Superfluous," December 6, 1941, A4.
21.   Lloyd Lehrbas, "Second Tokio Reply Awaited Here; Peace Talks Are Delayed," *Washington Evening Star*, December 6, 1941, 1X.
22.   Bertram D. Hulen, "Japanese Answer; Says Troops in Indo-China Do Not Exceed Limit in Pact with Vichy," *New York Times*, December 6, 1941, 1.
23.   Associated Press, "Joint U.S.-Japan Commission Is Proposed to End Deadlock," *Atlanta Constitution*, December 6, 1941, 1.
24.   *New York Times*, "Japan Institute Here Is Closing," December 6, 1941, 2.
25.   Associated Press, "Joint U.S.-Japan Commission Is Proposed to End Deadlock," *Atlanta Constitution*, December 6, 1941, 1.
26.   *Christian Science Monitor*, "Draft for Overseas Service Major Issue in Australia," December 6, 1941, 11.

27. Associated Press, "Australia Calls for Execution of 'ABCD' Military Measures," *Constitution*, December 6, 1941, 4.

28. Associated Press, "Britain Takes Up Battle Posts in Far East as Crisis Grows," *Christian Science Monitor*, December 6, 1941, 1.

29. Associated Press, "Singapore Alert Sounded; Manila Evacuation Seen," *Birmingham News*, December 6, 1941, 1.

30. Henry W. Harris, "Crisis Finds Foes of Japan Strong," *Boston Evening Globe*, December 6, 1941, 2.

31. Henry W. Harris, "Crisis Finds Foes of Japan Strong," *Boston Evening Globe*, December 6, 1941, 2.

32. Walter Robb, "Macarthur Prepared if Japan Strikes Blow," *Los Angeles Times*, December 6, 1941, 5.

33. Otto D. Tolischus, "Needn't Fear Air Attacks Japan Told," *Washington Post*, December 6, 1941, 2.

34. Henry W. Harris, "Crisis Finds Foes of Japan Strong," *Boston Evening Globe*, December 6, 1941, 2.

35. *Christian Science Monitor*, "House Votes Eight Billions for Defense," December 6, 1941, 1.

36. Associated Press, "Army Recreation Delay Ridiculed," *Christian Science Monitor*, December 6, 1941, 11.

37. Sheilah Graham, "Navy Air Cadets Talk Girls and Planes, Not War, Reporter Says." *Washington Evening Star*, December 6, 1941, 2X.

38. Associated Press, "State Drops Charges In Naval Plane Killing," *Washington Evening Star*, December 6, 1941, A2.

39. *Washington Evening Star*, "Temporary Buildings' Removal Following Emergency Indicated," December 6, 1941, A4.

40. *Wall Street Journal*, "Vinson Tries to Work Up Steam for Profits Limit Bill, But Congress Is Not Responsive," December 6, 1941, 2.

41. *Wall Street Journal*, "Vinson Tries to Work Up Steam for Profits Limit Bill, But Congress Is Not Responsive," December 6, 1941, 2.

42. *Wall Street Journal*, "Defense Contracts Awarded," December 6, 1941, 6.

43. *Baltimore Sun*, "Dr. Lazaron Tells of Britain at War," December 7, 1941, 8.

44. *Baltimore Sun*, "Germans Plan to Ask U.S. to Repay Blacklist," December 6, 1941, 1.

45. Honor Croome, "The Nazi Economy," *Christian Science Monitor*, December 6, 1941, 10.

46. Earl C. Behrens, "Propoganda Drive Centers in Schools," *Los Angeles Times*, December 6, 1941, 1.

47. *Baltimore Sun*, "Dies Group Probes Pro-Nazi Influence in America First," December 6, 1941, 1.

48. *Baltimore Sun*, "Dies Group Probes Pro-Nazi Influence in America First," December 6, 1941, 1.

49. F.R. Kent Jr., "Widening of Dies Probes Revealed," *Baltimore Sun*, December 7, 1941, 15.

50. *Washington Post*, "Youth Rally Hears Pepper Assail Hitler," December 6, 1941, 19.

51. Gordon William Prange, Donald M. Goldstein, Katherine V. Dillon, *At Dawn We Slept, The Untold Story of Pearl Harbor* (New York, New York, Penguin Books, 1991,) 70.

52. *New York Times*, "Nazis Bar Sales By Jews," December 6, 1941, 7.

53. *New York Times*, "Nazis Bar Sales By Jews," December 6, 1941, 7.

54. Jerome Frank, "Red-White-and-Blue Herring," *Saturday Evening Post*, December 6, 1941, 9.

55. Jerome Frank, "Red-White-and-Blue Herring," *Saturday Evening Post*, December 6, 1941, 9.

56. Jerome Frank, "Red-White-and-Blue Herring," *Saturday Evening Post*, December 6, 1941, 9.

57. Jerome Frank, "Red-White-and-Blue Herring," *Saturday Evening Post*, December 6, 1941, 9.

58. Jerome Frank, "Red-White-and-Blue Herring," *Saturday Evening Post*, December 6, 1941, 9.

59. Joe Morton, "American Concentration Camp," *Greeley (CO) Daily Tribune*," December 6, 1941, 4.

60. Frederick Kuh, "Britain Declares War on Finland, Hungary, Rumania," *Idaho Evening News*, December 6, 1941, 1.

61. *Hartford (CT) Courant*, "That Ickes Oil 'Shortage,'" December 6, 1941, 8.

62. *Hartford (CT) Courant*, "That Ickes Oil 'Shortage,'" December 6, 1941, 8.

63. J. H. Carmical, "10% Cut Is Likely In 'Gas' Efficacy," *New York Times*, December 6, 1941, 1.

64. *Saturday Evening Post*, "Partners in Power for the Nation's Defense," December 6, 1941, 33.

65. *Saturday Evening Post*, "I Keep 500 'Horses' on Their Toes." December 6, 1941, 90.

66. *Saturday Evening Post*, "All-out Aid for a Hungry Man!" December 6, 1941, 31.
67. *Saturday Evening Post*, "When You Have a Smokers Cough—It's Time to Change to Spuds," December 6, 1941, 75.
68. *Washington Post*, "Seasonal Sale! Brand New '41 Models," December 6, 1941, 18.
69. *Washington Post*, "Seasonal Sale! Brand New '41 Models," December 6, 1941, 18.
70. *Christian Science Monitor*, "War Dines Heartily at New World Table But Essential Foods Are Still Plentiful," December 6, 1941, 6.
71. *Christian Science Monitor*, "War Dines Heartily at New World Table But Essential Foods Are Still Plentiful," December 6, 1941, 6.
72. *Washington Evening Star*, "Work of Colored Artist in Library of Congress," December 6, 1941, A4.
73. *Atlanta Constitution*, "Todays Radio; Saturdays Local Program," December 6, 1941, 11.
74. Associated Press, "Honduran President Reveals Nazi Plots in Central America," *Washington Evening Star*, December 6, 1941, A1.
75. Associated Press, "Russian Armies Slash at Foe in Flank Attacks," *Washington Evening Star*, December 6, 1941, A1.
76. Associated Press, "Russian Armies Slash at Foe in Flank Attacks," *Washington Evening Star*, December 6, 1941, A1.
77. Associated Press, "British Submarine Sunk Off Norway, Nazis Claim," *Washington Evening Star*, December 6, 1941, A2.
78. *Christian Science Monitor*, "Prisoners: Pawns of Nazi Conquest," December 6, 1941, 7.
79. *Baltimore Sun*, "Cannibalism Is Reported in Germany's Prison Camp," December 7, 1941, 3.
80. *Baltimore Sun*, "Cannibalism Is Reported in Germany's Prison Camp," December 7, 1941, 3.
81. Angus Thuermer, "Prisoners Make Arms for Nazis," *Hartford (CT) Courant*, December 7, 1941, 5.
82. Associated Press, "British Free Admiral's Wife," *Christian Science Monitor*, December 6, 1941, 11.
83. Jesse A. Linthicum, "Sunlight on Sports," *Baltimore Sun*, December 1, 1941, 14.
84. Bill Dismer Jr., "Banta of Eagles Aims to Show Redskins They Passed Up Ace," *Washington Evening Star*, December 6, 1941, A18.
85. Associated Press, "Tommy Breaks Up With Fifth Wife," *Evening (OH) Independent*, December 6, 1941, 2.
86. Ida Jean Kain, "Rita Hayworth Does Not Diet; Stays Thin by Dancing, Sports," *Washington Evening Star* December 6, 1941, 15.
87. *Washington Post* "Bible for President," December 6, 1941, 8.
88. Edgar Ansel Mowrer, "Japan Believed Certain to Fight," *Los Angeles Times*, December 6, 1941, 5.
89. *Washington Post*, "U.S.-Japan at End of Talk, He Asserts," December 6, 1941, 4.
90. *Christian Science Monitor*, "World Golden Rule Week Calls For Self-Denial and Generosity," December 6, 1941, 14.
91. *Christian Science Monitor*, "Tokyo Regime Called Bluff; China Stiffer," December 6, 1941, 14.
92. *Christian Science Monitor*, "Tokyo Regime Called Bluff; China Stiffer," December 6, 1941, 14.
93. United Press, "Japanese Council Defies Effort of United States to Bar 'New Order,'" December 6, 1941, 1.

CHAPTER 7: THE SEVENTH OF DECEMBER

1. Joint Committee on the Investigation of the Pearl Harbor Attack, *Pearl Harbor Attack: Hearings Before the Joint Committee on the Investigation of the Pearl Harbor Attack*, 79th Cong., 1st sess., 1946, Government Printing Office, Exhibit no. 17, Memorandum for the President, "Subject: Far Eastern Situation," November 27, 1941, 1083.
2. Joint Committee on the Investigation of the Pearl Harbor Attack, *Pearl Harbor Attack: Hearings Before the Joint Committee on the Investigation of the Pearl Harbor Attack*, 79th Cong., 1st sess., 1946, Government Printing Office, Exhibit no. 17, Memorandum for the President, "Subject: Far Eastern Situation," November 27, 1941, 1083.

3. Joint Committee on the Investigation of the Pearl Harbor Attack, *Pearl Harbor Attack: Hearings Before the Joint Committee on the Investigation of the Pearl Harbor Attack*, 79th Cong., 1st sess., 1946, Government Printing Office, Exhibit no. 17, Memorandum for the President, "Subject: Far Eastern Situation," November 27, 1941, 1083.

4. Joint Committee on the Investigation of the Pearl Harbor Attack, *Pearl Harbor Attack: Hearings Before the Joint Committee on the Investigation of the Pearl Harbor Attack*, 79th Cong., 1st sess., 1946, Government Printing Office, Exhibit no. 17, Memorandum for the President, "Subject: Far Eastern Situation," November 27, 1941, 1083.

5. Joint Committee on the Investigation of the Pearl Harbor Attack, *Pearl Harbor Attack: Hearings Before the Joint Committee on the Investigation of the Pearl Harbor Attack*, 79th Cong., 1st sess., 1946, Government Printing Office, Exhibit no. 17, Memorandum for the President, "Subject: Far Eastern Situation," November 27, 1941, 1083.

6. Husband E. Kimmel, *Admiral Kimmel's Story* (Chicago, IL: 1955, Henry Regnery Company), 15.

7. Husband E. Kimmel, *Admiral Kimmel's Story* (Chicago, IL: 1955, Henry Regnery Company), 19.

8. Gerald Griffin, "President Makes Move As Convoys Are Sighted Bound for Gulf of Siam," *Baltimore Sun*, December 7, 1941, 1.

9. Doris Kerns Goodwin, *No Ordinary Time: Franklin and Eleanor Roosevelt: The Home Front in World War II* (New York: Simon and Schuster, 1955), 286.

10. *Honolulu Advertiser*, "Housing Aid Appeal Sent to Governor," December 7, 1941, 1.

11. *Honolulu Advertiser*, "See Santa Today," December 7, 1941, 1.

12. *Honolulu Advertiser*, "'Clean Shave' Drive Started," December 7, 1941, 1.

13. United Press, "Week's War Preview," *Honolulu Advertiser*, December 7, 1941, 7.

14. Associated Press, "Man Dies Without Learning His Identity," *Los Angeles Times*, December 7, 1941, 8.

15. United Press, "Japanese Herald 'Supreme Crisis,'" *New York Times*, December 7, 1941, 3.

16. United Press, "Singapore Forces Recalled to War Stations; Base Ready to Act in Any Emergency," *Honolulu Advertiser*, December 7, 1941, 7.

17. Associated Press, "Australia and Allies Reported in Accord on Pacific Defense," *Washington Evening Star*, December 7, 1941, A2.

18. Blair Bolles, "Roosevelt Sends Note to Hirohito; Japanese Convoys Near Thailand; U.S. Takes Over Finnish Vessels: President's Action Looked on Here As Last Step," *Washington Evening Star*, December 7, 1941, 1.

19. Franklin Delano Roosevelt Presidential Library and Museum, "Roosevelt's Appeal to Hirohito to Avoid War," December 6, 1941, Hyde Park, NY.

20. Franklin Delano Roosevelt Presidential Library and Museum, "Roosevelt's Appeal to Hirohito to Avoid War," December 6, 1941, Hyde Park, NY.

21. Franklin Delano Roosevelt Presidential Library and Museum, "Roosevelt's Appeal to Hirohito to Avoid War," December 6, 1941, Hyde Park, NY.

22. *New York Times*, "New Troop Moves," December 7, 1941, 1.

23. Blair Bolles, "Roosevelt Sends Note to Hirohito; Japanese Convoys Near Thailand; U.S. Takes Over Finnish Vessels: President's Action Looked on Here As Last Step," *Washington Evening Star*, December 7, 1941, 1.

24. Blair Bolles, "Roosevelt Sends Note to Hirohito; Japanese Convoys Near Thailand; U.S. Takes Over Finnish Vessels: President's Action Looked on Here As Last Step," *Washington Evening Star*, December 7, 1941, 1.

25. Associated Press, "F.D.R. Puts Jap Crisis Up to Emperor: Personal Message Sent to Mikado Amid Reports of Fresh Troop Moves," *Birmingham (AL) News*, December 7, 1941, 1.

26. Associated Press, "Japanese Head for Thailand," *Los Angeles Times*, December 7, 1941, 14.

27. Fredric L. Borch, Daniel Martinez, *Kimmel, Short, and Pearl Harbor* (Annapolis, MD: Naval Institute Press, 2005), 56.

28. United Press, "London Prepares for Fighting," *New York Times*, December 3, 1941, 4.

29. Associated Press, "Special Commission Urged," *New York Times*, December 7, 1941, 3.

30. Associated Press, "U.S. Stalling, Says Tokyo," *Los Angeles Times*, December 7, 1941, 1.

31. Associated Press, "U.S. Stalling, Says Tokyo," *Los Angeles Times*, December 7, 1941, 1.

32. Associated Press, "Roosevelt Insincere, Stalling in Talks, Japanese Press Says," *Washington Evening Star*, December 7, 1941, A4.

33. Associated Press, "U.S. Helps Guard South Pacific," *The Calgary* (Alberta, Canada) *Herald*, December 2, 1941, 3.

34. Associated Press, "Roosevelt Insincere, Stalling in Talks, Japanese Press Says," *Washington Evening Star*, December 7, 1941, A4.

35. Associated Press, "Australia and Allies Reported in Accord on Pacific Defense," *Washington Evening Star*, December 7, 1941, A1.

36. Associated Press, "British Forces Recalled to Singapore Posts," *Washington Evening Star*, December 7, 1941, A3.

37. Associated Press, "Britain Goes to War Against Finland Quietly and Formally," *Washington Evening Star*, December 7, 1941, A1.

38. Associated Press, "Move Synchronous With British War Declaration," *Washington Evening Star*, December 7, 1941, A1.

39. Associated Press, "Finn President Warns Britain and U.S. of Soviet Friendship," *Washington Evening Star*, December 7, 1941, A4.

40. Associated Press, "French Fleet Declared Active in Mediterranean," *Washington Evening Star*, December 7, 1941, A1.

41. Associated Press, "British Credit American Planes for Biggest Victory in Libya," *Washington Evening Star*, December 7, 1941, A1.

42. Associated Press, "Russia May Get Wheat From Pacific Northwest," *Washington Evening Star*, December 7, 1941, A1.

43. Associated Press, "Moscow Facing New Peril From Enemy Hordes," *Washington Evening Star*, December 7, 1941, A1.

44. *New York Times*, "Navy Is Superior to Any," December 7, 1941, 1.

45. *New York Times*, "Dentistry to Cut Army Rejections," December 2, 1941, 18.

46. Department of The Navy, Memorandum for the President, "Subject: Report on Enlisted Personnel, United States Navy," December 2, 1941, Washington, DC.

47. *Birmingham (AL) News*, "Experts With Radios Are Needed By Navy," December 7, 1941, 14.

48. *Washington Evening Star*, "21-Year-Olds Face Call to Army Duty At Least by July 1," December 7, 1941, A5.

49. Associated Press, "Doctor Scores His Profession," *Indiana* (PA) *Evening Gazette*, December 5, 1941, 1.

50. *Washington Evening Star*, "Revlon Nail Enamel," December 7, 1941, A7.

51. Martin Caidin, *Golden Wings* (New York: Random House, 1960), 104.

52. Martin Caidin, *Golden Wings* (New York: Random House, 1960), 104.

53. Drew Pearson and Robert S. Allen, "Merry-Go-Around," *Palm Beach (FL) Post-Times*, December 14, 1941, 4.

54. Martin Caidin, *Golden Wings* (New York: Random House, 1960), 104.

55. Associated Press, "Japs Strike at U.S.," *Emporia* (KS) *Gazette*, December 1941, 1.

56. Associated Press, "Eyewitness Report of Air Raid," *Baltimore Sun*, December 8, 1941, 2.

57. Martin Caidin, *Golden Wings* (New York: Random House, 1960), 106.

58. Bill Henry, "By the Way With Bill Henry," *Los Angeles Times*, December 9, 1941, A1.

59. Bernard C. Nalty, *War in the Pacific Pearl Harbor to Tokyo Bay: The Story of the Bitter Struggle in the Pacific Theater of World War II* (Norman, OK: University of Oklahoma Press, 1999), 32.

60. *Time*, "The U.S. at War, Tragedy at Honolulu," December 15, 1941, 22.

61. Thomas Yarbrough, "Writer Learns Hawaiian Raid No 'War Game,'" *Atlanta Constitution*, December 13, 1941, 1.

62. Jim Hopkins and Michelle Kessler, "Unlike Pearl Harbor, This Tragedy Was Live," *USA Today*, September 25, 2001, 8B; Geoffrey C. Ward and Ken Burns, *The War: an Intimate History, 1941–1945* (New York: A.A. Knopf, 2007), 1.

63. Jim Hopkins and Michelle Kessler, "Unlike Pearl Harbor, This Tragedy Was Live," *USA Today*, September 25, 2001, 8B; Geoffrey C. Ward and Ken Burns, *The War: an Intimate History, 1941–1945* (New York: A.A. Knopf, 2007), 1.

64. United Press, "Hawaii Under Martial Law, Islands Quiet; Blackout Enforced, Violators Punished," *New York Times*, December 11, 1941, 6.

65. Gerald Eckert, in discussion with the author.

66. Thomas E. Henry, "Capital Retains Outward Calm Despite Shock of War News," *Washington Evening Star*, December 8, 1941, A8.

67. Shirley Povich, "War's Outbreak Is Deep Secret to 27,102 Redskin Game Fans," *Washington Post*, December 8, 1941, 24.

68. Shirley Povich, "War's Outbreak Is Deep Secret to 27,102 Redskin Game Fans," *Washington Post*, December 8, 1941, 24.

69. Shirley Povich, "War's Outbreak Is Deep Secret to 27,102 Redskin Game Fans," *Washington Post*, December 8, 1941, 24.

70. Associated Press, "Struck Before Declaration, Tokyo Admits," *Washington Post*, December 8, 1941, 8.

71. Paul S. Dull, *A Battle History of the Imperial Japanese Navy, 1941–1945* (Annapolis, MD: Naval Institute, 1978), 16.

72. Paul S. Dull, *A Battle History of the Imperial Japanese Navy, 1941–1945* (Annapolis, MD: Naval Institute, 1978), 16.

73. Associated Press, "Japs Open War on U.S. With Bombing of Hawaii; Fleet Speeds Out to Battle Invader," *Los Angeles Times*, December 8, 1941, 1.

74. Associated Press, "Child Among the Dead," *New York Times*, December 8, 1941, 13.

75. Richard Haller, International New Service, "Honolulu Caught By Surprise Raid," *Charleston (SC) News and Courier*, December 8, 1941, 7.

76. Associated Press, "Eyewitness Report of Air Raid," *Baltimore Sun*, December 8, 1941, 2.

77. Associated Press, "Many Americans Die in Bombing of Hawaii; Fires Set in Honolulu," *Baltimore Sun*, December 8, 1941, 1.

78. Associated Press, "Eyewitness Report of Air Raid," *Baltimore Sun*, December 8, 1941, 2.

79. Associated Press, "Eyewitness Report of Air Raid," *Baltimore Sun*, December 8, 1941, 2.

80. *Newsday* (NY), "How Radio Reported '41 Attack," December 7, 1941, 15.

81. Video Material, *Tora! Tora! Tora!*, Craig Shirley Collection.

82. Associated Press, "2 Big U.S. Battleships Reported in Action Now," *Baltimore Sun*, December 8, 1941, 3.

83. Mark S. Watson, "Dawn Air Raid Finds U.S. Forces on Islands Not Ready for Action," *Baltimore Sun*, December 8, 1941, 4.

84. *Maryville (MO) Daily Forum*, "Japs Attack Manila," December 7, 1941, 1.

85. *Maryville (MO) Daily Forum*, "Reports Staggers London," December 7, 1941, 1.

86. *Maryville (MO) Daily Forum*, "Far East Crisis Explodes!" December 7, 1941, 1.

87. *Maryville (MO) Daily Forum*, "News Spreads," December 7, 1941, 1.

88. Associated Press, "Two Japanese Bombers Appear Over Honolulu; Unverified Report Says a Foreign Warship Appears Off Pearl Harbor," *Maryville (MO) Daily Forum*, December 7, 1941, 1.

89. *Washington Post*, "War Brings a Tense Day to White House Press Room," December 8, 1941, 4.

90. Margalit Fox, "Frank Tremaine, 92, Reporter Who Broke Pearl Harbor News, Dies," *New York Times*, December 27, 2006, C11.

91. Susan McShane, in discussion with the author, September 12, 2011.

92. Susan McShane, in discussion with the author, September 12, 2011.

93. Gerald Eckert, in discussion with the author.

94. Associated Press, "U.S. at War! Japan Bombs Hawaii, Manila." *Washington Post Extra*, December 7, 1941, 1.

95. *Washington Post*, "War Brings a Tense Day to White House Press Room," December 8, 1941, 4.

96. Edward T. Folliard, "Hawaii Attacked Without Warning With Heavy Loss; Philippines Are Bombed," *Washington Post*, December 8, 1941, 1.

97. Gerald Griffin, "Tempo of War Apparent at White House," *Baltimore Sun*, December 8, 1941, 3.

98. Frank L. Kluckhohn, "Guam Bombed; Army Ship Is Sunk," *New York Times*, December 8, 1941, 1.

99. *Washington Post*, "War Brings a Tense Day to White House Press Room," December 8, 1941, 4.

100. *Washington Post*, "War Brings a Tense Day to White House Press Room," December 8, 1941, 4.

101. *Washington Post*, "War Brings a Tense Day to White House Press Room," December 8, 1941, 4.

102. *Washington Post*, "War Brings a Tense Day to White House Press Room," December 8, 1941, 4.

103. *Washington Post*, "War Brings a Tense Day to White House Press Room," December 8, 1941, 4.

104. *Washington Post*, "War Brings a Tense Day to White House Press Room," December 8, 1941, 4.

105. Richard Haller, "Hawaii Attack Is Described By Eyewitness," *Washington Post*, December 8, 1941, 3.

106. *Washington Post*, "War Brings a Tense Day to White House Press Room," December 8, 1941, 4.

107. Edward T. Folliard, "Hawaii Attacked Without Warning With Heavy Loss; Philippines Are Bombed," *Washington Post*, December 8, 1941, 1.

108. Associated Press, "All Jap Nationals Ordered Arrested," *Maryville (MO) Daily Forum*, December 7, 1941, 1.

109. Thomas R. Henry, "Capital Retains Outward Calm Despite Shock of War News," *Washington Evening Star*, December 8, 1941, A6.

110. Scott Hart, "Crowds Gather at White House As News of Attack Spreads," *Washington Post*, December 8, 1941, 3.

111. *Washington Post*, "News of War With Nippon Stuns Civilians, Service Men Alike," December 8, 1941, 7.

112. Richard Turner, Associated Press, "Bursting Jap Bombs Bring War to Hawaii," *Boston Daily Globe*, December 8, 1941, 11.

113. *Washington Evening Star*, "Washington Quickly Turned Into a Wartime Capital." December 8, 1941, B19.

114. Richard L. Strout, "War Comes to Washington—On a Sunday Afternoon," *Christian Science Monitor*, December 8, 1941, C1.

115. Gerald Griffin, "Tempo of War Apparent at White House," *Baltimore Sun*, December 8, 1941, 3.

116. Richard L. Strout, "War Comes to Washington—On a Sunday Afternoon," *Christian Science Monitor*, December 8, 1941, C1.

117. Associated Press, "Bombers Attack Philippine Points," *New York Times*, December 8, 1941, 8.

118. Associated Press, "Army Bombers Roar North," *New York Times*, December 8, 1941, 8.

119. Royal Arch Gunnison, North American Newspaper Alliance, "No Bombing of Manila," *New York Times*, December 8, 1941, 8.

120. Associated Press, "Nichols Field Gas Supply Reported Destroyed," *Washington Post*, December 9, 1941, 3.

121. C. P. Trussell, "Congress Decided," *New York Times*, December 8, 1941, 1.

122. C. P. Trussell, "Congress Decided," *New York Times*, December 8, 1941, 1.

123. Robert Schlesinger, *White House Ghosts* (New York, Simon and Schuster, 2008), 26.

124. Franklin Delano Roosevelt Presidential Library and Museum, "FDR: Day by Day—The Pare Lorentz Chronology," December 7, 1941.

125. *Time*, "The U.S. at War: National Ordeal," December 15, 1941, 18.

126. Peter Grier, "Pearl Harbor Day: How FDR Reacted on December 7, 1941," *Christian Science Monitor*, December 7, 2010.

127. Franklin Delano Roosevelt Presidential Library and Museum, "Diary Entry of Agriculture Secretary Claude R. Wickard," December 7, 1941, Hyde Park, NY.

128. *Time*, "The U.S. at War: National Ordeal," December 15, 1941, 18.

129. *Baltimore Sun*, "Congress Leaders Take Part in Cabinet Session to Discuss U.S. Action," December 8, 1941, 2.

130. Edward T. Folliard, "Hawaii Attacked Without Warning With Heavy Loss; Philippines Are Bombed," *Washington Post*, December 8, 1941, 1.

131. Edward T. Folliard, "Hawaii Attacked Without Warning With Heavy Loss; Philippines Are Bombed," *Washington Post*, December 8, 1941, 1.

132. *Washington Evening Star*, "All-Night Vigil Kept at Navy Department; 1,000 at Decks," December 8, 1941, B8.

133. *Washington Evening Star*, "All-Night Vigil Kept at Navy Department; 1,000 at Decks," December 8, 1941, B8.

134. Franklin Delano Roosevelt Presidential Library and Museum, "Diary Entry of Agriculture Secretary Claude R. Wickard," December 7, 1941, Hyde Park, NY.

135. Associated Press, "Tojo Promises Japan Victory Over America," *Washington Post*, December 8, 1941, 3.

136. Associated Press, "Tokyo Acts First," *New York Times*, December 8, 1941, 1.

137. Associated Press, "Tokyo Acts First," *New York Times*, December 8, 1941, 1.

138. Blair Bolles, "Japanese Diplomats to Be Guaranteed Safe Return Home," *Washington Evening Star*, December 8, 1941, A5.

139. Paul W. Ward, "Japanese Embassy Guarded by Washington Police Squad," *Baltimore Sun*, December 8, 1941, 4.

140. Paul W. Ward, "Japanese Embassy Guarded by Washington Police Squad," *Baltimore Sun*, December 8, 1941, 4.

141. *Washington Post*, "Irish Mother of Six Can't Leave Embassy," December 8, 1941, 3.

142. Paul W. Ward, "Japanese Embassy Guarded by Washington Police Squad," *Baltimore Sun*, December 8, 1941, 4.

143. *New York Times*, "Burning of Papers Watched By 1,000," December 8, 1941, 5.

144. *Washington Post*, "Embassy Row Bustles as War Comes to U.S.," December 8, 1941, 3.

145. *Time*, "The U.S. at War, the Last Stage," December 15, 1941, 26.

146. *Washington Evening Star*, "F.B.I. Rounding Up Japanese Citizens Throughout Nation," December 8, 1941, B1.

147. *Baltimore Sun*, "Boys Hang Effigy," December 8, 1941, 11.

148. Associated Press, "Clipper Reaches Hawaii Safely," *Washington Post*, December 8, 1941, 2.

149. Thomas M. Coffey, *Hap: The Story of The U.S. Air Force and The Man Who Built It, General Henry "Hap" Arnold*, (New York, Viking Press, 1982), 242.

150. Elizabeth Henney, "Beautiful, Friendly Honolulu, Asking Only Peace, Is at War," *Washington Post*, December 8, 1941, 5.

151. Bill Henry, "Japan's Daring Attack on Hawaii Designed to Cripple U.S. Fleet; Suicide Bomb Raid Perfectly Timed," *Los Angeles Times*, December 8, 1941, 1D.

152. Franklin Delano Roosevelt Presidential Library and Museum, "Memorandum for The President," Box 1, December 7, 1941.

153. Franklin Delano Roosevelt Presidential Library and Museum, "Transcript of Telephone Conversation Between FDR and Treasury Secretary Henry Morgenthau, Jr." Box 515, December 7, 1941, Hyde Park, NY.

154. T. J. King, *Joint and Naval Intelligence Support to Military Operations* (Darby, PA: Diane Publishing 2011), V12.

CHAPTER 8: THE EIGHTH OF DECEMBER

1. Charles Hurd, "Stark's Report Stresses Speed, Day Before Japan Attacks," *Washington Post*, December 8, 1941, 27.

2. Frank L. Kluckhohn, "Guam Bombed; Army Ship Is Sunk," *New York Times*, December 8, 1941, 1.

3. George Fielding Eliot, "Jap Raid Believed Hindering Action," *Los Angeles Times*, December 8, 1941, 1C.

4. Editorial, "We Shall Win," *Baltimore Sun*, December 8, 1941, 16.

5. *Los Angeles Times*, "Public Believed First War Reports Only Gag," December 8, 1941, 2.
6. *Los Angeles Times*, "Air Guards, Attention!" December 8, 1941, 1.
7. Carroll Kilpatrick, "Visitor to White House Criticizes American Defense in Hawaii," *Birmingham (AL) News*, December 8, 1941, 8.
8. Gordon William Prange with Donald M. Goldstein and Katherine V. Dillon, *Dec. 7, 1941: The Day the Japanese Attacked Pearl Harbor* (New York: Wings Books, 1991), 376.
9. *Washington Evening Star*, "Gasoline Dump at Nichols Field Believed Fired," December 8, 1941, A1.
10. *Boston Daily Globe*, "Japan Strikes Over Wide Area," December 8, 1941, 4.
11. *Washington Evening Star*, "Gasoline Dump at Nichols Field Believed Fired," December 8, 1941, A1.
12. Bill Henry, "Japan's Daring Attack on Hawaii Designed to Cripple U.S. Fleet," *Los Angeles Times*, December 8, 1941, 1D.
13. *Washington Evening Star*, "Gasoline Dump at Nichols Field Believed Fired," December 8, 1941, A1.
14. United Press, "Japanese Premier's Story," *New York Times*, December 8, 1941, 5.
15. *Washington Evening Star*, "Gasoline Dump at Nichols Field Believed Fired," December 8, 1941, A1.
16. Woody Klein, *All the Presidents' Spokesmen: Spinning the News—White House Press Secretaries from Franklin D. Roosevelt to George W. Bush* (Westport, CT: Praeger Publishers, 2008), 38.
17. William L. O'Neill, *A Democracy at War: America's Fight at Home and Abroad in World War II* (Cambridge, MA: Harvard University Press, 1995), 5.
18. Hazel Rowley, *Franklin and Eleanor: An Extraordinary Marriage* (New York: Farrar, Straus and Giroux, 2010), 246.
19. Philip M. Seib, *Broadcasts from the Blitz: How Edward R. Murrow Helped Lead America Into War* (Dulles, VA: Potomac Books, 2006), 157.
20. James MacGregor Burns and Susan Dunn, *The Three Roosevelts: Patrician Leaders Who Transformed America* (New York: Grove Press, 2001), 442.
21. Dan Van Der Vat, *Pearl Harbor: The Day of Infamy—An Illustrated History* (New York: Basic Books, 2001), 74.
22. Peter Grier, "Pearl Harbor Day: How FDR Reacted on December 7, 1941," *Christian Science Monitor*, December 7, 2010, http://www.csmonitor.com/USA/2010/1207/Pearl-Harbor-day-How-FDR-reacted-on-December-7-1941; Emma Brown, "'Air raid, Pearl Harbor': Who Said It?," *Washington Post*, January 19, 2011, http://voices.washingtonpost.com/postmortem/2011/01/air-raid-pearl-harbor-who-said.html.
23. *New York Times*, "Army, Navy Order Wide Censorship," December 8, 1941, 8.
24. Associated Press, "Espionage Act Violators Face Death Penalty," *Boston Daily Globe*, December 8, 1941, 6.
25. *New York Times*, "Army, Navy Order Wide Censorship," December 8, 1941, 8.
26. John G. Norris, "All Dangerous Japanese Face Arrest by U.S.," *Washington Post*, December 8, 1941, 7.
27. John G. Norris, "All Dangerous Japanese Face Arrest by U.S.," *Washington Post*, December 8, 1941, 7.
28. Drew Person and Robert S. Allen, "Merry–Go–Round," *Birmingham (AL) News*, December 14, 1941, 5.
29. *Washington Post*, "Armed Plants Told to Work 24 Hours a Day," December 8, 1941, 23.
30. *Washington Post*, "Heavy Guard Thrown Around Capital's Most Vital Spots," December 8, 1941, 3; *New York Times*, "Patterson Asks All Plants Guard Against Sabotage," December 8, 1941, 4; Associated Press, "Emergency Measures Enforced in Nation," *Boston Daily Globe*, December 8, 1941, 20.
31. C.P. Trussel, "Congress Decided," *New York Times*, December 8, 1941, 1.
32. *New York Times*, "The Day in Washington," December 9, 1941, 4.

33. *New York Times,* "La Guardia Acts to Guard Cities," December 8, 1941, 3.
34. Associated Press, "Britain Declares War on Japs, Allying Herself With U.S.," *Washington Evening Star,* December 8, 1941, A2.
35. Associated Press, "Text of Address by Churchill," *Washington Post,* December 9, 1941, 19.
36. Associated Press, "Costa Rica at War With Japan," *Atlanta Constitution,* December 8, 1941, 1.
37. United Press, "China Goes to War With Axis States," *New York Times,* December 9, 1941, 9.
38. *New York Times,* "Australia Declares War on the Japanese," December 8, 1941, 2; Associated Press, "Netherlands Join in War on Japan," *New York Times,* December 8, 1941, 7.
39. Associated Press, "Nicaragua Takes Stand," *New York Times,* December 8, 1941, 15.
40. *New York Times,* "Canada Declares War Upon Japan," December 8, 1941, 14.
41. Associated Press, "Carpenter Union Declares War on Japanese as War Flares," *Atlanta Constitution,* December 8, 1941, 11.
42. *Atlanta Constitution,* "Island of Hilo Open to Attack, Says Atlantan," December 8, 1941, 11.
43. Associated Press, "North Borneo Attack Reported," *Washington Evening Star,* December 8, 1941, A1.
44. *Washington Evening Star,* "Gasoline Dump at Nichols Field Believed Fired," December 8, 1941, A1; Frank L. Kluckhohn, "Guam Bombed, Army Ship Is Sunk," *New York Times,* December 8, 1941, 1.
45. United Press and International News Service, "Jap 'Chute Troops Seen in Honolulu," *Washington Post,* December 8, 1941, 2.
46. John Franklin Carter, "Memorandum on Japanese Problem (West Coast, Mexican Border)," December 8, 1941, Franklin Delano Roosevelt Presidential Library and Museum, Hyde Park, NY.
47. United Press, "Jap Attack Under Way for 2 Weeks," *Washington Post,* December 8, 1941, 1.
48. Associated Press, "Believe May Have Used Suicide Squads," *Washington Post,* December 8, 1941, 3.
49. *Washington Post,* December 8, 1941, 1.
50. Associated Press, "Japan Strikes All Over Pacific," *Boston Daily Globe,* December 8, 1941, 1.
51. Associated Press, "1,500 Dead in Hawaii," *Boston Evening Globe,* December 8, 1941, 1.
52. Frank L. Kluckhohn, "Guam Bombed; Army Ship Is Sunk," *New York Times,* December 8, 1941, 1.
53. United Press, "Report Nazis to Act," *Boston Daily Globe,* December 8, 1941, 10.
54. *Washington Evening Star,* "Gasoline Dump at Nichols Field Believed Fired," December 8, 1941, A1.
55. Blair Bolles, "Japanese Diplomats to Be Guaranteed Safe Return Home," *Washington Evening Star,* December 8, 1941, A5.
56. Associated Press, "Wave After Wave of Japanese Planes Attack Hawaii," *Washington Evening Star,* December 8, 1941, A5.
57. *Washington Evening Star,* "Gasoline Dump at Nichols Field Believed Fired," December 8, 1941, A1.
58. United Press, "Jap Transport Hit," *Boston Daily Globe,* December 8, 1941, 15; Associated Press, "Aircraft Carrier Used in Attack on Pearl Harbor Reported Sunk," *Boston Daily Globe,* December 8, 1941, 1.
59. United Press, "Tokyo Bombers Strike Hard at Our Main Bases on Oahu," *New York Times,* December 8, 1941, 1.
60. Frank L. Kluckhohn, "Guam Bombed; Army Ship Is Sunk," *New York Times,* December 8, 1941, 1.
61. Associated Press, "Many Americans Die In Bombing of Hawaii; Fires Set in Honolulu," *Baltimore Sun,* December 8, 1941, 1.
62. Associated Press, "Wave After Wave of Japanese Planes Attack Hawaii," *Washington Evening Star,* December 8, 1941, A5.
63. Thomas R. Henry, "Capital Retains Outward Calm Despite Shock of War News," *Washington Evening Star,* December 8, 1941, A6.

64. Associated Press, "Rome Radio Denies Saying Axis Is at War With U. S.," *Washington Evening Star*, December 8, 1941, A2.
65. *Washington Evening Star*, "Gasoline Dump at Nichols Field Believed Fired," December 8, 1941, A1.
66. Blair Bolles, "Japanese Diplomats to Be Guaranteed Safe Return Home," *Washington Evening Star*, December 8, 1941, A5.
67. Blair Bolles, "Japanese Diplomats to Be Guaranteed Safe Return Home," *Washington Evening Star*, December 8, 1941, A5; United Press, "Japanese Consulate Booed in New Orleans," *Washington Post*, December 8, 1941, 3.
68. Associated Press, "Japanese Beaten Up by New York Trio," *Boston Evening Globe*, December 8, 1941, 2.
69. *New York Times*, "Plains Guard City From Air Attacks," December 9, 1941, 1.
70. Associated Press, "Huge Naval Stronghold Is Bombed," *Boston Daily Globe*, December 8, 1941, 2.
71. Associated Press, "1500 Dead In Hawaii," *Boston Evening Globe*, December 8, 1941, 1.
72. Associated Press, "Manila Planes Roar North," *New York Times*, December 8, 1941, 5.
73. Hedley Donovan, "Aid to Allies Won't Falter, U.S. Pledges," *Washington Post*, December 9, 1941, 1.
74. United Press, "Latest War Bulletins," *Los Angeles Times*, December 8, 1941, 1.
75. Louis P. Lochner, "Nazis Try to Put Blame on Roosevelt," *Washington Post*, December 9, 1941, 14;
76. Associated Press, "Germans, Blaming Roosevelt, Silent on Aid to Japanese," *Los Angeles Times*, December 9, 1941, 4.
77. *New York Times*, "The International Situation," May 28, 1941, 1.
78. Frank L. Kluchkhohn, "Fifth Column Curb," *New York Times*, June 17, 1941, 1.
79. John C. Henry, "Roosevelt Says Date of Attack in Pacific Will Live in Infamy," *Washington Evening Star*, December 1941, 1; *Washington Post*, "Roosevelt Message to Be Broadcast," December 8, 1941, 27.
80. Associated Press, "Oakland Schools Closed as Air Raid Precaution," *Washington Evening Star*, December 8, 1941, A4.
81. *Honolulu Star-Bulletin*, December 7, 1941, 1.
82. Associated Press, "Markets at a Glance," *Washington Evening Star*, December 8, 1941, A1.
83. *New York Times*, "A Pause on the Stock Exchange to Listen to The President," December 9, 1941, 53.
84. *Washington Evening Star*, "Tense Throng Fills Grounds as President Goes to Capitol," December 8, 1941, 1.
85. C.P. Trussel, "Congress Decided," *New York Times*, December 8, 1941, 1.
86. *Washington Post*, "Roosevelt Message to Be Broadcast," December 8, 1941, 27.
87. James B. Reston, "History Is Heard: Studies Here as President Asked for Declaration of War," *New York Times*, December 9, 1941, 5.
88. James B. Reston, "History Is Heard: Studies Here as President Asked for Declaration of War," *New York Times*, December 9, 1941, 5.
89. Frank L. Kluckhohns, "Unity in Congress," *New York Times*, December 9, 1941, 1.
90. Robert C. Albright, "Calm Congress Accepts Challenge with But One Dissenting Vote; Long Ovation Given President; Packed Galleries Applaud Speech," *Washington Post*, December 9, 1941, 1.
91. James B. Reston, "History Is Heard: Studies Here as President Asked for Declaration of War," *New York Times*, December 9, 1941, 5.
92. John C. Henry, "Roosevelt Says Date of Attack in Pacific Will Live in Infamy," *Washington Evening Star*, December 8, 1941, A1.
93. *Time*, "The U.S. At War: National Ordeal," December 15, 1941, 18.
94. *Time*, "The U.S. At War: National Ordeal," December 15, 1941, 18.
95. Associated Press, "Aids Twice in War Steps," *New York Times*, December 9, 1941, 5.
96. *Birmingham (AL) News*, "No Man's Land in Washington," December 14, 1941, 1.

97. F. R. Kent, Jr., "Notables Pack Capitol for War Declaration," *Baltimore Sun*, December 9, 1941, 2.

98. *Time*, "The U.S. At War: National Ordeal," December 15, 1941, 18.

99. Associated Press, "Administration Foes Issue Calls for Unity in War on Japan," *Washington Evening Star*, December 8, 1941, A8.

100. Louis M. Lyons, "Again a U.S. President Asks for Declaration of War," *Boston Daily Globe*, December 8, 1941, 20; F. R. Kent, Jr., "Notables Pack Capitol for War Declaration," *Baltimore Sun*, December 9, 1941, 2.

101. Louis M. Lyons, "Again a U.S. President Asks for Declaration of War," *Boston Daily Globe*, December 8, 1941, 20; Charles Mercer, "Service Chiefs, Envoys Attend Joint Session," *Washington Post*, December 9, 1941, 2.

102. Mona Dugas, "Wives of Cabinet Members and Diplomats Fill Gallery to Hear War Declaration," *Washington Evening Star*, December 8, 1941, B3.

103. James B. Reston, "History Is Heard: Studies Here as President Asked for Declaration of War," *New York Times*, December 9, 1941, 5.

104. Alistair Cooke, *The American Home Front: 1941–1942* (New York: Grove Press, 2007), 12.

105. Alistair Cooke, *The American Home Front: 1941–1942* (New York: Grove Press, 2007), 13.

106. James B. Reston, "History Is Heard: Studies Here as President Asked for Declaration of War," *New York Times*, December 9, 1941, 5.

107. Louis M. Lyons, "Again a U.S. President Asks for Declaration of War," *Boston Daily Globe*, December 8, 1941, 20.

108. Franklin D. Roosevelt, "To The Congress of the United States," The White House, December 8, 1941, Collection Grace Tully Archive, Franklin Delano Roosevelt Presidential Library and Museum, Hyde Park, NY.

109. The United States National Archives and Records Administration, "Teaching With Documents: 'A Date Which Will Live in Infamy,'" http://www.archives.gov/education/lessons/day-of-infamy/.

110. Ron Powers, *Dangerous Water: A Biography of the Boy Who Became Mark Twain* (Cambridge, MA: Da Capo Press, 2001), 174.

111. Lyle C. Wilson, "Senate's Vote Unanimous; House Ballots 388 to 1. Victory Pledged," *Pittsburgh (PA) Post-Gazette*, December 8, 1941, 1.

112. Louis M. Lyons, "Again a U.S. President Asks for Declaration of War," *Boston Daily Globe*, December 8, 1941, 20.

113. Gould Lincoln, "Jeannette Rankin Casts Only Vote Against War," *Washington Evening* Star, December 8, 1941, A2.

114. John C. Henry, "Roosevelt Says Date of Attack in Pacific Will Live in Infamy," *Washington Evening Star*, December 1941, 1.

115. Chesly Manly, "Congress Votes War on Japan in Speedy Session," *Chicago Tribune*, December 9, 1941, 7.

116. John C. Henry, "Roosevelt Says Date of Attack in Pacific Will Live in Infamy," *Washington Evening Star*, December 1941, 1.

117. Gould Lincoln, "Jeannette Rankin Casts Only Vote Against War," *Washington Evening* Star, December 8, 1941, A2.

118. Gould Lincoln, "Jeannette Rankin Casts Only Vote Against War," *Washington Evening* Star, December 8, 1941, A2; F. R. Kent, Jr., "Notables Pack Capitol for War Declaration," *Baltimore Sun*, December 9, 1941, 2.

119. *Boston Daily Globe*, "388 to 1," December 9, 1941, 18; Louis M. Lyons, "War Declared Swiftly After F.D. Speaks," December 9, 1941, 1.

120. F. R. Kent, Jr., "Notables Pack Capitol for War Declaration," *Baltimore Sun*, December 9, 1941, 2.

121. Ruth Cowan, "Republican Women Happy Over Victory," *Washington Post*, November 5, 1942, 4.

122. Associated Press, "55 Who Missed Vote on War Declaration All Approved It," *Washington Evening Star*, December 9, 1941, A2.

123. *New York Times*, "The President Signs the Declaration of War," December 9, 1941, 1; *Washington Post*, "Rep. Rankin Again Votes Against War," December 9, 1941, 2.

124. *New York Times*, "Four-Hour Chronology of Declaration of War," December 9, 1941, 3.

125. James B. Reston, "History Is Heard: Studies Here as President Asked for Declaration of War," *New York Times*, December 9, 1941, 5.

126. *Time*, "The U.S. at War: National Ordeal," December 15, 1941, 18.

127. *Washington Evening Star*, "Recruiting Offices Here Crowded With Men Eager to Enlist," December 8, 1941, B1.

128. *Washington Evening Star*, "Recruiting Offices Here Crowded With Men Eager to Enlist," December 8, 1941, B1.

129. *Washington Evening Star*, "Senator Chandler Volunteers for Army Duty," December 8, 1941, B1.

130. *Atlanta Constitution*, "Women Offered Defense Courses," December 8, 1941, 12.

131. Associated Press, "Ted Williams Is Still Rated in Class 3-A," *Atlanta Constitution*, December 8, 1941, 17.

132. Associated Press, "Hundreds of Women Offer Services for Defense Work," *Baltimore Sun*, December 9, 1941, 4.

133. C. P. Trussell, "Unanimous Senate Acts in 15 Minutes," *New York Times*, December 9, 1941, 6.

134. Franklin Delano Roosevelt Presidential Library and Museum, "FDR: Day by Day—The Pare Lorentz Chronology," December 8, 1941; John C. Henry, "White House Indicates War Crisis Is 'Bigger' Than Clash in Orient," *Washington Evening Star*, December 9, 1941, 1X.

135. Associated Press, "Emergency at San Francisco," *New York Times*, December 8, 1941, 6.

136. *Los Angeles Times*, "Jap Boat Flashes Messages Ashore," December 8, 1941, 6.

137. *Boston Globe*, "U.S. Government at the Panama Canal," December 8, 1941, 2.

138. *Christian Science Monitor*, "Outbreak of War Halts Strikes in New England Area," December 8, 1941, 2.

139. *Christian Science Monitor*, "Harvard's Role in Country at War Topic of Meeting," December 8, 1941, 2.

140. Associated Press, "Arrest of Japs Dangerous to U.S. Ordered," *Atlanta Constitution*, December 8, 1941, 1.

141. *Washington Evening Star*, "F. B. I. Rounding Up Japanese Citizens Throughout Nation," December 8, 1941, B1.

142. Associated Press, "Arrest of Japs Dangerous to U.S. Ordered," *Atlanta Constitution*, December 8, 1941, 1.

143. *Washington Evening Star*, "F. B. I. Rounding Up Japanese Citizens Throughout Nation," December 8, 1941, B1.

144. *Baltimore Sun*, "Judge Denies Citizenship to 34 Aliens," December 9, 1941, 28.

145. *New York Times*, "Japan, U.S. Close 88 Years Peace," December 8, 1941, 2.

146. *Washington Evening Star*, "F. B. I. Rounding Up Japanese Citizens Throughout Nation," December 8, 1941, B1.

147. Associated Press, "Japanese Firms Grabbed by U.S," *Spokesman-Review (WA)*, December 9, 1941, 2.

148. Associated Press, "U.S. Takes Over All Japanese Businesses and Funds, Rounds Up Nearly 1000 Nationals," *Washington Post*, December 9, 1941, 8.

149. Associated Press, "Morgenthau's Order Bans Communication With Japan or 'Allies,'" *Washington Evening Star*, December 8, 1941, A9.

150. Associated Press, "Communicating or Trading with Japanese Barred," *Washington Post*, December 8, 1941, 9; Associated Press, "U.S. Takes Over All Japanese Businesses and Funds, Rounds Up Nearly 1000 Nationals," *Washington Post*, December 9, 1941, 8.

151. *New York Times*, "Japan's Holdings Here Impounded," December 8, 1941, 7.

152. Associated Press, "Morgenthau Bans Dealings with Japanese," *Baltimore Sun*, December 8, 1941, 3.

153. *Los Angeles Times*, "Little Tokyo Banks and Concerns Shut," December 9, 1941, 4.

154. *Los Angeles Times*, "Little Tokyo Carries on Business as Usual," December 8, 1941, 2.

155. *Los Angeles Times*, "Troops Rush to Posts Here," December 8, 1941, 4.

156. *Washington Evening Star*, "Washington Quickly Turned Into a Wartime Capital," December 8, 1941, B14.

157. *Boston Daily Globe*, "Navy in New England Switches to War Basis," December 8, 1941, 6; *Boston Evening Globe*, "Antisabotage Moves by F. B. I. and Timilty," December 8, 1941, 5.

158. *Boston Daily Globe*, "America First Undecided About Lindbergh Rally," December 8, 1941, 16.

159. *New York Times*, "Isolation Groups Back Roosevelt," December 9, 1941, 44; *Washington Post*, "'Forced Upon, We Must Fight,' Hoover Says," December 8, 1941, 15; Associated Press, "America First Backs War, Says Gen. Wood en Route to Boston," *Boston Daily Globe*, December 8, 1941, 19; *New York Times*, "'No Choice,' Says Landon" December 8, 1941, 6.

160. United Press, "U. S. Provoked War, Nye Says," *Washington Post*, December 8, 1941, 8; *Time*, "The U.S. at War: Man Without a Cause," December 15, 1941, 19.

161. Associated Press, "War Fails to Halt Anti-War Rally," *Baltimore Sun*, December 9, 1941, 28.

162. *Boston Daily Globe*, "Cancel Permits for Ships Leaving Boston for Abroad," December 8, 1941, 15; *Boston Daily Globe*, "Railroads Won't Sell Japs Tickets," December 8, 1941, 15.

163. *New York Times*, "Entire City Put on War Footing," December 8, 1941, 1.

164. John MacCormac, "Tax Rise Hinted by Morgenthau," *New York Times*, December 9, 1941, 35.

165. *New York Times*, "Navy Acts Here to Guard Coast," December 8, 1941, 7.

166. *New York Times*, "Entire City Put on War Footing," December 8, 1941, 1.

167. Associated Press, "First Casualty List in War With Japan," *Washington Evening Star*, December 8, 1941, A2.

168. Associated Press, "Wave After Wave of Japanese Planes Attack Hawaii," *Washington Evening Star*, December 9, 1941, A5.

169. *New York Times*, "Drastic Control Marks War News," December 9, 1941, 7.

170. Associated Press, "Large U.S. Losses Clamed by Japan," *New York Times*, December 9, 1941, 1; *Washington Evening Star*, "'Dim Out' Is Tasted by Capital But 'Don't Walk' Signs Glow," December 8, 1941, A14; *Washington Evening Star*, "Nearby Communities Organize to Guard Against Sabotage," December 8, 1941, B1.

171. Associated Press, "Lindbergh Asks United Stand in War Effort," *Washington Evening Star*, December 8, 1941, A1; *Boston Daily Globe*, "Lindbergh Silent; All Callers Barred at Vineyard Estate," December 8, 1941, 7.

172. Associated Press, "America First Urges All-Out Hostilities Against Japanese," *Washington Evening Star*, December 8, 1941, B23.

173. *Washington Evening Star*, "The Christmas Campaign," December 8, 1941, A2.

174. *Washington Evening Star*, "National Airport Goes on Virtual Wartime Basis," December 8, 1941, A9.

175. *Washington Evening Star*, "Nearby Communities Organize to Guard Against Sabotage," December 8, 1941, B1.

176. *Washington Evening Star*, "'Dim Out' Is Tasted by Capital But 'Don't Walk' Signs Glow," December 8, 1941, A14.

177. *Washington Evening Star*, "Mrs. Roosevelt Challenges Women in War Crisis," December 8, 1941, A14.

178. *Washington Post*, "With All Uncertainty Gone, We're Ready, First Lady Says," December 8, 1941, 5.

179. Associated Press, "G. M. on War Basis," *Washington Evening Star*, December 8, 1941, A4.

180. Associated Press, "Welders Rescind Order Calling Off Nation-Wide Strike," *Washington Evening Star*, December 8, 1941, A4.

181. Associated Press, "Patterson Requests Munition Productions On 24-Hour Basis," *Washington Evening Star*, December 8, 1941, B23.

182. Associated Press, "45th's Only Japanese Soldier in Guardhouse," *Washington Evening Star*, December 8, 1941, A11.

183. Associated Press, "West Coast Musters Emergency Strength for Possible Attack," *Washington Evening Star*, December 8, 1941, A12.

184. Associated Press, "Canal Zone Guarded, Panama to Intern All Japanese Residents," *Washington Evening Star*, December 8, 1941, A12.

185. Associated Press, "Emergency at San Francisco," *New York Times*, December 8, 1941, 6; Associated Press, "Private Planes Except Airliners Are Grounded," *Washington Evening Star*, December 8, 1941, B1.

186. Associated Press, "West Coast Musters Emergency Strength for Possible Attack," *Washington Evening Star*, December 8, 1941, A12.

187. *Los Angeles Times*, "City Springs to Attention," December 8, 1941, 1.

188. *New York Times*, "West Coast Acts for War Defense," December 8, 1941, 6; *Los Angeles Times*, "Port Black-Out Ordered by Navy," December 8, 1941, 1C.

189. *Los Angeles Times*, "City's Airfield Blacked Out," December 8, 1941, 1E.

190. *Los Angeles Times*, "Terminal Island Isolated as Defense Precaution," December 8 ,1941, 1F.

191. *Washington Evening Star*, "500 Radio Amateurs in Washington Area Silenced by War," December 8, 1941, B18.

192. Garnett D. Horner, "Final Japanese Note, Flouting U. S. Offer, Rouses Hull's Anger," *Washington Evening Star*, December 8, 1941, A3.

193. Associated Press, "Secretary Hull's Statement, U.S. Note of Nov. 26 and Japan's Reply," *New York Times*, December 8, 1941, 10.

194. Garnett D. Horner, "Final Japanese Note, Flouting U. S. Offer, Rouses Hull's Anger," *Washington Evening Star*, December 8, 1941, A3.

195. Cordell Hull, *The Memoirs of Cordell Hull in Two Volumes Volume II* (New York: The McMillan Company, 1948), 1095.

196. *Time*, "The U.S. At War, In Mr. Hull's Office," December 15, 1941, 26.

197. Corbis Images, "Ambassadors Nomura and Kurusu on December 7, 1941," http://www.corbisimages.com/stock-photo/rights-managed/NA008645/ ambassadors-nomura-and-kurusu-on-december-7.

198. *Washington Evening Star*, "Japan's War Declaration," December 8, 1941, A11.

199. *New York Times*, "Entire City Put on War Footing," December 8, 1941, 1.

200. Hanson W. Baldwin, "War of the World," *New York Times*, December 8, 1941, 7.

201. Edward T. Folliard, "Hawaii Attacked Without Warning with Heavy Loss; Philippines Are Bombed," *Washington Post*, December 8, 1941, 1.

202. *New York Times*, "Entire City Put on War Footing," December 8, 1941, 1.

203. Associated Press, "3,000 Killed and Hurt in Jap Attack on Hawaii; Two U.S. Warships Sunk," *Birmingham (AL) News*, December 8, 1941, 1.

204. Doris Kearns Goodwin, *No Ordinary Time Franklin and Eleanor Roosevelt: The Home Front in World War II* (New York: Simon and Schuster, 1995), 289.

205. Peter Grier, "Pearl Harbor Day: How FDR Reacted on December 7, 1941," *Christian Science Monitor*, December 7, 2010, http://www.csmonitor.com/USA/2010/1207/ Pearl-Harbor-day-How-FDR-reacted-on-December-7-1941.

206. *Los Angeles Times*, "Death Sentence of a Mad Dog," December 8, 1941, A; *New York Times*, "Newspapers Call for Meeting Foe," December 8, 1941, 5.

207. Frank L. Kluckhohn, "Guam Bombed; Army Ship Is Sunk," *New York Times*, December 8, 1941, 1.

208. *Atlanta Constitution*, "Comment Here Flare Against Move by Japan," December 8, 1941, 2.

209. Editorial, "Death Sentence of a Mad Dog," *Los Angeles Times*, December 8, 1941, A.

CHAPTER 9: THE NINTH OF DECEMBER

1. Associated Press, "New York Has Two Air Raid Alarms; Planes Reported Near; Hostile Aircraft Said to Be Flying Toward East Coast," *Birmingham (AL) News*, December 9, 1941, 1.

2. *New York Times*, "City Nonchalant as Sirens Wail," December 10, 1941, 14.

3. *New York Times*, "City Nonchalant as Sirens Wail," December 10, 1941, 14.

4. *New York Times*, "2 False Air 'Raids' Upset New Yorkers," December 10, 1941, 14.

5. *New York Times*, "City Nonchalant as Sirens Wail," December 10, 1941, 14.

6. *New York Times*, "2 False Air 'Raids' Upset New Yorkers," December 10, 1941, 14.

7. *New York Times*, "What to Do in an Air Raid," December 10, 1941, 14.

8. *New York Times*, "What to Do in an Air Raid," December 10, 1941, 14.

9. *Los Angeles Times*, "Registration of Defense Volunteers Will Continue Throughout Week," December 9, 1941, A14.

10. *Boston Evening Globe*, "War Extra! Air Raid 'Dress Rehearsal,'" December 10, 1941, 1.

11. Associated Press, "New York Has Two Air Raid Alarms; Planes Reported Near; Hostile Aircraft Said to Be Flying Toward East Coast," *Birmingham (AL) News*, December 9, 1941, 1.

12. Associated Press, "New York Has Two Air Raid Alarms; Planes Reported Near; Hostile Aircraft Said to Be Flying Toward East Coast," *Birmingham (AL) News*, December 9, 1941, 1.

13. *Boston Daily Globe*, "Antiaircraft Guns Put on Coast," December 9, 1941, 14.

14. *Boston Daily Globe*, "Near-Panic Reported in Several Schools; Many Teachers Weep," December 9, 1941, 14.

15. *Boston Daily Globe*, "Boston-Bound Cars Stopped in Cambridge," December 9, 1941, 14.

16. *Boston Daily Globe*, "Raid Signals Go on in Eastern Mass.; Warning on Panic," December 9, 1941, 14.

17. Associated Press, "More Plains Off Frisco, New Raid Alarm Sounded; About 30 Craft Fly Over West Coast Sector, Then Leave, Army Says," *Baltimore Sun*, December 9, 1941, 1.

18. Associated Press, "Big Air Squadron Driven Back from San Francisco; Navy Sends Three Warships to Hunt Intercepted Planes," *Atlanta Constitution*, December 9, 1941, 1.

19. Lawrence E. Davies, "Turn Back To Sea," *New York Times*, December 9, 1941, 1.

20. Associated Press, "Army and Navy Are on Prowl for Pacific Aircraft Carrier," *Birmingham (AL) News*, December 9, 1941, 1.

21. Associated Press, "More Plains Off Frisco, New Raid Alarm Sounded; About 30 Craft Fly Over West Coast Sector, Then Leave, Army Says," *Baltimore Sun*, December 9, 1941, 1.

22. Associated Press, "Alaska Prepares Against Possible Attack by Japanese Fleet in Swing Northward," *New York Times*, December 9, 1941, 28.

23. *Birmingham (AL) News*, "Japs Believed Trying to Panic U.S. Into Calling Fleet Back Home," December 9, 1941, 2.

24. Associated Press, "Seattle City Scene of Wild Blackout Acts," *Cumberland (MD) Evening Times*, December 9, 1941, 1.

25. Associated Press, "All Pacific Northwest Feels Impact of War," *Birmingham (AL) News*, December 9, 1941, 15.

26. *Washington Evening Star*, "Alarms a Rehearsal Safety Officials Say; 'Alert' Ordered Here," December 9, 1941, A1.

27. Associated Press, "Reports of Japanese Planes Over Pacific Coast Stirs Alarms," *Washington Evening Star*, December 9, 1941, 1X.

28. John Barry, "War Diary 829th Day—Dec. 9, 1941," *Boston Evening Globe*, December 9, 1941, 12.

29. *Boston Evening Globe*, "War Extra! Air Raid 'Dress Rehearsal,'" December 10, 1941, 1.

30. Associated Press, "2 'Rehearsals' In N. Y.; General Still Dubious," *Boston Evening Globe*, December 1, 1941, 1.

31. Associated Press, "Hitler Reported Told Six Days Ago That War Was Coming in Pacific," *Birmingham (AL) News*, December 9, 1941, 1.

32. Associated Press, "Army Still Give Troops Yule Holidays," *Birmingham (AL) News*, December 9, 1941, 1.

33. Associated Press, "Tokyo Insists Planes Sunk 2 Battleships, *Boston Daily Globe*," December 9, 1941, 3.

34. Associated Press, "Reports 2 American Battleships Sunk, 4 Others Damaged," *Washington Post*, December 9, 1941, 7.

35. Associated Press, "Air Reinforcements Rushed to Hawaii," *Boston Daily Globe*, December 9, 1941, 3.

36. Edward E. Bomar, "Temporary Loss of Superiority by U. S. Fleet Seen," *Atlanta Constitution*, December 9, 1941, 7.

37. Associated Press, "F. D. R. to Talk on Japanese Attack Tonight," *Atlanta Constitution*, December 9, 1941, 9.

38. John C. Henry, "Plant Expansion Also Planned as War Measure," *Washington Evening Star*, December 9, 1941, A1.

39. Amy Porter, "Hundreds of Women Overrun Defense Centers Offering to Aid," *Atlanta Constitution*, December 9, 1941, 2.

40. *Atlanta Constitution*, "Women Rush to Offer Help in War Work," December 9, 1941, 7.

41. Associated Press, "Jap Troops Land on Island Near Philippine Capital," *Atlanta Constitution*, December 9, 1941, 1.

42. United Press, "10 R.A.F. Planes Lost in Raids Over France," *New York Times*, December 9, 1941, 7.

43. Associated Press, "U.S. May Have to Put Up 150 Billions in War," *Birmingham (AL) News*, December 9, 1941, 1.

44. Associated Press, "Army's First Casualty List Names 37 Killed in Honolulu," *Birmingham (AL) News*, December 9, 1941, 1.

45. Associated Press, "War Casualties," *Hartford Courant*, December 10, 1941, 13.

46. Associated Press, "Army Casualty List Released," *Los Angeles Times*, December 10, 1941, 1C.

47. *Washington Evening Star*, "News Operator Repeats Role in World War I," December 10, 1941, B6.

48. Associated Press, "Official Army Casualty List," *Baltimore Sun*, December 10, 1941, 4.

49. Associated Press, "House Acts Today to Send Army to Fight Anywhere," *Boston Daily Globe*, December 10, 1941, 19.

50. *Boston Evening Globe*, "A Message From the U.S. Treasury," December 9, 1941, 1.

51. Associated Press, "No Picnic, but Will Buy a Defense Bond," *Boston Evening Globe*, December 9, 1941, 12.

52. Associated Press, "Fighting Songs Call Sounded" *Los Angeles Times*, December 9, 1941, 7.

53. *Birmingham (AL) News*, "Alabamians Flock to Answer Nation's Summons to Defense," December 9, 1941, 12.

54. *Boston Daily Globe*, "Boston Recruiting Offices Swamped; '17 Mark Broken," December 9, 1941, 1.

55. *Los Angeles Times*, "Lindbergh Beacon on Top of City Hall Turned Off," December 9, 1941, A1.

56. Associated Press, "Volunteers Swamp Recruiting Offices Throughout Nation," *Washington Evening Star*, December 9, 1941, A4.

57. Associated Press, "Greenberg Gives up Plans for Baseball to Rejoin Army," *Washington Evening Star*, December 10, 1941, A21; Hugh Fullerton Jr., "Athletic Programs Held Sure to Be Curtailed by War," Washington Evening Star, December 9, 1941, A13.

58. John Lardner, "Louis Given New Song for Christmas Present," *Hartford Courant*, December 10, 1941, 17.

59. Associated Press, "American Eagles Ask Crack at Japs; Some May Leave England," *Birmingham (AL) News*, December 9, 1941, 15.

60. *Birmingham (AL) News*, "Merchants Are Urged to Help Government Catch Moonshiners," December 9, 1941, 6.

61. Associated Press, "280,000-Man Civil Air Patrol Is Asked," *Birmingham (AL) News*, December 9, 1941, 6.

62. Carroll Kilpatrick, "Call Issued for Alabama Farmers to Step Up Their Production," *Birmingham (AL) News*, December 9, 1941, 6.

63. Associated Press, "Union Vow Loyal Work," *Los Angeles Times*, December 9, 1941, 15.

64. Associated Press, "Union Vow Loyal Work," *Los Angeles Times*, December 9, 1941, 15.

65. Associated Press, "Prison Meted 18 Socialists," *Los Angeles Times*, December 9, 1941, 15.

66. Dorothy Thompson, "Declare War on All of Axis Partners Now," *Boston Daily Globe*, December 8, 1941, 14.

67. Possible Form of Declaration of War Against Japan, 1941 December 8, Henry Lewis Stimson Papers (Microfilm edition, reel 105), Manuscripts and Archives, Yale University Library, New Haven, Connecticut.

68. Telegram from William Loeb to Henry Stimson, 1941 December 8, Henry Lewis Stimson Papers (Microfilm edition, reel 105), Manuscripts and Archives, Yale University Library, New Haven, Connecticut.

69. Letter from Douglas Palmer to Henry Stimson, 1941 December 10, Henry Lewis Stimson Papers (Microfilm edition, reel 106), Manuscripts and Archives, Yale University Library, New Haven, Connecticut.

70. Henry Lewis Stimson, Council on Foreign Relations, Royal Institute of International Affairs, *The Far Eastern Crisis* (New York: Harper & Brothers, 1936), 1.

71. Jennet Conant, *Tuxedo Park: A Wall Street Tycoon and the Secret Palace of Science That Changed the Course of World War II* (New York: Simon and Schuster, 2003), 24.

72. *New York Times*, "Attack Long Planned, Evidence Indicates," December 8, 1941, 2.

73. Frank L. Kluckhohn, "Japan Wars on U.S. and Britain; Makes Sudden Attack on Hawaii; Heavy Fighting at Sea Reported," *New York Times*, December 8, 1941, 1.

74. Frank L. Kluckhohn, "Japan Wars on U.S. and Britain; Makes Sudden Attack on Hawaii; Heavy Fighting at Sea Reported," *New York Times*, December 8, 1941, 1.

75. Associated Press, "Tokyo Radio Broadcasts a Talk on 'Good Morals,'" *New York Times*, December 8, 1941, 5.

76. *New York Times*, "Text of Roosevelt's Message to Hirohito," December 8, 1941, 12.

77. James B. Reston, "Japan Out to Get Our Cargo Ships," *New York Times*, December 8, 1941, 5.

78. *Washington Post*, "What's Going On and Where," December 9, 1941, 32.

79. *New York Times*, "Wake and Guam Reported Taken," December 9, 1941, 12; *New York Times*, "Japanese Aerial and Ocean Forces Strike in Widening War in the Pacific," December 9, 1941, 4.

80. *New York Times*, "Wake And Guam Reported Taken," December 9, 1941, 12.

81. Hanson W. Baldwin, "Japan's War Pattern: Swift Blows Reveal the Grandiose Aims and Underline Our Defense Problem," *New York Times*, December 9, 1941, 20.

82. Associated Press, "Langley Not Bombed, Navy Advises Bulletins," *Washington Post*, December 10, 1941, 1.

83. Associated Press, "Nichols and Clark Air Fields, Fort McKinley Among Targets," *Washington Post*, December 9, 1941, 3.

84. F. Tillman Durdin, "Malaya Thwarts Push by Japanese," *New York Times*, December 9, 1941, 1.

85. *New York Times*, "Hong Kong Raided Twice in a Day," December 9, 1941, 11.

86. *New York Times*, "Japanese in Singapore Celebrate Before Attack," December 9, 1941, 11.

87. United Press, "Great American Navy Defeat Hinted by War Correspondent," *Los Angeles Times*, December 9, 1941, 1C.

88. Associated Press, "Navy's Pacific Chief Tough Customer," *Baltimore Sun*, December 8, 1941, 6.

89. Associated Press, "Move Is Brewing to Courtmartial Island Defenders," *Birmingham (AL) News*, December 9, 1941, 1.

90. Associated Press, "Move Is Brewing to Courtmartial Island Defenders," *Birmingham (AL) News*, December 9, 1941, 1.

91. Associated Press, "Move Is Brewing to Courtmartial Island Defenders," *Birmingham (AL) News*, December 9, 1941, 1.

92. Associated Press, "War at a Glance," *Birmingham (AL) News*, December 9, 1941, 1.

93. C.P. Trussell, "Navy Criticized as Caught Asleep," *New York Times*, December 10, 1941, 1.

94. *New York Times*, "Attack on Sunday Held to Show Study of West," December 8, 1941, 2.

95. *New York Times*, "Japan, U.S. Close 88 Years' Peace," December 8, 1941, 2.

96. Bill Henry, "Japan's Daring Attack on Hawaii Designed to Cripple U.S. Fleet: Suicide Bomb Raid Perfectly Timed," *Los Angeles Times*, December 8, 1941, 1D.

97. *New York Times*, "Hull Often Said 'Japan' in Hitting Croquet Ball," December 8, 1941, 7.

98. Hedley Donovan, "Japan Lied 'Infamously,' Hull Says," *Washington Post*, December 8, 1941, 1.

99. Hedley Donovan, "Japan Lied 'Infamously,' Hull Says," *Washington Post*, December 8, 1941, 1.

100. Associated Press, "Secretary Hull's Statement, U.S. Note of Nov. 26 and Japan's Reply," *New York Times*, December 8, 1941, 10.

101. *New York Times*, "Japan, U.S. Close 88 Years' Peace," December 8, 1941, 2.

102. Nobel Foundation, "The Nobel Peace Prize 1906," http://www.nobelprize.org/nobel_prizes/peace/laureates/1906/roosevelt-bio.html#.

103. Associated Press, "Bulletins," *Baltimore Sun*, December 9, 1941, 1.

104. Associated Press, "Canal Zone Seizes Nationals of Axis," *New York Times*, December 9, 1941, 7.

105. *Birmingham (AL) News*, "First Alien Roundup Is Begun in Alabama; Seven Nabbed By FBI," December 9, 1941, 12.

106. *Boston Daily Globe*, "Germans, Italians Taken by Federal Agents Here," December 10, 1941, 10.

107. *New York Times*, "Japanese Arrests in Country At 345," December 9, 1941, 40.

108. Associated Press, "Roundup; U. S. Seizes Enemy Businesses, Nationals," *Boston Daily Globe*, December 9, 1941, 30.

109. Craig Thompson, "Britain Joins U.S. Against Japanese," *New York Times*, December 9, 1941, 14.

110. *Washington Post*, "Bulletins," December 8, 1941, 1.

111. *New York Times*, "West Coast Acts for War Defense," December 8, 1941, 6.

112. *Los Angeles Times*, "Japanese Aliens' Roundup Starts," December 8, 1941, 1.

113. *New York Times*, "West Coast Acts for War Defense," December 8, 1941, 6.

114. Thomas J. Hamilton, "Japanese Seizure Ordered by Biddle," *New York Times*, December 8, 1941, 6.

115. Thomas J. Hamilton, "Japanese Seizure Ordered by Biddle," *New York Times*, December 8, 1941, 6.

116. Thomas J. Hamilton, "Japanese Seizure Ordered by Biddle," *New York Times*, December 8, 1941, 6.

117. Associated Press, "Support Pledges Flood Olson," *Los Angeles Times*, December 9, 1941, 9.

118. Associated Press, "Unimaginable," *Los Angeles Times*, December 8, 1941, 2.

119. *Los Angeles Times*, "Japan Consul 'Quite Sorry,'" December 8, 1941, 2.

120. *Los Angeles Times*, "Planes Guard City from Air Attack," December 9, 1941, 1.

121. *Washington Evening Star*, "Scientists Concede It's Difficult to Tell Japs from Chinese," December 10, 1941, A5.

122. Associated Press, "Chinese Get Buttons to Distinguish from Japs," *Boston Evening Globe*, December 9, 1941, 6.

123. *New York Times*, "United China Relief," December 9, 1941, 29.

124. *New York Times*, "Planes Guard City from Air Attacks," December 9, 1941, 1.

125. Thomas J. Hamilton, "Japanese Seizure Ordered by Biddle," *New York Times*, December 8, 1941, 6.

126. *Los Angeles Times*, "Disaster Plan Use Imminent," December 9, 1941, A1.

127. *Los Angeles Times*, "City Springs to Attention," December 8, 1941, 1.

128. *Los Angeles Times*, "City Springs to Attention," December 8, 1941, 1.

129. *Los Angeles Times*, "City Springs to Attention," December 8, 1941, 1.

130. *New York Times*, "Fire Siren Blast to Warn of Raids," December 9, 1941, 27.

131. *Los Angeles Times*, "Navy's Intelligence Office Hums in Night," December 8, 1941, 6.

132. Associated Press, "Censors Shut Off News to Axis; U. S. Papers Get Restrictions," *Chicago Daily Tribune*, December 9, 1941, 13.

133. *Chicago Daily Tribune*, "Army and Navy Act," December 9, 1941, 13.

134. *Los Angeles Times*, "Auxiliary Volunteers Swamp Police Stations," December 9, 1941, 7.

135.   Associated Press, "West Coast Marshals Forces to Meet Crisis," *Los Angeles Times*, December 9, 1941, 4.

136.   Associated Press, "West Coast Set to Meet New Danger," *Hartford Courant*, December 9, 1941, 10.

137.   Associated Press, "LaGuardia Issues Air Raid Instructions," *Atlanta Constitution*, December 9, 1941, 11.

138.   *Los Angeles Times*, "J.J. Haggarty," December 9, 1941, 2.

139.   *Birmingham (AL) News*, "Nash," December 9, 1941, 2.

140.   Malvina Lindsay, "The Gentler Sex," *Washington Post*, December 8, 1941, 17.

141.   Dorothy Dix, "Men Are Slaves to Beauty, Yet When Marry They Pass up Looks," *Baltimore Sun*, December 8, 1941, 25.

142.   H.I. Phillips, "The Once Over," *Washington Post*, December 8, 1941, 13.

143.   William F. Kerby, "All Consumption Curbs Due to Be Stiffened; Scarcity List Will Grow," *Wall Street Journal*, December 8, 1941, 1.

144.   William F. Kerby, "All Consumption Curbs Due to Be Stiffened; Scarcity List Will Grow," *Wall Street Journal*, December 8, 1941, 1.

145.   William F. Kerby, "All Consumption Curbs Due to Be Stiffened; Scarcity List Will Grow," *Wall Street Journal*, December 8, 1941, 1.

146.   Thomas J. Keller, "Civilian Uses of Copper, Lead, Zinc and Other Vital Metals to Disappear; Increased Output Will Be Pushed," *Wall Street Journal*, December 8, 1941, 2.

147.   Thomas J. Keller, "Civilian Uses of Copper, Lead, Zinc and Other Vital Metals to Disappear; Increased Output Will Be Pushed," *Wall Street Journal*, December 8, 1941, 2.

148.   Associated Press, "Welders End Strike at Ordnance Plant," *New York Times*, December 8, 1941, 18.

149.   Henry Rose, "Japan Almost Wholly Dependent on Imports for Oil; Her Supplies Are Sufficient for 1 to 2 Years," *Wall Street Journal*, December 8, 1941, 5.

150.   Alfred F. Flynn, "Ship Schedules, Priorities Being Revised Based on Longer Routes and Use of Convoys," *Wall Street Journal*, December 8, 1941, 4.

151.   *Wall Street Journal*, "Secret Plans to Protect Defense Plants Put in Immediate Operation," December 8, 1941, 4.

152.   Associated Press, "Free French Declare War on Japan," *Los Angeles Times*, December 9, 1941, 8.

153.   Editorial, "This, Too, Is War," *Birmingham (AL) News*, December 9, 1941, 8.

154.   Walter Lippmann, "U. S. Must Fight Axis Combination on All Fronts," *Boston Daily Globe*, December 9, 1941, 18.

155.   Uncle Dudley, "Dedication," *Boston Daily Globe*, December 9, 1941, 18.

156.   Uncle Dudley, "Dedication," *Boston Daily Globe*, December 9, 1941, 18.

157.   *Washington Evening Star*, "Smoke at German Embassy Indicates Burning of Papers," December 9, 1941, A1.

158.   Associated Press, "Reichstag May Meet Tomorrow to Hear Stand on New War," *Washington Evening Star*, December 9, 1941, A3.

159.   Garnett D. Horner, "Rumors of Nazi War on U.S. Heard By Hull," *Washington Evening Star*, December 9, 1941, 1X.

160.   John C. Henry, "White House Indicates War Crisis Is 'Bigger' Than Clash in Orient," *Washington Evening Star*, December 9, 1941, 1X.

161.   Associated Press, "Germany May Declare War at Any Moment," *Boston Evening Globe*, December 1, 1941, 1.

162.   Associated Press, "Reichstag May Meet Tomorrow to Hear Stand on New War," *Washington Evening Star*, December 9, 1941, A3.

CHAPTER 10: THE TENTH OF DECEMBER

1.   Ruth Cowan, "Roosevelt Shows Little Effect of Strain in Directing War," *Evening Star*, December 10, 1941, A3.

2. Ruth Cowan, "Roosevelt Shows Little Effect of Strain in Directing War," *Evening Star*, December 10, 1941, A3.

3. David Brinkley, *Washington Goes to War* (New York: Alfred A. Knopf, 1988), 105.

4. Ruth Cowan, "Roosevelt Shows Little Effect of Strain in Directing War," *Evening Star*, December 10, 1941, A3.

5. David Brinkley, *Washington Goes to War* (New York: Alfred A. Knopf, 1988), 252.

6. *Evening Star*, "President Defines Duties and Curbs on Resident Aliens," December 9, 1941, 2X.

7. *Evening Star*, "President Defines Duties and Curbs on Resident Aliens," December 9, 1941, 2X.

8. *Baltimore Sun*, "Full Navy Department Shakeup Demanded as Result of Hawaii Defeat," December 10, 1941, 2.

9. J. Edgar Hoover, "J. Edgar Hoover to Edwin M. Watson," December 10, 1941, Federal Bureau of Investigation, President's Official File 10-B: Justice Department; FBI Reports, 1941; Box 15, Franklin Delano Roosevelt Presidential Library and Museum, Hyde Park, NY, 1.

10. Henry N. Dorris, "Senate, House Groups Vote Bills to Keep All in Service During War," *New York Times*, December 10, 1941, 1.

11. *Evening Star*, "U.S. Control of All Radio Authorized," December 10, 1941, A-1.

12. Frank L. Kluckhohn, "Army, Navy Get Control of Radio," *New York Times*, December 11, 1941, 3.

13. *Evening Star*, "Gen. Pershing, 81, Offers Services to President," December 10, 1941, A1.

14. Associated Press, "President's Power Greatly Enlarged," *New York Times*, December 9, 1941, 7.

15. Associated Press, "President's Power Greatly Enlarged," *New York Times*, December 9, 1941, 7.

16. Associated Press, "President's Power Greatly Enlarged," *New York Times*, December 9, 1941, 7.

17. John C. Henry, "Roosevelt Summons State and Military Leaders to Parley," *Evening Star*, December 10, 1941, A1.

18. John C. Henry, "Roosevelt Summons State and Military Leaders to Parley," *Evening Star*, December 10, 1941, A1.

19. Associated Press, "Real Teeth in Price-Control Bill Urged," *Boston Daily Globe*, December 10, 1941, 19.

20. *Birmingham (AL) News*, "Strict Censorship Is on But Feverish Activity Is Apparent," December 9, 1941, 14.

21. Associated Press, "Alien Enemies in U.S. Under Rigid Rules," *Boston Daily Globe*, December 10, 1941, 19.

22. Lawrence E. Davies, "Carrier Is Hunted off San Francisco," *New York Times*, December 10, 1941, 20.

23. Associated Press, "Hawaii Calm Since Blitzkrieg, Governor Says; Food Control Planned to Conserve Supplies," *New York Times*, December 9, 1941, 13.

24. Associated Press, "Seek Exchange of American for Japanese," *Boston Evening Globe*, December 9, 1941, 3.

25. United Press, "Japan to Protect Enemy Nationals," *New York Times*, December 9, 1941, 15.

26. Associated Press, "Americans, Britons Rounded Up," *New York Times*, December 9, 1941, 15.

27. Associated Press, "U.S. Warships in Battle off Manila, Berlin Says," *Baltimore Sun*, December 10, 1941, 1.

28. Associated Press, "Superior Knowledge of Languages Seen as Aid to Japan," *Evening Star*, December 10, 1941, A15.

29. C.P. Trussell, "Navy Criticized as Caught Asleep," *New York Times*, December, 10, 1941, 1.

30. C.P. Trussell, "Navy Criticized as Caught Asleep," *New York Times*, December, 10, 1941, 1.

31. Associated Press, "Wheeler Calls for Support of Roosevelt," *Boston Daily Globe*, December 8, 1941, 11.

32. Winston S. Churchill, *The Grand Alliance* (New York: Houghton Mifflin, 1950), 652–655.

33. Walter Robb, "Clique Pushed Japan Into War, Says Writer," *Los Angeles Times*, December 8, 1941, 4.

34. Glenn Babb, "Japanese Run True to Form—Striking at U.S. Without Warning," *Birmingham News*, December 9, 1941, 13.

35. Glenn Babb, "Japanese Run True to Form—Striking at U.S. Without Warning," *Birmingham News*, December 9, 1941, 13.

36. *Boston Daily Globe*, "Madness Infects Japanese, President of Tufts Asserts," December 9, 1941, 7.

37. *Christian Science Monitor*, "U.S. Navy Suffers a 'Scapa Flow'; Allies Quick to Declare War on Japan," December 11, 1941, C1.

38. Carroll Kilpatrick, "Army Does Not Plan Expeditionary Force Against Japs at Once," *Birmingham News*, December 9, 1941, 14.

39. Carroll Kilpatrick, "Army Does Not Plan Expeditionary Force Against Japs at Once," *Birmingham News*, December 9, 1941, 14.

40. Helen Lombard, "Admiral Leahy's Warning on Japan Recalled, Wanted to 'Clean Up' After Panay Was Sunk," *Washington Evening Star*, A5.

41. David Lawrence, "U.S. Learns, Lesson in Attack," *Evening Star*, December 9, 1941, A11.

42. Jay G. Hayden, "U.S. Navy Caught off Guard," *Evening Star*, December 9, 1941, A11.

43. Associated Press, "Preparedness of Defenses Is Questioned: Capital Hears Queries About Functions of Hawaii Off-Shore Patrol," *Baltimore Sun*, December 9, 1941, 1.

44. *Baltimore Sun*, "Full Navy Department Shakedown Demanded as Result of Hawaii Defeat," December 10, 1941, 2.

45. *Baltimore Sun*, "Full Navy Department Shakedown Demanded as Result of Hawaii Defeat," December 10, 1941, 2.

46. *Baltimore Sun*, "Full Navy Department Shakedown Demanded as Result of Hawaii Defeat," December 10, 1941, 2.

47. Jack Bell, "Hitler Promised to Aid Japs, Says Senator Gillette," *Evening Independent*, December 9, 1941, 1.

48. Husband E. Kimmel, *"Admiral Kimmel's Story,"* (Chicago, IL, Henry Regnery Company, 1955) 32.

49. Husband E. Kimmel, *"Admiral Kimmel's Story,"* (Chicago, IL, Henry Regnery Company, 1955) 2.

50. *Washington Post*, "Strategy at Hawaii," December 8, 1941, 12.

51. *New York Times*, "The Rendezvous with Destiny," December 12, 1941, C24.

52. *New York Times*, "Drastic Control Marks War News," December 9, 1941, 7.

53. Associated Press, "Raid Manila; Seize Guam Call Hawaii Loss 'Disaster,'" *Chicago Daily Tribune*, December 9, 1941, 1.

54. Associated Press, "60 Years Later, Pearl Harbor Pilots Recall Attack," *Mount Airy News*, December 6, 2001, 8A.

55. *Washington Post*, "Strategy at Hawaii," December 8, 1941, 12.

56. *Washington Post*, "Strategy at Hawaii," December 8, 1941, 12.

57. Associated Press, "Reports Plane Mother Ship Sunk," December 9, 1941, 13.

58. *New York Times*, "Large U.S. Losses Claimed By Japan," December 9, 1941, 1.

59. Winston Churchill, *"The Grand Alliance."* (New York, NY, Rosetta Books, 1948), 551.

60. *New York Times*, "Japan Says Allies Are Broken at Sea," December 11, 1941, 1.

61. *New York Times*, "Japan Says Allies Are Broken at Sea," December 11, 1941, 1.

62. F. Tillman Durdin, "Japanese Ashore in Force in Malaya," *New York Times*, December 10, 1941, 1.

63. Associated Press, "Britain and Japan Hurl Reinforcements Into Malayan Jungle Battle," *Baltimore Sun*, December 10, 1941, 4.

64. Associated Press, "Heroism in Philippines," *Baltimore Sun*, December 10, 1941, 4.

65. Associated Press, "Tokyo Claims Seizure of 200 Merchantmen," *Baltimore Sun*, December 10, 1941, 4.

66. Associated Press, "Tokyo Claims Seizure of 200 Merchantmen," *Baltimore Sun*, December 10, 1941, 4.

67. Associated Press, "Tokyo Claims Seizure of 200 Merchantmen," *Baltimore Sun*, December 10, 1941, 4.

68. Franklin Delano Roosevelt Presidential Library and Museum, *"Halifax to FDR Letter Regarding Military Situation: Military Report from London, December 10, 1941,"* December 12, 1941, Hyde Park, NY.

69. Associated Press Wire Photo, "Casualty Error," *Evening Star*, December 10, 1941, A2.
70. *New York Times* "2 False Air 'Raids' Upset New Yorkers," December 10, 1941, 1.
71. *New York Times*, "Blackout Ordered for Capitol Dome," December 10, 1941, 18.
72. International News Service, "The Presidents Day," *Washington Post*, December 11, 1941, 2.
73. *New York Times*, "The President's Address," December 10, 1941, 1.
74. *New York Times*, "The President's Address," December 10, 1941, 1.
75. *New York Times*, "The President's Address," December 10, 1941, 1.
76. *New York Times*, "The President's Address," December 10, 1941, 1.
77. *New York Times*, "The President's Address," December 10, 1941, 1.
78. *New York Times*, "The President's Address," December 10, 1941, 1.
79. *New York Times*, "The President's Address," December 10, 1941, 1.
80. International News Service, "The Presidents Day," *Washington Post*, December 11, 1941, 2.
81. International News Service, "The Presidents Day," *Washington Post*, December 11, 1941, 2.
82. Associated Press, "New Air Raid Alarm Sounded in New York After 2 False Scares," *Evening Star*, December 10, 1941, A2.
83. Associated Press, "New Air Raid Alarm Sounded in New York After 2 False Scares," *Evening Star*, December 10, 1941, A2.
84. Associated Press, "New Air Raid Alarm Sounded in New York After 2 False Scares," *Evening Star*, December 10, 1941, A2.
85. Thomas R. Henry, "Innocent Inquiry 'Alerts' Northeast Seaboard," *Evening Star*, December 10, 1941, B1.
86. Lawrence R. Davies, "Carrier Is Hunted off San Francisco," *New York Times*, December 10, 1941, 20.
87. Lawrence R. Davies, "Carrier Is Hunted off San Francisco," *New York Times*, December 10, 1941, 20.
88. *New York Times*, "The Day in Washington," December 10, 1941, 7.
89. C. P. Trussell, "Navy Criticized as Caught Asleep," *New York Times*, December 10, 1941, 1.
90. C.P. Trussell, "Navy Criticized as Caught Asleep," *New York Times*, December 10, 1941, 1.
91. Associated Press, "Senate Committees Refuse to Question Defense Strategy," *Washington Evening Star*, December 10, 1941, A-5.
92. Paul W. Ward, "Navy and Army Criticized For Hawaii Defeat," *Baltimore Sun*, December 10, 1941, 3.
93. C.P. Trussell, "Navy Criticized as Caught Asleep," *New York Times*, December 10, 1941, 1.
94. *New York Times*, "Arrests of 12,850 Revealed in Vichy," December 10, 1941, 7.
95. *New York Times*, "Arrests of 12,850 Revealed in Vichy," December 10, 1941, 7.
96. *New York Times*, "Arrests of 12,850 Revealed in Vichy," December 10, 1941, 7.
97. Associated Press, "Germany Cuts Off Press Relations with America," *Washington Evening Star*, December 10, 1941, A-1.
98. *New York Times*, "Enlistments Rise to New Highs Here," December 10, 1941, 22.
99. Associated Press, "Bulletins: Report U.S. Burning Papers," *Hartford (CT) Courant*, December 10, 1941, 1.

CHAPTER 11: THE ELEVENTH OF DECEMBER

1. Associated Press, "Germany and Italy Declare War on U.S. and Sign New Axis Alliance," *Washington Evening Star*, December 11, 1941, A1.
2. Associated Press, "Dictators Give Views on Conflict," *Kingsport (TN) Times*, December 11, 1941, 1.
3. Associated Press, "Dictators Give Views on Conflict," *Kingsport (TN) Times*, December 11, 1941, 1.
4. Associated Press, "Dictators Give Views On Conflict," *Kingsport (TN) Times*, December 11, 1941, 1.
5. Associated Press, "Mussolini War Statement," *New York Times*, December 12, 1941, 4.

6.   Associated Press, "Dictators Give Views on Conflict," *Kingsport (TN) Times*, December 11, 1941, 1.

7.   Associated Press, "How Hitler Declared War on U.S.," *Christian Science Monitor*, December 11, 1941, 10.

8.   Associated Press, "How Hitler Declared War on U.S.," *Christian Science Monitor*, December 11, 1941, 10.

9.   Associated Press, "Germany and Italy Declare War on U.S. and Sign New Axis Alliance," *Washington Evening Star*, December 11, 1941, A1.

10. Michael Barone, *Our Country: The Shaping of America from Roosevelt to Reagan* (New York: Free Press, 1990), 145.

11. Brett Gary, *The Nervous Liberals: Propaganda Anxieties from World War I to the Cold War* (New York: Columbia Univ. Press, 1999), 301.

12. *Washington Evening Star*, "Axis Envoys Notifying U.S. of War Received By Under-Officials," December 11, 1941, A2.

13. Bertram D. Hulen, "Hull Very Frigid to Visiting Envoys," *New York Times*, December 12, 1941, 3.

14. *Washington Evening Star*, "Axis Envoys Notifying U.S. of War Received By Under-Officials," December 11, 1941, A2.

15. Associated Press, "Germany and Italy Declare War on U.S. and Sign New Axis Alliance," *Washington Evening Star*, December 11, 1941, A1.

16. *New York Times*, "Charges in German Note," December 12, 1941, 5.

17. Associated Press, "Sequence of Nazi Aggression Leading to Break With U.S.," *Christian Science Monitor*, December 11, 1941, 6.

18. *New York Times*, "Submarine Warfare," February 20, 1940, 18.

19. *Washington Evening Star*, "Axis Envoys Notifying U.S. of War Received By Under-Officials," December 11, 1941, A2.

20. *Washington Evening Star*, "Italian and German Embassies Are Calm at War Declaration," December 11, 1941, A3.

21. *New York Times*, "Our Declaration of War," December 12, 1941, 1.

22. *New York Times*, "City Calm and Grim as the War Widens," December 12, 1941, 1.

23. Frank L. Kluckhohn, "War Opened On Us," *New York Times*, December 12, 1941, 1.

24. Associated Press, "Miss Rankin Voted 'Present' in Weak Voice; Clerk Had to Call Her Name a Second Time," *New York Times*, December 12, 1941, 6.

25. *Chicago Daily Tribune*, "Montana G. O. P. Head Demands Rep. Rankin Change Vote on War," December 9, 1941, 4.

26. Robert C. Albright, "Declaration Laid On President's Desk Three Hours After Two Houses Meet," *Washington Post*, December 12, 1941, 1.

27. Associated Press, "U.S. Troops Released for War Abroad," *Kingsport (TN) Times*, December 11, 1941, 1.

28. Drew Pearson and Robert S. Allen, "Washington Merry-Go-Round," *Kingsport (TN) Times*, December 11, 1941, 4.

29. Associated Press, "Grim-Visaged F.D.R. Signs War Papers," *Atlanta Constitution*, December 12, 1941, 6.

30. Associated Press, "Proof Democracy Can Move Swiftly," *Atlanta Constitution*, December 12, 1941, 6.

31. Associated Press, "U. S. Answers Axis Challenge, Declares War," *Atlanta Constitution*, December 12, 1941, 1.

32. Associated Press, "U.S. Troops Released for War Abroad," *Kingsport (TN) Times*, December 11, 1941, 1.

33. Associated Press, "Tobey Renews Demands for Navy Inquiry," *Washington Evening Star*, December 11, 1941, A1.

34. Associated Press, "Tobey Renews Demands for Navy Inquiry," *Washington Evening Star*, December 11, 1941, A1.

35. Associated Press, "Senators of Both Parties Demand Investigation of Hawaii Attack," *Kingsport (TN) Times*, December 11, 1941, 4.

36. Drew Pearson and Robert S. Allen, "Washington Merry-Go-Round," *Kingsport (TN) Times*, December 11, 1941, 4.

37. *New York Times*, "Silent Galleries Watch War Vote," December 12, 1941, 5.

38. *Washington Evening Star*, "Roosevelt Accepts Offer of Parties to Drop Politics," December 1, 1941, A9.

39. Associated Press, "Democrats and Republicans Adjourn Domestic Politics," *Los Angeles Times*, December 11, 1941, 17.

40. Associated Press, "Japs May Have Timed Attack By U.S. Army's Down Patrol," *Washington Evening Star*, December 11, 1941, A8.

41. Gordon W. Prange, *At Dawn We Slept* (New York: McGraw-Hill, 1981), 70–77.

42. *New York Times*, "Stimson Asks Time for Facts on Hawaii," December 12, 1941, 11.

43. George Fielding Eliot, "Bomb Hits of Japanese Hint New Device Used," *Los Angeles Times*, December 11, 1941, 5.

44. *Washington Post*, "Suicide Pilots' Dove Straight Into Ships, U.S. Officers Think," December 11, 1941, 1.

45. *Washington Post*, "Congressmen Halt Hawaiian Investigation," December 11, 1941, 26.

46. Charles Hurd, "U.S. Fliers Score," *New York Times*, December 12, 1941, 1.

47. Associated Press, "Churchill Expects U.S. Losses to Cut Help for Britain," *Washington Evening Star*, December 11, 1941, A2.

48. Winston S. Churchill, *The Grand Alliance* (New York: Houghton Mifflin, 1950), 620.

49. Associated Press, "130 Officers Saved With 2,200 Men from Wales and Repulse," *Washington Evening Star*, December 11, 1941, A3.

50. Winston S. Churchill, *The Grand Alliance* (New York: Houghton Mifflin, 1950), 590.

51. Canadian Press, "British-U.S. Navies Still Superior To Joint Axis Fleets," *Lethbridge Herald* (Alberta, Canada), December 11, 1941, 1.

52. Associated Press, "Brown of CBS, Rescued from Sea," *Atlanta Constitution*, December 11, 1941, 1.

53. O. D. Gallagher, International News Service, "Repulse Survivor Walked Down to Sea as on Sloping Sidewalk," *Atlanta Constitution*, December 11, 1941, 1.

54. *New York Times*, "The Admiralty's Christmas Card of Good Cheer Becomes a Message of Sorrow," December 11, 1941, 7.

55. *Washington Evening Star*, "Officials Consider Air Raid Shelters for Washington," December 11, 1941, A1.

56. Associated Press, "Capitol Hums with War Activity; One Senator Blocks FDR Bill," *Atlanta Constitution*, December 11, 1941, 2.

57. *Washington Post*, "Navy to Clean Up Merchant Marine," December 11, 1941, 7.

58. Associated Press, "Late War Bulletins," *Washington Evening Star*, December 11, 1941, A1.

59. Alfred Friendly, "U.S. Bans Tire Sales; Will Seize All Imports," *Washington Post*, December 11, 1941, 1.

60. Alfred Friendly, "U.S. Bans Tire Sales; Will Seize All Imports," *Washington Post*, December 11, 1941, 1.

61. Associated Press, "Capitol Hums with War Activity; One Senator Blocks FDR Bill," *Atlanta Constitution*, December 11, 1941, 2.

62. Drew Pearson, Robert S. Allen, "Washington Merry-Go-Round," *Kingsport (TN) Times*, December 11, 1941, 4.

63. Doris Kearns Goodwin, *No Ordinary Time* (New York: Simon & Schuster, 1994), 291.

64. Doris Kearns Goodwin, *No Ordinary Time* (New York: Simon & Schuster, 1994), 265–266.

65. Frank L. Kluckhohn, "Army, Navy Get Control of Radio," *New York Times*, December 11, 1941, 3.

66. Franklin Delano Roosevelt Presidential Library and Museum, "Memo from Chief of Naval Operations Harold Stark to President Roosevelt" December 12, 1941, Hyde Park, NY.

67. Clark Lee, Associated Press, "Landings in North Are 'In Heavy Force'," *Washington Post*, December 11, 1941, 6.

68. Constantine Brown, "This Changing World," *Washington Evening Star*, December 11, 1941, A13.

69. *Washington Post*, "Bulletins: Japs Seize U.S. Consuls at Hanoi," December 11, 1941, 4.

70. United Press, "U.S. Bombs Fire Japanese Battleship; Army Smashes Main Philippine Invasion," *Washington Post*, December 11, 1941, 1.

71. United Press, "Philipines Fight; Army Reports Invasion Under Control, With a New Effort Repulsed," *New York Times*, December 11, 1941, 1.

72. William Safire, Leonard Safir, *Words of Wisdom* (New York: Simon & Schuster, 1989), 54.

73. William Manchester, *American Caesar, Douglas MacArthur 1880–1964* (Boston: Little, Brown and Company, 1978), 152.

74. *Life*, "Commander of the Far East," December 8, 1941, 1.

75. *Life*, "Commander of the Far East," December 8, 1941, 8.

76. *Washington Evening Star*, "Navy Calls Member of House for Duty," December 11, 1941, A13.

77. Robert A. Caro, *Means of Ascent: The Years of Lyndon Johnson* (New York: Alfred A. Knopf, 1990), 20.

78. Robert A. Caro, *Means of Ascent: The Years of Lyndon Johnson* (New York: Alfred A. Knopf, 1990), 24–25.

79. *Kingsport (TN) Times*, "Go Ahead—Surprise Her! With a Diamond," December 11, 1941, 5.

80. *Kingsport (TN) Times*, "Give Her Glamour . . . You Can Do So With . . .," December 11, 1941, 6.

81. *Kingsport (TN) Times*, "To Show Your Devotion Nothing Will Thrill Her More Than a Gorgeous . . .," December 11, 1941, 6.

82. *Washington Evening Star*, "Jordan's Corner 13th & G Sts.," December 11, 1941, A3.

83. *Washington Evening Star*, "Haley's Photo Album," December 11, 1941, A3.

84. Ovid A. Martin, Associated Press, "Housewives Assured Food Supplies Ample for Nation," *Kingsport (TN) Times*, December 11, 1941, 7.

85. *Los Angeles Times*, "Vegetables Found Free of Poisons," December 11, 1941, Part II, 2.

86. *Washington Evening Star*, "Grand Opening! Bladensburg D.G.S. Mkt.," December 11, 1941, A15.

87. *Washington Post* "'Give Gifts That Pour'; Clark's," December 11, 1941, 7.

88. Gladwyn Hill, Franklin Mullin, Wide World, "Nation's Corn Crop Will Be Basic Factor in Deciding War End," *Birmingham (AL) News*, December 11, 1941, 2.

89. Associated Press, "Government Okays New Army Helmets," *Washington Post*, December 11, 1941, 10.

90. Associated Press, "1,000 Heavy Bombers Monthly New Goal of U.S. Industry," *Atlanta Constitution*, 3.

91. Associated Press, "War Brings Peace to Labor Front: Threatens Propeller Output," *Washington Post*, December 11, 1941, 10.

92. *Birmingham (AL) News*, "Two Alabamians Die in Fighting Around Hawaii," December 12, 1941, 1.

93. *Boston Globe*, "Lynn, Hingham Youths Killed at Honolulu," December 12, 1941, 1.

94. *Washington Evening Star*, "Army List of 87 Killed," December 11, 1941, A4.

95. *Washington Evening Star*, "More Victims," December 11, 1941, A4.

96. Associated Press, "This Soldier Is Very Much Alive," *Washington Post*, December 11, 1941, 12.

97. Associated Press, "Admiral Kidd Dead in Action in Hawaii," *New York Times*, December 11, 1941, 4.

98.   *New York Times*, "Award 62 Medals to Heroes of Navy," March 15, 1942.

99.   Associated Press, "Eleven Frenchmen Shot By Germans," *Kingsport (TN) Times*, December 11, 1941, 2.

100. Associated Press, "U.S. Writers Restrained in Germany," *Hartfort (CT) Courant*, December 11, 1941, 13.

101. Associated Press, "Nazis Seize Americans Equal to Number Arrested in U.S.," *Washington Evening Star*, December 11, 1941, A4.

102. *Washington Evening Star*, "Italian Embassy Staff Stocks Up With Vitamins," December 12, 1941, B21.

103. *New York Times*, "U.S. to Exchange Axis Reporters," December 12, 1941, 7.

104. *Washington Post*, "Navy to Clean Up Merchant Marine," December 11, 1941, 7.

105. Associated Press, "5th Columnist Hunt Started by F.B.I.," *Boston Globe*, December 11, 1941, 18.

106. Associated Press, "Justice Department Starts Check on Potential Quislings," *Los Angeles Times*, December 12, 1941, Part-1, 8.

107. *Washington Post*, "Navy to Clean Up Merchant Marine," December 11, 1941, 7.

108. *Los Angeles Times*, "Axis Aliens Have Citizenship Right," December 14, 1941, 11.

109. *Washington Post*, "Navy to Clean Up Merchant Marine," December 11, 1941, 7.

110. United Press, "U.S. Bombs Fire Japanese Battleship; Army Smashes Main Philippine Invasion," *Washington Post*, December 11, 1941, 1.

111. *New York Times*, "Bulletins: N.Y. Harbor Mined, Navy Warns Shipping," December 11, 1941, 33.

112. Associated Press, "Navy Will Bury Dead Where They Lost Lives," *Atlanta Constitution*, December, 11, 1941, 4.

113. *Washington Evening Star*, "Army Mounts Guns to Protect U.S. Buildings and Workers," December 12, 1941, A3.

114. *Atlanta Constitution* "City Defense Corps Formed; Blackout Planned Next Week," December 11, 1941, 1.

115. *Boston Globe*, "Japanese War Propaganda Here, Says Speaker," December 11, 1941, 5.

116. *Los Angeles Times*, "Everything Normal in Hawaii, Brother Phones Angelino," December 11, 1941, Part-1, 9.

117. *Washington Evening Star*, "D.C. Emergency Don'ts," December 11, 1941, A9.

118. F.R. Kent, Jr., "A Blitz Veteran Writes On: Air Raid Behavior," *Baltimore Sun*, December 11, 1941, 30.

119. Howard W. Blakeslee, Wide World, "Here's How to Teach Yourself to See Better in Blackouts," *Birmingham (AL) News*, December 11, 1941, 2.

120. *Washington Post*, "Skip War Talk with Children, OCD Urges," December 11, 1941, 25.

121. *Washington Post*, "Capital Eager to Do Its Share: We Can Be of Great Service By Observing These Don'ts," December 11, 1941, 1.

122. *Washington Post*, "Tin Pan Alley Declares War on Japan," December 12, 1941, 11.

123. *Washington Post*, "Japan's Mark Is Taboo," December 11, 1941, 8.

124. David Brinkley, *Washington Goes To War* (New York: Alfred A. Knopf, 1988), 25.

125. *Washington Post*, "Japan's Mark Is Taboo," December 11, 1941, 8.

126. *Washington Post*, "Military Guard's Shot in Air Stops Thief; U.S. Buildings Install Blackout Curtains," December 11, 1941, 25.

127. Mark Eliot. *Walt Disney: Hollywood's Dark Prince* (New York: Carol Publishing, 1993), 163-166.

128. Louella O. Parsons, International News Service, "Cheers for Cartoons," *Washington Post*, December 11, 1941, 17.

129. Hedda Hopper, "So They Take Busmen's Holidays," *Washington Post*, December 11, 1941, 16.

130. John Lardner, "Slapsie Maxie Gets Set For Babe Ruth's Arrival," *Hartford (CT) Courant*, December 11, 1941, 19.

131. Associated Press, "Axis Powers Pledge No Separate Peace, Japan Announces," *Washington Evening Star*, December 11, 1941, A6.

132. International News Service, "The President's Day," *Washington Post*, December 11, 1941, 2.

133. "Employment Status of the Civilian Noninstitutional Population, 1940s to date," Last Modified: April 11, 2011, http://www.bls.gov/cps/cpsaat1.pdf.

134. *Washington Post*, "Valuable U.S. Documents May Be Hidden in Maryland," December 11, 1941, 7.

135. Doris Kearns Goodwin, *No Ordinary Time* (New York: Simon & Schuster, 1994), 298.

136. Associated Press, "Panama Canal Closed From 6 P.M. to 6 A.M.," *Boston Globe*, December 11, 1941, 9.

137. *Los Angeles Times*, "Planes Search Skies for Japs," December 11, 1941, 1.

138. Associated Press, "Unidentified Planes Circle Los Angeles," *Washington Post*, December 11, 1941, Part-1, 9.

139. *Los Angeles Times*, "Plans Made to Provide Bomb Shelters Here," December 11, 1941, Part-1, 9.

140. *Los Angeles Times*, "San Diegan Killed in Black-out Crash," December 11, 1941, Part-1, 12.

141. *Los Angeles Times*, "Thunderbolts During Storm Cause Bomb Scare," December 11, 1941, Part-2, 1.

142. *New York Times*, "End of Air Raid Alarm Confusion Sought by Army, Navy and City," December 11, 1941, 1.

143. *Boston Globe*, "N.E. Rectifies Mistakes of Its First Air Raid Alarm," December 11, 1941, 1.

CHAPTER 12: THE TWELFTH OF DECEMBER

1. *Washington Evening Star*, "Strong Jap Attacks Dent British Lines on Malayan Border," December 12, 1941, 1.

2. *Washington Evening Star*, "Strong Jap Attacks Dent British Lines on Malayan Border," December 12, 1941, 1.

3. Associated Press, "Vessels Slip Away; Attacks on Luzon at Increased Fury," *Birmingham (AL) News*, December 12, 1941, 1.

4. Dewitt Mackenzie, "The War Today:," *Birmingham (AL) News*, December 12, 1941, 49.

5. *Boston Daily Globe*, "Must Teach Axis Lesson to Remember 1000 Years," December 12, 1941, 24.

6. Richard Overy, *Why The Allies Won* (New York: Norton, W.W. & Company, Inc., 1995), 249.

7. Richard Overy, *Why The Allies Won* (New York: Norton, W.W. & Company, Inc., 1995), 32.

8. David M. Kennedy, *The Library of Congress World War II Companion* (New York: Simon & Schuster, 2007), 480.

9. Associated Press, "Pilot, Killed Sinking Haruna, Called First U.S. Hero in New War," *Washington Evening Star*, December 12, 1941, A6.

10. Associated Press, "Pilot, Killed Sinking Haruna, Called First U.S. Hero in New War," *Washington Evening Star*, December 12, 1941, A6.

11. *New York Times*, "Liners and Carrier Escape Invaders," December 11, 1941, 1.

12. *Washington Evening Star*, "Lone Code Word Puts Pan American Planes on Wartime Plan," December 12, 1941, A15.

13. *Washington Evening Star*, "Our Trial Begins", December 12, 1941, A12.

14. Hanson W. Baldwin, "Air Power Pacific Key," *New York Times*, December 11, 1941, 6.

15. Ernest Lindley, "A Bad Beginning," *Washington Post*, December 10, 1941, 17.

16. *Los Angeles Times*, "If the Battleship is Doomed—," December 11, 1941, 4.

17. Cecil Brown, "Dramatic Death of Battle Cruiser Repulse," *Washington Evening Star*, December 11, 1941, A7.

18. Cecil Brown, "Dramatic Death of Battle Cruiser Repulse," *Washington Evening Star*, December 11, 1941, A7.

19. *Birmingham (AL) News*, "Optimists Warned Japs No Pushover," December 12, 1941, 6.

20. Associated Press, "The Japanese Aren't Any Pushover," *Birmingham (AL) News*, December 12, 1941, 39.

21. *New York Times*, "This Is an Air War," December 11, 1941, 26.
22. David Lawrence, "America's Courage Faces Test," *Washington Evening Star*, December 12, 1941, A13.
23. Associated Press, "Closer British Watch Kept on Nazi Fleet," *Washington Evening Star*, December 12, 1941, 1.
24. *Boston Evening Globe*, "All Men and Women May Be Registered for Defense," December 12, 1941, 1.
25. *Boston Evening Globe*, "All Men and Women May Be Registered for Defense," December 12, 1941, 1.
26. Associated Press, "Bill to Draft Men 18 to 65 to Get Swift House Action," *Washington Evening Star*, December 12, 1941, A1.
27. *Washington Evening Star*, "Recruiting Stations Report Little Letup in Enlistments," December, 12, 1941, A14.
28. *Baltimore Sun*, "Son Gives His Navy Father a Surprise," December 12, 1941, 30.
29. *Telegraph-Herald*, "Sees Need for 10,000 Nurses," December 11, 1941, 8.
30. *Washington Evening Star*, "D.C. Man Jailed for Attempting to Dodge Draft," December 12, 1941, B1.
31. David Brinkley, *Washington Goes to War* (New York: Knopf, 1988), 81.
32. *Atlanta Daily World*, "S.C. Soldiers Given Bibles," December 13, 1941, 1.
33. *New York Times*, "From Jobs to Marines, 'Privilege' to Serve," December 11, 1941, 4.
34. *New York Times*, "From Jobs to Marines, 'Privilege' to Serve," December 11, 1941, 4.
35. Associated Press, "Billions in War Taxes to Be Sought at Once by Legislators," *Washington Evening Star*, December 12, 1941, A6.
36. *Washington Evening Star*, "Model Air-Raid Shelter Planned in Alexandria," December 12, 1941, B1.
37. *New York Times*, "Making the Rounds with a New York City Air-Raid Warden," December 14, 1941, 64.
38. Grace Tully, *F. D. R. My Boss* (Peoples Book Club: Chicago, IL, 1949), 259.
39. *Washington Evening Star*, "Boat Owners Help 24-Hour Patrols on Potomac Bridges," December 12, 1941, B1.
40. *Boston Daily Globe*, "Air Raid Rules for Autoists: Stop, Park at Curb, Lights Out," December 12, 1941, 3.
41. *Washington Evening Star*, Woodward & Lothrop ad, December 12, 1941, B20.
42. *Los Angeles Times*, "Roundup of Aliens Called Nearly Over," December 11, 1941, 8.
43. *Los Angeles Times*, "Roundup of Aliens Called Nearly Over," December 11, 1941, 8.
44. *Hartford (CT) Courant*, "Local Chinese Has His Troubles Proving It On New York Trip," December 11, 1941, 22.
45. Associated Press, "Body of Chinese, Slain by Headsman, Found in Seattle," *Washington Evening Star*, December 12, 1941, A2.
46. *Los Angeles Times*, "Filipino Knifes Japanese in Car," December 13, 1941, B1.
47. *New York Times*, "Warns Americans of 'Split Loyalty,'" December 11, 1941, 7.
48. *New York Times*, "Warns Americans of 'Split Loyalty,'" December 11, 1941, 7.
49. *New York Times*, "Warns Americans of 'Split Loyalty,'" December 11, 1941, 7.
50. Associated Press, "Hitler Admirer and Aides Seized by F. B. I. on Coast," *Washington Evening Star*, December 12, 1941, A2.
51. *Washington Evening Star*, "Congress Is Warned of Sabotage Danger; F. B. I. Calls 'Alumni,'" December 12, 1941, A4.
52. *Washington Evening Star*, "Army Mounts Guns to Protect U. S. Buildings and Workers," December 12, 1941, A3.
53. *Washington Evening Star*, "Congress Is Warned of Sabotage Danger; F. B. I. Calls 'Alumni,'" December 12, 1941, A4.
54. Frank L. Kluckhohn, "Army, Navy Get Control of Radio," *New York Times*, December 11, 1941, 8.

55. *Atlanta Constitution*, "General Motors Defense Output Beats Schedule," December 12, 1941, 20.

56. Frank L. Kluckhohn, "Army, Navy Get Control of Radio," *New York Times*, December 11, 1941, 8.

57. *Washington Post*, "Blue Pencil," December 13, 1941, 14.

58. *Atlanta Constitution*, "Criticism," December 12, 1941, 16.

59. Walter Lippmann, "On Rising to the Occasion," *Birmingham (AL) News*, December 12, 1941, 16.

60. *Pittsburgh Post-Gazette*, "Raid Alarms to Silence Radio Quickly," December 13, 1941, 6.

61. *Birmingham (AL) News*, "Another Chance to Do Your Bit," December 12, 1941, 39.

62. *New York Times*, Jailed in Charity Scheme; Five Men Also Fined in Lottery at Paterson Elks Club," December 13, 1941, 12.

63. Robert Quillen, "No Man's Right to Liberty Transcends Another's Right to Life," *Atlanta Constitution*, December 12, 1941, 16.

64. Will Swift, Ph.D, *The Roosevelts and the Royals* (Hoboken, New Jersey: John Wiley & Sons, Inc., 2004), 133.

65. Associated Press, "Van Nuys Introduces Bill Giving President Extra War Powers," *Washington Evening Star*, December 12, 1941, A6.

66. *Washington Evening Star*, "Tobey Knows Nothing of Hawaiian Battle, Roosevelt Declares," December 12, 1941, A14.

67. *Washington Evening Star*, "Upper House Votes to Give Each Senator $4,500 Assistant," December 12, 1941, A2.

68. *Saturday Evening Post*, "Happy Birthday to You," December 13, 1941, 34.

69. Associated Press, "Five Auto Plants Close Under O. P. M. Order for Curtailment," *Washington Evening Star*, December 12, 1941, A2.

70. Associated Press, "Production of Automobiles May Be Halted Entirely After February 1," *Washington Evening Star*, December 12, 1941, A20.

71. Associated Press, "Ford and G. M. Plan War Operations on Seven-Day Week," *Washington Evening Star*, December 13, 1941, A12.

72. Associated Press, "President Asks Press and Radio Not to List War Casualties," *Washington Evening Star*, December 12, 1941, A2.

73. *Washington Evening Star*, "Army Death List From Hawaii Reaches 155, Still Incomplete," December 12, 1941, A6.

74. *Washington Evening Star*, "Tobey Knows Nothing of Hawaiian Battle, Roosevelt Declares," December 12, 1941, A14.

75. *Washington Evening Star*, "40-Hour Work Week and Overtime Stand, President Declares" December 12, 1941, A14.

76. Associated Press, "Kimmel, Bloch Commend Valor Shown at Hawaii," *Washington Evening Star*, December 12, 1941, B28.

77. Associated Press, "Would-Be Hero Admits Hoax in Blast Scare," *Washington Evening Star*, December 12, 1941, A14.

78. David Brinkley, *Washington Goes to War* (New York: Knopf, 1988), 21.

79. Lamar Q. Ball, "Atlanta's Santa Claus Is in War Up to His Ears, on U. S. Side," *Atlanta Constitution*, December 12, 1941, 1.

80. U. S. Census Bureau, Educational Attainment, "A Half Century of Learning: Historical Census Statistics on Educational Attainment in the United States, 1940 to 2000: Detailed Tables," Last Revised: September 22, 2010, http://www.census.gov/hhes/socdemo/education/data/census/half-century/tables.html.

81. U. S. Census Bureau, Educational Attainment, "A Half Century of Learning: Historical Census Statistics on Educational Attainment in the United States, 1940 to 2000: Detailed Tables," Last Revised: September 22, 2010, http://www.census.gov/hhes/socdemo/education/data/census/half-century/tables.html.

CHAPTER 13: THE THIRTEENTH OF DECEMBER

1. Associated Press, "Californians 'Lose Pants' in Jap Cleaning Shop," *Birmingham (AL) News*, December 12, 1941, 1.
2. *Los Angeles Times*, "Census Bureau Tells Reason for Crowded Clothes Closets," December 12, 1941, 13.
3. Associated Press, "Sees Open Season on 'Japs," *New York Times*, December 12, 1941, 21.
4. *Washington Evening Star*, "Ship, Japan Mail, Has Name Changed to China Mail," December 13, 1941, A12.
5. *Boston Globe*, "Axis Nationals Being Taken Off American Ships," December 13, 1941, 2.
6. Associated Press Wire Photo, "Alien Detention Camp in Canal Zone," *Washington Evening Star*, December 13, 1941, A12.
7. Associated Press Wire Photo, "Alien Detention Camp in Canal Zone," *Washington Evening Star*, December 13, 1941, A12.
8. Associated Press, "Total of 2,541 Enemy Aliens Are Arrested," *Atlanta Constitution*, December 13, 1941, 5.
9. *New York Times*, "Central America Now Fully in War," December 13, 1941, 7.
10. Associated Press, "Housewife's 'Doorstop' Proves to Be 50-Pound Aerial Bomb," *Atlanta Constitution*, December 13, 1941, 2.
11. *Los Angeles Times*, "Gloria Vanderbilt Will Be Married to Di Cicco," December 12, 1941, 1-Part II.
12. *Atlanta Constitution*, "To Amuse Us Today," December 12, 1941, 19.
13. *Atlanta Constitution*, "War Takes Play in Newsreels Showing at Movie Houses Here," December 12, 1941, 19.
14. Associated Press, "A Tokyo Claim—It's Suspect," *San Francisco Chronicle*, December 13, 1941, 1.
15. Associated Press, "Japanese Claim U.S. Battleship Arizona Is Sunk," *Birmingham (AL) News*, December 13, 1941, 1.
16. Constantine Brown, "This Changing World," *Washington Evening Star*, December 13, 1941, A9.
17. Associated Press, "Knox Returns From Hawaii; Hurries Here," *Washington Evening Star*, December 13, 1941, 1.
18. *Washington Post*, "Rain and Sleet Slow Washington Traffic; Many Late to Work," December 13, 1941, 2.
19. John C. Henry, "High Naval Officials Called to White House for Consultation," *Washington Evening Star*, December 13, 1941, A3.
20. Associated Press, "Capital Moves to Tap Vast War Reserves," *Atlanta Constitution*, December 13, 1941, 1.
21. Associated Press, "Bombers and More Bombers Likely to Be Cry in War of Pacific," *Birmingham (AL) News*, December 13, 1941, 2.
22. International News Service, "The President's Day," *Washington Post*, December 13, 1941, 2.
23. International News Service, "The President's Day," *Washington Post*, December 13, 1941, 2.
24. *Washington Evening Star*, "Encircled Axis Troops Attacked by British West of Tobruk," December 13, 1941, A2.
25. Associated Press, "Army Cancels Coast Blackout to Avoid Hysteria," *Boston Globe*, December 12, 1941, 31.
26. Associated Press, "Warnings Wear Out Fire Engine Sirens," *Washington Evening Star*, December 13, 1941, A9.
27. *Los Angeles Times*, "Man Glows in Blackout," December 13, 1941, 5.
28. *Los Angeles Times*, "Black-out Hint on Calling Doctor," December 12, 1941, D.
29. *Los Angeles Times*, "Windows Dim at Plane Plants," December 12, 1941, 5.
30. *Los Angeles Times*, "Alien Rules Tightened," December 12, 1941, 2-Part II.
31. Associated Press, "Blackout Extended 100 Miles Eastward from San Francisco," *Washington Evening Star*, December 13, 1941, A12.

32. *Los Angeles Times*, "Blue Car Lights Under Ban; Autos Must Halt in Blackouts," December 13, 1941, 1.

33. *San Francisco Chronicle*, "FDR Slaps a 'Keep Out' Order on S.F. Harbor; Navy's in Charge," December 13, 1941, 2.

34. *San Francisco Chronicle*, "FDR Slaps a 'Keep Out' Order on S.F. Harbor; Navy's in Charge," December 13, 1941, 2.

35. *Baltimore Sun*, "Blackout of Baltimore Within 10 Days Planned; Westminster Has Drill," December 13, 1941, 24.

36. Associated Press, "3d Blackout in San Diego; 'Something' Off the Coast," *Boston Globe*, December 12, 1941, 22.

37. Associated Press, "Brief Alert Is Sounded on New England Coast," *Washington Evening Star*, December 13, 1941, A2.

38. *New York Times*, "Veteran Briton Gives Us Raid Pointers; Says Police and Fire Autos Should Use Bells," December 12, 1941, 20.

39. *New York Times*, "Veteran Briton Gives Us Raid Pointers; Says Police and Fire Autos Should Use Bells," December 12, 1941, 20.

40. *Los Angeles Times*, "Weather Bureau Halts Forecasts," December 13, 1941, 1.

41. Associated Press, "New Orleans Won't Have Mardi Gras," *Los Angeles Times*, December 13, 1941, D.

42. *New York Times*, "Churches Prepare for Raids on City," December 12, 1941, 21.

43. *New York Times*, "Theatres to Test Blackout Tonight; Lights in 45th Street Are to Go Out," December 13, 1941, 12.

44. Paul Mallon, "Huge Increase in Army Now Is Imperative," *Birmingham (AL) News*, December 12, 1941, 1.

45. Eugene Burns, "Six Vicious Raids by Japs Leave Oahu's Defenders Fighting Mad," *Washington Evening Star*, December 12, 1941, A8.

46. Associated Press, "Japanese Populace Told New York Was Bombed Twice," *Los Angeles Times*, December 13, 1941, A.

47. *Washington Evening Star*, "Day Parking Banned For Christmas Season," December 13, 1941, A7.

48. *Washington Evening Star*, "War Won't Stop D.C. Christmas Tree Program," December 13, 1941, A16.

49. Christine Sadler, "Guns Mounted, D.C. Wardens on 24-Hr. Shift," *Washington Post*, December 13, 1941, 8.

50. Eleanor Roosevelt, "My Day," *Atlanta Constitution*, December 13, 1941, 14.

51. *New York Times*, "City Calm As The War Widens," December 12, 1941, 1.

52. *Boston Globe*, "Says Jap Attack Brings Unanimity of Action to U.S.," December 12, 1941, 4.

53. *Boston Globe*, "National Peace Group Disbands, Votes Funds for Defense Bonds," December 12, 1941, 31.

54. *Los Angeles Times*, "America First to Be Dissolved," December 12, 1941, 8.

55. *Boston Globe*, "Hemisphere Solidarity," December 12, 1941, 26.

56. *New York Times*, "City Calm as the War Widens," December 12, 1941, 1.

57. *New York Times*, "14 Convicted Here as German Spies," December 13, 1941, 1.

58. *New York Times*, "14 Convicted Here as German Spies," December 13, 1941, 1

59. Associated Press, "'Loyalty' Probe Before Civil Pilots Can Fly Again," *Boston Globe*, December 12, 1941, 5.

60. *New York Times*, "Ban Lifted By CAA on Private Airplanes," December 12, 1941, 12.

61. *Boston Globe*, "Manual Cautions Against Pollution of Water Supply," December 12, 1941, 31.

62. Gene R. Casey, "Crack Army Crews Are Constantly Alert at Guns, Searchlights," *Boston Globe*, December 12, 1941, 31.

63. Gene R. Casey, "Key Cities Armed Camps in Greater Boston Now," *Boston Globe*, December 12, 1941, 14.

64. *Boston Globe*, "State Bans Cameras at Boston's Airport Following Complaint," December 12, 1941, 33.
65. Gene R. Casey, "Key Cities Armed Camps in Greater Boston Now," *Boston Globe*, December 12, 1941, 14.
66. *Boston Globe*, "Good for You, Food for You, Guinness," December 12, 1941, 31.
67. *Boston Globe*, "Norman Thomas Tells His Stand on War at Harvard University," December 12, 1941, 33.
68. *Boston Globe*, "Museum Closes to Public Its Jap Art Treasures," December 12, 1941, 23.
69. *Boston Globe*, "Pilgrim Monument Beacon Blacked Out at Provincetown," December 13, 1941, 2.
70. Associated Press, "Lloyd's Discontinues War Risk Insurance on Property in U.S.," *Boston Globe*, December 12, 1941, 22.
71. Associated Press, "Price-Fixing Fines Levied," *Los Angeles Times*, December 12, 1941, 12.
72. Associated Press, "Price Ceilings Are Placed on Fats and Oils," *Atlanta Constitution*, December 13, 1941, 4.
73. *New York Times*, "Japanese Farmers Exempt," December 12, 1941, 3.
74. *New York Times*, "City Votes $25,000 for Raid Sirens," December 12, 1941, 20.
75. United Press, "Japanese Pounded in Luzon, Warships Chased; Russians Rout Nazi Armies on Moscow Front; House Gets Bill to Register All Men 18 to 64," *New York Times*, December 13, 1941, 1.
76. *Saturday Evening Post*, "Smoker's Hack!" December 13, 1941, 60.
77. *Saturday Evening Post*, "Greetings from Philip Morris," December 13, 1941, 64.
78. *Saturday Evening Post*, "Something New has been added!," December 13, 1941, 67.
79. *Saturday Evening Post*, "Merry Crispness," December 13, 1941, 94.
80. *Saturday Evening Post*, "Thirst Asks Nothing More," December 13, 1941, 126.
81. Associated Press, "Guam Probably Taken By Japs, Navy Says, Conferees O.K. 10 Billion For Defense," *Washington Evening Star*, December 13, 1941, 1.
82. Associated Press, "Enemy Is Wiped Out North of Manila by Stubborn Defenders," *Washington Evening Star*, December 13, 1941, 1.
83. Associated Press, "Army Concludes Mopping Up in Lingayen Sector," *Washington Evening Star*, December 13, 1941, 1.
84. Associated Press, "Japs Claim Sinking of Battleship Arizona at Hawaii Sunday," *Washington Evening Star*, December 13, 1941, A2.
85. Associated Press, "4000 Japs Drown," *Boston Globe*, December 13, 1941, 1.
86. David M. Nichol, "'Human Torpedoes' Story Denied by Jap Naval Attache at Vichy," *Boston Globe*, December 13, 1941, 17.
87. Associated Press, "Tokyo Admits Using 'Human Torpedoes'," *Washington Post*, December 13, 1941, 6.
88. Associated Press, "Pearl Harbor War Widows to Get More," *Pittsburg Post-Gazette*, December 18, 1941, 2.
89. Associated Press, "'I Know He's Happy,' Mrs. Kelly Says on Death of Hero Husband," *Washington Evening Star*, December 13, 1941, A3.
90. United Press, "First Gold Star of 1942 Awarded," *Los Angeles Times*, December 14, 1941, 9.

CHAPTER 14: THE FOURTEENTH OF DECEMBER

1. Associated Press, "Line-Up of Countries Now at War," *Evening Star*, December 13, 1941, A6.
2. Associated Press, "Line-Up of Countries Now at War," *Evening Star*, December 13, 1941, A6.
3. *Washington Post*, "Eire's Stand Unchanged," December 1, 1941, 11.
4. David Brinkley, *Washington Goes to War* (New York: Alfred A. Knopf, 1988), 93.
5. *Baltimore Sun*, "Transit Visas Restricted By Portugal," December 13, 1941, 4.
6. Associated Press, "German Army in Headlong Retreat From Moscow After Utter Defeat," *Atlanta Constitution*, December 13, 1941, 1.
7. Hanson W. Baldwin, "Philippines Delaying Foe," *New York Times*, December 13, 1941, 4.

8. Associated Press, "Nazis Shoot 4 in Paris," *New York Times*, December 13, 1941, 4.

9. By Telephone, "100 Hostages Shot By Nazis in France," *New York Times*, December 14, 1941, 1.

10. *New York Times*, "Reich to Register Americans Over 50," December 13, 1941, 7.

11. W. H. Shippen, "Wherein He Found 'Sanctity of Space,'" *Evening Star*, December 13, 1941, 17.

12. *Washington Evening Star*, "Bolles Urges Dimming Lights to Guard City," December 13, 1941, A16.

13. Associated Press, "U.S. Flyers Battle Japs in Manila Raid," *Sunday Star*, December 14, 1941, 1.

14. Associated Press, "War Insurance Firm Created By Government," *Atlanta Constitution*, December 14, 1941, 9B.

15. David Brinkley, *Washington Goes to War* (New York: Alfred A. Knopf, 1988), xiv.

16. David Brinkley, *Washington Goes to War* (New York: Alfred A. Knopf, 1988), 20.

17. Private Walter Weisbecker, "War and Washington: Soldiers Made to Feel They Belong," *San Francisco Chronicle*, December 14, 1941, 8.

18. *Sunday Star*, "Where to Go What to Do," December 14, 1941, B6.

19. *Atlanta Constitution*, "Attack on Flag Stirred Troops, Atlantan Says," December 13, 1941, 11.

20. *Lethbridge Herald*, "Censor Puts Ban on Kisses in a Row," December 15, 1941, 2.

21. Associated Press, "Plan No Censorship of Domestic Mail," *Boston Sunday Globe*, December 14, 1941, 10.

22. *Los Angeles Times*, "Less Talk Urged on Navy Actions," December 13, 1941, 5.

23. *San Francisco Chronicle*, "U.S. Worried About Gas Protection, Says Mrs. FDR," December 14, 1941, 7.

24. Thomas R. Henry, "Civilian Gas Mask Bill Action Scheduled in Congress Tomorrow," *Sunday Star*, December 14, 1941, A3.

25. *Los Angeles Times*, "Report of Labor Exodus Denied," December 14, 1941, 24.

26. George Gallup, "Air Raid Sentiments Sounded in Gallup Poll," *New York Times*, December 13, 1941, 4.

27. *Washington Post*, "Do's and Don'ts for Handling Fire Bombs," December 13, 1941, 8.

28. *Atlanta Constitution*, "Skull Practice Held Here on Handling Incendiary Bombs," December 14, 1941, 12A.

29. *Sunday Star*, "The Volunteer Overlax of Army Here," December 14, 1941, A4.

30. *Los Angeles Times*, "Draft Objector Ready to Serve," December 13, 1941, 1D.

31. *Atlanta Constitution*, "Georgian Killed in Hawaii Attack," December 13, 1941, 2A.

32. *Birmingham News*, "Lauderdale Negro Killed In Naval Engagement," December 14, 1941, 1.

33. *Boston Sunday Globe*, "Military Honors for Lynn Private Killed in Hawaii," December 14, 1941, 7.

34. *Boston Sunday Globe*, "Schools Asked to Make Stretchers and First Aid Chests," December 14, 1941, 7.

35. Associated Press, "Blind Man Offers Self and Seeing-Eye Dog as Blackout Guides," *The Sunday Star*, December 14, 1941, A3.

36. *Birmingham News*, "Boy Scouts to Help," December 14, 1941, 16.

37. *Birmingham News*, "Class at Millport Will Call Off Tour, Buy Defense Bond."

38. *The Atlanta Constitution*, "War Writes New Corus to Song," December 14, 1941, 1A.

39. *The Atlanta Constitution*, "Auto Clubs Helping Defense," December 14, 1941, 6B.

40. *The Sunday Star*, "Gen. Wood Volunteers Services During War," December 14, 1941, A5.

41. *New York Times*, "America First Unit Quits," December 13, 1941, 10.

42. *Sunday Star*, "Gen. Wood Volunteers Services During War," December 14, 1941, A4.

43. Associated Press, "Provisions of Draft Bill," December 13, 1941, 14.

44. *Los Angeles Times*, "Worker Surplus Now Wiped Out," December 13, 1941, 1 Part I.

45. Associated Press, "Studies No Reason For Not Serving," *Evening Star*, December 14, 1941, C1.

46. Associated Press, "Army Officer Urges Rose Bowl Football Game Be Cancelled," *Atlanta Constitution*, December 13, 1941, 1A.

47. Walter McCallum, "Ban on Big-Time Competitive Golf by U.S.G.A. for Duration of War Expected," *The Sunday Star*, December 14, 1941, C2.

48. *Sunday Star*, "Riggs, Sarah Cooke Get Top Rankings In U.S. Tennis," December 14, 1941, C2.

49. Associated Press, "Frank Capra Quits Films to Join the Signal Corps," *New York Times*, December 13, 1941, 24; Joseph McBride. *Frank Capra: The Catastrophe of Success* (New York: St. Martins Griffin, 2000), 448-460.

50. *Los Angeles Times*, "Frank Capra Awaiting Summons from Army," December 13, 1941, 2.

51. Hedda Hopper, "What Will Public Say?" *Washington Post*, November 2, 1942, B6.

52. *Los Angeles Times*, "Fox West Coast Theaters," December 15, 1941, A15.

53. Associated Press, "Defense Plant Where Explosion Killed Nine," *New York Times*, December 13, 1941, 10.

54. *Lost Angeles Times*, "Drowned Man's Body Found, Probable Victim of Blackout," December 14, 1941, A2.

55. *Christian Science Monitor*, "Oregon Sinking Described at Federal Probe," December 12, 1941, 5.

56. *New York Times*, "Canada to Ration Gasoline April 1," December 12, 1941, 12.

57. Henry E. Rose, "Public to Get Lower Quality Fuel, Means Higher Motorists' Bills," *Wall Street Journal*, December 13, 1941, 1.

58. *Wall Street Journal*, "Heavy Food Buying in Some Areas Forces Grocers to Impose Informal Curbs," December 13, 1941, 2.

59. Associated Press, "O.P.M. Act Bars Sugar Hoarding or Speculation," *Boston Daily Globe*, December 13, 1941, C3.

60. *San Francisco Chronicle*, "OPM Order: Deliveries of Sugar to Big Users Curbed," December 14, 1941, 9.

61. J.S. Armstrong, "Major Shift Seen In War Financing," *Baltimore Sun*, December 13, 1941, 17.

62. George Gallup, "Price, Wage Control Favored," *Atlanta Constitution*, December 14, 1941, 2.

63. Drew Pearson, "President's Bodyguard Strips Jap Newsmen of Their White House Passes; Living Costs Continue Upward Trend," *Birmingham News*, December 14, 1941, 1.

64. *San Francisco Chronicle*, "New York Wrecks Symbol of Goodwill," December 14, 1941, 13.

65. *Baltimore Sun*, "Baltimore Army Nurse 'Well, Safe' in Hawaii," December 13, 1941, 6.

66. *Baltimore Sun*, "Baltimore Army Nurse 'Well, Safe' in Hawaii," December 13, 1941, 6.

67. *Sunday Star*, "Six U.S. Flyers Cited by Army for 'Spectacular Heroism' in Battle to Save Honolulu," December 14, 1941, A1.

68. Celestine Sibley, "54 Women Learning Meaning of Dot-Dash in Classes Here," *Atlanta Constitution*, December 14, 1941, 4B.

69. *San Francisco Chronicle*, "This World" Cover, Col. 5, No. 38, December 14, 1941.

70. Richard H. Minear, *Dr. Seuss Goes to War* (New York: The New Press, 2001).

71. Franklin Delano Roosevelt Presidential Library and Museum, "Report By The Secretary of the Navy to the President," December 14, 1941, Hyde Park, NY.

72. Glen Babb, "There Is No 'One Man' in Japan But Adml. Yamamoto New Hero," *Birmingham News*, December 14, 1941, 8.

73. United Press, "Rear Admiral Kimmel's Death, Reported by Japan, Doubted," *Los Angeles Times*, December 14, 1941, 1.

74. Clarke Beach, "America's Strategic Islands Are Keys to Victory in Pacific," *Sunday Star*, December 14, 1941, B5.

75. Owen L. Scott, "U.S. Facing Long Hard-Fought War," *Boston Sunday Globe*, December 14, 1941, 7.

76. *Sunday Star*, "Kann's Toyland" Advertisement, December 14, 1941, B6.

77. *New York Times*, "Dance Lessons Cost No More at Arthur Murray's," December 14, 1941, X4.

78. *Boston Sunday Globe*, "Gilchrist's" Advertisement, December 14, 1941, 7.

79. *New York Times*, "Saks-34th" Advertisement, December 14, 1941, 17.

80. *Sunday Star*, "Best Sellers," December 14, 1941, E7.

81. *Sunday Star*, "The President" Advertisement, December 14, 1941, D15.

82. Jay Carmody, "Another Year, Another 10-Best List," *Sunday Star*, December 14, 1941, E1.

83. Carolyn Anspacher, "Neediest Families: You Can Help Keep the Home Fires Burning," *San Francisco Chronicle*, December 14, 1941, 9.

84. Blair Bolles, "Total War Between the Democracies and Berlin-Rome-Tokyo Axis Engulfs War," *Sunday Star*, December 14, 1941, B3.

CHAPTER 15: THE FIFTEENTH OF DECEMBER

1. W. E. Lucas, "Fading of Lisbon 'Liberty Beacon' Halts Exodus to America," *Christian Science Monitor*, December 16, 1941, 7.
2. *Boston Daily Globe*, "Hundreds Lose Out on Last U.S. Liner Sailing From Lisbon," December 14, 1941, 10.
3. W. E. Lucas, "Fading of Lisbon 'Liberty Beacon' Halts Exodus to America," *Christian Science Monitor*, December 16, 1941, 7.
4. W. E. Lucas, "Fading of Lisbon 'Liberty Beacon' Halts Exodus to America," *Christian Science Monitor*, December 16, 1941, 7.
5. *New York Times*, "Many Missionaries Listed in War Zone," December 14, 1941, 4.
6. *Life*, "War," December 15, 1941, 27.
7. Associated Press, "Tojo Tells Japanese Diet U.S.-British Fleets 'Crushed,'" *Christian Science Monitor*, December 16, 1941, 7.
8. Franck L. Kluckhohn, "Serious Setback," *New York Times*, December 10, 1941, 1; Charles Hurd, "Two U.S. Isles Holding Out, But Guam Is Believed Lost," *New York Times*, December 14, 1941, 1.
9. *Time*, "The U.S. at War," December 15, 1941, 17.
10. Frank L. Kluckhohn, "Roosevelt Holds Navy Conference," *New York Times*, December 14, 1941, 22.
11. *Time*, December 15, 1941.
12. Waldo Heinrichs, *Threshold of War: Franklin D. Roosevelt and American Entry Into World War II* (Oxford, UK: Oxford University Press, 1990), 18.
13. *Time*, "Labor: Hip & Thigh," November 10, 1941; *Time*, "Letters," December 15, 1941, 4.
14. *Life*, "War," December 15, 1941, 27.
15. United Press, "President Studies First Report on Japs' Surprise Raid on Pearl Harbor," *Yuma (AZ) Daily Sun*, December 15, 1941, 1.
16. Franklin D. Roosevelt Presidential Library and Museum, "Report by the Secretary of the Navy to the President," December 14, 1941.
17. United Press, "President Gives Background of War With Japan," *Yuma (AZ) Daily Sun*, December 15, 1941, 1.
18. Associated Press, "F.D.R. Declares Jap Attack Case of Horror," *Birmingham (AL) News*, December 15, 1941, 1.
19. Associated Press, "Legion Asks Tobey to Demonstrate His Allegiance to U.S.," *Birmingham (AL) News*, December 15, 1941, 6.
20. United Press, "Knox Reveals Six U.S. Warships Lost in Hawaii Attack," *Yuma (AZ) Daily Sun*, December 15, 1941, 2.
21. United Press, "President Gives Background of War With Japan," *Yuma (AZ) Daily Sun*, December 15, 1941, 1.
22. *Time*, "The U.S. At War," December 15, 1941, 18.
23. *Washington Evening Star*, "Secretary Knox's Account of Surprise Attack on Hawaii," December 15, 1941, A1.
24. United Press, "Knox Reveals Six U.S. Warships Lost in Hawaii Attack," *Yuma (AZ) Daily Sun*, December 15, 1941, 1.
25. United Press, "President Studies First Report On Jap's Surprise Raid on Pearl Harbor," *Yuma (AZ) Daily Sun*, December 15, 1941, 1.
26. Charles Hurd, "Heroic Acts Cited," *New York Times*, December 16, 1941, 1.
27. United Press, "Knox Reveals Six U.S. Warships Lost in Hawaii Attack," *Yuma (AZ) Daily Sun*, December 15, 1941, 1.

28. United Press, "Knox Reveals Six U.S. Warships Lost in Hawaii Attack," *Yuma (AZ) Daily Sun*, December 15, 1941, 1.

29. *Washington Evening Star*, "Secretary Knox's Account of Surprise Attack on Hawaii," December 15, 1941, A1.

30. *Washington Evening Star*, "Secretary Knox's Account of Surprise Attack on Hawaii," December 15, 1941, A1.

31. *Washington Evening Star*, "Secretary Knox's Account of Surprise Attack on Hawaii," December 15, 1941, A1.

32. Turner Jordan, "President Roosevelt on All Stations Over Bill of Rights Program," *Birmingham (AL) News*, December 15, 1941, 7.

33. *Los Angeles* Times, "City Unites Today to Honor Bill of Rights Anniversary," December 15, 1941, A1; United Press, "President to Speak Tonight at 8:00 M.S.T.," *Yuma (AZ) Daily Sun*, December 15, 1941, 1.

34. Associated Press, "Bill of Rights Exercises to Be Observed," *Atlanta Constitution*, December 14, 1941, 3.

35. Associated Press, "Allies Are Expected to Take Solemn Vow of No Separate Peace," *Birmingham (AL) News*, December 14, 1941, 1.

36. German Radio received by Associated Press, "Axis Powers Hold Parley," *Lethbridge Herald* (Alberta, Canada), December 15, 1941, 1.

37. Associated Press, "On Warpath Again," *Lethbridge Herald* (Alberta, Canada), December 15, 1941, 6.

38. United Press, "White House Under Guard; No Longer Goldfish Bowl," *Los Angeles Times*, December 14, 1941, 8.

39. *Los Angeles Times*, "Closed Forest Area Patroled," December 14, 1941, 27.

40. Associated Press, "Patrols to Halt All Ships Nearing Naval Academy," *Washington Evening Star*, December 15, 1941, B20.

41. *New York Times*, "One Plate for New York Autos in 1942, The Other to Be Kept for Use in 1943," December 14, 1941, 1.

42. *New York Times*, "Nazi Citizens are Barred From Liquor Licenses," December 14, 1941, 13.

43. Associated Press, "Stove Firms' Use of Metals Is Cut," *Milwaukee Journal*, December 15, 7.

44. *New York Times*, "11,000 Small Firms Rally for Work," December 21, 1941, 9.

45. *Time*, "Weld It!," December 15, 1941, 44.

46. *Washington Post*, "Coast Guard Takes Over Swedish Liner," December 14, 1941, 1; *New York Times*, "The International Situation," December 13, 1941, 1.

47. *Birmingham (AL) News*, "Sandusky, Ohio, Firm Awarded High Honors for Defense Efficiency," December 14, 1941, 13.

48. *Christian Science Monitor*, "Two Refuse Salute; Dismissed From Jobs," December 15, 1941, 3.

49. *New York Times*, "GE Works on Sunday," December 15, 1941, 13.

50. Associated Press, "Jersey Factory Blast Checked by F.B.I., Navy and Police," *Washington Evening Star*, December 15, 1941, A-14.

51. *Baltimore Sun*, "War Boosts Total of Blood Donors," December 14, 1941, 16.

52. *Life*, "Movie of the Week: Ball of Fire," December 15, 1941, 89.

53. Associated Press, "Few Things Escape Slang In U.S. Army," *Baltimore Sun*, December 1941, 7.

54. *Life*, "Movie of the Week: Ball of Fire," December 15, 1941, 89.

55. *Life*, "Do You Tell Yourself You Smoke Too Much?" December 15, 1941, 24 and 128.

56. *Los Angeles Times*, "Body of Japanese Found in Canal," December 14, 1941, 27.

57. *Birmingham (AL) News*, "Americans Reminded Most Aliens in U.S. Still Loyal Citizens," December 14, 1941, 19.

58. *Birmingham (AL) News*, "Americans Reminded Most Aliens in U.S. Still Loyal Citizens," December 14, 1941, 19.

59. *Los Angeles Times*, "Little Tokyo Lid Clamped," December 14, 1941, 1D.

60. Hyung-chan Kim, edit., *Asian Americans and the Supreme Court: A Documentary History* (Westport, CT: Greenwood Publishing Group, 1992), 44.

61. Associated Press, "Japanese Report All-Out Land and Air Offensive Aimed to Capture Hongkong," *Baltimore Sun*, December 15, 1941, 2; United Press, "Enemy Force In Northern Luzon Halted," *Washington Post*, December 11, 1941, 1.

62. Associated Press, "Japanese Drive Forcing British to Quit Kowoloon," *Christian Science Monitor*, December 15, 1941, 1.

63. Associated Press, "King George Marks 46th Birthday," *Los Angeles Times*, December 15, 1941, 2.

64. Canadian Press, "Jungle Fight Is Confused in Malaya," *Lethbridge Herald* (Alberta, Canada), December 15, 1941, 1.

65. Associated Press, "Philippines Declare Emergency State," *Lethbridge Herald* (Alberta, Canada), December 15, 1941, 3; Canadian Press, "Thailand Is Enemy Occupied Country," *Lethbridge Herald* (Alberta, Canada), December 15, 1941, 3.

66. United Press, "How Tables Turned," *Lethbridge Herald* (Alberta, Canada), December 15, 1; Robert C. Freeman and Jon R. Felt, *German Saints at War* (Springville, UT: Cedar Fort, 2008), 205.

67. Associated Press, "New Gains Reported, British Forces Seek Showdown in Libya," *Washington Evening Star*, December 15, 1941, B15; Associated Press, "Indian Troops Reported Repulsing Nazi Forces," *Washington Evening Star*, December 15, 1941, B15.

68. Associated Press, "Marines Are Holding Firm on Tiny Island Despite Air Attacks," *Atlanta Constitution*, December 15, 1941, 1.

69. Associated Press, "80,000 Serbs Hold Germans," *Lethbridge Herald* (Alberta, Canada), December 15, 1941, 2.

70. Associated Press, "Guerrillas Immobilize 24 Axis Divisions, Greeks Report," *Washington Evening Star*, December 15, 1941, A4.

71. Richard L. Strout, "Key Post Seen in Government Seen Probable for Wilkie," *Christian Science Monitor*, December 15, 1941, 3.

72. Richard L. Strout, "Key Post Seen in Government Seen Probable for Wilkie," *Christian Science Monitor*, December 15, 1941, 3.

73. *Washington Evening Star*, "Arnold Named to Be Lieutenant General; 14 Others Promoted," December 15, 1941, B9.

74. Eleanor Roosevelt, "My Day: Ingenuity Replaces Lack of Material," *Atlanta Constitution*, December 15, 1941, 14.

75. Franklin Delano Roosevelt Presidential Library and Museum, "FDR: Day by Day—The Pare Lorentz Chronology," December 15, 1941.

76. Joseph C. Harsch, "Blackouts Find Honolulu Ready for Any Challenge," *Christian Science Monitor*, December 15, 1941, 1.

77. Associated Press, "First Air Passengers Arrive from Hawaii," *Washington Evening Star*, December 15, 1941, B18; United Press, "Honolulu Back on Air," *New York Times*, December 15, 1941, 4.

78. Associated Press, "Rose Bowl Game to Be Played at Duke," *Washington Evening Star*, December 15, 1941, A1.

79. Associated Press, "Launchings Lose Fanfare to Save Money and Time," *Washington Evening Star*, December 15, 1941, A8.

80. *Washington Evening Star*, "Two Men From District Area Killed in Pacific, Navy Says," December 15, 1941, A2.

81. Associated Press, "City Which Gave One Son in '18 Lost Three in Hawaii," *Washington Evening Star*, December 15, 1941, A7.

82. David Lawrence, "Hawaii Attack Held Jap Blunder," *Washington Evening Star*, December 15, 1941, A11.

CHAPTER 16: THE SIXTEENTH OF DECEMBER

1. *Time*, "Wandering Jews," December 15, 1941, 67.
2. *Time*, "Wandering Jews," December 15, 1941, 67.
3. *Time*, "Wandering Jews," December 15, 1941, 67.
4. *Christian Science Monitor*, "Fading Lisbon 'Liberty Beacon' Halts Exodus to America," December 15, 1941, 7.
5. *Christian Science Monitor*, "Fading Lisbon 'Liberty Beacon' Halts Exodus to America," December 15, 1941, 7.
6. *Washington Evening Star*, "Stores Here Report Brisk Demand for Blackout Cloth," December 15, 1941, B1.
7. *Christian Science Monitor*, "Air Shelter Market Booms in New York," December 16, 1941, 6.
8. *Boston Globe*, "Parents! Read This!" December 15, 1941, 11.
9. *Christian Science Monitor*, "Child Registration Planned by U.S.," December 16, 1941, 6.
10. *Christian Science Monitor*, "Strict Wartime Restrictions Imposed on All Ship Traffic in and Out of Boston; Departures and Arrivals Banned During Night Hours," December 16, 1941, 2.
11. *Christian Science Monitor*, "Weather Data Restricted As 'War Secret,'" December 16, 1941, 2.
12. *Christian Science Monitor*, "Birth Control Hearing Jan. 29," December 15, 1941, 2.
13. *Christian Science Monitor*, "Replanning of South End Urged," December 16, 1941, 5.
14. *Christian Science Monitor*, "Great Throng Gives $35,000 to Aid Russia," December 15, 1941, 5.
15. *Christian Science Monitor*, "Great Throng Gives $35,000 to Aid Russia," December 15, 1941, 5.
16. Ella Winter, *Red Virtue: Human Relations in the New Russia* (New York: Harcourt Brace & Company, 1933).
17. *Boston Globe*, "Firewomen of Bay State Lead Nation," December 15, 1941, 1.
18. *Washington Evening Star*, "Dartmouth Speedup to End School Year by May 10," December 15, 1941, B9.
19. *Birmingham (AL) News*, "University Students Urged to Keep Calm During War Crisis," December 15, 1941, 6.
20. *New York Times*, "Yale Pledges Support of War," December 15, 1941, 17.
21. *New York Times*, "War Work Rushed at City Colleges," December 15, 1941, 14.
22. *Atlanta Constitution*, "Wants U.S. to Win If It Can—But Don't Deprive Her of a Man," December 15, 1941, 2.
23. *Washington Evening Star*, "Snow Clearance Parking Ban Goes into Effect," December 15, 1941, B1.
24. *Christian Science Monitor*, "U.S. Jews to Rally to Full Aid of Allies" December 15, 1941, 9.
25. James W. Fawcett, "3,000 Here Join in Prayers for Victory, Peace," *Washington Evening Star*, December 15, 1941, B1.
26. James W. Fawcett, "3,000 Here Join in Prayers for Victory, Peace," *Washington Evening Star*, December 15, 1941, B1.
27. *Los Angeles Times*, "Catholics End Prayer Ritual: Processional Honoring Our Lady of Guadalupe Climaxes Peace Services," December 15, 1941, A1.
28. *Atlanta Constitution*, "Minister Resigns; Opposed to War," December 15, 1941, 8.
29. *New York Times*, "Kerrl, Dictator of Reich Churches," December 15, 1941, 19.
30. *Christian Science Monitor* "Draft Unlikely for Men over 35," December 15, 1941, 8.
31. Associated Press, "After All, It Seems Swimming Might Be Handy for Sailors," *Birmingham (AL) News*, December 15, 1941, 13.
32. *New York Times*, "Sunday Recruiting Amazes Officers," December 15, 1941, 17.
33. *Atlanta Constitution*, "Domei Writer Denounces Jap Attack on U.S.," December 15, 1941, 8.
34. *Atlanta Constitution*, "Domei Writer Denounces Jap Attack on U.S.," December 15, 1941, 8.
35. Associated Press, "Boy, 16, Army Veteran, Gets His Discharge," *Atlanta Constitution*, December 15, 1941, 9.
36. United Press, "Roads Drop Leave Plan," *New York Times*, December 17, 1941, 30.

37. *Washington Evening Star*, "Defense Sidelights," December 15, 1941, B21.

38. *New York Times*, "'Date Seekers' Are Barred at Enrollment of Boys and Girls for Service in Air Raids," December 15, 1941, 16.

39. Associated Press, "Work Exemption," *Christian Science Monitor*, December 16, 1941, 5.

40. *Wall Street Journal*, "The Electrical Industry," December 16, 1941, 7.

41. *New York Times*, "All Help Pledged by Organizations," December 15, 1941, 15.

42. *New York Times*, "Chief Boatswain Killed," December 15, 1941, 15.

43. *Christian Science Monitor*, "More Japs," December 6, 1941, 8.

44. Associated Press, "Leahy Is Mentioned as Pacific Coordinator," *Birmingham (AL) News*, December 15, 1941, 7.

45. *Los Angeles Times*, "Daylight Plan for City Advocated," December 16, 1941, 1.

46. *Christian Science Monitor*, "Short Wave Listening Posts Vital Sources of War News," December 16, 1941, 8.

47. Dewey L. Fleming, "Half of U.S. Income to Go for War Effort Under Roosevelt Plan," *Baltimore Sun*, December 31, 1941, 1.

48. Dewey L. Fleming, "Half of U.S. Income to Go for War Effort Under Roosevelt Plan," *Baltimore Sun*, December 31, 1941, 1.

49. *New York Times*, "Display Ad 21," December 15, 1941, 17.

50. Wide World, "Figuring Your Income Tax (No. 1)," *Birmingham (AL) News*, December 15, 1941, 13.

51. *New York Times*, "Held Under Sedition Act," December 15, 1941, 8.

52. *Christian Science Monitor*, "Moviegoer Is Fined for Booing President," December 16, 1941, 3.

53. *Christian Science Monitor*, "Children Spurn Flag, Mother Gets a Year," December 16, 1941, 9.

54. Associated Press, "U.S. Prepares to Seize Billion in Enemy Assets," *Washington Post*, December 16, 1941, 15.

55. *Christian Science Monitor*, "Office of Bund Seized by U.S.," December 16, 1941, 9.

56. Franklin Delano Roosevelt Presidential Library and Museum, "Memorandum of Summary of West Coast and Honolulu Reports by Munson Etc.," December 16, 1941, Hyde Park, NY.

57. *Christian Science Monitor*, "'Ad Men' Told of Hug Task of Business," December 16, 1941, 2.

58. *Christian Science Monitor*, "Price Curb Vital to Win War Declares Senate," December 16, 1941, 1.

59. Associated Press, "Farm Bloc Endangers Price Controls," *Wall Street Journal*, December 16, 1941, 3.

60. *Los Angeles Times*, "Live Projectile Falls in Yard," December 15, 1941, 1.

61. *Yuma (AZ) Daily Sun*, "New Powers Voted For President," December 16, 1941, 1.

62. Franklin Delano Roosevelt Presidential Library and Museum, "FDR: Day by Day—The Pare Lorentz Chronology," December 10, 1941.

63. Associated Press, "Blast Hongkong as British Defy Surrender Edict," *Chicago Daily Tribune*, December 15, 1941, 4.

64. Associated Press, "Blast Hongkong as British Defy Surrender Edict," *Chicago Daily Tribune*, December 15, 1941, 4.

65. *Christian Science Monitor* "Fading Lisbon 'Liberty Beacon' Halts Exodus to America," December 16, 1941, 7.

66. *Christian Science Monitor* "Tojo tells Japanese Diet U.S. & British Fleets 'Crushed,'" December 16, 1941, 7.

67. *Christian Science Monitor* "Plan for Joint War Council Speeded by Allied Nations,'" December 16, 1941, 10.

68. *Christian Science Monitor* "Tojo tells Japanese Diet U.S. & British Fleets 'Crushed,'" December 16, 1941, 7.

69. *Christian Science Monitor*, "Yamamoto Planned Assault; Seeks to Take Whitehouse," December 16, 1941, 7.

70. *Christian Science Monitor*, "Army Flier Tells How He Downed Four Enemy Planes in Hawaii Attack," December 16, 1941, 8.

71. *Christian Science Monitor*, "Yamamoto Planned Assault; Seeks to Take Whitehouse," December 16, 1941, 7.

72. *Christian Science Monitor*, "Educators Take Up Project of Planning World Peace," December 16, 1941, 3.

CHAPTER 17: THE SEVENTEENTH OF DECEMBER

1. *Christian Science Monitor*, "A Penny a Plane Bad News for Axis," December 16, 1941, 8.

2. *New York Times*, "Start Fund for a New Arizona," December 17, 1941, 3.

3. *Christian Science Monitor*, "Donations of Cash to Beat Japan Range From One Cent Up to $200," December 17th, 1941, 3.

4. *Christian Science Monitor*, "Reading Girl to Santa: Every Nation Be Free," December 17, 1941, 4.

5. *Christian Science Monitor*, "Aviation Books Free to All Young Fliers," December 17, 1941, 3.

6. *New York Times*, "Congress Speeds Huge War Effort," December 17, 1941, 7.

7. *Baltimore Sun*, "Big Defense Fees Told By Corcoran," December 17, 1941, 8.

8. Robert De Vore, "Large Arms Manufacturer Is Linked to Defense Lobby," *Washington Post*, December 3, 1941, 1.

9. *Washington Evening Star*, "Corcoran Reveals $65,000 Contract Fee," December 16, 1941, 1.

10. *Christian Science Monitor*, "Corcoran Denies Any Fee Concerning Defense Contracts," December 16, 1941, 10.

11. Merrel W. Whittlesey, "Tee to Green . . ." *Washington Post*, April 19, 1942, 5.

12. Gibson, Truman K.; Steve Huntley, *Knocking Down Barriers: My Fight for Black America*. (Chicago: Northwestern University Press, 2005).

13. Francis E. Stan, "Baseball's Old Fox Picks Up a Package," *Washington Evening Star*, December 16, 1941, A-17.

14. *Los Angeles Times*, "Shrine Game to New Orleans," December 17, 1941, 21.

15. Bill Boni, "Tom Harmon Chosen Outstanding Male Athlete of Year in Poll," *Atlanta Constitution*, December 10, 1940, 21.

16. Hy Hurwitz, "Fear Baseball Leagues Will Suspend in '42," *Boston Globe*, December 17, 1941, 1.

17. Larry Wolters, "W-G-N Program Features Oath by Six Recruits," *Chicago Tribune*, December 20, 1941, 14; Larry Wolters, "Theme of Radio in 1942: 'Keep 'Em Rolling!'" *Chicago Tribune*, January 4, 1942, S4.

18. *Christian Science Monitor*, "Pearl Harbor Widows' Pension to Be Raised to Wartime Level," December 17, 1941, 9.

19. *Christian Science Monitor*, "Pearl Harbor Widows' Pension to Be Raised to Wartime Level," December 17, 1941, 9.

20. *New York Times*, "German-Born Parents Lose Sons in Hawaii," December 17, 1941, 11.

21. *New York Times*, "Midget Submarine Has 2 Torpedoes", December 17, 1941, 8.

22. Franklin Delano Roosevelt Presidential Library and Museum, "Memorandum for the President From the Secretary of the Navy Regarding Assets in the Pacific," December 20, 1941, Hyde Park, NY.

23. Franklin Delano Roosevelt Presidential Library and Museum, "Memorandum for the President From the Secretary of the Navy Regarding Assets in the Pacific," December 20, 1941, Hyde Park, NY.

24. Associated Press, "New Air Attack by Japanese Aimed at Philippine Sea Base," *Christian Science Monitor*, December 16, 1941, 8.

25. *Christian Science Monitor*, "Americans in Air and Sea Attacks but Foe Gains in Borneo and Hong Kong," December 17, 1941, 1.

26. *Christian Science Monitor*, "Hong Kong and Singapore in Serious Danger?" December 16, 1941, 1.

27. Hanson W. Baldwin, "The Threat to Singapore," *New York Times*, December 17, 1941, 8.

28. Walter Trohan, "Enemy Warships Shell 2 Isles in Hawaiian Area," *Chicago Tribune*, December 17, 1941, 2.

29. Associated Press, "Hong Kong Is Facing Threat," *Rock Hill Herald*, December 16, 1941, 1.
30. Franklin Delano Roosevelt Presidential Library and Museum, "First Priority of Military Strategy," December 19, 1941, Hyde Park, NY.
31. Hanson W. Baldwin, "The Threat to Singapore," *New York Times*, December 17, 1941, 8.
32. *Washington Post*, "Bomb Kills 6 Gestapo Men in Paris," December 17, 1941, 3.
33. Associated Press, "Indian Heroes, British Officer Stem Japanese," *Atlanta Constitution*, December 15, 1941, 4.
34. *Washington Post*, "Singapore and Hongkong Peril Admitted," December 17, 1941, 4.
35. United Press, "Hitler at Berchtesgaden, Nerves Torn, Turks Hear," *New York Times*, December 17, 1941, 13.
36. Associated Press, "Germans Wreck Shrines of Three Famed Russians," *Chicago Tribune*, December 17, 1941, 14.
37. Franklin Delano Roosevelt Presidential Library and Museum, "Memorandum from the British Embassy to President Roosevelt Regarding Operational Events Covering the 4th to 11th December, 1941," December 17, 1941, Hyde Park, NY.
38. Porter Barclay, "Nazis Take Stern Measures to Nazify Conquered Youth; Polish Children Executed," *Lethbridge (CA) Herald*, December 17, 1941, Back Page.
39. Hanson W. Baldwin, "The Threat to Singapore," *New York Times*, December 17, 1941, 8.
40. *New York Times*, "Tokyo Version of U.S. 'Losses,'" December 17, 1941, 11.
41. *New York Times*, "4 Young Ensigns Take Ship to Sea in Pursuit of Japs," December 17, 1941, 10.
42. *New York Times*, "1917 Powers Voted," December 17, 1941, 1.
43. *Washington Evening Star*, "Congress Expected to Delay Inquiry on Pearl Harbor," December 16, 1941, A-6.
44. Associated Press, "News by Knox Held Amazing," *Los Angeles Times*, December 16, 1941, 1A.
45. *New York Times*, "Hawaiian, With Three Bullet Wounds, Beats Japanese Airman to Death Against a Wall," December 17, 1941, 7.
46. Clarice B. Taylor, "Hawaiian Woman Slays Jap Pilot," *Washington Post*, December 17, 1941, 1.
47. Joseph G. Harrison, "War Powers Granted President; Army-Navy Shake-Up in Pacific?" *Christian Science Monitor*, December 17, 1941, 1.
48. Joseph G. Harrison, "War Powers Granted President; Army-Navy Shake-Up in Pacific?" *Christian Science Monitor*, December 17, 1941, 1.
49. Associated Press, "Pearl Harbor Raid Probers Appointed," *Atlanta Constitution*, December 17, 1941, 1.
50. Husband E. Kimmel, *Admiral Kimmel's Story* (Chicago, IL: Henry Regnery Company, 1955), 78.
51. Joseph G. Harrison, "War Powers Granted President; Army-Navy Shake-Up in Pacific?," *Christian Science Monitor*, December 17, 1941, 1.
52. International News Service, "The President's Day," *Washington Post*, December 17, 1941, 2.
53. *New York Times*, "1917 Powers Voted," December 17, 1941, 1.
54. *New York Times*, "1917 Powers Voted," December 17, 1941, 1.
55. Arthur Krocks, "Hull Warning Unheeded?" *New York Times*, December 17, 1941, 4.
56. *Boston Globe*, "F.D. Labor-Industry Address," December 18, 1941, 9.
57. *New York Times*, "Aid in War Voted By Longshoremen," December 17, 1941, 22.
58. *Boston Globe*, "Rationing Starts on Jan. 4 for Automobile Tires," December 18, 1941, 33.
59. *Christian Science Monitor*, "Don't Neglect Your Pets During Air Raids," December 17, 1941, 3.
60. *New York Times*, "Siren Tests Today; Blast of 15 Minutes Real Raid Warning," December 17, 1941, 1.
61. *Los Angeles Times*, "Daylight Time Plan for City Advocated," December 16, 1941, 1.
62. *Christian Science Monitor*, "Australians Give Up Liberty to Assure Defense of Liberty," December 17, 1941, 9.

63. *New York Times*, "1917 Powers Voted," December 17, 1941, 1.
64. *Nevada State Journal*, "Censor Plan on Out-Going Data Slated," December 17, 1941, 1.
65. *Los Angeles Times*, "Prompt War Censorship Planned by President," December 17, 1941, 11.
66. International News Service, "The President's Day," *Washington Post*, December 17, 1941, 2.
67. David Brinkley, *Washington Goes to War* (New York; Alfred A. Knopf, 1988), 105.
68. Associated Press, "No More Arrests Coming for Alleged Sedition," *Christian Science Monitor*, December 17, 1941, 9.
69. *New York Times*, "1917 Powers Voted," December 17, 1941, 1.
70. Everett R. Holles, "Roosevelt Finds Military Strategy Doing Very Well," *Washington Post*, December 17, 1941, 1.
71. International News Service, "The President's Day," *Washington Post*, December 17, 1941, 2.
72. *New York Times*, "1917 Powers Voted," December 17, 1941, 1.
73. *Atlanta Constitution*, "All Divisions Participate in Bonds' Rally," December 17, 1941, 13.
74. *Wall Street Journal*, "Plans Being Drafted for Wartime Control of Capital if Need Arise," December 17, 1941, 3.
75. "History: B-17 Flying Fortress," *Boeing.com*, 1995–2011. http://boeing.com/history/boeing/b17.html.
76. Associated Press, "First 'Fabricated' Bomber Ready Soon After Jan. 1," *New York Times*, December 17, 1941, 16.

CHAPTER 18: THE EIGHTEENTH OF DECEMBER
1. *Wall Street Journal*, "U.S. Flag Prices Up; Material Scarcities Slow Down Production," December 17, 1941, 1.
2. Associated Press, "Hawaii Buries U.S. Dead Until Peace," *Washington Post*, December 18, 1941, 11.
3. *Chicago Daily Tribune*, "Army, Navy Dead Buried in Hawaii Until War's End," December 17, 1941, 1.
4. *Chicago Daily Tribune*, "Army, Navy Dead Buried in Hawaii Until War's End," December 17, 1941, 1.
5. Associated Press, "Hawaii Buries U.S. Dead Until Peace," *Washington Post*, December 18, 1941, 11.
6. Eugene Burns, "In the Quiet Hills of Honolulu America's Finest Laid to Rest," *Birmingham (AL) News*, December 17, 1941, 1.
7. Eugene Burns, "In the Quiet Hills of Honolulu America's Finest Laid to Rest," *Birmingham (AL) News*, December 17, 1941, 1.
8. Eugene Burns, "In the Quiet Hills of Honolulu America's Finest Laid to Rest," *Birmingham (AL) News*, December 17, 1941, 1.
9. *Washington Evening Star*, "Mass at Georgetown Honors First Alumnus to Die in War," December 18, B1.
10. *Birmingham (AL) News*, "Birmingham Youth on U.S.S. Arizona," December 17, 1941, 21.
11. *Birmingham (AL) News*, "Tarrant Couple Told of Son's Death in Conflict With Japs," December 17, 1941, 22.
12. *Birmingham (AL) News*, "Birmingham Negro is Killed in Action," December 17, 1941, 29.
13. *Birmingham (AL) News*, "Julius Ellsberry," December 18, 1941, 14.
14. *Christian Science Monitor*, "To the Future: A Tribute to U.S. War Hero," December 18, 1941, 1.
15. United Press, "Hawaii Raid Inquiry Opens," *Los Angeles Times*, December 18, 1941, 1A.
16. John G. Norris, "Nimitz Replaces Kimmel; Emmons Made Successor to Gen. Short" *Washington Post*, December 18, 1941, 1.
17. William Manchester, *American Caesar: Douglas MacArthur 1880–1964* (New York: Little, Brown and Company, 1978), 149 to Go for War Effort152.
18. Husband E. Kimmel, *Admiral Kimmel's Story* (Chicago: Henry Regnery Company, 1955), v.
19. David Brinkley, *Washington Goes to War*, (New York: Alfred A. Knopf, 1988), 86.

20. Richard M. Ketchum, *The Borrowed Years* (New York: Random House, 1989), 730.

21. Mark S. Watson, "Three Highest Officers Relieved of Commands; Successors Appointed," *Baltimore Sun*, December 18, 1941, 1.

22. United Press, "Two Generals Also Removed," *Los Angeles Times*, December 18, 1941, 1.

23. Associated Press, "Army, Navy Oust Commanders in Charge During Hawaii Attack," *Atlanta Constitution*, December 18, 1941, 1.

24. Walter Trohan, "Oust Pearl Harbor Chiefs," *Chicago Daily Tribune*, December 18, 1941, 1.

25. Franklin Delano Roosevelt Presidential Library and Museum, "FDR: Day by Day—The Pare Lorentz Chronology," December 18, 1941.

26. Associated Press, "Allies Occupy Portuguese Base as Japan Gains," *Christian Science Monitor*, December 18, 1941, 1.

27. Associated Press, "Allies Occupy Portuguese Base as Japan Gains," *Christian Science Monitor*, December 18, 1941, 1.

28. Frank Hewlett, "Motorized Force Lured to Trap; Foe's Casualties Heavy," *Washington Post*, December 18, 1941, 1.

29. *Christian Science Monitor*, "Sarawak and North Borneo: Rich Lands in Vast Jungle," December 18, 1941, 6.

30. *Christian Science Monitor*, "Sarawak and North Borneo: Rich Lands in Vast Jungle," December 18, 1941, 6.

31. *Wall Street Journal*, "OPM "Freezes" All U.S. Tin Supplies in Sweeping Control Over Imports and Deliveries; Year's Stock on Hand," December 18, 1941, 3.

32. *Wall Street Journal*, "U.S. Assumes Control of California's Oil Industry to Safeguard War Supplies," December 18, 1941, 2.

33. *Wall Street Journal*, "Laundry Machinery Firms Will Receive Large War Orders," December 18, 1941, 6.

34. *Wall Street Journal*, "Business Bulletin," December 18, 1941, 1.

35. *Washington Post*, "Storm Battered North California," December 18, 1941, 6.

36. *New York Times*, "Golf Ball Rush Causes Rationing," December 19, 1941, 27.

37. Bob Smyser, "Scene of Pro Bowl Game Shifted to New York," *Los Angeles Time*, December 19, 1941, 19.

38. *New York Times*, "Ship Is Here With Exiles," December 17, 1941, 24.

39. Associated Press, "6 Die as Navy Plane Crashes in No. Carolina," *Washington Post*, December 18, 1941, 7.

40. *Washington Post*, "Hunt Pressed for Plane Lost with General," December 19, 1941, 1.

41. Associated Press, "Submarine Attacked on Pacific Coast, General Discloses," *Los Angeles Times*, December 18, 1941, 1.

42. Franklin Delano Roosevelt Presidential Library and Museum, "Memorandum for the President from J.R. Beardall on Naval Aircraft Bombs," December 18, 1941, Hyde Park, NY.

43. Franklin Delano Roosevelt Presidential Library and Museum, "Memorandum for the President from J.R. Beardall on Naval Aircraft Bombs," December 18, 1941, Hyde Park, NY.

44. Associated Press, "Cubans Discover German Plot to Signal Planes," *Washington Post*, December 18, 1941, 2.

45. Hedley Donovan, "Conference at Rio Set for January 15," *Washington Post*, December 18, 1941, 5.

46. *Washington Evening Star*, "Defense Bond Sales Soar 146% in Week," December 18, 1941, D6.

47. Harlan V. Hadley, "Auto Series," *Wall Street Journal*, December 18, 1941, 5.

48. Harlan V. Hadley, "Auto Series," *Wall Street Journal*, December 18, 1941, 5.

49. *Christian Science Monitor*, "Status of Enemy Aliens Is Given by U.S. Attorney," December 18, 1941, 2.

50. *New York Times*, "Trade Promoter for Reich Seized," December 20, 1941, 7.

51. David Brinkley, *Washington Goes to War*, (New York: Alfred A. Knopf, 1988), 27.

52. *Christian Science Monitor*, "Status of Enemy Aliens Is Given by U.S. Attorney," December 18, 1941, 2.
53. *Christian Science Monitor*, "Status of Enemy Aliens Is Given by U.S. Attorney," December 18, 1941, 2.
54. *Christian Science Monitor*, "Status of Enemy Aliens Is Given by U.S. Attorney," December 18, 1941, 2.
55. *Christian Science Monitor*, "Status of Enemy Aliens Is Given by U.S. Attorney," December 18, 1941, 2.
56. *Lethbridge Herald* (Alberta, Canada), "Compulsory Registration of All Japanese Is Now Provided For," December 18, 1941, 13.
57. Associated Press, "1,035 Jap Boots Tied Up in British Columbia," *Washington Evening Star*, December 18, 1941, A20.
58. Associated Press, "FBI Seizes Jap Aide In Chicago," *Baltimore Sun*, December 18, 1941, 2.
59. David Brinkley, *Washington Goes to War*, (New York: Alfred A. Knopf, 1988), 87.
60. Associated Press, "Nazi Diplomats Held in Hotel," *Christian Science Monitor*, December 18, 1941, 9.
61. Associated Press, "Swiss Now Represent U.S. in All Belligerent Countries," *Christian Science Monitor* December 18, 1941, 9.
62. Associated Press, "Husbands of Working Wives Face Induction Into Army," *Christian Science Monitor*, December 18, 1941, 3.
63. Associated Press, "Husbands of Working Wives Face Induction Into Army," *Christian Science Monitor*, December 18, 1941, 3.
64. Associated Press, "Husbands of Working Wives Face Induction Into Army," *Christian Science Monitor*, December 18, 1941, 3.
65. Associated Press, "University to Credit Students in Services," *Christian Science Monitor*, December 18, 1941, 3.
66. United Press, "Japanese-Americans Enlist in U.S. Army," *Christian Science Monitor*, December 18, 1941, 3.
67. *Washington Post*, "Nurses May Be Drafted to Meet Greatest War-Time Demand in Nation's History," December 18, 1941, 9.
68. *Christian Science Monitor*, "Snapshots in Color for All," December 18, 1941, 8.
69. *Christian Science Monitor*, "Toy Makers Race to Fill Yule Orders," December 18, 1941, 5.

CHAPTER 19: THE NINETEENTH OF DECEMBER

1. Associated Press, "Allies are Holding Conferences," *Lethbridge Herald* (Alberta, Canada), December 19, 1941, 1.
2. Franklin Delano Roosevelt Presidential Library and Museum, "Memorandum of Agreement: Supreme War Council," December, 19, 1941, Hyde Park, NY, 1–4.
3. Franklin Delano Roosevelt Presidential Library and Museum, "Memorandum of Agreement: Supreme War Council," 1-4, December, 19, 1941, Hyde Park, NY, 1.
4. *Washington Post*, "Nimitz, War Chiefs Map New Strategy," December 19, 1941, 2.
5. International News Service, "The President's Day," *Washington Post*, December 19, 1941, 2.
6. *Los Angeles Times*, "Camps in West to House Aliens," December 19, 1941, 9.
7. *Christian Science Monitor*, "Enemy Aliens Will Be Kept in Camps in the Southwest," December 19, 1941, 8.
8. *Christian Science Monitor*, "Enemy Aliens Will Be Kept in Camps in the Southwest," December 19, 1941, 8.
9. *Los Angeles Times*, "Roundup of Axis Aliens Jails 442," December 19, 1941, 8.
10. *Christian Science Monitor*, "Enemy Aliens Will Be Kept in Camps in the Southwest," December 19, 1941, 8.
11. *Washington Post*, "Laura Ingalls Jailed in D.C. as Nazi Agent," December 19, 1941, 1.

12. *Washington Post*, "Laura Ingalls Jailed in D.C. as Nazi Agent," December 19, 1941, 1.

13. Royal Arch Gunnison, "Japanese to Find Navy Using Offensive Defense in Far East," *Washington Evening Star*, December 18, 1941, A-21.

14. *Lethbridge Herald* (Alberta, Canada), "War Shots from Far East: Manila," December 19, 1941, 5.

15. Associated Press, "Hit-and-Run Planes Raid Vital Area," *Baltimore Sun*, December 19, 1941, 1.

16. Associated Press, "U.S. Subs Sink Transport, Torpedo Jap Destroyer," *Boston Globe*, December 19, 1941, 1.

17. Canadian Press, "News Contact With Island Now Cut Off," *Lethbridge Herald* (Alberta, Canada), December 19, 1941, 1.

18. Associated Press, "Japs Meanwhile Strike Fierce New Blows in Pacific," *Birmingham (AL) News*, December 18, 1941, 1.

19. *New York Times*, "Japanese Advance in Malayan Drive," December 19, 1941, 6.

20. Franklin Delano Roosevelt Presidential Library and Museum, "Memorandum from Dillon to FDR," Box 2, a1bb01, December 19, 1941, Hyde Park, NY.

21. *Christian Science Monitor*, "British Garrison Evacuates Penang; Cavite and Wake Attacked Again; U.S. Troops reported at Singapore," December 19, 1941, 1.

22. *New York Times*, "American Flier Crashed His Plane Into Enemy Ship Off Philippines," December 19, 1941, 6.

23. *Christian Science Monitor*, "Two Cruisers, Destroyer Lost By Italians," December 19, 1941, 7.

24. Jack B. Beardwood, Associated Press, "If Canal Is Bombed—Pacific War Focuses New Attention on Historic Straits of Magellan," *Washington Post*, December 19, 1941, 9.

25. United Press, "Macarthur Is Nominated for General's Rank," *Yuma (AZ) Daily Sun*, December 19, 1941, 1.

26. *Washington Post*, "MacArthur's Promotion," December 21, 1941, 6.

27. Associated Press, "Dogfish Harassed Dunedin Survivors," *Washington Post*, December 19, 1941, 12.

28. Edward Shorter, *Bedside Manners* (New York: Simon and Schuster, 1985), 181.

29. Paul Mallon, "Civilian Life Change Seen in 60 Days," *The Hartford Courant*, December 18, 1941, 3.

30. *Boston Globe*, "Eels for Hyphenated Americans Arrive to Christmas Marts," December 19, 1941, 12.

31. *Lethbridge Herald* (Alberta, Canada), "War Dries Up Imported Liquers," December 19, 1941, 2.

32. *Los Angeles Times*, "Fake Wardens Hit for Tactics in Blackout," December 18, 1941, 6.

33. *Los Angeles Times*, "Crack Riflemen Form Corps of Minute Men," December 18, 1941, Part II-5.

34. *Washington Post*, "First Official U.S. War Poster," December 19, 1941, 10.

35. *New York Times*, "Poster Depicting Army Pursuit Ship Wins 'Keep 'Em Flying' Contest to Aid Recruiting," December 19, 1941, 5.

36. *Washington Post*, "Need Stressed for Chaplains," December 19, 1941, 16.

37. *Washington Post*, "Catholics Back 'War for Peace,'" December 19, 1941, 16.

38. *Washington Evening Star*, "Pictures," December 18, 1941, A10.

39. David Lawrence, "Money Dims Halo About New Dealers," *Washington Evening Star*, December 18, 1941, D-8.

40. Robert De Vore, "Firm With $42,500 Capital Shared $34,000,000 War Jobs," *Washington Post*, December 19, 1941, 1.

41. Harold Heffernan, "A Moving Performance: Stars Applaud Jimmy Stewart's Bill of Rights Radio Stint," *Washington Evening Star*, December 18, 1941, D4.

42. *Wall Street Journal*, "Washington Wire," December 19, 1941, 1.

43. Charles Hurd, "Army Will Close Volunteer Rolls," *New York Times*, December 19, 1941, 5.

44. *Baltimore Sun*, "Men and Women Stenographers Sought for War Office Jobs," December 19, 1941, 7.

45.   *Baltimore Sun*, "Senate Passes 19-to-45 Draft With Only Two Dissenting," December 19, 1941, 12.
46.   *Christian Science Monitor*, "North Carolina Town Entertains the Army," December 19, 1941, 3.
47.   Harold Martin, "Doesn't Take Book Learning to Shoot a Rifle, Says York," *Atlanta Constitution*, December 19, 1941, 8.
48.   Ruth Cowan, Associated Press, "Roosevelts to Have Christmas as Usual Despite A.A. Guns," *Birmingham (AL) News*, December 19, 1941, 49.
49.   *Birmingham (AL) News*, "More Alabamians Killed in Jap War," December 19, 1941, 51.
50.   *Wall Street Journal*, "Future of Television Discussed in Capital," December 19, 1941, 6.
51.   *Christian Science Monitor*, "State Governments Mobilize Strength Behind War Effort," December 19, 1941, 1.
52.   *New York Times*, "Wire Control Approved," December 19, 1941, 6.
53.   Associated Press, "Senators Urge Daylight Savings," *New York Times*, December 19, 1941, 4.
54.   *New York Times*, "Laws To Enforce Blackouts Urged," December 19, 1941, 18.
55.   *New York Times*, "Mayor Off to Washington; Defense Job Under Fire," December 19, 1941, 22.
56.   United Press, "War Costing U.S. $729 Per Second; Next Year, $1400," *Yuma (AZ) Daily Sun*, December 19, 1941, 1.
57.   Louis M. Lyons, "New England Colleges Move to War Footing," *Boston Evening Globe*, December 19, 1941, 5.
58.   Associated Press, "30 Minutes Warning and Japs Would Have Lost at Honolulu," *Birmingham (AL) News*, December 19, 1941, 1.
59.   United Press, "Know Warns Japs Have Largest Naval Force in Western Pacific," *Yuma (AL) Daily Sun*, December 19, 1941, 1.

CHAPTER 20: THE TWENTIETH OF DECEMBER
1.   *Boston Evening Globe*, "Hong Kong Doomed," December 20, 1941, 1.
2.   Winston Churchill, *The Gathering Storm* (New York: Rosetta Books, 2002), 562.
3.   *Boston Daily Globe*, "Flying Santa Claus Grounded by War," December 20, 1941, 6.
4.   Franklin Delano Roosevelt Library and Museum, "Memorandum For The President from the Director of the Selective Service Regarding Men in Defense-Related Jobs, Recruiting and the Draft," December 20, 1941, Hyde Park, NY.
5.   Franklin Delano Roosevelt Library and Museum, "Summary of Report on Program For Loyal West Coast Japanese from John Franklin Carter," December 19, 1941, Hyde Park, NY.
6.   Franklin Delano Roosevelt Library and Museum, "Secretary of the Navy Knox to President Roosevelt Regarding Trans-Pacific Netherlands Shipping," December 20, 1941, Hyde Park, NY.
7.   Franklin Delano Roosevelt Library and Museum, "Memorandum Regarding Sharing Information From Moscow Between London and Washington," December 20, 1941, Hyde Park, NY.
8.   Franklin Delano Roosevelt Library and Museum, "Memorandum Regarding the Soviet Post-War Desire to Expand into the Baltic States and Further West," December 20, 1941, Hyde Park, NY.
9.   Franklin Delano Roosevelt Library and Museum, "Memorandum from the Office of the Legal Advisor of the State Department Regarding Legalities Surrounding Declarations of War and Peace," December 20, 1941, Hyde Park, NY.
10.   *Baltimore Sun*, "Bares Axis Spying in Latin America," December 20, 1941, 9.
11.   Associated Press, "Thousands of Enemy Agents Are Active in Southern Continent," *Atlanta Constitution*, December 20, 1941, 1, 87
12.   *Boston Evening Globe*, "United Press Editors Place Soviet War High," December 20, 1941, 1.
13.   Associated Press, "Marshall, Wife Get Full Custody of Girls," *Washington Post*, December 20, 1941, 15.
14.   Associated Press, "National Debt Tops 57 Billion," *Los Angeles Times*, December 20, 1941, 2.

15. *Washington Evening Star,* "Workers Are Wanted to Help Fix Damage at Pearl Harbor," December 19, 1941, B-1.
16. *New York Times,* "Plant to Produce New Dive Bombers," December 19, 1941, 17.
17. *Washington Post,* "Navy Seizes Scarce Materials Worth a Million," December 20, 1941, 15.
18. *Washington Evening Star,* "Navy Takes Over Four of Gulf's Finest Yachts," December 20, 1941, 16.
19. *Wall Street Journal,* "Roosevelt's Powers Already Greater Than Any Previous President's With More On the Way," December 20, 1941, 1.
20. *Wall Street Journal,* "Streamlining of OPM Activities to Speed Arms Work Taking Form," December 20, 1941, 4.
21. *Washington Post,* "Many More to Go; Government Will Aid Those Moving," December 20, 1941, 1.
22. *Washington Post,* "Senior Scouts Start Civilian Defense Move," December 20, 1941, 15.
23. *New York Times,* "Air Training Plan for U.S. Boys Seen," December 20, 1941, 5.
24. *Washington Post,* "D.C. Committee of 70 Set Up to Direct Salvage of Scrap," December 20, 1941, 17.
25. *New York Times,* "Blind Now Aiding Defense Program," December 19, 1941, 21.
26. Associated Press, "Coast Harbor Defender Calls For Dog Recruits," *Baltimore Sun,* December 20, 1941, 8.
27. *New York Times,* "Public Notices and Commercial Notices," December 19, 1941, 2.
28. *New York Times,* "Japanese Bomb Philippine Port," December 19, 1941, 4.
29. *Yuma Daily Sun,* "San Quentin Men Volunteer for Suicide Squad," December 20, 1941, 1.
30. *Wall Street Journal,* "Factories to Hum on Christmas Day Where Operations Aid War Effort," December 20, 1941, 2.
31. Associated Press, "Christmas in Honolulu," *Baltimore Sun,* December 20, 1941, 4.
32. Associated Press, "Christmas in Honolulu," *Baltimore Sun,* December 20, 1941, 4.
33. *Wall Street Journal,* "Industrial Output Up, Reserve Board Says; BAE Forecasts Rise in '42 Buying Power," December 20, 1941, 2.
34. *Wall Street Journal,* "Spiegel Adopts New Sales Policy; Adds Credit Service Charge," December 20, 1941, 3.
35. *Wall Street Journal,* "Shirley Temple Again," December 20, 1941, 7.
36. *Lethbridge Herald,* "War Shots From Here and There," December 20, 1941, 12.
37. *Lethbridge Herald,* "War Shots From Here and There," December 20, 1941, 12.
38. *Wall Street Journal,* "What's News," December 20, 1941, 1.
39. *Baltimore Sun,* "British Take Derna Airport in Quick Sally," December 20, 1941, 3.
40. *Baltimore Sun,* "German Division Wipe Out, Reds Say; Other Casualties Inflicted," December 20, 1941, 1.
41. *Yuma Daily Sun,* "American Pilots Down Four Jap Bombers, China," December 20, 1941, 1.
42. *Washington Post,* "Embattled Wake Fights Off 2 More Jap Air Attacks," December 20, 1941, 1.
43. *Boston Sunday Globe,* "MacArthur's Army," December 21, 1941, 8.
44. *Baltimore Sun,* "New Marine Poster Will Be Out Next Week," December 20, 1941, 3.
45. *Baltimore Sun,* "Thinks He Knows Causes of Physical Defects," December 20, 1941, 9.
46. Associated Press, "Navy and Marine Corps Relax Recruiting Rules," *Los Angeles Times,* December 20, 1941, 5.
47. *Boston Sunday Globe,* "MacArthur's Army," December 21, 1941, 8.
48. Associated Press, "More U.S. War Aid Sought by Quezon," *Baltimore Sun,* December 20, 1941, 9.
49. *Boston Sunday Globe,* "MacArthur's Army," December 21, 1941, 3.
50. Associated Press, "Jap Fifth Columnists Do It With Mirrors," *Washington Post,* December 20, 1941, 3.
51. International News Service, "The President's Day," *Washington Post,* December 20, 1941, 2.
52. *Washington Post,* "Hull Denies He Asked Navy to Lift Patrol," December 20, 1941, 1.
53. *Washington Post,* "Hull Denies He Asked Navy to Lift Patrol," December 20, 1941, 4.

CHAPTER 21: THE TWENTY-FIRST OF DECEMBER

1. *Hartford Courant*, "Enemy Subs Active off East, West Coasts," December 21, 1941, 1.
2. Joseph J. Cloud, "Enemy Subs Lurking off Bothe U.S. Coasts; Two Vessels Attacked in California Waters; Adm. King Named Chief of All Our Naval Forces," *Washington Post*, December 21, 1941, 1.
3. *Los Angeles Times*, "Jap Subs Raid California Ships," December 21, 1941, 1.
4. Foster Hailey, "West Coast Eyes South for Enemy," *New York Times*, December 22, 1941, 3.
5. Foster Hailey, "West Coast Eyes South for Enemy," *New York Times*, December 22, 1941, 3.
6. Foster Hailey, "West Coast Eyes South for Enemy," *New York Times*, December 22, 1941, 3.
7. Joseph J. Cloud, "Enemy Subs Lurking off Bothe U.S. Coasts; Two Vessels Attacked in California Waters; Adm. King Named Chief of All Our Naval Forces," *Washington Post*, December 21, 1941, 1.
8. Associated Press, "Gen. MacArthur Out of Touch With Davao Defenders," *Boston Daily Globe*, December 21, 1941, 1.
9. Associated Press, "Davao Cut Off by Jap Air and Land Attack," *Chicago Daily Tribune*, December 21, 1941, 6.
10. Associated Press, "Bolo-Swinging Moros Rally to Fight Japs," *Boston Daily Globe*, December 21, 1941, A10.
11. *Chicago Daily Tribune*, "Reveal 20 Jap Ships Engaged in Philippine Raid," December 21, 1941, 8.
12. United Press, "Japanese Wreck Ship at Guam," *Los Angeles Times*, December 21, 1941, 1A.
13. Associated Press, "Fight of British for Hongkong Wins Jap Praise," *Chicago Daily Tribune*, December 21, 1941, 6.
14. *Washington Post*, "Allies Merge to Preserve Singapore," December 21, 1941, 4.
15. *Washington Post*, "Allies Merge to Preserve Singapore," December 21, 1941, 4.
16. Arthur Griffin, "Guns Over Boston," *Boston Daily Globe*, December 21, 1941, B7.
17. Harry W. Hannery, "Germany Faces a Five-Year War," *Saturday Evening Post*, December 20, 1941, 6.
18. Terry Goldsworthy, *Valhalla's Warriors: A History of the Waffen-SS on the Eastern Front 1941–1945* (Indianapolis, IN: Dog Ear Publishing, 2010), 231.
19. International News Service, "Capt. Kelly Gave Life to Save Flaming Bomber's Crew of 6," *Washington Post*, December 21, 1941, 1.
20. Associated Press, "Burma Road: American Flyers Down 4 Jap Planes in First Battle for Chinese," *Boston Daily Globe*, December 21, 1941, A9.
21. Joseph L. Myler, "Supreme Council on War Planned," *Washington Post*, December 21, 1941, 5.
22. Franklin Delano Roosevelt Presidential Library and Museum, "Telegram From Thurston to Hull," December 21, 1941, Hyde Park, NY.
23. James B. Reston, "Allies Link Plans in Talks This Week," *New York Times*, December 22, 1941, 1.
24. James B. Reston, "Allies Link Plans in Talks This Week," *New York Times*, December 22, 1941, 1.
25. *New York Times*, "Spartan Days Face Us, Willkie Warns," December 21, 1941, 13.
26. Associated Press, "Willkie Boosters Suspend for War," *Washington Post*, December 22, 1941, 6.
27. *Washington Post*, "Martin Puts Off GOP Meetings Because of War," December 22, 1941, 18.
28. W. H. Lawrence, "Britain-U.S. Confer," *New York Times*, December 21, 1941, 1.
29. Russell Hill, "Arab Cheers Greet British at Derna," *Washington Post*, December 21, 1941, 10.
30. *Baltimore Sun*, "McNutt Asks Nation to Conserve Its Food," December 20, 1941, 8.
31. Associated Press, "Price of Sugar Is 'Frozen' at Current Level," *Chicago Daily Tribune*, December 21, 1941, 1.
32. Associated Press, "Chicago Flag Trade Booms," *Washington Post*, December 21, 1941, S6.
33. George Gallup, "Defense Labor Ready to Work Longer Hours," *Washington Post*, December 21, 1941, B5.
34. *New York Times*, "Effort of States in War Expanded," December 20, 1941, 9.
35. Gerald G. Gross, "Washington in Wartime," *Washington Post*, December 21, 1941, B3.

36. *Baltimore Sun*, "Plants Under Control of Axis Nationals Seized," December 20, 1941, 8.

37. *Chicago Daily Tribune*, "Ships, More Ships Launched to Aid U.S. War on Seas," December 21, 1941, 3.

38. *Chicago Daily Tribune*, "Makers of War Needs to Work Christmas Day," December 20, 1941, 23.

39. Jack Bell, "Criticism in Order Still, Senators Say," *Washington Post*, December 21, 1941, 13.

40. *Chicago Daily Tribune*, "'U.S. Will Regain Pacific Control'—Col. M'Cormick," December 21, 1941, 4.

41. *Chicago Daily Tribune*, "Japanese Tricks," December 21, 1941, 14.

42. *Boston Daily Globe*, "There's No Better Gift Than an Album of Columbia Records," December 21, 1941, C8.

43. *Washington Post*, "Gay Caroling Ushers in Christmas Week," December 22, 1941, 6.

44. *Leithbridge Herald* (Alberta, Canada) "How Would You Like to Bomb Germany?" December 22, 1941, 2.

45. *Washington Post*, "Board Selects 'Citizen Kane' As Best Movie of the Year," December 22, 1941, 7.

46. *Chicago Daily Tribune*, "Buy Defense Bonds," December 21, 1941, 14.

47. *Chicago Daily Tribune*, "350 Licenses to Wed Issued in Day, A Record," December 21, 1941, 16.

48. *Lethbridge Herald* (Alberta, Canada) "Christmas Mail Sets Record," December 22, 1941, 6.

49. Associated Press, "Son Is Not Dead, Navy Apologizes; Gloom Vanishes," *Boston Daily Globe*, December 21, 1941, A9.

50. United Press, "Navy to Give Yule Leave to All of Its Recruits," *New York Times*, December 21, 1941, 13.

51. *Washington Evening Star*, "Admiral King New Chief of U.S. Fleet," December 20, 1941, 1.

52. Associated Press, "Air Man Given New Navy Post; Outranks Stark," *Boston Daily Globe*, December 21, 1941, C1.

53. Marshall Andrews, "New Head Noted for Strategy; Ingersoll Gets Atlantic Post," *Washington Post*, December 21, 1941, 1.

54. Marshall Andrews, "New Head Noted for Strategy; Ingersoll Gets Atlantic Post," *Washington Post*, December 21, 1941, 1.

55. Gerald G. Gross, "Washington in Wartime," *Washington Post*, December 21, 1941, B3.

CHAPTER 22: THE TWENTY-SECOND OF DECEMBER

1. *Washington Post*, "Biddle Appoints Alien Enemy Board for D.C.," December 21, 1941, 18.

2. *Washington Post*, "Biddle Appoints Alien Enemy Board for D.C.," December 21, 1941, 18.

3. *New York Times*, "Hawaii Holds 273 as 5th Columnists," December 22, 1941, 4.

4. *Washington Post*, "Enemy Aliens," December 22, 1941, 12.

5. *New York Times*, "The Slanting Eye," December 22, 1941, 16.

6. *New York Times*, "Gun Battle Routs Coast Saboteurs," December 22, 1941, 3.

7. *Los Angeles Times*, "Car Believed Used by Gunmen Against Soldiers Located," December 22, 1941, A1.

8. Franklin Delano Roosevelt Presidential Library and Museum, "Full Report on Program For Dealing With West Coast Japanese Problem," December 22, 1941, Hyde Park, NY.

9. Franklin Delano Roosevelt Presidential Library and Museum, "FDR: Day by Day—The Pare Lorentz Chronology," December 22, 1941, Hyde Park, NY.

10. *Life*, "How To Tell Japs From The Chinese," December 22, 1941, 81.

11. *Life*, "How To Tell Japs From The Chinese," December 22, 1941, 81.

12. *Washington Evening Star*, "Patent Office Removal Assailed as Costly And Unwise by Congress Leaders and Lawyers," December 21, 1941, 1.

13. Jerry Kluttz, "Several Agencies to Remain Permanently From Capital," *Washington Post*, December 22, 1941, 1.

14. Scott Hart, "Raid Alarm Test Works Well, Except for Sirens," *Washington Post*, December 22, 1941, 1.

15. *Washington Post*, "Yesterday's Fiasco," December 22, 1941, 12.

16. Blair Bolles, "Press No Longer Wholly Free Under War Censorship Order," *Washington Evening Star*, December 21, 1941, 10.

17. Associated Press, "Broadcasters Adopt Guide for Handling America's War News," *Birmingham (AL) News*, December 22, 1941, 8.

18. *New York Times*, "Radio to Outlaw Rumors on War," December 22, 1941, 14.

19. Associated Press, "She's Looking for a Jap," *Washington Post*, December 22, 1941, 8.

20. *Yuma (AZ) Daily Sun*, "Local Fliers Are Grounded by CAA," December 22, 1941, 1.

21. *Life*, "Japanese Planes; How to Identify Enemy Craft That Might Attack the U.S.," December 22, 1941.

22. Associated Press, "U.S. Vessels Are Attached," *Lethbridge Herald* (Alberta, Canada) December 22, 1941, 1.

23. United Press, "30 Survivors of Tanker Reach Coast; Freighter Sunk Dec. 11," *Yuma (AZ) Daily News*, December 22, 1941, 1.

24. United Press, "30 Survivors of Tanker Reach Coast; Freighter Sunk Dec. 11," *Yuma (AZ) Daily News*, December 22, 1941, 1.

25. Associated Press, "U.S. Tanker Captain Tries to Ram Sub," *Washington Post*, December 22, 1941, 2.

26. Associated Press, "Reports Received of Enemy U-Boats off The West Coast," *Nevada Mail*, December 22, 1941, 8.

27. Walter V. Nessly, "14 U-Boats Sunk or Hit in Atlantic Knox Says," *Washington Post*, December 22, 1941, 1.

28. Walter V. Nessly, "14 U-Boats Sunk or Hit in Atlantic Knox Says," *Washington Post*, December 22, 1941, 1.

29. Marshall Andrews, "Survivors of U.S. Ship Are Shelled," *Washington Post*, December 22, 1941, 2.

30. Associated Press, "Tokyo Claims Navy Has Sunk 9 Enemy Subs," *Washington Post*, December 22, 1941, 8.

31. Associated Press, "Japs May Have 40 Subs Able to Reach U.S.," *Washington Post*, December 22, 1941, 2.

32. Associated Press, "Japs May Have 40 Subs Able to Reach U.S.," *Washington Post*, December 22, 1941, 2.

33. Clark Lee, Associated Press, "Japs Try Big Landing Near Manila," *Lethbridge Herald* (Alberta, Canada) December 22, 1941, 1.

34. Associated Press, "U.S. Forces Ready For Attack; Control of Islands at Stake," *Washington Post*, December 22, 1941, 1.

35. H. Ford Wilkins, Copyright by the *New York Times*, "Bombing of Quezon's Home Solidifies Filipinos for U.S.," *Washington Post*, December 22, 1941, 8.

36. *Time*, "The U.S. At War," December 22, 1941, 10.

37. United Press, "King George Sends Defenders Praise and Encouragement," *Washington Post*, December 22, 1941, 8.

38. United Press, "King George Sends Defenders Praise and Encouragement," *Washington Post*, December 22, 1941, 8.

39. Associated Press, "British in Malaya Smash at Japanese from New Positions," *Washington Evening Star*, December 22, 1941, A4.

40. *Washington Post*, "Heroes on Wake Hold Firm Despite Two New Attacks," December 22, 1941, 1.

41. Associated Press, "Nazis Execute 5 Jews in Occupied France," *Boston Daily Globe*, December 22, 1941, 26.

42. Associated Press, "Germany Pulling Troops Out of Occupied Norway, Sending Them to Russia And Libya," *Lethbridge Herald* (Alberta, Canada) December 22, 1941, 5.

43. Daniel T. Brigham, "Brauchitsch Is Out," *New York Times*, December 22, 1941, 1.

44. International News Service, "Sailor Still Lives, Parents Learn After Rites Are Held," *Washington Post*, December 21, 1941, 5.

45. Associated Press, "Parents of Son Killed in World War Lose 2 More at Pearl Harbor," *Baltimore Sun*, December 22, 1941, 3.

46. Associated Press, "Town Mourns Deaths of Three Brothers in Honolulu Attack," *Birmingham (AL) News*, December 22, 1941, 13.

47. *Birmingham (AL) News*, Youth Would Avenge Death of His Brother," December 21, 1941, 1.

48. Associated Press, "Birthday Felicitations For Stalin, This Time By Allies, Not Hitler," *Baltimore Sun*, December 22, 1941, 11.

49. *Birmingham (AL) News*, "Alabama Press," December 22, 1941, 12.

50. Associated Press, "General Sales Tax Proposal Gains in Favor," *Washington Post*, December 22, 1941, 1.

51. Associated Press, "General Sales Tax Proposal Gains in Favor," *Washington Post*, December 22, 1941, 1.

52. *Washington Post*, "Public Told What Foods It Should Stock," December 22, 1941, 6.

53. Jane Driscoll, "No Glove Shortage Is Foreseen, But Wise Buying Is Advised," *Washington Post*, December 22, 1941, 15.

54. *Washington Post*, "New Research Shows Food Value of Milk," December 22, 1941, 15.

55. *Birmingham (AL) News*, "What Every Woman Wants to Know About a Man," December 22, 1941, 3.

56. United Press, "Makes 'War Tires' For 35 M.P.H. Tops," *New York Times*, December 22, 1941, 7.

57. Associated Press, "'War Tire' Ready for Market, But Don't Drive Over 35," *Washington Post*, December 22, 1941, 6.

CHAPTER 23: THE TWENTY-THIRD OF DECEMBER

1. Associated Press, "What? A War? Dixie 'Cracker' Rarin' to Crack a 'Danged Jap,'" *Atlanta Constitution*, December 22, 1941, 5.

2. United Press, "28,363 Join Army In 2 Weeks After War Declaration," *Yuma (AZ) Daily Sun*, December 23, 1941, 1.

3. *Washington Post*, "Sen. Truman's Ready for Army, But Army's Not Ready for Him," December 22, 1941, 8.

4. *Los Angeles Times*, "Women May Drive Taxis," December 22, 1941, 16.

5. Associated Press, "Prison Labor Urged for Use on war Goods," *Atlanta Constitution*, December 22, 1941, 8.

6. Associated Press, "Former Steelers Star Dudley Dies at 88," ESPN NFL, February 4, 2010. http://sports.espn.go.com/nfl/news/ story?id=4887025&campaign=rss&source=NFLHeadlines.

7. Associated Press, "Miller of 'Four Horsemen' Named U.S. Attorney," *The Evening Star*, December 23, 1941, A2.

8.

9. *New York Herald-Tribune*, "35,000 Press Agents," *Birmingham (AL) News*, December 23, 1941, 6.

10. Walter Winchell, "Walter Winchell: Man About Town," *Birmingham (AL) News*, December 23, 1941, 6.

11. *Atlanta Constitution*, "Margaret Mitchell En Route for Commissioning of Atlanta," December 23, 1941, 6.

12. Associated Press, "Subs Sink U.S. Tanker," *Lethbridge Herald* (Alberta, Canada) December 23, 1941, 2.

13. Associated Press, "Subs Sink U.S. Tanker," *Lethbridge Herald* (Alberta, Canada), December 23, 1941, 2.

14. Associated Press, "Heavy Gunfire Heard Off California Coast," *Birmingham (AL) News*, December 23, 1941, 1.

15. *Los Angeles Times*, "Freighter's Smoke Causes Alarm Along Coast Cities," December 22, 1941, 1.

16. *Los Angeles Times*, "Four Lose Lives Serving Country," December 22, 1941, B16.

17. *Birmingham* (AL) *News*, "War Victim," December 22, 1941, 14.

18. *Los Angeles Times*, "Eagle Rock Holds Memorial For Lieut. Comdr. Michael," December 22, 1941, 8.

19. *Los Angeles Times*, "Sons of 'Times' Man Missing," December 22, 1941, Part I, 8.

20. Tom Yarbrough, Associated Press, "Japs Not Suicidal at Pearl Harbor, Witnesses Declare," *Washington Post*, December 23, 1941, 5.

21. Tom Yarbrough, Associated Press, "Japs Not Suicidal at Pearl Harbor, Witnesses Declare," *Washington Post*, December 23, 1941, 5.

22. Associated Press, "U.S. Pilot Fired On By Jap Flyers While 'Chuting from Sky," *Baltimore Sun*, December 23, 1941, 3.

23. Associated Press, "U.S. Flyer Is Saved From Savage When They See His Hair," *Baltimore Sun*, December 23, 1941, 4.

24. Frank L. Kluckhohn, "2 Leaders Confer," *New York Times*, December 22, 1941, 1.

25. Associated Press, "Churchill In Washington Big Surprise," *Lethbridge Herald* (Alberta, Canada) December 23, 1941, 1.

26. Associated Press, "Nazis Placed Churchill in Middle East," *Boston Daily Globe*, December 23, 1941, 3.

27. United Press, "Steve Early's Desk Will Never Look the Same Again," *Boston Evening Globe*, December 23, 1941, 26.

28. Associated Press, "Churchill Wears Life Saver's Garb," *New York Times*, December 23, 1941, 5.

29. Associated Press, "Leaders of Democracy at White House to Plan War Against Axis," *New York Times*, December 23, 1941, 16.

30. Dewey L. Fleming, "Prime Minister Makes Sudden, Dramatic Trip; Parleys Start at Once," *Baltimore Sun*, December 23, 1941, 1.

31. Associated Press Photo, *Washington Post*, December 23, 1947, 16.

32. *Washington Evening Star*, "Churchill Says Allies Plan Complete Unity of Action in Pacific," December 23, 1941, A6 continued from A1.

33. Jon Meacham, *Franklin and Winston: An Intimate Portrait of an Epic Friendship* (New York: Random House, 2003), xii.

34. *New York Times*, "The Day in Washington," December 23, 1941, 5.

35. Franklin Delano Roosevelt Presidential Library and Museum, "Memorandum From FDR to Jack Carter on The Summary of Preliminary Intelligence Problems in New York Area," December 23, 1941, Hyde Park, New York.

36. International News Service, "The President's Day," *Washington Post*, December 23, 1941, 2.

37. Associated Press Wirephoto Caption, "Discussing War Strategy," *Boston Evening Globe*, December 23, 1941, 23.

38. International News Service, "The President's Day," *Washington Post*, December 24, 1941, 2.

39. Associated Press, "Japs Meanwhile Effect Landing On Wake Island," *Birmingham* (AL) *News*, December 23, 1941, 1.

40. *Washington Post*, "Hongkong's Valiant Defenders Sink Two Ships; Siege Goes On," December 24, 1941, 2.

41. Associated Press, "Japs Obtained No Oil From Borneo Wells," *Baltimore Sun*, December 23, 1941, 4.

42. *Atlanta Constitution*, "Japs Hurled Into Sea by Luzon Defenders," December 23, 1941, 1.

43. United Press, "Resists Invaders," *New York Times*, December 23, 1941, 2. (Dateline: December 22, 1941).

44. Associated Press, "U.S. Mechanized Forces Rushed Into Luzon Battle," *Birmingham* (AL) *News*, December 23, 1941, 1.

45. Franklin Delano Roosevelt Presidential Library, "Radiogram from Manila to the Adjutant General," December 22, 1941, Hyde Park, NY.

46. *Time*, "The U.S. at War," December 22, 1941, 10.
47. *New York Times*, "Last Guam Message Received on Dec. 10," December 23, 1941, 3.
48. Dr. George Gallup, "The Gallup Poll: Germany Considered Greater Threat to U.S. Thank Japan, Survey of Attitudes Shows," *Washington Post*, December 23, 1947, 2.
49. International News Service, "British Carrier Sunk in Atlantic By Sub, Nazis Say," *Washington Post*, December 23, 1941, 4.
50. Canadian Press, "Casualties of Canadians Said 'Heavy,'" *Lethbridge Herald* (Alberta, Canada) December 23, 1941, 1.
51. United Press, "Gallant Few Still Hold Out at Hongkong," *Washington Post*, December 23, 1941, 1.
52. Associated Press, "British in Hongkong Still Fighting, They Report by Radio to Chungking: Communication Maintained," *New York Times*, December 23, 1941, 4.
53. Frank Oliver, "Prize of War: Hong Kong, Garden of South China," *Washington Post*, December 23, 1941, 19.
54. Associated Press, "Churchill in Washington; Confers With Roosevelt," *Atlanta Constitution*, December 23, 1941, 1.
55. Lloyd Lehrbas, Associated Press, "Introducing Winston Churchill," *Birmingham* (AL) *News*, December 23, 1941, 5.
56. Jon Meacham, *Franklin and Winston* (New York: Random House, 2003), 42.
57. Jon Meacham, *Franklin and Winston* (New York: Random House, 2003), 8.
58. Lloyd Lehrbas, "Introducing Winston Churchill," *Birmingham* (AL) *News*, December 23, 1941, 5.
59. *Washington Post*, "President Asks Country to Pray," December 23, 1941, 4.
60. *Time Magazine*, "The U.S. at War, Full Blast," December 22, 1941, 9.
61. *New York Times*, "No Strikes in War, Spellman Pleads," December 22, 1941, 15.
62. *New York Times*, "No Strikes in War, Spellman Pleads," December 22, 1941, 15.
63. *New York Times*, "Four Freedoms Aim of War Hit by Taft," May 26, 1943, 20.
64. Associated Press, "Fall Schedule Helps Ease Worry For Mrs. Roosevelt," *Sarasota* (FL) *Herald-Tribune*, December 23, 1941, 6.
65. *Washington Post*, "Photo," December 24, 1941, 5.
66. Associated Press, "White House to Have Turkey and Trimmin's," *Los Angeles Times*, December 25, 1941, 10.
67. John C. Henry, "Round Table Talks By War Council to Fix Command," *Washington Evening Star*, December 23, 1941, 1.
68. John C. Henry, "Roosevelt and Churchill Mix Showmanship With Democracy," *Washington Evening Star*, December 24, 1941, A3.
69. John C. Henry, "Roosevelt and Churchill Mix Showmanship With Democracy," *Washington Evening Star*, December 24, 1941, A3.
70. Frank L. Kluckhohn, "Churchill Talks," *New York Times*, December 24, 1941, 4 continued from page 1.
71. John C. Henry, "Roosevelt and Churchill Mix Showmanship With Democracy," *Washington Evening Star*, December 24, 1941, A3.
72. John C. Henry, "Roosevelt and Churchill Mix Showmanship With Democracy," *Washington Evening Star*, December 24, 1941, A3.
73. International News Service, "The President's Day," *Washington Post*, December 24, 1941, 2.
74. John C. Henry, "Roosevelt and Churchill Mix Showmanship With Democracy," *Washington Evening Star*, December 24, 1941, A3.
75. John C. Henry, "Roosevelt and Churchill Mix Showmanship With Democracy," *Washington Evening Star*, December 24, 1941, A3.
76. Associated Press, "Transportation Office Created," *Los Angeles Times*, December 24, 1941, 4.
77. Frank L. Kluckhohn, "2 Leaders Confer," *New York Times*, December 23, 1941, 1.
78. United Press, "F.D. and Churchill Divide War Into 4 Major Actions," *Boston Evening Globe*, December 23, 1941, 3.

79. *Washington Evening Star*, "Churchill, President Studying War Roles For Other Allies," December 24, 1941, 1.

80. Associated Press, "'War Council' to Confer with Churchill: Allied Chieftains Discuss Means of Crushing Axis," *Birmingham* (AL) *News*, December 23, 1941, 1.

81. Associated Press, "'War Council' to Confer with Churchill: Allied Chieftains Discuss Means of Crushing Axis," *Birmingham* (AL) *News*, December 23, 1941, 2 continued from page 1.

82. Associated Press, "'War Council' to Confer with Churchill: Allied Chieftains Discuss Means of Crushing Axis," *Birmingham* (AL) *News*, December 23, 1941, 1.

CHAPTER 24: THE TWENTY-FOURTH OF DECEMBER

1. Associated Press, "Churchill Gets 2-Week Ration of Eggs on His Breakfast Tray," *Washington Evening Star*, December 24, 1941, A2.

2. Associated Press, "Churchill Gets 2-Week Ration of Eggs on His Breakfast Tray," *Washington Evening Star*, December 24, 1941, A2.

3. Associated Press, "Churchill Gets 2-Week Ration of Eggs on His Breakfast Tray," *Washington Evening Star*, December 24, 1941, A2.

4. Edward T. Folliard, "Prime Minister Fences Press U.S. Style," *Washington Post*, December 24, 1941, 4.

5. Associated Press, "Santa Claus To Visit Sing Sing Prison," *Birmingham (AL) News*, December 24, 1941, 7.

6. *Washington Post*, "Ceremony at White House on Christmas Eve to Highlight Varied Program of Yule Activity," December 22, 1941, 19.

7. Associated Press, "8-Lb. Baby Boy Born to Mrs. F. D. Roosevelt Jr.," *Boston Daily Globe*, December 22, 1941, 1.

8. *Washington Evening Star*, "Churchill, President Studying War Roles For Other Allies," December 24, 1941, A1.

9. Franklin Delano Roosevelt Presidential Library and Museum, "Telegram from Kirk to Hull," December 24, 1941, 1-2, Hyde Park, NY.

10. Franklin Delano Roosevelt Presidential Library and Museum, "Telegram from Kirk to Hull," December 24, 1941, 2, Hyde Park, NY.

11. Franklin Delano Roosevelt Presidential Library and Museum, "Memorandum for Grace," December 24, 1941, Hyde Park, NY, 1.

12. Franklin Delano Roosevelt Presidential Library and Museum, "Memo From C.V. Munson," Hyde Park, NY.

13. *Washington Evening Star*, "Churchill, Roosevelt Will Attend Church Together Tomorrow," December 24, 1941, B1.

14. Associated Press, "Churchill Gets 2-Week Ration of Eggs on His Breakfast Tray," *Washington Evening Star*, December 24, 1941, A2.

15. *Washington Post*, "Ceremony at White House on Christmas Eve to Highlight Varied Program of Yule Activity," December 22, 1941, 19.

16. Associated Press, "Film Studio Ready if War Should Hit," *Baltimore Sun*, December 23, 1941, 2.

17. *Los Angeles Times*, "Studio Builds Raid Shelters," December 23, 1941, 7.

18. Ronald J. Schmidt, *This is The City: Making Model Citizens in Los Angeles* (Minneapolis, MN, University of Minnesota Press, 2005), 46.

19. International News Service, "Jap Ambassador Buys Drawers," *Washington Post*, December 24, 1941, 1.

20. Franklin Delano Roosevelt Presidential Library and Museum, "Telegram to the President from Generalissimo Chiang Kai-shek, Chungking," December 24, 1941, Hyde Park, NY.

21. Associated Press, "Shells and Carols Mix on Kent Coast," *Washington Post*, December 25, 1941, 6.

22. Associated Press, "RAF Suspends Activity," *New York Times*, December 27, 1941, 8.

23.   Associated Press, "Nazis Finish Bases for Use Against Britain," *Washington Evening Star*,
      December 24, 1941, A1.
24.   Associated Press, "35 in Crew Take to Lifeboats in View of Shore," *Washington Evening Star*,
      December 24, 1941, A1.
25.   Associated Press, "Tanker, Turned Back in Pacific, Reaches Port," *Washington Evening Star*,
      December 24, 1941, A1.
26.   *Los Angeles Times*, "Santa Catalina Island Ships Halt Service Temporarily," December 24, 1941, A.
27.   Associated Press, "30 Gaunt Survivors of Lahaina Safe After 20 Days in Lifeboat," *Washington
      Evening Star*, December 24, 1941, A5.
28.   United Press, "Wake Island All Now in Jap Hands," *Lethbridge Herald* (Alberta, Canada)
      December 24, 1941, 9.
29.   *Washington Evening Star*, "385 Americans There Led by Maj. Devereux," December 24, 1941, A1.
30.   *Washington Evening Star*, "385 Americans There Led by Maj. Devereux," December 24, 1941, A1.
31.   *Washington Evening Star*, "Communiques: U.S. Contact With Wake Island," December 24, 1941,
      A4.
32.   Associated Press, "Success Claimed By British in Hong Kong Battle," *Washington Evening Star*,
      December 24, 1941, A4.
33.   Associated Press, "Canadians Hold in Last Stand Fight," *Hartford (CT) Courant*, December 24,
      1941, 1.
34.   Associated Press, "Dutch Report Sea Victories," *Milwaukee (WI) Journal*, December 24, 1941, 2.
35.   *Washington Evening Star*, "Communiques: U.S. Contact With Wake Island," December 24,
      1941, A4.
36.   Associated Press, "Strong Units Reported in Coast Area," *Hartford (CT) Courant*, December
      24, 1941, 1.
37.   *Washington Evening Star*, "Japs, Off Batangas, Now Menace Manila from Two New Points,"
      December 24, 1941, A1.
38.   Royal Arch Gunnison, "Flying Fortress Defies 18 Foes; Returns With 1,500 Bullet Holes," *New
      York Times*, December 24, 1941, 3.
39.   *Washington Evening Star*, "Spectacular Pacific Flight Wins Flying Cross for 75," December 24,
      1941, A2.
40.   Whitney Martin, "Louis-Conn Fight Chosen As Year's Best in Roundup," *Washington Post*,
      December 24, 1941, 21.
41.   Sigrid Arne, Associated Press, "Mickey Rooney Loses Heart Under Hollywood's Nose and No
      One Had Even an Inkling of It," *Washington Post*, December 24, 1941, 23.
42.   Associated Press, "Roosevelt to Avoid Film Censorship," *Washington Post*, December 24,
      1941, 23.
43.   *Birmingham (AL) News*, "An Urgent Appeal," December 24, 1941, 7.
44.   Tom Yarbrough, Associated Press, "Ruined Hangars Stand As Mute Evidence o Fury of Jap
      Raid," *Birmingham (AL) News*, December 24, 1941, 4.
45.   *Washington Post*, "Army Rushes Repair Work on Oahu Isle," December 25, 1941, 2.
46.   Alfred Friendly, "Labor-Industry Parley Accepts Stoppage Ban," *Washington Post*, December 24,
      1941, 1.
47.   Associated Press, "Congress May Seek Every Possible Dollar for Taxes Next Year," *Birmingham
      (AL) News*, December 24, 1941, 7.
48.   Associated Press, "Unlimited' Tax Bill Considered to Meet War Expenditures," *Washington
      Evening Star*, December 24, 1941, A5.
49.   Associated Press, "Petain Tells France Peace Is Farther Off Than Ever," *Washington Evening
      Star*, December 24, 1941, A5.
50.   Associated Press, "New Efforts to Push Into North Africa," *Hartford (CT) Courant*, December
      24, 1941, 1.
51.   Associated Press, "Pope Lays Down plan For Peace Based on Arms Limitation," *Washington
      Evening Star*, December 24, 1941, A2.

52. Associated Press, "On the Radio Today," *Baltimore Sun*, December 24, 1941, 1.
53. Gerald G. Gross, "Leaders of Democracies Key Their Speeches to Christmas Spirit at Tree Lighting," *Washington Post*, December 25, 1941, 1.
54. *Washington Post*, "Impatient Comment Stops as Churchill Speaks," December 25, 1941, 5.
55. *Washington Post*, "Impatient Comment Stops as Churchill Speaks," December 25, 1941, 5.
56. John C. Henry, "Churchill Tells U.S. Sacrifice Will Win War," *Washington Evening Star*, December 24, 1941, 1.
57. John C. Henry, "Churchill Tells U.S. Sacrifice Will Win War," *Washington Evening Star*, December 24, 1941, A1.
58. *Washington Post*, "Churchill Text," December 25, 1941, 5.
59. *Washington Post*, "Impatient Comment Stops as Churchill Speaks," December 25, 1941, 5.
60. *Washington Post*, "President's Text," December 25, 1941, 5.
61. *Washington Post*, "President's Text," December 25, 1941, 5.
62. Associated Press, "FDR and Churchill Call for Courage, Predict Victory in Yuletide Messages," *Boston Daily Globe*, December 25, 1941, 1.
63. Associated Press, "Churchill Gets 2-Week Ration of Eggs on His Breakfast Tray," *Washington Evening Star*, December 24, 1941, A2.

CHAPTER 25: THE TWENTY-FIFTH OF DECEMBER

1. *New York Times*, "Government Quits Manila," December 26, 1941, 4.
2. Frank Hewlett, "Foe Gains Two Beachheads 55 Miles from Capital, One Periling Cavite; MacArthur Takes Field Command; Fierce Battles Raging at Two Points," *Washington Post*, December 25, 1941, 1.
3. Frank Hewlett, "Foe Gains Two Beachheads 55 Miles from Capital, One Periling Cavite; MacArthur Takes Field Command; Fierce Battles Raging at Two Points," *Washington Post*, December 25, 1941, 1.
4. John G. Norris, "Marines Held Base 14 Days with 12 Planes, 6 Cannon," *Washington Post*, December 25, 1941, 1.
5. Associated Press, "Colony Governor Meets with Foes, Tokyo Declares," *Washington Evening Star*, December 25, 1941, 1.
6. Associated Press, "Hongkong Surrenders to Japanese," *Los Angeles Times*, December 26, 1941, 1.
7. Associated Press, "Hongkong Colony Falls When Water Mains Blasted," *Daily Boston Globe*, December 26, 1941, 1.
8. Franklin Delano Roosevelt Presidential Library and Museum, "Optel. No. 48," December 25, 1941, Hyde Park, NY.
9. Associated Press, "Guest Churchill Is Sleeping and Eating Well at White House," *Washington Evening Star*, December 25, 1941, A-3.
10. Jon Meacham, *Franklin and Winston: An Intimate Portrait of an Epic Friendship* (New York: Random House, 2003), xvi–xvii.
11. John C. Henry, "Churchill Joins Roosevelt in Victory Prayer," *Washington Evening Star*, December 25, 1941, A1.
12. Associated Press, "President Too Busy to Open Presents," *Los Angeles Times*, December 27, 1941, 2.
13. *Washington Post*, "Traditional Dinner Awaits Churchill," December 25, 1941, 5.
14. Associated Press, "White House to Have Turkey and Trimmins," *Los Angeles Times*, December 25, 1941, 10.
15. Associated Press, "White House to Have Turkey and Trimmins," *Los Angeles Times*, December 25, 1941, 10.
16. Franklin Delano Roosevelt, Joseph P. Lash, *F.D.R.: His Personal Letters* (New York: Duell, Sloan, And Pearce, 1950), 1260.

17. Franklin Delano Roosevelt Presidential Library and Museum, "Message from Clementine Churchill to Roosevelts 12/27/41," December 27, 1941, Hyde Park NY.

18. Franklin Delano Roosevelt Presidential Library and Museum, "Message from Lord Halifax to Franklin Delano Roosevelt 12/25/41," December 25, 1941, Hyde Park, NY.

19. Associated Press, "Philippines, Only Christian Nation in Orient, Swarms with Invading Hordes on Christmas Day," *Washington Post*, December 25, 1941, 8.

20. United Press, "Pilgrims Steam to Town of Bethlehem for Traditional Christmas Ceremonies," *Washington Post*, December 25, 1941, 11.

21. Associated Press, "War Goes on But Yuletide Touches All," *Hartford Courant*, December 25, 1941, 23.

22. Associated Press, "War Goes on But Yuletide Touches All," *Hartford Courant*, December 25, 1941, 23.

23. Associated Press, "Christmas a Memory in Many World Capitals, but Moscow Enjoys It at Nazis' Expense," *Washington Evening Star*, December 25, 1941, 5.

24. Associated Press, "War Goes on But Yuletide Touches All," *Hartford Courant*, December 25, 1941, 23.

25. Christine Sadler, "Justice Holmes' House Will Be Haven For Girls," *Washington Post*, December 25, 1941, 17.

26. *Washington Evening Star*, "Thousands of Christmas Gifts Distributed Among Needy Here," 25, 1941, 6.

27. *Washington Evening Star*, "Children Talk Over Radio With Army Officers in London," December 25, 1941, B-1.

28. *Baltimore Sun*, "65 Negro Children Patients Are Given Christmas Party," December 25, 1941, 5.

29. *Los Angeles Times*, "Navy Santa Doesn't Forget Children Who Lost Fathers," December 25, 1941, 1.

30. *Washington Evening Star*, "Party Honors 125 Soldiers Quartered at Treasury," December 25, 1941, A-5.

31. Associated Press, "1,500,000 Pounds of Turkey Destined for Army's Tables," *Baltimore Sun*, December 20, 1941, 8.

32. Associated Press, "1,500,000 Pounds of Turkey Destined for Army's Tables," *Baltimore Sun*, December 20, 1941, 8.

33. Associated Press, "1,500,000 Pounds of Turkey Destined for Army's Tables," *Baltimore Sun*, December 20, 1941, 8.

34. *Washington Post*, "Many Parties Arranged for Service Men," December 24, 1941, 17.

35. Associated Press, "Honolulu's Christmas Eve Dry as Army Bans All Hard Liquor," *Washington Evening Star*, December 25, 1941, A1.

36. Associated Press, "Japanese Took Pop, Candy on Hawaii Raid," *Washington Evening Star*, December 25, 1941, A-2.

37. *Baltimore Sun*, "Wounded and Evacuees Reach San Francisco From Hawaii," December 24, 1941, 1.

38. *Baltimore Sun*, "Wounded and Evacuees Reach San Francisco From Hawaii," December 24, 1941, 1.

39. Lawrence E. Davies, "Hawaii Wounded Home, Tell How Defenders Dared Death," *New York Times*, December 26, 1941, 1.

40. *Washington Evening Star*, "For His Christmas!," December 20, 1941, 2.

41. *Atlanta Constitution*, "Dickens Story of Christmas on Vallee Hour," December 25, 1941, 31.

42. *Birmingham* (AL) *News*, "Strongest Stars at the Box Office," December 25, 1941, 15.

43. Vincent Townsend, "'Men of Boys Town' Is Best Box office Picture," *Birmingham* (AL) *News*, December 25, 1941, 15.

44. *New York Times*, "Beware of Women Spies, Navy Men Are Warned," December 25, 1941, 22.

45. *New York Times*, "War Casts Shadow Over Christmas Joy Throughout Land," December 25, 1941, 1.

46. *Washington Post,* "Congressman Now Must Carry Identity Cards," December 25, 1941, 24.

47. *New York Times,* "Congress to Use Identity Cards," December 25, 1941, 10.

48. Associated Press, "U.S. Plane's Direct Hits Filled Air with Debris, Army Says," *Washington Evening Star,* December 25, 1941, A1.

49. John C. Henry, "Churchill Joins Roosevelt in Victory Prayer," *Washington Evening Star,* December 25, 1941, A5.

50. *Baltimore Sun,* "Eire to Stay Neutral, DeValera Declares, Unless Under Attack," December 25, 1941, 2.

51. *Los Angeles Times,* "Dawn of Another Christmas Hailed," December 25, 1941, A1.

52. *Washington Post,* "Christmas," December 25, 1941, 10.

53. Henrt Wadsworth Longfellow, *The Complete Poetical Works of Henry Wadsworth Longfellow* (London: George Routledge & Sons, 1871), 544.

54. *Evening Star,* "Christmas, 1941," December 25, 1941, A8.

55. *Washington Post,* "Christmas," December 25, 1941, 10.

56. John Meachan, *Franklin and Winston* (New York: Random House, 2004), 134.

CHAPTER 26: THE TWENTY-SIX OF DECEMBER

1. *Washington Evening Star,* "Churchill Forecast Allies Will Take War Initiative in 1943," December 26, 1941, A2.

2. *Washington Evening Star,* "Churchill to Make Speech to Congress in Senate Chamber," December 25, 1941, A1.

3. *Baltimore Sun,* "Churchill Captures Capital With Speech," December 27, 1941, 1.

4. *Baltimore Sun,* "Churchill Captures Capital With Speech," December 27, 1941, 1.

5. *Washington Evening Star,* "War Tide to Turn by 1943, Churchill Says," December 26, 1941, A2.

6. *Baltimore Sun,* "Honor to Churchill Single Precedent Found," December 27, 1941, 4.

7. *Washington Evening Star,* "War Tide to Turn by 1943, Churchill Says," December 26, 1941, A2.

8. *Baltimore Sun,* "Churchill With Half an Hour of Oratory Captures Nation's Capital," December 27, 1941, 5.

9. The Churchill Center and Museum at the Churchill War Rooms, London, Speeches, Speeches of Winston Churchill, "Winston Churchill Addresses a Joint Session of Congress on December 26, 1941," http://www.winstonchurchill.org/learn/speeches/speeches-of-winston-churchill/1941-1945-war-leader/288-us-congress-1941.

10. The Churchill Center and Museum at the Churchill War Rooms, London, Speeches, Speeches of Winston Churchill, "Winston Churchill Addresses a Joint Session of Congress on December 26, 1941," http://www.winstonchurchill.org/learn/speeches/speeches-of-winston-churchill/1941-1945-war-leader/288-us-congress-1941.

11. The Churchill Center and Museum at the Churchill War Rooms, London, Speeches, Speeches of Winston Churchill, "Winston Churchill Addresses a Joint Session of Congress on December 26, 1941," http://www.winstonchurchill.org/learn/speeches/speeches-of-winston-churchill/1941-1945-war-leader/288-us-congress-1941.

12. The Churchill Center and Museum at the Churchill War Rooms, London, Speeches, Speeches of Winston Churchill, "Winston Churchill Addresses a Joint Session of Congress on December 26, 1941," http://www.winstonchurchill.org/learn/speeches/speeches-of-winston-churchill/1941-1945-war-leader/288-us-congress-1941.

13. Sydney J. Harris, "Thoughts at Large," *Sarasota Harold-Tribune,* December 28, 1941, 4.

14. Stuart Ball, *Winston Churchill* (New York: NYU Press, 2003), 63.

15. The Churchill Center and Museum at the Churchill War Rooms, London, Learn, Speeches, Quotation, "Famous Quotations and Stories," http://www.winstonchurchill.org/learn/speeches/quotations.

16. Sir Winston Churchill, Martin Gilbert, *The Churchill War Papers: The Ever Widening War, 1941* (New York, W. W. Norton & Company, 2001), 1685.

17. The Churchill Center and Museum at the Churchill War Rooms, London, Speeches, Speeches of Winston Churchill, "Winston Churchill Addresses a Joint Session of Congress on December 26, 1941," http://www.winstonchurchill.org/learn/speeches/speeches-of-winston-churchill/1941-1945-war-leader/288-us-congress-1941.

18. The Churchill Center and Museum at the Churchill War Rooms, London, Speeches, Speeches of Winston Churchill, "Winston Churchill Addresses a Joint Session of Congress on December 26, 1941," http://www.winstonchurchill.org/learn/speeches/speeches-of-winston-churchill/1941-1945-war-leader/288-us-congress-1941.

19. The Churchill Center and Museum at the Churchill War Rooms, London, Speeches, Speeches of Winston Churchill, "Winston Churchill Addresses a Joint Session of Congress on December 26, 1941," http://www.winstonchurchill.org/learn/speeches/speeches-of-winston-churchill/1941-1945-war-leader/288-us-congress-1941.

20. The Churchill Center and Museum at the Churchill War Rooms, London, Speeches, Speeches of Winston Churchill, "Winston Churchill Addresses a Joint Session of Congress on December 26, 1941," http://www.winstonchurchill.org/learn/speeches/speeches-of-winston-churchill/1941-1945-war-leader/288-us-congress-1941.

21. Associated Press, "Churchill Phones Senator's Wife Too Ill to See Him," *Chicago Daily Tribune*, December 27, 1941, 6.

22. *Baltimore Sun*, "Churchill Captures Capital With Speech," December 27, 1941, 1.

23. *New York Times*, "40 Billion Is '42 Arms Goal; Churchill Is Going to Canada," December 27, 1941, 1.

24. *New York Times*, "Fort Dix to Open 2 Target Ranges," December 27, 1941, 9.

25. Associated Press, "National Lottery Urged in New Senate Bill," *Washington Evening Star*, December 27, 1941, A3.

26. Associated Press, "National Lottery Urged in New Senate Bill," *Washington Evening Star*, December 27, 1941, A3.

27. Franklin Delano Roosevelt Presidential Library and Museum, "Memorandum for the President: Subject Victory Program," December 26, 1941, Hyde Park, NY.

28. Franklin Delano Roosevelt Presidential Library and Museum, "Memorandum for the President: Subject: North Africa," December 26, 1941, Hyde Park, NY.

29. Associated Press, "Plans to Curb Spending Hit," *Los Angeles Times*, December 27, 1941, 2.

30. *Hartford Daily Courant*, "New Red Cross By Flagg," December 26, 1941, 13.

31. *Atlanta Constitution*, "A Good Reminder," December 26, 1941, 2.

32. The Churchill Center and Museum at the Churchill War Rooms, London, Speeches, Speeches of Winston Churchill, "Winston Churchill Addresses a Joint Session of Congress on December 26, 1941," http://www.winstonchurchill.org/learn/speeches/speeches-of-winston-churchill/1941-1945-war-leader/288-us-congress-1941.

33. *Washington Evening Star*, "1,000 Civilians on Wake, Navy Announces," December 26, 1941, A3.

34. Associated Press, "Christmas Assaults Retake 100 Villages, Red Army Claims," *Washington Evening Star*, December 26, 1941, A2.

35. Walter B. Kerr, "Nazi Resistance Appears Stiffer," *Baltimore Sun*, December 26, 1941, 1.

36. Associated Press, "Bulletins," *Baltimore Sun*, December 26, 1941, 1.

37. Craig Thompson, "British Garrison Ends 16-Day Siege," *New York Times*, December 26, 1941, 1.

38. *New York Times*, "'We Are Still Here,' Is Midway Greeting," December 26, 1941, 1.

39. *Washington Evening Star*, "Midway Marines Still Holding Out," December 26, 1941, A1.

40. Associated Press, "War Tide to Turn By 1943, Churchill Says Japs Intensify Two-Way Drive on Manila," *Washington Evening Star*, December 26, 1941, A1.

41. John G. Doll, *Battling Bastards of Bataan* (Bennington, VT: Merriam Press, 1988), 24.

42. *Atlanta Constitution*, "Loss of Philippines Considered Possible by Gloomy Capital," December 26, 1941, 1.

43. United States Constitution, Article 3, Section 3.

44. David Nasaw, *The Chief: The Life of William Randolph Hearst* (Boston, MA: Houghton Mifflin Harcourt, 2001), 268.

45. *Boston Daily Globe*, "Gettysburg Eternal Light Extinguished As Raid Precaution," December 26, 1941, 2.

46. *Washington Evening Star*, "4,900 Soldier Dinners Go Uneaten Here on War Zone Order," December 26, 1941, B1.

47. Associated Press, "Accidents Kill 429 in 40 States During Two-Day Period," *Washington Evening Star*, December 26, 1941, B2.

48. Associated Press, "Accidents Kill 429 in 40 States During Two-Day Period," *Washington Evening Star*, December 26, 1941, B2.

49. *Boston Daily Globe*, "Isabbele Hallin, Saugus Beauty, Is N.Y. Suicide," December 26, 1941, 2.

50. *Boston Daily Globe*, "Isabbele Hallin, Saugus Beauty, Is N.Y. Suicide," December 26, 1941, 2.

51. *Boston Daily Globe*, "Isabbele Hallin, Saugus Beauty, Is N.Y. Suicide," December 26, 1941, 2.

52. *Baltimore Sun*, "Traveler's Aid Gets Sad Message," December 26, 1941, 4.

CHAPTER 27: THE TWENTY-SEVENTH OF DECEMBER

1. *Daily Boston Globe*, "Former Slave, 107, Combines Birthday, Yule Celebrations," December 26, 1941, 17.

2. *Atlanta Constitution*, "Fighting Spirit," December 26, 1941, 1.

3. *The Atlanta Constitution*, "Ex-Slaves Offer Victory Prayer At Annual Christmas Party," December 26, 1941, 3.

4. *Chicago Daily Tribune*, "Refuses To Seat Negro Named To Bench By Green," December 27, 1941, 9.

5. Gould Lincoln, "The Political Mill," *Washington Evening Star*, December 27, 1941, 9.

6. Ralph McGill, "One Word More," *Atlanta Constitution*, December 27, 1941, 4.

7. Franklin Delano Roosevelt Presidential Library and Museum, "Memorandum from Ambassador Winant to Secretary Hull Summarizing German and Italian Press Comment on Prime Minister Churchill's Address to the Congress," December 27, 1941, Hyde Park, NY.

8. Associated Press, "Text of Address Delivered by Winston Churchill," *Baltimore Sun*, December 27, 1941, 4.

9. David Lawrence, "Churchill Sets Sights for Victory," *Washington Evening Star*, December 27, 1941, 9.

10. *Washington Evening Star*, "War Strategy Talks Rushed at White House," December 27, 1941, 1.

11. Associated Press, "Death Toll Put at 50 in 3-Hour Air Attack; Property Loss Heavy," *Washington Evening Star*, December 27, 1941, 1.

12. Associated Press, "Helpless People Without a Gun Die Amid Terror," *Birmingham* (AL) *News*, December 27, 1941, 1.

13. Associated Press, "Helpless People Without a Gun Die Amid Terror," *Birmingham* (AL) *News*, December 27, 1941, 1.

14. R.P. Cronin, Jr., "Manila Sky Filled with Terror During Unmerciful Jap Attack," *Birmingham* (AL) *News*, December 27, 1941, 3.

15. Associated Press, "Hull Says Japan Follows Hitler's Cruelty Methods," *Birmingham* (AL) *News*, December 27, 1941, 1.

16. Associated Press, "Hull Says Japan Follows Hitler's Cruelty Methods," *Birmingham* (AL) *News*, December 27, 1941, 1.

17. Associated Press, "Helpless People Without a Gun Die Amid Terror," *Birmingham* (AL) *News*, December 27, 1941, 1.

18. Franklin Delano Roosevelt Presidential Library and Museum, "War Department Communique on Lingayen Gulf & Lamon Bay" December 26, 1941, Hyde Park, NY.

19. Associated Press, "Bulletin," *Baltimore Sun*, December 27, 1941, 1.

20. Mark S. Watson, "Retreat in the Philippines," *Baltimore Sun*, December 27, 1941, 1.

21. Vicente A. Pacis, "Fear for Safety of MacArthur on Philippine Front," *Chicago Daily Tribune*, December 27, 1941, 2.

22. Associated Press, "Fighting Is Bitter," *New York Times*, December 27, 1941, 1.

23. Associated Press, "Japanese Expect to Restore 70 Borneo Oil Wells in Month," *Washington Evening Star*, December 27, 1941, 1.

24. Associated Press, "Sarawak and the Brookes," *Washington Evening Star*, December 27, 1941, 8.

25. Associated Press, "Japs in Gilbert Islands; Fear for Europeans," *Chicago Daily Tribune*, December 27, 1941, 2.

26. *Baltimore Sun*, "U.S. Daily Newspapers Reach Circulation High," December 27, 1941, 4.

27. *Chicago Daily Tribune*, "GoodYear," December 28, 1941, 8.

28. Associated Press, "Rules Deny New Tires to Private Cars," *Los Angeles Times*, December 27, 1941, 1.

29. Associated Press, "Tire Rationing Rules Released; They Are Tough," *Birmingham* (AL) *News*, December 27, 1941, 1.

30. *Life*, "Schwinn-Built Bicycles," December 29, 1941, 36.

31. Associated Press "Tire Rationing Rules Released; They Are Tough," *Birmingham* (AL) *News*, December 27, 1941, A1.

32. Associated Press, "O.P.M. Relaxes Rubber Ban to Allow Making of Fire Hose," *Los Angeles Times*, December 27, 1941, A1.

33. Associated Press, "Vast Dandelion Planting Urged for Production of Rubber," *Los Angeles Times*, December 27, 1941, A1.

34. *Life*, "On The Newsfronts of the World," December 29, 1941, 20.

35. Associated Press, "Detroit May Revert to Trolleys in Tire Crisis," *Portsmouth* (VA) *Times*, December 28, 1941, 2.

36. Associated Press, "British Ban Making Rubber Articles," *Los Angeles Times*, December 27, 1941, A1.

37. Associated Press, "Princes Stage One-Round Bout at Gloria Vanderbilt's Party," *Birmingham* (AL) *News*, December 27, 1941, 1.

38. *Los Angeles Times*, "Ralph's the Year Ahead . . . ," December 27, 1941, 4.

39. *Baltimore Sun*, "Seeking to Fill Up Skilled Labor Gap," December 27, 1941, 4.

40. Associated Press, "Enemy Aliens Must Turn in Radios, Cameras," *Washington Evening Star*, December 27, 1941, 1.

41. Associated Press, "Aliens En Route to Montana Camp," *Los Angeles Times*, December 27, 1941, A2.

42. Associated Press, "Mexico Travelers Halted In Search for Letters," *Los Angeles Times*, December 27, 1941, A2.

43. *Los Angeles Times*, "Identification Cards Needed for Entrance to Water Front," December 27, 1941, B.

44. *Los Angeles Times*, "Identification Cards Needed for Entrance to Water Front," December 27, 1941, B.

45. *Los Angeles Times*, "Where to Cut to Save Money for War," December 27, 1941, 4.

46. Associated Press, "Nazi Envoys to U.S. Housed at Hotel," *Baltimore Sun*, December 27, 1941, 4.

47. Lloyd Lehrbas, "Geneva Pact Governs American Treatment of Jap War Prisoners," *Washington Evening Star*, December 27, 1941, A4.

48. *New York Times*, "U.S. Outlines Stand on War Prisoners," December 27, 1941, 8.

49. *New York Times*, "U.S. Outlines Stand on War Prisoners," December 27, 1941, 8.

50. United Press, "Coastal Subsea Raiding Falls Off," *Los Angles Times*, December 27, 1941, A2.

CHAPTER 28: THE TWENTY-EIGHTH OF DECEMBER

1. *New York Times*, "Support for U.S. Urged in Sermons," December 28, 1941, 11.

2. Rev. John Evans, "Pray Against Godless Foes, Archbishop Says," *Chicago Daily Tribune*, December 28, 1941, 13.
3. *New York Times*, "Support for U.S. Urged in Sermons," December 28, 1941, 11.
4. Associated Press, "Market Commissioner says Dispute Topped List of Incidents," *Washington Evening Star*, December 28, 1941, A2.
5. *Time*, "Civilian Defense," December 29, 1941, 11.
6. *Time*, "Civilian Defense," December 29, 1941, 11.
7. *Bulletin of International News*, Vol. 19, No. 1, (Royal Institute of International News, London, England, 1942) 23.
8. *New York Times*, "Australia Warned of More Reverses," December 27, 1941, 5.
9. *New York Times*, "40 Billion is '42 Arms Goal," December 27, 1941, 1.
10. *New York Times*, "Australia Warned of More Reverses," December 27, 1941, 5.
11. *New York Times*, "For Anglo-American Unity," December 27, 1941, C18.
12. United Press, "Gilbert Islands Believed Seized," *Los Angeles Times*, December 28, 1941, 3.
13. Associated Press, "Publisher Assails Removal of Manila's Defenses," *Sunday* (DE) *Star*, December 28, 1941, A3.
14. Associated Press, "Australia Reliance in U.S., Premier Declares," *Washington Evening Star*, December 28, 1941, A2.
15. John C. Henry, "Parleys Bolster Allies' Position, Roosevelt Says," *Washington Evening Star*, December 28, 1941, A1.
16. John C. Henry, "Parleys Bolster Allies' Position, Roosevelt Says," *Washington Evening Star*, December 28, 1941, A1.
17. Associated Press, "Has Busy Day of Conferences With Churchill," *Boston Daily Globe*, December 28, 1941, C1.
18. John C. Henry, "Parleys Bolster Allies' Position, Roosevelt Says," *Washington Evening Star*, December 28, 1941, A1.
19. Maj. George Fielding Elliot, "French Still Play Vital Part in War," *Los Angeles Times*, December 28, 1941, 4.
20. John C. Henry, "Parleys Bolster Allies' Position, Roosevelt Says," *Washington Evening Star*, December 28, 1941, A1.
21. John C. Henry, "Parleys Bolster Allies' Position, Roosevelt Says," *Washington Evening Star*, December 28, 1941, A1.
22. *Washington Evening Star*, "Henderson Acts to Block Cigarette Price Increase," December 28, 1941, A3.
23. *Life*, "We Want Camels!," December 29, 1941, 70.
24. Associated Press, "Has Busy Day of Conferences With Churchill," *Boston Daily Globe*, December 28, 1941, C1.
25. Associated Press, "O.P.M. Limits Output of All Types of New Farm Machinery," *Washington Evening Star*, December 28, 1941, A4.
26. *Life*, "Toke Raid Would be Costly and Futile," December 29, 1941, 56.
27. *Life*, "Perspiration Is Acid . . . It Cuts Stocking Life!" December 29, 1941, 68.
28. *Los Angeles Times*, "Tommy Dorsey," December 28, 1941, 4.
29. *Honolulu Advertiser*, "Prescriptions for Liquor Under Control," December 28, 1941, 8.
30. *Honolulu Advertiser*, "Hawaii Defense Act," December 28, 1941, 12.
31. United Press, "Hawaii Boys Flew for Japs," *Los Angeles Times*, December 28, 1941, 2.
32. *Honolulu Advertiser*, "KGMB," December 28, 1941, 12.
33. *Los Angeles Times*, "Aliens Evacuated From Federal Jail," December 28, 1941, 8.
34. *Los Angeles Times*, "Welder Union Votes to Stop Work Today," December 20, 1941, 1.
35. *New York Times*, "Short-wave Sets of Aliens Curbed," December 28, 1941, 4.
36. International News Service, "Nab Alleged Coast Bund Leader," *Honolulu Advertiser*, December 29, 1941, 4.

37. *Life*, "Nazi Spies," December 29, 1941, 24.
38. *Time*, "Civilian Defense," December 29, 1941, 11.
39. *Los Angeles Times*, "End of Curbs in Prospect," December 28, 1941, 3.
40. Associated Press, "Defense Plants Asked to Work on New Year's," *Baltimore Sun*, December 28, 1941, 12.
41. *Los Angeles Times*, "Don't Let Tongue Slip," December 28, 1941, 3.
42. *Los Angeles Times*, "A Word to Amateur War Critics," December 28, 1941, 4.
43. *Los Angeles Times*, "We Shall Not Forget This, Yellow Men," December 28, 1941, 4.
44. *New York Times*, "Washington Asks Revenge Bombings," December 28, 1941, 1.
45. United Press, "Old Area in Ruins," *New York Times*, December 28, 1941, 1.
46. United Press, "Old Area in Ruins," *New York Times*, December 28, 1941, 1.
47. *New York Times*, "The International Situation," December 28, 1941, 1.
48. Associated Press, "Nipponese Broadcast Is Quickly Scorned by Angry Islanders," *Atlanta Constitution*, December 28 1941, 1A.
49. United Press, "Japanese Advance Slowly on Manila," *New York Times*, December 28, 1941, 1.
50. *Honolulu Advertiser*, "Japanese Launch Fresh Manila Attack from Air," December 28, 1941, 1.
51. *Honolulu Advertiser*, "Japanese Launch Fresh Manila Attack from Air," December 28, 1941, 1.
52. F. Tillman Durdin, "New Malaya Push by Japan Starts," *New York Times*, December 28, 1941, 6.
53. *New York Times*, "Barkley Predicts Bombing of Tokyo," December 30, 1941, 3.

CHAPTER 29: THE TWENTY-NINTH OF DECEMBER

1.   United Press, Frank Hewlett, "Filipino Police Hunt Chutists in Manila Area," *Honolulu Advertiser*, December 29, 1941, 1.
2.   United Press, Frank Hewlett, "Filipino Police Hunt Chutists in Manila Area," *Honolulu Advertiser*, December 29, 1941, 1.
3.   Associated Press, "Famed Holy Statue Saved in Manila," *Los Angeles Times*, December 29, 1941, 3.
4.   United Press, "Priceless Library in Manila Is Lost," *New York Times*, December 29, 1941, 4.
5.   *New York Times*, "Tokyo Is Firm on Manila," December 29, 1941, 2.
6.   *Honolulu Advertiser*, "FDR Pledges Full Aid to Filipinos," December 29, 1941, 1.
7.   *New York Times*, "Messages on Philippines," December 29, 1941, 1.
8.   Associated Press, "Philippines Given Pledge By F.D.R. for 'Redemption,'" *Birmingham* (AL) *News*, December 29, 1941, 1.
9.   *Honolulu Advertiser*, "Don't Be Impatient, Navy Urges America," December 29, 1941, 4.
10. *Honolulu Advertiser*, "Don't Be Impatient, Navy Urges America," December 29, 1941, 4.
11. Associated Press, "Philippines Given Pledge By F.D.R. for 'Redemption,'" *Birmingham* (AL) *News*, December 29, 1941, 1.
12. Associated Press, "Philippines Given Pledge By F.D.R. for 'Redemption,'" *Birmingham* (AL) *News*, December 29, 1941, 1.
13. *Life* "College Men Wanted," December 29, 1941, 57.
14. Paul Mallon, "Reverses in Far East May Be Expected," *Birmingham* (AL) *News*, December 29, 1941, 1.
15. United Press, Frank Hewlett, "Filipino Police Hunt Chutists in Manila Area," *Honolulu Advertiser*, December 29, 1941, 1.
16. Associated Press, "War Office Says Attacks Will Continue," *Baltimore Sun*, December, 29, 1941, 4.
17. *New York Times*, "10-to-1 Toll Taken on Southeast," December 29, 1941, 3.
18. *New York Times*, "10-to-1 Toll Taken on Southeast," December 29, 1941, 3.
19. *New York Times*, "Washington Is Hopeful," December 29, 1941, 3.
20. *Honolulu Advertiser*, "British Holding Foe Firmly in North Malaya," December 29, 1941, 2.
21. *Chicago Daily Tribune*, "Jap 'Friendship' Leaflets Lure Many to Death," December 29, 1941, 4.

22. *New York Times*, "Australian Force Ready in Malaya," December 29, 1941, 4.
23. Associated Press, "War Office Says Attacks Will Continue," *Baltimore Sun*, December 29, 1941, 4.
24. *Atlanta Constitution*, "Japs in China Seize U.S. Consul, Others," December 28, 1941, 1.
25. Franklin Delano Roosevelt Library and Museum, "Memorandum from Hull to FDR," December 29, 1941, Hyde Park, NY.
26. Franklin Delano Roosevelt Library and Museum, "Memorandum from FDR to H. Hopkins," December 29, 1941, Hyde Park, NY.
27. Franklin Delano Roosevelt Library and Museum, "Progress Report on Intelligence Problems in the New York Area," December 27, 1941, Hyde Park, NY.
28. Franklin Delano Roosevelt Library and Museum, "Progress Report on Intelligence Problems in the New York Area," December 27, 1941, Hyde Park, NY.
29. Franklin Delano Roosevelt Library and Museum, "Letter from FDR to John Carter," December 29, 1941, Hyde Park, NY.
30. Franklin Delano Roosevelt Library and Museum, "Memorandum Regarding Alien Activity in Great Britain," December 29, 1941, Hyde Park, NY.
31. Franklin Delano Roosevelt Library and Museum, "Memorandum from FDR to H. Hopkins," December 29, 1941, Hyde Park, NY.
32. *Honolulu Advertiser*, "13 Survivors of SS Prusa Arrive Here," December 29, 1941, 1.
33. *Life*, "Attack on Hawaii," December 29, 1941, 11.
34. *Life*, "Attack on Hawaii," December 29, 1941, 18.
35. *Life*, "Troops on the Move," December 29, 1941, 23.
36. *Life*, "Anatomy of Bombs," December 29, 1941, 50.
37. Boyd D. Wagner, "'Buzz' Wagner's Story," *Life*, December 29, 1941, 36.
38. *Life*, "U.S. Marines," December 29, 1941, 43.
39. *Life*, "Anatomy of Bombs," December 29, 1941, 50.
40. Oliver Jensen, "Ensign Weems," *Life*, December 29, 1941, 55.
41. *Time*, "World Battlefronts," December 29, 1941, 16.
42. *Time*, "The U.S. at War," December 29, 1941, 7.
43. *Time*, "The U.S. at War," December 29, 1941, 7.
44. *Time*, "The U.S. at War," December 29, 1941, 11.
45. *Birmingham* (AL) *News*, "Russia, England Agree on Method of War Conduct," December 29, 1941, 1.
46. *Honolulu Advertiser*, "Eden-Stalin Conference Covers Conduct of War," December 29, 1941, 2.
47. *Birmingham* (AL) *News*, "Russia, England Agree on Method of War Conduct," December 29, 1941, 1.
48. *Time*, "The U.S. at War," December 29, 1941, 8.
49. *Time*, "World Battlefronts," December 29, 1941, 9.
50. *Time*, "World Battlefronts," December 29, 1941, 12.
51. *Time*, "World Battlefronts," December 29, 1941, 12.
52. Associated Press, "Churchill Is Cheered Wildly by Canadians on Arrival at Ottawa," *Birmingham* (AL) *News*, December 29, 1941, 2.
53. Associated Press, "Churchill Is Cheered Wildly by Canadians on Arrival at Ottawa," *Birmingham* (AL) *News*, December 29, 1941, 2.
54. *New York Times*, "Churchill in 'Coveralls,'" December 30, 1941, 3.
55. Associated Press, "35 Per Cent Slash in Gas Consumption Studied For Civilians," *Birmingham* (AL) *News*, December 29, 1941, 2.
56. Associated Press, "Californians Warned of Jap Raid Reports," *Birmingham* (AL) *News*, December 29, 1941, 2.
57. Lawrence E. Davies, "Foes Spread 'News' of a Fake Bargain," *New York Times*, December 29, 1941, 7.

58.   *Birmingham* (AL) *News*, "Venereal Disease in Wartime," December 29, 1941, 6.
59.   Associated Press, "Lady Barflies a Prime Target As Anti-Profanity Week Opens," *Baltimore Sun*, December 29, 1941, 13.
60.   *Birmingham* (AL) *News*, "Guilty Flag Defiler," December 29, 1940, 7.
61.   *Los Angeles Times*, "Gloria Vanderbilt Wed to Pasquale Di Cicco," December 29, 1941, Part B1.
62.   *New York Times*, "National Philosophy Found Lacking Here," December 29, 1941, 12.
63.   *New York Times*, "Enlistments Begin In 'Spiritual Army'," December 29, 1941, 12.
64.   Associated Press, "Woman Air Spotter 97; Nursed Soldiers in 1865," *New York Times*, December 29, 1941, 8.
65.   *Chicago Daily Tribune*, "A Lonely Yank, a Note, and Wow!" December 29, 1941, 1.
66.   Associated Press, "She Refuses to Believe Son Killed and Navy Acknowledges Mistake," *Birmingham* (AL) *News*, December 29, 1941, 7.
67.   *Time*, "People: Pluggers & Donors," December 29, 1941, 40.
68.   *Honolulu Advertiser*, "Defense Stamps Free!," December 30, 1941, 2.
69.   *Time*, "People: Pluggers & Donors," December 29, 1941, 40.
70.   *New York Times*, "Britain to Join U.S. in Prayers Thursday," December 28, 1941, 2.
71.   *Los Angeles Times*, "Axis Aliens Surrender Radio Sets and Cameras," December 29, 1941, 1.
72.   *Time*, "Music: Of Thee I Sing, Baby," December 29, 1941, 46.
73.   *Time*, "Music: Of Thee I Sing, Baby," December 29, 1941, 46.
74.   A) *Honolulu Advertiser*, "Buses Black," December 30, 1941, 2.
75.   *Honolulu Advertiser*, "At the Theaters," December 30, 1941, 4.
76.   *New York Times*, "Flier, Shot Down, Resumed Battle in Another Plane as Wife Watched," December 30, 1941, 5.
77.   *New York Times*, "Flier, Shot Down, Resumed Battle in Another Plane as Wife Watched," December 30, 1941, 5.

CHAPTER 30: THE THIRTIETH OF DECEMBER

1.   Associated Press, "Eiffel Tower May Be Melted to Scrap Metal," *Birmingham* (AL) *News*, December 30, 1941, 2.
2.   Associated Press, "Eiffel Tower May Be Melted to Scrap Metal," *Birmingham* (AL) *News*, December 30, 1941, 2.
3.   Associated Press, "How War News Gets Around and Why Editors Go Nuts," *The Atlanta Constitution*, December 31, 1941, 1.
4.   Churchill Center and Museum, Speeches, Speeches of Winston Churchill, "Preparation-Liberation-Assault," December 30, 1941, Chicago, IL, http://www.winstonchurchill.org/learn/speeches/speeches-of-winston-churchill/106-preparation-liberation-assault.
5.   *Hartford* (CT) *Courant*, "U.S. Expenditures . . . December Top World War Record," December 30, 1941, 1.
6.   *Honolulu Advertiser*, "Bulletins," December 31, 1941, 1.
7.   *Time*, "Mr. Paul's Ideas," December 29, 1941, 54.
8.   *Time*, "Mr. Paul's Ideas," December 29, 1941, 54.
9.   Dewey L. Fleming, "Half of US Income to Go for War Effort Under Roosevelt Plan," *Baltimore Sun*, December 31, 1941, 1.
10.   Gerald Griffin, "President Plans Daylight Saving," *Baltimore Sun*, December 31, 1941, 3.
11.   Associated Press, "Defense Bond Sales Reach Highest Mark," *Birmingham* (AL) *News*, December 30, 1941, 3.
12.   *Birmingham* (AL) *News*, "Defense Bond Sales Reach Highest Mark," December 30, 1941, 1.
13.   *Birmingham* (AL) *News*, "11 Billion Dollar Tax Increase Is Proposed," December 30, 1941, 4.
14.   *Baltimore Sun*, "Financial Sacrifice Must Come to Win, Morgenthau Warns," December 30, 1941, 1.
15.   *Birmingham* (AL) *News*, "Women Volunteers in Uniforms Given Approval Of U.S. Army," December 30, 1941, 2.

16. *Birmingham* (AL) *News*, "Women Volunteers in Uniforms Given Approval Of U.S. Army," December 30, 1941, 2.

17. *Los Angeles Times*, "Cigarette Price Ceiling Slated," December 30, 1941, 1.

18. *Los Angeles Times*, "Hoarding of Fats and Oils Banned," December 30, 1941, 5.

19. *New York Times*, "Allocation Plan Held Inadequate," December 30, 1941, 12.

20. Ernest Lindley, "Tire Rationing to Serve as Test of Democratic Administration," *Birmingham* (AL) *News*, December 30, 1941, 10.

21. Harvey S. Firestone, Jr., "The Rubber Situation," *Baltimore Sun*, December 30, 1941, 4.

22. George Gallup, "The Gallup Poll: Survey Shows Majority of Americans Do Nothing to Keep Physically Fit," *Baltimore Sun*, December 30, 1941, 13.

23. Associated Press, "Tire Curb Sells Horses," *New York Times*, December 30, 1941, 11.

24. Paul Gesner and John Beckley "Round-Clock Defense Work in Sight at Most All Plants," *Birmingham* (AL) *News*, 10.

25. Associated Press, "Nazi Launch Air Assault on Coastal Area," *Baltimore Sun*, December 30, 1941, 1.

26. Associated Press, "Mikado's Troops Move on Capital From Southeast," *Birmingham* (AL) *News*, December 30, 1941, 1.

27. AP, "R.A.F. Blows Climax British Land, Sea and Air Assaults," *Los Angeles Times*, December 30, 1941, 1.

28. Pierre J. Husk, "F.D.R. 'Pushed Europe Into War Against Me,' Nazi Dictator Complains," *Birmingham* (AL) *News*, December 30, 1941, 1.

29. Pierre J. Husk, "F.D.R. 'Pushed Europe Into War Against Me,' Nazi Dictator Complains," *Birmingham* (AL) *News*, December 30, 1941, 1.

30. Pierre J. Husk, "F.D.R. 'Pushed Europe Into War Against Me,' Nazi Dictator Complains," *Birmingham* (AL) *News*, December 30, 1941, 4.

31. United Press, "Planes Blast Luzon's Base for Three Hours," *Los Angeles Times*, December 30, 1941, 1.

32. Rear Admiral Yates Sterling, Jr., "Manila Bay Protected by Mighty Corregidor," *Honolulu Advertiser*, December 30, 1941, 1.

33. Associated Press, "Tribe of Philippine Pygmies Joins Allies in War on Japs," *Los Angeles Times*, December 30, 1941, 3.

34. *Birmingham* (AL) *News*, "Gen. MacArthur Urges Reprisals for Manila Raids," December 30, 1941, 1.

35. United Press, "U.S. Volunteer Pilots Bag 26 Enemy Planes," *Honolulu Advertiser*, December 30, 1941, 5.

36. United Press, "FDR to Call War Council," *Honolulu Advertiser*, December 30, 1941, 1.

37. United Press, "Enemy Suffers Heavy Losses in Far East," *Honolulu Advertiser*, December 30, 1941, 1.

38. Associated Press, "Churchill Says War Not To End Until Attack on Nazi Homeland," *Birmingham* (AL) *News*, December 30, 1941, 1.

39. Churchill Center and Museum, Speeches, Speeches of Winston Churchill, "Preparation-Liberation-Assault," December 30, 1941, Chicago, IL, http://www.winstonchurchill.org/learn/speeches/speeches-of-winston-churchill/106-preparation-liberation-assault.

40. Churchill Center and Museum, Speeches, Speeches of Winston Churchill, "Preparation-Liberation-Assault," December 30, 1941, Chicago, IL, http://www.winstonchurchill.org/learn/speeches/speeches-of-winston-churchill/106-preparation-liberation-assault.

41. *New York Times*, "U.S. Lists 29 Nations at War With the Axis; Figure Differs From Churchill's in Speech," December 31, 1941, 6.

42. Churchill Center and Museum, Speeches, Speeches of Winston Churchill, "Preparation-Liberation-Assault," December 30, 1941, Chicago, IL http://www.winstonchurchill.org/learn/speeches/speeches-of-winston-churchill/106-preparation-liberation-assault.

43. Associated Press, "Red Men Bury Hatchet to Aid War on Axis," *Baltimore Sun*, December 30, 1941, 4.
44. Associated Press, "Hard Blows at Foe Urged By Einstein," *Baltimore Sun*, December 30, 1941, 4.
45. *New York Times*, "Bid Astronomers, Navigate Bombers," December 30, 1941, 1.
46. Associated Press, "Astronomy Called Aid to War Effort," *New York Times*, December 30, 1941, 13.
47. Associated Press, "Astronomer Inclined to Doubt Theory Universe Is Exploding," *Baltimore Sun*, December 31, 1941, 13.
48. International News Service, "Scientists Say Water Exists on Red Planet," *Atlanta Constitution*, December 31, 1941, 6.
49. *Honolulu Advertiser*, "Important Notice to All Residents Of Oahu," December 30, 1941, 2.
50. *Honolulu Advertiser*, "Bakery Goods Sale Regulated By Governor," December 31, 1941, 2.
51. *Honolulu Advertiser*, "Sought By Relatives," December 30, 1941, 3.
52. *Honolulu Advertiser*, "General Orders," December 30, 1941, 6.
53. *Honolulu Advertiser*, "Alarm System Will Warn Four Isles of Raids," December 30, 1941, 6.
54. Wallace Carroll, "Fifth Column Exposed," *Boston Evening Globe*, December 30, 1941, 1.
55. *Los Angeles Times*, "Long Lines of Enemy Aliens Deliver Banned Articles," December 30, 1941, 8.
56. Franklin Delano Roosevelt Presidential Library and Museum, "Second Progress Report on Intelligence Problems in the New York Area," December 31, 1941, Hyde Park, NY.
57. *Los Angeles Times*, "Patriotic Raffles Robs Vanderbilts of Jewelry," December 30, 1941, 1.
58. *Baltimore Sun*, "Newlywed Gloria Gets More Money," December 30, 1941, 1.
59. *Los Angeles Times*, "Whales Fool Fort Gun Crew; Report Submarines Offshore," December 30, 1941, 8.
60. Associated Press, "Bulletins," *Baltimore Sun*, December 30, 1941, 1.
61. *New York Times*, "The Texts of the Day's Communiqués on Fighting in Various Zones," December 30, 1941, 2.
62. F. Tillman Durdin, "Foe Seeks to Ring Singapore; Plan to Take It Intact Seen," *New York Times*, December 30, 1941, 1.
63. *New York Times*, "U.S. Freighter Sunk in Atlantic Dec. 3," December 30, 1941, 13.
64. Franklin Delano Roosevelt Presidential Library and Museum, "Memorandum for the Naval Aide to the President," December 26, 1941, Hyde Park, NY.
65. United Press, "Lindy's Offer to Serve May Be Accepted," *Honolulu Advertiser*, December 31, 1941, 6.
66. Associated Press, "Lindbergh Volunteers Servicesin Air Corps; Reaction Is Indefinite," *Birmingham* (AL) *News*, December 30, 1941, 1.
67. James P. Duffy, *Lindbergh Vs. Roosevelt* (Washington DC: Regnery, 2010), 209.
68. *Baltimore Sun*, "A Darkened Liberty," December 30, 1941, 3.
69. *Baltimore Sun*, "A Darkened Liberty," December 30, 1941, 3.

CHAPTER 31: THE THIRTY-FIRST OF DECEMBER

1. Anne O'Hare McCormick, "The Outstanding Fact in a Fateful Year," *New York Times*, December 31, 1941, 16.
2. Franklin Delano Roosevelt Presidential Library and Museum, "Memorandum from Ambassador Winant to Secretary Hull Requesting a Presidential Message from President Roosevelt for the National Day of Prayer on New Year's Day 1942," December 30, 1941, Hyde Park, NY.
3. Franklin Delano Roosevelt Presidential Library and Museum, "Memorandum from Ambassador Winant to Secretary Hull Requesting a Presidential Message from President Roosevelt for the National Day of Prayer on New Year's Day 1942," December 30, 1941, Hyde Park, NY.
4. *New York Times*, "The Plaza for New Year's Eve," December 31, 1941, 18.

5. *Los Angeles Times*, "Police Warn New Year's Celebrants," December 30, 1941, 1.

6. *New York Times*, "Mayer Assails Critics," December 31, 1941, 10.

7. *Boston Daily Globe*, "Boisterous Greeting Ready for 1942's Boston Arrival," December 31, 1941, 1.

8. Geoffrey Parsons Jr., "Slim Santa This Year In Britain," *Baltimore Sun*, December 23, 1941, 13.

9. *Honolulu Advertiser*, "License Suspensions Face Speeders Here," December 31, 1941, 2.

10. *Honolulu Advertiser*, "Banana Supply Plentiful Here," December 31, 1941, 3.

11. *Honolulu Advertiser*, "Leis for Dead to Be Received New Year's Day," December 31, 1941, 2.

12. *Honolulu Advertiser*, "Leis for Dead to Be Received New Year's Day," December 31, 1941, 2.

13. *Baltimore Sun*, "It's a Treat to Dine Out," December 31, 1941, 5.

14. *Los Angeles Times*, "New Year's Eve," December 31, 1941, 12.

15. Mary Harris, "Ringside Table," *Washington Post*, December 31, 1941, 16.

16. Jane Holt, "News of Food," *New York Times*, December 30, 1941, 14.

17. *New York Times*, "Rest-Period Demand Costs Hours at Ford," December 31, 1941, 9.

18. *New York Times*, "Rest-Period Demand Costs Hours at Ford," December 31, 1941, 9.

19. *Atlanta Constitution*, "Big California Telescope to Be Barred to Public," December 31, 1941, 10.

20. Ben Gilbert, "War Casts Deep Shadow on New Years Parties Here," *Washington Post*, January 1, 1941, 1.

21. *Birmingham* (AL) *News*, "Don't Throw Anything Away, Save Everything for Defense," December 31, 1941, 3.

22. Martin Lide, "2,800 Tanks a Month Is Goal Soon in View; Gun Totals Are Secret," *Birmingham* (AL) *News*, December 31, 1941, 5.

23. *Los Angeles Times*, "County Ordered to Save Salvage," December 31, 1941, 6.

24. John MacCormac, "Railroads Expect Aid from Tire Ban," *New York Times*, December 31, 1941, 9.

25. *Baltimore Sun*, "Whither Fashion in 1942," December 31, 1941, 10.

26. *Honolulu Advertiser*, "Ted Williams Is Voted Baseball's Man of Year," December 31, 1941, 8.

27. Joan Fontaine Female, "'Citizen Kane' Picked as Top Movie of '41," *Birmingham* (AL) *News*, December 31, 1941, 19.

28. *Honolulu Advertiser*, "No Messages Received Since Late Last Night," December 31, 1941, 1.

29. *Honolulu Advertiser*, "No Messages Received Since Late Last Night," December 31, 1941, 1.

30. Associated Press, "Indies Papers Ask Public to be Patient," *Baltimore Sun*, December 31, 1941, 3.

31. Husband E. Kimmel, *Admiral Kimmel's Story* (Chicago, IL: Henry Regnery Company, 1955), v.

32. Husband E. Kimmel, *Admiral Kimmel's Story* (Chicago, IL: Henry Regnery Company, 1955), 169.

33. *Hartford Courant*, "Short Dies at His Home in Texas," September 5, 1949, 1.

34. Associated Press, "Line South of Manila," December 31, 1941, 1.

35. Hanson W. Baldwin, "What Navy Is Doing," *New York Times*, December 31, 1941, 4.

36. Martin Caidin, *Golden Wings* (New York: Bramhall House, 1960), 108.

37. Associated Press, "Hope Fades in Gotham," *Birmingham* (AL) *News*, December 31, 1941, 2.

38. R. P. Cronin Jr., "Outnumbered Forces of Allies Being Pushed Back by Invader," *Birmingham* (AL) *News*, December 31, 1941, 2.

39. Dewitt MacKenzie, "The War Today: Strengthening of Singapore Now Is Squarely Up to U.S.; Weakness in Air Power Is Cited," December 31, 1941, 2.

40. Associated Press, "Japanese Dive Bombers Control Roads as Tanks Smash Closer to Capital," *Baltimore Sun*, December 31, 1941, 1.

41. Associated Press, "Sailor in Hawaii Sees Grave Marked as His," *Baltimore Sun*, December 31, 1941, 2.

42. Leland Stowe, "Burma Road Scandal," *Boston Evening Globe*, December 30, 1941, 1.

43. *New York Times*, "Gandhi Steps Down in War Policy Rift," December 31, 1941, 6.

44. *Birmingham* (AL) *News*, "Lynchings in 1941," December 31, 1941, 6.

45. *New York Times*, "The Day in Washington," December 31, 1941, 9.

46. Dewy L. Fleming, "Half of U.S. Income to Go for War Effort Under Roosevelt Plan," *Baltimore Sun*, December 31, 1941, 1.

47. Associated Press, "Washington Holds Partial Blackout," *Baltimore Sun*, December 31, 1941, 7.

48. Franklin Delano Roosevelt Presidential Library and Museum, "Memorandum To President Roosevelt From Rome Regarding Covert Conversation with Goering," January 31, 1942, Hyde Park, New York.

49. Pierre J. Huss, "Jap Attack Was Nazis' Secret Weapon Against U.S., Writer Discloses," *Birmingham* (AL) *News*, December 31, 1941, 1.

50. Franklin Delano Roosevelt Presidential Library and Museum, "Memorandum for the Naval Aide to the President, Regarding Factional Strife in Germany; Possible Peace Moves," September 26, 1941, Hyde Park, NY.

51. United Press, "'Frau Roosevelt Named by Hitler," *Boston Evening Globe*, December 31, 1941, 2.

52. Canadian Press, "Prime Minister Churchill's Address to Canadian Parliament," *New York Times*, December 31, 1941, 6.

53. Jon Meacham, *Franklin and Winston* (New York: Random House 2004), 5.

54. Jon Meacham, *Franklin and Winston* (New York: Random House 2004), xvii.

55. David Brinkley, *Washington Goes to War* (New York: Alfred A. Knopf, 1988), xiv.

56. David Brinkley, *Washington Goes to War* (New York: Alfred A. Knopf, 1988), 27.

57. Franklin Delano Roosevelt Presidential Library and Museum, "Memorandum to Rear Admiral Ross T. McIntire, (MC) U.S. Navy, The Surgeon General, Bureau of Medicine and Surgery, Navy Department, Washington, D.C., from Elphege A.M. Gendreau, Captain, (MC), U.S. Navy Flight Surgeon, United States Pacific Fleet, U.S.S. Pennsylvania," December 11, 1941, Hyde Park, NY.

58. Martin Caidin, *Golden Wings* (New York: Bramhall House, 1960), 89.

59. Studs Terkel, *The Good War* (New York: Pantheon Books, 1984,) 1.

60. *Baltimore Sun*, "Special Prayers Planned for U.S., December 31, 1941, 6.

61. Franklin Delano Roosevelt Presidential Library and Museum, "Message From President Roosevelt to the American Embassy London, Triple Priority, National Day of Prayer Message," December 31, 1941, Hyde Park, NY.

EPILOGUE

1. Fred Pulis, *The Impact and Legacy Years, 1941, 1947, 1968* (Victoria, BC: Trafford, 2000), 15.

2. Carl Jung Resources, "What Is Synchronicity?," Last Modified: 2011, http://www.carl-jung.net/synchronicity.html.

3. Martin Caidin, *Golden Wings* (New York: Bramhall House, 1960), 102.

4. David Brinkley, *Washington Goes to War* (New York: Alfred A. Knopf, 1988), 43.

5. Walter Trojan, "Blame 2 for Pearl Harbor!" *Chicago Tribune*, January 25, 1942, 1.

6. *Hilo Tribune Herald*, "Japan May Strike Over The Weekend," November 30, 1941, 1.

7. *New York Times*, "Medals Given to 9 by Admiral Nimitz," May 28, 1942, 8.

BIBLIOGRAPHY

BOOKS

Ball, Stuart. *Winston Churchill*. New York: NYU Press, 2003.

Bankhead, Tallulah. *Tallulah: My Autobiography*. New York: Harper, 1952.

Barone, Michael. *Our Country: The Shaping of America from Roosevelt to Reagan*. New York: Free Press, 1990.

Bartsch, William H. *December 8, 1941 Macarthur's Pearl Harbor*. College Station, TX: Texas A&M University Press, 2003.

Bassett, James. *Harms Way*. New York: The World Publishing Company, 1962.

Beschloss, Michael R. *The Conquerors: Roosevelt, Truman and the Destruction of Hitler's Germany, 1941-1945*. New York: Simon & Schuster, 2002.

Bildner, Phil. *The Unforgettable Season: The Story of Joe DiMaggio, Ted Williams, and the Record-Setting Summer of '41*. New York: Penguin Books, 2011.

Billingsley, Kenneth Lloyd. Hollywood Party: How Communism Seduced the American Film Industry in the 1930s and 1940s. Rocklin, CA: Forum, 1998.

Black, Conrad. *Franklin Delano Roosevelt: Champion of Freedom*. New York: Public Affairs, 2003.

Borch, Fredric L., and Daniel Martinez. *Kimmel, Short, and Pearl Harbor*. Annapolis, MD: Naval Institute Press, 2005.

Braeman, Joe. *American Politics in the Twentieth Century*. New York: Thomas Y. Cromwell Company, 1969.

Brinkley, David. *Washington Goes to War: The Extraordinary Story of the Transformation of a City and a Nation*. New York: Random House, 1988.

Brinkley, Douglas. *The World War II Memorial: A Grateful Nation Remembers*. Washington, DC: Smithsonian Books, 2004.

Buchanan, Patrick J. *Churchill, Hitler, and the Unnecessary War: How Britain Lost Its Empire and the West Lost the World*. New York: Three Rivers Press, 2008.

Bulletin of International News, vol. 19, no. 1. Royal Institute of International News, London, UK, 1942.

Burns, James MacGregor, and Susan Dunn, *The Three Roosevelts: Patrician Leaders Who Transformed America*. New York: Grove Press, 2001.

Caidin, Martin. *Golden Wings: A Pictorial History of the United States Navy and Marine Corps in the Air*. New York: Bramhall House, 1960.

Caro, Robert A. *Means of Ascent: The Years of Lyndon Johnson*. New York: Alfred A. Knopf, 1990.

Chaplin, George. *Presstime In Paradise: The Life and Times of The Honolulu Advertiser, 1856-1995*. Honolulu, HI: University of Hawai'I Press, 1998.

Churchill, Winston S. *The Grand Alliance*. New York: Houghton Mifflin, 1950.

Churchill, Winston S. *The Second World War: Their Finest Hour*. Boston, MA: Houghton Mifflin, 1949.

Churchill, Winston S., and Martin Gilbert. *The Churchill War Papers: The Ever Widening War, 1941*. New York, W. W. Norton & Company, 2001.

Churchill, Winston. *The Gathering Storm*. New York: Rosetta Books, 2002.

Coffey, Thomas M. *Hap: The Story of The U.S. Air Force and The Man Who Built it, General Henry "Hap" Arnold*. New York: Viking Press, 1982.

Cohen, Adam. *Nothing to Fear FDR's Inner Circle and the Hundred Days that Created Modern America*. New York: Penguin Press, 2009.

Conant, Jennet. *Tuxedo Park: A Wall Street Tycoon And the Secret Palace of Science That Changed the Course of World War II*. New York: Simon and Schuster, 2003.

Connaughton, Richard. *Macarthur and Defeat in the Philippines*. New York: The Overlook Press, 2001.

Cooke, Alistair. *The American Home Front: 1941-1942*. New York: Atlantic Monthly Press, 2006.

Costello, John. *The Pacific War: 1941-1945*. New York: HarperCollins, 1981.

Courtney, Richard D. *Painting the Milkweeds: How One American Family Coped with the Great Depression*. Raleigh, NC: Lulu Press, 2008.

Craig, Gordon A. *Europe Since 1914: Third Edition*. Hillsdale, IL: Dryden Press, 1972.

Cressman, Robert. *The Official Chronology of the U.S. Navy in World War II*. Annapolis, MD, Naval Institute Press, 2000.

Diehl, Lorraine B. *Over Here! New York City During World War II*. New York: Harper Collins, 2010.

Doll, John G. *Battling Bastards of Bataan*. Bennington, VT: Merriam Press, 1988.

Donovan, Hedley. *Roosevelt to Reagan: A Reporter's Encounters with Nine Presidents*. New York: Harper & Row, 1985.

Drea, Edward J. *Japan's Imperial Army: Its Rise and Fall, 1853-1945*. Lawrence, KS: University Press of Kansas, 2009.

Duffy, James P. *Lindbergh Vs. Roosevelt: The Rivalry That Divided America*. Washington, DC: Regnery, 2010.

Dull, Paul S. *A Battle History of The Imperial Japanese Navy (1941-1945)*. Annapolis, MD: Naval Institute Press, 1978.

Edey, Maitland A., ed. *Time Capsule 1941*. New York: Time Life Books, 1967.

Edey, Maitland A., ed. *Time Capsule 1942*. New York: Time Life Books, 1968.

Edwards, Anne. *Early Reagan: The Rise to Power*. New York: William Morrow, 1987.

Eliot, Mark. *Walt Disney: Hollywood's Dark Prince*. New York: Carol Publishing, 1993.

Ensign, Clint W. *Inscriptions of a Nation: Collected Quotations from Washington Monuments*. Washington, DC: Elliott & Clark, 1994.

Evans, David C. and Mark R. Peattie. *Kaigun: Strategy, Tactics, and Technology in the Imperial Japanese Navy, 1887-1941*. Annapolis, MD: Naval Institute Press, 1997.

Farago, Landislas. *The Broken Seal: "Operation Magic" and the Secret Road to Pearl Harbor.* New York: Random House, 1967.

Freeman, Robert C. and Jon R. Felt. *German Saints at War.* Springville, UT: Cedar Fort, 2008.

Gallagher, Hugh Gregory. *FDR's Splendid Deception: The Moving Story of Roosevelt's Massive Disability-And the Intense Efforts to Conceal It from the Public.* Arlington, VA: Vandamere Press, 1995.

Gary, Brett. *The Nervous Liberals: Propaganda Anxieties From World War I to the Cold War.* New York: Columbia Univ. Press, 1999.

Gibson, Truman K. with Steve Huntley. *Knocking Down Barriers: My Fight for Black America.* Chicago: Northwestern University Press, 2005.

Gill, Bob. *Jackie Robinson: Pro Football Prelude.* Warminster, PA: Professional Football Researchers Association, 1987.

Goff, Kenneth. *Red Betrayal of Youth.* Enterprise Print, 1946.

Goldstein, Donald M. and Katherine V. Dillon. *The Pearl Harbor Papers: Inside The Japanese Plans.* Dulles, VA: Brasseys, 1993.

Goldsworthy, Terry. *Valhalla's Warriors: A History of the Waffen-SS on the Eastern Front 1941-1945.* Indianapolis, IN: Dog Ear Publishing, 2010.

Goodwin, Doris Kearns. *No Ordinary Time Franklin and Eleanor Roosevelt: The Home Front in World War II.* New York: Simon and Schuster, 1994.

Greenstein, Fred I. *The Presidential Difference: Leadership Style from FDR to George W. Bush.* Princeton, NJ: Princeton University Press, 2004.

Hart, Jeffrey. *From This Moment On.* New York: Crown Publishers, 1987.

Hayes, Carlton J.H. and Margareta Faissler. *Modern Times: The Fresh Revolution to the Present.* New York: The Macmillan Company, 1965.

Heinrichs, Waldo. *Threshold of War: Franklin D. Roosevelt and American Entry Into World War II.* Oxford, UK: Oxford University Press, 1990.

Holmes, Wendell, and Richard A. Posner. *The Essential Holmes: Selections From the Letters, Speeches, Judicial Opinions, and Other Writings of Oliver Wendell Holmes, Jr.* Chicago: University of Chicago Press, 1997.

Hull, Cordell. *The Memoirs of Cordell Hull.* vol. 1. New York: Macmillan, 1948.

Hull, Cordell. *The Memoirs of Cordell Hull.* vol. 2. New York: Macmillan, 1948.

Jacobson, Matthew Frye, and Gaspar González. *What Have They Built You To Do? The Manchurian Candidate and Cold War America.* Minneapolis: University of Minnesota Press, 2006.

James, D. Clayton. *The Years of MacArthur Volume 1: 1880-1941.* Boston, MA: Houghton Mifflin, 1970.

Japanese Demobilization Bureaux Records. *Reports of General MacArthur: Japanese Operations in the Southwest Pacific Area.* vol. II, pt. I. Tokyo, Japan: U.S. Department of the Army, 1950.

Kass, Amy A. and Leon R. Kass. *What so Proudly We Hail: The American Soun in Story, Speech, and Song.* Wilmington, DE: ISI Books, 2011.

Kennedy, David M. *The Library of Congress World War II Companion.* New York: Simon & Schuster, 2007.

Kennedy, Kostya. *56: Joe DiMaggio and the Last Magic Number in Sports.* New York: Sports Illustrated Books, 2011.

Ketchum, Richard M., *The Borrowed Years 1938-1941.* New York: Random House, 1989.

Kim, Hyung-chan, ed. *Asian Americans and the Supreme Court: A Documentary History.* Westport, CT: Greenwood Publishing Group, 1992.

Kimmel, Husband E., *Admiral Kimmel's Story*. Chicago: Henry Regnery Company, 1955.

King, T. J. *Joint and Naval Intelligence Support to Military Operations*. Darby, PA: Diane Publishing, 2011.

Klein, Jonas. *Beloved Island: Franklin & Eleanor And the Legacy of Campobello*. Forest Dale, VT: Paul S. Eriksson, 2000.

Klein, Woody. *All the Presidents' Spokesmen: Spinning the News - White House Press Secretaries from Franklin D. Roosevelt to George W. Bush*. Westport, CT: Praeger Publishers, 2008.

Kluger, Richard. *Ashes to Ashes: America's Hundred-Year Cigarette War, The Public Health, And The Unabashed Triumph of Philip Morris*. New York: Random House, 1997.

Klurth, Peter. *American Cassandra: The Life of Dorothy Thompson*. New York: Little Brown & Co., 1991.

Kotani, Ken. *Japanese Intelligentce in World War II*. New York: Osprey Publishing, 2009.

Lapica, R.L. and Charles Freedhand, ed. Facts on File Yearbook, 1941: Persons index of World Events. vol. 1. New York: Facts on File, 1942.

Lash, Joseph P. *Eleanor and Franklin: The Story of Their Relationship Based on Eleanor Roosevelt's Private Papers*. New York: W.W. Norton & Company, 1971.

Leonard, Thomas M. *Day by Day: The Forties*. New York: Facts on File, 1977.

Longfellow, Henrt Wadsworth. *The Complete Poetical Works of Henry Wadsworth Longfellow*. London, UK: George Routledge & Sons, 1871.

Lundstrom, John B. *The First Team: Pacific Naval Air Combat From Pearl Harbor to Midway*. Annapolis, MD, Naval Institute Press, 2005.

Lyons, Eugene. *Herbert Hoover: A Biography*. Garden City, NY: Doubleday & Company, 1964.

MacArthur, Douglas. *Reminiscences*. New York: McGraw-Hill, 1964.

Manchester, William. *American Caesar: Douglas MacArthur 1880 – 1964*. Boston, MA: Little, Brown and Company, 1978.

McBride, Joseph. *Frank Capra: The Catastrophe of Success*. New York: St. Martins Griffin, 2000.

McCullough, David. *Truman*. New York: Simon and Schuster, 1992.

McElvaine, Robert S. *The Great Depression: America 1929-1941*. New York: Three Rivers Press, 1984.

McGuire, Edna, and Thomas B. Portwood. *The Rise of Our Free Nation*. New York: The Macmillan Company, 1947.

Meacham, Jon. *Franklin And Winston: An Intimate Portrait of an Epic Friendship*. New York: Random House, 2003.

Meachan, John. *Franklin and Winston*. New York: Random House, 2004.

Middleton, K.W.B. *Britain and Russia*. London, UK: Hutchinson, 1947.

Mills, Walter, and E.S. Duffield. *The Forestall Diaries*. New York: Viking Press, 1951.

Minear, Richard H. *Dr. Seuss Goes To War: The World War II Editorial Cartoons of Theodore Seuss Geisel*. New York: The New Press, 1999.

Monaghan, Frank. *World War II An Illustrated History*. vol. 1. Chicago: J.G. Ferguson, 1943.

Monaghan, Frank. *World War II An Illustrated History*. vol. 2. Chicago: J.G. Ferguson, 1943.

Morton, Louis. *U.S. Army in World War II The War in The Pacific: The Fall of the Philippines*. Washington, DC: Department of The Army, 1953.

Nalty, Bernard C. *War in the Pacific Pearl Harbor to Tokyo Bay: The Story of the Bitter Struggle in the Pacific Theater of World War II*. Norman, OK: University of Oklahoma Press, 1999.

Nasaw, David. *The Chief: The Life of William Randolph Hearst*. Boston, MA: Houghton Mifflin Harcourt, 2001.

Neustadt, Richard E. *Presidential Power and the Modern Presidents: The Politics of Leadership from Roosevelt to Reagan*. New York: The Free Press, 1991.

Notley, David. *Winston Churchill: Quotations*. Norwich, UK: Jarrold Publishing, 1977.

O'Neill, William L. *A Democracy At War: America's Fight at Home and Abroad in World War II*. Cambridge, MA: Harvard University Press, 1995.

Overy, Richard. *War in the Pacific*. Long Island City, NY: Osprey Publishing, 2010.

Overy, Richard. *Why The Allies Won*. New York: W.W. Norton, & Company, 1995.

Peattie, Mark R. *Sunburst: The Rise of Japanese Naval Air Power 1909-1941*. Annapolis, MD: Naval Institute Press, 2001.

Pietrusza, David. *1948: Harry Truman's Improbable Victory and the Year That Transformed America*. New York: Union Square Press, 2011.

Polenberg, Richard. *The Era of Franklin D. Roosevelt 1933-1945*. Boston, MA: Bedford/St. Martin's, 2000.

Powers, Ron. *Dangerous Water: A Biography of the Boy Who Became Mark Twain*. Cambridge, MA: Da Capo Press, 2001.

Prange, Gordon William, Donald M. Goldstein, and Katherine V. Dillon. *At Dawn We Slept: The Untold Story of Pearl Harbor*. New York: McGraw-Hill, 1981.

Prange, Gordon William, Donald M. Goldstein, and Katherine V. Dillon. *Dec. 7, 1941: The Day the Japanese Attacked Pearl Harbor*. New York: Wings Books, 1991.

Raucher, Herman. *Summer of '42*. New York: G.P. Putnam's Sons, 1971.

Richler, Mordecai, ed. *Writers on World War II: An Anthology*. New York: Alfred A. Knopf, 1991.

Rickenbacker, Edward V. *Rickenbacker*. New York: FawcettWorld Library, 1969.

Roosevelt, Eleanor. *This I Remember*. New York: Dolphin Books, 1961.

Roosevelt, Elliott and James Brough. *A Rendezvous with Destiny: The Roosevelts of the White House*. New York: G.P. Putnam's Sons, 1975.

Roosevelt, Elliott and Joseph P. Lash. *F.D.R. His Personal Letters 1928-1945 I*. New York: Duell, Sloan and Pearce, 1950.

Roosevelt, Elliott and Joseph P. Lash. *F.D.R. His Personal Letters 1928-1945 II*. New York: Duell, Sloan and Pearce, 1950.

Roosevelt, Franklin D. *The War Messages of Franklin D. Roosevelt, December 8, 1941, to April 13, 1945: The President's War Addresses to the People & to the Congress of the United States of America*. Lexington, KY: HP, 2011.

Rowley, Hazel. *Franklin and Eleanor: An Extraordinary Marriage*. New York: Farrar, Straus and Giroux, 2010.

Safire, William and Leonard Safir. *Words of Wisdom*. New York: Simon and Schuster, 1989.

Satterfield, Archie. *The Home Front: An Oral History of The War Years in America: 1941-1945*. Chicago: Playboy Press, 1981.

Schlesinger, Arthur M. Jr. *The Crisis of the Old Order: 1919-1933*. Boston, MA: Houghton Mifflin, 1957.

Schlesinger, Robert. *White House Ghosts: Presidents and their Speechwriters; From FDR to George W. Bush*. New York: Simon and Schuster, 2008.

Schmidt, Ronald J. *This Is the City: Making Model Citizens in Los Angeles*. Minneapolis: University of Minnesota Press, 2005.

Seib, Philip M. *Broadcasts from the Blitz: How Edward R. Murrow Helped Lead America Into War*. Dulles, VA: Potomac Books, 2006.

Shales, Amity. *The Forgotten Man A New History of the Great Depression.* New York: Harper Collins, 2007.

Shirer, William L. *The Rise and Fall of The Third Reich.* New York: Simon and Schuster, 1960.

Shogan, Robert. *Hard Bargain: How FDR Twisted Churchill's Arm, Evaded the Law, and Changed the Role of the American Presidency.* Boulder, CO: Westview Press, 1999.

Shorter, Edward. *Bedside Manners.* New York: Simon and Schuster, 1985.

Shrirer, William L. *20th Century Journey: A Memoir of a Life and the Times: The Start: 1904-1930.* New York: Simon and Schuster, 1976.

Smith, Jean Edward. *FDR.* New York: Random House, 2007.

Smith, Page. *America Enters the World: A People's History of the Progressive Era and World War I.* vol.VII. New York: McGraw-Hill, 1985.

Steinhoff, Johannes, Peter Pechel, and Dennis Showalter. *Voices From The Third Reich: An Oral History.* Washington, DC: Regnery Gateway, 1989.

Stille, Mark. *Imperial Japanese Navy Heavy Cruisers 1941-1945.* Long Island City, NY: Osprey Publishing, 1969.

Stimson, Henry Lewis, and McGeorge Bundy. *On Active Service in Peace and War.* New York: Harper & Brothers, 1948.

Stimson, Henry Lewis, Council on Foreign Relations, and Royal Institute of International Affairs. *The Far Eastern Crisis.* New York: Harper & brothers, 1936.

Swift, Will. *The Roosevelts and the Royals.* Hoboken, NJ: John Wiley & Sons, 2004.

Tansill, Charles Callan. *Back Door to War: Roosevelt Foreign Policy: 1933-1941.* Chicago: Henry Regnery Company, 1952.

Taylor, Robert Lewis. *Winston Churchill: An Informal Study of Greatness.* Garden City, NY: Doubleday, 1952.

Terkel, Studs. *The Good War: An Oral History of World War Two.* New York: Pantheon Books, 1984.

Thomas, Evan. *Sea of Thunder: Four Commanders and the Last Great Naval Campaign 1941-1945.* New York: Simon and Schuster, 2006.

Thompson, Robert Smith. *A Time For War: Franklin D. Roosevelt and The Path to Pearl Harbor.* New York: Prentice-Hall, 1991.

Tremaine, Frank and Kay Tremaine. *The Attack on Pearl Harbor: By Two Who Were There.* Fredericksburg, TX: The Admiral Nimitz Foundation, 1997.

Tuchman, Barbara. The Guns of August. New York: Dell Publishing, 1973.

Tully, Grace. *F.D.R. My Boss.* New York: Charles Scribner's Sons, 1949.

Vaccaro, Mike. *1941--The Greatest Year In Sports: Two Baseball Legends, Two Boxing Champs, and the Unstoppable Thoroughbred Who Made History in the Shadow of War.* New York: First Anchor Books, 2007.

Van Der Vat, Dan. *Pearl Harbor: The Day of Infamy - An Illustrated History.* New York: Basic Books, 2001.

Ward, Geoffrey C., and Ken Burns. *The War: an Intimate History, 1941-1945.* New York: A.A. Knopf, 2007.

Winter, Ella. *Red Virtue: Human Relations in the New Russia.* New York: Harcourt Brace & Company, 1933.

PERIODICALS

Albuquerque (NM) Journal
Atlanta Constitution
Atlanta Daily World
Bakersfield (CA) Californian
Baltimore Sun
Beatrice (NE) Daily Sun
Birmingham (AL) News
Bismarck (ND) Tribune
Boston Daily Globe
Boston Evening Globe
Boston Sunday Globe
Brainerd (MN) Daily
Calgary Herald (Alberta, Canada)
Charleston (SC) Gazette
Charleston (SC) News and Courier
Chicago Daily Tribune
Christian Science Monitor
Coshocton (OH) Tribune
Cumberland (MD) Evening Times
Dunkirk (NY) Evening Observer
Emporia (KS) Daily Gazette
Fitchburg (MA) Sentinel
Greeley (CO) Daily Tribune
Hartford (CT) Courant
Hilo (HI) Tribune Herald
Honolulu (HI) Advertiser
Idaho Evening Times
Ironwood (MI) Daily Globe
Kingsport (TN) Times
Lethbridge Herald (Alberta, Canada)
Life

Long Island (NY) Newsday
Look
Los Angeles Times
Maryville (MO) Daily Forum
Middlesboro (KY) Daily News
Milwaukee Journal
Mount Airy (NC) News
Nevada Mail
Nevada State Journal
New York Times
Pittsburgh Post-Gazette
Portsmouth (NH) Herald
Portsmouth (VA) Times
Rock Hill (SC) Herald
San Francisco Chronicle
Sarasota (FL) Herald-Tribune
Saturday Evening Post
Spokane (WA) Spokesman-Review
St. Petersburg (FL) Evening Independent
St. Petersburg (FL) Times
Sunday (DE) Star
Sunday Star
Telegraph-Herald (IA)
Time
Tucson (AZ) Daily Citizen
Wall Street Journal
Washington Evening Star
Washington Post
Washington Times Herald
Yuma (AZ) Daily Sun

NEWS WIRES
Associated Press
Canadian Press
Chicago Tribune Service
International News Service
United Press

ELECTRONIC MEDIA
Tora! Tora! Tora! The Attack on Pearl Harbor. 1970. Craig Shirley Collection.
Midway. 1976. Craig Shirley Collection.
MacArthur. 1977. Craig Shirley Collection.
The March of Time: News Reels. Time. 1931 – 1967. HBO Archives.
FOX News Reels.

OTHER MATERIALS
Claude Wickard. Secretary of Agriculture Claude Wickard's Diary. Wickard Collection. Franklin D.
    Roosevelt Presidential Library.
Presidential Records. Franklin Delano Roosevelt Presidential Library and Museum.
Joint Committee on the Investigation of the Pearl Harbor Attack.
Henry Lewis Stimson Papers, Manuscripts and Archives, Yale University Library.
The Churchill Center and Museum at the Churchill War Rooms, London, Speeches,

INTERVIEWS
Gerald Eckert, Interview by Craig Shirley.
McShane, Susan. Interview by Craig Shirley. September 12, 2011.

ABOUT THE AUTHOR

Craig Shirley is the author of the critically praised bestsellers about President Reagan, *Rendezvous with Destiny: Ronald Reagan and the Campaign that Changed America* and *Reagan's Revolution: The Untold Story of the Campaign That Started It All.* He is the president of Shirley & Banister Public Affairs, was chosen in 2005 by Springfield College as their Outstanding Alumnus, and has been named the First Reagan Scholar at Eureka College, Ronald Reagan's alma mater.

His books have been hailed as the definitive works on the Gipper's campaigns of 1976 and 1980. He is a member of the Board of Governors of the Reagan Ranch and has lectured at the Reagan Library.

Shirley, a widely sought after speaker and commentator, has written extensively for the *Washington Post*, the *Washington Examiner*, the *Washington Times*, the *Los Angeles Times*, *Town Hall*, the *Weekly Standard*, and many other publications. He also edited the book, *Coaching Youth Lacrosse*, for the Lacrosse Foundation.

Shirley and his wife, Zorine, are the parents of four children. They reside at "Trickle Down Point" on the Rappahannock River in Lancaster, Virginia. His varied interests include sailing, waterskiing, sport shooting, renovating buildings, and scuba diving. He was a decorated contract agent for the Central Intelligence Agency.

Shirley is now working on three more books on Reagan as well as a political biography of Newt Gingrich.

ACKNOWLEDGMENTS

During the final course of writing this book, my editor and friend at Thomas Nelson, Joel Miller, was in the middle of doing a wonderful thing. He and his wife Megan were in Uganda adopting two young boys. While there for several weeks, he edited *December 1941* on a laptop on a table in the bathroom of his hotel. Their magnificence of kindness and charity and sacrifice puts book writing into perspective. Thank you, Joel.

Thank you also to the marvelous professionals at Nelson: Dave Schroeder, Heather Skelton, Kristen Parrish, Jason Jones, Julie Faires, Brian Hampton, Debbie Eicholtz, Rosie Colvin, and Dean Nelson. In addition to their skills and patience, they also have a very necessary sense of humor.

As in the case of my previous books, this one would not have been possible without the tender ministries, patience, tough editing, long hours, and superior suggestions of my wife and best friend, Zorine. Nor would this have been possible without the encouragement and support of my business partner and our friend, Diana Banister. Thank you, Zorine. Thank you, Diana.

Andrew Shirley was superb in his research, editing, fact-checking, and advice. He has dedicated, literally, thousands of hours to this book. This is as much Zorine's and Andrew's book as it is mine. Thank you. Thanks also to Borko and Andreja Komnenovic for their superb work.

Thanks also to our other children, Matthew, Taylor, and Mitchell for their encouragement and love and help and support. Our children are simply the most important people in Zorine's and my life.

Special thanks to four dear friends: Vic Gold, Fred Barnes, Michael McShane and Gay Hart Gaines for their support, advice, and wise council. The same goes for Gary Maloney.

And thanks to John Persinos for his advice and input on edits as well as cultural and historical suggestions and many thanks also to my mother, Barbara Eckert and my sister Rebecca Sirhal, for digging up family history for the Dedication, as well as their advice and counsel and love.

In the last two weeks, because of the press of time and the reams of research material, a group of professional researchers came to my assistance to help finish the job, like the Marines coming in over the hill just in the nick of time. Thank you to Kate Maxwell, Kristen Helmstetter, Linda Emery, Inez Feltscher, Jasmina Zahirovic, Scott Whitlock, Megan Higgins, Anna Hyde and Joseph S. Catapano, Queenie Bui, Lauren Elizabeth Merz, Mirah Johnston, Sakari Deichsel, Mark Hensch, and Alex B. Weisman. Each was dedicated and their work invaluable.

In no particular order, thanks also to the following friends: Mark Levin; Tony Fabrizio, Ken Cuccinelli, Jennifer Harper, Michael Barone, Bill Kristol, Mark Masters, Robert Schlesinger, Charles Pratt, John McLaughlin, Matthew Dallek, Jim McLaughlin, Grover Norquist, Mark Tapscott, Michael Phelps, Shannon Bream, Ken Cuccinelli, Tom McDevitt, Ralph Hallow, Rob and Robert Meyne, Paul Begala, Ricky Greenfield, Chuck Todd, Mark Allen, Matt Continetti, Jay Test, Peggy Noonan, Bill Clark, Joanne Herring, Stephen Moore, Roger Stone, Richard Viguerie, Michele Davis, John Fund, Paul and Carole Laxalt, Bill Schulz, Fred Eckert, David Marks, George and Mari Will, Cleta Mitchell, Tom Loringer, Fred Barbash, David Alpern, Newt and Callista Gingrich, Cheryl Rampy, Lee Edwards, Del Quentin Wilber, John Heubusch, Dave Arnold, Mike Murtaugh, Philip Cavalier, John Morris, Joanne Drake, Jewell and Pal Horning, Rick Perry, Ken Cribb, Jim Burnley, Dick Allen, Ken Khachigian, Stu Spencer, Karen Spencer, Fred Ryan, Carl Cannon, Carolyn Hauer, Pat Nolan, Dennis LeBlanc, Quin Hilyer, Brent and Norma Bozell, Susan McShane, Rick and Sue Johnson, Bruce Baker and Rhonda Lognon, Llewellyn King and Linda Gasparello, Ron Robinson,

Frank and Becki Donatelli, Dave Roberts, Peter and Irene Hannaford, Jed Donahue, Dick and Mary Snyder, Lou Cannon, Tom and Lyn Finnigan, Ed Meese, Bill Pascoe, Al Regnery, Tish Leonard, Bob Tyrrell, Jim Pinkerton, Howard Fineman, Kevin and Chris Kabanuk, Dan, Soona, Jinnyn, Dan III, Coury and Raymond Jacob, Ross, Candy, Elizabeth and Katherine Bhappu, Manek Bhappu, Dr. Roshan and Perin Bhappu, and Homee Schroff. And to Ellen and Wayne Masters and Nathan, Todd, Eric and Margaret Shirley. And to Human, Stephanie, Laura and Ethan Sirhal Karen Howard and Michelle and John Bae.

Thanks to Tish Leonard, Kevin McVicker, Courtney Nolan, Jameson Cunningham and Dan Wilson at Shirley & Banister Public Relations. And thanks to Matthew C. Hanson, Archives Specialist at the Franklin D. Roosevelt Presidential Library and to everybody at the Library of Congress.

In the course of writing and researching this book, I discovered many things including things about my family I did not know until the papers from the Daughters of the American Revolution were given to me by my mother and sister.

I knew about the many sacrifices of many men in the Shirley, Cone, Abbott, Westbook, Watkins, and McGiveron families in all the wars of America but did not know about Henry Cone of Haddam, Connecticut—on my mother's side—who enlisted in May 1775 in the 1st Company, 1st Regiment. He was "at the siege of Boston in May, and at Bunker Hill in June. . . ." Under George Washington's command, our grandfather then "wintered at Valley Forge, 1777–8; was at the battles of Brandywine, Monmouth, and Long Island. In 1781, while still in service, he lost an eye by smallpox. In 1793, he was granted a pension and [died] at Lyme Dec. 15, 1827, aged 83." Henry's son Andrew Diodate Cone—another grandfather—served in the War of 1812.

On my father's side, Private William Watkins was one of the "men who marched from Connecticut Town for the relief of Boston in the Lexington Alarm of April 1775. . . ." Watkins was in the "Third Regiment, under General Putnam, 1775, fifth company."

To all the aforementioned, I am in your debt.